COOK'S
ILLUSTRATED

~ 1995 ~

Published by
Boston Common Press Limited Partnership
17 Station Street
Brookline, MA 02445

ISBN: 0-9640179-3-8
ISSN: 1068-2821

To get home delivery of future issues of *Cook's Illustrated*
magazine, call 800-526-8442. To order any of the book titles
from the *Cook's Illustrated* Library, call 800-611-0759,
or write to the address above.

$29.95

Key: BC = Back Cover

COOK'S ILLUSTRATED INDEX

NUMBER TWELVE

JANUARY/FEBRUARY 1995

COOK'S
ILLUSTRATED

Rustic Country Bread
The Secret to
Big-League Chew

Foolproof Polenta
Less Stirring, More
Consistent Results

The Magic of Pudding Cakes
How One Batter Makes
Both Cake and Sauce

Rating House Blend Coffees
Supermarket Brands
Finish Dead Last

SPICE-INFUSED OILS

TASTING CALIFORNIA'S
BEST REDS

QUICK-COOKING
STRONG-FLAVORED GREENS

THE BEST ROESTI

BRAISING LAMB SHANKS

$4.00 U.S./$4.95 CANADA

"Kale and Turnips"
See page 12 for the best way to cook kale.

ILLUSTRATION BY
BRENT WATKINSON

Banana-Papaya Fool, adapted from *Big Flavors of the Hot Sun* (Morrow, 1994) by Chris Schlesinger and John Willoughby

ILLUSTRATION BY
CAROL FORTUNATO

COOK'S
ILLUSTRATED

Publisher and Editor CHRISTOPHER KIMBALL

Executive Editor MARK BITTMAN

Senior Editor JOHN WILLOUGHBY

Food Editor PAM ANDERSON

Senior Writer JACK BISHOP

Articles Editor ANNE TUOMEY

Managing Editor MAURA LYONS

Assistant Managing Editor TRICIA O'BRIEN

Copy Editor KURT TIDMORE

Editorial Assistant KIM N. RUSSELLO

Test Cook VICTORIA ROLAND

Art Director MEG BIRNBAUM

Food Stylist MARIE PIRAINO

Special Projects Designer AMY KLEE

Marketing Director ADRIENNE KIMBALL

Circulation Director ELAINE REPUCCI

Circulation Assistants JENNIFER L. KEENE
JONATHAN VENIER

Production Director JAMES McCORMACK

Production Assistants SHEILA DATZ
PAMELA SLATTERY

Publicity Director CAROL ROSEN KAGAN

Treasurer JANET CARLSON

Accounting Assistant MANDY SHITO

Office Manager JENNY THORNBURY

Office Assistant SARAH CHUNG

Special Projects FERN BERMAN

Cook's Illustrated (ISSN 1068-2821) is published bimonthly by Boston Common Press, 17 Station Street, Box 569, Brookline, MA 02147-0569. Copyright 1995 Boston Common Press. Application to mail at second-class postage rates is pending at Boston, MA, and additional mailing offices. Editorial office: 17 Station Street, Box 569, Brookline, MA 02147-0569; (617) 232-1000, FAX (617) 232-1572. Editorial contributions should be sent to: Editor, *Cook's Illustrated*, 17 Station Street, Box 569, Brookline, MA 02147-0569. We cannot assume responsibility for manuscripts submitted to us. Submissions will be returned only if accompanied by a large self-addressed stamped envelope. Subscription rates: $24.95 for one year; $45 for two years; $65 for three years. (Canada: add $3 per year; all other countries: add $12 per year.) Postmaster: Send all new orders, subscription inquiries, and change of address notices to *Cook's Illustrated*, P.O. Box 59046, Boulder, CO 80322-9046. Single copies: $4 in U.S., $4.95 in Canada and foreign. Back issues available for $5 each. PRINTED IN THE U.S.A.

PHOTOGRAPH BY JIM THOMAS

EDITORIAL

BREAD AND WATER

CHRISTOPHER KIMBALL

The Greek philosopher Epicurus established an informal school of philosophy in ancient Athens that was devoted to the pursuit of happiness. For Epicurus, happiness was a life of simplicity and ease. Water was the preferred drink and barley bread the primary food. In later centuries, Epicurus's "happiness" was misinterpreted as "pleasure," hence the modern term epicurean. Today, an epicure shuns the simplicity of bread and water for the thrill of luxury and the new—a package tour of the latest Pacific rim culinary experiments.

But perhaps the true epicure is a different sort altogether. In *Honey From a Weed*, Patience Gray notes, "The island Greek has the habit of going for long periods ... on a crust of home-baked bread, a hunk of hard goat's cheese, and wild pears, honey sweet, stuffed inside his shirt. He then makes the most of a providential event, a ripe fruit tree, a sudden haul of fish, or the killing of a pig."

My wife and I have an odd assortment of urban and rural friends; architects and dairy farmers, financial consultants and carpenters. Most of us would not consider the farmers epicures, but perhaps, like the Greek from Naxos, they know more about the appreciation of food than their urban counterparts. In our village, hidden high in a valley in Vermont's Green Mountains, neighbors have fed us venison steaks and roast heifer, watermelon pickles and pickled tongue, goat's milk ice cream and dandelion greens. We have even been served a spur-of-the-moment stew starring a luckless woodchuck who had been caught early that morning in a neighbor's garden.

Gourmet cooking? No, but perhaps it's a whole lot closer to the true notion of the epicurean life. The bunch of peppery watercress growing near the horse trough, the quarts of Taxi tomatoes put up on Labor Day, the still-tender fiddlehead ferns that provide the first taste of spring—these foods are appreciated more because they are not plucked from the produce aisle of the local supermarket. Each bite has a taste of history because someone in the family grew it, picked it, hunted it, or canned it.

But simple foods are rarely simple. In developing this issue's recipe for country bread, I spent six months of weekends baking various combinations of flour, water, yeast, and salt. After the first few loaves, slight variations in the recipe took on increasing importance. A bit too much salt. A dough that was slightly too wet. A crust that was a tad too thin. I began to appreciate the subtleties of bread and the complex relationship between technique and end result. Practiced familiarity with the simplest of recipes breeds a deeper understanding of the notion of epicurean. At first glance, nothing is more basic than bread, yet with experience you find that nothing is more complex.

Many years ago I was helping a local Vermont dairy farmer during haying season. After filling up the wagon, he stopped the tractor and asked me to join him for a walk. We hiked down the dusty river road until we came to a spring running down a shale embankment. The water was stony cool and flinty, with a sweet aftertaste of fern and mint. He eased his cap back from his pale forehead, as white as the belly of a brook trout, and said, "Good water."

Well, it wasn't just good, it was the best darn drink I've ever had. It was more subtle than Sancerre, more refreshing than a chilled Chardonnay, and sweeter than Tokay. It was also free for the taking. I know that farmer is familiar with every spring and brook in town, and this is his favorite—after sixty years of sipping the local waters, his palate is fine-tuned to the subtle differences between the spring by Gene Kennedy's up in Beartown, and the taste of the Green River by the old Baptist hole behind the Methodist church. Would Epicurus have considered this simple farmer an epicure? I'd like to think so.

Maybe it is better to spend a lifetime fully appreciating just one thing than to know many things only by their first names. Perhaps that is the true definition of an epicure. ∎

NOTES
FROM READERS

PARBOILING RIBS

*A*s a Kansas City native, I was very interested in your article "How to Make Authentic Barbecued Ribs at Home" (July/August 1994). I offer a few comments to the author of your article, A. Cort Sinnes, as it is obvious he is a rib-lover, and I have found that as a group rib-lovers are always ready to share information that will improve the art of "doing" ribs.

I am a fan of parboiling but not to cut cooking time, although that is a beneficial side effect. My experience is that parboiling ribs allows the meat to literally be sucked off the bone; it tends to detach the flesh of the rib where it connects to the bone and gristle. I find this creates a better dining experience. Parboiling also renders most of the fat from the ribs. I use a different method and timing for parboiling than the one offered in your article. I put my ribs in the pot, bone end down. This reduces the possibility of inadvertently burning the ribs' flesh during the process. I cover the ribs with water and cook them over high heat until the water boils. I then reduce the heat and skim off the scum. I cook the ribs until the flesh turns gray, turn off the heat, and let them sit uncovered for five to ten minutes. Finally, I remove the ribs from the pot, wash them in cold water, and pat them dry with paper towels.

On the subject of direct versus indirect cooking methods, I prefer direct cooking if the distance between the coals and meat is such that flare-ups will not singe the meat. If ribs are parboiled, cooking time with the direct method will be about one hour. If ribs are not parboiled, cooking time should be doubled. With direct cooking, the cook must be alert for flare-ups, and the ribs must be turned every fifteen minutes or so to promote even cooking. Indirect cooking slows things down, eliminates the need to be alert for flare-ups, and permits turning every half hour or so.

ROBERT RUSSELL
Aurora, CO

CHINESE TIP FOR RIBS

*T*he article on cooking authentic barbecued ribs was certainly interesting, and I would like to add some additional comments. A Chinese cook once told me that the very first step in preparing ribs should be to remove the thin membrane found underneath the ribs. Most people don't realize it's there, but if you take a paper towel and start from one end of the slab, first pulling a little piece of the membrane up with your fingers and then grab-

bing it with the paper towel and pulling it carefully across the slab, the whole membrane comes off in one piece. Once you see what is removed, you would not want that stuff in your stomach.

As for parboiling, I start my ribs in cold water and keep the temperature low for only as long as it takes for the scum to appear. Then I take the ribs out, drain them, and prepare them as described in your article.

RAIMAR VOGELSANG
Bloomfield Hills, MI

POTATO STARCH

*I*s there a difference between potato starch and cornstarch? I have a number of recipes, especially from cookbooks by Jacques Pépin, that call for potato starch, but I ordinarily only have cornstarch in my pantry. Can cornstarch be substituted in the same quantities for the potato starch?

NANCY SUMMERS
Durham, NC

Culinary starches are used to thicken purees, broths, and sauces. The most common culinary starches are extracted from potatoes, cassava (the tuber that tapioca comes from), arrowroot, wheat, rice, and corn. All of them can be used as thickeners, although they vary in their ability to thicken as well as in other ways.

Like cornstarch, potato starch, which is sometimes known by its French name *fecula*, makes translucent sauces. (Flour, the most common thickener in American kitchens, makes opaque sauces.) Both potato starch and cornstarch are twice as powerful as flour.

You can substitute cornstarch in recipes that call for potato starch and vice versa, but you should be aware of differences and make appropriate adjustments in your cooking technique.

For instance, potato starch gelatinizes at a lower temperature than either cornstarch or flour and also tends to break down at a lower temperature. Therefore, sauces thickened with potato starch should be watched carefully and removed from the heat as soon as they reach the proper consistency. In addition, potato starch does not have as much holding power as cornstarch, so sauces thickened with potato starch should be served promptly.

On the positive side, potato starch is flavorless, making it the choice of many chefs for delicate sauces. Also, since potato starch is tasteless, there is no need to "cook out" the raw flavor of the thickener, as you have to do with flour and even

cornstarch. This means that potato starch can be added much later in the cooking process. If you substitute cornstarch for potato starch, you should allow more time for the sauce to thicken and for the raw flavor of the starch to fade.

Arrowroot, a root starch that comes from a West Indian plant, is more similar to potato starch and is probably a better substitute for it than cornstarch. Unfortunately, arrowroot is not as easily available as cornstarch. Your best bet for recipes calling for potato starch may be to head to the local health food store, which may stock potato starch since it is a gluten-free product. Otherwise, use cornstarch, but be aware of the differences outlined above.

POLISHING COPPER

*I*nstead of using expensive polishes to brighten up tarnished copper pots and pans, simply use a fresh lemon (or lime) and salt. Squeeze the juice of half a lemon over the copper surface and sprinkle it with a tablespoon of salt. Then, using the lemon half as a scrubber, buff the copper until it shines. It's the simplest and safest method I've found for cleaning copper.

SANDRA NEWMAN
Garden Grove, CA

Peter George, a reader from Granada Hills, California, also wrote to us with the same idea. When finished with the lemon half, he tosses it into the sink disposal unit to keep the drain sweet-smelling.

CLOTTED CREAM

I recently returned from a trip to Great Britain, where I fell in love with the clotted cream served with berries and scones. I can't find clotted cream in any of my local markets and was wondering if there is a way to make it at home.

SHEILA EWING
Rockport, ME

Like sour cream and crème fraîche, clotted cream is traditionally made by adding lactobacilli (lactic acid-producing bacteria) to raw milk. To make clotted cream, the unpasteurized milk is first heated until some of the liquid evaporates and a layer of cream forms on top. The bacteria is then added to this thick cream. Unless you live on a dairy farm, you will have to use heavy cream as your base for making clotted cream. When you add a small amount of buttermilk to heavy cream, the lactobacilli in the buttermilk multiply and co-agulate, causing the mixture to thicken.

Unfortunately, not all heavy creams can be used to make clotted cream. Ultra-pasteurized cream, as opposed to regular pasteurized cream, often will not thicken properly. Even when ultra-pasteurized cream does thicken, it is sometimes grainy, lumpy, and/or gelatinous. According to Todd Klaenhammer, director of the Southeast Dairy Foods Research Center in Raleigh, North Carolina, this happens because the heat treatment used in ultra-pasteurization leaves the cream with too little food for the bacteria, thus producing less consistent coagulation.

Klaenhammer recommends that you look for pasteurized cream, often sold in old-fashioned glass bottles at natural foods stores. Check the dates, and buy the freshest cream possible to reduce the chances of getting unwanted bacteria that sometimes appear in older cream and may create a gelatinous or grainy product. Klaenhammer generally doesn't recommend leaving dairy products at room temperature, but because the cream will not thicken if immediately put into the refrigerator, he suggests leaving it on the counter just until the reaction begins. Don't leave it out any longer than a day.

HOMEMADE CLOTTED CREAM
Makes 2 cups
This recipe can be halved or doubled as needed.

   1½   cups pasteurized (not ultra-
         pasteurized) heavy cream
   ½   cup buttermilk

Combine cream and buttermilk in jar or measuring cup. Stir, cover, and let stand at room temperature until mixture has thickened to the consistency of softly whipped cream, 12 to 24 hours. Refrigerate; cream will continue to thicken as it chills. Clotted cream can be kept refrigerated and covered for up to 10 days.

FRIED CHICKEN COMMENTS

There are two points that I would like to make about your article "Rediscovering Fried Chicken" (May/June 1994).

You mention in the story that several recipes you tried recommend drying the coated chicken on a rack for several hours before frying, in an attempt to get the flour to adhere better to the chicken. While you said that you were unimpressed with the effects this technique had on the coating when it was fried, you neglected to mention that this technique is also unsafe. Room temperature provides the optimum conditions for the growth of bacteria like salmonella. It's fine to let battered chicken dry out in the refrigerator for several hours, but don't let raw chicken sit at room temperature for any length of time.

My second point has to do with your discussion of frying chicken in Crisco and the notion that "it all comes back." When frying a whole chicken you ended up with almost three cups of fat, the same amount of Crisco you started with. But what about the fat in the chicken? For example, when I bake a chicken that size, I usually end up with one-quarter to one-half cup of fat in the pan. Frying may not add fat, but it does not seem to allow for the release of the fat in the chicken either.
DIANE BIANCHINI
Belle Mead, NJ

BETTER FRENCH FRIES

When fixing French fries, I use a little trick to keep the temperature of the oil from going down when the potatoes are added. I first heat the potato slices (for chips) or sticks in the microwave. This way the oil temperature does not drop too much when the potatoes are added, so the potatoes don't absorb too much oil and become soggy or greasy.
MRS. V. ROBERTSON
Centerville, MO

WHAT IS IT?

Can you tell me what this glass bottle is for? It was given to me as a gift some time ago, and I can't remember how it should be used.
ANNALIESE CREFELD
Whippany, NJ

This is an all-in-one oil and vinegar cruet designed for dressing salads at the table. The vinegar should be poured into the inner container; the oil is poured into the outer compartment. The cruet can be tilted to one side to drizzle oil over salad, and to the other side to drizzle vinegar. This unusual cruet is available from Liguori & Hunt (Colts Towne Plaza, Route 34, Colts Neck, NJ 07722; 908-462-4014) for $19.95 including shipping costs.

RINSING RICE

I'm confused about when to rinse rice, when to soak it, and when to use it straight from the box or bag. Are there some guidelines you could give me?
TRIXIE CHATTMAN
Fairfield, CT

The U.S. Rice Council recommends that you never rinse or soak white rice. Laws in six states require that white rice be enriched with iron, niacin, and thiamine. Since states with enrichment requirements include New York and California, most domestic millers enrich rice for the entire U.S. market. Consequently, roughly 95 percent of all domestically milled white rice is enriched. These nutrients are usually applied in a topical coating (you can sometimes feel and see this powdery layer on the rice) that will easily wash off if the rice is rinsed. Therefore, rinsing or washing white rice is not advised.

White rice that is milled abroad is less likely to be enriched, although if it is sold in a state that requires fortification it must be enriched. In Asia and Latin America, rice is usually washed to remove any impurities and prepare the rice for cooking. You will see recipes in many ethnic cookbooks that recommend this practice, but for maximum nutrient retention you may wish to skip this step. Also, note that soaking rice before cooking will decrease overall cooking time. You may need to make adjustments to recipes if they call for soaking and you omit that step.

As for brown rice, it is not enriched, so there is less to be concerned about with regard to rinsing or washing. However, small quantities of some water-soluble nutrients that occur naturally in the grain can be lost through prolonged soaking, so you may want to avoid it.

SUBSTITUTING BAKING PANS

I have a favorite blueberry buckle recipe from my mother that calls for a nine-inch-square glass baking dish. I can't seem to find a glass dish this size anywhere, but I was wondering if I could use a round glass pie plate instead. Is there some formula for figuring out how to use a different baking pan from the one specified in a recipe?
LIA BARRETT
Chapel Hill, NC

Of course, your first choice should always be a pan that is the specified size and made from the specified material. That said, it is possible to make some adjustments.

As far as the material of the pan is concerned, recipes with acidic ingredients, especially berries, are usually baked in nonreactive pans made from glass or ceramic. This is particularly important if the berries are to come in direct contact with the surface of the pan during cooking. (In a double-crust pie, for instance, this is less crucial than when making a buckle or cobbler.)

As for the size of the pan, you can use any pan with a similar depth that has an equivalent surface area. For instance, a nine-inch glass baking dish is usually about two inches deep. Therefore, if you needed to use another pan, it should have the same depth so that the baking time and appearance of the finished dish will be similar. To determine the surface area of a square or rectangular dish, simply multiply the length of the pan by its width, in this case nine by nine, or eighty-one square inches. The surface area of a circular pan can be computed by multiplying half the diameter by itself (the radius squared) and then multiplying that sum by 3.14 (pi). For instance, a ten-inch round pan has a surface area of seventy-eight and one-half square inches—five times five, times 3.14. Therefore, a round glass pie plate that is at least two inches deep and ten inches across is an equivalent substitution for a nine-inch-square glass pan ∎

Quick Tips

CLEANING CULTIVATED MUSHROOMS

Mushrooms need to be cleaned, but brushing them leaves dirt behind and washing changes the texture. Betsey Orman of Arlington Heights, Illinois, suggested this excellent method.

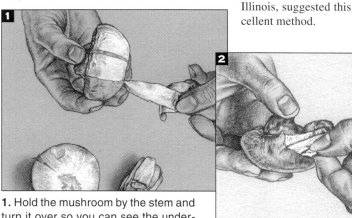

1. Hold the mushroom by the stem and turn it over so you can see the underside of the cap. Grasp a piece of the fringe around the cap border; pull this very thin layer up and over the cap.

2. Repeat until the cap is completely clean.

PRESSING CRUMB CRUSTS

Carol Spence of Roselle Park, New Jersey, has found an easy way to press graham cracker crumb crusts into the bottoms of pans.

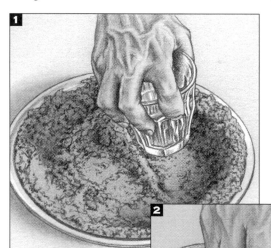

1. For larger crusts, use the bottom of a glass to press the crumb mixture into the pan.

2. When making miniature tarts and cheesecakes, use the bottom of a cordial glass or the cork from a cordial bottle.

MAKING A FOIL COVER FOR PIE CRUSTS

When covering the edge of a pie crust with foil for a portion of the baking time, it can be frustrating to piece together long strips of foil. Instead, follow this tip from Susan Reynolds of Newton, Massachusetts.

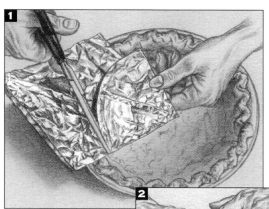

1. Lay out a square of foil large enough to cover the pie. Fold the square in half and then in half again to form a smaller square. Place the closed corner point in the center of the pie and cut an arc as shown.

2. When you unfold the foil, you will have cut out a circle from the middle of the sheet. This open circle exposes the pie, while the remaining ring of foil covers the crust.

HALVING CRANBERRIES

Some recipes call for halved rather than chopped cranberries. To make this task easy, follow the advice of Cheryl McNabb of Vacaville, California. Place the cranberries in the gutter of a cutting board, then use a large knife to halve them all at once.

LOADING A PASTRY BAG

When loading a pastry bag for piping, follow this tip from Leo Gallager of Elegant Events Catering in Wallingford, Connecticut. Simply roll the top of the bag down about 2 inches, then use an ice cream scoop for easy loading with no mess.

ILLUSTRATIONS BY ALAN WITSCHONKE

SEPARATING AND PEELING LARGE AMOUNTS OF GARLIC

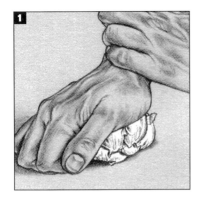

When a recipe calls for lots of garlic, separating the individual cloves from the head and then peeling them can be a time-consuming chore. Rhoda Bukzin of Charlotte, North Carolina, sent this tip to make the task much faster and easier.

1. Press down on the garlic head with the heel of your hand to loosen the cloves.

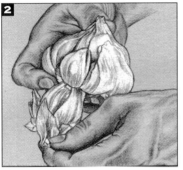

2. Remove as much of the papery skin from the outside of the head as possible.

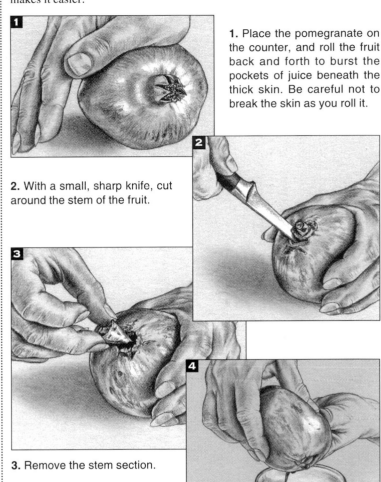

3. Place the head of garlic in a very lightly oiled mixing bowl of an electric mixer and fit the mixer with a paddle attachment.

4. Mix until the cloves are separate and the peels are removed.

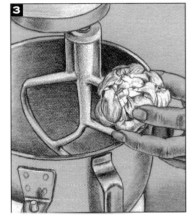

JUICING A POMEGRANATE

Pomegranate juice is delicious by itself and makes a wonderful tart-sweet addition to many dishes. However, getting the juice out of the fruit can be difficult. Here's a tip from Kelly Salloum of Los Angeles, California, that makes it easier.

1. Place the pomegranate on the counter, and roll the fruit back and forth to burst the pockets of juice beneath the thick skin. Be careful not to break the skin as you roll it.

2. With a small, sharp knife, cut around the stem of the fruit.

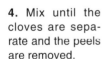

3. Remove the stem section.

4. Carefully turn the fruit upside down into a glass, and squeeze the pomegranate until all the juice is expelled.

WEIGHTING FOOD EVENLY

When weighting salted eggplant or cucumber to extract the liquid, it is difficult to apply weight evenly all across the surface of the food. Louis Schanerman of Verona, New Jersey, suggested this method: Place the vegetable in a colander. Fill a gallon-size plastic bag one half to two thirds full of water. Twist-tie the bag closed and use it as a weight.

CUTTING BUTTER INTO FLOUR

When you don't want to use the food processor to cut in butter, follow this tip from Linda McBrearty of Portland, Oregon. Using the large holes of your grater, grate frozen butter into the bowl containing the flour and other dry ingredients, then finish cutting in the butter with forks or a pastry cutter.

ATTENTION READERS: FREE SUBSCRIPTION FOR PUBLISHED TIPS. Do you have a unique tip you would like to share with other readers? We will provide a one-year complimentary subscription for each quick tip that we print. Send a description of your special technique to *Cook's Illustrated,* P.O. Box 569, Brookline Village, MA 02147-0569. Please write "Attention: Quick Tips" on the envelope and include your name, address, and daytime phone number. Unfortunately, we can only acknowledge receipt of tips that will be printed in the magazine. In case the same tip is received from two readers, the one postmarked first will be selected.

Rustic Country Bread

The secret to a well-muscled country loaf with a big-league chew and great crust is a very wet dough.

Flour, water, yeast, and salt. That's about as simple as it gets in the kitchen—or so I thought when I set out to discover a reliable home recipe for a crusty, rough-textured country bread. I was looking for the kind of bread that is a main course all by itself; the kind where the first bite hits you with a heady burst of crackle and chew, an inspired whiff of yeast, and a hint of sourness. I didn't want a tea party sandwich loaf; I wanted peasant cooking, the kind of bread that, when sliced and stuffed into a basket at a white-tablecloth restaurant, looks like Hercules at a tea party.

My first task was to determine which of the four types of country bread to test. The four different types result from four different methods of leavening the bread: with a natural starter (a mixture of flour and water left out for twenty-four hours, during which time the mixture attracts yeast spores from the air); a mixed starter (a piece of dough reserved from a previously made batch); a standard yeast starter (packaged yeast mixed into the dough at the beginning); or a sponge starter (a "sponge" of flour, water, and yeast, left to ferment and then combined with additional flour, water, and other ingredients).

The first and second methods are inconvenient for home cooks. The third method lacks the flavor I was looking for because there's no time for the flavor to develop. The last method proved to be a good compromise.

Finding the Secret to a Great Chew

In *Chez Panisse Cooking* (Random House, 1988), Paul Bertolli suggests making a sponge, covering it, and letting it sit out overnight before making the dough. I decided to follow this method. In his recipe, however, Bertolli uses only one quarter of the sponge as a starter, reserving the rest for use in future loaves. Since most home cooks don't have the patience to keep a starter going in the refrigerator, I decided to deviate from his recipe by using the entire sponge.

A muslin-lined wicker basket is an ideal place for bread to rise.

It worked well. As I had expected, there was more flavor than with a quick rise using a greater amount of packaged yeast. In fact, I only used half a teaspoon of dry yeast (most recipes call for up to a tablespoon) for six cups of flour. I also varied Bertolli's sponge recipe by increasing the amount of whole wheat flour to 50 percent for added flavor and texture.

Having figured out my sponge recipe, the next step was a trip to California, where I visited with Steve Sullivan at the Acme Bakery in Berkeley. Steve, formerly the bread baker for Chez Panisse, is no French-cuff yuppie. I was immediately struck by his total focus on the very *idea* of bread, to the exclusion of his physical surroundings, which consisted of a disheveled room above the bakery stuffed with an industrial-size washer and dryer, empty detergent bottles, and a garage sale–quality sofa and chair.

Steve echoed what many experts had told me: Bread with a high water content produces a chewier texture. However, like most bread professionals, Steve threw around water percentages like softballs.

Ed Behr, editor and publisher of the newsletter *The Art of Eating,* finally sat me down and explained it. To figure out the amount of water as a percentage of the flour (by weight), simply calculate the weight in grams of the water in the recipe (each cup of water weighs 237.5 grams) and divide that by the weight of the flour (a cup of flour weighs 130 grams), then multiply by 100.

From this conversation and from a seminar I attended in San Francisco led by Joe Ortiz, author of *The Village Baker* (Ten Speed Press, 1992) and Daniel Leader, author of *Bread Alone* (Morrow, 1993), I concluded that a water content of 68 percent would be about right. The theory was that the higher percentage of water—most bread recipes run around sixty percent—would make the bread chewier. I tried it, but with mediocre results. It was good bread, but it lacked the big-league chewiness I was seeking.

About this time, my wife came across Iggy's Bakery just outside of Boston. Their bread was perfect: very chewy, very crusty, and very flavorful. I rushed out to meet Igor, the chief baker, who reinforced my ideas about a wet dough. When I stuck my hand into his plastic vats of dough, I

Wet dough can be tricky to work with, but it results in bread with a texture so rough, chewy, and substantial that it is a meal all by itself.

found a sticky mass that would just about pour. Eureka! My idea of bread dough had always been a nonstick, satiny ball, easy to handle and more solid than liquid. But this stuff puddled and pulled; it shimmered and shook. Igor also told me that he used a mixture of three flours—high-protein, whole wheat, and rye—for reasons having to do with both flavor and texture. I rushed home to duplicate what I had seen.

First, I increased the water to near-dangerous levels, using two and one-half cups of water to six cups of flour, which brought the percentage of water to flour up to a whopping 76 percent, a percentage so high it borders on heresy. However, this high water content was slightly counteracted by the fact that 25 percent of the flour was whole wheat and rye. I had chosen them for flavor, but both flours also absorb more water than white flour does. The other 75 percent of the flour was a high-protein white flour borrowed from Igor.

Professional bakers use giant mixers and special shaping machines that can easily handle very moist dough. At home, the dough stuck to my hands, to the wooden counter, to the bowl, to the damp dishtowel, and even to the heavily floured peel (the long-handled paddle used to move

6 • COOK'S ILLUSTRATED • JANUARY/FEBRUARY 1995

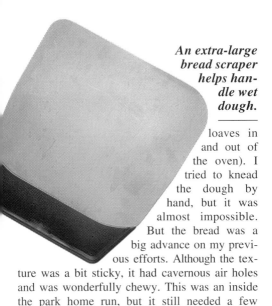

An extra-large bread scraper helps handle wet dough.

loaves in and out of the oven). I tried to knead the dough by hand, but it was almost impossible. But the bread was a big advance on my previous efforts. Although the texture was a bit sticky, it had cavernous air holes and was wonderfully chewy. This was an inside the park home run, but it still needed a few refinements.

High-Protein Flour Versus All-Purpose

I now turned my attention to the flour. Previously I had been using the high-protein flour (13.8 percent protein) that professional bakers use. Now I decided to try an all-purpose flour and a regular bread flour to see if the protein content had a noticeable effect on the finished loaf.

The results were fascinating. The dough made with regular bread flour, while wetter than that made with the high-protein flour, was workable; the all-purpose flour yielded a dough so wet that it couldn't be handled at all. After additional testing, it became clear that the higher-protein flour can absorb more water, so the recipe must be adjusted for different flours. When I reduced the amount of water to two and one-third cups for the bread flour and to two and one-quarter cups for the all-purpose flour, the results were fine. In fact, the regular bread flour was best, yielding a good, chewy crumb. In general, lower-protein flour produced a chewier, crustier loaf, while higher-protein flour produced a slightly more refined loaf. Dough made with all-purpose flour produced a loaf that was unpleasantly tough.

How to Knead and Handle a "Stickum" Dough

While it can be done (*see* instructions on page 9), kneading by hand was not my first choice. To get around it, I first tried using a food processor with the metal blade. This worked fine, except that my $250 machine sounded like a lawn mower in a dense patch of weeds; all that was missing was the curl of blue smoke and the smell of burning rubber. The machine simply could not handle eight and a half cups of quicksand. So I divided the recipe into two batches and tried again. This worked pretty well. I found that leaving the metal blade in the processor between batches is best (although you won't get all of the first batch out of the processor bowl). Otherwise your hands will get sticky, and dough may ooze out around the center core of the bowl during the second batch. Also, I found that the machine worked fine for the first twenty-five to thirty seconds and then started to slow down. My processor can *just* handle the

load (although it seemed compelled to walk across the counter like a dog off its leash). I recommend you process for no more than thirty seconds, which is enough time to knead the dough. And I recommend this method only if you have a good-quality, heavy-duty processor.

The best way to knead the dough was with a heavy-duty countertop mixer with a dough hook. Using this, I simply threw in the ingredients, mixed them briefly with a large, stiff rubber spatula, and then turned the machine on at its lowest setting for fifteen minutes. When the kneading was done, I transferred the dough to an oiled bowl and let it rise for about two hours until it tripled in volume. Allowing the dough to triple in volume improves its flavor and helps it develop more "muscle" so that it maintains its shape.

Even after the dough was mixed and kneaded, it was a problem to handle. For the first rise, you can use a rubber spatula to transfer the wet dough to an oiled bowl or plastic tub. After letting the dough rise, use the same spatula to transfer the dough onto a lightly floured surface. Flour both the dough (lightly) and your hands, then press the dough very gently into a disk and fold it over (*see* steps 1 through 5, page 8). Note that you should handle the dough as little as possible at this point, both because it is still a little sticky (you'll be tempted to add extra flour) and because excessive handling is bad for rustic bread—you want an irregular texture with lots of air holes. This goes for all bread making: Strong kneading after the first rise will harm the dough's delicate structure.

Incidentally, from here on out, the best way

to move the dough is to use a large dough scraper (*see* Sources and Resources, page 32, for mail-order information), two metal spatulas, or a thin, floured cookie sheet.

Line a colander or basket with a piece of muslin or linen or a cotton pastry cloth into which plenty of flour has been rubbed to prevent sticking (*see* "Shortcuts, Tips, and Advice," below). (You can also purchase a *banneton* that is pre-lined with linen—*see* Sources and Resources, page 32.)

The dough now needs to be covered during the second rise. I tried using a damp dish towel as a cover, but it stuck to the dough, and unwrapping it was like unwrapping a piece of saltwater taffy on a hot day. Aluminum foil works best for two reasons: The dough is less likely to stick to it, and, since it is laid loosely over the bowl and does not form a tight seal like plastic wrap, it allows the dough to breathe. This in turn causes the dough to rise less, which is important because allowing the dough to rise too much at this point will produce a dough with a fluffy texture that will lose its shape when transferred to the peel.

Salt and Honey

I also wanted to experiment with varying the amount of salt as well as testing the effect of other ingredients. Most recipes with six cups of flour

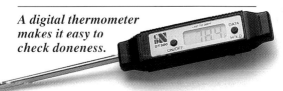

A digital thermometer makes it easy to check doneness.

SHORTCUTS, TIPS, AND ADVICE

➣ Cornmeal is vastly better than flour for coating a peel, especially when working with a wet dough. Use a very quick backward jerk to slide the loaf off the peel.

➣ For an even denser bread, let the dough rise only about 75 percent during the second rise (not double). In my kitchen, where the bread rises on a rack on top of a warm oven, this takes thirty to forty-five minutes.

➣ You can experiment with this recipe by adding or subtracting flour. A wetter dough always produces a better crust and more air holes. A drier dough is easier to handle but also gives you a thinner crust and a more refined texture. Try adding or subtracting white flour a quarter-cup at a time from the dough recipe.

➣ Muslin comes in differ-

ent grades from fine (about $2.99 per yard) to coarse (about $1.50 per yard). To line your bread-rising basket, use the cheaper variety and make sure that it is 100 percent cotton and unbleached. A real *banneton* has the linen or muslin sewn to the basket. The basket I used was four inches high, seven inches wide across the bottom, and twelve inches wide across the top. A colander also works well because it allows air to reach all sides of the dough (the dough is more likely to stick to the muslin when it's sitting in a bowl).

➣ In place of a muslin cloth, you can use a 100 percent cotton pastry cloth (*see* Sources and Resources, page 32, for a supplier) to line the colander. The cloth that I used measures twenty-four by nineteen inches.

Simply lay it out on a flat surface and then rub three-quarters of a cup of flour into it. Make sure that the entire cloth is covered and that the flour is really worked in. Then lay it in the colander.

➣ Inevitably, the crust will start to lose its crunch, especially in humid weather. Just pop the loaf back into a 400-degree oven for up to ten minutes to restore it.

➣ Rising times vary a great deal depending on temperature and other factors, including the amount of yeast spores in the air. A professional bakery is always humid and is crawling with yeast, so the bread will rise far more quickly there than in a home kitchen.

➣ A serrated knife works well for slashing the top of a large loaf of bread before baking.

SHAPING THE DOUGH FOR RISING

To form this wet dough into a disk for rising, simply fold the dough into the middle from the top, right, bottom, and left sequentially, then gather it loosely together.

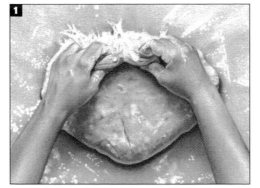

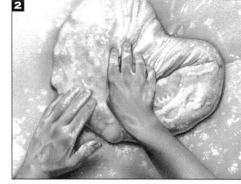

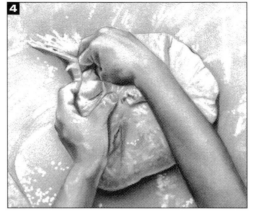

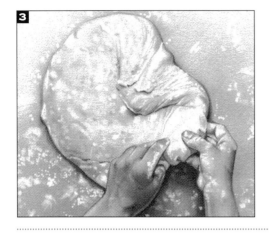

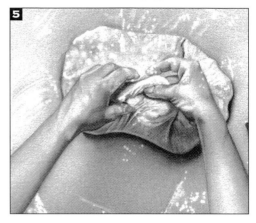

use two teaspoons of salt. I found this amount of salt insufficient and boosted it to a full tablespoon. I use kosher salt, not regular table salt, and there is a difference; if you have only regular table salt, use two teaspoons.

Next, I decided to try a little sweetness to boost flavor and promote browning. I added two tablespoons of barley malt (which I subsequently changed to honey for the sake of convenience). The flavor was better with the sweetener, and the crust was a rich nut-brown.

Does Steam Make a Better Crust?

The last major issue was the texture of the crust. The key to a great crust, according to most of the experts, is steam. To test this theory, we baked one loaf with no steam at all. The crust was thin and unappealing.

The truth is that bread does need steam, but there are many options. Some bakers throw ice cubes on the floor of the oven. Others pour hot water into a pan in the oven at the beginning of baking. Some use a spritzer to mist the outside of

the dough every few minutes.

My tests showed that hot water is the best option. This was confirmed by Steve Sullivan, who noted that it takes 225 calories to turn a gram of ice into steam but only 120 calories to turn an equal amount of tap water into steam. So why throw ice into an oven, where you want lots of heat? Our tests confirmed that ice cubes lower oven temperature much more than hot water. A head-to-head test also proved that you get a better crust with hot water than with ice cubes.

As a side note, if you count yourself among the ice cube flingers, be aware that you could blow out the heating element in an electric oven if you don't throw the ice cubes into a container (this also goes for throwing tap water onto the floor of the oven).

And speaking of containers, I place my water for steaming in a small *preheated* pan placed on a separate, lower rack in the oven. The theory among bread pros is that you want steam immediately, in the first few minutes of baking. A cold pan will not do the trick—the hot water will just sit there. A preheated pan, however, will vaporize some of the hot water the second it is poured in. By using two cups of water, you get both instant steam and enough residual water to keep a nice steamy environment throughout the baking process.

Since water vaporizes as soon as it hits the heated pan, wear thick oven mitts and a long-sleeved shirt when pouring the hot water into the pan.

Finally, we tested spritzing the bread every few minutes. The results were poor—a thin, pliable crust. So use hot water, preheat the pan, and, most important of all, no peeking! If you open the door in the first twenty minutes of baking, you'll let out the steam.

WHAT ABOUT LA CLOCHE?

La cloche is an ancient tool for baking. It consists of a "bell" eleven inches wide by five inches high. It is made of unglazed pottery and sits on a one-inch-high tart-shaped pan made of the same material. It was designed as a portable oven; embers were placed around the cloche, which created a moist, even cooking environment inside. Although the cloche method was mentioned by a number of professional bakers I interviewed, only one had tried it.

The theory is that a closed environment is moister than a regular oven and therefore the crust should be superior. I started by soaking the bell portion of the cloche for half an hour to add extra moisture. I then transferred the risen dough to the bottom section of the cloche, which had been liberally coated with cornmeal, then put on the top. I then set the contraption in the oven.

The results were disappointing. The bread cooked much more slowly than in a standard oven, and the resulting loaf had a thin, pliable crust. The color of the crust was uneven, more of an orange-brown than the desired deep blackish-brown. Although I have heard bakers recommend this device (James Beard approved of it, and Steve Sullivan tried it once with excellent results), the cloche, as tested, does not ring any bells in my kitchen.

ILLUSTRATIONS BY MICHELE AMATRULLA

Oven Temperature and Baking Time

Most bread recipes say that bread should be baked to an internal temperature of 190 degrees. This produces undercooked bread, at least with this very wet recipe. This bread needs to reach 210 degrees. You can measure this by pushing an instant-read thermometer halfway into the loaf from the bottom. When the bread reaches this temperature, it should also have a very dark brown crust. If you do not have an instant-read thermometer, just bake the bread until the crust starts to turn brownish-black in spots.

I also tried starting the bread off in a 500-degree oven and then immediately turning the oven down to 400 degrees, on the theory that the higher temperature offsets the drop in temperature caused by opening the oven door (the dough absorbs a great deal of heat quickly). The resulting crust was thin and disappointing. So I tried starting the bread off at 500 degrees for fifteen minutes and then reducing the temperature to 400. This time the crust was scorched—it cooked so fast that the interior did not have time to cook properly. The best baking temperature turned out to be a constant 450 degrees.

RUSTIC COUNTRY BREAD
Makes 1 large round loaf

Whole wheat and rye flours contribute to this bread's full flavor, and extra oven time gives the bread its thick crust. Because of its high water content, the bread will be gummy if it is undercooked. To check doneness, make sure its internal temperature has reached 210 degrees by inserting an instant-read thermometer halfway through the loaf from the bottom. Also look at the crust—it should be very dark brown, almost black. Because the dough is so sticky, a heavy-duty countertop mixer is best for kneading, but food processor and hand-kneading instructions follow this recipe. Keep in mind that rising times vary, and the times listed below are minimums. You can vary the bread's texture by increasing or decreasing the amount of flour. For bread with a finer crumb and a less chewy texture, experiment with increasing the flour in one-fourth-cup increments. For coarser, chewier bread, decrease the flour one-fourth cup at a time. Your oven will give a much

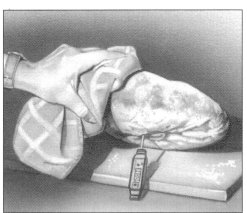

To check bread for doneness, remove it from the oven and use a digital thermometer to check the temperature.

To help ensure a good crust, preheat a pan, fill it with warm water, and set it on the oven's lower rack.

more even heat if you lay out a baking platform of quarry tiles on the rack before preheating. If you decide to do this, preheating will take longer.

The Sponge
- ½ teaspoon active dry yeast (not rapid-rise)
- 1 cup bread flour
- 1 cup whole wheat flour

The Dough
- 3½ cups bread flour
- ½ cup rye flour
- 2 tablespoons honey
- 1 tablespoon kosher salt or 2 teaspoons table salt
  Coarse cornmeal for sprinkling on peel

1. *For the sponge,* dissolve yeast into 1 cup tap water in medium-size bowl. Mix in flours with rubber spatula to create stiff, wet dough. Cover with plastic wrap; let sit at room temperature for at least 5 hours, preferably overnight. (Can be refrigerated up to 24 hours; return to room temperature before continuing with recipe.)

2. *For the dough,* mix flours, 1⅓ cups tap water, honey, and sponge with rubber spatula in the bowl of an electric mixer. Knead, using dough hook attachment, on lowest speed until dough is smooth, about 15 minutes, adding salt during final 3 minutes. Transfer dough to large, lightly oiled bowl. Cover with plastic wrap; let rise until tripled in size, at least 2 hours.

3. Turn dough onto lightly floured surface. Lightly dust hands and top of dough with flour. Following illustrations 1 through 5, on page 8, lightly press dough into a large disk. Fold toward center, overlapping edges slightly. Using a large metal dough scraper or two metal spatulas, transfer dough, smooth side down, to colander or basket lined with heavily floured muslin. Cover loosely with large sheet of aluminum foil; let rise

until almost doubled in size, at least 45 minutes.

4. As soon as dough begins to rise, adjust oven rack to low-center position and arrange quarry tiles on rack to form 18-by-12-inch surface (or larger). On lowest oven rack, place small baking pan or cast-iron skillet to hold water. Heat oven to 450 degrees.

5. Sprinkle coarse cornmeal liberally over entire surface of peel. Invert dough onto peel and remove muslin. Use scissors or serrated knife to cut three slashes on top of dough.

6. Slide dough from peel onto tiles. Wearing oven mitts and a long-sleeved shirt, carefully add 2 cups hot water to pan or cast-iron skillet. Bake until instant-read thermometer inserted in bread registers 210 degrees and crust is very dark brown, 35 to 40 minutes, turning bread around after 25 minutes if not browning evenly. Turn oven off, open door, and let bread remain in oven 10 minutes longer. Remove from oven, then let cool to room temperature before slicing, about 2 hours. To crisp crust, warm in 400-degree oven for 10 minutes.

To knead in food processor, mix half of sponge, half of flours, and half of honey in food processor fitted with the metal blade. Pulse until roughly blended, three or four 1-second pulses. With machine running, slowly add ⅔ cup water through the feed tube; process until dough forms a ball. Let sit for 3 minutes, then add half the salt, and process to form smooth dough, about 30 seconds longer. Transfer dough to large, lightly oiled bowl, leaving metal blade in processor (some dough will remain under blade). Repeat process with remaining half of ingredients. Proceed with recipe.

To knead by hand, place sponge and all dough ingredients, except 2 cups of bread flour, in large bowl. Stir mixture with a wooden spoon, about 5 minutes. Work in reserved flour and turn dough out onto floured board. Knead by hand 5 minutes, incorporating no more than ¼ cup additional flour. Dough will be *very* wet and sticky. Proceed with recipe.

Note: Regular supermarket bread flour has 12 percent protein content, whereas the flour I prefer to use is closer to 14 percent. If you wish to use this high-protein flour, increase the water in the dough from 1⅓ cups to 1½ cups. You might also try making this recipe with King Arthur all-purpose flour (11 percent protein content) by decreasing the water from 1½ cups to 1¼ cups. The results are good, although I find the bread to be a bit tougher than I like. ■

How to Quick-Cook Strong-Flavored Greens

For best results with assertive greens such as mustards, collards, turnips, and kale, give them a rough chop and a quick plunge into shallow boiling water before quick-cooking.

~ BY PAM ANDERSON WITH KAREN TACK ~

As a Southerner, I grew up on mustard greens, collard greens, and turnip greens. Like all respectable southern vegetables back then, these greens weren't considered properly cooked unless they had simmered all morning on the back burner. In fact, they were considered done only when the tough rind on the fatback had cooked to the soft texture of the fat itself.

I live in the North now, but like my southern accent, my craving for greens and cornbread kicks in at the Virginia border. Nevertheless, I no longer cook greens like my mother did. It has nothing to do with health. According to food scientist and cooking teacher Shirley Corriher, the vitamin loss from slow-cooked greens is the pot likker's gain, and as for fat, the average ham hock (enough to flavor a huge pot of greens) releases only two and one half tablespoons of fat when boiled. Nor does it have anything to do with flavor—braised greens with pot likker and cornbread still rate high on my list of favorite dishes.

Instead, my change in cooking technique has to do with time and place. Right or wrong, I associate southern-style, slow-cooked greens with an era when cooks spent all morning in the kitchen, served the big meal at lunch, and a bowl of greens was only one of the many seasonal vegetables on a table laden with meats, cornbread, and sweet tea. This style of greens just doesn't go with the food I serve these days. For years I avoided them except on New Year's Day, when even lapsed Southerners eat them—as the ritual goes—to ensure prosperity in the coming year. I needed to find a new way to cook greens.

Bone Dry, Burned, and Bitter

As I pointed out in "Cooking Tender Greens" (September/October 1994), greens divide themselves quite naturally into two categories. In one camp are the tender greens like spinach, Swiss chard, and beet greens, which cook quickly over high heat and take to almost any spice or aromatic. Then there are the more assertively flavored greens like mustard greens, turnip greens, collards, and kale. These present more of a challenge—they demand a different cooking method, and to my taste their strong flavors clash with all but a select few seasonings.

I discovered early on that kale, turnips, collards, and mustards were too tough, too bitter, and too dry to be wilted in a skillet with only the clinging rinse water for liquid. This method, which worked perfectly with tender greens, often scorched the bottom leaves of these tougher greens and left the leaves on top uncooked. Placing the greens on a steamer basket over simmering water kept the leaves from burning, but it didn't help leach out their bitterness nor did it prevent them from turning a much duller shade of green.

The microwave was even worse than steaming, accentuating rather than taming the negative features of the tough greens. After five minutes, two cups of packed greens partially covered with plastic film were leathery, bitter, and dry. The microwave seemed to suck out their moisture without actually wilting them. Oddly, it also turned them an unattractive, jaundice green.

After unsuccessful attempts at wilting, steaming, and microwaving, I finally decided these tougher greens needed to be cooked with liquid. The question was how *much* liquid? And how long did they need to cook in it?

Greens blanched in large quantities of salted water had a lot going for them. They were tender,

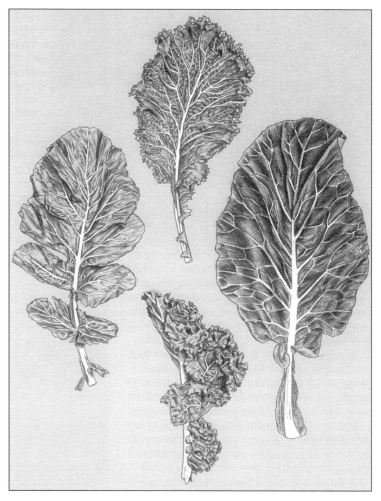

Kale, turnip, mustard, and collard greens (clockwise from bottom) all share certain basic characteristics. Unlike their more tender cousins—such as spinach, Swiss chard, and beet greens—these more assertive greens need to be softened and have some of their bitterness removed before being sautéed.

brilliantly colored, and less bitter than those cooked by other methods; also the salt in the water rounded out their flavor. However, blanching was not ideal. Once boiled, drained, rinsed, and squeezed, the greens had lost much of their individual character and tasted rather pallid and generic.

So I tried cooking them in small quantities of

ILLUSTRATION BY ALAN WITSCHONKE/PHOTOGRAPHS BY ERIC ROTH

water. I started by cooking leaves from one pound of greens in one cup salted water, checking at five and then again at seven minutes. The five-minute leaves had a sharp, raw bite and were starting to acquire that dull look. The seven-minute greens were fully cooked, but still tasted bitter. I therefore decided to double the water from one to two cups. The greens cooked in this quantity of water weren't as grossly bitter as those cooked in only one cup of liquid, but they were still a bit too bold. On the verge of settling for conventional blanching, I decided to give this shallow-cook method one more shot by once again doubling the water from two cups to a quart, and cooking the greens the full seven minutes. The resulting greens offered the balance I was looking for: good color, full flavor without bitterness, and a tender green, ready for a quick, final cooking to unite them with other flavorful ingredients.

When you think about it, it stands to reason that a shallow blanch would work best with these greens. The more water you use when blanching porous vegetables, the more diluted the flavor of the vegetable becomes. That's one reason why steaming is the preferred way to cook so many vegetables—you want as little of the flavor as possible to escape into the cooking liquid. These greens are different. You want to rid them of some of their bitterness, but not all of it. A shallow blanching erases enough bitterness to make these assertive greens palatable, but not so much as to rob them of their character.

Shallow blanching not only preserves the greens' color and flavor, it also saves time. I was surprised to learn that, on our stove, a gallon of water took almost twenty minutes to boil. Two quarts (the amount you need to cook greens for four) could be brought to boil in half that time.

I found that cut leaves cook faster than whole ones, but the leaves are much easier to cut when cooked. The tremendous bulk of the raw greens meant that, if I wanted to chop them in the food processor, I had to do it in several batches. It was a messy, clumsy process, and in the end the greens were chopped much too fine for my taste. However, the alternative—tediously stacking two gallons of leaves in batches, rolling them up like big cigars, and cutting them into ribbons with a knife—seemed like a waste of time when seven minutes later the same leaves would be boiled down to a far more manageable two cups. I found it much simpler to rough-chop them with a knife before blanching. Then after blanching it was easy to cut the dramatically shrunken greens with a knife as fine as I liked in order to speed up their cooking the second time around. Speeding up their cooking time was important because greens start to lose their color if they're cooked too long.

Once assertive greens have been shallow blanched, they can be cooked in five minutes following one of the recipes below. Serve them with roast pork or lamb. They're great with chicken and meaty, firm-fleshed fish as well. Quick-cooked greens, as the following recipes demonstrate, can also be tossed with pasta or stirred into beans for a quick and satisfying meal.

BASIC SHALLOW-BLANCHED GREENS
Makes about 2 cups

1½ teaspoons salt
2 pounds assertive greens, such as kale, collards, mustard, or turnip greens; stemmed, washed in 2 or 3 changes of clean water, and coarsely chopped

Bring 2 quarts water to boil in soup kettle or large, deep sauté pan. Add salt and greens; stir until wilted. Cover and cook until greens are just tender, about 7 minutes; drain in colander. Rinse kettle or pan with cold water to cool, then refill with cold water. Pour greens into cold water to stop cooking process. Gather handful of greens, lift out of water, and squeeze until only droplets fall from them. Repeat with remaining greens. Roughly cut each bunch of greens. Proceed with one of the following recipes.

QUICK-COOKED GREENS WITH GARLIC AND RED PEPPER FLAKES
Serves 4

2 large garlic cloves, thinly sliced
¼ teaspoon hot red pepper flakes
3 tablespoons vegetable oil
2 cups Basic Shallow-Blanched Greens (see above)
⅓–½ cup chicken stock or low-sodium chicken broth
Salt
Lemon wedges

In a large sauté pan, heat garlic and pepper flakes with oil over medium heat until garlic starts to sizzle. Add greens; sauté to coat with oil. Add ⅓ cup stock; cover and cook over medium-high heat, adding more stock during cooking if necessary, until greens are tender and juicy and most of stock has been absorbed, about 5 minutes. Serve.

QUICK-COOKED GREENS WITH PROSCIUTTO
Serves 4

Follow recipe for Quick-Cooked Greens with Garlic and Red Pepper Flakes (see above), but after garlic starts to sizzle stir in 1 ounce thin-sliced prosciutto cut crosswise into thin strips. Add greens and continue with recipe, stirring ¼ teaspoon minced lemon zest into greens just before serving.

QUICK-COOKED GREENS WITH RED BELL PEPPER
Serves 4

Follow recipe for Quick-Cooked Greens with Garlic and Red Pepper Flakes (see above), but heat the oil and sauté ½ thinly sliced red bell pepper, until softened, about 4 minutes. Then add garlic and hot red pepper flakes, and continue with recipe.

QUICK-COOKED GREENS WITH BLACK OLIVES AND LEMON ZEST
Serves 4

Follow recipe for Quick-Cooked Greens with Garlic and Red Pepper Flakes (see above), but after garlic starts to sizzle stir in ⅓ cup pitted, coarse-chopped black olives (oil-cured or brine-soaked). Add greens and continue with recipe, stirring in ¼ teaspoon minced lemon zest just before serving.

QUICK-COOKED GREENS WITH BACON AND ONION
Serves 4

2 bacon slices (about 2 ounces), cut crosswise into thin strips
Vegetable oil
½ medium onion, chopped fine
2 garlic cloves, minced
2 cups Basic Shallow-Blanched Greens (see above), chopped medium
⅓–½ cup chicken stock or low-sodium chicken broth
2 teaspoons cider vinegar
Salt

1. Fry bacon in a large sauté pan over medium-low heat until crisp, 4 to 5 minutes. Remove bacon with slotted spoon and set aside. If necessary, add oil to bacon drippings to bring up to 2 tablespoons. Add onion and garlic; sauté until softened, 4 to 5 minutes.

2. Add greens; sauté, stirring, to coat with oil. Add stock, cover and cook over medium high heat until greens are tender and most of stock has been absorbed, about 5 minutes. Sprinkle greens

with vinegar and bacon bits; season with salt if necessary. Serve.

PENNE WITH QUICK-COOKED GREENS AND PROSCIUTTO
Serves 4

This pasta dish is equally good if made with Quick-Cooked Greens with Black Olives and Lemon Zest (*see* page 13), increasing the chicken broth from one-third to two-thirds cup.

- 1 recipe Quick-Cooked Greens with Prosciutto (*see* page 13), increasing prosciutto from 1 to 2 ounces and chicken stock from ⅓ to ⅔ cup
- 1 tablespoon salt
- 12 ounces dried penne or rigatoni
- ¼ cup grated Parmesan cheese

Prepare Quick-Cooked Greens with Prosciutto. Meanwhile, in large soup kettle, bring 1 gallon water to boil. Add salt and pasta; cook until al dente, 9 to 10 minutes. Drain pasta, then return to soup kettle; add greens and toss. Transfer portion of pasta to each of four pasta bowls; pass Parmesan cheese separately.

QUICK-COOKED GREENS WITH BACON AND BLACK-EYED PEAS
Serves 4 as a main course

- 1 recipe Quick-Cooked Greens with Bacon and Onion (*see* page 13), increasing bacon to 4 slices
- 1 recipe Cooked Dried Beans (*see* below), using black-eyed peas and reserving 1 cup liquid from beans

Prepare Quick-Cooked Greens with Bacon and Onion. Just before adding vinegar and bacon, stir in black-eyed peas and 1 cup reserved cooking liquid. Bring to simmer; cover and cook to blend flavors, about 5 minutes. Adjust seasoning. Ladle portion of beans and greens into each of four soup plates; dress each with portion of vinegar and bacon bits. Serve.

QUICK-COOKED GREENS WITH WHITE BEANS AND ROSEMARY
Serves 4 as a main course

If you're short on time, you can substitute two cans (nineteen ounces total) drained and rinsed cannellini beans and one cup chicken stock for the cooked dried beans called for in the recipe.

- 1 recipe Quick-Cooked Greens with Garlic and Red Pepper Flakes (*see* page 13)
- 1 teaspoon fresh rosemary, minced
- 1 recipe Cooked Dried Beans (*see* below), using Great Northern beans and reserving 1 cup liquid from beans
  Grated Parmesan cheese (optional)

Prepare Quick-Cooked Greens with Garlic and Red Pepper Flakes, adding rosemary with garlic and red pepper flakes. Stir in beans and 1 cup reserved cooking liquid. Bring to simmer; cover and simmer to blend flavors, about 5 minutes. Adjust seasoning. Ladle a portion of beans and greens into each of four soup plates; pass Parmesan cheese separately.

COOKED DRIED BEANS
Makes 3 cups drained beans

- ½ pound dried black-eyed peas or large white beans (such as Great Northern beans), soaked until rehydrated, overnight or at least 4 hours
- 1 bay leaf
- 4 whole garlic cloves
- 1½ teaspoons salt

Bring peas or beans, bay leaf, garlic, and 7 cups water to simmer in large saucepan. Simmer, partially covered, until beans are just tender, 30 to 40 minutes. Remove from heat, stir in salt, cover, and let beans stand until completely tender, about 15 minutes. Drain, reserve cooking liquid, and discard bay leaf and garlic. (Beans in liquid can be cooled, covered, and refrigerated up to 5 days.) ∎

HOW MUCH IS A POUND OF GREENS?

The following measurements are based on one pound of uncleaned greens.

Greens	Quantity	Yield	Yield Cooked
Kale	9 ounces stems 7 ounces leaves	7 cups lightly packed raw leaves	1¼ cups cooked and lightly squeezed leaves
Mustard Greens	7½ ounces stems 8½ ounces leaves	7 cups lightly packed raw leaves	Scant 1 cup cooked and lightly squeezed leaves
Collard Greens	9½ ounces stems 6½ ounces leaves	7 cups lightly packed raw leaves	1 cup cooked and lightly squeezed leaves
Turnip Greens	8 ounces stems 8 ounces leaves	7 cups lightly packed raw leaves	Scant 1 cup cooked and lightly squeezed leaves

---

STEMMING ASSERTIVE GREENS

Collard, kale, and mustard greens are best stemmed by holding the leaves over a sink of clean water and slashing down each side of the stem with a sharp knife.

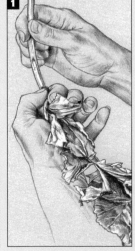

1. Turnip greens have many leaves on the stem. They are most easily stemmed by grasping the leaves between your thumb and index finger at the base of the stem and stripping them off by hand.

2. When using this method, the very tip of the stem will break off along with the leaves. It is tender enough to cook along with the leaves.

ILLUSTRATIONS BY ALAN WITSCHONKE

Spice-Infused Oils

Infusions with deep, vibrant flavors depend on using the right temperature oil with each individual spice.

∽ BY MINDY SCHREIL ∽

We've all seen flavored oils in gourmet shops. By making your own versions, however, you can save money and end up with oils with superior flavor.

But why make these oils at all? Why not just chop herbs, grate citrus peel, or grind some spices while you're cooking? Well, once you've taken the time to make a range of infused oils tailored to your cooking needs, it's not necessary to chop, roast, or grind anything—just add a drizzle of oil and you will have instant flavor. A little infused oil may be all you need to season a dish, and it also gives you a quick way to enliven vinaigrettes, sauces, and marinades.

When herbs are in season, creating infused oils is an excellent method of preserving their flavor. During winter months, make oils infused with dried spices, which are always readily available.

The Keys: Oil Type and Temperature

In developing recipes for infused oils, I wanted to showcase each infusion's distinct flavoring. Therefore, it made sense to choose oils that were fairly neutral. I started with the oils I was most familiar with: canola, olive, corn, and peanut.

Some spices worked well with olive oil, but ginger tasted strange when made with this oil; it needed a more neutral base. Corn and peanut oils worked well too, but my favorite base turned out to be canola oil. It complimented every flavoring and had a clean taste and consistency that appealed to me. As an added bonus, it has the least saturated fat of all the oils.

Once I knew which oil to use, I faced the task of finding the best method for infusing it. I started out assuming that hot oil would best bring out the flavors, so I ground every spice I could get my hands on and measured them all into bubbling pots of oil. But I was not happy with the results. The high heat made ground spices bitter.

So I stopped heating the oil and went to the other extreme. Again I chopped the spices, this time pouring room-temperature oil over everything. This time, my patience was rewarded, as ground spices responded perfectly when treated in this gentle manner.

There were some exceptions, though. Oils made using the cold-oil method with ginger, chile peppers, and peppercorns were bland. Heat was required to activate these ingredients. For them the winning method turned out to be a middle-of-the-road approach. Starting with oil heated to 350 degrees, I worked my way down to 140 degrees, which turned out to be hot enough to release the flavors in peppers and ginger, but low enough that it did not make them bitter.

I also experimented with roasting whole spices in a skillet, then grinding them and infusing the oil. This worked well. However, I also found that I got very good results by using high-quality spices that I ground without roasting. So my advice is that you can skip the roasting step if you wish, but buy your spices whole and grind them at home in a spice grinder, coffee mill, or with a mortar and pestle.

MASTER METHOD FOR WARM OIL INFUSING

1. Combine oil and flavorings from chart below in noncorrosive, heavy-bottomed pan. Starting on lowest heat possible, bring oil temperature to 140 degrees (use deep-fry or candy thermometer to gauge temperature), and maintain temperature for 10 minutes as oil weakly bubbles.

2. Carefully transfer oil and flavorings to bowl and cool to room temperature. Let sit for at least 1 day before using. Pour into a clean, tightly sealed glass jar and refrigerate. Use within 1 month.

MASTER METHOD FOR COLD OIL INFUSING

In stainless steel, glass, or ceramic bowl, combine oil and flavorings from chart below. Leave loosely covered with plastic wrap in a cool, dry place for 3 days. The oil may be used at this point. If making a ground spice oil, strain through two layers of cheesecloth and discard spice sediment. Pour oil into clean glass jars with snug-fitting lids. Keep refrigerated and use within 1 month. ∎

Mindy Schreil cooks professionally in the San Francisco Bay area and contributed to the *China Moon Cookbook* (Workman, 1993).

RECIPES FOR SPICE-INFUSED OILS

Each recipe uses 3 cups of oil. Any of the oils listed will work well.

FLAVORING	METHOD	TYPE OF OIL	AMOUNT OF SPICE
Allspice	cold oil	canola, corn, peanut, or olive	3 tablespoons ground allspice
Caraway	cold oil	canola, corn, peanut, or olive	¼ cup ground caraway seeds
Cardamom	cold oil	canola, corn, peanut, or olive	¼ cup ground cardamom
Clove	cold oil	canola, corn, peanut, or olive	3 tablespoons ground cloves
Coriander	cold oil	canola, corn, peanut, or olive	¼ cup ground coriander
Cumin	cold oil	canola, corn, peanut, or olive	3 tablespoons ground cumin
Curry	cold oil	canola, corn, peanut, or olive	¼ cup curry powder
Dried Hot Chile	warm oil	canola, corn, peanut, or olive	¼ cup dried, crushed red chiles
Fennel	cold oil	canola, corn, peanut, or olive	¼ cup ground fennel seeds
Ginger	warm oil	canola, corn, or peanut	1 cup peeled and very finely chopped fresh ginger
Peppercorn	warm oil	canola, corn, peanut, or olive	⅓ cup mixed cracked peppercorns (black, white, red, or green)

Forming Bread Shapes

Many bread loaf shapes have been developed over the centuries, evolving as regional variations, festive expressions, or simply as ways for one baker to distinguish his bread from that of a fellow baker down the road. Follow these step-by-step instructions from Joe Ortiz, author of *The Village Baker* (Ten Speed Press, 1993), to form five different shapes.

There are certain factors you might want to consider when choosing a loaf shape. The crown loaf, like the baguette, is designed for those who prefer more crust with their bread. The *épi* (ear of wheat) is a shape that makes it easy for guests to pull off a section as the loaf is passed around the table. *La tabatière* (the hat), a regional loaf from the Jura region of France, is traditionally made with sourdough. The *fers à cheval* (horseshoe) and the begonia are particularly decorative loaves suitable for centerpieces.

Make sure that you use a firm dough for most of these shapes, as it will help them keep a vivid, distinctive appearance. Very wet doughs, such as the dough for Rustic Country Bread (*see* page 9) are not suitable. ∎

CROWN LOAF

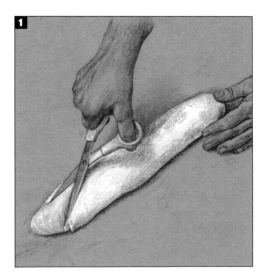

1. Begin with a round ball of dough that has been allowed to rest for 5 minutes after the initial shaping. Generously flour your elbow and press it down into the center of the loaf. When your elbow has gone through the dough to the table, make a circular motion to slowly expand the diameter of the hole through the dough.

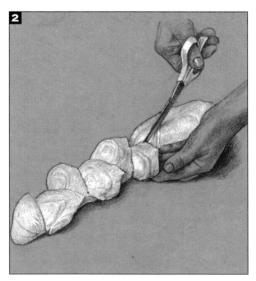

2. Use both hands to stretch the now-doughnut-shaped loaf so that the hole is 4 to 5 inches in diameter.

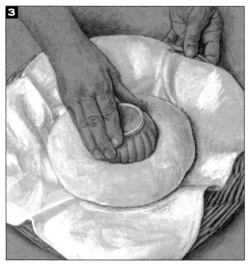

3. To help the dough keep its shape as it rises, place it in a basket lined with a floured dish towel made of linen or cotton, and place a teacup or round ramekin in the center hole.

EAR OF WHEAT

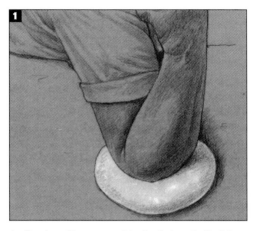

1. Shape the dough into a baguette. Using a sharp pair of scissors, cut down into the dough at a 45-degree angle, cutting almost through to the work surface.

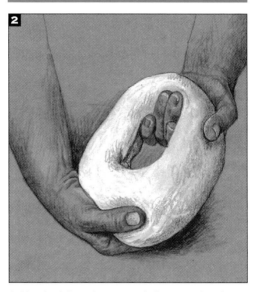

2. Make cuts about every 2 inches for the entire length of the loaf. Turn sections alternately to the left or right.

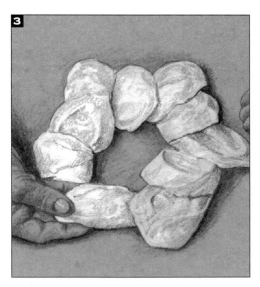

3. You can either bake the loaf straight or formed into a circle with the ends joined, as shown.

ILLUSTRATIONS BY ANATOLY

THE HAT	HORSESHOE	BEGONIA

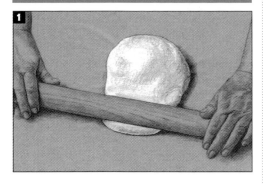

1. Start with a spherical loaf that has been allowed to rest for 5 minutes after the initial shaping. Push a rolling pin down into the middle of the loaf, and flatten out one side of the dough so that it is about ⅛ inch thick.

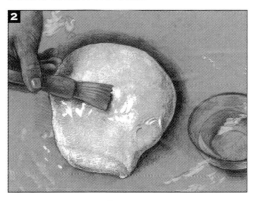

2. Using water or a glaze made of water and egg white, wet the unflattened part of the loaf.

3. Fold the flattened part of the loaf over the unflattened part.

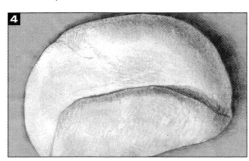

4. The flattened part should extend over slightly more than half of the unflattened part. The top will slide open an inch or two during baking.

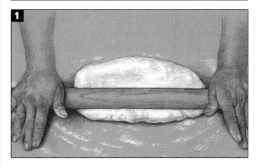

1. Roll out a baguette, let it rise, then dust it with a bit of flour. Push a rolling pin down across the middle of the loaf until it is tight against the work surface, then roll it forward slightly.

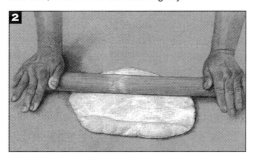

2. Roll the rolling pin back and forth several times in each direction, until you have formed a 3- to 4-inch flat section between two narrow baguette shapes.

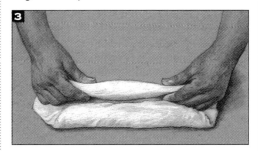

3. Use your hands to roll the two baguette shapes into the flat section so that they almost touch.

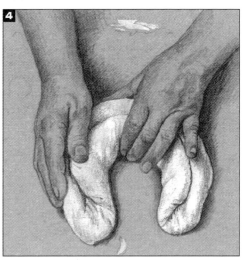

4. Form the loaf into a horseshoe shape, and dust it lightly with flour.

1. Start with a round loaf. Using a razor blade, make two curved slices directly down into the bread in the middle of the loaf; the two cuts should be about ½ inch apart and at least ½ inch deep.

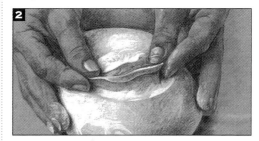

2. Using your thumb and forefinger, grasp the section of bread between the two cuts and pinch it together until it resembles a thin flower petal.

3. Make two more similar cuts on the opposite side of the loaf from the first cuts, and pinch the petals of dough together in a similar manner. Continue to make concentric cuts and pinch the dough into thin petal shapes, moving out toward the edge of the loaf.

4. When you're finished, the dough will resemble a begonia.

Braising Lamb Shanks

For shanks that are fall-off-the-bone tender and deeply flavorful, oven-braise in a mixture of wine and stock.

~ BY STEVE JOHNSON ~

One of the great pleasures of cooking is to take a relatively tough cut of meat and turn it into a meltingly tender dish. Among the most richly flavored of these tougher cuts is the lamb shank, which is simply the lower portion of a lamb's leg (see "Lamb Shank Types and Availability," page 19).

Like other cuts of meat from joints, such as oxtails or short ribs, lamb shanks are extremely flavorful when properly cooked. This is because they contain a high proportion of connective tissue and fat, which breaks down during cooking and adds flavor to the meat.

However, the presence of all this connective tissue and fat means that shanks can only be cooked using a long, slow, moist cooking method that will disintegrate the connective tissue and render the fat without drying out the meat. The only practical cooking method to achieve all this is braising, which means cooking the meat partially covered in liquid, usually in a closed container. Braising keeps the temperature of the meat relatively low—around the boiling point of water—for a long period of time, which is exactly what is needed to convert the tough collagen to tender gelatin.

Braising Details

While satisfactory results can be obtained by braising shanks on top of the stove, I prefer braising in the oven because in the enclosed space the heat comes from all directions. This provides more even heat, which is a particular advantage given that many pans have "hot spots" that cause them to heat unevenly on a burner.

Because of the high fat content of this particular cut of meat, it makes sense for the cook to take several precautions to keep the fat in the final

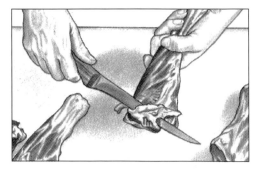

To minimize the amount of fat in the final product, be sure that before cooking you remove any excess fat as well as the white fell from the exterior of the shanks.

product to a minimum.

First, if your butcher hasn't already done so, it is helpful to take the time to trim off any excess fat that may be left on the exterior of the meat (see illustration, below). Even a long, slow braising will not successfully render all of the external fat on a lamb shank. Trimming it helps you get a jump on that potential problem.

If the shanks are well browned before you braise them, this also helps render some of the exterior fat. Browning has the added advantage of providing a great deal of flavor to the dish. When you brown the meat over high heat, a chemical change called the Maillard reaction takes place; carbohydrates react with amino acids to create a whole range of new compounds that not only turn the food brown, but also add many new flavors.

Be sure to drain the fat from the pan after browning. You should also remove the fat from the braising liquid after the shanks have been cooked. To do this, take the shanks out of the braising liquid, strain out the vegetables, and allow the liquid to rest undisturbed for a short while. Then, using a ladle, carefully skim off and discard the fat that rises to the surface. This process is easier if you transfer the liquid to a taller, narrower container before setting it aside to rest. If, after skimming the liquid, you find that it still contains too much fat, you can let the liquid rest for ten minutes and skim it again, although with most shanks this will not be necessary. If the meat is braised well in advance of serving, you can refrigerate the braising liquid and then simply lift the solidified fat from the top of the liquid.

Balancing the Acid

The braising liquid, along with the aromatics you include in it, will greatly enhance the flavor of the entire dish. Stock has traditionally been used as the braising liquid because it adds a textural richness as well as depth of flavor. I recommend using chicken stock rather than beef or veal stock, because these heartier stocks compete too much with the flavor of the lamb and tend to make the

Because it is a slow-cooked dish, one of the great pleasures in preparing lamb shanks comes midway through the cooking process, when your kitchen fills with the aroma of the dish.

sauce overly rich. A good chicken stock complements the flavor, and lamb shanks, because of their marrow, tend to "make their own sauce" as they cook.

Wine is a particularly good addition to the braising liquid, adding complexity and acid to the sauce. In this dish, the acid balance is particularly important. Too little acid creates a dull, rather flat dish. On the other hand, too much acid results in a rather harsh, off-putting flavor. After trying many different ratios, I find that two parts wine to three parts stock gives the flavor I like best.

Either white wine or red works, the difference being that red wine will give you a richer, deeper finish. You can also vary the choice of herbs and spices according to your taste. I have included several suggestions in the following recipes.

Whatever liquid you use for braising, it should cover all but the top inch of the shanks. This differs somewhat from classical braising, in which only a small amount of liquid is used. I adopted this method after leaving some shanks braising in the oven, then returning some time later to find that the liquid had boiled away and the shanks were burned. I had forgotten that, unless you use

ILLUSTRATION BY WENDY WRAY/PHOTOGRAPH BY ERIC ROTH

a true braising pan with an extremely tight-fitting lid, a fair amount of liquid will escape. Unless you're cooking with a professional-quality braising pan, I recommend you use the larger amount of liquid. In this department, it is better to have too much than too little.

Lamb shanks need not be served whole, though I prefer them this way for their dramatic appeal. But if you prefer, once the shanks have been cooked and cooled, you can remove the meat from the bone before re-incorporating it into the vegetables and sauce. The resulting stewlike dish will be less dramatic, but equally delicious.

LAMB SHANKS BRAISED IN RED WINE WITH HERBES DE PROVENCE
Serves 6

If you can't locate *herbes de Provence*, substitute a mixture of one teaspoon each of dried thyme, rosemary, and marjoram. If you're using smaller shanks than the ones called for in this recipe, reduce the braising time from one and one-half hours to one hour.

 6 lamb shanks (¾ to 1 pound each), trimmed of excess fat and fell (*see* illustration, page 18)
    Salt
 1 tablespoon canola oil
 2 medium onions, sliced thick
 3 medium carrots, peeled and cut crosswise into 2-inch pieces
 2 celery ribs, cut crosswise into 2-inch pieces
 4 garlic cloves, minced
 2 tablespoons tomato paste
 1 tablespoon herbes de Provence
 2 cups dry red wine
 3 cups chicken stock or low-sodium chicken broth
    Ground black pepper

1. Heat oven to 350 degrees. Sprinkle shanks with salt. Heat oil in a large, nonreactive sauté pan over medium-high heat. Add shanks to pan in batches if necessary to avoid overcrowding. Sauté until browned on all sides, 5 to 7 minutes. Using tongs, transfer shanks to a plate as they brown.

2. Drain all but 2 tablespoons of fat from pan; add onions, carrots, celery, garlic, tomato paste, 1 teaspoon of herbes de Provence, and light sprinkling of salt; sauté vegetables to soften slightly, 3 to 4 minutes. Add red wine, then chicken stock to pan, stirring with wooden spoon to loosen browned bits from bottom. Bring liquid to simmer; transfer vegetables and liquid into deep braising pan large enough to hold shanks in a single layer. Add shanks, season with salt, pepper, and remaining 2 teaspoons herbes de Provence.

3. Cover pan (with foil if pan has no lid) and transfer it to the oven; braise shanks for 1½ hours. Uncover and continue braising until shank tops are browned, about 30 minutes. Turn shanks and braise until other side is browned and shanks are fall-off-the-bone tender.

4. Remove pan from oven; let shanks rest for at least 15 minutes. With tongs, carefully transfer a shank to each of 6 plates. Arrange a portion of vegetables around each shank. Skim excess fat from braising liquid and adjust seasoning. Spoon braising liquid over each shank and serve.

BRAISED LAMB SHANKS WITH WHITE BEANS, SWISS CHARD, AND MARJORAM

Follow recipe for Lamb Shanks Braised in Red Wine with Herbes de Provence, making the following changes: Substitute 2 teaspoons minced fresh marjoram leaves (or 1 teaspoon dried) for the herbes de Provence and dry white wine for the red wine. After skimming excess fat from braising liquid, return the liquid and cooked vegetables to the braising pan. Add 1 recipe Cannellini Beans (*see* below); 3 ounces Swiss chard, cleaned, stemmed, and chopped coarse; and 1 additional teaspoon minced fresh marjoram. Cook over medium heat until greens wilt and flavors meld, about 5 minutes.

CANNELLINI BEANS
Makes 3 cups drained beans

 ½ pound dried cannellini beans, soaked until rehydrated, overnight or at least 4 hours
 1 bay leaf
 4 whole garlic cloves
 1½ teaspoons salt

Bring beans, bay leaf, garlic cloves, and 7 cups water to simmer in large saucepan. Simmer, partially covered, until beans are just tender, 30 to 40 minutes. Remove from heat, stir in salt, cover, and let beans stand until completely tender, about 15 minutes longer. Drain beans; discard bay leaf and garlic cloves; reserve cooking liquid.

BRAISED LAMB SHANKS WITH LEMON AND MINT

Follow recipe for Lamb Shanks Braised in Red Wine with Herbes de Provence, making the following changes: To the braising liquid, add 1 lemon, quartered, with zest removed, minced, and set aside. Substitute 1 tablespoon minced fresh mint leaves for the herbes de Provence and substitute dry white wine for the red wine. After skimming excess fat from braising liquid, stir in lemon zest and 1 additional tablespoon minced fresh mint leaves. Serve, if you like, with garlic-flavored mashed potatoes. (*See* "Making Perfect Mashed Potatoes," November/December 1993.)

BRAISED LAMB SHANKS WITH NORTH AFRICAN SPICES

Follow recipe for Lamb Shanks Braised in Red Wine with Herbes de Provence, making the following changes: Substitute 2 tablespoons *ras al hanout* (*see* recipe below) for herbes de Provence. Add 2 ancho chile peppers (or 2 or 3 jalapeños), stemmed, seeded, and minced, to the sautéing vegetables. Serve, if you like, with steamed couscous seasoned with one or more of the following: sautéed onion, lemon zest, parsley, mint, toasted almonds, or ras al hanout.

RAS AL HANOUT
Makes about ½ cup

 ½ teaspoon anise seeds
 1 teaspoon fennel seeds
 8 allspice berries
 8 cardamom pods
 15 black peppercorns
 1 cinnamon stick, about ½ inch long
 1 teaspoon coriander seeds
 ½ teaspoon cumin seeds
 ⅛ teaspoon red pepper flakes
 ⅛ teaspoon mace
 1 tablespoon ground ginger
 1 teaspoon ground nutmeg

In a spice grinder, combine all ingredients; grind to a fine powder. Transfer to small bowl. ∎

Steve Johnson is the chef at Mercury Bar in Boston.

LAMB SHANK TYPES AND AVAILABILITY

Logically enough, shanks can come either from the front legs (fore shanks) or back legs (hind shanks) of the lamb. The two shanks are basically interchangeable as far as cooking technique is concerned.

After speaking with a half dozen butchers, the consensus is that the hind shank is slightly more desirable. This is because, even though it is somewhat smaller (typically about one pound instead of one and one quarter pounds for a fore shank), the hind shank has more meat on it.

The forequarter has a higher proportion of bone. According to John Dewar, a wholesale/retail meat purveyor in Boston, Massachusetts, this is typical of four-legged animals.

However, this may be a moot point. Because hind shanks are usually sold as part of a leg of lamb, they are difficult to find. The fore shank is what you will almost always find in the grocery store.

Years ago lamb, like most other products, was seasonal, with the best lamb available only in the spring. Today lamb is available in a standard quality year-round. You should never have much of a problem finding it in the grocery store. However, Dewar also noted that lamb processing is primarily conducted on the East and West Coasts and in Chicago. Lamb is in high demand there and in larger cities, but the demand is less elsewhere in the country. Because of this, a consumer may be hard-pressed to locate lamb shanks in the Deep South.

Foolproof Polenta

The traditional method for preparing polenta is time-consuming and fraught with danger. Double-boiler polenta is still time-consuming—but it's foolproof.

~ BY SARAH FRITSCHNER ~

If your mother ever complained about slaving over a hot stove, she was probably talking about making polenta. Nothing more than cornmeal mush, polenta is made from dried, ground corn cooked in liquid until the starches in the corn have had enough time to hydrate and swell into soft, balloonlike structures. For many purposes, this soft stage is the most delicious way to serve polenta.

The stiff polenta you often see in restaurants starts out as a soft mass but is spread into a thin layer on a baking sheet or marble surface, cooled until stiff, sliced, and then sautéed, fried, or grilled to become croutonlike. These crisp rectangles are rarely more than a garnish. A smooth, piping-hot mound of soft polenta can be a meal. More commonly, soft polenta is used in Italy as a filler to stretch out meager game birds like quail, or to cut the rich earthiness of meats like sausages. Most stews and braised dishes—everything from ratatouille to braised rabbit—can also be ladled over a bowl of soft polenta.

Although making polenta sounds easy enough, the mixture can seize up during cooking, refusing to budge even when well-developed biceps are applied to the task. Cornmeal is a starch, and starch thickens when it's mixed with water and heated. On a warm day it doesn't take long to work up a sweat just trying to stir it. This is one reason why polenta is always served in cool weather and why cooks are always seeking ways to make preparing it easier.

Traditional Method Is Unreliable
The traditional Italian method for cooking polenta starts out as follows: Bring water to a boil in a heavy saucepan, add salt, bring the water to a boil again, stir it with a wooden spoon to create a vortex, then add the cornmeal gradually while continuing to stir to maintain the vortex. It can take up to ten minutes to add the polenta, but this stir-and-sprinkle method prevents lumps.

I found I could speed up this portion of the process—going from a painfully slow sprinkle to a relatively quick pour, but not to an instant dump—by using a whisk instead of the traditional wooden spoon.

Unfortunately, the whisk could not solve my real beef with polenta. Once the cornmeal has been added to the water, you must stir the mixture constantly, and I mean *constantly*, for thirty to forty-five minutes or "until it pulls away from the sides of the pan." (Cooking time will vary depending on how fast the water is boiling, the type and grind of cornmeal, and the ratio of water to corn.) In any case, within minutes you'll feel like you've been arm-wrestling Arnold Schwarzenegger, and thirty to forty-five minutes will begin to feel like forever.

Of course, this assumes you have avoided the biggest pitfall of all, the "seizing" problem at the beginning of cooking that indicates the cornmeal has cooked too fast. If you're new at polenta, you may think it's so thick (and difficult to stir) that it must be finished. More than likely, though, your polenta has cooked unevenly because the cornmeal was added too quickly or because the water was above a simmer. Seized polenta will be gummy and have a raw corn flavor; it is best tossed in the garbage.

Varying the Ingredients
To see if I could take some of the guesswork out of the traditional technique, I first tried playing around with the ingredients. There are only three ingredients in conventional polenta: water, salt, and cornmeal. I experimented by changing the temperature and amount of the water, the amount of salt, and the grind of the cornmeal. While varying these factors will affect the quality of the finished product, no ingredient changes make polenta any easier to prepare.

Some details on my work: I've seen polenta recipes that call for two parts water to one part cornmeal as well as those with four and one half parts water to one part cornmeal. I found that lesser amounts of water yielded consistently gummy polenta. Though the mixture may cook in as little as twenty minutes, it is usually tacky, sticky, and starchy, because there simply isn't enough liquid to hydrate the swelling starches. More water makes better polenta but takes much longer—up to forty-five minutes—to cook.

Dumping polenta into cold (that is, not boiling) water, a method touted in several cookbooks, eliminates some up-front work, but still requires constant stirring for forty-five minutes and delivers inferior results.

Besides adding flavor, salt slows the swelling of the starch so that the surface of the cornmeal doesn't overcook before the interior is done. Properly salted water allows the cornmeal to cook evenly and helps prevent seizing. Good polenta requires a teaspoon of salt per cup of cornmeal. More salt only makes the polenta inedible and can't prevent seizing if the cornmeal is added too quickly or if the water is boiling too fast.

The size of the cornmeal granules will affect the texture of the cooked polenta, but it doesn't seem to alter the cooking process. Determining how finely the cornmeal is ground can be difficult, since one company's coarse grind may be identical to another company's medium. When cornmeal is coarsely ground, sharp pieces of corn (rather than smoother spherical granules) make the polenta too gritty. Finely ground cornmeal (like the Quaker brand commonly sold in supermarkets) is too powdery and makes a gummy polenta. In general, I found that cornmeal with a texture more akin to sugar than table salt delivered the best results.

Easier Methods
After failing to make any headway by playing around with the ingredients, I began experimenting with alternative cooking techniques. I followed a number of recipes in microwave cookbooks and made polenta that ranged from passable to inedible. If you insist on making polenta in the microwave, avoid any recipe that requires less than three parts water to one part cornmeal; too little water yields a raw, sticky, starchy mass. Even when made with enough water, microwave polenta will never become a fluffy, corny mound, and is not recommended.

Pressure cookers combine the worst of all worlds. The polenta takes a long time to prepare—you still have to bring water to a boil, you still have to be ultra-careful about adding the cornmeal, you still have to stir, then you have to bring the cooker up to pressure—meanwhile, you lose a large part of the polenta to the bottom of the pan (where some of it may remain forever), and what you end up with still doesn't have the round, corny taste of longer-cooked polenta. The only thing you eliminate by using a pressure cooker is the stirring, but you make up for that with scouring time after dinner.

The nontraditional method I prefer uses a double boiler and requires only occasional stirring. To my mind, polenta prepared this way has a

Creamy, soft polenta makes an ideal side dish.

softer, lighter texture than even well-made traditional polenta (something most cooks will not achieve without a lot of practice, concentration, and luck). I think this is because the constant stirring of the traditional method breaks up some of the starch balloons and makes the mixture pastier. Double boilers give polenta a softer mouth-feel because you don't have to stir so often (the simmering water in the bottom of the double boiler keeps the polenta from overheating) and more balloons stay swollen.

I also think that cooking polenta in a double boiler makes it more flavorful; to me it tastes more like fresh corn. Much of the flavor comes from the bonding of proteins and sugars in the cornmeal. The longer polenta cooks, the more time there is for these elements to come together and to increase the sweetness and rich corn flavor of the polenta.

Besides better texture and flavor, the double-boiler method has an asset that no other method I tried can claim—it's foolproof. You can't overcook the polenta this way, and it will never seize up. There is only one drawback; the double-boiler method takes twice as long as the constant-stir method, fully one and one half hours. However, since you need only stir once every ten or fifteen minutes, this is not a really a hassle if you're going to be around the kitchen anyway. Double-boiler polenta can also be made several hours in advance and reheated at serving time. Given the advantages, it's the method I'll use from now on.

DOUBLE-BOILER POLENTA
Serves 4
This method is foolproof and requires minimal attention. Serve polenta underneath any of the Quick-Cooked Greens (*see* recipes on page 13), with lamb shanks (*see* recipes on page 19), or with one of the four simple toppings that follow. When stirring the polenta, there's no need to beat it vigorously; just move the cornmeal around, scraping the sides and bottom of the pan.

- 4 cups boiling water
- 1 teaspoon salt
- 1 cup medium-grind cornmeal

1. Bring about 2 inches of water to boil in bottom of double boiler; reduce to simmer and maintain throughout cooking process.
2. Set top of double boiler over simmering water, and add 4 cups boiling water. Add salt, then gradually sprinkle cornmeal into water, whisking constantly to avoid lump formation.
3. Cover and cook until polenta is very soft and smooth, 1¼ to 1½ hours, stirring for several seconds every 10 to 15 minutes. (Once cooked, polenta can be covered and saved up to 4 hours and reheated; stir in a bit of water if necessary.)

POLENTA WITH PARMESAN AND BUTTER
Serves 4 as a first course or side dish

- 1 recipe Double-Boiler Polenta
    (*see* above)
- 4 tablespoons unsalted butter, softened, plus 4 pats for garnish
- ½ cup grated Parmesan cheese, plus more for passing

Prepare Double-Boiler Polenta. Stir in butter and ½ cup Parmesan cheese. Divide polenta among four bowls. Top each with a pat of butter and sprinkle generously with Parmesan cheese to taste.

POLENTA WITH WILD MUSHROOMS AND ROSEMARY
Serves 4 as a main course
In this recipe, you may use any fresh wild mushrooms (such as cremini, shiitakes, or oysters), either alone or in combination.

- 1 recipe Double-Boiler Polenta
    (*see* above)
- 2 tablespoons unsalted butter
- 2 tablespoons olive oil
- 1 small onion, chopped
- 2 garlic cloves, minced
- 2 teaspoons minced fresh rosemary
- 1 pound wild mushrooms (cremini, shiitakes, or oysters), cleaned and sliced
- ⅓ cup chicken or vegetable stock
    Salt and ground black pepper
    Grated Parmesan cheese, for passing

1. Prepare Double-Boiler Polenta.
2. Meanwhile, heat butter and oil in large skillet. Add onion; sauté over medium heat until softened, about 5 minutes. Stir in garlic and rosemary; sauté until fragrant, about 1 minute longer.
3. Add wild mushrooms; sauté, stirring occasionally, until juices release, about 6 minutes. Add stock, and salt and pepper to taste; simmer briskly until sauce thickens, 5 to 10 minutes depending on mushroom variety. Adjust seasonings.
4. Divide polenta among four bowls; top each with portion of mushrooms and sauce. Garnish with Parmesan cheese, and serve immediately.

POLENTA WITH ITALIAN SAUSAGES AND TOMATO SAUCE
Serves 4 as a main course

- 1 recipe Double-Boiler Polenta
    (*see* above)
- 2 tablespoons olive oil
- 1 pound sweet Italian sausage, cut into 3-inch lengths
- ½ small onion, chopped (3 tablespoons)
- ½ small carrot, peeled and chopped (3 tablespoons)
- ½ small celery stock, chopped (3 tablespoons)
- 1 can (16 ounces) whole tomatoes, juice reserved, and tomatoes chopped coarse
    Salt and ground black pepper

1. Prepare Double-Boiler Polenta.
2. Meanwhile, heat oil in large sauté pan; add sausage, and cook, turning occasionally, until browned on all sides, about 10 minutes.
3. Add onion, carrot, and celery; sauté over medium heat until vegetables soften, about 5 minutes. Add tomatoes with their juice; simmer gently, until sauce thickens, 20 to 25 minutes. Season with salt and pepper to taste.
4. Divide cooked polenta among four bowls; top each with a portion of sausage and tomato sauce; and serve immediately.

POLENTA WITH GORGONZOLA
Serves 4 as a substantial first course or a light entree
Choose a *dolcelatte* Gorgonzola or other mild, creamy blue cheese such as Saga Blue. Do not use an aged Gorgonzola for this dish. Other aged blue cheeses will also be too salty, crumbly, and pungent.

- 1 recipe Double-Boiler Polenta
    (*see* above)
- 2 tablespoons unsalted butter, softened
- 4 ounces Gorgonzola cheese in four 1-ounce slices

Prepare Double-Boiler Polenta. Stir in butter. Divide polenta among four bowls. Top each with a slice of cheese. Serve immediately. ∎

Sarah Fritschner is the Food Editor of the *Louisville Courier-Journal.*

How to Make Roesti

For the best version of this classic Swiss potato pancake, use high-starch potatoes and pure butter—and don't bother to precook the potatoes.

∽ BY MARIE PIRAINO ∽

In Switzerland, a fried potato cake known as *roesti* has a daily place at the table. Like the potato omelette of Spain, it's a quick, easy, and delicious dish suitable as a weekday accompaniment to meats and stews, or as a meal in itself, topped with eggs or cheese.

Finding the best recipe for roesti seemed like a simple task. The only ingredients are potatoes, butter, salt, and pepper, and all I wanted was a crisp, golden crust around moist buttery potatoes. But after reviewing dozens of recipes, the variables and subtle differences seemed endless.

The Ingredients

I began by searching for the best potato. I found that the high starch content of baking potatoes such as russets, Yukon Golds, and "all-purpose" baking potatoes, helped the potato strands hold together into a cake during cooking. Waxy potatoes such as Red Bliss produced a less cohesive potato cake with a less satisfying mouth feel.

Most recipes for roesti suggested boiling the potatoes a day ahead. So I tried making roesti with potatoes boiled the previous day, potatoes boiled the same day, and potatoes that hadn't been boiled at all. Somewhat to my surprise, raw potatoes made the best roesti, a moist cake with a thick, crisp crust and a buttery, fresh potato flavor. As an added benefit, raw potatoes are much easier to grate.

The one constant during my initial tests was unsalted butter. To satisfy my culinary curiosity, however, I tried cooking roesti in three different kinds of fat: clarified butter, a combination of butter and oil, and extra virgin olive oil. The roesti made with clarified butter had a less buttery taste than I'd grown accustomed to; similarly, a combination of butter and oil gave a good but bland roesti. Extra virgin olive oil made a rich, full-flavored roesti, but it was

still not as rich as when made with butter, and that remained my first choice. In fact, you might say that a potato pancake made without butter is not roesti at all. Advancing this view, food writer Laurie Colwin once wrote that roesti "in reality, is an excuse for eating a quarter of a pound of butter." But is this much butter necessary? Not really. Using a nonstick skillet, I found that one ounce of butter for each pound of potatoes was enough to give the roesti a pronounced buttery flavor and a crisp crust that didn't stick to the pan.

The Method

The Swiss have a special grater for making roesti, but you can grate your potatoes using the large-hole side of a hand grater or, more quickly, with the shredding disc of a food processor. After grating, dry the potatoes with paper towels and quickly add them to the melted butter to prevent them from turning brown. (Don't rinse the shredded potatoes; the water will wash away some of the starch, which is the adhesive that holds the roesti together.) Mixing the salt and pepper with the raw potatoes ensures that the roesti will be well seasoned throughout.

Cooking the roesti over moderate heat is important because it ensures that the center will be tender by the time the crust has turned a crisp golden brown. A well-cooked crust will help hold the pancake together when it is turned over.

Other Root Vegetables

The Swiss are very conservative with their roesti. Other than some regional variations which include cheese or bacon and onions, they prefer their roesti simple. Wondering if other root vegetables would work with the same Master Recipe, I explored several options. Some root vegetables, such as sweet potatoes, proved unsuitable due to their high sugar content, which caused the crust to brown too much and stick to even a nonstick pan. Other vegetables, such as beets and celery root, lacked enough starch on their own to cook into a moist, compact cake. However, by combining them with white potatoes I could make roesti with both great taste and texture.

MASTER RECIPE FOR ROESTI
Serves 4 to 6

If you want, you can substitute an equal amount of olive oil for the butter in this recipe and in the variations which follow. If necessary, move the pan around on the burner to make certain that the crust browns evenly. The roesti is best served immediately, but it can be kept on a cooling rack,

loosely covered, in a warm oven for up to one hour.

- 4 tablespoons unsalted butter
- 2 pounds high-starch potatoes (russets, all-purpose, or Yukon Golds), peeled, coarsely shredded, and patted dry
- ¾ teaspoon salt
- ¼ teaspoon ground black pepper

1. Melt butter in 10-inch nonstick or well-seasoned cast-iron skillet over medium heat.

2. Season shredded potatoes with salt and pepper. Spread potatoes evenly in skillet; press with spatula to form compact cake. Cook until bottom crust is golden brown, pressing on potatoes occasionally with spatula, about 15 minutes.

3. Shake skillet or use spatula to loosen roesti. Place large plate or platter over skillet and carefully invert. Slide roesti back into skillet and cook until bottom crust is golden brown, 10 to 15 minutes longer. Serve immediately.

HERBED ROESTI WITH SMOKED CHEDDAR

Follow Master Recipe for Roesti, adding 1 tablespoon each minced fresh parsley, dill, and chives to shredded potatoes. Cook as in Master Recipe. About 5 minutes before roesti is done, sprinkle top crust with ¾ cup shredded smoked cheddar cheese. Cover and cook until cheese melts.

BEET AND POTATO ROESTI WITH CHIVES

Follow Master Recipe for Roesti, substituting 4 medium beets, peeled and shredded, for 1 pound of the potatoes, and adding 3 tablespoons of minced fresh chives or scallions to shredded potato-beet mixture. Serve with sour cream flavored to taste with horseradish.

CELERY ROOT AND POTATO ROESTI WITH LEMON AND PARSLEY

Follow Master Recipe for Roesti, substituting 1 pound celery root, peeled and shredded, for 1 pound of the potatoes; increase butter from 4 to 5 tablespoons, and add 2 teaspoons grated lemon zest and 2 tablespoons minced fresh parsley to the shredded potato-celery root mixture. Serve with sauce made from equal parts mayonnaise and Dijon-style mustard. ∎

Marie Piraino is a Boston-based food stylist and recipe developer.

PHOTOGRAPH BY ERIC ROTH

Savory Dried Fruit Compotes

Dried fruits, herbs, and spices transform a dessert into an unusual but easy-to-make savory accompaniment.

～ BY ANDY HUSBANDS AND KEN GOODMAN ～

Mention fruit compote and most people think of a sort of sweet stew of fresh fruit intended for dessert, either by itself or spooned over ice cream. This is certainly one type of fruit compote, but there are many others as well. Basically, a compote refers to fresh or dried fruit that has been slowly cooked in a sugar syrup; the syrup may also contain liquor or liqueur along with spices or herbs.

We found that fresh fruits work best in dessert compotes. The somewhat heavier and spicier flavors of compotes made with dried fruits, on the other hand, make them excellent accompaniments for hearty dishes such as roast or grilled meats or game.

Strongly flavored aromatic herbs and spices seem to us to work best in dried fruit compotes, because all have rather aggressive flavors and therefore provide distinct taste counterpoints to the concentrated sweetness of the dried fruits and the sugar syrup. The high sugar content of compotes also makes it important that you cook them in a heavy-bottomed pan to prevent them from sticking to the bottom of the pan and burning.

After cooking, compotes should be cooled to room temperature and then kept refrigerated or frozen, tightly covered. Stored this way, they will last three to four weeks and sometimes longer.

Many of the compote recipes that we came across suggested allowing them to sit for at least a week before eating them, so that the flavors could meld. We found that, with the compotes based on dried peaches, raisins, and dried apricots, we preferred the flavor of the mixture when eaten within the first two or three days. After that, the progressive blending of the flavors tended to lessen the intensity of the whiskey (in the dried peach compote), the herbs (in the raisin compote), and the balsamic vinegar (in the dried apricot compote). The compote of dried pears with

fresh oranges and lemons, on the other hand, definitely benefited from sitting at least a week after cooking. This flavor-melding period allowed the citrus peels to soften and their sharp tastes to mellow.

DRIED PEACH COMPOTE WITH MINT AND WHISKEY
Makes about 3 cups
This compote goes particularly well with lamb.

- 2½ cups dried peaches (about 14 ounces), cut into ¼-inch strips
- 2 tablespoons honey
- 1 cup fresh mint leaves, minced
- ⅓ cup bourbon or rye whiskey

Bring peaches, honey, and 2 cups water to simmer in a medium-size, heavy-bottomed saucepan over medium heat. Reduce heat to low and simmer uncovered, stirring frequently, until peaches plump and liquid thickens to slightly thinner than applesauce, about 20 minutes. Stir in mint and whiskey; simmer until alcohol evaporates, 2 to 3 minutes. Cool to room temperature. Serve warm or at room temperature.

RAISIN COMPOTE WITH ROSEMARY AND THYME
Makes about 3 cups
Serve this herbed fruit compote in place of cranberry relish with roast turkey, chicken, or pork.

- 1 cup golden raisins (about 7 ounces)
- 1 cup dark raisins (about 7 ounces)
- 1 cup juice from 3 to 4 oranges
- ¼ cup juice from 1 to 2 lemons
- ¼ cup sugar
- 1 teaspoon cayenne pepper
- 1½ teaspoons minced fresh rosemary leaves
- 1½ teaspoons minced fresh thyme leaves
- 1 teaspoon minced fresh sage leaves
- ¼ cup minced fresh parsley leaves
  Salt and ground black pepper

Bring first six ingredients, along with 1½ cups water, to simmer in a medium-size, heavy-bottomed saucepan over medium heat. Reduce heat to low and simmer, stirring frequently, until raisins plump, about 15 minutes. Add next four ingredients; simmer to blend flavors, about 5 minutes. Cool to room temperature, season to taste with salt and pepper, then refrigerate. Serve chilled.

DRIED APRICOT COMPOTE WITH BALSAMIC VINEGAR AND JUNIPER BERRIES
Makes about 3 cups
Try this compote with grilled or roast chicken.

- 2½ cups dried apricots (about 14 ounces), cut into ¼-inch strips
- ½ cup juniper berries, crushed
- ½ cup loose-packed brown sugar
- ½ cup balsamic vinegar
  Salt and ground black pepper

Bring first four ingredients, along with 2¼ cups water, to simmer in a medium-size, heavy-bottomed saucepan over medium heat. Reduce heat to low and simmer uncovered, stirring often, until apricots plump and liquid thickens to slightly thinner than applesauce, about 20 minutes. Cool to room temperature and season to taste with salt and pepper. Serve warm, at room temperature, or chilled.

DRIED PEAR AND ORANGE COMPOTE WITH HONEY AND SAGE
Makes about 1 quart
Try this rather tart fruit compote with roast duck, quail, or other game. Make it ahead and let it sit for at least a week, covered and refrigerated, so that the flavors meld and the rinds soften.

- ½ cup honey
- 1 large navel orange, ends removed, fruit (including zest) sliced very thin
- ½ lemon, ends removed, fruit (including zest) sliced very thin
- 2 cups dried pears (about 12 ounces), cut into ¼-inch strips
- 2 tablespoons minced fresh sage leaves
- 2 tablespoons Grand Marnier or other orange-flavored liqueur

Bring honey and 2 cups water to boil in a large, heavy-bottomed saucepan over medium heat, stirring frequently. Add orange, lemon, and pears; reduce heat to low and simmer uncovered, stirring often, until pears plump, about 20 minutes. Stir in sage and liqueur; simmer to evaporate alcohol, 1 to 2 minutes. Cool, then refrigerate until citrus peels soften, about 1 week. Serve chilled or at room temperature. ■

Andy Husbands and **Ken Goodman** are the chef and sous chef, respectively, at the East Coast Grill in Cambridge, Massachusetts.

The Magic of Pudding Cakes

The secret to a light, puffy pudding cake, which separates into cake and pudding layers during baking, is an extra egg white.

~ BY STEPHEN SCHMIDT ~

When baked in ramekins, pudding cakes can be inverted after baking and served upside down, with the gooey pudding layer on top. They can be served either hot or cold.

Pudding cakes are basically egg custards, but with two clever improvements. Unlike ordinary egg custards, pudding cakes contain a little flour and some beaten egg whites. During baking, the beaten egg whites float to the top, forming a spongy, cakelike cap. Meanwhile, the remainder of the batter settles to the bottom to make a puddinglike layer.

Based on recipes that date back to colonial times, pudding cakes have existed in their present form for at least one hundred and fifty years (*see* "Pudding Cake Genealogy," page 25). Lemon and orange are the classic flavors, although other versions also appear fairly regularly. Historic and modern formulas are surprisingly similar. One cookbook that I consulted presented a version supposedly made in Shaker kitchens. Sure enough, the same recipe turned up in a Shaker cookbook that I own—but it also appeared, verbatim, in the 1975 edition of *Joy of Cooking*.

In preparing this article, I baked some fifteen pudding cakes. I immediately noticed that those made with lemon or orange juice came out especially well, while those flavored in other ways tended to have flimsy, fast-dissolving tops and rubbery, dense bottoms. I eventually deduced that it was the acidity of the citrus juices that made the difference. Because the juice lightly clabbered the milk-based batter, causing it to thicken, the frothy upper layer became stiffer and more stable and thus was better able to puff. At the same time, the acidic juice undercut the thickening power of the flour, making for a more tender custard.

To shore up the cake part of those variations made with coffee, chocolate, and vanilla, I tried adding an extra egg white. I liked the results so much that I ended up using the extra white in all the recipes. The excessive thickness of the pudding layer in the nonacidic variations was easily fixed by reducing the amount of flour.

As a lover of rich desserts, I could not keep myself from trying to make pudding cakes with extra butter and with cream instead of milk. I discovered, however, that the added fat caused the whipped egg whites to collapse, making for a thin top. In any case, the extra richness didn't really improve the desserts—in fact, it was barely discernible. What a surprise!

Finally, while I find baking things in a *bain marie*, or water bath, just as much of a nuisance as the next person, I'm afraid that there is no way to do without it here. Because water cannot get hotter than its boiling point, it insulates the custard and prevents it from curdling. I tried baking a pudding cake without the water bath and got scrambled eggs!

Be sure to let pudding cakes stand in the water bath for ten minutes after removing them from the oven. Like other custards, pudding cakes need to finish cooking outside the oven; if left in the oven long enough to make their centers completely firm, pudding cakes may become rubbery and overcooked around the edges.

To give us a fresh, contemporary perspective on the subject, *Cook's Illustrated* asked master baker Catherine Cunningham to develop some pudding cake recipes of her own. Ms. Cunningham came up with excellent coffee, chocolate, and vanilla versions, all of which are represented in the variations below. Any of the following pudding cakes can be made in any of the following: six three-quarter-cup custard cups; four one-and-one-third-cup ramekins or miniature soufflé cups; one nine-inch round cake pan; or one eight-inch square cake pan. All pudding cakes, regardless of pan size, require the same baking time.

LEMON PUDDING CAKE
Serves 4 to 6

2 tablespoons unsalted butter, softened, plus enough to grease the baking pan
½ cup plus 2 tablespoons sugar
⅛ teaspoon salt
3 large egg yolks
3 tablespoons all-purpose flour
2–3 teaspoons grated zest and ¼ cup strained juice from 1 or 2 lemons
1 cup milk
4 large egg whites, at room temperature

1. Adjust oven rack to center position and heat oven to 325 degrees. Lightly butter pan or baking molds of choice. Lay folded dish towel in bottom of a roasting pan and set molds or pan inside. Bring several quarts of water to boil for water bath.

2. Meanwhile, in mixing bowl mash 2 tablespoons butter together with sugar and salt with back of wooden spoon until crumbly. Beat in yolks, then flour, mixing until smooth. Slowly beat in lemon zest and juice, then stir in milk. Beat egg whites to stiff, moist peaks. Gently whisk whites into batter just until no large lumps remain.

3. Immediately ladle (don't pour) batter into pan, custard cups, or ramekins. Set baking pan on oven rack. Pour enough boiling water into roasting pan to come halfway up sides of baking pan or molds. Bake until pudding cake center is set and springs back when gently touched, about 25 minutes. Remove roasting pan from oven and let pan or molds continue to stand in water bath for 10 minutes. Pudding cakes can be served warm, at room temperature, or even chilled.

ORANGE PUDDING CAKE
Serves 4 to 6

Follow the recipe for Lemon Pudding Cake, making the following changes: Substitute the juice (¼ cup) and zest from 1 medium navel orange for the lemon juice and zest. Add 2 tablespoons lemon juice along with the orange juice.

COFFEE PUDDING CAKE
Serves 4 to 6

This cake tastes best when made with superstrong coffee. The easiest way to make the strong coffee needed for this recipe is to cover one-third cup finely ground coffee with two-thirds cup boiling water and let it stand for five minutes, then drip through a coffee filter.

Follow the recipe for Lemon Pudding Cake, making the following changes: For lemon juice and zest, substitute ⅓ cup cooled strong coffee and 2 tablespoons coffee-flavored liqueur. Decrease sugar from ½ cup plus 2 tablespoons to ½ cup, and decrease flour from 3 to 2 tablespoons.

CHOCOLATE PUDDING CAKE
Serves 4 to 6

Follow the recipe for Lemon Pudding Cake, making the following changes: Make a rather thick cocoa paste by slowly stirring ½ cup boiling water into ⅓ cup unsweetened cocoa. Cool the paste slightly, then stir in 1 tablespoon dark rum. Substitute cocoa paste for lemon juice and zest. Decrease flour from 3 to 2 tablespoons.

VANILLA-BOURBON PUDDING CAKE
Serves 6

This delicious version is rich enough to serve six amply. If possible, bake it in cups rather than a pan, and eat it warm.

Follow the recipe for Lemon Pudding Cake, making the following changes: Decrease flour from 3 to 2 tablespoons, substitute 1 tablespoon pure vanilla extract and 1 tablespoon bourbon whiskey for lemon zest and juice, and increase milk from 1 to 1⅓ cups. Serve with Bourbon Butter Sauce (below).

BOURBON BUTTER SAUCE

    8 tablespoons unsalted butter
    ⅔ cup sugar
    2 tablespoons bourbon
    ½ teaspoon grated nutmeg
    ⅛ teaspoon salt
    1 large egg, beaten until foamy

Heat first five ingredients plus 2 tablespoons

PUDDING CAKE GENEALOGY

Pudding cakes trace their origins to a simple dish called "flour pudding" or "plain pudding," a recipe for which appears in the first American cookbook, published in 1796. This pudding was really nothing more than an egg custard containing a small amount of flour. The flour changed the texture, making the custard firm and somewhat dense. Flavored with wine or rose water, the pudding was always served with a sweet sauce. In *The Carolina Housewife*, published in 1847, Sara Rutledge adds a refinement, probably already long current, to her version of the pudding. Instead of merely mixing all the ingredients together, she whips the egg whites separately and folds them in at the end. This causes the batter to separate into a cakelike layer on the top and a custardy pudding on the bottom—in other words, a pudding cake. In the 1850s lemon-flavored pudding cakes rapidly became the standard, replacing the earlier ones flavored with wine or roses.

water in small, heavy-bottomed saucepan over medium-low heat, stirring occasionally, until bubbly around the edges. Remove from heat. Beat egg into hot butter mixture. Return to burner, bring to boil over medium-low heat, stirring constantly. Cook until thickened, about 1 minute. Spoon sauce over each pudding cake. Pass leftover sauce separately. ∎

Stephen Schmidt is the author of *Master Recipes* (Ballantine, 1987).

PUDDING CAKE HINTS

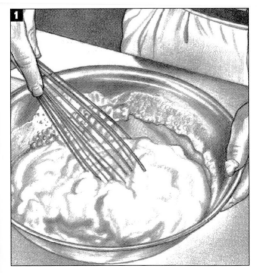

1. Be sure to *whisk* the egg whites into the batter instead of folding them in. Since the batter is about the consistency of milk, folding would flatten the fluffy whites.

2. Rather than pouring the batter, ladle it; otherwise the first cups get all the froth and the later cups get all the batter.

3. Set the roasting pan on an oven rack and pour boiling water into the pan until it comes halfway up the sides of the molds. This water bath keeps the temperature low enough to prevent the eggs from curdling.

ILLUSTRATIONS BY WENDY WRAY

House Blend Coffee Tasting Finds Wide Divergence of Styles

Starbucks takes top honors as mail-order coffees leave supermarket brands in the dust.

~ BY JACK BISHOP ~

"Gourmet" coffee now seems to be everywhere, but many consumers are confused by the hype and pretension that surrounds this suddenly trendy drink. Most consumers have heard that it is better to buy whole beans than preground coffee, but they are not really sure which beans it is best to buy. To provide some guidance, we held a tasting of eleven house blends from specialty roasters around the country, along with the two best-selling supermarket brands.

As might be expected, even the "premium" brands from Maxwell House and Folger's fared poorly against whole beans ground just before brewing. That said, not all mail-order coffees were great, and many received decidedly mixed reviews, in part because personal preferences play such an important part in the coffee-drinking experience. As with wine, there is no such thing as "the best." However, we did find some specialty coffees with great appeal to a diverse group of coffee aficionados.

There are two major categories of coffee beans, called arabica and robusta. Arabica beans have a richer flavor profile. Robusta beans have twice the caffeine of arabicas and also tend to have a grassy flavor that becomes unpleasant when these beans comprise a high proportion of a coffee blend. Unfortunately, arabica beans are not very hardy and grow at high elevations—between 2,000 and 6,000 feet above sea level, often on the sides of mountains—where cultivation is an expensive proposition. Arabicas are used by the specialty roasters mentioned in this story, but they are too costly for supermarket brands. Supermarket coffees therefore rely on the cheaper robusta beans, which are often blended with a small amount of arabica beans for flavor.

A single-origin variety, like Kenya AA or Kona, will generally present strong distinctive characteristics. By blending top beans from various growing regions, a roaster can create a coffee with more complexity and better overall balance than could ever be achieved with just one variety of bean. "Certain coffees have accentuated properties such as tremendous acidity, good body, or potent aroma," says Ted Lingle, executive director of the Specialty Coffee Association. "The knowledgeable roaster tries to a create a synergistic blend where the whole is greater than the sum of the parts."

For this article, we tested house blends (or, in cases where the company does not sell anything called "house blend," a popular, medium-roast blend). Although our panel enjoyed most of these coffees (hence the large group of "recommended coffees"), the general consensus was that these middle-of-the-road blends often lack the character of an intriguing varietal or a more unusual blend. House blends may not represent the most exciting products, but we did find them to be a good gauge of the skill and style of each roaster.

Professionals use a process called "cupping" to evaluate roasted beans. In this process, almost-boiling water is poured directly over grounds in a cup, and the brew is allowed to steep for several minutes before it is slurped and sampled. Since we wanted to taste in a way that was more consistent with home conditions, we did not follow the cupping method. However, we used the same four criteria to evaluate our drip-brewed coffees that professionals use when cupping.

Aroma is the first clue to which of the five hundred or so essential oils found in coffee are most prevalent in a given sample. *Flavor*, which is related to aroma, may include such characteristics as sweetness or earthiness or may remind the taster of flowers, chocolate, nuts, and/or spices. The growing conditions (soil, climate, etc.) are all reflected in flavor. *Body* is viscosity or mouth-feel. Think of the difference between a rich, "chewy" red wine and a young, thin white. In general, coffee with more body provides a more pleasurable drinking experience. The final criteria is *acidity*—the sharp, snappy quality found in many coffees. Acidity should not be confused with bitterness, which is due to dark roasting. Acidity is the brightness or bite in a good cup of coffee, not the taste of carbon or charcoal.

Tasting Procedures

Our tasting was held at the Rainbow Room in New York. In addition to the author, the panel included Fern Berman, president of Fern Berman Communications; Mark Bittman, executive editor of *Cook's Illustrated;* Oren Bloostein, president and roast master at Oren's Daily Roast, a chain of New York coffee stores; David Michael Cane, host of the "The Food Show" on WABC Radio in New York; Elizabeth Friedmann, director of marketing and sales in New York for Illy Caffe; Renee Gerson, co-owner of Espresso Madison, a espresso bar in New York; and Alan Reyburn, CEO of the Rainbow Room.

With the exception of the two supermarket brands (which were purchased several days before the tasting), coffees were ordered one week in advance in whole bean form and ground an hour before the tasting. The coffee was brewed through Melitta drip cones lined with paper filters and consumed immediately. All coffees were brewed with the equivalent of two rounded tablespoons per six ounces of water to highlight each coffee's particular characteristics. ∎

COFFEE FRESHNESS

Everyone we spoke with in the industry agreed that the best beans and roasting techniques mean little if coffee is not absolutely fresh. While grinding coffee speeds up oxidation and should not be done until the coffee is needed for brewing, even whole beans begin to deteriorate noticeably several weeks after they are roasted.

Therefore, beans sold in bins at a gourmet shop or supermarket may in fact be inferior to vacuum-packed ground coffee unless there is a high enough turnover rate to keep the bins replenished with freshly roasted beans.

The best way to guarantee consistently good coffee is to buy from a source that only sells freshly roasted beans.

Many of the companies listed on page 27 have numerous retail stores across the country.

Ordering by mail is also an excellent option for coffee lovers who live outside the coffee belt. All the specialty roasters in our tasting ship just-roasted beans in vacuum-packed bags to maintain freshness.

Coffees are listed in order of preference based on the scores awarded by our panel. Place of origin refers to the site of the roasting plant or company headquarters. Prices do not include shipping and are subject to increases due to recent shortages in the world coffee market. Some roasters operate retail outlets, in some cases one hundred or more shops, where their coffee can be purchased. All roasters will send a free catalog at your request.

HIGHLY RECOMMENDED COFFEES
Only one coffee received uniformly positive comments.

Starbucks Coffee House Blend (Seattle), $8.95/pound. A favorite of all eight tasters and the top choice of four panelists. Dark brown beans with oily sheen yield coffee with a "very sophisticated aroma and flavor." Brew described as "nicely bitter" with a "good balance between mellowness and acidity." Tasters felt this coffee was "full-bodied" with a "rich mouthfeel," relying on adjectives like "earthy," "round," and "smooth" to describe it. *Available in Starbucks stores nationwide and by mail by calling 800-782-7282.*

RECOMMENDED COFFEES
The majority of coffees garnered mixed reviews and are recommended with varying degrees of enthusiasm. Coffees earning mostly positive reviews are at the top of this group; those receiving some positive responses but as many, or slightly more, negative reviews are at the bottom.

The Coffee Connection CC Special (Boston), $8.25/pound. Medium-colored, matte beans make coffee with "exceptional nose" and "seductive aroma." Coffee is "well-balanced" and "mellow" but still "pleasantly tangy." Very full body with "thick, almost chewy" mouth-feel. One of two tasters who gave this coffee a top vote felt it "finishes like coffee bean candies." "Pleasant, nice" coffee wowed most tasters, although two deemed it merely "fair" or "acceptable." *Available in Coffee Connection stores in the Northeast and by mail by calling 800-284-5282.*

Thanksgiving Coffee Company, Paul's Special House Blend (Fort Bragg, California), $8.25/14 ounces. Oily, dark brown (almost black) beans drew very enthusiastic comments from most tasters but prompted several strong dissents. Aroma and flavor described as "roasty, toasty" and "heavily spiced." Acidity and body deemed average. Dark roast was not universally appreciated, with comments ranging from "excellent, clean, and bitter" to "carbony" and "smells like cigarette smoke." Obviously, this dark roast appeals to many but not all. *Available by mail by calling 800-648-6491.*

Caravali Coffees House Blend (Seattle), $7.95/14 ounces. Dark brown beans with light, oily sheen. "Mild but rich" aroma and "strong but still smooth" acidity are hallmarks of this "round, full" brew. Several tasters felt this cup had more body than most. Dissenters complained it was "too mild" or "unfocused." Most tasters judged this "a well-made mouthful of coffee." *Available by mail by calling 800-942-5282.*

The Coffee Beanery Blend (Flushing, Michigan), $8.99/pound. Medium brown, matte beans make coffee with "full, rich aroma" that is neither harsh nor bitter. Medium acidity judged to give coffee "nice bite." Flavor is "earthy but sweet" or "deep and rich," depending on taster. A few thought "toasted quality" was "a bit flat" or "lacking dimension." *Available in Coffee Beanery stores nationwide and by mail by calling 800-441-2255.*

Barnie's Coffee and Tea Company Special Blend (Orlando), $8.99/-pound. Beans medium brown in color and lack oily sheen. "Decent" was the universal assessment of this coffee. "Clean and interesting" also interpreted as "round" and "mild." This "good if unremarkable" coffee typified the panel's overall finding that house blends are "least common denominator coffees." *Available in Barnie's stores in the East and by mail by calling 800-284-1416.*

Torrefazione Italia Perugia Blend (Seattle), $9.75/pound. Dark brown beans with light, oily sheen. Coffee has "pleasant, earthy" aroma that intrigued some tasters ("interesting floral note") but left others nonplussed ("mild verging on weak"). Most tasters felt acidity was at "pleasant level" but body was "too thin." General comments ranged from "pleasant enough" to "nice blend with some, but not all, dark-roasted notes." *Available by mail by calling 800-827-2333.*

Green Mountain Coffee Roasters Breakfast Blend (Waterbury, Vermont), $9.99/pound. Medium brown beans with very light oily sheen earned slightly more negative comments than positive ones. Some tasters complained about "narrow flavor profile" while others detected hints of chocolate and berries. Average acidity and body. Some tasters appreciated "mellow character," but most thought it "underroasted" and "boring." *Available in Green Mountain stores in New England and by mail by calling 800-223-6768.*

Seattle's Best Coffee Seattle's Best Blend (Vashon Island, Washington), $8.25/pound. Very dark brown beans have glossy sheen. Fans of this coffee slightly outnumbered by its detractors. Most everyone agreed that flavor was "mild" and "slight." This translated to "weak" and "bland" for some, a "good morning brew" for others. *Available in Seattle's* Best Coffee stores in Washington and by mail by calling 800-962-9659.

COFFEES NOT RECOMMENDED
These coffees received uniformly negative assessments.

Millstone Coffee Breakfast Blend (Everett, Washington), $6.49/12 ounces. Medium brown beans lack an oily sheen or gloss. Several tasters commented on "sour" aroma and flavor, while others were thrown off by "acrid," "medicinal" taste. Most assessments fell between "awful" and "very unpleasant," with a few more charitable tasters offering weak endorsements like "pleasant enough—just barely." *Available by mail by calling 800-466-0300.*

Peet's Coffee and Tea House Blend (Emeryville, California), $6.95/pound. Dark brown beans with oily sheen. Several tasters detected "woody" or "nutty" overtones in this "full-bodied" brew, while others felt flavors were closer to "charcoal." Even tasters who wrote some favorable notes were unimpressed. "Unremarkable" was the kindest comment offered. *Available in Peet's stores in the San Francisco area and by mail by calling 800-999-2132.*

Maxwell House Colombian Supreme (White Plains, New York), $4.39/12 ounces. Ground coffee slightly lighter in color than Folger's but noticeably lighter than coffee from whole beans. "Sour, weak" flavor with "no aroma at all" caused tasters to downgrade this coffee. Very high acidity is "too sharp" for most, while body is "so thin I can't find any." Overall impression—"flat," "flabby," "awful" and "uninteresting." *Available in supermarkets nationwide.*

Folger's Gourmet Supreme (Cincinnati), $4.25/13 ounces. Medium brown ground coffee. "Muddy" or "grassy" with no aroma. Acid level "out of control." Coffee "extremely bitter." "Weak," "underdeveloped" brew also "very thin." Most positive comment offered was "undistinguished." Negative reviews ranged from "not worth the effort" to "battery acid." *Available in supermarkets nationwide.*

Rating Electric Coffee Grinders

After testing seventeen coffee grinders, we find that mills definitely outperform choppers and are a must for those who brew espresso.

∾ BY SHARON K. BARRETT ∾

Coffee is far more flavorful when fresh beans are ground just before brewing. However, the process of grinding beans in your own kitchen is not always pleasant. In addition to the roaring noise, the inconsistent grind and the mess produced by many coffee grinders can be very annoying.

To find the best coffee grinders, we tested seventeen different models—seven blade grinders and ten burr grinders. We wanted to find out not only which model was best in each category, but also whether expensive burr grinders really are better than cheap blade grinders, as is often claimed.

Mills versus Grinders

Coffee mills, also called burr grinders, use grinding stones or wheels to grind beans (*see* illustration, right). The closer the stones or wheels are to each other, the finer they grind the coffee. As soon as a few beans have been ground, the coffee is immediately dispensed into a container to prevent it from being overheated, and more beans are pushed between the wheels. The idea is that each bean will be ground in exactly the same manner, creating a truly consistent grind at any desired consistency.

Instead of wheels or grinding stones, blade grinders, also known as choppers, use a blade that rotates through the beans, chopping them into smaller pieces with each rotation—basically, it's a small version of the steel blade in a food processor. You press a button to control how long the blade rotates, and chopping is complete when the

grounds reach the desired consistency. As a side effect of their design, choppers do their work a bit unevenly and tend to warm the beans as friction builds up, since the beans remain in the chopping area for a longer time. Excess heat from too much friction can cause some of the coffee's flavorful oils to evaporate.

Of course, the differences between mills and blade grinders would be moot if you couldn't taste any difference in the coffee. Therefore we held a mini-tasting with several coffee buffs at which we ground coffee in a our top-rated mill and top-rated chopper. When we brewed the coffee and tasted it blind, the difference between the two coffees was striking. All tasters uniformly agreed that the mill-ground coffee had a cleaner, more robust, more nuanced flavor.

Two main factors account for the superior taste of coffee made with mill-ground beans—a more consistent texture and less coffee dust. The latter is an especially important consideration when making espresso, since the water is forced through the grounds much more quickly than when making drip-brewed coffee. "The goal is to have an evenly resistant bed of ground coffee to produce even brewing," explains Corby Kummer, senior editor at *Atlantic Monthly* and author of the forthcoming *The Joy of Coffee* (Chapters, 1995). "Coffee dust and finer particles will trap water flowing through the filter, while coarser particles can form sluices from which the water drips too fast." Coffee ground in a chopper may be less flavorful (as we found in our top chopper), or it may be bitter or weak if the grind is very uneven.

By using wheels to grind beans, which are then removed from the grinding area, mills produce an even-textured grind.

Setting Standards

After grinding pounds and pounds of coffee, we developed the following standards for the perfect grinder: It should produce a very evenly textured grind; it should allow for easy removal of the grounds and easy cleanup after use; it should be reasonably quiet; it should heat the beans only a minimal amount; and it should produce very little dust while grinding.

Unfortunately, we had trouble removing grounds and cleaning up all of the mills we tested. Even on our top-rated $200 mill, grounds stuck in the dispensing chute. Because of these problems, we failed to find what we would consider the "ideal" coffee grinder.

However, several machines performed admirably, delivering an excellent range of grinds. In general, we found a correlation between the cost of a mill and its quality. If you want the best brewed coffee at any cost, we recommend the Saeco Model 2002 mill ($200). If cost is an important consideration, we recommend the Braun or Xcell mills, which can be bought for around $50 each.

Even if you are not an espresso drinker, if you are using ground coffee, you should at least invest $20 in a chopper and switch to whole beans. The improvement will be obvious. Our recommended Bosch model was a slight favorite in our testing, although all the other choppers were deemed acceptable; there were only minor differences among the various models. ■

Sharon K. Barrett recently graduated from Peter Kump's New York Cooking School.

WHAT A RACKET

Most people want fresh-ground coffee early in the morning or as a peaceful end to dinner. But grinding coffee can sound like a cat fight taking place over the roar of a jet engine. We used a meter to measure the noise of each grinder, testing the A-weighted overall sound level, more commonly referred to as the decibel level and written as the dBA. A five or six dBA difference is clearly noticeable—a male voice at six feet averages sixty dBA; a raised voice measures about sixty-six dBA.

With their high-pitched whine, no coffee grinder is quiet, but we did find real differences among them.

Among the blade grinders, the top-rated Bosch measured eighty-three dBA. Among the mills, the Saeco topped out at seventy-six dBA and reached this volume only after all of the beans had gone through the wheels. On the basis of their other qualities, both grinders had secured their places in the ratings even before their sound

levels were tested; their relative quiet came as a bonus. On the other end of the scale, the Black & Decker blade grinder blared out at eighty-nine dBA, with the Krups and Braun just behind at eighty-eight dBA. The Maxim mill hit an earsplitting ninety dBA.

To our surprise, the mills didn't measure significantly louder than the choppers (and our favorite was actually quieter), although they often sound louder at the end of their cycle, with an annoying high-pitched scream.

ILLUSTRATIONS BY DAN KROVATIN

**PENNE WITH QUICK-COOKED GREENS
AND PROSCIUTTO**
page 14

POLENTA WITH GORGONZOLA
page 21

RECIPE INDEX

ORANGE PUDDING CAKE
page 25

LAMB SHANKS BRAISED IN RED WINE
page 19
WITH ROESTI page 22

PAELLA, CRIOLLA'S STYLE
page 11

RUSTIC COUNTRY BREAD
page 0

Banana-Papaya Fool

In a medium bowl, mix the following: two ripe bananas that have been peeled and cut into ½-inch dice; one papaya that has been peeled, halved, seeded, and cut into ½-inch dice; 1 tablespoon of dark rum; and 2 tablespoons of sugar. Puree half of this mixture in a food processor fitted with a metal blade; return the puree to the bowl and mix it with the remaining diced fruit. Whip 1 cup cream to soft peaks; add ¼ cup of sugar to the cream, 1 tablespoon at a time, and continue to whip it until it forms stiff peaks. Fold the fruit mixture into the whipped cream until it is fully incorporated. Serve in individual bowls or goblets or a large serving bowl. Garnish with ½ pint of raspberries and ½ cup of toasted coconut. *Serves 8.*

RATING COFFEE GRINDERS

We tested both mills and blade grinders for four grinds: coarse (for plunger pots), medium (for flat-bottomed drip filters), fine (for cone-shaped drip filters), and extra-fine (for espresso). We put slightly more emphasis on getting a good fine grind, a must for espresso, than a good coarse one. The differences among the mills, from best to worst, are considerably more pronounced than the differences among the blade grinders. Ratings are listed in order of preference within each category. Sound ratings (in dBA) are given for the loudest noise each machine produced. Prices are suggested retail and will vary. *See* Sources and Resources on page 32 for information on purchasing the top-rated models.

BEST MILL

Saeco Model 2002

BEST BUY: MILLS

Braun Aromatic Coffee Mill Model KMM 20

BEST BLADE

Bosch Model MKM 6

HIGHLY RECOMMENDED MILLS

Very few design flaws. Worked well on all grinds from coarse to fine.

Saeco Model 2002
Price: $200 **Noise:** 76 dBA
Features: 15 grind settings
Performance: Excellent range of grinds, quick grinding, good construction, and reasonable noise level put this model in first place. Mess caused when grounds container is detached and grounds sticking in chute keep it from being ideal.

Gaggia Coffee Grinder Model MDF
Price: $235 **Noise:** 77 dBA
Features: 34 grind settings
Performance: Excellent range of grinds, but no container from which to spoon out grounds. Gives nice coarse grind for plunger pot, but to remove grounds you must dose them out as you would for espresso, with something underneath to catch them. Grinder has great appeal, but only for espresso drinkers.

RECOMMENDED MILLS

Worked fairly well but did not produce a full range of grinds. Note low price of the Braun, a best buy for all but users of plunger pots.

Braun Aromatic Coffee Mill Model KMM 20
Price: $81 **Noise:** 86 dBA
Features: 9 grind settings; timed portion regulator
Performance: Tall, narrow machine is very easy to clean and produces evenly textured grinds from medium-fine to slightly gritty espresso, but no coarse grind. On the down side, it's loud, gets hot, and grounds stick. Dollar for dollar, an excellent choice.

Xcell Emide Burr Grinder Model KM-51
Price: $49 **Noise:** 89 dBA
Features: 3 grind settings plus inter-mediate settings

Performance: Ranks just below the Braun because it makes more noise and more of a mess when you remove the grounds. "Coarse" grind is even finer than that from the Braun.

Gaggia Model MM
Price: $85 **Noise:** 83 dBA
Features: 9 grind settings
Performance: Good grinds from drip to espresso, but trendy design gets in the way. Fineness markings are black on black and hard to see; hopper is too dark to see beans inside. Grounds container doesn't have hinged lid for coffee removal, so coffee spills. "On" button must be held down for grinding.

Bosch "Columbia" Coffee Grinder Model MKM700070
Price: $90 **Noise:** 83 dBA
Features: 12 grind settings plus intermediate settings; timed portion regulator
Performance: Cleaning instructions left us in a fog, but machine produces grinds from drip to espresso. Timer runs only to 30 seconds, often not long enough. Location of fineness dial is annoying.

La Pavoni Electric Coffee Grinder Model PGC
Price: $110 **Noise:** 85 dBA
Features: 9 grind settings
Performance: Produces evenly textured grinds from medium to powdery-fine, and has a nice pour spout from which the grounds can drop into container or directly into filter without spilling; unfortunately it can't produce a coarse grind. Fineness knob is annoying to turn, spout is difficult to clean, and both coffee and exterior of mill get very hot. It took four minutes to grind just 3 ounces of beans.

DeLonghi Coffee Grinder and Doser Model DCG-3
Price: $109 **Noise:** 85 dBA
Features: 15 grind settings plus in-

termediate settings
Performance: Produces nice grinds from drip to espresso but is awkward and messy to use. Arrow marking the grind setting is hard to see, grounds container is difficult to unlock and detach, and grounds clog up spout.

MILLS NOT RECOMMENDED

These two machines were unable to produce a fine grind for espresso.

Waring Coffee Grinder Model CG110-1
Price: $48 **Noise:** 89 dBA
Features: 12 grind settings plus intermediate settings; measurement markings on hopper correspond to tablespoons of ground coffee
Performance: Only produces grinds from coarse to medium. Wheel cover can be unlocked and removed for cleaning under hopper, but getting cover back in place is difficult—lock is deceptive and cover can come loose as next batch is being ground.

Maxim Coffee Mill Model GC-30
Price: $45 **Noise:** 90 dBA
Features: 18 grind settings; timed portion regulator
Performance: Loud machine that doesn't produce as evenly textured a grind as others tested; range runs from coarse to medium. Grinding wheel unlocks for easy cleaning.

HIGHLY RECOMMENDED BLADE GRINDER

The wide range of grinds and low noise level separate this model from the rest of the pack.

Bosch Model MKM 6
Price: $25 **Noise:** 83 dBA
Performance: Produced the most evenly textured grind of all choppers; not too much powder. Easy to operate, but impossible to remove grounds cleanly, as neither base nor lid are deep enough to hold grounds without spilling.

RECOMMENDED BLADE GRINDERS

Performance of remaining blade grinders was acceptable with only minimal differences between models.

Braun Aromatic KSM 4
Price: $29 **Noise:** 88 dBA
Performance: Machine rates high because of evenly textured, fine grind; less proficient at coarse grinds. Loud. Coffee clings to sides and under blade. Machine is easy to hold and operate.

Krups Fast-Touch Coffee Mill Model 203
Price: $20 **Noise:** 88 dBA
Performance: Works well for medium-fine to extra-fine grinds, but cannot produce coarse grinds.

Melitta Select-Grind Model CG-2
Price: $20 **Noise:** 87 dBA
Performance: Decent grind at all stages—even texture, without too much powder—but not top-notch. At 27 seconds grind is even and fine but sticks badly.

DeLonghi Electronic Coffee Grinder Model DCG-1
Price: $39 **Noise:** 84 dBA
Performance: Grind control is accurate, but coarse and medium grinds are unevenly textured. Inconvenient to operate: one button must be popped into place to lock lid, and another button must be depressed to grind.

Mr. Coffee Mill Model IDS50
Price: $15 **Noise:** 84 dBA
Performance: Produces unevenly textured grind with a lot of dust; takes too long to achieve fine grind.

Black & Decker Coffee Mill Model CBM1
Price: $20 **Noise:** 89 dBA
Performance: Produces fairly evenly textured grind, but is unable to get truly fine grind without also getting hot. Some grinds stick.

Rating California's Best Reds

The best California reds are blended wines, and although they're expensive, our tasters thought them worth the price.

∼ BY MARK BITTMAN ∼

The work of a winemaker involves many choices, none more important than deciding whether to use an individual grape or to blend those that are complementary. Both traditions are entirely legitimate. The great Burgundies, both red and white, are almost exclusively nonblended wines; the great Bordeaux are almost always blends. Most German and Alsatian wines are of the single-grape variety; most Champagne and Rhone wines are blended.

When California winemakers began making world-class red wines in the sixties and seventies, most of the best were single-grape wines—also called varietals—and most of those were made from cabernet sauvignon, one of the two most important grapes of Bordeaux (the other is merlot). The best of these wines had character, but most lacked the depth that experienced wine drinkers seek in top-notch reds. The Bordelaise tradition of using cabernet sauvignon softened by merlot (or merlot "stiffened" by cabernet sauvignon) and further enhanced by cabernet franc and other "lesser" grapes, provided a direction, and California winemakers began to concentrate on blended wines.

The first well-known California blend is still the best-known. Called Opus One, it is the product of a joint venture begun in 1979 by well-known California winemaker Robert Mondavi and Baron Phillippe de Rothschild, owner of one of Bordeaux's greatest wineries. Opus One was a marketing hit from the start, but it was expensive (usually about $70 a bottle) and did not always perform well in blind tastings.

It didn't take long, however, for other California winemakers to begin making and marketing superpremium blended red wines. By 1988, these wines were given a semi-official name: Meritage (which rhymes with *heritage*). Not all wineries call their best red blends Meritage, but at this point about forty of them do. There are probably another forty cabernet-merlot-cabernet franc blends that would meet the criteria used to define the term: the wine is a blend of two or more traditional Bordeaux varieties, it is the best wine made by the winery, it is made in the United States, and its production is limited to 25,000 cases. One might add that the wines are, as a group, quite expensive.

We began our tasting of Meritage and Meritage-style California reds by selecting those that were readily available nationwide, then we held a pretasting to narrow the field to fourteen wines. Our list included two ringers: One, the De Lorimier, was tasted twice (it finished in seventh place and in a four-way tie for eighth); the other, the 1990 Pavillon Rouge du Chateau Margaux, a wine from

Bordeaux, finished dead last. Overall, the tasting was sensational.

The celebrated Opus One finished in fourth place, a solid member of the first pack of wines, but also the most expensive of that group. The top-ranked finisher, Justin "Isoceles," costs about $25, just over a third of what you'd pay for a bottle of Opus; I'd consider it a best buy. Ranked second was the rather pricey Dominus, weighing in at about $50 a bottle. The third-place wine, Langtry Meritage (made by Guenoc winery), costs about

$35.

Unlike many of our tastings, those wines that did not score in the top of the range were still roundly enjoyed. Therefore you should not rule out trying some of those that are quite favorably priced. "Marlstone" from Clos du Bois is quite good and sells for about $22. The Meritage from Estancia, despite an eighth-place finish, was described as the "class of the tasting" by our most experienced taster; yet it sells for only $15. ∎

BLIND TASTING RESULTS

"**H**ighly Recommended" wines received raves from several tasters and positive comments from all testers; "Recommended" wines received positive comments with a rave or two; "Not Recommended" wines received few or no positive comments.

1991 Justin "Isoceles"

1990 Dominus Estate

1990 Langtry Meritage

1990 Opus One

HIGHLY RECOMMENDED:

1991 Justin "Isoceles," $25. "Big, well-structured wine with an abundance of fruit." Most tasters found this "smooth," but a number thought it was "closed" or "too tannic."

1990 Dominus Estate, $52. It was almost unanimously agreed that this wine was "smooth, approachable, and sweet."

1990 Langtry Meritage, $37. "Unctuous." "Full, rich, and intense." A wine that will improve with time. Some downgraded it for its "rubbery" nose.

1990 Opus One, $70. "Smooth, complex, and rich, very drinkable with lots of nuances." Many saw this as a "wine for future drinking."

RECOMMENDED:

1990 Clos du Bois "Marlstone," $22. "Real style and balance;" "delicious and luscious." Roundly enjoyed; the main reservation was "Does this wine have the structure to last?" Drink it now and don't worry about it.

1990 Lyeth Meritage, $13. "Harshness up front belies overall sweetness; enjoyable now, better in a couple of years," wrote one taster.

1990 De Lorimier "Mosiac," $18. "Sweet fruit; very approachable; nice wine for the short term." "There is class and there is balance."

1991 Estancia Meritage, $15. Our most experienced taster found this "full-flavored, overwhelming, a world-class wine." Others found it "supple" and "lush," but some called it "weak" and "without potential."

1991 Flora Springs "Trilogy," $25. "Lovely, minty nose, with beautiful fruit," wrote this wine's top fan. "Nice depth and texture; very classy," wrote another. Some found it "unremarkable."

1991 Geyser Peak Reserve "Alexandre," $26. One taster found this "bursting with fruit and tannins, wonderful right now." Others found it "low in flavor."

1991 Concannon "Assemblage," $15. "Spicy and minty nose, with flavor about the same," wrote one fan. But some tasters found it "flabby" and "a bit soft."

1990 Phelps "Insignia," $38. Its one fan found it "big and structured, with a background of concentrated fruit." But most others thought this wine was "unremarkable" or "too harsh."

NOT RECOMMENDED:

1990 Cosentino "The Poet," $28. "Not totally clean but good" was the nicest thing anyone said about this wine.

1990 Pavillon Rouge du Chateau Margaux, $33. Not a ranking which should necessarily reflect badly on this wine; it is austere compared to most California reds.

BOOK
REVIEWS

Bitter Almonds
Maria Grammatico and Mary Taylor Simeti
William Morrow, $20

Mary Taylor Simeti is a gifted cook, a gifted oral historian, and most important, a gifted writer with great respect for her subject. Her first cookbook, *Pomp and Sustenance: Twenty-five Centuries of Sicilian Food* (Knopf, 1989), was a masterful blending of delicious recipes and cultural history. Now, in *Bitter Almonds*—a collaboration with Maria Grammatico, the proprietor of a famous bakery in Erice, Sicily—Simeti takes a further step down the rewarding road on which literature and cooking instructions merge.

The book is divided into two parts. The first is a compelling narrative of Grammatico's life, told in her own very distinctive, powerful voice and accompanied by Simeti's insightful commentary. The second part comprises a collection of Grammatico's recipes for Sicilian pastries.

Like many novels, the narrative portion of the book begins in mid-story. This is a daring technique for a cookbook, but it works. Within a few pages, I was completely caught up in the unfolding story of this strong-willed woman, who at age eleven was shut away from the world in a cloistered convent/orphanage. With Simeti's deft commentary as a guide, I eagerly followed Grammatico's tale as it segued from anger at the harshness of orphanage life, to joy in early memories of her family, to wonder at the redemptive power she found in fashioning the intricate pastries that the nuns sold to raise money.

In the second part of the book, we are given forty-six recipes for those pastries. Some of them—a Pascal lamb fashioned of marzipan, for example—are beyond the reach of all but the most dedicated culinary artists. Many, however, are surprisingly simple, with few ingredients. Sighs and Desires, for instance, are intensely rich, tender cookies fashioned from the almond pastry on which many of the recipes are based. Orange Balls—almonds and sugar ground up with a whole orange and perfumed with rum—are simple in concept and execution but complex in taste. A cake soaked in rum and topped with almond pastry seems the very embodiment of Sicilian dessert tradition. Readers should be aware, though, that these are not confections to be consumed by the handful; instead, they are intensely sweet treats to be doled out on special occasions.

Whether for cultural insight, for recipes that will turn your kitchen into a traditional Sicilian bakery, or simply for a good read, *Bitter Almonds* is a book that should not be missed.

—*John Willoughby*

The Essential Thai Cookbook
Vatcharin Bhumichitr
Clarkson Potter, $32.50

The principle behind this book is simple: Knowing how to buy and use ingredients is the key to mastering an unfamiliar cuisine. As the owner of one of London's leading Thai restaurants, Vatcharin Bhumichitr has witnessed the growing availability of Thai staples in markets in the West. The superb recipes he has collected here demonstrate that most Thai dishes are easy to execute.

The book is divided into four chapters, one for each region of Thailand. Each chapter is subdivided into sections based on ingredients. In each chapter an introductory travelogue with photographs is followed by short essays containing shopping information, lists of English and Thai names, and photographs that enable you to recognize a half dozen chiles, for example, in markets where labelling may not be uniform.

Since recipes are authentic, most require one or two ingredients that can only be purchased in an Asian grocery. Shoppers who mail-order staples (like fish sauce) will be able to prepare about half of the recipes with supermarket ingredients. However, recipes that require ingredients like fresh lemon grass or tiny red Thai chiles will pose a challenge since no substitutes are suggested.

Ingredients aside, the recipes are remarkably simple. Directions are brief and assume basic knowledge of cooking. This style, characteristic of cookbooks for chefs, served me well, but I did run into problems with the Grilled Eggplant with Dried Shrimp and ended up cooking the eggplant twice as long as indicated.

The six other dishes I tested came off without a hitch. Fried Chicken with Garlic and Sesame Seeds is similar to the fiery chopped chicken dishes served in Thai restaurants, only much less greasy and considerably hotter. (The author says he toned down the heat but cautions readers that the food is still quite spicy). Shrimp and Lychee Spring Rolls are easy to assemble and are accompanied by one of the best (and most incendiary) dipping sauces I've ever tasted. Pad Thai—the famous noodle dish with dried shrimp, peanuts, and eggs—is authentic and thankfully not swimming in oil as is often the case.

Given the lack of comprehensive Thai cookbooks in English, this volume is the best I have seen and arguably lives up to the promise of its title. The recipes allow the diligent shopper and confident cook to duplicate traditional dishes, while well-written culinary tours of Thailand provide a background on the history of this cuisine.

—*Jack Bishop*

Mesa Mexicana
Mary Sue Milliken and Susan Feniger,
with Helene Siegel
William Morrow, $17.95

Mesa Mexicana is the second book by Mary Sue Milliken and Susan Feniger, co-chefs of Border Grill in Los Angeles. Their first, *City Cuisine*, defined a hip, restrained, multiethnic style, and *Mesa Mexicana*, while limited to a single cuisine, expresses again the ebullient spirit, high flavor, and uncomplicated procedures for which these two women are known.

Although there are some recipes (like Squash Flower Soup) that few outside the trade will cook, most seem to be easily executed and sound dead-on appealing. I considered, but did not make, Quesadillas with Roasted Garlic and Carnitas; Bread Soup, which is laced with bananas and fresh herbs; and Roast Duck with Chipotle Glaze, all of which are on my list to try this winter.

I did sample Grilled Turkey Breast with Vinegar and Cracked Pepper, which is sort of like a solid version of hot-and-sour soup. It was delicious. I couldn't resist Poached Eggs in Chile Broth, a warmly spiced dish with poblanos and tomatoes; my only objection was the cheese topping, which detracted from the dish's clarity. I also tried the Anticuchos (grilled beef heart, although I used veal). I find it difficult to resist new recipes for unusual meats, and this one didn't disappoint; marinated and grilled on skewers, it was a big hit. Finally, I made Flan, not because I wanted to see if the recipe worked (it did) but for the chance to make homemade condensed milk. Like Milliken and Feniger, I have often wondered if it was possible to make lower-sugar condensed milk; unlike them, I had never figured out how. Well, it *is* possible, it's easy, and it's better.

The food in this book is not strictly authentic, but it is simple to make and powerfully flavorful. That's enough for me. ■

—*Mark Bittman*

SOURCES
AND RESOURCES

Most of the ingredients and materials needed for the recipes in this issue are available at your local supermarket, gourmet store, or kitchen supply shop. The following are mail-order sources for particular items. Prices listed below are current at press time and do not include shipping or handling unless otherwise indicated. Contact companies directly to confirm prices and availability.

COFFEE GRINDERS
Among the burr grinders tested for the article on page 28, our top choice is the Saeco Model 2002, which is available through the Front Gate catalog (800-537-8484) for $199.95. For budget-conscious shoppers who want a burr grinder, we also have a recommended best buy, the Braun Aromatic Coffee Mill Model KMM 20. The Braun grinder retails for $81, but is often sharply discounted since it is being phased out in 1995. To find a local store that carries this grinder, contact Braun's customer service department at 800-272-8611. Our favorite blade chopper was the Bosch Model MKM 6. This grinder retails for about $25, but the Starbucks catalog (800-782-7282) sells it under their own label for $19.95. It is also available at Starbucks stores.

BOTTLES FOR INFUSED OILS
You may want to store homemade infused oils (see page 15) in attractive glass bottles. The Williams-Sonoma catalog (800-541-2233) imports slender glass bottles from Italy. The bottles, which cost $24 for a set of six, have four sides and gently rounded corners and can hold one liter each. Williams-Sonoma also sells smaller green glass bottles with a capacity of sixteen ounces. These hand-blown bottles have a raised vineyard motif and are priced at $24 for a set of six.

PURCHASING POLENTA
Any medium-grind cornmeal will make good polenta, but the author of the polenta story on page 20 raved to us about the medium-grind yellow cornmeal from Arrowhead Mills. We were also consistently pleased with this product, which is sold in two-pound bags in some supermarkets as well as in health food stores across the country. If you have trouble finding it, Arrowhead Mills will ship directly to consumers. For more information, call 806-364-0730 and ask for their catalog. Minimum order $5.

DOUBLE BOILERS
We found that preparing polenta in a double boiler eliminates the guesswork. Double boilers also prevent scorching of delicate sauces and allow sauces to be held without separating. If money is no object, Sur La Table (410 Terry Avenue North, Seattle, WA 98109-5229; 800-243-0852) imports an attractive and functional French double boiler with a copper base, a thick white porcelain insert, and polished bronze handles. It comes in two sizes, one quart and one and three-quarters quarts. We recommend the larger size, which costs $134.95. For less expensive double boilers, A Cook's Wares (211 37th Street, Beaver Falls, PA 15010; 412-846-9490) sells double boiler inserts from All-Clad that are made from stainless steel and aluminum and are designed to fit various All-Clad saucepans. For instance, the All-Clad Master Chef three-quart aluminum insert costs $55 and will fit into either the three-and-one-half- or four-and-one-half-quart Master Chef saucepan. A Cook's Wares also sells double boiler inserts for Cuisinart and Le Creuset saucepans.

CHORIZO SAUSAGE
Chorizo, the spicy pork sausage used in the paella recipe on page 11, is a common ingredient in the cooking of Spain and Portugal. The Massachusetts city of Fall River is known for its large population of immigrants from the Iberian Peninsula. A local store, Sardinha's Gourmet Sausages (206 Brownell Street, Fall River, MA 02720; 800-678-0178), sells more than a dozen types of chorizo. Varieties are based on spiciness—mild, medium, and hot—as well as size—large half-pound links, smaller frankfurter-size links, patties, ground, and chopped. Regular chorizo products cost $4.50 per pound. Sardinha's also makes an unusual chicken chorizo for sausage lovers looking for lighter links. Note that there is a seven-pound minimum but that prices include shipping in vacuum-sealed bags that keep sausages fresh for about ten days. Sausages can be frozen once they arrive at your home.

SPECIALTY FLOURS AND BAKING EQUIPMENT
The King Arthur Flour Baker's Catalogue (P.O. Box 876, Norwich, VT 05055; 800-827-6836) carries dozens of flours, from a special high-protein flour priced at $3.50 for a five-pound bag to white wheat flour (which has the nutritional benefits of whole wheat but is lighter in color) at a cost of $3.95 for a five-pound bag. They also carry a giant spatula with a nine-and-one-fifth-by-10-inch blade for $14.95, which is wonderful for moving up to six cups of sticky bread dough from a bread board to a bowl. They also have the Thermapen pocket thermometer ($62.95) with a stainless steel probe that is perfect for checking a thick-crusted country loaf or for roast turkey. The extra-large digital display measures up to 550 degrees. Although we find that small, round-faced instant thermometers are sometimes hard to read, they certainly are the better buy for budget-conscious shoppers. King Arthur carries a stainless steel thermometer with a good-size dial that costs just $12.95. The catalog also carries a twelve-inch-round muslin-lined basket, called a *banneton*, which is the ideal place to let a sticky dough rise. Unfortunately, these imported French baskets are rather expensive at $79.95 each. You can make your own banneton by lining any willow basket with muslin, which is available at most any fabric store.

WEST COAST SPECIALTY FLOURS
In addition to products from King Arthur, we highly recommend flours from Giusto's Vita-Grain. Flours from this small California miller are available through a catalog put together by Pamela's Products (156 Utah Avenue, South San Francisco, CA 94080; 415-952-4546). The catalog sells specialty items such as whole wheat, high-protein, coarse flour, lima bean flour, and spelt flour, as well as an array of brans, cereals, and pancake mixes. Flour comes in packages ranging from two pounds to fifty pounds. Prices are a bit lower than King Arthur flours, especially for bakers on the West Coast since shipping costs will be lower.

COTTON PASTRY CLOTH
The country bread (see page 9) rises in a metal colander so that air can circulate around the dough. We use a large cotton pastry cloth to prevent this wet dough from sticking to the metal. If you can't find a pastry cloth locally, Wilton Enterprises (2240 West 75th Street, Woodbridge, IL 60517; 708-963-7100) sells one that mesures twenty-four by twenty inches. The cloth comes in a set with a rolling pin cover and costs $4.99.

PAELLA PAN
The paella recipe on page 11 can be prepared in a twelve-inch skillet. However, a traditional paella pan makes a more attractive vessel for bringing the finished dish to the table. We especially like the enameled-steel paella pan carried by the Williams-Sonoma catalog (800-541-2233) that can go from stovetop to oven to table. The pan costs $12.

PUDDING CAKE RAMEKINS
The pudding cakes on page 24 can be baked in one large pan or in individual glass or ceramic dishes. If you are someone who can't seem to own enough porcelain, you should know about the catalog from Sisson Imports (32718 193rd Avenue S.E., Kent, WA 98042; 800-423-2756), a company that imports white porcelain bakeware and serving pieces from France. Either their six-ounce ramekins that measure three and one-half inches across and one and one-half inches deep, or the individual deep soufflé cups that are four inches across and two and one-half inches deep and hold just over one cup, are perfect for baking small portions of pudding cake batter. The ramekins cost $2 each and come in sets of six. The soufflé cups cost $4.50 each and come in sets of four. ∎

COOK'S
ILLUSTRATED

Juicy, Flavorful Beef Brisket

We Find the Perfect Balance of Cooking Time and Oven Temperature

Smooth, Rich Crème Brûlée

Use Chilled Cream for Best Texture

Tasting Balsamic Vinegars

Best-Selling Brands Finish Last

Tricks to Steaming Fish

Quick, Healthful Techniques

SECRETS OF GNOCCHI

•

RATING RICE COOKERS

•

ITALIAN VEGETABLE PASTA SAUCES

TASTING INEXPENSIVE RHÔNE WINES

$4.00 U.S./$4.95 CANADA

"Leeks"
See page 14 for the best way to cook leeks.

ILLUSTRATION BY
BRENT WATKINSON

Garlic and Sage Soup adapted from *Mediterranean the Beautiful Cookbook* (Collins, 1994), by Joyce Goldstein

ILLUSTRATION BY
CAROL FORTUNATO

COOK'S
ILLUSTRATED

Publisher and Editor CHRISTOPHER KIMBALL

Executive Editor MARK BITTMAN

Senior Editor JOHN WILLOUGHBY

Food Editor PAM ANDERSON

Senior Writer JACK BISHOP

Articles Editor ANNE TUOMEY

Managing Editor MAURA LYONS

Assistant Managing Editor TRICIA O'BRIEN

Copy Editor KURT TIDMORE

Editorial Assistant KIM N. RUSSELLO

Test Cook VICTORIA ROLAND

Art Director MEG BIRNBAUM

Food Stylist MARIE PIRAINO

Special Projects Designer AMY KLEE

Marketing Director ADRIENNE KIMBALL

Circulation Director ELAINE REPUCCI

Circulation Assistant JENNIFER L. KEENE

Customer Service JONATHAN VENIER

Production Director JAMES MCCORMACK

Production Assistants SHEILA DATZ
PAMELA SLATTERY

Publicity Director CAROL ROSEN KAGAN

Treasurer JANET CARLSON

Accounting Assistant MANDY SHITO

Office Manager JENNY THORNBURY

Office Assistant SARAH CHUNG

Special Projects FERN BERMAN

Cook's Illustrated (ISSN 1068-2821) is published bimonthly by Boston Common Press, 17 Station Street, Box 569, Brookline, MA 02147-0569. Copyright 1995 Boston Common Press. Application to mail at second-class postage rates is pending at Boston, MA, and additional mailing offices. Editorial office: 17 Station Street, Box 569, Brookline, MA 02147-0569; (617) 232-1000, FAX (617) 232-1572. Editorial contributions should be sent to: Editor, *Cook's Illustrated*, 17 Station Street, Box 569, Brookline, MA 02147-0569. We cannot assume responsibility for manuscripts submitted to us. Submissions will be returned only if accompanied by a large self-addressed stamped envelope. Subscription rates: $24.95 for one year; $45 for two years; $65 for three years. (Canada: add $3 per year; all other countries: add $12 per year.) Postmaster: Send all new orders, subscription inquiries, and change of address notices to *Cook's Illustrated*, P.O. Box 59046, Boulder, CO 80322-9046. Single copies: $4 in U.S., $4.95 in Canada and foreign. Back issues available for $5 each. PRINTED IN THE U.S.A.

EDITORIAL

COMMON GROUND

CHRISTOPHER KIMBALL

William James is a writer and critic for *Time* and the author of a provocative book entitled *In Defense of Elitism*. In it he raises the issue of the American melting pot—a society where immigrants unite under the banner of common interest to create a homogenous culture— and asks the obvious question: What have we lost by exchanging the notion of a common set of values for a rampant cultural individualism?

The comparison with America's culinary history is clear and immediate. In reaction to both our homogenized culture and our declining cuisine, Americans have embarked on a commendable search for improvement. But in this search for satisfying culture and cuisine, many of us have opted for an archeological pursuit of cuisines from around the world. We want to discover the true culinary heritage of Tuscany or the real method for making couscous from scratch (which takes most of your day and all of your patience—the recipe on page 12 is more suited to modern times). These culinary expeditions set out with romantic notions about other cultures, past or present, and often disregard the realities of modern American life.

Perhaps we feel that our own culinary history is somehow lacking. But according to Evan Jones in *American Food*, the Pilgrims often dined royally on beach plum jam and soft-shelled crab. Summer succotash was common New England fare, made from shell beans stewed with bacon and onions and then mixed with fresh corn, black pepper, and rich, sweet cream. Deliciously crisp, golden corn oysters, which are no more than fried corn pulp, were made from freshly harvested ears. Authentic baked beans came in as many varieties as cassoulet and were every bit as good. Country-cured hams could match any prosciutto and were no less a measure of culinary artistry. "The making of a ham dinner," one Southerner wrote, "like the making of a gentleman, starts a long, long time before the event." And don't forget plantation skillet cakes, boiled lobsters, maple syrup, beaten biscuits, hominy grits, clambakes, and pandowdies.

At the heart of all good, populist cooking is economy, forthrightness, and a good measure of common sense. Today, New England cooking may seem unduly heavy, but without central heating, Pilgrim fare had to be substantial. The Puritan heritage also engendered Yankee frugality. Out of strict religious observance came the notion of good, plain food made with the ingredients at hand, a notion that is at the core of any good cuisine. And since the Sabbath lasted from sundown on Saturday to sundown on Sunday, early cooks had to devise dishes that could be baked ahead and then simply reheated. If nothing else, American cooking was practical.

As we race to reinvent our culinary present, let's remind ourselves of our own history of practicality and economy. Just as the Puritans had to work around the realities of daily life, we should do the same. Instead of importing ingredients, let's use what is grown locally. Let's once again eat with the seasons, when the produce is both cheapest and at its best. With two working parents, most households have to prepare a meal in less than an hour. That means more quick, high-heat cooking and less slow roasting or stewing. It calls for one-dish meals instead of chicken and two vegetables. It also calls for economy of technique—finding new ways to make great food with less fuss. And most of us need lighter fare, since we spend our days sitting at desks instead of clearing fields.

It is my belief that at six o'clock in the evening most adult Americans are standing on common ground. We need to get a good dinner on the table, and it makes little difference where we live or who our ancestors were. For better or worse, we share a modern lifestyle and therefore share the need for a modern American cuisine. Let's stop running helter-skelter down the road to diversity, a path that leads to culinary anarchy. Culinary elitism offers no answers to our culinary dilemma.

Anyone who doubts the value of a melting-pot cuisine should consider Thanksgiving, the one holiday most Americans cherish. In the simplest terms, Thanksgiving is about 240 million people eating the same menu on the same day. We compare notes on how the turkey was cooked, on the flakiness of the pumpkin pie crust, and on the components of the stuffing. It feels good to share the menu with our neighbors. Despite the abundance of the table, it's also a meal that has echoes of our ancestral frugality; the leftovers are eagerly consumed over the long weekend.

As a culture, we gain much from a shared cuisine. It helps to bind us together in a time when we are constantly being urged to pull apart by expressing our individuality. We should heed the lessons of Thanksgiving. Let's give thanks for our own foods, reflect on the practical legacy of our culinary past, and then set out to retool American cooking for the next century. But let's do it together. We are in desperate need of common ground. ∎

NOTES FROM READERS

PRESERVED LEMONS

I recently ran across several recipes that called for preserved lemons. Is this something I can make at home?

BRUCE HAINLEY
New Haven, CT

Preserved lemons are a popular pantry item in many parts of the Mediterranean, especially North Africa. Salt pickles and preserves the lemons, which plump and soften over time. This condiment is frequently added to salads (particularly those with olives) or dishes made with chicken or fish. While it may be possible to find a specialty store that prepares and sells preserved lemons, it's probably easier to make them yourself. Simply scrub two large lemons under cold running water and pat them dry. Cut the lemons into eight or so wedges (or slice them into thick circles) and toss these with one-fourth cup of coarse salt. Place the salted lemons in a sterilized glass jar with a lid. Pour enough fresh lemon juice into the jar to cover the lemons, and seal it tightly. Let the lemons stand at room temperature for a week to ten days, shaking and turning the jar over once a day to redistribute the contents. Rinse the salted lemons and use them immediately, or cover them with oil and store them in the refrigerator for several weeks.

HOW TO MEASURE

A discussion of wet and dry measures in the September/October 1994 issue of Cook's Illustrated *(Notes from Readers) strongly implied that the two types are somehow inherently different. This would be astonishing if true. As Gertrude Stein might have said, a cup is a cup is a cup. It's eight fluid ounces, whether of water carefully added right up to the eight-ounce mark in a glass measuring cup, or of sugar leveled off flush with the rim of an eight-ounce metal cup. The two measuring containers hold exactly the same volume.*

*But as your note pointed out, it's inconvenient to fill a metal cup precisely to the rim with a liquid. We use a "wet" measuring cup, which allows the liquid to level itself while remaining well below the rim; it's made of glass or transparent plastic so we can see exactly where that level is. We must level the solids, however, by scraping them off across the flat rim of the cup, which can be made of opaque plastic or metal. That's the only difference between "wet" and "dry" mea-*suring cups.

What contradicted all common sense, therefore, was your statement that a leveled-off metal measuring cup of sugar fell short of the one-cup mark when transferred to a glass measure. But baffling as it may sound, this observation is perfectly correct. So what's going on? The answer lies in the nature of liquids and solids, not the measuring cups themselves.

When you pour a liquid into a container it flows down into every crevice, leaving no spaces, not even microscopic ones. But granulated solids can settle unpredictably, depending on the shape and size of the grains and of the container into which they are poured. When poured into a wide container, the grains can spread out and settle down more tightly than when they are stacked up in a narrow container. When settled more densely, they occupy less volume, so that the same amount of sugar will actually occupy less volume in a wide container than in a narrow one.

Since most glass measures are wider than "dry" metal ones, sugar as well as flour (which is notorious for its erratic settling) will occupy less volume in the glass cups. To confirm this phenomenon, I poured a level measuring cup of sugar into a chemist's graduated cylinder—a tall, narrow, glass measuring vessel. As expected, the sugar filled the cylinder quite a bit higher than the eight-ounce mark.

The moral of all this is that granulated or powdered solids are most accurately measured by weight. If you choose to measure them by volume, use metal or plastic dry measures since that's what the recipe developer probably used.

ROBERT L. WOLKE
Professor Emeritus of Chemistry
University of Pittsburgh
Pittsburgh, PA

COOKING IN BED

This past summer I had guests from Denmark, and they told me about an intriguing cooking method—cooking in bed. At first, I thought that perhaps my friend sat in bed while preparing vegetables. No, she told me that she literally cooks her food in bed while she goes to the beach. For example, she starts potatoes on the stove and, once the water is boiling, removes the pot from the stove, places it in the bed, and surrounds it with blankets. The potatoes are done when she returns a few hours later.

My Danish friend ran a restaurant and said she used the same technique to prepare roast beef, *and it was never overcooked. She says this is an old cooking method that she learned from other chefs, some of whom used hay or loose blankets, but I wonder how safe this can be. I am a home economist by profession and am concerned about bacterial buildup.*

LUCILLE PANTEL
South Fallsburg, NY

This cooking method is certainly unusual but not necessarily unique. In many cultures, food has traditionally been slow-cooked in places where heat could be trapped. For instance, some barbecue recipes call for burying wrapped meat in the ground with hot coals. Cooking under blankets in the bed certainly seems related to other ancient, low-fuel cooking methods.

However, you are right to be concerned about food-borne illnesses. While bacteria grow quite slowly when food is chilled in the refrigerator and are killed by high temperatures (such as those in a conventional oven), bacteria thrive in just the kind of warm environment you are describing. While this is not a problem with vegetables, we would not recommend preparing meat in bed. "Cooking" meat at such a low temperature may prevent an overdone roast but will allow bacteria to multiply rapidly and can cause illness. In any case, cooking between the sheets sounds like a messy proposition to us, especially if you plan on sleeping in that bed.

DUNGENESS CRABS

I have recently moved from the East Coast to California so I am now easily able to buy the famed Dungeness crab. Can you tell me a little about this species and how it differs from the crabs I ate when I lived in Maine?

KURT KRUGER
San Francisco, CA

The Dungeness is a Pacific crab found in waters from Alaska to Baja California. A member of the rock crab family, the Dungeness takes its name from a small town on the Olympic Peninsula in Washington, where it was first commercially caught. By law, only adult males at least six and one-quarter inches long can be harvested. Therefore, Dungeness are particularly meaty crabs, weighing at least two pounds and often more. The meat of the crabs, which are in their prime season during the winter, is so rich and firm-textured it is perhaps more akin to the lobster meat you enjoyed in Maine than to the blue crab that inhabits Atlantic and Gulf waters. While you should be able to buy live Dungeness crabs in San Francisco, most of the country has to rely on cooked and frozen whole crabs. Live crabs can be boiled in water or a seasoned crab boil. Simply crack the claws and body to eat them. Cooked and frozen crabs can be defrosted, cracked, dressed with vinaigrette, and tossed over salad greens.

DUALIT TOASTER

*B*ack in 1993, I bought the Dualit toaster that you reviewed in your September/October 1994 issue. I knew that these expensive toasters ($215) are restaurant standard in the United Kingdom (where they are made) and that they work very well there. However, I was both disappointed and curious when I got such lousy results with the toaster I purchased here in New York.

I faxed a note to the company and learned that U.S. safety regulations limit the toaster to 1650 watts for the four-slice model, while the original design exceeds 2000 watts. The note I received from the company assured me that they had done much research and development to get the toaster to work as well as possible on American current. But these assurances were empty, given the poor performance, so naturally I returned the toaster.

EDWARD SCHNEIDER
New York, NY

INSTANT YEAST

I have a breadstick recipe that calls for instant yeast, which is added directly to the dough without first proofing. How is instant yeast different from regular active dry yeast, and where can I buy it?

PAT REBUCCI
Mountain Lakes, NJ

Instant yeast was developed in Europe during the late 1960s as an alternative to the active dry yeast that comes in small packets and is sold in American supermarkets. Instant yeast contains a different strain of yeast that is more vigorous.

Both types of yeast undergo a drying process during which live yeast cells become encapsulated inside dead ones. Adding water to the yeast releases the live cells from their "coffins" and allows them to work. The drying process used with active dry yeast involves higher temperatures and results in about 25 percent dead weight in the final product. Warm water is needed to free the live cells before the yeast is added to the dough. This is why recipes with active dry yeast usually call for proofing—a step that involves dissolving the yeast in water between 105 and 115 degrees. This also allows the baker to test (or *proof*) the strength of the yeast. Old or dead yeast will not bubble and can be discarded before being added to the dough.

In contrast, instant yeast is dried at a much lower temperature and has just 5 percent dead cells. Instant yeast is also more granular and porous—all traits that permit the quick absorption of water. Therefore, instant yeast does not need to be soaked in water before use and can be added directly to the flour. Soaking in water does no harm to instant yeast). Instant yeast also has a considerably wider temperature tolerance than active dry yeast; it is activated between 80 and 120 degrees.

You may use instant yeast in recipes that call for active dry yeast, but decrease the quantity of yeast by 25 percent to account for its added strength. (Replace every packet of active dry yeast with two teaspoons of instant yeast.) You also may notice that doughs made with instant yeast rise more quickly because the yeast works more consistently. SAF Instant Yeast from France is available through the Williams-Sonoma catalog (800-541-2233). A 5.3-ounce package contains the equivalent of fifteen individual packets of active dry yeast and costs $7.

CONFECTIONERS' SUGAR

*W*hat's the difference between various confectioners' sugars? Does it matter whether I buy one labeled XXXX or 10X? They are the same price in my supermarket, but I assume there must be a difference.

SUSAN OTTEN
Charleston, SC

You are right; there is a difference between these sugars, but it is fairly minor and rarely matters, according to the experts we spoke with at Domino Sugar and Dixie Crystals. The higher the number on the box—those commonly available are 4X (or XXXX), 6X, and 10X—the finer the sugar has been ground. The amount of cornstarch (which is added to all confectioners' sugar to prevent clumping) remains the same.

The only time that you may want to pay attention to the fineness of your confectioners' sugar is when you are making frostings. A finer grind (10X) will make the smoothest icing for cakes. However, there are times when you want a thicker, firmer frosting, such as for the flowers on a wedding cake. In that case, a 4X confectioners' sugar would provide the additional strength you are looking for.

FREEZING LEMON ZEST

*I*s it possible to save the zest from lemons that I am about to juice and then use the zest later? If so, should I freeze the lemon zest or keep it in the refrigerator?

SCOTT GEWIRTZ
New York, NY

Your question intrigued us so we zested several lemons (both with a grater and with a zester to make long strips of peel). We then wrapped the zest in plastic and then in aluminum foil. We put several of these wrapped packages into the refrigerator and several into the freezer. After three days, we removed one package from the refrigerator and one from the freezer. The refrigerated zest had lost most of its flavor and aroma and was not usable. However, zest that had been frozen and thawed tasted almost as good as fresh, even though it had lost some of its color. After three weeks, frozen zest still had a bright lemon flavor. Although we would not use frozen zest as a garnish (the color is too anemic), the flavor of zest frozen up to three weeks is fine, so you can use it in cooking with no qualms. ∎

WHAT IS IT?

I own a large assortment of kitchen utensils and recently purchased this whisk to add to my collection. I was wondering if it has a special purpose?

BUDDY GOLD
New York, NY

Your new purchase is a flat or spiral sauce whisk, most likely from Europe or at least based on a European design. The principle behind this whisk is simple. A regular wire whisk is great for whipping egg whites to stiff peaks but is not the best tool for mixing sauces, soups, or custards in a pan. That's because very little of a regular whisk actually comes in contact with the bottom of the pan. The curved design also makes stirring around the sides of a pan difficult and can lead to some burning and scorching.

The coil on a flat or spiral sauce whisk is offset from the handle and stem so that when the coil is parallel to the bottom of the pan the handle stands up and can be used to move the whisk around the sides of the pan. La Cuisine Kitchenware (323 Cameron Street, Alexandria, VA 22314; 800-521-1176) carries two spiral sauce whisks. An eleven-inch-long spiral whisk from Denmark is identical to the one pictured above and costs $8. This whisk can handle large quantities of sauce or gravy and is perfect for whisking thin batters for crepes or popovers. A smaller eight-inch whisk with a teardrop-shaped coil that is completely closed is best for beating a few eggs in a bowl or whisking a small quantity of sauce on top of the stove. This whisk is imported from France and also costs $8.

Quick Tips

TO CHOP FENNEL SEEDS

Small, hard seeds like fennel do not grind well, and they are seemingly impossible to chop because they scatter all over the counter when you bear down on them. To overcome this problem, follow this tip from cooking teacher, cookbook author, and regular *Cook's Illustrated* contributor Stephen Schmidt.

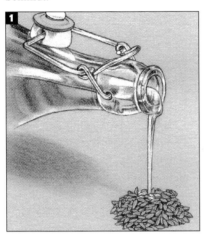

1. Pour just enough water or oil on a small pile of the seeds to moisten them.

2. Seeds can then be chopped with a chef's knife without flying all over the kitchen.

TO KEEP CAKE FILLING FROM BLEEDING INTO FROSTING

When a cake filling differs in color from the outer frosting, it often seeps through the frosting and mars the appearance of the cake. To prevent this from happening, follow this tip from Patricia Marino of Rutherford, New Jersey.

1. Fill a pastry bag with the outer frosting and fit it with a plain, round tip. Pipe a circle of the frosting around the top edge of all the layers except the one that will form the top of the cake.

2. Spread the filling inside this frosting ring. The frosting ring will seal the layers of the cake together and prevent the filling from seeping out.

TO CLEAN A FOOD PROCESSOR BOWL

The easiest way to clean bowls is to soak them with water prior to washing them. However, the hole in the center of a food processor bowl makes this impossible to do. Cooking teacher, author, and master baker Flo Braker of Palo Alto, California, has come up with a way to circumvent this problem.

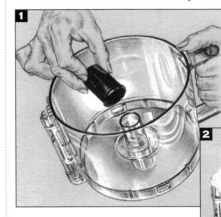

1. Remove the bowl cover and blade from the bowl. Set an empty 35mm film canister upside down over the hole in the food processor bowl.

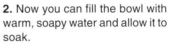

2. Now you can fill the bowl with warm, soapy water and allow it to soak.

TO MAKE A COOKBOOK HOLDER

In many kitchens, counter space is at a premium, and there is no room for an open cookbook. G. Grant of Framingham, Massachusetts, has devised this homemade cookbook holder made of coat hangers.

1. Cut the hooks off of two coat hangers just below their twists.

2. Use pliers to straighten the coat hanger wire. Then bend a hook into each end of each piece of wire, making sure that the hooks bend in opposite directions on each piece of wire and that the bottom hook is longer than the top hook.

3. Hang the wires by their top hooks over a cabinet door, spacing them to accommodate the size book or magazine you're using.

ILLUSTRATIONS BY ALAN WITSCHONKE

To Form Icebox Cookies

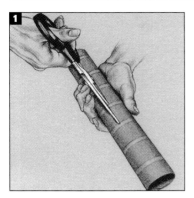

When making icebox cookies, follow this tip from Betty Roan of Westminster, Colorado, to form perfectly round cookies.

1. Use scissors to cut down the length of a cardboard tube, such as the core of a roll of paper towels.

2. Line the inside of the tube with waxed paper.

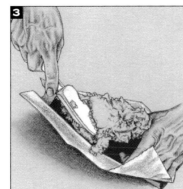

3. Pack the cookie dough into the tube.

4. When the tube is full, close it, wrap a rubber band around each end, and refrigerate it. After the dough is chilled, unwrap it and slice it for baking. The dough will be perfectly shaped.

To Replicate Magi-Cake Strips

Moistened Magi-Cake Strips prevent cakes from peaking, cracking, and overbrowning. One of Stephen Schmidt's cooking students from New Jersey has come up with a way to make these strips in your kitchen using newspaper.

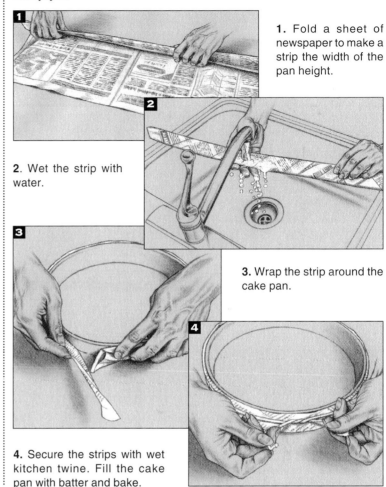

1. Fold a sheet of newspaper to make a strip the width of the pan height.

2. Wet the strip with water.

3. Wrap the strip around the cake pan.

4. Secure the strips with wet kitchen twine. Fill the cake pan with batter and bake.

To Easily Skin Tomatoes

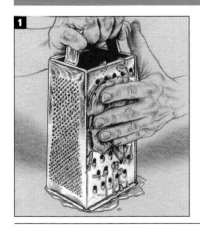

While traveling in the Eastern Mediterranean gathering material for her latest book, culinary historian and cookbook author Paula Wolfert (*see* Master Class on page 12) discovered this quick and easy way to skin tomatoes.

1. Cut the tomatoes in half, remove the seeds, and grate the tomatoes on the side of the grater with the largest holes.

2. You will end up with grated pulp and no skin.

To Grease Pans, Mess-Free

Dawn Mason of Madison, Wisconsin, suggests purchasing a bottle moistener with a sponge tip, filling it with oil, and using it to grease baking pans. No more greasy paper towels or fingers.

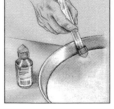

Perfect Crème Brûlée

Slow, gentle heat is the key to perfect custard, so for the best crème brûlée, use chilled cream, a protective water bath, and a low oven temperature.

~ BY GENE FREELAND ~

My objective was simple—find the perfect recipe for classic crème brûlée. My standards were high—I wanted a custard that was light, firm, smooth, creamy, sweet, fragrant, and slightly eggy, with a brown sugar crust that was both delicate and crisp. And, of course, making the process easy and quick was also a consideration.

As I attempted to reach this elusive goal, trying some thirty-six variations along the way, I found that the process was one of exclusion, not inclusion. The fewest ingredients, fewest steps, and simplest cooking techniques delivered the best results.

The Custard

Probably the biggest challenge to making crème brûlée is getting the texture of the custard right. In consulting dozens of recipes, I found a surprising number of options for the custard ingredients, in-cluding variations on the eggs (either yolks only or whole eggs), the sugar (white, brown, or none at all), the flavorings (vanilla, rum, kirsch, various liqueurs, instant espresso, cinnamon, and grated nutmeg), and most importantly, the cream (heavy, whipping, or half-and-half). Further variations could be found in the cooking techniques, such as the temperature of the cream (from boiling to chilled) and whether to cook the custard on the stove or in the oven.

I experimented with every possible variation, but found that the most crucial were the type of cream, the cooking time and temperature, and where the custard was cooked. (The results of my experiments with other ingredients are listed in "Searching for Perfect Crème Brûlée," page 7.)

I started with a simple, traditional crème brûlée recipe that calls for two cups of heavy cream to be boiled for one minute, beaten into four egg yolks, returned to the fire over low flame (in a double boiler if desired), then stirred until nearly boiling. The mixture is then poured into a greased baking dish, chilled, covered with a thin layer of brown sugar, caramelized under the broiler, chilled again, and served.

I began by making separate versions of this recipe using all three types of cream, and cooking them in the oven, on top of the stove in a pan, and on top of the stove in a double boiler.

The custard made with heavy cream, which contains between 36 and 40 percent fat, was way too rich; half-and-half, with between 10½ and 18 percent fat, made a watery custard. Whipping cream (sometimes called light whipping cream), which is between 30 and 36 percent fat, gave the custard the smooth, sweet, balanced flavor and texture I wanted.

After this first set of tests, I also dismissed cooking the custard on the stovetop in a saucepan, since the results were so poor. The double boiler was not much better, but I decided to try some variations before giving up on this more forgiving method.

I also decided to call Shirley Corriher, cooking teacher and resident food science advisor for *Cook's Illustrated*, to discuss the results of my tests. Corriher started with some basic custard science. She explained that when egg yolks are heated, the bonds that hold together the proteins in the yolks begin to break. The proteins then unwind with their bonds sticking out, run into other unwound proteins, and bind together to form a three-dimensional mesh. This is what causes a custard to thicken. When a custard reaches 180 degrees, the proteins bond together so extensively that they form clumps and the eggs curdle—in effect, they become scrambled eggs.

Because of this dynamic, the speed with which you heat the custard mixtures is very important. "If the eggs are heated quickly, they won't thicken until well into the 170-degree range, sometimes just before 180 degrees, leaving little time for thickening before curdling," Corriher warned me. "If the eggs are heated slowly, though, thickening can start at 150 degrees and continue slowly as the custard heats past 160 and 170 degrees." Slow, gentle heat, then, is the best—and probably the only—way to succeed with custards. Given that explanation, it was obvious that cooking the custard directly over heat was the worst possible way, as it heated the custard most quickly.

Custard science also explains why, in my next set of tests, I discovered that using up to a tablespoon of granulated sugar per egg yolk improved

---

SEARCHING FOR PERFECT CRÈME BRÛLÉE

In my search for the perfect crème brûlée, I tried dozens of possible variations with the basic ingredients of cream, eggs, and sugar. The following list highlights some of my failures along the road to successful crème brûlée.

EXPERIMENT	CONCLUSION
Heavy cream used in custard	Too rich for its own good
Half-and-half used in custard	Weak flavor and watery texture
Whole eggs used in custard	Too dense and firm
Flavorings such as vanilla, cinnamon, nutmeg, and instant espresso	Extracts and spices detract from the sweet cream and egg flavors
Caramelized white sugar used in custard	Flavor is burned and texture is grainy
Brown sugar used in custard	Texture is grainy, flavor too sweet
Salt added to the custard	Odd and out of place
Cornstarch added to custard cooked in double boiler	May help prevent curdling, but leaves behind a grainy texture and makes custard very dense
⅓-inch brown sugar topping	Forms thick barrier that is too difficult to penetrate
Powdered sugar used to dust buttered ramekins	Even small amounts make the custard too sweet

---

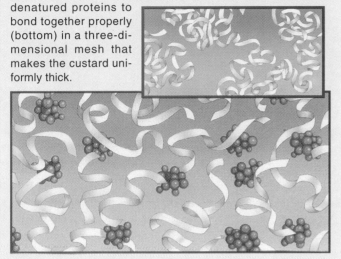

When eggs are heated too quickly or with too hot a flame, the proteins in the eggs, denatured by the heat, bond together too extensively and form clumps (top), curdling the mixture. Proper heating technique and the presence of large sugar molecules, which inhibit bonding to some degree, cause the denatured proteins to bond together properly (bottom) in a three-dimensional mesh that makes the custard uniformly thick.

the texture of the custard, while cornstarch made it extremely dense, grainy, and sticky.

Corriher explained that sugar molecules are very large—she calls them "Mack trucks"—and therefore come between unwound egg proteins during cooking, in effect blocking, at least temporarily, their attempts to bond. As my tests confirmed, adding sugar improves the texture of the custard. Cornstarch works in a similar fashion, but unfortunately it also gives the custard an unpleasant graininess.

Corriher also mentioned that stirring constantly, which is necessary to keep the heat evenly distributed in a double boiler, where the heat all comes from the bottom, makes thickening more difficult. As you stir, you actually break apart the egg proteins as they attempt to bond to each other. While this is fine for a custard like crème anglaise that should be thin enough to pour, crème brûlée has to be dense. At this point, it seemed time to move on to the oven.

I first tried placing uncooked and uncovered custards in a warm water bath, called a *bain marie*, in a cold oven, turned the heat to 250 degrees, and baked for eighty minutes. This first attempt at oven-cooking was a disaster. The custard did not set right, cooked unevenly, and was too runny, and the brown sugar toppings absorbed moisture when they caramelized and turned into iron plates. More lessons learned.

I next tried covering and cooking the custard in a warm water bath in a preheated, 350-degree oven for fifteen minutes. When these custards had been cooked, chilled, topped and caramelized, chilled again, and finally served, I knew I was getting close to reaching my goal.

As a final test, I compared uncovered custards cooked in a bain marie with those cooked without a water bath in 300-degree oven. Dry heat caused the baked custards to set like omelets. Cooking the custards in a bain marie keeps their temperature from rising above 212 degrees; this low temperature guarantees that the custard approaches its set point slowly and therefore thickens gradually. At this lower temperature, the custards cooked in the water bath were also silkier than those baked in a 350-degree oven. As a final refinement, I lowered the oven temperature to 275 degrees and increased the cooking time to forty-five minutes. Even better.

Had I exhausted all the custard options? Not yet! I decided to fiddle with the temperature of the cream. Until now, I'd always boiled the cream for a minute or so and then mixed it into the yolk-sugar mixture. Now, I tried my recipe with scalded cream, room temperature cream, and chilled cream straight from the fridge. I was pleasantly surprised to find that the chilled cream sample was richer, smoother, and more velvety than its scalded or room temperature counterparts.

When I mentioned this to Corriher, she was a bit surprised. To my thinking, adding boiling or scalded cream to the yolks would raise their temperature too quickly. Corriher said this was correct but that dairy products are usually scalded to cause some of their proteins to unwind and help promote thickening. After some thought, she said this was essential when making ice cream, which has a high proportion of milk. Unlike milk, however, high-fat cream does not have all that much protein, so the benefits of scalding or boiling the cream would be minor. Also, adding hot cream certainly raises the temperature of the eggs very quickly. Since the secret to perfect crème brûlée is very slow heat, using chilled cream fit in with the rest of my results.

The Topping

While working on the custard variations, I also experimented with the caramelized sugar topping. The first recipe I had tried called for a brown sugar topping so thick that it formed a barrier difficult to penetrate with a spoon. I soon realized that two teaspoons of brown sugar per crème brûlée gave the best coverage and depth for even, controllable, and consistent caramelization.

I also tested the relative merits of light and dark brown sugar for the topping. On my first try, the dark brown sugar topping burned quickly, was too hard, and didn't taste as good as the topping made with light brown sugar. However, the light brown sugar topping was not perfect either, so I decided to try drying both light and dark brown sugar for fifteen minutes in a 250-degree oven before sprinkling them over the chilled custards. Pre-drying the brown sugar significantly improved its taste, texture, and appearance when caramelized. Pre-dried dark brown sugar gave the topping a richer flavor that was superior to the light brown sugar topping, just the reverse of when the sugars were not pre-dried.

It seems that drying brown sugar in the oven removes moisture as well as some of the lumps, which makes it easier to sprinkle and allows it to coat more evenly. Also, since the caramelization process involves melting the sugar and then evaporating some of its water, having less water in the brown sugar before it is run under the broiler undoubtedly helps get the process going. A dried sugar topping needs less time under the broiler, so the dark brown sugar, with its richer flavor, can be used without the danger of burning or becoming too hard.

PERFECT CRÈME BRÛLÉE
Serves 6

- 1 tablespoon unsalted butter, softened
- 6 large egg yolks, chilled
- 6 tablespoons white sugar
- 1½ cups whipping cream, chilled
- 4 tablespoons dark brown sugar

1. Adjust oven rack to center position and heat oven to 275 degrees. Butter six ½-cup ramekins or six ⅔-cup custard cups and set them in a glass baking pan.

2. Whisk yolks in a medium bowl until slightly thickened. Add white sugar and whisk until dissolved. Whisk in cream, then pour mixture into prepared ramekins.

3. Set baking dish on oven rack and pour warm water into baking dish to come halfway up the ramekins. Bake uncovered until custards are just barely set, about 45 minutes.

4. Remove baking pan from oven, leaving ramekins in the hot water; cool to room temperature. Cover each ramekin with plastic wrap and refrigerate until chilled, at least 2 hours (can be covered and refrigerated overnight).

5. While custards are cooling, spread brown sugar in a small baking pan; set in turned-off (but still warm) oven until sugar dries, about 20 minutes. Transfer sugar to a small zipper-lock freezer bag; seal bag and crush sugar fine with a rolling pin. Store sugar in an airtight container until ready to top custards.

6. Adjust oven rack to the next-to-the-highest position and heat broiler. Remove chilled ramekins from refrigerator, uncover, and evenly spread each with 2 teaspoons dried sugar. Set ramekins in a baking pan. Broil, watching constantly and rotating pan for even caramelization, until toppings are brittle, 2 to 3 minutes, depending on heat intensity.

7. Refrigerate crème brûlées to re-chill custard, about 30 minutes. Brown sugar topping will start to deteriorate in about 1 hour. ■

Gene Freeland writes about food and art collecting from his home in Rancho Santa Fe, California.

The Secrets of Gnocchi

For light, fluffy gnocchi, bake and thoroughly mash the potatoes so they require the least possible amount of flour to form a coherent dough.

∿ BY JACK BISHOP ∿

Gnocchi's traditional shape is not coincidental—it causes these little dumplings to cook more evenly and also makes the sauce adhere to them.

The classic Italian potato dumplings known as gnocchi should be light, airy, and fluffy. Unfortunately, they too often resemble the heavy, stick-to-your-ribs potato dumplings of Central Europe. So my mission was clear: Figure out what makes potato dumplings heavy, then develop a recipe that avoids these pitfalls.

After conducting thirty-six tests, I have concluded that the real culprit in leaden gnocchi is not the potatoes but the amount of flour. While it is certainly important to use the right kind of potato (*see* "Which Potato Is Best?", page 9), even gnocchi made with the proper potato will be terrible if too much flour is added. The trick to light, fluffy gnocchi lies in preparing the potatoes so that they require the least possible amount of flour to form a coherent dough.

Baking Is Best

Before I started my kitchen work, I gathered about seventy-five gnocchi recipes and analyzed them for the type of potato used and the way the potatoes were cooked. The majority of these recipes called for boiling the potatoes with their skins on, peeling and mashing them, and then combining them with flour and salt. A smaller number of recipes advocated peeling the potatoes before boiling, or steaming them (with or without skins). I also ran across a few recipes that sug-

gested baking the potatoes in their skins. After working with four kinds of potatoes (reds, Yukon Golds, Idaho baking potatoes, and russets), I concluded that all potatoes respond best to baking.

In my tests, boiled peeled potatoes made the heaviest, gummiest gnocchi, followed by boiled unpeeled potatoes. Steamed potatoes (peeled or unpeeled) made less-doughy gnocchi, but they were no match for gnocchi made from baked potatoes. I attributed this to the presence or absence of moisture during cooking. Boiling and steaming are wet cooking methods that leave potatoes quite moist. Baking in a hot oven, however, seemed likely to dry out the potatoes.

To see if my hunch was correct, I weighed several kinds of potatoes before and after cooking them. Boiling and steaming had a negligible effect—boiling increased the potatoes' weight by about 0.5 percent, while steaming decreased their weight by about 2 percent. However, after fifty minutes in the oven, baked potatoes shed between 15 percent and 20 percent of their weight, depending on their variety. This weight loss was caused by the evaporation of water.

With so much less water, baked potatoes need far less flour to form a coherent dough. As an added benefit, gnocchi made with baked potatoes have a stronger potato flavor. The elimination of water during cooking not only makes the potatoes drier, it also concentrates their flavor; I could easily pick out by taste the gnocchi made with baked potatoes.

Making the Dough

After deciding baking was the best cooking method, I experimented with a number of methods for peeling and mashing the potatoes. While it is more convenient to peel potatoes after they cool, I found that the skin, which lifts and separates from the flesh during baking, reattaches fairly quickly as the potatoes cool. It is possible to peel cooled potatoes, but you lose more flesh than if you peel them as soon as they come out of the oven. To avoid scorching my hand, I wear an oven mitt to hold the hot potatoes. A swivel vegetable peeler or a paring knife can be used to lift the skin, but fingers are best for carefully peeling and removing it.

Once the potatoes are peeled, they must be mashed. It quickly became clear that lumps had to be avoided at all costs because they caused the gnocchi to come apart when they were cooked. The shredding disk on the food processor, a hand-held masher, and a fork all left lumps; the food processor also made the potatoes slightly gummy. I found that a $9 ricer (*see* Sources and Resources, page 32) was the best tool for mashing potatoes. This device gets its name from the tiny, rice-shaped pieces it produces. Simply place peeled potatoes in the round compartment fitted with the fine disk, press down on the clamp, and perfectly riced potatoes are extruded through the disk.

After mashing, the next step is to add the salt and flour to make the dough. Again, working from the premise that less flour makes better gnocchi, I found it helpful to allow the steam from the riced potatoes to dissipate. By adding flour to potatoes that were only warm, I could prevent the gumminess that sometimes resulted when flour was sprinkled over steaming hot potatoes.

Kneading is the enemy of light gnocchi. When I combined the potatoes and flour in a countertop mixer, the dough was incredibly sticky, and the gnocchi cooked up like little Super Balls that bounced right off the plate. Working the dough by hand until it just comes together is the easiest and safest way to combine the flour and potatoes.

As a side note: I felt compelled to try gnocchi made with an egg, a common addition to northern European dumplings and a trick espoused by some Italian cookbook authors to bind the dough more tightly. (Several usually reliable sources argued that eggs were anathema to light gnocchi, so I had my doubts from the start.) After trying whole eggs, whites, and yolks, I concluded that while eggs make firmer gnocchi, they also make them gummier and heavier. I also felt that the egg overwhelmed the delicate potato flavor.

Final Thoughts on Flour

Throughout most of my testing, I concentrated on adding as little flour as possible. However, when I began to roll and shape the gnocchi, I realized it was possible to add too little flour. First of all, the potatoes need enough flour to make a dough that is not sticky and that will roll easily. If the dough comes apart (*see* illustration 3, page 9), you must add more flour.

There were also times when I added barely enough flour to bind the dough and allow it to be rolled and shaped. While the dough looked fine, the gnocchi cooked up a bit soft and mushy. I realized I was taking my obsession with flour too far and that my gnocchi would have been more resilient if I had added a few more tablespoons of flour after the dough first came together.

Since the moisture level of each potato varies according to variety and how long it has been out of the ground, it is impossible to write a recipe giving an exact ratio of potatoes to flour. I found that two pounds of baked potatoes could require as little as one-and-one-quarter cups of flour or as much as one-and-one-half cups. As a general rule, I worked one-and-one-quarter cups of flour into the riced potatoes. In most cases, the dough seemed to be just barely bound so I added another two tablespoons of flour as a kind of insurance policy. First-time gnocchi cooks may also want to boil a few quickly shaped gnocchi as a test before shaping and rolling out dozens.

Shaping Gnocchi

Speaking of shaping, a fair amount of mystique surrounds the cutting and shaping of these little dumplings. Traditionally, the dough is rolled into long ropes and cut into small pieces which are then imprinted with ridges on one side and indented in the center on the other.

Rolling the dough into long ropes (I found a three-quarter-inch thickness to be ideal) and then slicing the ropes into individual gnocchi seems unavoidable to me. In any case, the process is fairly quick. However, I wondered if the final shaping process—which can become tedious when a hundred gnocchi are involved—was necessary. The answer is yes.

I cooked traditionally formed gnocchi and compared them to gnocchi that were simply cut from the dough ropes and then dropped into the boiling

water. The indentation in the center of the gnocchi serves two purposes. First, it decreases the thickness of the gnocchi and allows the center to cook more evenly. Gnocchi without this indentation were often a bit underdone in the center. Second, the indentation traps sauce on the otherwise smooth surface. As for the grooves, they are also for the sauce; in my tests, traditionally formed gnocchi did a better job of holding onto the sauce than gnocchi without creases or crevices.

Although I judged the traditional shape to be

essential, I wanted to see if I could improve upon the process of forming it. Most sources use the tines of a fork to imprint ridges. I found that simply pressing the fork against the cut gnocchi, much as you'd press a fork against peanut butter cookie batter, squashes the gnocchi and is not advisable. Holding the tines of a fork parallel to a work surface and rolling little balls of dough down and off the tines imprints ridges and gives gnocchi their characteristic indentation if pressure is applied as the dough is flipped. The prob-

TIPS ON MAKING GNOCCHI

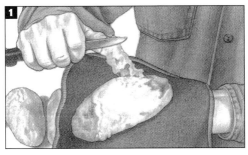

1. Hold the hot potato with a pot holder and use a vegetable peeler or paring knife to remove the skin.

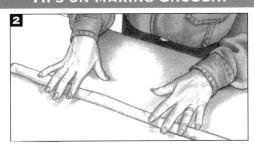

2. Break off a portion of the dough and roll it into a rough rope. Glide your hands over the dough to thin the rope evenly to about ¾-inch thick.

3. If the rope won't hold together when it's rolled, there is not enough flour in the dough. Return the rope to the bowl with the remaining dough and work in more flour as needed.

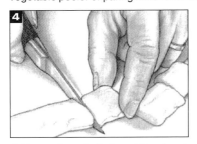

4. Use a sharp knife to cut the dough ropes into ¾-inch-long pieces.

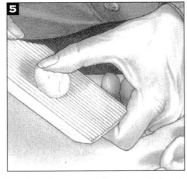

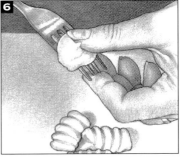

5. Hold a wooden butter paddle in one hand and press each piece of dough against its ridged surface with your index finger to make an indentation in the center. Roll the dough down and off the ridges and let it to drop to the work surface.

6. and 7. If you would rather shape the gnocchi with a fork, hold the fork so that the tines are parallel to the work surface. Flip the gnocchi off the ends of the fork to imprint the ridges, applying some pressure as you do this in order to make a shallow indentation in the center.

ILLUSTRATIONS BY WENDY WRAY

lem is that the dough tends to stick to the fork.

After looking around my kitchen for a better solution, I noticed the ridges on my butter paddle (*see* Sources and Resources, page 32). When I rolled and flipped gnocchi off this surface, I was pleasantly surprised. Not only was it easier because the surface I was working against was so much bigger, but the gnocchi did not stick. The bigger surface also meant the entire length of the gnocchi was covered by thin grooves, whereas the fork-rolled gnocchi had only a few crevices. More grooves translates into a more attractive appearance and better sauce retention.

MASTER RECIPE FOR POTATO GNOCCHI
Makes about 100 gnocchi

To insure that gnocchi are the right texture, bring a small saucepan of water to simmer while mixing the dough. Roll a small piece of the dough into the rope shape. Cut off a small piece or two from the rope, shape them into gnocchi, then drop them into the simmering water. If the gnocchi are too mushy, put the dough rope back into the potato mixture and add in another tablespoon or two of flour. It's better to take the time to test one or two gnocchi than to ruin the whole batch. Also, be careful not to overwork or overknead the dough; you simply want to incorporate the flour into the potatoes. Avoid cooking the gnocchi at a rolling boil since violently churning water makes it difficult to determine when the gnocchi are floating. Even gently boiling gnocchi may bob temporarily to the surface, but don't lift them out until they float.

   2 pounds russet or baking potatoes, washed
1¼ cups flour, plus more as needed
   1 teaspoon salt, plus more for cooking liquid

1. Heat oven to 400 degrees. Bake potatoes until a metal skewer slides easily through them, 45 minutes to 1 hour, depending on size.
2. Hold potato with a pot holder or kitchen towel and peel it with a vegetable peeler or paring knife (*see* illustration 1, page 9); rice peeled potato into a large bowl. Peel and rice remaining potatoes. Cool until potatoes are no longer hot, about 15 minutes.
3. Sprinkle 1¼ cups flour and 1 teaspoon salt over warm potatoes. Using your hands, work mixture into a soft, smooth dough. If dough is sticky (which is often the case), add more flour as needed, up to 1½ cups total.
4. Roll about one-quarter of dough into a long ¾-inch-thick rope (illustration 2). If rope won't hold together (illustration 3), return it to bowl with remaining dough and work in more flour as

GNOCCHI HISTORY

In one form or another, gnocchi have been eaten since Roman times. At one time, the most basic recipe for this Italian dumpling called for just flour and water—in effect, soft pieces of boiled dough. Other versions, which are still made today, use ricotta cheese and spinach, or a mixture of semolina, milk, butter, eggs, and Parmesan cheese. Potatoes began to gain wide culinary acceptance in the eighteenth century and have since replaced much of the flour in simple dumpling recipes.

needed. Repeat until all dough is rolled.

5. Cut rope of dough into ¾-inch lengths (illustration 4). Holding butter paddle or fork in one hand, press each piece of cut dough against ridged surface with index finger to make an indentation in center. Roll dough down and off ridges and allow it to drop to work surface (illustrations 5, 6, and 7). (Gnocchi can be placed in a single layer on a baking sheet and refrigerated for several hours. Or, baking sheet can be placed in freezer for about 1 hour. Partially frozen gnocchi can be transferred to plastic bag or container, sealed, and frozen for up to 1 month.)

6. Bring 4 quarts of water to low boil in large pot. Add 2 teaspoons salt or to taste. Add about one-third of the gnocchi and cook until they float, 1½ to 2 minutes (about 3 minutes for frozen gnocchi). Retrieve gnocchi with slotted spoon and transfer to warm, shallow serving bowl or platter. Repeat cooking process with remaining gnocchi, following specific topping and tossing instructions in recipes below.

POTATO GNOCCHI WITH BUTTER, SAGE, AND PARMESAN CHEESE
Serves 8 as a first course or 4 to 6 as a main course

Although sage is the classic herb choice in this preparation, other fresh herbs such as oregano, thyme, chives, or marjoram can be substituted.

   6 tablespoons unsalted butter
12 fresh sage leaves, cut into thin strips
   1 Master Recipe for Potato Gnocchi
 ½ cup grated Parmesan cheese, plus extra for passing

1. Melt butter in small skillet. When butter foams, add sage. Remove pan from heat and set aside.
2. Cook gnocchi according to Master Recipe and transfer to warm platter. Top each batch with a portion of herbed butter and cheese. When last batch has been sauced, gently toss gnocchi and serve immediately with more cheese passed separately.

POTATO GNOCCHI WITH TOMATO-MINT SAUCE
Serves 8 as a first course or 4 to 6 as a main course

Two cups of any smooth tomato sauce can be used with a full recipe of gnocchi. An equal amount of ragù, the slow-simmering meat sauce that hails from Bologna, is also appropriate.

   3 tablespoons olive oil
 ½ small onion, chopped
 ½ small carrot, peeled and chopped
 ½ small celery rib, chopped

   1 can (14.5 ounces) crushed tomatoes
   8 fresh mint or basil leaves
     Salt
   1 Master Recipe for Potato Gnocchi
     Grated Parmesan cheese for passing

1. Heat oil in a medium saucepan. Add onion, carrot, and celery; cook over medium heat until vegetables soften slightly, about 5 minutes. Add tomatoes and mint. Simmer until sauce thickens and vegetables soften completely, about 30 minutes. Puree sauce in food processor or blender. Adjust seasonings, adding salt if necessary, and keep sauce warm.
2. Cook gnocchi according to Master Recipe and transfer to warm serving platter. Gently toss with tomato sauce and serve immediately with cheese passed separately.

POTATO GNOCCHI WITH PESTO
Serves 8 as a first course or 4 to 6 as a main course

This recipe makes a scant cup of pesto. Feel free to use an equal amount of any favorite type of pesto as sauce for a full recipe of gnocchi.

   2 cups packed fresh basil leaves
   2 medium garlic cloves
   2 tablespoons pine nuts
 ½ cup olive oil
 ¼ cup grated Parmesan cheese
     Salt
   1 Master Recipe for Potato Gnocchi

1. Place basil, garlic, and pine nuts in workbowl of food processor. Process, scraping down sides as needed, until minced. With motor still running, slowly pour oil through feed tube and process until smooth. Scrape pesto into bowl. Stir in cheese and salt to taste.
2. Cook gnocchi according to Master Recipe and transfer to warm platter. Gently toss gnocchi with pesto and serve immediately.

POTATO GNOCCHI GRATINÈED WITH FONTINA CHEESE
Serves 8 as a first course or 4 to 6 as a main course

One cup of freshly grated Parmesan cheese can be substituted for the fontina cheese in this recipe.

   5 tablespoons unsalted butter
   1 Master Recipe for Potato Gnocchi
   4 ounces fontina cheese, shredded

1. Adjust oven rack to highest position and heat broiler. Smear 2 tablespoons butter on a gratin dish large enough to hold gnocchi in a single layer. Melt remaining butter in small skillet and set aside.
2. Cook gnocchi according to Master Recipe and transfer to buttered dish. When last batch has been cooked, toss gnocchi with melted butter and sprinkle evenly with cheese.
3. Broil gnocchi until cheese melts and just begins to brown, no more than 3 or 4 minutes. Serve immediately. ∎

Country Italian Vegetable Pasta Sauces

Take a cue from Italian cooks, who transform common spring vegetables into quick, healthy pasta sauces.

~ BY JACK BISHOP ~

Italian cooks know that spring vegetables such as artichokes, fennel, asparagus, and arugula can be turned into quick pasta sauces with minimal cooking. Although some American cooks may be unfamiliar with some of these Italian staples, they will have no trouble making these quick and healthful sauces.

BRAISED ARTICHOKE SAUCE WITH WHITE WINE, GARLIC, AND LEMON
Enough for 1 pound of pasta
The total cooking time is fairly long for this dish, but you can be finished with the actual work in about 20 minutes. Toss this sauce with linguine or other long, thin pasta.

- 1 small lemon, 1 teaspoon of zest removed and reserved; lemon halved
- 4 medium artichokes
- 6 medium garlic cloves, cut into thin slivers
- ¼ cup olive oil
- 2 cups dry white wine
  Salt
- ¼ cup minced fresh parsley leaves

1. Squeeze lemon juice into large bowl filled with cold water; drop in lemon halves. Remove stems, tough outer leaves, and tips from the artichokes, cut artichokes into quarters, remove chokes, and cut quarters into ¼-inch wedges. Drop wedges into acidulated water when cut.
2. Heat garlic with oil in large braising pan or deep skillet. When garlic starts to sizzle and color, stir in lemon zest, drained artichokes, and wine; bring to simmer; season to taste with salt. Cover pan and simmer until artichokes are tender when pierced with fork, about 40 minutes. Stir in parsley; adjust seasonings.

TOMATO SAUCE WITH ARUGULA AND BLACK OLIVES
Enough for 1 pound of pasta
Toss with 1 pound fusilli or other short, curly pasta and pass grated Parmesan cheese at the table.

- 1 tablespoon minced garlic
- ½ teaspoon hot red pepper flakes or to taste

- 2 tablespoons olive oil
- 1 can (28 ounces) crushed tomatoes
- 20 oil-cured black olives, pitted and chopped
  Salt
- 1 large bunch arugula (⅓ pound), stemmed and washed thoroughly

Heat garlic and pepper flakes with oil in large saucepan. When garlic starts to color, stir in tomatoes and olives; simmer over medium heat until sauce thickens a bit, about 10 minutes. Season to taste with salt, if necessary. Stir in arugula when ready to toss with pasta.

ASPARAGUS AND MUSHROOM SAUCE WITH CARAMELIZED SHALLOTS
Enough for 1 pound of pasta
If pencil-thin asparagus are available, they don't need to be halved, but thicker asparagus should be sliced in half, and very thick pieces need to be quartered. You may add ¼ cup Parmesan cheese when you toss the sauce with pasta, preferably linguine, then offer extra Parmesan at the table.

- 1 pound medium asparagus, tough ends snapped off; spears halved lengthwise, then cut diagonally into 1-inch pieces
- ¼ cup olive oil
- 4 large shallots, thinly sliced
- ½ pound button or cremini mushrooms, brushed clean and thinly sliced
  Salt and ground black pepper

1. Bring 1 inch of water to boil in large pot. Put asparagus in steamer basket, then carefully place steamer basket in pot. Cover and steam over medium-high heat until asparagus is just tender, about 2 minutes. Remove asparagus and set aside. Reserve ¾ cup of the asparagus steaming liquid.
2. Heat oil in large skillet over medium heat. Add shallots; sauté, stirring occasionally to separate rings, until crisp and light brown, about 10 minutes. Add mushrooms, increase heat to medium-high, and sauté until they soften and release their juices, about 5 minutes longer. Season with 1 teaspoon salt and ½ teaspoon pepper or to taste.
3. Add asparagus and reserved cooking liquid. Simmer until asparagus is heated through and

sauce has thickened a bit, about 2 minutes longer. Adjust seasonings.

BRAISED FENNEL AND BITTER GREENS SAUCE WITH BALSAMIC VINEGAR
Enough for 1 pound of pasta
The natural sweetness of fennel makes it a good partner for bitter greens like kale, mustard, turnip, or beet. Flowering kale adds color as well as earthy flavor.

- ¼ cup olive oil
- 1 medium onion, minced
- 1 medium fennel bulb (about 1 pound), fronds removed, minced, and reserved (1 tablespoon); bulb trimmed, halved, and thinly sliced
  Salt and ground black pepper
- 2 tablespoons balsamic vinegar
- 1 pound spaghetti
- ¾ pound kale or other bitter greens, washed thoroughly and chopped coarsely
- ¼ cup grated Parmesan cheese, plus more for passing

1. Heat oil in a large braising pan or skillet with a cover. Add onion; sauté over medium heat until softened, about 5 minutes. Stir in fennel; sauté until golden, about 10 minutes. Add ½ cup water and season to taste with salt and pepper. Cover and simmer over medium-low heat until fennel is tender, about 8 minutes longer. Stir in vinegar; simmer to blend flavors, 1 minute longer. Adjust seasonings.
2. Meanwhile, bring 4 quarts water to boil in large pot. Add 1 tablespoon salt and the pasta; return to boil. Add kale; continue to cook until pasta is al dente, about 7 minutes
3. Drain pasta and greens; toss with fennel mixture and cheese. Transfer portions to warm pasta bowls. Garnish with reserved minced fennel fronds. Serve immediately with more cheese passed separately. ∎

Jack Bishop is the author of the forthcoming *Vegetarian Pasta Sauces* (HarperCollins, 1996).

Moroccan Lamb Couscous

For the proper texture, steaming couscous is essential—it fluffs this North African pasta to twice the volume of mere soaking.

"Lightness and fluffiness are the charms of good couscous, just like al dente is the charm of properly cooked pasta," says Paula Wolfert, author of five Mediterranean cookbooks, including *Couscous and Other Good Food from Morocco* (Harper & Row, 1973) and the recently revised *Mediterranean Cooking* (HarperCollins, 1994). Most American cooks prepare couscous according to the directions on the package. While this instant method is easy—couscous is stirred into boiling liquid, covered, allowed to rest off heat for five minutes, and then fluffed with a fork—Wolfert says the results are "inferior" and "heavy." She believes we're missing out on truly great couscous.

Misconceptions about what couscous actually is add to the confusion. Many cooks think couscous is a grain like barley or bulgur. Actually, it is made from semolina and water, just like spaghetti or linguine; it is a pasta. But in addition to couscous the pasta, there is also couscous the dish, a specialty in Morocco, Tunisia, and Algeria. In these North African countries, couscous granules are steamed over a simmering stew, and the two are then served together. Since it has meat, vegetables, and starch, couscous can be a one-dish meal.

Buying Couscous

All couscous is precooked and dried at the factory. The job of the home cook is to rehydrate the tiny pellets and make them swell, soften, and lighten in color. Wolfert demonstrates the difference between steamed and quick-cooked couscous by simply comparing the volume of each. One pound of couscous (about two and one-half cups) will swell to five or six cups when soaked in hot water according to the instant method. When steamed, this same quantity grows to twelve cups. Wolfert says quick-cooking does not give couscous the chance to swell fully, and warns that half-cooked couscous expands in your stomach, making for a heavy eating experience.

When shopping for couscous, ignore labels that say "instant" or "quick-cooking." All couscous has been precooked and all couscous can be steamed. Wolfert offers only two purchasing caveats—look for medium couscous (some Middle Eastern stores may sell fine

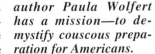

Mediterranean cookbook author Paula Wolfert has a mission—to demystify couscous preparation for Americans.

or coarse couscous, which have different uses; however, supermarkets generally carry only medium couscous) and make sure that couscous is made from pure semolina instead of regular wheat flour. As with other pastas, 100 percent semolina makes the best couscous.

Steaming Options

Wolfert recommends a traditional North African regimen for rehydrating couscous, which involves steaming it twice. There are several possible steamer setups. In North Africa, most cooks use a *couscoussier*—a steamer with plenty of head room between the bottom of the steamer basket and the bottom of the pot. A traditional couscoussier is earthenware although metal versions are now used in many homes. (*See* Sources and Resources, page 32, for details on purchasing a metal couscoussier.) A conventional flat-bottomed steamer insert and a deep pot can be used as long as the steamer basket is at least four inches above the simmering liquid.

If you don't own a steamer, you can rig one up with a deep pot and a metal colander. Simply put water in the pot and suspend the metal colander above it. Ideally the colander should fit snugly against the sides of the pot and sit no closer than about four inches above the water. Once the water comes to a rolling boil, the couscous can be put into the colander and steamed. Even if the holes on the steamer are fairly large, the couscous will not slip through as long as there is enough steam. For this reason, it's imperative that the steam rise through the holes in the colander, not around the edges. If your colander doesn't fit tightly into your pot and steam comes up through the gap between them, wrap a piece of damp cheesecloth around the rim of the pot to seal this space (*see* illustration 2, page 13).

Ideally, couscous should be served in a wide, flat bowl that slopes down gently to the center. At the table, allow each person to take some of the couscous as well as the meat and sauce.

North African cooks usually steam couscous above a simmering stew to conserve fuel and minimize the number of pots needed. However, steaming the couscous over a separate pot filled with water is probably easier for Americans, and is recommended unless you are using a couscoussier.

The stew component in couscous can be varied almost infinitely. Any fish, meat, poultry, or vegetable mixture with a fairly thin broth is suitable. The broth must be well seasoned with aromatic spices since it flavors the couscous as well. Couscous can be quite spicy, especially when served with hot sauces, or it can be only mildly spicy, as is the case with the Moroccan recipe that follows, in which a peppery broth is combined with a sweet caramelized onion topping.

STEAMED COUSCOUS WITH MOROCCAN LAMB BROTH, GLAZED ONIONS, AND FRIED ALMONDS
Serves 10

1 recipe Steamed Couscous
1 recipe Moroccan Lamb Broth with Chickpeas and Vegetables
1 recipe Glazed Onions with Raisins
1 recipe Fried Almonds
2 tablespoons unsalted butter

1. Prepare Steamed Couscous, Moroccan Lamb

Broth with Chickpeas and Vegetables, Glazed Onions with Raisins, and Fried Almonds. Pour couscous onto large flat serving dish with sloping sides and toss with butter. Use fork to smooth out any remaining lumps. Form couscous into a large ring, leaving a small opening in the center for meat. Pour 3 cups reserved broth over couscous. Cover, and let stand 10 minutes.

2. Remove meat from broth and place in center opening. Scatter vegetables over couscous (*see* illustration 4). Spread glazed onions over meat and vegetables, then sprinkle with almonds. Serve immediately. (Leftovers can be stored in covered container and refrigerated up to 2 days. Reheat individual portions in microwave.)

STEAMED COUSCOUS
Makes about 12 cups

4 cups medium couscous (1½ pounds)
1 teaspoon salt

1. Place couscous in a fine strainer and rinse under cold running water (*see* illustration 1, below). Dump couscous into large bowl and let stand until grains swell, about 10 minutes. Break up lumps with your fingers.

2. Fill a large steamer pot or stockpot with water. Set up steamer (illustration 2), making sure there are 4 inches between simmering water and steamer basket. Carefully pour couscous into steamer or colander. Steam couscous, uncovered, over simmering water for 15 minutes.

3. Pour couscous onto large, rimmed baking sheet. Sprinkle with 1 cup cold water and salt; use long fork or oiled hands to spread couscous and break up any lumps (illustration 3). Set aside for at least 5 minutes. (Couscous can be covered with paper towels and stored at room temperature up to 8 hours.)

4. Add water to pot, making sure there is enough room between simmering water and steamer bottom. Carefully pour couscous into perforated steamer or colander; steam couscous, uncovered, over simmering water for 20 minutes. For assembly, *see* Steamed Couscous with Moroccan Lamb Broth, Glazed Onions, and Fried Almonds, page 12.

MOROCCAN LAMB BROTH WITH CHICKPEAS AND VEGETABLES
Serves 8 to 10
An equal amount of lamb neck, if available, can be substituted for the shanks, and butternut squash is a fine stand-in for the pumpkin.

1 cup dried chickpeas (about 7 ounces), soaked in water until rehydrated (at least 4 hours)
2 lamb shanks (about 1½ pounds)
2 teaspoons salt
1 tablespoon ground black pepper
1 teaspoon ground ginger
¼ teaspoon saffron threads
3 medium onions, quartered
2 sprigs each fresh parsley and cilantro, all tied together into bundle

3 tablespoons unsalted butter
6 small carrots, peeled and quartered
6 small turnips, peeled and quartered
1½ pounds pumpkin, peeled, seeded, and cut into 2-inch chunks
5 very small zucchini, halved crosswise

1. Bring chickpeas and 7 cups water to simmer in medium saucepan. Simmer, covered, until chickpeas are just tender, about 1 hour. Drain chickpeas, then pour into bowl of cold water. Gently rub chickpeas between fingers to remove skins. Discard skins, drain chickpeas, and set aside.

2. Place lamb, salt, pepper, ginger, saffron, onions, parsley and cilantro, and butter in soup kettle. Melt butter over low heat, swirling pan once or twice to let spices and meat mix gently. Add 3 quarts of water and bring to simmer. Add chickpeas; cover, and simmer until meat is tender, about 1¼ hours.

3. Cool lamb broth, skimming fat that rises to the surface. Remove 2 cups of broth and strain it; reserve for glazed onion topping. Remove and discard herb bundle. Remove shanks and separate meat from bone; return meat to broth. (Can be covered and refrigerated up to 2 days.)

4. About 30 minutes before serving, bring lamb broth to simmer. Add carrots, turnips, pumpkin, and zucchini. Cover and simmer until vegetables are tender, about 20 minutes. Adjust seasonings. Remove another 3 cups of broth and strain it; reserve for moistening couscous. (There will be only a little broth left in meat and vegetables at this point.) For assembly, *see* Steamed Couscous

with Moroccan Lamb Broth, Glazed Onions, and Fried Almonds, page 12.

GLAZED ONIONS WITH RAISINS
Makes about 2 cups

2 cups strained lamb broth (*see* step 3 of Moroccan Lamb Broth with Chickpeas and Vegetables)
1 large Spanish onion, quartered and sliced thin, lengthwise
½ teaspoon ground cinnamon
½ cup raisins
¼ cup sugar
3 tablespoons unsalted butter
   Salt and ground black pepper

Bring broth to boil in saucepan. Add remaining ingredients, including salt and pepper to taste. Simmer, covered, for 45 minutes. Uncover and simmer until liquid boils away and onions have glazed appearance, 30 to 45 minutes. (Can be covered and refrigerated up to 2 days.) Warm before serving.

FRIED ALMONDS
Makes 1 cup

2 tablespoons vegetable oil
1 cup whole blanched almonds

Heat oil in large skillet over medium-high heat. Add almonds; fry until golden brown, 3 to 4 minutes. Drain on paper towels and set aside. (Can be stored in airtight container up to 2 days.) ∎

PREPARING COUSCOUS

1. Rinse the couscous in a fine-mesh strainer.

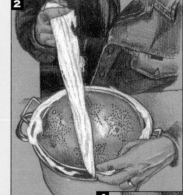

2. If you do not have a traditional steamer or couscoussier, set a metal colander over a deep pot of water, leaving 4 inches between water and bottom of colander. Use a damp cheesecloth to seal the gap around the rim of the pot.

3. Spread the steamed couscous over a large, rimmed baking sheet, sprinkle with water, and use a long fork to break up any lumps.

4. After the couscous has been steamed the second time, assemble the dish in a large flat bowl that slopes gently down toward the center.

How to Cook Leeks

A two-step cooking process, starting with presteaming, is the secret to perfectly prepared leeks.

∽ BY MINDY SCHREIL ∽

The unique, onion-like sweetness of leeks makes them a delicious vegetable side dish, equally good whether served hot or cold. However, to use these delicately flavored vegetables to best effect, you must take some care in selecting, trimming, and cleaning them. I also found, after cooking leeks in almost every possible manner, that they are best when presteamed to soften them. After that, they can either be dressed and served, or cooked further.

After choosing your leeks (see "Buying and Storing Leeks," below), the next step is trimming them. Trimming is essential because it is the only way to expose the many layers of the leek and clean it properly.

Instead of following the often recommended technique of slicing off the leaves right where they lighten into the white base of the leek, I found you could move about two inches upward into the leaves, to the point at which the light green part turns dark green, without any ill effect. To finish trimming, cut a very thin slice off the base, slit the leek in half lengthwise, leaving the two halves attached at the base, and trim off the tough dark green parts of the leaves (see steps 1 through 4, page 15).

The next step is to clean the leeks. Since leeks grow underground, during the process of pushing upward they collect dirt between their layers. I've come across leeks that had only a few grains of dirt between the layers, but I've also found leeks with mud jammed in the crevices.

I was skeptical of the cleaning directions in most recipes, which usually recommend either swishing trimmed leeks in a bowl of water or simply rinsing them under running water. I tried both of these methods, but when I took the leeks apart I discovered a lot of dirt left. Some recipe books advocated soaking trimmed leeks. I discovered that time spent soaking in water did loosen a lot of dirt from the leeks, but this should be followed by a quick rinse under cold running water, pulling apart the layers with your fingers to expose any persistent grime (see step 5, page 15).

I also wanted to see if prolonged soaking in water affected leeks' flavor. To test this, I sliced some leeks and soaked them in bowls of water, tasting them for loss of flavor after ten minutes, thirty minutes, one hour, two hours, and overnight. Apart from a slight but noticeable flavor loss in ones soaked overnight, I felt that soaking did not diminish the flavor.

Finding the Best Way to Cook Leeks

In researching the best way to cook leeks, I found that, apart from a few chefs who braised leeks in the oven, most advocated boiling them.

My first test was to boil leeks in water for ten to fifteen minutes. The resulting leeks were moist and their color was good. They were a bit misshapen, however, so I tried tying them in bundles the way one recipe book suggested. The results didn't justify the trouble. All you really need to do, I found, is arrange the leeks on the plate or platter after cooking, taking care to coax them into shape. I also tried boiling the leeks in chicken stock instead of water. This, too, produced delicious results. But I was looking for a stronger leek flavor, not one dominated by the stock.

The next cooking process I tried was braising, defined as first browning in fat then covering tightly and continuing to cook with a small amount of liquid at low heat for a long time. I went the traditional route of browning and simmering in chicken stock. Again I got delicious results, but not the assertive leek flavor that I was seeking, so I tried braising in water, which gave very nice results. In both cases, the browning process sealed the leek from flavor loss, while the liquid cushioned the leek from the harsh oven heat. However, this method involved more work than I wanted, so I moved on to baking.

I tried baking the leeks three ways: wrapping them in foil with butter, wrapping them in foil with a bit of water, and brushing them with butter and baking them unwrapped. None of the methods proved satisfactory. In all three cases, the texture suffered. The wrapped leeks were tough and dry, while the naked ones were too tough to chew.

Next I turned to the sauté pan. This method yielded leeks that were well browned on the outside, which provided an initial flavor boost that I liked; however, when I cut into the leek, I found that the center was not cooked and the outer layers were tough. The leeks also needed to cook in a generous amount of butter to keep them sizzling without burning. I rolled out my grill and threw some leeks on it, brushing them first with butter. No matter how much butter I lavished on them, though, the leeks came out charred on the outside but still uncooked, tough, and stringy inside.

Fortunately, the last method that I tried turned out to be the hands-down winner. When I steamed leeks, the results were full-flavored, moist, and tender. Steamed leeks not only tasted better than boiled leeks, with a stronger and sweeter onion-like flavor, they also retained more of their nutritional value; as an added bonus, no butter, oil, or complicated cooking techniques were required

---

TESTING STORAGE METHODS

To find the best way to store leeks at home, I tried just leaving them on the refrigerator shelf; putting them on the refrigerator shelf in a plastic bag; putting them in the vegetable crisper bin both unwrapped and wrapped in plastic; and refrigerating them, wrapped in paper bags, thinking that this method might allow the leeks to breathe and not "sweat," as sometimes happens when they're wrapped in plastic. I also tried "misting" the leeks to keep them moist.

After a few days, all of the leeks had become somewhat limp and dry except those wrapped in plastic and kept in the vegetable crisper. There-fore, I recommend you store your leeks completely enclosed in plastic bags in the crisper. However you store them, leeks should be used within five days of purchase.

Leeks come in all sizes, but in most stores they are bundled together without regard for this. To ensure even cooking times, it is best to make your own bundles of same-size leeks if possible.

I didn't find any difference between larger and smaller leeks, either in taste or texture. As long as the leeks are firm and have sprightly, unblemished leaves, bulbs two inches in diameter should be just as tender as smaller ones only one-half inch thick. Try to buy the leeks with the longest white stems, since you get more usable, tender parts that way. The white parts can vary from four inches long up to eight inches long.

Some supermarkets sell leeks trimmed down to the lighter base part. At first, this seems like a good deal because you aren't paying for the upper leaves, which are discarded anyway. However, after buying and cooking these trimmed-down leeks, I found the actual purpose of this procedure was to trim away aging leaves and make tough, old leeks look fresher to the unwary consumer.

when leeks were steamed.

Steaming turned out to be not only an excellent method of cooking leeks, but also a very useful intermediate step when cooking leeks by other methods. The steaming softens the leeks and leaves them better suited to grilling, sautéing, braising, or baking.

MASTER RECIPE FOR STEAMED LEEKS
Serves 4

4   leeks (preferably small to medium thickness), trimmed, soaked, and rinsed thoroughly (*see* illustrations 1 through 5, at right)

Arrange leeks in a single layer in a steamer basket or steamer insert. Carefully place basket over pot of vigorously boiling water; cover and steam until tip of knife inserted in thickest part of leek meets no resistance, about 10 minutes for leeks ¾ inch thick, about 12 minutes for leeks 1¼ inch thick.

GRILLED LEEKS WITH ORANGE-CHIVE BUTTER
Serves 4

Orange-Chive Butter
2   tablespoons unsalted butter, softened
1½ teaspoons zest and 1 teaspoon juice from 1 small orange
2   teaspoons snipped fresh chives
¼   teaspoon salt
⅛   teaspoon ground black pepper

1   Master Recipe for Steamed Leeks

1. Heat grill. Mix Orange-Chive Butter ingredients together in a small bowl; set aside.
2. Grill steamed leeks over hot coals until lightly browned on one side, about 2 minutes. Turn leeks with tongs and grill until lightly browned on other side, about 2 minutes longer.
3. Arrange leeks on plates or serving platter, evenly distribute bits of butter over leeks, and serve immediately.

STEAMED LEEKS GLAZED WITH CRUNCHY SEEDS
Serves 4

1   tablespoon red wine vinegar
2   teaspoons sugar
¼   teaspoon salt
⅛   teaspoon ground black pepper
1   teaspoon yellow mustard seeds
½   teaspoon fennel seeds
1   teaspoon sesame seeds
3   tablespoons unsalted butter
1   Master Recipe for Steamed Leeks

1. Mix vinegar, sugar, salt, pepper, mustard seeds, fennel seeds, and sesame seeds together in small bowl; set aside.
2. Heat butter in large skillet over medium-high heat. Add leeks and spice mixture. Cook,

shaking skillet constantly and turning leeks to coat all sides, until mixture thickens to glaze, about 2 minutes.
3. Arrange leeks on individual plates or serving platter; pour remaining glaze over leeks and serve.

BAKED LEEKS WITH BACON AND GRUYÈRE
Serves 1 2

1   ounce bacon, cut into small dice
1   large egg
¼   cup milk
¼   cup chicken stock or low-sodium chicken broth
    Salt and ground white pepper
1   ounce Gruyère cheese, grated (about ⅓ cup) More
1   Master Recipe for Steamed Leeks
1   tablespoon dry bread crumbs
1   tablespoon minced fresh parsley leaves

1. Adjust oven rack to center position and heat oven to 350 degrees. Fry bacon in small skillet over medium-high heat until fat is rendered and bacon is crisp, 3 to 5 minutes. Drain fat and set bacon aside to cool.
2. Whisk egg, milk, chicken stock, and salt and pepper to taste in small bowl. Stir in Gruyère cheese.
3. Arrange leeks in a single layer in baking

dish. Pour egg mixture over leeks; sprinkle with bacon bits and bread crumbs. Bake until top is browned and egg mixture is set, about 30 minutes. Sprinkle with parsley and serve immediately.

STEAMED LEEKS WITH MUSTARD VINAIGRETTE
Serves 4
This can be served warm or chilled.

Mustard Vinaigrette
1   tablespoon cider vinegar
1   tablespoon Dijon mustard
½   teaspoon salt
⅛   teaspoon ground black pepper
1   teaspoon sugar
¼   cup olive oil

1   Master Recipe for Steamed Leeks, warm or chilled

1. Whisk vinegar, mustard, salt, pepper, and sugar together in small bowl until well blended; slowly whisk in olive oil so that vinaigrette emulsifies.
2. Arrange leeks on individual plates or serving platter; drizzle with vinaigrette and serve. ∎

Mindy Schreil cooks professionally in the San Francisco area and contributed to the *China Moon Cookbook* (Workman, 1993).

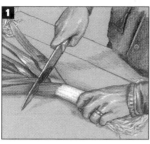

1. Trim leeks about 2 inches beyond the point where the leaves start to darken.

2. Trim the root end, keeping the base intact.

3. Slit the leek lengthwise upward through the leaves, leaving the base intact.

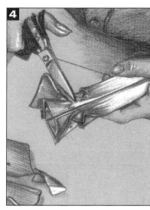

4. By trimming only the dark, green parts of each half, more of the leek can be saved.

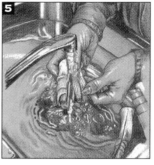

5. Soak the trimmed leeks in a sinkful of cold water to loosen excess dirt, then rinse the leeks in cold running water, pulling apart the layers with your fingers to expose any clinging dirt.

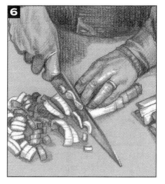

6. To slice leeks, follow steps 1 through 4, completely halving the leek lengthwise. Slice the leek halves to the desired thickness.

How to Clean Whole Fish

Most of us buy our fish cut to order—if we want a fillet, we buy one; if we want a whole fish, scaled and gutted, that's what we ask for. But there are times when you may want to "butcher" a fish yourself; and although it's difficult to do as good a job of filleting as someone who practices all day long, there is no single aspect that you can't do adequately with a minimum of practice.

What follow here are general rules for most finfish. For tools, you will need three knives: a sharp ten- or twelve-inch chef's knife; a paring knife; and a boning or fillet knife with a six- to eight-inch-long blade that may be either flexible or rigid. ∎

SCALING

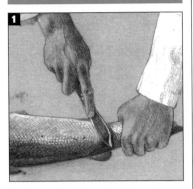

1. Rinse the fish and place it on a flat surface. Holding the fish by the tail, use the back of a knife, a spoon, or a fish scaler, and begin scraping from the tail toward the head with short, authoritative strokes. Scale the whole fish, including the belly and back, and rinse it well.

REMOVING FINS

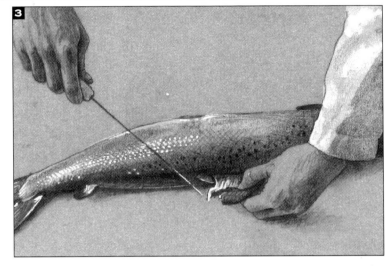

2. Use a boning or paring knife to make a ⅛-inch-long cut on each side of the fin. Make both cuts on an angle, so that you form a V with the fin in the middle.

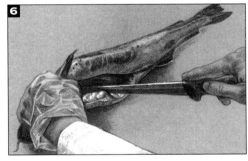

3. Use your hands or a pair of pliers to pull out the fin, along with the bones that attach it to the fish.

GUTTING

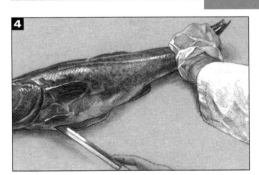

4. With a sharp, small knife, cut a slit from the fish's anal opening to the gill openings.

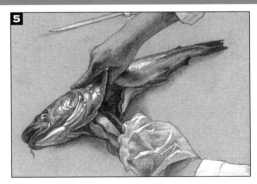

5. Pull out the innards with your fingers.

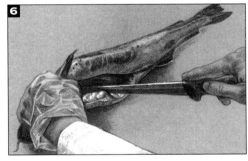

6. Use a spoon or knife to scrape out any innards that remain. Rinse the fish.

BEHEADING

7. Make a cut on either side of the fish's head just above the pectoral fin.

8. Hit the back of your knife with a rubber mallet if you have trouble cutting through the fish's thick neck bones.

GILLING

(Don't bother if beheading.)

9. Snip the gills at the bottom with a knife or scissors to detach them.

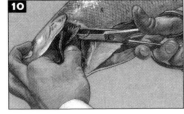

10. Next, snip the gills at the top and remove with your fingers. They can be sharp, so be careful.

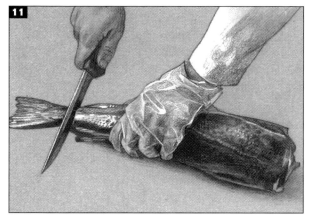

11. Cut off the tail.

12. Using a sharp, heavy knife or cleaver, cut through the fish to make steaks of the desired thickness, usually an inch or so. Try to make the cuts even and clean. If the central bone gives you trouble, rest the knife against it and whack the back of the knife with a wooden or rubber mallet, as pictured in illustration 8.

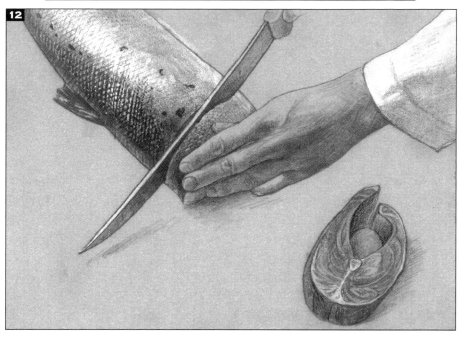

13. Lay the fish on its side, and make a top-to-bottom cut behind the gill cover.

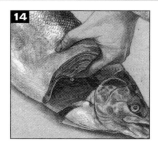

14. With the back of the fish toward you, make a long cut along the back from the gill cover to the tail, following the line of the central bone. Lift the flesh as you cut, to reveal the central bone and make the job easier.

15. Turn the fish so that the belly is toward you and, again, make a long cut from gill to tail. The tip of the knife should meet the first cut at the central bone, and the fillet will be released.

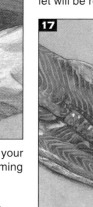

17. Lift the V out entirely.

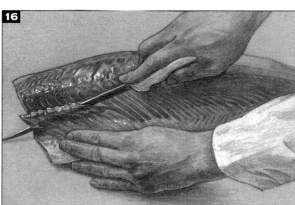

16. The thin belly flap may contain a row of bones. Use your fillet knife to cut underneath them from each side, forming a V shape.

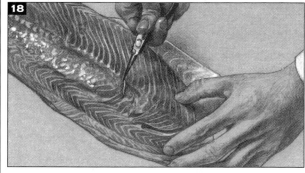

18. Remove pin bones with needle-nose or similar pliers, as shown, or by cutting a "zip-strip," making a V-shaped cut on either side of the bones and pulling out the V with your fingers.

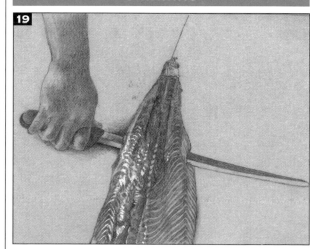

19. Make a small cut at the narrow end of the fillet and grab the skin. Use a sharp knife, held parallel to the skin, to run between the skin and flesh.

ILLUSTRATIONS BY ALAN WITSCHONKE

Steaming Fish Fillets and Steaks

The key to this quick, healthful cooking method is judging cooking time, which is most affected by the thickness and texture of the individual fish.

~ BY STEPHANIE LYNESS ~

I hadn't steamed much fish until last year when I began work on a translation of a French cookbook devoted exclusively to steaming. Since then, I've steamed all types of fish and found it to be a terrific method. Not only is it easy and quick, but it also keeps the fish moist and its flavor pure. Generally—with the exception of wild striped bass and sturgeon, both of which toughen when steamed—if you like a fish cooked by another technique, you'll enjoy it steamed as well.

Calculating Steaming Time

Steaming fish is really very easy, but there is one factor that is a bit tricky, and that is how long to steam.

In my testing, I hoped to find a simple timing rule that would hold true for all varieties of fish. I was looking for something like the Canadian rule that fish should be cooked ten minutes per inch of thickness. Unfortunately, I discovered no such rule of thumb. Instead, I found that giving cooking times is a risky business; there are so many variables that no time given can be completely reliable for every cook. However, I did find that there are certain variables that are very important in determining cooking times, while others turned out to be less important than I had expected. By paying attention to the proper variables, a very close approximation of perfect cooking time can be made for each type of fish.

In my testing, I found the two most important variables affecting steaming time to be the thickness and the texture of the individual fish. Times are more affected by the thickness of the fillet or steak, for example, than by weight or size; as long as they are roughly the same thickness, an eight-ounce salmon fillet and a one-pound salmon fillet take the same amount of time to cook. The texture of the flesh varies considerably among different fish, and this makes a real difference when it comes to cooking time. A flaky cod fillet steams much more quickly, for example, than a meaty monkfish fillet of the same thickness. After a while I got pretty good at estimating what the steaming time of a fillet or steak might be by comparing it to a fish with a similar texture for which I already had a steaming time. Using the chart on page 20, you should be able to do the same.

When it comes to heat, I have always steamed fish at a rapid simmer rather than at a full boil because that is the French method as I learned it. Therefore, times in the chart are given for cooking over rapidly simmering water. If you prefer to cook over a rolling boil, you should slightly reduce the times since the increased amount of steam will cook the fish slightly more quickly.

Two factors that I expected to influence cooking times—the tightness of the seal on the steamer and the quantity of fish being steamed—turned out to be irrelevant.

When you are dealing with most foods, a steamer with a tight-fitting lid and a tight seal between pot and steamer basket steams food faster than a steamer with a less effective seal and lid. This is not true, however, when steaming fish; even in a pot covered with foil instead of a lid, the fish steams at the same rate.

The quantity of fish in the pot does not seem to influence the steaming time, either. I discovered that as long as the fish is not jammed up against the side of the pot or the lid and is arranged in a single layer so that the steam can circulate freely, four fillets or steaks take the same amount of time as one fillet or steak.

This led to an interesting possibility: Could fillets be steamed stacked one on top of another, to save space? I found that they could indeed. I tried this technique with thin fillets such as bluefish, snapper, cod, and tail ends of salmon fillets, stacked skin-sides to the outside. Since steam cannot circulate on all sides of the fish, however, the steaming time must be increased to about one minute less than double the time for a single fillet. The stacked fillets can stick together so I separated them with a leaf of lettuce, spinach, or cabbage to prevent this.

Knowing that steam cooks with a relatively low, moist heat, I wondered whether there was a greater margin of error when steaming fish than when cooking by other methods. Except for oily fish such as bluefish and mackerel, which remained moist even when overcooked, the answer was no; even steaming dries out fillets and steaks if they are allowed to overcook. Since the fish continues to cook after it is removed from the

You can use steaming as a method to keep the flavor of the fish pure, or you can steam the fish on a thick bed of herbs or other aromatics to add flavor.

steamer, I found it best to take the steaks out when they were still medium-rare at the bone; by the time I ate the fish, it had cooked through. Fillets should still be slightly translucent in the center when they're removed from the steamer; if the fish is flaking apart, it's overcooked.

I also found that I could hold the cooked fish in the steamer for a few minutes while I made a sauce, wrote up my notes, or set the table, by turning off the heat and setting the steamer lid at an angle.

Adding Flavor

The easiest and most effective way to add flavor to fish while it is cooking is to steam it on a thick bed of herbs or other aromatics such as onion, lemon, or ginger. This has the added advantage of preventing the fish from sticking to the steamer basket. Using an aromatic steaming liquid will also flavor the fish, but it needs to be very strongly flavored because the fish doesn't steam for long.

You can also add flavor and make a sauce at

PHOTOGRAPHS BY ERIC ROTH

the same time by putting the fish in a deep plate with aromatics such as shallot, ginger, or fresh herbs, and a liquid such as soy sauce, mirin, fresh lemon juice, or cream, and then putting this plate in the steamer.

If you do this in a metal steamer, cover the plate with aluminum foil so that the condensed steam won't drip into it and dilute the sauce. Because the fish is covered, it will take about half again as long to cook as it otherwise would. If you are using a bamboo steamer, condensation will not collect on the underside of the lid, so the aluminum foil won't be necessary.

Removing and Serving the Fish

For a long time, the way I moved fish out of the steamer after it was done was to turn off the fire, open the steamer and, battling the heat of the steam, use a spatula to lift the fish out of the steamer and onto a serving plate. Finally I realized that it was much easier to remove the entire steamer basket or perforated insert from the steamer pot, setting it on a plate to catch the drips, before lifting out the fish itself with a spatula.

However, I found that steamed fillets of delicate fish like snapper, bluefish, and pompano flake apart when moved. A "tray" made with a single sheet of aluminum foil cut to size and placed under each fillet made it easy to move them. This also kept the fillets from sticking to the steamer and was especially useful when using a rack in a roasting pan. To move the cooked fish, simply grasp opposite corners of the foil and lift it, with the fillet, out of the steamer. Then with a spatula, gently slide the fillet onto a plate.

I find that I often want a little something on top of steamed fish for added flavor, even if it's just a drizzle of olive oil and lemon juice and a sprinkling of chopped fresh herbs. Below are some quick sauces that complement many of the steamed fish in the chart.

Steamed fish is not as wet as poached fish, but as it sits it gives off juices. The juices are welcome if I'm just using oil and lemon juice, but they'll dilute a "real" sauce. Blot them with paper towels or drain the fish for a minute on clean cloth towels before putting it on serving plates.

WHITE WINE–BUTTER SAUCE WITH CAPERS

Makes about ⅔ cup (enough to serve 4)
This quick, rather thin pan sauce is made with reduced white wine and a little of the liquid the fish was steamed with. It bathes the fish rather than thickly coating it.

- ½ cup white wine
- ¼ cup of liquid used for steaming
- 1 rounded tablespoon capers, drained and coarsely chopped
- 4 tablespoons unsalted butter, chilled and cut into small pieces
- ½ teaspoon caper brine
- 1 teaspoon chopped fresh parsley leaves
- Salt and ground black pepper

Over high heat, reduce wine to ¼ cup in a small saucepan. Add steaming liquid and reduce combined liquids to ⅓ cup. Add capers and whisk in butter pieces a few at a time to incorporate. When all butter has been added, remove sauce from heat and whisk in remaining ingredients, including salt and pepper to taste. Serve immediately.

BLACK OLIVE PASTE
Makes scant 1 cup
A little of this paste goes a long way. You only need a tablespoon or so per serving of fish, but making a smaller quantity doesn't make sense considering that whatever is leftover can be spread on toast rounds and served as appetizers. Only strong-flavored fish like tuna and bluefish can stand up to this assertive paste. For tuna, cut the steaks into thin slices and lay them in a fan shape on each plate, serving a small mound of tapenade alongside. If you use Kalamata olives, smack them with the flat side of a chef's knife blade to loosen the pits. If you use Niçoise olives, put them in a zip-lock bag and roll a rolling pin over them to make pitting easier.

- 1 cup olives, such as Kalamata or Niçoise, pitted
- 1 large garlic clove, chopped coarse

STEAMING EQUIPMENT

All you really need for steaming is some kind of pot and a perforated steamer rack that stands up off the bottom of the pot so that the fish is above the water. You probably already have something suitable in your kitchen.

I experimented with steaming fish in various pieces of kitchen equipment, some actually marketed as steamers and some just contraptions that I improvised. There are also a number of electric steamers on the market that steam fish beautifully, although they may do so somewhat more slowly than stove-top arrangements.

I found that most non-electric steamers steam fish at about the same rate, except for bamboo steamers set over a wok, which take significantly longer. Since I wanted to give steaming times that would be consistent between steamers, I excluded bamboo steamers from my testing.

Here are some options for steaming equipment:

Collapsible Steamer Baskets
These are useful and convenient for steaming steaks and smallish fillets. They are cheap, easy to wash and store, and are sold everywhere. I prefer to use them in a deep sauté pan rather than a pot because it is easier to get the basket in and out. The disadvantage these baskets have is that they tip easily and are tricky to handle when loaded with fish.

Pasta Cookers and Stackable Steamers
Deep pasta cookers are cheap and readily available, but it's hard to get the fish out of them because there isn't room to maneuver the spatula under the fish.

I prefer two-tiered stackable steamers, which are very useful not only for steaming but also for making stocks and stews. With its two steaming baskets, this type of steamer can accommodate steaks for up to eight people and even fairly large fillets for four. However, I found that, if steaming in two layers, the fish in the top layer sometimes steamed a little slower than the fish in the bottom layer. Also, these steamers are large and fairly expensive.

Roasting Pan and Rack
My second-favorite steaming apparatus (after my enameled steamer from France) is an oval, dome-lidded roasting pan fitted with an oval roasting rack. I like this set-up because it is multipurpose and very inexpensive to buy, only about $12. It's also large enough to steam four fairly large fillets or six steaks. To use it, simply set the rack on two empty tuna cans to raise it farther off the bottom of the pan, and thus assure that the water doesn't touch the fish. You can use any roasting pan as long as it has a rack. The pan needn't have a lid; I have often resorted to covering a pan with aluminum foil. When using this setup, it is best to put the pan over two burners.

Fish Poachers
A fish poacher, particularly useful for steaming whole fish, can also be used for steaks and fillets. Raise the rack off the bottom with empty cans and cover the poacher with a lid or with aluminum foil, as when steaming in a roasting pan. Again, it is best to steam over two burners.

2 anchovy fillets (optional)
1 tablespoon capers
½ teaspoon minced fresh thyme leaves
Pinch cayenne pepper
3 tablespoons olive oil

Place all ingredients in work bowl of a food processor fitted with steel blade; process to a paste. Scrape into a small bowl. (Can be refrigerated in an airtight container for at least 1 month.)

SPICY RED PEPPER BUTTER
Serves 8 to 10
This compound butter is flavored with steamed red pepper; steaming accentuates both the sweet and bitter tastes of the pepper. It's easy to make—

if the butter is softened to room temperature, the whole thing can be done in the blender. One-half teaspoon Tabasco may seem like a lot of hot sauce, but the butter is only mildly spicy. Serve the butter with any white fish such as monkfish, cod, snapper, flounder, or halibut. The fish must be hot; the butter should melt over it. The compound butter holds a few days in the refrigerator or several weeks in the freezer and is great on vegetables as well as fish.

½ red bell pepper, stemmed and cored
1 large garlic clove, chopped
½ teaspoon red wine vinegar
½ teaspoon Tabasco sauce
½ teaspoon salt

¼ pound unsalted butter, at room temperature

1. Set the half pepper on a steamer rack over boiling water, cover, and adjust heat so that water simmers. Steam until tender, about 15 minutes. Remove from steamer and let cool at room temperature or in refrigerator.

2. Put cooled pepper along with garlic, vinegar, Tabasco, and salt in blender or work bowl of food processor fitted with steel blade and process until smooth. Add butter and blend until smooth. Finished butter will be very loose. If using immediately, spoon about 1 tablespoonful onto each piece of steamed fish and serve. Or roll into a log in parchment paper and refrigerate or freeze. When ready to serve, cut ¼-inch-thick medallions of chilled butter and place one on each serving of hot, steamed fish.

BLACK PEPPER–MUSTARD SAUCE
Serves 4
This sauce couldn't be simpler and is particularly nice with monkfish.

¼ cup light cream
2 tablespoons Dijon mustard
¼ teaspoon ground black pepper
2 tablespoons of liquid used for steaming

Whisk cream and mustard together in small saucepan; stir in pepper and set aside. Once fish has steamed, add steaming liquid to pan. Bring sauce to boil, remove from heat, and serve immediately.

TOMATO SAUCE WITH BELL PEPPERS AND BALSAMIC VINEGAR
Serves 4
Try this simple sauce with cod, salmon, swordfish, tuna, or even shrimp or chicken.

1 tablespoon olive oil
1 garlic clove, minced
½ medium onion, chopped
½ red bell pepper, halved, stemmed, cored, and thinly sliced lengthwise
½ green bell pepper, halved, stemmed, cored, and thinly sliced lengthwise
1½ cups canned tomatoes with juice
1 teaspoon balsamic or red wine vinegar
Salt and ground black pepper

Heat olive oil over medium heat in medium saucepan; add garlic, onion, and bell peppers. Cover and cook until vegetables soften, about 5 minutes. Add tomatoes and juice; simmer, uncovered, until thickened, about 15 minutes. Stir in vinegar, and season to taste with salt and pepper. Serve. ■

Stephanie Lyness is a freelance food writer and cooking teacher living in New York. She has recently translated *Cuisine a la Vapeur: The Art of Cooking with Steam* by Jacques Manière (Morrow, 1995).

STEAMING TIMES FOR FISH FILLETS AND STEAKS

Although I have found the cooking times listed here to be very reliable (seven minutes has been perfect for every one-and-one-quarter-inch-thick salmon fillet I have ever steamed, for example), keep in mind that because the heat, thickness, and perhaps the quality of the fish affects the steaming time, these times should be used as guidelines. I prefer to err on the side of undercooking; check the fish for doneness early and continue steaming it if it isn't cooked enough for your taste. You can always cook it a little longer, but once fish is overcooked, it's overcooked.

If you are steaming a fish not listed on the chart, find a fish on the chart that has a similar texture and thickness and use the time shown for it.

Species	Type of Cut	Time
Arctic Char	Fillet (1 inch thick)	5 minutes
Bluefish	Fillet (¾ to 1 inch thick)	7 to 8 minutes
Cod	Steak (1 inch thick) Fillet (1 inch thick)	6 to 8 minutes 6 minutes
Flounder and Gray Sole	Fillet (¼ to ½ inch thick, folded in half so the tail end is under the wide end)	4 to 6 minutes
Grouper	Fillet (1 to 1½ inches thick)	10 to 12 minutes
Halibut	Steak (1 inch thick)	6 minutes
Monkfish	Fillet (1 inch thick)	10 to 12 minutes
Pompano	Fillet (½ to ¾ inch thick)	6 to 8 minutes
Salmon	Steak (1¼ to 1½ inches thick)	7 to 8 minutes for medium-rare 8 to 9 minutes for medium
	Fillet (1½ inches thick)	7 to 8 minutes for medium-rare 8 to 9 minutes for medium
Snapper	Fillet (¾ inch thick)	5 minutes
Swordfish	Steak (¾ to 1 inch thick)	6 minutes
Tilefish	Steak (1 to 1¼ inches thick)	6 to 8 minutes
Tuna	Steak (¾ to 1 inch thick)	2 minutes for rare 4 minutes for medium-rare
Wolffish	Fillet (½ to ¾ inch thick)	5 minutes

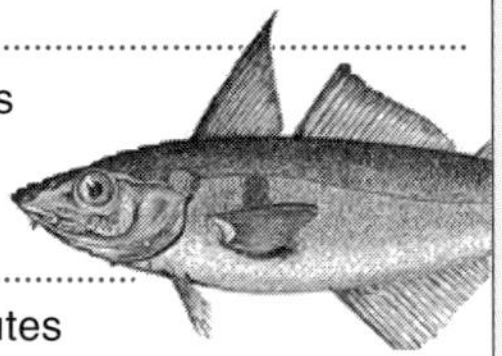

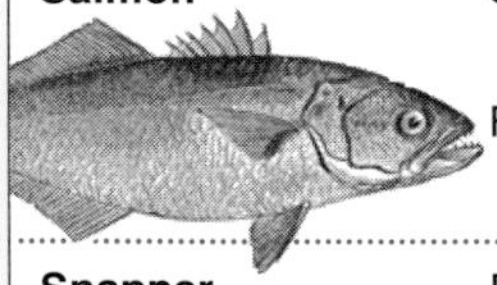

Quick Crumb Coffee Cake

The trick is to use the same mixture for both batter and topping.

~ BY STEPHEN SCHMIDT ~

Serving a freshly baked coffee cake for brunch on a Sunday morning is a splendid idea, but the fantasy quickly fades when you contemplate the actual baking. Yeast coffee cakes require that you get up at dawn, while baking powder–types rarely prove tasty enough to merit even a modest effort.

There is, however, one coffee cake that is both delicious and quick enough for the bleary-eyed Sunday morning baker—crumb coffee cake.

At first glance, the recipe seems a bit dubious, since the same flour-sugar batter mixture is used for the topping and as the basis of the batter. Actually, recipes of this kind have been around for years and make perfect sense. Cake batters and crumb toppings are composed of the same basic ingredients, namely flour, sugar, and butter. The main difference between the two is that cake batters contain liquid, which binds the protein and starch in flour into a springy, cohesive mass, while crumb toppings are made without liquid and thus remain loose. A recipe that derives both cake and crumbs from the same basic mixture is merely making use of a fact of baking life.

I had to bake my way through several cookbook recipes before I came up with my ideal crumb coffee cake. First I added more crumbs, then I devised a two-tone cake (a yellow cake topped with dark brown crumbs) by making the initial crumb mixture with white sugar and then adding brown sugar to the topping crumbs only.

Other problems proved trickier, however. None of the cookbook recipes that I tested were quite buttery enough for my taste, but when I tried adding more butter to the batter the cake became too weak to support the crumbs and collapsed in the center. Increasing the flour shored up the cake but also made it dry and puffy, sort of like a bland, yellow layer cake.

I knew that adding a bit more buttermilk would strengthen the structure by promoting the gelatinization of the starch in the flour, but I resisted this because I thought that the resulting batter would be too liquid to hold fruit in suspension. When I finally bit the bullet and put a little more buttermilk in, I was pleasantly surprised. The batter was less stiff and easier to beat, and I found that a thorough beating aerated and emulsified the ingredients, making the batter wonderfully thick and fluffy. Even with a goodly quantity of butter added, the cake with more buttermilk rose perfectly, and the solids stayed firmly suspended.

QUICK CRUMB COFFEE CAKE
Serves 8 to 10

This cake is best eaten on the day it is baked, though it may be made a day ahead. The batter is quite heavy, so you may prefer to beat it with an electric mixer at medium-high speed for a minute or so, rather than whisk it by hand.

- 1 tablespoon dry bread crumbs
- 2 cups all-purpose flour
- 1 cup plus 2 tablespoons sugar
- 1 teaspoon salt
- 10 tablespoons (1¼ sticks) unsalted butter, softened
- 1 teaspoon baking powder
- ½ teaspoon baking soda
- ¾ cup unsalted buttermilk or low-fat (but not nonfat) plain yogurt, at room temperature
- 1 large egg, at room temperature
- 1 teaspoon pure vanilla extract
- ¾ cup (3 ounces) walnuts or pecans, finely chopped
- ½ cup firmly packed dark brown sugar
- 1 teaspoon ground cinnamon

1. Adjust oven rack to center position and heat oven to 350 degrees. Generously grease bottom and lightly grease sides of 10-inch springform pan. Sprinkle bottom of pan with dry bread crumbs, then shake lightly to coat. Tap out excess crumbs.

2. Whisk flour, sugar, and salt in large mixing bowl until blended. Add butter and cut with whisk until mixture resembles coarse crumbs. Remove 1 cup of crumbs to separate bowl.

3. Whisk baking powder and soda into mixture remaining in large mixing bowl. Add buttermilk or yogurt, egg, and vanilla; whisk vigorously until batter is thick, smooth, fluffy, and frostinglike, 1½ to 2 minutes. Using a rubber spatula, scrape batter into prepared pan and smooth top.

4. Add nuts, brown sugar, and cinnamon to reserved crumbs; toss with a fork or your hands until blended. Sprinkle crumbs over batter, pressing lightly so that mixture adheres. Bake cake until center is firm and cake tester comes out clean, 50 to 55 minutes. Transfer cake to rack; remove pan sides. Let cake cool completely, about 2 hours, before serving. When completely cooled, cake can be slid off pan bottom onto serving plate.

APPLE-CINNAMON COFFEE CAKE

Peel and core 2 medium-large Granny Smith apples and cut into ¼-inch dice. Heat 1 tablespoon butter in a 10-inch skillet (preferably nonstick) over high heat until golden. Add apples, cover, and cook over high heat, stirring frequently, until they are dry and very tender, 2 to 3 minutes. Remove from heat, sprinkle apples with 2 table-

Do not insert a skewer into this cake to test for doneness until the center appears firm when the pan is shaken. If you do, the topping may squeeze air out, and the middle of the cake may sink.

spoons sugar, and lightly toss until glazed. Cool to room temperature. Follow recipe for Quick Crumb Coffee Cake, adding 1 teaspoon cinnamon with the baking powder and soda, and folding the apples into the finished batter.

COCONUT CHOCOLATE CHIP COFFEE CAKE

Follow recipe for Quick Crumb Coffee Cake, substituting firm-packed light brown sugar for white sugar and stirring 1 cup miniature chocolate chips into finished batter. For topping, decrease nuts to ½ cup, substitute light brown sugar for dark, omit cinnamon, and add 1 cup sweetened flaked coconut.

RASPBERRY-ALMOND COFFEE CAKE

Follow recipe for Quick Crumb Coffee Cake, adding 1 teaspoon pure almond extract along with vanilla. Turn batter into pan. Beat ½ cup *seedless* raspberry jam until smooth and fluid, then carefully spread it over the batter with the back of a teaspoon. For crumble topping, substitute ¾ cup (4 ounces) ground almonds for walnuts or pecans and ½ cup white sugar for dark brown sugar; omit cinnamon. Add 1 large egg yolk and 1 teaspoon pure almond extract to crumbs and mix with a fork. Thoroughly knead mixture with your fingers until the color is uniform. ∎

Stephen Schmidt is the author of *Master Recipes* (Ballantine, 1987).

Juicy, Flavorful Brisket

The perfect balance of oven heat and cooking time yields a beef brisket that is both juicy and flavorful.

~ BY IAN DICKSON SMITH AND TINA WILSON ~

Proper cooking can turn tough beef brisket into a dish that is juicy and quite tender. To maximize this tenderness, slice the beef very thin and across the grain.

C ooking beef brisket has traditionally been a lesson in compromise. Nature supplies the cut with a hearty taste, so producing flavor is not difficult. The tricky part is the delicate balance between toughness and moisture—you can have one or you can have the other, but it is very difficult to get both in the same piece of meat. Even today, it seems the standard practice in most recipes is to cook the meat to the point of complete dehydration in an effort to make tough meat seem tender.

We wanted to lessen the need for compromise—that is, to make a brisket that had really big beef flavor and was both reasonably tender and still moist. After cooking over a hundred pounds of beef according to a cross-referential system of time, temperature, and technique, we have found that you can make a better brisket than the one produced by following most recipes, but you can't completely escape the need to compromise.

The Nature of Beef Brisket

Because the brisket is cut from a load-bearing portion of the steer, right next to the foreleg (*see* "Choosing the Proper Cut," page 23), this cut has a much higher concentration of the connective tissue protein collagen than is found in a less active section of the steer, such as the loin. This collagen is what makes the meat tough, but if it is cooked long enough, the connective tissue will break down into gelatin, causing the meat to become more tender. This is the standard practice called for in most recipes. The losses incurred during this long cooking, however, include most of the juice in the meat, and a majority of the fat as well. What one has, then, is beef that is tender but too dry.

This results from the unfortunate fact that the process of converting collagen to gelatin—solubilization—occurs in exactly the temperature range that coincides with the expulsion of most of the moisture out of the meat. Collagen begins to convert to gelatin at about 150 degrees, but it doesn't really dissolve rapidly until above 200 degrees. Cooking beef to an internal temperature of 180 degrees, however, will drive out almost every bit of moisture that can be released from the meat. So the fact that the beef reaches an internal temperature high enough to convert the collagen is vital in promoting tenderness, but the amount of time spent at that temperature is important as well.

For example, a five-pound brisket in a 350-degree oven will reach an internal temperature of 175 degrees in under two hours. But this does not produce the same outcome in terms of collagen breakdown, or tenderness, that you would get cooking a five-pound brisket to 175 degrees over three to four hours in a cooler oven. The quickly cooked brisket, although moist, is very tough, while the slowly cooked brisket is far more tender and still retains a significant amount of moisture. The compromise is to cook the brisket within the collagen-converting temperature range for a sufficient time to tenderize the meat, but without heating the meat past 180 degrees and cooking away all the moisture.

The Nature of the Compromise

To achieve the best balance of moisture and tenderness, we saw three promising directions to take: adjusting the relationship of cooking time and oven temperature; brining prior to cooking for increased moisture retention; and marinating prior to cooking for increased tenderness.

Since cooking, at its most basic level, is a function of time and heat, we began our tests by focusing on the relationship of these two factors in cooking the beef.

Traditional recipes suggest pan browning a well-trimmed four- to five-pound brisket, then braising it with vegetables in broth in a 350-degree oven for three to four hours. We tried this, and found that the process results in well-browned meat with an internal temperature in excess of 205 degrees, and over 40 percent weight loss. The beef was easily cut with a fork, and could be eaten hot from the pan with a generous coating of pan juices, but when it was allowed to rest for more than fifteen minutes, it became dry and grainy. The amount of moisture retained in beef cooked to internal temperatures of over 200 degrees is negligible. When you slice overcooked beef, you will see steam escaping; that is the last of the moisture being forced out of the meat. The only juiciness you may have left will be from liquefied internal fat. If you don't eat the meat immediately or coat it liberally with a fat, a gelatin, or a rich sauce, it will be very dry and grainy.

We tried the same basic technique with a partially trimmed brisket, homemade chicken stock, and the oven set at 250 degrees. The meat was juicier, but it was poorly browned, and the sauce was pale. The internal temperature of the meat averaged 180 degrees. We concluded that the majority of the deep, flavorful browning of not only the surface of the brisket, but the vegetables as well, is accomplished in the high heat of the oven, rather than in the sauté pan.

Our next test was to brown the meat in a 350-degree oven for an hour, then slice it and return it to the pan to finish cooking. The slices quickly overcooked in the broth; they became coarse, and yet remained tough.

Comparing the results of our first tests, we found that all the briskets lost 33 to 40 percent of their weight as the internal temperature of the meat increased from 100 degrees to about 170 degrees. From the visual evidence of shrinkage and all the unmelted fat on the beef, it was clear that the majority of the weight loss was from lost water. But since the low heat method had produced the least moisture loss, we concluded that slow cooking and starting with a generous layer of fat on top of the brisket was the right direction. We decided that it was possible for the meat to be heated to a temperature sufficient to promote tenderness and liquefy some of the fat, yet not quite hot enough to drive out all the moisture.

We then worked on optimizing the time-to-temperature ratio. To do this, we ran a careful series of tests, checking the amount of weight lost and the internal temperature as cooking time progressed (see "Cooking Secret: A Window of Stabilization," page 24).

Since we removed the brisket from the oven every 15 minutes to check internal temperature and weight, the actual cooking time was longer than it would be under ordinary conditions. However, the relationship of time, internal temperature of the meat, and moisture loss from the brisket is the same. We found a consistent pattern of moisture loss: As the internal temperature of the thickest section of the meat stabilized at about 160 degrees, the rate of moisture loss decreased. But when most of the moisture had escaped, the internal temperature of the meat began to rise again. It is within the window of stabilization that the balance of tenderness to moistness is found. After 120 minutes the brisket was not tender; after 285 minutes it was very tender but dry, even though the internal temperature difference was only fifteen degrees. The compromise that suited our tastes for this particular dish was in the region of 210 to 225 minutes: There the meat was tender but still moist; not juicy like a rare steak (which is usually about 125 degrees) but moist.

Through all of this testing, we arrived at a method that produced deep browning, retained some moisture, and adequately tenderized the meat. Our method involves pan browning followed by a short time in a very hot oven with a small amount of prewarmed stock to complete the browning of both the meat and the vegetables.

The heat is then reduced, and the meat slowly comes to an internal temperature between 160 and 175 degrees. Using this method, the weight loss is limited to about 30 percent, which is a slight but perceptible improvement.

In terms of flavor, the browning from the hot oven accounts for most of it, but a good homemade stock was also helpful, especially in terms of providing a gelatin-rich sauce. Using a food processor or a blender to extract the essence of the vegetables will also greatly improve the sauce.

Other Cooking Variables

After searching out the proper balance of cooking time and oven temperature for cooking brisket, we experimented with other variables, including brining, marinating, and larding the meat.

In an effort to add and retain more moisture, we brined the beef in a mixture of salt, sugar, and spice. The average weight gain of the raw beef after forty-eight hours in the brine was 15 percent. However, we found that this extra weight was eliminated within the first hour of cooking, as the meat reached an internal temperature of 145 degrees. The cooked brined meat had a salty flavor and a firm texture, similar to ham. All our attempts at brining yielded the same results: None of the added moisture survived the cooking, and the meat seemed less tender.

The next effort at possible improvement was to marinate the beef prior to cooking to get a head start on breaking down the connective tissue. Using a mildly acidic red wine–based marinade, we cooked a series of briskets: plain, with twenty-four-hour marination, and with forty-eight-hour marination. The marinated raw beef was altered in both appearance and texture, turning a dull gray and becoming soggy. The change in texture, however, seemed to penetrate only about a quarter of

an inch into the meat. When we cooked the marinated beef, we were not able to discern any increased tenderness

Next we tested two different grades of beef, select and choice, suspecting that one would be better suited to the long cooking process. The superiority of choice beef was quickly evident, as the higher fat content gave the brisket extra juiciness, and a richer flavor. Select grade beef seemed a little less moist and a lot more chewy. Since brisket is never graded prime, you should look for the best-marbled choice beef available.

Using some excessively trimmed briskets, we also explored the possibility of adding fat through larding. We tried small slivers and long sections of both beef fat and pork fat either inserted through the brisket or stuck in little pockets cut into the surface of the brisket. The most noticeable effect of larding is that you have a lot more fat to skim off the braising liquid when you prepare the sauce. The meat in direct contact with the added fat did seem more moist, but the effect did not seem to permeate the rest of the brisket at all.

BRAISED BEEF BRISKET
Serves 8

It is important to have a good quality, instant-read thermometer with a scale of 0 to 220 degrees. An accurate oven thermometer is useful as well. Basting with the braising liquid produces a rich, flavorful glaze. Follow the instructions on page 4 for chopping the fennel seeds. All the other spices can be crushed by rolling the bottom of a heavy sauté pan back and forth over them.

1 tablespoon black peppercorns
2 teaspoons whole fennel seeds
1 teaspoon whole coriander seeds
½ teaspoon whole allspice

CHOOSING THE PROPER CUT

The brisket is cut from a well-exercised portion of the steer between the foreleg and the plate, running down the chest just below the short ribs. It could be thought of as breast of beef, or even as beef bacon, since those cuts come from the corresponding parts of the anatomy of a veal calf and a pig.

A full, untrimmed beef brisket (see illustration 1) can weigh as much as fourteen pounds, of which about 10 percent is surface fat. The brisket is usually separated into two sections called the first cut and the second cut (illustration 2). The two pieces are divided by a thick layer of fat that slants through the large end of the meat. Most of the brisket available at supermarkets and meat

markets is first cut; second cut is so fatty and coarse that it usually ends up as ground meat.

If you can find what is called whole brisket (illustration 3), it is absolutely your best choice. This is usually a six- or seven-pound, partially trimmed brisket with the coarse, fatty part of the second cut removed and the remainder of the second cut still attached. It should be very well marbled and have at least a quarter-inch-thick layer of surface fat covering most of one side. Leave the fat on rather than trimming it off as it will do a lot to prevent the brisket from becoming too dry as it cooks.

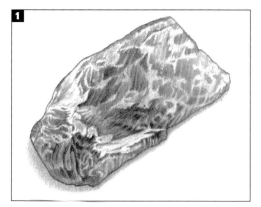

1. The full brisket.

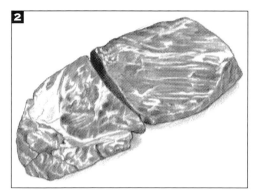

2. The whole brisket cut into the first cut (right) and the second, or point, cut (left).

3. The whole brisket with the small, fatty piece removed from the second cut.

1 whole choice beef brisket (about 5 pounds), surface fat retained
3 tablespoons vegetable oil
1 cup dry red wine
4–6 cups chicken stock or low-sodium chicken broth
 Salt
2 medium onions, quartered and separated into sections
1 head garlic, halved crosswise
3 celery stalks, chopped coarsely
2 medium carrots, peeled and chopped coarsely
 Parsley sprigs for garnish

1. Heat oven to 500 degrees. Crush spices or grind them coarsely; press them into brisket and set aside.

2. Using two burners if necessary, heat oil in large, heavy roasting pan long and wide enough to hold brisket and at least 2 inches deep. Add brisket; cook over medium-high heat, turning once with tongs, until brown on both sides, about 10 minutes. Remove brisket and set aside. Add wine; bring to boil, scraping bottom of pan with wooden spoon to loosen brown bits; reduce by half. Add 2 cups chicken stock; bring to simmer. Remove pan from heat. Season brisket lightly with salt, and return to roasting pan. Scatter vegetables around brisket.

3. Put roasting pan in oven and cook, stirring vegetables occasionally to avoid burning, until thickest part of brisket reaches an internal temperature of around 130 degrees, about 20 minutes.

4. Remove pan from oven; reduce oven temperature to 250 degrees. Do not return brisket to oven until temperature drops to 250 degrees. Add enough chicken stock to pan so that liquid comes about halfway up side of meat, baste brisket, and return to oven. Braise brisket, basting and turning every ½ hour or so, until meat just gives when pierced with meat thermometer and brisket's internal temperature registers around 175 degrees, 1½ to 2½ hours.

5. Remove brisket from braising liquid and wrap in foil. Strain braising liquid into large mixing bowl. Reserve vegetables, squeezing garlic cloves from heads. Transfer braising liquid to tall, narrow container, and let stand until fat rises. Skim and discard fat. Puree vegetables, including garlic, with ½ cup braising liquid in food processor or blender. Add pureed vegetables and braising liquid to a sauté pan and simmer until reduced to thin sauce consistency.

6. Meanwhile, cut brisket across the grain into thin slices (about ⅛ inch thick). Arrange slices of meat on warm plates; generously ladle sauce over meat. Garnish with parsley, and serve immediately.

BRAISED BRISKET, SOUTHERN ITALIAN STYLE
Serves 8 to 10

Follow the recipe for Braised Beef Brisket, omitting the coriander seeds and allspice and adding 1 teaspoon hot red pepper flakes to the spice rub. Decrease the wine to ¼ cup and add it to the pan, along with 1 cup chicken stock, and 2 pounds peeled and chopped Italian plum tomatoes (or one 28-ounce can). Bring to a simmer. (If using fresh tomatoes, simmer until the tomatoes release their juices.) When seasoning the brisket with salt, sprinkle 2 teaspoons dried rosemary and 2 teaspoons dried oregano over it. Add 4 ounces chopped, sliced bacon or pancetta and the braising vegetables, adding one extra onion and omitting celery and carrots. Once the brisket has reached an internal temperature of 130 degrees, add enough stock to the pan to come about halfway up the side of the meat (another 1 to 3 cups). Continue with the recipe, removing the brisket from the braising liquid when it is fully cooked. Add ½ cup pitted Kalamata olives to the braising liquid (which is thickened with the pureed braising vegetables as in the Braised Beef Brisket recipe) and reduce it to a thin, pasta-sauce consistency, 15 to 20 minutes. Slice the brisket and serve it and the sauce with pasta or creamy polenta.

BRAISED BRISKET, OAXACAN STYLE
Serves 8

Follow the recipe for Braised Beef Brisket, omitting the fennel seeds and allspice and adding 2 teaspoons cumin seeds and 1 tablespoon chili powder to the spice rub. Omit the wine and add 1 cup chicken stock, 2 pounds peeled and chopped Italian plum tomatoes (or one 28-ounce can), and 2 ounces dried, seeded Pasilla chiles to the pan once the browned brisket has been removed. Bring to a simmer. (If using fresh tomatoes, simmer until the tomatoes release their juices.) When seasoning the brisket with salt, sprinkle 2 teaspoons dried thyme and 2 teaspoons dried oregano over it. Add the braising vegetables, adding one extra onion and omitting celery and carrots. Once the brisket has reached an internal temperature of 130 degrees, add enough stock to the pan to come about halfway up the side of the meat (another 2 to 4 cups). Continue with the recipe, reducing the braising liquid (which is thickened with the pureed braising vegetables as in the Braised Brisket recipe) to a thick sauce consistency, about 20 minutes. Slice the brisket and serve it and the sauce with warm flour tortillas and fresh salsa. ■

Ian Dickson Smith is a Los Angeles–based food writer; **Tina Wilson** is the chef at Campanile restaurant in Los Angeles.

COOKING SECRET: A WINDOW OF STABILIZATION

This chart shows the relationships of cooking time, internal temperature of the meat, and weight (moisture) loss as brisket is cooked. Brisket stabilizes for some time at an internal temperature of 160 degrees. In this window of stabilization, the rate of moisture (weight) loss also drops dramatically. The optimum "doneness point" occurs just at the end of this plateau, when the temperature begins to rise and the rate of moisture loss begins to increase, as well. By taking meat out of the oven at this point, you optimize both tenderness and moistness.

Since the meat was removed from the oven every fifteen minutes to measure internal temperature and weight, the actual cooking time shown here is longer than it would be under normal cooking conditions. However, the relationship of time, temperature, and weight (moisture) loss from the brisket that this test reveals will hold true during ordinary cooking.

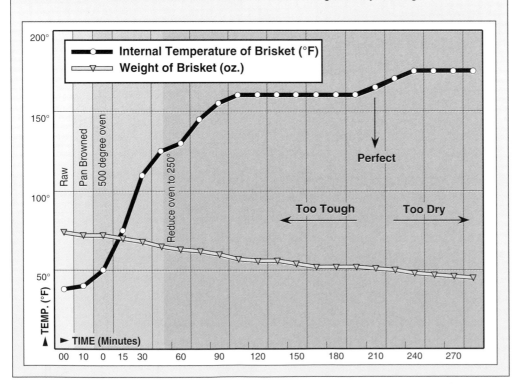

CHART DESIGNED BY SUE DAHL

How to Cook Lentils

All types of lentils are best when cooked with salt but without acid.

～ BY KATHERINE ALFORD ～

The conventional practice when cooking dried legumes is to soak them before cooking, and avoid salt or acidic ingredients during cooking. One of the charms of lentils is that they don't need to be soaked. I wondered if this nonconformist status would also apply to the restrictions on salt and acid. Therefore, I set out to test these factors and also to determine the best cooking times and uses for the four main varieties of lentils—French Le Puy, common green or brown, peeled red, and whole red masoor (red lentils with the brownish seed coat left on).

Before cooking, all lentils need to be inspected for stones, seeds, or foreign objects. After sorting, lentils should be rinsed in water to remove any residual dirt.

To determine how long it takes the lentils to cook to tenderness without any graininess, I cooked half a cup of each kind of cleaned lentils in three cups of plain water. After bringing the water to a boil, I skimmed any foam off the surface of the liquid, turned the heat down, and let the lentils simmer.

As they cooked, each kind of lentil showed its unique character. Peeled red lentils almost immediately lost their shape and turned into a rough mush; this no doubt explains why these lentils are most often used in purees. The common green or brown lentils and the masoors became tender and creamy in about twenty to twenty-five minutes; however, at this point these lentils also started to lose their seed coats, which caused them to disintegrate slightly. The French Le Puy took the longest to get tender, about thirty minutes, but they also kept their original shape better than any other variety, a real advantage for salads.

There was a dramatic difference in the tastes of the types of lentils. The common green lentils were dull and bland; the red lentils had a slight sweetness to them but were basically neutral; the flavor of the whole red masoors was delightful, with a hint of cumin and coriander. The French lentils had the most robust, down-to-earth flavor.

My next test was to follow the same procedure but to add one teaspoon of kosher salt to the water. The green and brown, peeled red, and masoor lentils all cooked in about the same amount of time as they had in plain water, but the Le Puy took about ten minutes longer. The taste of each lentil, and in particular of the common green and brown types, was much more developed and clearer. Lentils are definitely better when cooked with salt.

Next, I cooked each lentil in the same amount of water, substituting one tablespoon of vinegar for the salt. The vinegar had a striking effect on the lentils, doubling their cooking time and giving them a rather grainy texture. Subsequent tests with wine and tomato yielded similar results. According to Barry Swanson, Ph.D., professor of Food Science at Washington State University, this is because acids interfere with lentils' ability to bind with water. This in turn causes them to take longer to soften and to have a rather dry taste. So unless you're using lentils in a slow-cooking dish and want to lengthen their cooking time, avoid cooking them with acidic ingredients.

INDIAN-SPICED LENTILS WITH KALE
Serves 4

 1 cup masoor lentils (*see* Sources and Resources, page 32), picked over and rinsed
 1 teaspoon salt
 1 pound kale, stemmed, washed, and leaves coarsely chopped
 2 tablespoons unsalted butter
 1 teaspoon ground coriander
 ½ teaspoon ground cumin
 ½ teaspoon ground mustard
 ¼–½ teaspoon hot red pepper flakes
 2 garlic cloves, minced
 2 teaspoons minced fresh ginger

1. Bring lentils, 6 cups water, and salt to boil in medium saucepan; boil for 5 minutes. Reduce heat; simmer until lentils are tender but still hold their shape, 20 to 25 minutes, adding kale during last 5 minutes of cooking. Drain, reserving 1 cup cooking liquid.

2. Meanwhile, heat butter in large skillet over medium heat. Add next four ingredients; sauté to develop flavors, about 1 minute. Add garlic and ginger; sauté until softened and fragrant, about 2 minutes. Add lentils and kale and reserved cooking liquid. Simmer to blend flavors, about 5 minutes. Adjust seasonings and serve.

FRENCH LENTIL SALAD WITH CARAWAY AND RADISH
Serves 4

Serve this hearty, piquant salad with grilled sausage, pâté, or roast duck.

 1 cup French Le Puy lentils, picked over and rinsed
 ½ onion, halved and studded with 2 whole cloves
 1 carrot, peeled and cut in half
 1 celery stalk, cut into thirds
 1 bay leaf
 ½ teaspoon salt
 2 tablespoons sherry wine vinegar
 3 tablespoons whole-grain mustard
 1 tablespoon caraway seeds, lightly crushed
 2 garlic cloves, minced
    Salt and ground black pepper
 ½ cup extra virgin olive oil
 4 radishes, minced
 ¼ cup minced fresh parsley

1. Bring first six ingredients plus 4 cups water to boil in medium saucepan; boil for 5 minutes. Reduce heat; simmer until lentils are tender but still hold their shape, 25 to 30 minutes.

2. Meanwhile, mix vinegar, mustard, caraway seeds, garlic, and salt and pepper to taste in a small bowl. Slowly whisk in oil to make vinaigrette; set aside.

3. Drain lentils, discarding vegetables. Add warm lentils to vinaigrette; toss to coat. Cool to room temperature; stir in radishes and parsley. Serve.

RED LENTIL PUREE WITH CUMIN AND ANISE
serves 4

 1½ cups red lentils, picked over and rinsed
 1½ tablespoons minced fresh ginger
 2 garlic cloves, minced
 ½ teaspoon turmeric
 ½ teaspoon salt
 2 tablespoons unsalted butter
 ½ teaspoon cumin seeds
 ½ teaspoon anise seeds
 3 tablespoons juice from 1 lemon
    Ground white pepper

1. Bring first five ingredients plus 4 cups water to boil in medium saucepan; boil for 5 minutes. Reduce heat; simmer until lentils lose their shape, 15 to 20 minutes. Whisk lentils to make a puree; set aside.

2. Heat butter in a small sauté pan. Add cumin and anise seeds; sauté until butter is nutty brown. Remove from heat; add lemon juice. Stir mixture into lentil puree. Season with pepper, adjust other seasonings, and serve. ■

Katherine Alford is a cooking teacher and food writer living in New York.

With Balsamic Vinegar, Price Equals Quality

The most popular supermarket brand comes in last.

~ BY JACK BISHOP ~

Balsamic vinegar is the trendy condiment of choice for everything from salad dressings to sauces. However, most Americans would be surprised to learn they have never tasted "real" balsamic vinegar. Even more shocking, balsamic vinegar is more popular here than in Italy, where its culinary uses are actually quite limited. Contrary to what the chef at your local restaurant may think, balsamic vinegar is not Italy's answer to soy sauce.

Until twenty years ago, balsamic vinegar was an obscure condiment made at home by wealthy families in the Emilia-Romagna region of north-central Italy. This artisanal product starts with the unfermented juice of local white grapes, which is then aged for decades in wood casks. Barrels of vinegar were often passed down from one generation to the next, sometimes as part of a dowry. Production has always been extremely limited, and costs have always been prohibitive. Traditional balsamic vinegar is a labor of love, not a money-making venture. (*See* "The Real Thing," below, for more information.)

All this changed when savvy Italian marketers realized that Americans would buy endless amounts of sweet-and-sour, commercially made balsamic vinegar. Although fewer than ten thousand bottles of traditional balsamic vinegar are released every year, annual American consumption of balsamic vinegar now stands at several million bottles. To turn a family tradition into an international business, manufacturers first had to create the supply to meet the demand. The solution? Sell a bastardized product.

"Most commercial balsamic vinegar on the market today is inexcusably bad," says Lynne Rossetto Kasper, author of *The Splendid Table* (Morrow, 1992), and the leading American expert on the cuisine of Emilia-Romagna. "The quality of commercial balsamic vinegar has declined in equal relation to its increasing popularity," she warns. While five or six drops of the real stuff can give "more pleasure than any other food I know," Kasper notes that most of the balsamic vinegar Americans buy is "inferior."

Since there is no legal definition for *aceto balsamico di Modena* (balsamic vinegar of Modena), even shoppers who read labels can end up with bad balsamic. Many cheap brands are simply red wine vinegar with caramel added for color and sweetness. Some brands that say "di Modena" on the label are actually made in other cities, most often Naples. Even among expensive commercial brands, there is a wide range of manufacturing techniques; some companies employ industrial methods, while others blend traditional artisanal production, like aging in a series of wood casks, with modern technologies.

Aged for decades in small wooden casks, true balsamic vinegar is an artisanal product made only by wealthy families.

Tasting to Judge Quality

To make sense of this muddle, we held a tasting of fourteen balsamic vinegars in a range of price categories. We included one traditional balsamic vinegar from Modena, which set us back $150 for 100 ml (just over three ounces); the leading commercial brands that sell in supermarkets for $3 to $4 per 500 ml bottle; as well as a number of more expensive commercial brands ($6 to $30 per 250 ml bottle) that try to duplicate the quality of traditional balsamico at a fraction of the cost.

The tasting was designed to answer one basic question: Does more money buy better vinegar? With few exceptions, our panel found that quality and price go hand-in-hand. Most of the higher-priced brands displayed a gentle sweetness combined with a low-to-moderate acidity; a complex, woody bouquet; a flavor reminiscent of fruit; and a dense, syrupy consistency—all qualities revered in traditional balsamic vinegar. While few tasters would confuse even the best commercial products with the real thing, several moderately priced brands were deemed excellent.

If this is the good news, the bad news is that supermarket brands are generally overly acidic and devoid of character. In fact, the two leading brands, which between them account for more than three-quarters of U.S. sales, finished last and next-to-last in the tasting. Our advice, then, is to visit your local gourmet store or pick up the phone when buying balsamic vinegar. Expect to spend $15 to $30 for an outstanding vinegar.

If $15 seems like a lot for vinegar, remember that a little goes a long way. Even quality commercial balsamic vinegars are not used straight in

---

THE REAL THING

Before reaching the public, all authentic balsamic vinegars have been aged for a minimum of twelve years in a series of small casks made from various woods and evaluated by one of the two consortia of producers. The larger one is located in Modena, the smaller in nearby Reggio. After passing a rigorous taste test, vinegars receive a consortium seal and are packaged in distinctive bottles. Only vinegars that meet all the requirements may be called *aceto balsamico tradizionale di Modena*. The key word is "tradizionale," which signals that the vinegar contains 100 percent cooked, aged, white grape must.

So why do three ounces of traditional balsamic vinegar cost $150? The answer is low yield and high storage costs. An acre of a typical vineyard might produce enough juice to make 800 gallons of wine vinegar. Once the juice from those same grapes has been cooked down and aged, during which time massive evaporation occurs, just twenty or thirty gallons of balsamic vinegar remain. The high storage costs—as one expert said, "just keeping water that long is expensive"—add to the final price, which is rarely less than $60 per bottle and can climb to $200.

Is any vinegar worth that much? The traditional balsamic vinegar in our tasting was the clear favorite of almost every panelist. Its high viscosity, intense but pleasant sweetness, heady aroma, and minimal acidity easily distinguished it from commercial vinegars. But these characteristics also restrict its uses. Wealthy Italians sip traditional balsamico after dinner or sprinkle a few drops over sliced strawberries. For most other culinary purposes, a good commercial balsamic vinegar is fine.

---

salad dressings in Italy but are usually combined with aged red wine vinegar. Other traditional uses—such as sprinkling over steamed asparagus, sliced Parmesan, or vanilla gelato—require very small quantities. Italians do not generally cook with balsamic vinegar because heat destroys its subtle qualities. To use balsamic vinegar in savory foods, add a few drops to a sauce just before serving, or drizzle some over a piece of grilled fish. ■

RATING BALSAMIC VINEGARS

Thirteen commercial vinegars were tasted blind and are listed in order of preference based on scores awarded by our judges. We also tasted one traditional balsamic vinegar, which was so clearly superior to the commercial vinegars and so much more expensive ($50 an ounce) that we did not include it in the chart.

All samples were poured into small cups and sipped directly from the cups or from demitasse spoons. Water and bread were available to cleanse the testers' palates. The tasting was held at Felidia restaurant in New York and was conducted by the author; Mark Bittman, Executive Editor of *Cook's Illustrated;* Anna Teresa Callen, Julia

della Croce, Nick Malgieri, and Michele Scicolone, all leading Italian cooking teachers and cookbook authors; Joanna Saliani, manager of Felidia; Philip Teverow, buyer for Dean & DeLuca; and Bill Toll, principal of Taste of the World and an importer of balsamic vinegar for ten years.

With the exception of the Cavalli, Rienzi, and Vine Hill Farms vinegars, all samples were bottled in Modena. Prices are based on purchases in supermarkets and gourmet stores in New York and Connecticut or on mail-order sources where indicated.

Compagnia del Montale Aceto Balsamico di Modena

Cavalli Condimento Balsamico

Cibo di Lidia Aceto Balsamico di Modena

Fiorucci Riserva Balsamic Vinegar

Fini Balsamic Vinegar

Masserie di Sant'Eramo Balsamic Vinegar of Modena

HIGHLY RECOMMENDED VINEGARS

These vinegars received uniformly positive comments from all nine tasters.

Compagnia del Montale Aceto Balsamico di Modena, $30/250 ml. Six first-place votes plus a second and third made this entry the clear winner. "Chewy" texture and "dynamite flavor" that was described as "rich," "perfume-y," and "sweet with very little acidity" set this vinegar apart from the pack. *Available by mail from Dean & DeLuca (560 Broadway, New York, NY 10012; 800-221-7714).*

Cavalli Condimento Balsamico, $14.95/250 ml. The only entry that hails from Reggio, Italy's "second" city for balsamic vinegar production, snared two first-place votes plus two seconds and four lower votes. Tasters described it as "quite sweet and tart at once" with a strong "grape" or "prune" flavor and "medium viscosity." Overall, a "pleasant, well-balanced" vinegar. *Available in gourmet stores and by mail from Dean & DeLuca (see address above).*

Cibo di Lidia Aceto Balsamico di Modena, $20/250 ml. Although this vinegar received only one first-place vote, all nine tasters ranked it among their favorites. The adjectives "mild" and "mellow" best describe this "fruity" five-year-old vinegar with "good density." *Available from Cibo de Lidia (243 E. 58th Street, New York, NY 10022; 212-758-1479).*

RECOMMENDED VINEGARS

These vinegars were well regarded by a majority of tasters.

Fiorucci Riserva Balsamic Vinegar, $5.79/250 ml. This vinegar has an "enticing berry flavor" with "strong wood" and "earthy character" that was described as "chocolate-y" or "like old barrels." A few tasters felt it was "too harsh," but it is an excellent choice given the low price. *Available in supermarkets.*

Fini Balsamic Vinegar, $10.50/250 ml. This vinegar was "not nearly as sweet" as the top vinegars and "perceptibly thinner," and received some complaints that its "acidity is too much." However, many panelists liked the "aromatic," "woody nose" on this "round" vinegar that was judged "pleasant but not very complex." *Available in gourmet stores and by mail from Williams-Sonoma (800-541-2233).*

Masserie di Sant'Eramo Balsamic Vinegar of Modena, $6.95/250 ml. This "fragrant" vinegar reminiscent of "yeast" and "wood" gets high marks for its "agreeable balance between sweetness and acidity" and "average viscosity." Although "pleasant," this vinegar lacks the complexity and nuances of the top choices. Still a great value. *Available in gourmet stores and by mail from Dean & DeLuca (see address above).*

VINEGARS NOT RECOMMENDED

These vinegars were poorly regarded by most tasters.

Giuseppe Giusti Gran Deposito Aceto Balsamico di Modena, $15.99/250 ml. Although a few tasters gave this vinegar decent marks, with comments like "winey, if too acidic" and "pungent," the majority felt it was "harsh," "sour," and "fake." Several complained of a "chemical quality." *Available in gourmet stores and by mail from Dean & DeLuca (see address at left).*

Modenaceti Balsamic Vinegar of Modena, $3.39/500 ml. "Comparatively little flavor" was the consensus about this "watery" vinegar. Because of its "extremely sharp vinegar quality" that "burned the back of the throat," several tasters felt it was "indistinguishable from cheap red wine vinegar." *Available in supermarkets.*

Mazzetti Balsamic Vinegar of Modena, $3.39/500 ml. "Sharp," "thin," and "acidic" sums up the panel's take on this "watery" and "harsh" vinegar. "Flat and not as fruity as others" and "decent, if too mild" was as charitable as our tasters got. *Available in supermarkets.*

Rienzi Balsamic Vinegar of Modena, $1.99/500 ml. Despite what the label says, the production codes indicate this vinegar actually comes from Naples. "Lots of acid and little else" was the panel's assessment of this least-expensive entry. *Available in supermarkets.*

Aceto Balsamico di Sonoma, $17/250 ml. Although made from 100 percent must and aged for six years in wood, the only balsamic vinegar made in this country did not show well. "Mild but one-dimensional" with "decent, if not overwhelming" body. The acid was "in check at first taste" but then "overwhelmed" the palate with "excessive sharpness." *Available by mail from Vine Hill Farms (Box 153, Sonoma, CA 95476; 707-664-6699).*

Duke's Balsamic Vinegar of Modena, $3.89/500 ml. The second-best-selling brand in the United States comes from a large Modena operation called Grosoli, which packages many private-label vinegars as well. The adjectives "sharp," "thin," and "coarse" sum up the panel's judgment of this vinegar that is "short on everything but color." *Available in supermarkets.*

Monari Federzoni Balsamic Vinegar of Modena, $3.79/500 ml. The best-selling brand in this country (with at least two-thirds of the market) was the only entry to receive no score at all. "Bitter" and "caustic" with a "burning finish" was the consensus. It "made me contort my face" wrote one taster. *Available in supermarkets.*

Rating Rice Cookers

Just load it up, and the top-rated Rival rice cooker will make perfect rice every time with no watching—and keep it warm until you're ready to eat.

~ BY SHARON KEBSCHULL BARRETT ~

It should be so easy: take water, add rice, and cook until done. However, many good cooks report that perfect rice eludes them every time. For them, rice cookers are a dream come true. With a good cooker, perfect rice *is* as simple as mixing rice and water and cooking until done. The result is never crunchy or scorched.

Rice cookers house an inner pot that rests above a heating element. Set ratios of water and rice are added to the pot and heated until the water has been completely absorbed. The cookers have no timers; rather, they work by sensing the temperature in the inner pot. When the water is all gone, the temperature rises, signaling the cooker to turn off. A decent cooker then switches to a "keep warm" setting at which it should hold the rice, without drying it, at a constant temperature of about 180 degrees for several hours.

Virtually every major housewares company now makes some sort of rice cooker, although some have combined them with steamers. We tested what the manufacturers consider to be their "latest and best" models. After cooking seventy pounds of rice, we can recommend several machines. Most of the cookers worked well, but the Rival was the clear winner, turning out excellent batches of rice every time.

When a Cup Is Not a Cup

To start, we made four batches of rice in each machine. Rather than using a standard amount of rice, we made two tests with each machine's minimum and maximum amounts of dry rice. For the first test we used short-grain rice and for the second we used long-grain rice. The amounts varied from one and one-half cups to twenty cups of cooked rice.

This leads to a complaint that applies to almost all the cookers. Few of them list the amount of cooked rice they produce. The boxes say "ten-cup capacity," but that turns out to mean neither ten standard eight-ounce cups of dry rice nor ten cups of cooked rice. What it means is ten of the plastic cups or scoops included with the cooker. These scoops aren't a standard measurement; usually they're about six ounces. You use them to measure the dry rice; then you add water to the pot up to the line marked with the number of scoops of rice you dumped in. If you lose the scoop, you can no longer follow the manufacturer's recipe.

To take this possibility into account, we also tested the machines using a ratio of one standard, eight-ounce cup of rice to two cups of water. The machines performed virtually the same as they had in the first tests. The moral is, if you think you

have the perfect formula for making rice on the stove, use it in your cooker and it should work the same way.

Most of the directions that come with the cookers advise letting the rice stand for fifteen minutes after the machine switches from "cook" to "keep warm" so the rice can finish steaming. We checked the rice as soon as the machines switched to "keep warm," and then we checked again fifteen minutes later. Extra points were given to those machines that produced ready-to-eat rice as soon as the keep-warm light came on. Some cookers were able to do this consistently; others re-

quired the extra wait.

Even when making rice on the stove goes well, cleaning the pot is always a chore. Some rice cookers have nonstick pots that eliminate this problem. This is the one category in which the winning Rival cooker lost, although it wasn't terrible. Some cookers without nonstick pans require soaking and scrubbing. To minimize this, before adding the rice and water, try coating the pan with cooking oil spray.

In addition to making rice, we also steamed eight ounces of green beans in each machine, noting the cooking time, convenience of use (are the

---

RATING RICE COOKERS

Seven standard rice cookers were evaluated based on the following characteristics and are listed in order of preference. A full rice cooker means the machine performed well in that category. A half-full rice cooker indicates average performance, and an empty rice cooker signals poor performance. (For information on purchasing the top models, *see* Sources and Resources, page 32.)

CAPACITY: Minimum and maximum amounts of cooked rice that can be prepared in machine.
COOKING TIME: Longest time recorded for preparing rice, without rest period.
QUALITY OF RICE: Models in which rice was ready to eat immediately after cooking cycle were given preference.

KEEP WARM: Rice cooled from 16 to 50 degrees after four hours; models are rated accordingly.
STEAMING: Machines with automatic shut-off for steaming are preferred.
CLEANING: Nonstick pans clean up in seconds and are preferred; models without nonstick pans require some soaking and scrubbing.

= very good performance

= average performance

= poor performance

Name	Price	Capacity	Cooking Time	Quality of Rice	Keep Warm	Steaming	Cleaning
Rival 4310	$58	2 to 11 cups	24 minutes	very good	very good	very good	average
Oster 3811-20	$59	3 to 20 cups	29 minutes	very good	very good	average	average
Hitachi RD-4053	$35	1.5 to 9.5 cups	22 minutes	average	average	very good	poor
Zojirushi NHR-G18	$72	4 to 17 cups	35 minutes	average	very good	poor	very good
National SR-SE10N	$100	1.75 to 9 cups	24 minutes	poor	very good	average	average
Sanyo EC23	$49	3 to 16 cups	33 minutes	average	very good	average	average
Salton RA-10	$60	3 to 20 cups	32 minutes	average	average	average	very good

beans done when the timer goes off?), and size of the steaming plates, as well as the beans' taste. On the best of the cookers, such as the Rival and the Oster, steaming worked just like rice cooking; when the specified amount of water boiled away, the machine clicked off and the beans were done. But many cookers give only vague guidelines for the amount of water and length of time needed, so the vegetables would end up being either over- or undercooked when the machine shut off. For this reason, we judged most of the rice cookers to be somewhat impractical for steaming vegetables.

Trying Steamers

For cooks who rarely make rice but who like steamed foods, a steamer may have more appeal than a rice cooker. Steamers have one or two cooking baskets set over a water reservoir. To use them, you either set a timer and then turn off the machine when it rings, or with some machines, wait for the water to boil away, which automatically turns off the machine. The latter design is more desirable. Because we set out to test rice cookers, we tested steamers only from companies that do not make a separate rice cooker.

Steamers not only take longer to make rice than rice cookers, they also require more attention. You have to remove the rice basket instantly to stop the cooking process, and steamers do not have keep-warm functions. In the end, the only steamer we can recommend is the Hamilton Beach, which shuts off automatically and makes good rice as well as steamed vegetables. We tested steamers from West Bend, Black & Decker, and Farberware, but all of them require guesswork for making rice, and the guidelines and directions are incomplete or confusing.

Rice-Only Cookers

We also tested the jar-type cookers that are most popular in Asia. We found they made great rice, but for most consumers we are hard pressed to find justification for a $165 rice cooker that can't do anything else. As fabulous as these deluxe cookers can be, they are so expensive and so limited that we can't really recommend them.

Of the two models we did test, the Sanyo ECJ PF18F ($120) slightly outperformed the Zojirushi NRC-18 ($165) in keeping rice warm, but otherwise the machines were virtually identical. They both feature a five-foot retractable cord, a condensation collector to keep water from dripping onto the rice when you raise the hinged lid, a nonstick interior, a nineteen-cup cooked rice capacity, and a flower-painted exterior. In both, the rice came out perfect almost every time—especially when it was allowed to rest for fifteen minutes after the cooking cycle.

If a pretty machine with fancy extras—but no steaming ability—appeals to you, buy the deluxe Sanyo. Otherwise, purchase the more versatile Rival; the $62 you save will buy rice for years to come. ∎

Sharon Kebschull Barrett recently graduated from Peter Kump's New York cooking school.

Rival: Consistently makes the best rice and does not require a rest period after the cooking cycle. Has the best keep-warm function in the pack and an automatic timer for steaming, but is a bit hard to clean.

Oster: Rice is usually ready without resting, but keep-warm function is poor, with fifty-degree drop after four hours. Steamer does not have automatic shut-off.

Hitachi: Rice must rest after cooking cycle. Automatic shut-off for steaming, but pot is the most difficult to clean.

Zojirushi: Rice is wet after cooking cycle and must rest. Steaming directions are unclear.

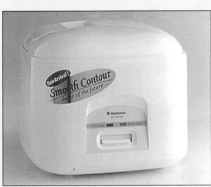

National: Timing is erratic—rice is sometimes overdone and sometimes needs resting period. Steaming must be timed manually, and too much steam escapes around lid.

Sanyo: Rice always needs rest period to finish cooking. Steaming directions are unusably vague. Very hard to clean.

Salton: Rice is never done after cooking cycle and is sometimes not even done after rest period. Steaming directions are sketchy; steaming plate is too small.

Sanyo ECJPF18F (Unrated): Because they cost twice as much as other rice cookers, deluxe jar-type cookers were not included in our ratings. If you want to spend that much for a machine that does only one thing, we recommend this model.

American "Rhône" Wine Wins Tasting

When we tasted the inexpensive wines of Southern France, we threw in a couple of California wines just for fun—one stole the show.

∼ BY MARK BITTMAN ∼

The red wines of Southern France—sometimes known collectively as "Rhône wines," although they are not all from the Rhône region—have become the darlings of much of the wine trade and of certain aficionados. The best wines, such as top-quality Hermitage and Châteauneuf-du-Pape, now command prices comparable to the classified Bordeaux. This well-publicized upgrade, deserved or not, has increased demand for the area's lesser wines, and we have seen a virtual flood of new labels from heretofore-unheard-of appellations such as Vacqueyras, which is a wine from the Rhône, and Roussillon and Minervois, which are from the Southwest.

The good news is that many of these wines sell for under $10; the bad news is that many are rough-and-tumble, the kind of *vin ordinaire* that you don't mind drinking out of a pitcher or a jug with pizza or ribs but that simply isn't worth even $5 or $6. The grapes one winemaker turns into a delicate wine of simple charm another transforms into a rough drink you might think of using for soaking paint-brushes. The labels and relative cost give little indication of what you are likely to find.

When we decided to try to find the inexpensive gems among the reds of Southern France our first challenge was to define the region. We opted for the broadest possible definition, choosing to taste those wines made from the grapes traditionally used in the region: the grenache and syrah, which usually make wines destined to be aged; the carignan, used mostly in wines meant to be drunk young; and a few others. These are indigenous grapes that are used in only a few other places in the world. Since one of those places happens to be California—where there's always someone willing to make wine from *any* grape—we threw in what experience had taught us was the best of the lot from there. To everyone's surprise, a California wine based primarily on carignan was the winner.

To see whether we drew the cost line too low, we also included two $15 wines in the tasting: the 1990 Gigondas from the esteemed firm of Guigal, and a relatively inexpensive Châteauneuf-du-Pape (1988, du Domaine Grand Tinel). The results were mixed: Experienced tasters recognized the more aggressive, bolder Gigondas and determined that it was not yet ready to drink; the Châteauneuf simply tasted like another one of the wines in the middle of the pack.

So, with the exception of the Gigondas, none of these wines is going to send you running to the local wine merchant begging for cases to store in your cellar. But that was hardly the goal; we wanted to identify very inexpensive reds for you to enjoy in the coming year. ∎

BLIND TASTING RESULTS

As usual, the wines in our tasting were judged blind by a panel made up of both wine professionals and amateur wine lovers. In the judging, seven points were awarded for each first-place vote; six for second; five for third; and so on. These wines were all purchased in the Northeast, and prices will vary somewhat throughout the country. Within each category, the wines are listed in order, based on the number of points scored.

1990 Cline Côtes d'Oakley Contra Costa County

1990 Vieille Ferme Reserve Côtes de Rhône

HIGHLY RECOMMENDED:

1990 Cline Côtes d'Oakley Contra Costa County, $7. This little gem, from a producer specializing in Rhône-style wines, is a light blend made primarily of grapes taken from older vines, and it shows. Every taster ranked it in the top five, and although one said it "lacked freshness," other comments were uniformly positive. At this price, it would be hard to do better.

1990 Vieille Ferme Reserve Côtes de Rhône, $9. A deeper, more complex wine than our winner, this was the one of the few entries that made a stab at greatness and nearly achieved it. Loved by some ("spicy and fruity—yum"), downgraded by others ("murky"), it's a good example of the high levels that the wines of this region can achieve at relatively low prices. It will probably improve with time.

RECOMMENDED:

1991 Guigal Côtes de Rhône, $9. A reliable wine from one of the area's leading producers. "Clean and fruity," but "lacks definition." A solid choice, widely available.

1990 Vidal Fleury Côtes de Rhône, $8. The name is that of an old southern Rhône firm, but the wine is also made by Guigal, which took it over some years ago. It's very similar to the wine above; both were judged to be "good quality" by most tasters.

1990 Domaine de Gautiere Provence, $8. This is organically grown wine from a new estate and is light in style. Some found it "strange," but for others that translated into "peppery and complex."

1992 Château St. Estephe Corbières, $5.50. One of the new breed of very inexpensive wines from the Southwest of France, this one appears to be consistent from year to year and always a decent buy.

1990 Vieille Ferme Côtes de Ventoux, $6. From a different area than the second-place finisher, this wine is also made differently. It's fruitier and less complex: "Lots of fruit, little spine."

1990 Guigal Gigondas, $15. More than any of the others, this is a wine to cellar. "Lots of tannin, loads of fruit; good now, better later." This is not a wine to buy for dinner tonight, however.

1991 Clos de Gilroy, Bonny Doon, $9. This is made by Randall Grahm, who pioneered the making of Rhône-style wines in California. Very light in color and style, this would make a "good picnic wine."

1988 Châteauneuf-du-Pape du Domaine Grand Tinel, $15. This is a middle-of-the-road Châteauneuf-du-Pape that suffered from an abundance of sulfur ("phew!") and alcohol.

NOT RECOMMENDED:

1990 Domaine le Couroulu Vacqueyras, $9. This is a "sweet, fruity, simple" wine that "lacks structure."

1992 Jaboulet Parallel 45, $7.50. This brand-name Côtes de Rhône has been made for years by this well-known producer; obviously 1992 was not a good one. "Dusty" and "bitter" were two of the less-harsh comments.

1993 Château de Paraza Minervois, $6. This comes from one of the new appellations responsible for cheap table wine. It was called "thin" and "not interesting" but "not unpleasant."

Clos de Pape Petit vin d'Avril, $6.50. This is a non-vintage blend of grenache, syrah, and cabernet. "Chemical" was the word used to describe it.

Chocolate and the Art of Low-Fat Desserts
Alice Medrich
Warner Books, $35

I've never been enthusiastic about low-fat cooking, and "low-fat dessert" has always struck me as a cheap oxymoron. Why try to "lighten" classics like fettuccine alfredo, cassoulet, or chocolate mousse? Eat them full strength, savor every bite, then eat lean the next day. The trouble with many writers of low-fat recipes is they go too far. They're not content with a 25 percent decrease in the amount of fat. Whether it's pressure from the publisher or demand from the public, they try to bring the grams of fat as close to zero as possible—flavor and texture be damned. The resulting dishes are unnatural and unsatisfying.

I'm happy to report that Alice Medrich does not fall into this no-fat trap. After trying six of her low-fat desserts, all of which have popular high-calorie counterparts, I have to admit that I am impressed.

I boasted rather than apologized, for example, as I served Medrich's Raspberry Tartlets with Chocolate Pastry Cream (a mere 3.5 grams of fat per serving) to dinner guests. Instead of lightening the pastry dough for this dish, she successfully reinvents it. A mixture of Wondra flour, sugar, egg, baking powder, a touch of oil, and flavorings starts off batterlike but bakes up into a flavorful, crisp disk. The resulting crust tastes more like crisped cake, but it makes a pleasant, substantial base for low-fat pastry cream and fresh raspberries. Similarly, her version of flourless chocolate cake, called Chocolate Decadence, has no butter and less bittersweet chocolate and fewer eggs than its rich counterpart. This makes it lighter and softer-textured, but it still delivers an impressive chocolate flavor and a satisfying texture, with only 6 grams of fat per serving. I had similar reactions to Frozen Hot Chocolate, a rich, lush frozen chocolate shake with only 2.3 grams of fat, and reduced-fat brownies that offered the chew and goo most brownie lovers want. I did draw the line at The New Cheesecake, however; relying on cottage cheese to lighten it, the cheesecake had a chalky, grainy finish.

Medrich's recipes work and taste great because her priorities are mostly right—taste and texture are more important than achieving zero grams of fat. I could sense with every satisfying bite that Medrich had taken each dessert to the edge of leanness, without crossing the boundary.

—Pam Anderson

Roger Verge's Vegetables in the French Style
Roger Verge
Artisan, $35

Has everything come full circle? Tired of "fresh vegetables, simply prepared," I turned to a book that dares to use exotic, arcane, even heretical ingredients: cream, butter, and eggs. The results were not only refreshingly different, they seemed new.

Verge, whose personal and not-so-simple Provençal cooking has been around for some time, usually seems like a reasonable chef. Yes, he instructs us to peel walnuts every now and then, a task no sane home cook would tackle. But on the whole he keeps things pretty reasonable. In quick succession over several days, I made Potato-Celeriac Pancakes with Cream and Celery, which took about a half hour (and my guests were suitably impressed); Spinach Coconut Flan, which was amazingly simple despite an instruction to dry the spinach in a towel, immediately succeeded by an instruction to plunge the spinach into boiling water; a soup made from broccoli stalks, a potato, a leek, and not much else, the kind of frugality one likes to see in French chefs; and my favorite, Turnip Galettes with Cardamom, crisp little turnip pies nicely caramelized thanks to the addition of sugar.

These recipes all had several things in common: They were not difficult to make; they did not contain too many ingredients (and none were hard to find); they didn't take too long; they were almost surprisingly delicious; and, as I've already said, they were rather different.

In fact, I have only two minor complaints about this book. One, some of the recipes did not deliver. The Carrot Flans with Cinnamon, for example, were underseasoned and definitely not sweet enough for dessert, as Verge claimed they would be; and two, the price seemed steep. This is a lovely book, printed on heavy, glossy stock and replete with beautiful photos by Bernard Touillon (whose work graced Richard Olney's Provence book)—but $35 for something personal and not at all definitive seems a bit much to me.

As for the butter, cream, and eggs, I use so little of them in my cooking these days that I felt justified in eating them. They sure do jazz up a dish. The amounts Verge uses are not excessive, and the results were unlike anything you can get using olive oil, yogurt, and pureed tofu. What's next? Pâté de compagne?

—Mark Bittman

Flatbreads and Flavors
Jeffrey Alford and Naomi Duguid
William Morrow, $30

Jeffrey Alford and Naomi Duguid met on a hotel rooftop in Lhasa, Tibet, in 1985 and have been traveling the world ever since, indulging their passion for flatbreads and the stories of the bakers from whom they learned about these breads. The result is a vast collection of authentic recipes for everything from crackers to pitas to pizzas to matzo. While they were at it, Alford and Duguid also collected recipes for the dishes that are most often served alongside flatbreads in their countries of origin. The result of all this globe-trotting culinary research is a book that is as fascinating to read as it is to cook from.

The authors emphasize cuisines unfamiliar to most Americans, but most of the breads can be made with supermarket staples. Afghan Home-style Naan, for example, is a doughy, whole wheat flatbread studded with sesame seeds and given a bit of tang by yogurt. Xichuan Pepper Breads, Chinese pancakes seasoned with scallions and Xichuan peppercorns, require a simple rolling and shaping process and are then cooked one at a time in a skillet until crisp. Cumin-scented Puri, deep-fried Indian whole wheat breads, balloon as promised on contact with hot oil. Although all three of these recipes seem exotic, all were easy to shop for and execute, as well as just plain delicious.

While the true passion of the authors is flatbreads, the traditional accompaniments that follow each flatbread recipe—the "flavors" part of the title—are just as interesting and useful. Besides making meal planning easier, this organization gives the reader a better understanding of the role each bread plays in its culture.

Recipes are clearly written and offer enough detail for novice cooks without being so basic that they bore experienced bread bakers. Most breads call for mixing and kneading by hand, but many can be made with a countertop mixer; this is something the authors mention in the introduction but don't repeat in most recipes. Of course, many readers will figure out how to knead doughs in a machine, but detailed instructions would have been nice.

Given the diversity of cultures and breads covered in this book, *Flatbreads and Flavors* is remarkably coherent—a testament to the strong, sure voice of this writing team. ∎

—Jack Bishop

SOURCES
AND RESOURCES

Most of the ingredients and materials needed for the recipes in this issue are available at your local supermarket, gourmet store, or kitchen supply shop. The following are mail-order sources for particular items. Prices listed are current at press time and do not include shipping or handling unless otherwise indicated. Contact the companies directly to confirm up-to-date prices and availability.

RICE COOKERS
We tested a dozen rice cookers and steamers for the article on page 28 and have a number of recommendations. Our favorite rice cooker is the Rival 4310, which is available at Ace Hardware and Caldor stores nationwide for about $58. We also recommend the Oster 3811-20 rice cooker, which has a suggested retail price of $59. To find a local source, contact Oster's customer service department at 800-528-7713. The manufacturer tells us that the model we tested is the same (except for slight cosmetic changes) as two other Oster rice cookers, models 4702 and 4703. Although steamers are our second choice for making rice, they are excellent if you only cook rice occasionally and are mainly interested in steaming vegetables. Among the steamers tested, our top choice is the Hamilton Beach Model 36520, which retails for about $58. To find a local source, call the company's customer service department at 800-851-8900.

TRADITIONAL BALSAMIC VINEGARS
While there is plenty of confusion when it comes to buying commercial balsamic vinegar (see story on page 26), purchasing traditional balsamic vinegar is a straightforward proposition. That's because two Italian consortia—one in Modena, the other in Reggio—regulate the sale of all traditional balsamic vinegar. All vinegars approved by the consortia (every year many vinegars are rejected to guarantee high quality) are packaged in distinctive 100 ml bottles. The Modena bottle has a globelike base; the Reggio bottle is narrower and curved like a vase. The bottles bear one of two labels: "Aceto Balsamico Tradizionale di Modena Consorzio Produttori," or "Consortium of Producers of Aceto Balsamico Tradizionale di Reggio Emilia." While Modena recognizes only one level of quality, Reggio has three grades indicated by colored labels: gold, silver, and red, in descending order of quality and price. If you are interested in Reggio vinegars, Zingerman's Delicatessen (422 Detroit Street, Ann Arbor, MI 48104; 313-663-3354) stocks three grades from Cavalli, the producer of a top-rated commercial vinegar. Cavalli red label costs $59, silver label is $89, and gold label is $119. Rogers International (44 Taunton Lake Drive, Newtown, CT 06470; 203-426-0216) imports traditional balsamic vinegar from the Modena consortium. Depending on which vinegars have recently been approved, the company carries vinegars from four to six different families at any given time, each priced at $110 for a 100 ml bottle.

COUSCOUSSIER
Although couscous (see page 12) can be steamed in a metal colander set over a pot of boiling water, you may want to invest in an authentic couscoussier from France. This efficient cooking method keeps the number of pots and burners needed to a minimum. Moroccan cooks have traditionally used earthenware pots to make couscous, but more and more cooks in North Africa and France, where couscous is quite popular, have turned to aluminum steamers. La Cuisine Kitchenware (323 Cameron Street, Alexandria, VA 22314; 800-521-1176) sells an aluminum steamer that comes with a large eight-and-one-half-quart base and a flat-bottomed steamer insert that holds five and one-fourth quarts. The broth is prepared in the larger pot, and then, while it finishes cooking, couscous is steamed in the insert. Because of its large size, this steamer, which costs $102, can be used to prepare other foods as well, such as the steamed fish on page 20.

RAMEKINS
Custards like the crème brûlée on page 7 are best made in individual ramekins. The Williams-Sonoma catalog (800-541-2233) is currently discounting a set of 4-ounce white porcelain ramekins from France. A set of 6 ramekins, usually $30, is on sale for $18. A 72-ounce tall souffle dish and a set of 2 individual 8-ounce souffle dishes, both made of the same white Apilco porcelain, are on sale in the catalog for $18 and $12 respectively.

EXOTIC LENTILS
The recipes on page 25 rely on a number of common and not-so-common lentils. Tiny green lentils from France, called lentils Le Puy, are available in gourmet stores and by mail from Dean & DeLuca (560 Broadway, New York, NY 10012; 800-221-7714). A nine-ounce box costs $3. Masoors, whole brown Indian lentils, are available at most Indian markets. If you cannot find a local source, Foods of India (120 Lexington Avenue, New York, NY 10016; 212-683-4419) sells masoors for $2.29 for two pounds.

GNOCCHI TOOLS
Hand-formed Italian potato dumplings require a few basic kitchen items. In order to mash potatoes with absolutely no lumps, we recommend that you use a ricer. The Colonial Garden Kitchens catalog (P.O. Box 66, Hanover, PA 17333; 800-258-6702) carries an inexpensive plastic ricer ($8.95) with two stainless-steel disks, one for fine and one for coarse textures. We used the fine disk and found it worked well for ricing potatoes for gnocchi. Gnocchi are traditionally shaped by rolling them off the tines of a fork. We found that the ridges on a wooden butter paddle were actually better suited to this task. A butter paddle, which is traditionally used to knead homemade butter, has many more grooves so that the gnocchi made with it are covered with ridges from end to end. The potato dough also tends to stick less to wood than to metal. Lehman's Non-Electric Catalog (4779 Kidron Road, Kidron, OH 44636; 216-857-5757) sells German-crafted butter paddles in two sizes. The smaller version, which is seven inches long, including the handle, and just shy of two and one-half inches wide, is perfect for forming gnocchi. The paddle costs $2.95.

MULTIPURPOSE POT
There are a number of recipes in this issue that call for some sort of steamer setup. We purchased a multipurpose, stainless-steel pot that could be used to steam couscous, fish, and leeks. This eight-quart pot comes with a large pasta insert with two handles so it's easy to lift and drain the pasta without having to pour the boiling water into the sink. A smaller steamer insert, which looks like a colander, comes with a fold-down handle and can hold a whole fish, numerous leeks, or many cups of couscous. The pot itself has a glass lid with a metal knob. This multipurpose pot is available from the Williams-Sonoma catalog (800-541-2233) for $59.

ROASTING PAN
Beef brisket (see recipes on page 23) requires a large, deep roasting pan that can accommodate this substantial cut of meat and the large quantity of liquid it cooks in. We particularly like a deep roasting pan with metal handles that allow for its easy removal from the oven. The Williams-Sonoma catalog (800-541-2233) is currently discounting aluminum roasting pans with durable nonstick coatings. The large roasting pan, which measures sixteen and one-fourth inches long, eleven and three-quarters inches wide, and three inches deep, should be right for cooking brisket. Normally this pan costs $120, but the price has been reduced to $89. ∎

COCONUT CHOCOLATE CHIP COFFEE CAKE
page 21

PERFECT CRÈME BRÛLÉE
page 7

POTATO GNOCCHI WITH PESTO
page 10

STEAMED FISH WITH WHITE WINE-BUTTER SAUCE WITH CAPERS
page 19

STEAMED COUSCOUS WITH MOROCCAN LAMB BROTH, GLAZED ONIONS, AND FRIED ALMONDS
page 12

STEAMED LEEKS GLAZED WITH CRUNCHY SEEDS
page 15

Garlic and Sage Soup

Bring 6 minced garlic cloves, 6 sage leaves, 2 thyme sprigs, and 6 cups of water to simmer in a medium saucepan. Simmer, uncovered, to blend the flavors, about 20 minutes. Whisk a cup or so of the hot liquid into 6 egg yolks to temper them. Then whisk the egg mixture into the saucepan of hot soup. Immediately ladle a portion of soup into each of six soup plates containing a slice of toasted bread. Drizzle each serving with olive oil and garnish with Parmesan cheese to taste. Season to taste with salt and pepper. Serve immediately. *Serves 6.*

**COCONUT CHOCOLATE CHIP
COFFEE CAKE**
page 21

POTATO GNOCCHI WITH PESTO
page 10

PERFECT CRÈME BRÛLÉE
page 7

**STEAMED FISH WITH WHITE
WINE-BUTTER SAUCE WITH CAPERS**
page 19

**STEAMED COUSCOUS WITH MOROCCAN LAMB BROTH,
GLAZED ONIONS, AND FRIED ALMONDS**
page 12

STEAMED LEEKS GLAZED WITH CRUNCHY SEEDS
page 15

Garlic and Sage Soup

Bring 6 minced garlic cloves, 6 sage leaves, 2 thyme sprigs, and 6 cups of water to simmer in a medium saucepan. Simmer, uncovered, to blend the flavors, about 20 minutes. Whisk a cup or so of the hot liquid into 6 egg yolks to temper them. Then whisk the egg mixture into the saucepan of hot soup. Immediately ladle a portion of soup into each of six soup plates containing a slice of toasted bread. Drizzle each serving with olive oil and garnish with Parmesan cheese to taste. Season to taste with salt and pepper. Serve immediately. *Serves 6.*

NUMBER FOURTEEN

MAY/JUNE 1995

COOK'S
ILLUSTRATED

Foolproof Birthday Cake
For Ideal Texture, Don't Beat Egg Whites

Perfect Pork Roast
Double-Roasting Method Yields a Juicy Roast

Professional Pizza At Home
The Best Crust, Methods, and Toppings

Imitation Versus Pure Vanilla
In Baking, It Makes No Difference

RATING "VACATION" WHITE WINES

TEA-SMOKED CHICKEN

HOW TO COOK SOFT-SHELL CRABS

TESTING HANDHELD MIXERS

$4.00 U.S./$4.95 CANADA

TABLE
OF CONTENTS

"Fennel"
Fennel is great in everything from salads (page 23) to pizza toppings (page 11).

ILLUSTRATION BY
CAROL FORTUNATO

Frozen Hot Chocolate, adapted from *Chocolate and the Art of Low-Fat Desserts* (Warner Books, 1994) by Alice Medrich

ILLUSTRATION BY
CRAIG NELSON
(based on a photograph by
Michael Lamotte)

COOK'S ILLUSTRATED

Publisher and Editor CHRISTOPHER KIMBALL

Consulting Editor MARK BITTMAN

Senior Editor JOHN WILLOUGHBY

Food Editor PAM ANDERSON

Senior Writer JACK BISHOP

Articles Editor ANNE TUOMEY

Managing Editor MAURA LYONS

Assistant Managing Editor TRICIA O'BRIEN

Copy Editor GARY PFITZER

Editorial Assistant KIM N. RUSSELLO

Test Cook VICTORIA ROLAND

Art Director MEG BIRNBAUM

Food Stylist MARIE PIRAINO

Special Projects Designer AMY KLEE

Marketing Director ADRIENNE KIMBALL

Circulation Director ELAINE REPUCCI

Ass't Circulation Manager JENNIFER L. KEENE

Customer Service JONATHAN VENIER

Production Director JAMES McCORMACK

Production Assistants SHEILA DATZ
PAMELA SLATTERY

Ass't Computer Admin. MATTHEW FRIGO

Production Artist KEVIN MOELLER

V.P./Business Manager JEFFREY FEINGOLD

Controller LISA A. CARULLO

Accounting Assistant MANDY SHITO

Office Manager JENNY THORNBURY

Office Assistant SARAH CHUNG

Special Projects FERN BERMAN

Cook's Illustrated (ISSN 1068-2821) is published bimonthly by Boston Common Press, 17 Station Street, Box 569, Brookline, MA 02147-0569. Copyright 1995 Boston Common Press. Application to mail at second-class postage rates is pending at Boston, MA, and additional mailing offices. Editorial office: 17 Station Street, Box 569, Brookline, MA 02147-0569; (617) 232-1000, FAX (617) 232-1572. Editorial contributions should be sent to: Editor, Cook's Illustrated, 17 Station Street, Box 569, Brookline, MA 02147-0569. We cannot assume responsibility for manuscripts submitted to us. Submissions will be returned only if accompanied by a large self-addressed stamped envelope. Subscription rates: $24.95 for one year; $45 for two years; $65 for three years. (Canada: add $3 per year; all other countries: add $12 per year.) Postmaster: Send all new orders, subscription inquiries, and change of address notices to Cook's Illustrated, P.O. Box 59046, Boulder, CO 80322-9046. Single copies: $4 in U.S., $4.95 in Canada and foreign. Back issues available for $5 each. PRINTED IN THE U.S.A.

EDITORIAL

EASY DOES IT

Floyd Bentley was a Vermonter who never did anything quickly. He was the common-law husband of Marie Briggs, the town baker, and they lived in the weathered yellow farmhouse just over the town line from Arlington. As a kid, I'd swing open the battered screen door and rush breathlessly into the dark front room, and there would be Floyd, quietly hunched over in the shadows, a lit cigarette in his hand. He'd look up at you with rheumy eyes and never utter the first word. When he did get around to saying something, it took time; it was like watching

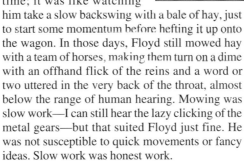

Floyd Bentley as painted by his neighbor Norman Rockwell in *Breaking Home Ties*

him take a slow backswing with a bale of hay, just to start some momentum before hefting it up onto the wagon. In those days, Floyd still mowed hay with a team of horses, making them turn on a dime with an offhand flick of the reins and a word or two uttered in the very back of the throat, almost below the range of human hearing. Mowing was slow work—I can still hear the lazy clicking of the metal gears—but that suited Floyd just fine. He was not susceptible to quick movements or fancy ideas. Slow work was honest work.

In those days cooking, too, was slow work. In that small yellow farmhouse, the roast was started early in the morning for midday dinner and was cooked over very low heat, usually in the woodstove. People had the time for a slow-cooked roast—there was always somebody around to check on it. I hadn't thought much of those tender, moist roasts until a few years ago when my own mother started serving her slow-roast turkey for the holidays.

Her recipe is simple. She cooks the tightly covered bird at 300 degrees for an hour and then leaves it in the oven overnight with the heat turned down to 200. The results are spectacular: moist, tender meat with great texture. She based her recipe on *Let's Cook It Right* (N.A.L. Dutton, 1970) by Adelle Davis, the sixties health guru. The author advocates cooking any roast for one hour at 300 degrees to kill off surface bacteria and then roasting for up to twenty-four hours, depending on the size of the roast, at the final temperature that you want the meat (if you want a turkey cooked to 165 degrees, for example, cook it at that temperature). I went home and tried out the slow-roast method on two turkeys and a pork roast, the latter at somewhat higher temperatures,

with fabulous results.

In the process, I learned that slowness has its benefits. In the kitchen as in life, some things take time. My most vivid memories are connected to times of inaction. Waiting for the cut and raked hay to dry in our lower meadow. Waiting in the frozen Vermont woods for my neighbor's beagle to pick up the scent of a rabbit. Waiting for the school bus with my six- and four-year-olds, our backs to the wind. Waiting in the hospital for my wife to give birth to our third child, a son.

Perhaps like the last of the old-time Vermont dairy farmers, slow-cooking has no place in modern times. You can't milk a herd of only twenty cows and get by; you can't take all day to roast meat, either. Neither is practical, yet with their passing we strip our lives of the subtleties, of those moments in life when we are freed from action and live for a brief moment suspended in the heightened awareness of expectation. A cake baking. A conversation about to be started.

The last time I saw Floyd was in the summer of 1968. His lungs were bad from the smoking, but, contrary to expectations, he had made it through another winter. It was the last day of summer vacation, and I had stopped by the yellow farmhouse for what turned out to be a final farewell. It was midday, almost time for dinner, and Floyd was hunkered down on the dull-green sofa with a cigarette. He looked up and didn't say much. He didn't have to. I knew he was busy taking his time.

SEND US YOUR COOKING PROBLEMS
So far, we at *Cook's Illustrated* have tackled a number of the problems most frequently encountered by home cooks, such as roasting a turkey evenly, creating the perfect pie crust, or making a meringue that doesn't weep. We want to continue to find the best ways to overcome the most common problems that you, our readers, face in your kitchens. So let us know what they are, and future issues will include articles on the problems mentioned most often. Unfortunately, we can only publish so many, and we do not have time to answer any questions personally. Write to: Cooking Challenges, *Cook's Illustrated*, 17 Station Street, Box 569, Brookline, MA 02147-0569. Thanks for your help. ∎

NOTES

FROM READERS

MEASURING SHORTENING

In the September/October 1994 issue, a letter from a reader invokes Archimedes' principle as a way to measure a volume of shortening. While this suggestion is useful, it is not entirely accurate.

Archimedes' principle states that an object floating in a fluid is buoyed upward by a force equal to the weight of the displaced fluid. If you put sufficient shortening in a measuring cup filled with water to raise the water level by a half cup, you have put in about a quarter pound of shortening, which is the weight of a half cup of water. Whether you have put in a half cup of shortening depends on the density of the shortening.

As it turns out, ordinary shortening is slightly less dense than water. (This is why it just barely floats.) Thus, it will take slightly more than a half cup of shortening to displace a half cup of water. As a practical matter, the difference is probably not large enough to affect most recipes.

An alternative would be to put a half pound of shortening for every cup desired on a piece of wax paper on a kitchen scale. This method would involve less cleanup than the water displacement method and would be slightly more accurate.

BILL BARKER
Arlington, TX

RECIPES THAT MIX OIL AND OTHER LIQUIDS

When a recipe calls for adding a lot of liquid ingredients to oil (pancake batter is a good example), the oil does not combine well with the other ingredients because it tends to float. I always combine the oil with an egg (most recipes call for at least one egg) since the egg can absorb an almost unlimited amount of oil. Once the oil and egg have been combined, the other liquids can be whisked in without the oil separating.

JULIE DAVIS
Dallas, TX

HOMEMADE YOGURT CHEESE

I have a much easier way to make yogurt cheese at home that does not involve chopsticks or a rubber band (see Quick Tips, September/October 1994 issue). The only special equipment you need is an old-fashioned colander covered with fine mesh, like the kind you find on a screen door.

Line a mesh colander with three pieces of paper towel. Dump a thirty-two-ounce container of
nonfat yogurt into the lined colander and cover it with a piece of aluminum foil. Set the colander over a bowl to catch the whey. I find that eight hours, which was the time you suggested, is not enough time to get the texture thick enough to resemble cream cheese. Twenty-four hours is better, and the bowl will have to be drained at least twice. (I save the whey for use in soups.) The yogurt cheese can be stored in a covered container for a good two weeks.

MARGE TEILHABER
Fort Lee, NJ

COOKING PORK SAFELY

A recipe in a local newspaper suggested cooking pork to medium, and a new Italian cookbook shows pictures of rare pork. Overcooking can make pork dry, but we are worried about reaching an internal temperature that will be sufficient to kill the trichinosis parasite. Is cooking pork to medium safe, and can you give us some actual numbers? Also, we have heard that freezing before cooking can kill parasites in pork. Is this true?

BEN & QUAY
Montegut, LA

The U.S. Department of Agriculture (USDA) recommends cooking pork to an internal temperature of 160 degrees. At this temperature, the pork is no longer pink and is in fact quite white, or "medium-well done." Cooking pork to an internal temperature above 160 degrees will cause almost all the moisture to be lost and should only be done if you prefer "well-done" meat.

Trichinosis is a disease caused by ingesting a worm parasite called trichina, or *Trichinella spiralis*. Although trichina is much less common than it was a generation ago (the USDA finds the parasite in less than 0.1 percent of all tested samples), it is still a concern. The parasite is killed at a temperature of 137 degrees, when pork is still pink and underdone to our thinking. The USDA recommendation to cook pork to 160 degrees includes a wide margin of error to compensate for inaccurate thermometers or thermometers that are not being used correctly, for instance by allowing the thermometer to touch bone when the temperature is taken.

The USDA recommendation regarding the cooking of pork also ensures that any other bacteria that may occasionally be present in pork will be killed. In rare cases, salmonella can be introduced to pork through cross-contamination with
raw poultry. Salmonella is killed at 160 degrees, which partly explains the USDA's high cooking temperature for pork. Since salmonella in pork is quite uncommon, you may choose to cook pork to 150 degrees, which is what we would call "medium." Pork cooked to this temperature will be white with perhaps a tinge of pink, and the juices will be pink. Although pork cooked to 150 degrees is much juicer than pork cooked to 160 degrees, this temperature guarantees that trichinae only, and not other possible pathogens, have been destroyed.

Freezing pork for long periods of time at a very low temperature can also kill trichinae. However, since the temperatures needed to kill the parasite are rarely reached in a home setting (for instance, holding pork at minus thirteen degrees for twenty days will kill the parasite), this method is not recommended.

BRINING THAWED SHRIMP

In the July/August 1994 issue, you discussed brining and cooking shrimp. I was wondering if brining does anything for shrimp that will be boiled or steamed? I usually boil shrimp in their shells for two or three minutes in seasoned water for "peeling and eating." Will boiling negate the effects of brining?

Also, your article recommended brining shrimp during thawing, but I wonder about brining thawed shrimp that have been purchased loose. Is this worth doing? If so, how?

SKIP LEWIS
Marlborough, CT

Although we recommend buying frozen shrimp in a large block and brining them at the same time they are thawing, you certainly can brine already-thawed shrimp that you have purchased loose. Frozen shrimp are brined in a room-temperature solution, but you should brine thawed shrimp in ice-cold water. Dissolve two cups kosher salt into two cups boiling water, cool the liquid to room temperature, and then add three and one-half quarts of ice-cold water. Add two pounds shrimp to the icy solution and let stand for about forty-five minutes, adding more ice as needed to keep the water very cold. Drain and rinse the shrimp, and then proceed with your recipe.

As for shrimp that are to be boiled, brining can't hurt them, but it is probably not worth the effort since cooking in water will lessen much of the benefits of brining. Brining causes shrimp to retain more water and to taste firmer for grilling or sautéing, the dry heat cooking methods we recommended in the article. However, much of the liquid that brining adds to shrimp will be lost if they are boiled.

STIR-FRYING KALE

*M*y favorite way to cook kale (see "How to Quick-Cook Strong-Flavored Greens," January/February 1995) is to wash the whole leaves, cut them crosswise (stems and all) into one-eighth-inch pieces, then stir-fry the kale in a wok with a little peanut or olive oil that has been heating with a cut garlic clove. I stir-fry the kale over high heat until the greens wilt, making sure to watch out for splatters since the leaves are still wet from washing. At the end of cooking, I cover the wok with a lid and turn the heat off. The greens continue to steam for a short time. The technique gives the greens a very mild flavor and refreshing crunch due to the presence of the stems.

Betsy Fuller
Syracuse, NY

VERTICAL ROASTERS

I have seen vertical roasting racks advertised and was wondering how they work with chickens and Cornish hens. Do they cut cooking time, as promised in the ads, and do they promote the loss of fat?

SIOBAHN SOMERVILLE
West Lafayette, IN

If you are interested in low-fat cooking, vertical roasting racks are a good idea. A hen, chicken, duck, or turkey can rest upright on these contraptions as it roasts and because the metal conducts heat inside the bird's cavity, cooking times are shorter than when birds are roasted conventionally. Even small birds such as Cornish hens will be done fifteen minutes before birds roasted on a regular rack.

To measure how much fat was lost with various cooking methods, we roasted Cornish hens on a vertical roaster, on a regular roasting rack, and directly in the pan. We brushed all the hens with a half tablespoon of oil before roasting, but did not baste them while in the oven. Hens cooked on a regular rack or in the pan lost between one-third and one-half pound of their original weight. In contrast, birds roasted on a vertical rack lost between two-thirds and three-quarters of a pound. In addition, there were slightly more drippings (i.e., fat) in the pan under the hens that were roasted on vertical racks. Hens cooked on the vertical roasters were surprisingly moist and their skin was a deeper golden color and more crisp than the skin on birds roasted on a regular rack or in a pan.

There are several kinds of vertical roasting racks on the market. Some are chromed steel, while others are coated with a nonstick surface. The nonstick surface did not make that much of a difference at serving time; birds came off both types of rack fairly easily. The nonstick racks were easier to clean though.

Nonstick vertical roasting racks are available from the Williams-Sonoma catalog (800-541-2233). They come in three sizes for turkeys, chickens or ducks, and Cornish hens. The largest rack costs $25 and can hold birds that weigh up to eighteen pounds; the medium rack costs $19 and can hold a seven-pound bird; the smallest rack is best for birds under three pounds and costs $17.

PEELING HARD-BOILED EGGS

*P*eeling hard-boiled eggs can be a chore, but here is a quick and easy way to do it. This works well no matter how many eggs you need.

After the eggs are cooked, cooled, and drained, leave them in the pot. Now raise and lower the pot quickly to make the eggs "jump." You want the eggs airborne so that when they come down, they will crack. Keep doing this until you no longer hear a crack—when you have reached the proper point, the sound will be more like a thud.

Now fill the pot with cold water and allow it to stand. The longer the eggs stand in the water, the easier they will be to peel. Overnight is ideal, but even one hour works well. Because the eggs have been cracked, the water seeps in between the egg and the shell, which makes the egg very easy to peel. As a matter of fact, if left overnight, the egg actually falls out of the shell when you go to pick it up. And don't worry, no water actually gets into the egg itself.

Michael Kelemen
Cheshire, CT

STORING ROASTED PEPPERS

*W*hen I roast red peppers, I sometimes prepare more than I need. What is the best way to store any that I don't use right away, and how long will they last?

ALEXANDRA FISCHMAN
Sag Harbor, NY

We roasted a number of red bell peppers under the broiler until charred, cooled them in a covered bowl, peeled away the wrinkled skin, and then cored and seeded them. We then took the large strips of roasted pepper and stored one batch in olive oil, a second batch in balsamic vinegar, and a third batch in a mixture of two parts water to one part white wine vinegar. (This last mixture is similar to the packing liquid used in many commercial bottles of roasted peppers.)

All three batches of refrigerated peppers remained free of mold for several weeks, but the flavors were markedly different. The peppers stored in olive oil retained their pure roasted pepper flavor, with the oil contributing little more than a silky texture, which could be rinsed off if desired. The peppers stored in balsamic vinegar had a strong vinegar flavor that could be partially lessened by rinsing the peppers. Because the flavor of balsamic vinegar complements roasted peppers nicely, this added flavor wasn't off-putting, but it would pose a problem in some recipes. The batch of peppers packed in white wine vinegar solution were way too acidic and lacked any real pepper flavor.

We also tried freezing roasted peppers in a tightly covered container. This worked surprisingly well. When thawed, the peppers tasted virtually the same as freshly roasted ones, with perhaps a slight loss of texture.

Our recommendation for storing peppers is simple. If you are roasting many and want to store them indefinitely, try freezing them (layer the peppers between sheets of wax paper in a plastic container for easy removal) and thaw as many as needed. Stored this way, roasted peppers should last for several months. If you have a small amount of leftover peppers that you plan to use within a week or two, place them in a small container, cover them with olive oil, and refrigerate them. ∎

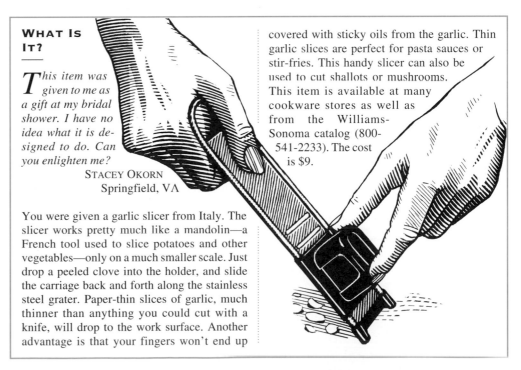

WHAT IS IT?

*T*his item was given to me as a gift at my bridal shower. I have no idea what it is designed to do. Can you enlighten me?
STACEY OKORN
Springfield, VA

You were given a garlic slicer from Italy. The slicer works pretty much like a mandolin—a French tool used to slice potatoes and other vegetables—only on a much smaller scale. Just drop a peeled clove into the holder, and slide the carriage back and forth along the stainless steel grater. Paper-thin slices of garlic, much thinner than anything you could cut with a knife, will drop to the work surface. Another advantage is that your fingers won't end up covered with sticky oils from the garlic. Thin garlic slices are perfect for pasta sauces or stir-fries. This handy slicer can also be used to cut shallots or mushrooms. This item is available at many cookware stores as well as from the Williams-Sonoma catalog (800-541-2233). The cost is $9.

ILLUSTRATION BY DAN KROVATIN

Quick Tips

TO ROAST BELL PEPPERS EASILY

Roasting bell peppers gives them a rich, sweet, smoky flavor, but it can also be something of a chore to roast them whole and then peel and seed them. Ben Gilmore, of Chicago, recommends this easier procedure.

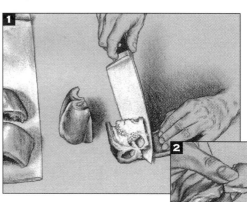

1. Stem, seed, and halve the peppers, then lay them on a cookie sheet, skin side up, and put them under the broiler until the skin is well blackened, 5 to 8 minutes.

2. The blackened skins will peel off easily, and you don't have to deal with the mushy seeds and interior.

TO SAVE "BROKEN" HOLLANDAISE

It is fairly easy to "break" a butter sauce such as hollandaise or bernaise. One way to fix it is by processing it in a food processor or blender. Stirring in a bit of ice is an easier method.

1. When a hollandaise is heated or mixed improperly, the sauce "breaks" and the butter comes out of the emulsion.

2. Add a couple of tablespoons of ice water (with ice) to the mixture and whisk it briskly.

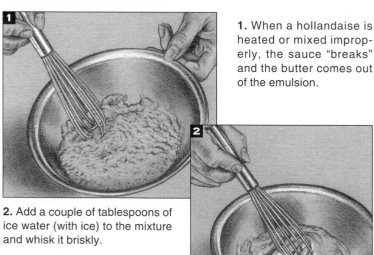

3. The sauce will soon have regained the proper smooth consistency.

TO SQUEEZE WATER FROM COOKED GREENS

Sometimes even steamed greens have too much water. Try this easy way to squeeze water from cooked greens.

1. Place the cooked greens on a dinner plate and put a second plate on top of them.

2. Squeeze the plates together over the sink (or a bowl, if you're reserving the liquid) until the greens are dry.

TO REMOVE SPICES EASILY

When cooking a soup, stew, or sauce that requires the removal of spices, garlic, or bay leaves at the end of cooking, you might follow this tip from Richard Wilson of Dayton, Ohio, and place the spices in a mesh tea ball for easy removal.

TO MAKE EVEN LAYER CAKE

Bea Murray, of Grand Rapids, Michigan, offers this tip to help you realign the layers of a cake after you cut and fill them.

1. Use a serrated knife to make a ⅛-inch cut down the side of the cake, perpendicular to the top.

2. Cut the cake horizontally into the desired number of layers, fill them as desired, then replace the layers, realigning the vertical cut. By putting the layers back in their original orientation to each other, any unevenness in the way you cut them will be concealed.

ILLUSTRATIONS BY ALAN WITSCHONKE

TO MAKE THE BEST USE OF DRIED HERBS

Paula Wolfert, cookbook author and expert on Mediterranean cuisines, shares a technique used frequently by cooks in the eastern Mediterranean. Before using dried herbs, place them in a mesh sieve and push down on them with your fingertips as you shake the sieve back and forth over a bowl. This process not only breaks the leaves into smaller pieces for easier use, it also helps release their flavor.

TO TEST A MEAT THERMOMETER

Follow this tip from frequent contributor Stephen Schmidt to make sure your meat thermometer is accurate.

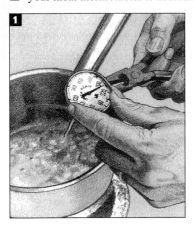

1. Hold the stem in boiling water for 15 seconds. Assuming you are at sea level, the thermometer should register 212 degrees.

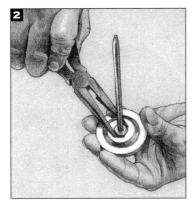

2. If your thermometer does not register 212 degrees, twist the small nut beneath the thermometer face with pliers until the temperature is correct.

TO MAKE WORKING WITH PIE CRUST EASIER

Susan Antonacci, of New Cumberland, Pennsylvania, advises placing your pie plate on a cake stand when placing the pastry in it and fluting the pastry edges. The cake stand makes it easier to turn the pie plate around and keeps you from having to stoop over as you work.

TO PULVERIZE SAFFRON

Recipes often call for saffron to be pulverized so that it diffuses throughout the dish. Libby Hayes, of Overland Park, Kansas, points out that saffron threads can be difficult to pulverize and recommends this process.

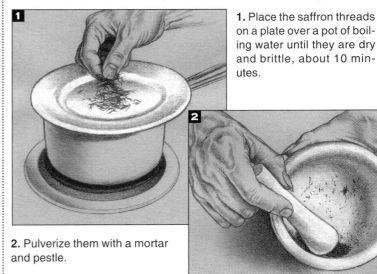

1. Place the saffron threads on a plate over a pot of boiling water until they are dry and brittle, about 10 minutes.

2. Pulverize them with a mortar and pestle.

TO GET QUICK, SEEDLESS LEMON JUICE

To juice lemons directly into your work bowl without getting seeds into the food, Elizabeth Fielding, of Wilmot Flat, New Hampshire, advises squeezing them with a wooden reamer directly over a slotted spoon or strainer. When the lemons have been squeezed, simply lift the spoon or strainer and discard the seeds.

TO STORE VIDALIA ONIONS

The high sugar content of Vidalia onions, which is what endears them to cooks, also makes them spoil more quickly if they are stored touching each other. Marilyn Broder, of Moldel, New Jersey, suggests this tip for storing Vidalia onions longer: Place one in the leg of an old but clean pair of pantyhose. Tie a knot in the hose, just above the onion. Repeat this process up the entire leg of the pantyhose.

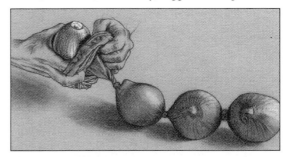

Thanks to our readers for Quick Tips: The editors of *Cook's Illustrated* would like to thank all of the readers who have sent us their quick tips. We have enjoyed reading every one of them, and have learned a lot. Keep them coming. We will provide a one-year complimentary subscription for each quick tip that we print. Send a description of your special technique to *Cook's Illustrated,* P.O. Box 569, Brookline Village, MA 02147-0569. Please write "Attention: Quick Tips" on the envelope and include your name, address, and daytime phone number. Unfortunately, we can only acknowledge receipt of tips that will be printed in the magazine. In case the same tip is received from two readers, the one postmarked first will be selected. Also, be sure to let us know what particular cooking problems you would like us to investigate in upcoming issues.

How to Cook Soft-Shell Crabs

To get the sea-fresh taste and crisp texture of soft-shells, buy them fresh, clean them yourself, and fry them immediately.

∾ BY STEPHANIE LYNESS ∾

Soft-shell crabs are blue crabs that have been taken out of the water just after they have shed their shells. At this brief stage of its life, the whole crab, with its new, soft, gray skin, is almost completely edible and fabulously delicious. For the cook, soft-shells are a wonderfully immediate experience. Once cleaned, they demand to be cooked and eaten on the spot, so they offer a very direct taste of the sea. Because they must be cooked so quickly after they are killed and cleaned, home cooks have an advantage over restaurants. I'm convinced that the best way to enjoy soft-shells is to cook them at home, where you can be sure to eat them within minutes of preparing them.

To my mind, the whole point of soft-shells is that they must be crisp. The legs should crunch delicately, like perfectly cooked whitebait, while the body should provide a contrast between its thin, crisp outer skin and the soft, rich interior that explodes juicily in the mouth. The only way to achieve this is by frying. My favorite way to eat a soft-shell crab is deep-fried, but true deep-frying is hardly ever practical for home cooks—it's messy, it uses a lot of oil, and it can be dangerous if you're not paying strict attention.

To avoid these problems, I tried playing around with various cooking methods (including roasting, which didn't get the crabs crisp enough) and came up with a method for panfrying lightly floured crabs that gives a satisfyingly crisp result without the mess of deep-frying.

Coatings and Fats for Frying

A coating of some kind helps crisp the crab. I tried flour, cornmeal, bread crumbs, and even Cream of Wheat coatings, and ended up opting for flour. It's a shame to hide the unique, essential flavor of the crab with a heavy coating, and flour provides a crisp crust without adding flavor. It also has the advantage of nearly always being on hand.

I also tried soaking the crabs in milk for two hours before applying the coating, since I had read that this process sweetens the crab. However, I found that milk takes away from the just-out-of the-water flavor that I like.

The type of fat you use for frying is largely a matter of personal preference. I tried frying floured crabs in whole butter, clarified butter, vegetable and peanut oils, and a combination of whole butter and olive oil. Whole butter gave the crabs a delicious, nutty

taste and browned them well. Clarified butter didn't brown them significantly better and is more work, so it offers no advantage over whole butter. Vegetable and peanut oils got the crab a hair crisper than butter and added no taste; peanut oil crispened the crabs particularly well because it fries very hot without burning. The combination of butter and oil didn't give a better result than either fat used separately, and I was surprised to find that the flavor of butter and even the flavorlessness of the other oils complement the crab better than the olive oil. My preference is to fry with either peanut oil or butter, depending on the taste I want and the kind of sauce I'm making.

Whether you opt for peanut oil, vegetable oil, or butter, the crab fries best in quite a lot of fat. Count on at least one tablespoon of butter per crab depending on the size of the pan; the crabs actually seem to absorb the butter as they cook. When cooking with oil, I add the oil to a depth of one-eighth to one-quarter inch. You can cook in any kind of pan, but a cast-iron pan holds even heat particularly well and practically guarantees a crispy critter.

Saucing and Serving the Crabs

Once you've cooked the crabs, they should be sauced and served immediately. In a pinch, you can hold crabs for a few minutes in a 300-degree oven, but they're really better eaten practically out of the pan. Therefore, if you're serving a main course for four (count on two crabs per person), you'll need two pans, each at least eleven inches in diameter, if you expect everyone to sit down to eat together. If you've only got one pan, your best bet is to let two people start on the first batch of crabs when they're cooked, while you start cooking the second batch. Or serve crabs as an appetizer—one per person is plenty. Because they're fried, the crabs don't need much of a sauce, just a drizzle of something acidic.

Buying, Cleaning, and Storing

Not surprisingly, considering how perishable they are, soft-shells can be quite difficult to locate. Fresh soft-shells are available only "in season," which used to mean a few short months during the summer. Now the "season" can extend from February all the way

through to September and maybe into October, depending on the weather.

Unfortunately, fresh crabs rarely show up in fish markets away from the eastern seaboard. Frozen crabs may be available in other parts of the country, but they are somewhat like organic produce was a few years ago—the consumer has to ask for them, and they may be very expensive. Also, they will not be anywhere near as tasty as fresh crabs. My advice is, if you can't get fresh, you should forego making soft-shells yourself, and restrict your enjoyment of them to restaurants. If you are willing to pay the price, however, there are suppliers who will send you fresh crabs by next-day air (*see* Sources and Resources, page 32).

For those who live in soft-shell territory, the standard advice for purchasing them is similar to that given for lobsters: They must be alive and, if possible, feisty. Sometimes it's hard to tell if a crab is dead or just not feeling active. A foolproof way to judge is to lift the pointy sides of the crab and smell the spongy, white gills underneath. The gills should have absolutely no odor. Once the crab is dead, the gills quickly take on a mild, fishy smell. Unfortunately, the crab begins to die once it's been manhandled this way, so some fish stores may not be too keen to have you do it.

Once you buy the crabs, the fish store will probably offer to clean them for you. It's a gener-

ILLUSTRATIONS BY NEVERNE COVINGTON

ous offer—cleaning defenseless soft-shells tests even my professionally hardened mettle—but if you like the crabs juicy, as I do, you'll be happier if you clean them yourself. The reason is that, like lobsters, the way a crab grows is to shed its hard shell periodically. After shedding, the crab swells with water to fill out its new skin, and the skin immediately begins to harden into a new, larger shell. When you clean a live crab, juice pours out of it. The longer the crab sits before cooking, the more liquid it loses. I found that a crab that is cooked immediately after cleaning is much plumper and juicier than a crab cleaned several hours before cooking. To clean a live crab, follow steps 1 through 3 at right.

My advice is that you not try to store soft-shells. Even a live crab won't stay that way very long in your refrigerator; they're better off at the fish store, where they are kept cool, not cold, so that they do not die of the cold.

But most books say to clean the crabs and refrigerate them if you're not eating them immediately, so I tried a couple of experiments. I refrigerated several whole live crabs overnight, piled one on top of another in the paper and plastic wrapping in which I had brought them home. The next day, the gills of the crabs on top smelled slightly, while the gills of the crabs on the bottom didn't smell at all. From this I concluded that crabs don't spoil as quickly if you keep them covered. My fishmonger keeps his covered with eel grass, but damp newspaper or a damp paper towel will also do the trick.

Next I tried refrigerating two more crabs overnight, one cleaned and one alive. I cleaned the second crab just before frying both crabs the next day. The crab that was refrigerated whole was significantly juicier than the cleaned crab. Therefore, if I'm not eating the crabs immediately, I refrigerate them whole, covered with damp newspaper or paper towels to keep them fresh, and I clean them just before cooking.

PANFRIED SOFT-SHELL CRABS WITH LEMON, CAPERS, AND HERBS
Serves 4

The pan sauce is tart and powerfully flavored; you only need about one tablespoon per serving.

    8   medium-to-large soft-shell crabs,
            cleaned (see illustrations at right)
            and patted dry with paper towels
        All-purpose flour for dredging
    10 tablespoons butter
    1   teaspoon juice from a small lemon
    1   teaspoon sherry vinegar
    1   teaspoon drained tiny capers, chopped
    1½ tablespoons minced fresh parsley
            leaves
    1   teaspoon minced fresh tarragon leaves
    1   scallion, minced
        Ground black pepper

1. Dredge crabs in flour; pat off excess. Heat two 11- or 12-inch heavy-bottomed frying pans over medium-high heat until pans are quite hot, about 3 minutes. Add 4 tablespoons of butter to each pan, swirling pans to keep butter from burning as it melts. When the foam subsides, turn heat to high and add four crabs, skins down, to each pan. Cover each pan with splatter screen and cook, adjusting heat as necessary to keep butter from burning, until crabs turn reddish brown, about 3 minutes. Turn crabs with spatula or tongs and cook until second side is browned, about 3 more minutes. Drain crabs on paper towel–lined plate.

2. Set one pan aside. Pour off butter from other pan and remove from heat. Add all remaining ingredients (including remaining 2 tablespoons butter and pepper to taste) to this still warm pan; swirl pan to melt butter. Arrange two crabs on each of four plates. Spoon about 1 tablespoon of sauce over each plate of crabs and serve immediately.

PANFRIED SOFT-SHELL CRABS ON A BED OF SPINACH
Serves 4

You can substitute mustard greens or collard greens for the spinach in this recipe—just make sure they are cooked in boiling, salted water until tender, then drained, rinsed in cold water, and squeezed dry. Roughly chop them, then proceed with the recipe.

    2   pounds fresh spinach, stemmed and
            thoroughly washed
    8   medium-to-large soft-shell crabs,
            cleaned (see illustrations at
            right) and patted dry with paper
            towels
        All-purpose flour for dredging
    10 tablespoons butter
    4   medium garlic cloves, minced
    ½   teaspoon salt
        Juice of 1 lemon (2 to 3 tablespoons)
        Ground black pepper

1. Place collapsible steamer basket or large steaming insert in large pot. Add enough water to come to bottom of basket; bring to boil. Add spinach, cover and steam, stirring once, until just tender, about 4 minutes. Drain spinach, refresh under cold water, then squeeze out excess liquid. Roughly chop spinach and set aside.

2. For coating and sautéing crabs, follow step 1 in Panfried Soft-Shell Crabs with Lemon, Capers, and Herbs.

3. Set one pan aside. Pour off butter from remaining skillet and return to burner set at medium-high. Melt remaining 2 tablespoons butter, add half the garlic, and cook until fragrant, about 30 seconds. Add spinach and salt; sauté to heat through, 1 to 2 minutes. Add remaining garlic; sauté to partially cook garlic, 30 seconds longer. Remove from heat and stir in lemon juice and pepper to taste. Divide spinach among four plates; arrange two crabs on each bed of spinach. Serve immediately. ■

Stephanie Lyness is the translator of Cuisine à la Vapeur: The Art of Cooking with Steam by Jacques Manière (Morrow, 1995).

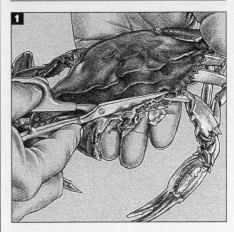

1. To clean a soft-shell, first cut off its mouth with kitchen scissors; the mouth is the first part of the shell to harden. You can also cut off the eyes at the same time, but this is purely aesthetic; the eyes are edible.

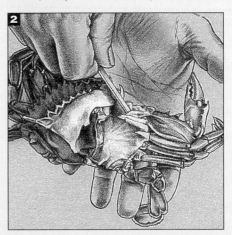

2. Next lift the pointed sides of the crab, and cut out the spongy off-white gills underneath; the gills are fibrous and watery and unpleasant to eat.

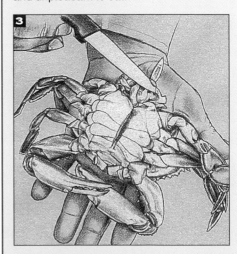

3. Finally, turn the crab on its back and cut off the triangular or T-shaped "apron" flap.

Overcoming the Obstacles of Homemade Pizza

Make your dough with bread flour, stretch it instead of rolling, and line your oven with quarry tiles for the best, easiest homemade pizza.

~ BY PAM ANDERSON WITH KAREN TACK ~

Pizza may be called fast food, but you've got plenty to do before you get it in the oven. There's dough to knead, allow to rise, and stretch; tomato sauce to make; cheese to grate; and toppings to prepare. Little wonder that so many people have surrendered to shredded mozzarella and premade pizza disks (not to mention frozen pizzas).

The real problem with take-out and frozen pizzas is that very few of them are very good—or good by the time they get to you. While we all settle for convenience over quality on occasion, the difference here is extreme: Homemade pizza really is superb. Besides, the actual cooking takes little time. If you could shortcut the tomato sauce and dough, homemade pizza could practically be made in the time it takes to heat the oven.

Since lining my oven with quarry tiles for breadmaking a few years back, I've started making pizza fairly frequently. In addition to looking for ways to streamline the process, I developed a list of pizza questions. Does dough crispness have to do with the ratio of flour to water or is it determined by some extra ingredient? Can the same dough, rolled differently, be used for cracker-crisp crusts and thick, chewy crusts?

I also wondered if I could find a foolproof method for shaping a ball of dough into a disk, particularly a thin disk. Depending on the stretching method I followed, my dough always ended up full of holes, incredibly misshapen, or tough and leathery before I could get it to the right thickness.

I already knew that quarry tiles produced a darker, thicker, crisper crust than dough pressed into a pan, but what about a pizza stone? Was there a difference, or were they interchangeable? Or was all this stone and tile stuff just a big hype? Would a "pizza screen"—a perforated pizza pan—work just as well?

I was curious about the sauce and the cheese as well. When fresh tomatoes weren't in season, I topped my pizzas with a quick-cooked sauce made from canned tomatoes, garlic, and oil. But I never forgot an interview with a pizza maker who skipped sauce making entirely, stirring herbs directly into uncooked canned tomatoes and counting on oven time alone to make the sauce. If this worked, it would eliminate one step in the process. I also wanted to know when it was best to sprinkle on the cheese—at the beginning, with everything else, or towards the end of baking?

Bread Flour Makes Good Dough

Armed with these questions, I began looking through cookbooks in search of a dough recipe. Carlo Middione, author of *The Foods of Southern Italy* (William Morrow, 1987) was the only source I came across who specifically linked bread and pizza dough. He wrote one recipe for both, instructing the cook to add oil to the dough if making pizza. Further recipe research confirmed that pizza dough is, in fact, nothing more than bread dough enriched with oil. Based on previous experience with bread dough (*see* "How To Make Bread," November/December 1992) as well as a review of scores of pizza recipes, I developed a basic recipe using all-purpose flour and a couple of tablespoons of oil. I then tried substituting different flours and liquids, increasing and decreasing the amount of oil, and trying both a quick and a long-rising sponge (*see* "Testing Pizza Doughs," page 9, for details).

Not surprisingly, the dough made from bleached all-purpose flour was disastrous as both a dough and a crust. The dough was soft and difficult to stretch, threatening to tear with every pull. The resulting crust was tough and leathery—limp instead of crisp and chewy. Although unbleached all-purpose flour was a step up from bleached, I found that bread flour delivered the best pizza crust. The semolina-enriched dough delivered a respectably denser crust, while the cornmeal-flavored crust was pleasing enough to become a recommended variation. Neither a quick- nor a long-rising sponge produced a pizza worth the extra trouble.

Next I tackled the problem that prevents most cooks from making pizza for a weeknight dinner—the time involved in letting the dough rise. Here I found two answers, each of which solved the problem with a different approach. I discovered that by decreasing the yeast, I could make the dough in the morning and let it rise slowly during the day so that it was ready to stretch just in time to make dinner. Or, for those who would rather speed up than slow down the process, publisher Christopher Kimball found that by using rapid-rise yeast and proofing it in warm water, he could cut the rising time down to a mere forty minutes (*see* "Pizza in a Hurry," page 10).

Stretch, Don't Roll

In working with the various doughs, I determined that, indeed, the same dough could be stretched a little to make a medium-thick pizza, or a lot to make a thin and crispy one. I wanted to figure out the best way to transform it from that fat little ball to a thin disk.

While for some people sliding the pizza from peel to stone is the most difficult step in making pizza, for me it's stretching the dough. What finally worked was a technique my coworker Karen picked up at a cooking class a few years back. The reason this technique works so well, at least for me, is that the dough never leaves the work surface (*see* "Stretch, Don't Roll," page 9).

Following this technique, the dough can easily be stretched to a medium thickness. Getting a thin disk, however, was another matter. I found that regardless of how much stretching and pulling I did, the dough would mischievously shrink back to its medium-thick size; it simply refused to get thin. Eventually, though, I found that to get the dough thinner, you can't fight with it. Instead, you simply need to give it a rest. Start flattening another piece of dough, open the wine, watch the

The same bread dough can be used to make thick- or thin-crust pizza, depending on how much it is stretched.

news—do anything, but just leave the dough alone for a few minutes. Given a rest, the dough relaxes and is easily stretched those extra few inches.

I tried using a rolling pin to make disks. I found that rolled pizza crusts were more uniform than those that had been stretched, but they were also noticeably tougher. I suspect that the rolling action presses the air out of the dough, causing it to be denser.

Tile Your Oven
After baking pizzas in a pan, on a pizza screen, on a pizza stone, and on quarry tiles, I found I preferred the tiles. Pizzas baked on a perforated screen, let alone a solid pan, just don't crisp and brown the way they do on stones and tiles. Between these two finalists, I opted for the quarry tiles, because the tiles consistently delivered pizza with darker, crisper bottoms.

Tile has it over stone for another reason. If you don't slide the pizza onto the stone just right—especially if you're making a large pizza—part of it always ends up hanging off the stone, and toppings fall to the oven floor. Lining the oven rack with quarry tiles allows you to bake on the entire rack. My oven, lined with tiles, is large enough to bake two medium pizzas at a time.

When buying tiles to line your oven, make sure you get unglazed quarry tiles, which are made of terra-cotta (red clay) and generally come from Mexico or Spain. These porous tiles are commonly available in six-inch squares and are either one-quarter- or one-half-inch thick. Take your oven rack with you to the store, and line the rack with tiles. If the tiles don't fit perfectly, ask the salesperson to cut them to fit. The store should have tile cutters on hand.

I tested both thicknesses of tiles by baking pizzas at 500 degrees, and found that the pizzas took two minutes longer to cook on the thinner tiles. Although the differences were very slight, I suggest that you buy the thicker tiles if you can. I checked several sources and found half-inch-thick tiles priced between 30¢ and $1 each.

You can leave the tiles in the oven all the time, but be careful not to splash cold water on them when they're hot or they may crack. Use warm water (but no detergent) to clean them. If necessary, you can scrub them with salt. Dry them with paper towels since they may stain dish towels.

Since I preferred baking pizza on tiles rather than in pans, I needed to work out the best way to get the dough onto the peel and then off the peel and into the oven. I sprinkle coarse cornmeal on the peel when making bread, so I tried using it for the pizzas, too. What's good for bread, though, isn't necessarily good for pizza. Because of the extremely large surface area of pizza, the ratio of coarse cornmeal to crust is too high; I didn't like the coarse, raw grain taste with every bite. I switched to a finer grind of cornmeal, but the finer grind seemed to attract the moisture from the damp dough, causing some of the topped doughs to stick. Nothing's worse than bringing a pizza to this point, then having it stick to the peel. Semolina, with its fine, sandy texture was perfect

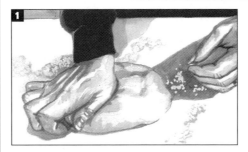

1. Flatten the dough into a disk using the palm of your hand.

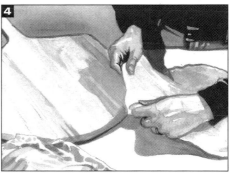

2. Starting at the center and working outward, use your fingertips to press the disk to about ¼-inch thick.

3. Using one hand to hold the dough in place, use your other hand to stretch the dough outward. For a medium-thick pizza crust, repeat the stretching by turning the dough a quarter turn after each pull, until it is the correct diameter. For a thinner pizza, let the dough relax for 5 minutes, then continue stretching it until it has reached the correct diameter.

4. Carefully lift the dough and transfer it to a peel dusted with semolina; proceed with the toppings.

TESTING PIZZA DOUGHS

In trying to find the best pizza crust, the following dough variations were tested. All the doughs were brushed with oil, topped with chopped, fresh tomatoes that had been seasoned with salt, and sprinkled with shredded fresh basil. All the pizzas were topped with mozzarella cheese during the last few minutes of baking.

• *Bleached all-purpose flour:* Dough was baby soft, almost sticky. Risen dough was soft and pliable but difficult to stretch. Untopped portion of crust was tough, while topped crust was hard, tough, and leathery.

• *Bread flour:* Muscular dough, substantial and tight, with good body but still quite easy to stretch. Crust was crisp and chewy but not tough. Exposed outer crust was crispy, while interior and covered portions were bready with the right amount of chewiness.

• *Part all-purpose flour, part semolina:* Tight, hard ball with a sandy, rough texture that neither helped nor hurt medium-thick dough. Thin pizzas made with semolina were denser and chewier, not as light and crisp as those made with bread flour.

• *Part all-purpose flour, part cornmeal:* Cornmeal flavor was very nice, but this soft dough tore easily and lacked the bubble-gum stretchiness of bread flour dough. Cornbready smell. A little extra crunch on the exterior, and a distinct corn flavor to the bready part.

• *No oil:* Dough was tacky and very sticky. Kept having to flour my hands during stretching. Dough stuck to the peel rather than sliding off easily.

• *Increased quantity of olive oil:* Dough was tender and too rich. If you ate meal's worth, you'd feel the effects. Much like many oil-laden pizzas that are made by national chains.

• *Slow-rising sponge:* Subtle flavor differences in crust are lost when tasted with toppings.

• *One-hour sponge:* No obvious taste or textural differences from regular-rise dough.

• *Milk dough:* Replaced one-half cup of water in the dough with milk, but found no improvement.

• *Egg dough:* Contrary to claims that replacing one-quarter cup of water with an egg would make a crisp crust, this crust was soft. Pleasant, but not what most of us have come to think of as pizza crust.

for sprinkling on the peel. It was fine enough to blend with the pizza texture without absorbing the dough's moisture (*see* Sources and Resources, page 32).

Toppings

Of all the pizzas I made, the ones topped with fresh tomatoes were everyone's favorite. But good tomatoes are available for only about three months out of the year. I found that a no-cook tomato sauce, enlivened with olive oil, garlic, and herbs and spread on the pizza, tasted almost as good as a cooked tomato sauce.

Cheese sprinkled on top of the pizza at the beginning of baking shriveled into the pizza and disappeared. But when added during the last few minutes of baking, it remained moist and lush, which meant that I could get away with using far less.

Bad news for those who want to make homemade pizza for a crowd and think it's possible to prebake the dough. While it is possible to prick the dough and partially bake it before topping, I found the fully baked crust to be tough and have a distinctly leftover flavor. To get the best crust, top it before baking, and add the cheese only for the last couple of minutes.

MASTER RECIPE FOR PIZZA DOUGH

This dough can be used for any size pizza with thick or thin crust; simply adjust the cooking time to fit the pizza.

Make sure you heat the oven to 500 degrees for thirty minutes before you start cooking. Your tiles or stone need at least that long to heat up; if they're not properly heated, your pizza crust will be thin, blond, and limp. Once the dough for the crust has been topped, use a quick jerking action to slide it off the peel and onto the hot tiles or stone; make sure that the pizza lands far enough back so that its front edge does not hang off.

For a cornmeal-flavored dough, substitute three-quarters cup of cornmeal for three-quarters cup of the bread flour.

> ½ cup warm water
> 1 envelope (2¼ teaspoons) active dry yeast
> 2 tablespoons olive oil, plus extra for brushing stretched dough
> 4 cups bread flour
> 1½ teaspoons salt
> Vegetable oil or spray for oiling bowl
> Semolina for peel

1. Measure ¼ cup of warm water into 2-cup measuring cup. Sprinkle in yeast; let stand until yeast dissolves and swells, about 5 minutes. Add remaining ¼ cup warm water plus 1 cup tap water and olive oil. Meanwhile, pulse flour and salt in workbowl of large food processor fitted with steel blade to combine. Add liquid ingredients (holding back a tablespoon or so) to flour and pulse together. If dough does not readily form into ball, stop machine, add remaining liquid, and continue to pulse until ball forms. Process until dough is smooth and satiny, about 30 seconds longer.

2. Turn dough onto lightly floured work surface; knead by hand with a few strokes to form smooth, round ball. Put dough into medium-large, oiled bowl, and cover with damp cloth. Let rise until doubled in size, about 2 hours.

3. Turn dough out onto lightly floured work surface and use chef's knife or dough scraper to halve, quarter, or cut dough into eighths, depending on number and size of pizzas desired. Form each piece into ball and cover with damp cloth. Working with one piece of dough at a time, shape as shown in illustrations 1 through 4, page 9. Transfer to pizza peel that has been lightly coated with semolina, brush dough very lightly with olive oil, then add topping. Proceed to cook topped pizza in preheated 500-degree oven for time indicated on "Pizza Cooking Time Chart," page 11.

EIGHT-HOUR PIZZA DOUGH

Follow Master Recipe for Pizza Dough, but decrease yeast to ½ teaspoon. In step 2, let dough stand at cool room temperature (about 68 degrees) until doubled in size, about 8 hours.

QUICK TOMATO SAUCE FOR PIZZA
Makes 3 cups

If you don't have time to cook this sauce, simply mix these ingredients together and let them stand while you stretch the dough. If you're using crushed tomatoes, I recommend either Red Pack or Glen Muir brands. Most other brands are full of seeds and skin. If you're using canned tomatoes packed in juice, you may want to drain off some of the liquid if you're not cooking the sauce.

> 2 large garlic cloves, minced
> 2 tablespoons olive oil
> 1 can (28 ounces) crushed tomatoes or tomatoes packed in puree, chopped coarse
> Salt and ground black pepper

Heat garlic with oil in saucepan over medium heat. When garlic starts to sizzle, add tomatoes. Simmer, uncovered, until sauce is thick enough to mound on spoon, about 15 minutes. Season to taste with salt and pepper.

CARAMELIZED ONION PIZZA WITH OIL-CURED OLIVES AND PARMESAN
Serves 4 to 6 as a main course or 8 as a substantial appetizer

Though substantial enough for a main course, this pizza is particularly nice as an hors d'oeuvre when cooked thin and cut into small pieces.

> 2 tablespoons olive oil
> 1 pound yellow onions, halved and sliced thin
> 1 teaspoon fresh thyme leaves
> Salt and ground black pepper
> 1 recipe Pizza Dough
> 1½ cups Quick Tomato Sauce for Pizza
> ¼ cup oil-cured olives, pitted and quartered
> 6 anchovies, chopped coarse (optional)
> ¼ cup grated Parmesan cheese

> ### PIZZA IN A HURRY
>
> **S**ometimes you don't have the time to let pizza dough rise at night, nor do you have the forethought to use the slow-rise process and start the dough rising in the morning (using only a fraction of the ordinary amount of yeast).
>
> For those occasions, try this especially fast recipe. By using rapid-rise yeast, a warm oven, warm water, and a little sugar, you can make a dough that will rise in only forty minutes. This means the entire process of making a pizza can be done in about seventy-five minutes from start to finish. Since convenience is the watchword here, all-purpose flour is used instead of bread flour.
>
> Although it does not have quite the tenderness or full flavor of dough made using the Master Recipe, this dough makes a very good pizza in very little time.
>
> **75-MINUTE PIZZA DOUGH**
>
> > 1⅓ cups warm water (about 105 degrees)
> > 1 envelope rapid-rise dry yeast
> > 1 tablespoon sugar
> > 2 tablespoons olive oil
> > 4 cups all-purpose flour, plus extra as needed
> > 1½ teaspoons salt
> > Vegetable oil for oiling bowl
>
> 1. Set oven to 200 degrees for 10 minutes, then turn oven off.
>
> 2. Meanwhile, in bowl of food processor fitted with either metal or plastic blade, add water and sprinkle in yeast and sugar. Pulse twice to dissolve yeast. Add all remaining ingredients and process until mixture forms cohesive mass. Dough should not be sticky (if it is, add 2 more tablespoons flour and pulse briefly) nor should it be dry and crumbly (if it is, add 1 more tablespoon water and pulse briefly). Let rest for 2 minutes. Process for another 30 seconds.
>
> 3. Remove dough from food processor and knead by hand on floured work surface for 1 minute or until dough is smooth and satiny (dough will feel a bit tough at this point).
>
> 4. Very lightly oil large bowl with vegetable oil. Place dough in bowl (do not coat dough with oil) and cover with plastic wrap. Place in warm oven. Let rise for 40 minutes or until doubled. Remove from oven, punch down, remove from bowl, and separate into two round pieces. Let rest for 10 minutes under damp dish towel, then shape, top, and bake according to directions on pages 9 to 11.
> *—Christopher Kimball*

This chart indicates the cooking time for pizza crust with topping but without cheese. All pizzas need to be cooked an **additional** two to three minutes after adding **cheese,** or until cheese is completely melted.

THIN CRUST

14-inch pizzas (Master Recipe makes 2)	7 to 8 minutes
12-inch pizzas (Master Recipe makes 4)	5 minutes
8-inch pizzas (Master Recipe makes 8)	3 minutes

MEDIUM-THICK CRUST

12-inch pizzas (Master Recipe makes 2)	9 to 10 minutes
8-inch pizzas (Master Recipe makes 4)	5 minutes
6-inch pizzas (Master Recipe makes 8)	4 minutes

1. Heat oil over medium-high heat in a large skillet. Add onions; sauté, stirring frequently until onions are softened and somewhat caramelized, about 10 minutes. Stir in thyme; season to taste with salt and pepper.

2. Top pizza dough with a portion of sauce. Scatter a portion of cooked onions over sauce. Sprinkle with olives and optional anchovies. Immediately slide dough onto heated quarry tiles or pizza stone. Follow cooking time on chart (*see* above), adding a portion of cheese at appropriate time.

SAUSAGE AND BELL PEPPER PIZZA WITH BASIL AND MOZZARELLA

Serves 4 to 6 as a main course or 8 as a substantial appetizer

If bulk sausage is not available, just buy cased sausage, remove the casing, and break meat into bite-size chunks.

- ¾ pound bulk mild Italian sausage, broken into bite-size pieces
- 1½ teaspoons olive oil (approximately)
- 1 red or yellow bell pepper, halved, cored, seeded, and cut into thin strips
  Salt and ground black pepper
- 1 recipe Pizza Dough
- 1½ cups Quick Tomato Sauce
- ¼ cup shredded fresh basil leaves
- 4 ounces mozzarella cheese, shredded (1 cup)

1. Put sausage and ¼ cup water in medium-large skillet. Cook over medium-high heat until water evaporates and sausage cooks through and browns, about 7 minutes. Remove sausage with slotted spoon. Add enough oil so that amount in skillet equals about 1 tablespoon. Add peppers and sauté until softened slightly, about 5 minutes. Season to taste with salt and pepper. Remove and set aside.

2. Top pizza dough with a portion of sauce. Scatter a portion of basil, sausage pieces, and peppers over sauce. Immediately slide dough onto heated quarry tiles or pizza stone. Follow cooking time on chart (*see* above), adding a portion of cheese at appropriate time.

WILD MUSHROOM PIZZA WITH SAGE, FONTINA, AND PARMESAN

Serves 4 to 6 as a main course or 8 as a substantial appetizer

- 2 large garlic cloves, minced
- 2 tablespoons olive oil
- 1 pound wild or domestic mushrooms, trimmed and sliced thin
- 1 teaspoon minced fresh sage leaves
  Salt and ground black pepper
- 1 recipe Pizza Dough
- 1 cup Quick Tomato Sauce
- 4 ounces fontina cheese, shredded (1 cup)
- ¼ cup grated Parmesan cheese

1. Heat garlic with oil in large skillet. When garlic begins to sizzle, add mushrooms; sauté, stirring frequently, until mushrooms release their liquid and most of it evaporates, about 5 minutes. Stir in sage and season to taste with salt and pepper. Set aside.

2. Top pizza dough with a portion of sauce. Scatter a portion of mushrooms over sauce. Immediately slide dough onto heated quarry tiles or pizza stone. Follow cooking time on chart at left, adding a portion of cheeses at appropriate time.

FRESH TOMATO PIZZA WITH ARUGULA AND PROSCIUTTO

Serves 4 to 6 as a main course or 8 as a substantial appetizer

When tossing the arugula with oil, you may also sprinkle on a teaspoon or so of balsamic vinegar if you like.

- 1 pound tomatoes, cored and sliced thin
- 1 recipe Pizza Dough
  Salt and ground black pepper
- 4 teaspoons olive oil, plus 2 teaspoons more for arugula
- 4 ounces thin-sliced prosciutto, about 8 slices
- 4 ounces (1 cup) shredded mozzarella cheese
- 2 cups arugula, washed thoroughly and spun dry

Arrange a portion of tomatoes in concentric circles over prepared pizza dough. Season with salt and pepper. Drizzle with a portion of oil. Immediately slide dough onto heated quarry tiles or pizza stone. Follow cooking time on chart (*see* above), adding prosciutto along with cheese at appropriate time. Toss arugula with remaining 2 teaspoons oil. As pizzas come out of oven, top each with a portion of arugula. ■

PIZZA BELLA DELIVERS PIZZA BRUTTA

In the past year I've noticed countertop pizza ovens making their debut in cooking catalogs. Though pricey and a bit bulky for the average kitchen counter, these ovens could prove useful for frequent pizza makers because of their speedy heat-up time, so I decided to give one a try. I ordered the Pizza Bella Model 2000 ($160 plus shipping) from Keystone Manufacturing.

The first machine malfunctioned before it ever cooked its first pizza, so I called the company; they promptly sent me a replacement. The replacement oven at least baked a pizza, but I don't recommend the investment.

These machines are expensive, potentially dangerous, and most important, don't deliver a well-cooked pizza.

First of all, these are nothing more than a pizza stone sandwiched between two heating coils. Nothing stands between the coils and the metal housing, so when the coils get hot, the metal surface gets equally hot. There is a "Caution: Hot Surface" sticker on the machine, but

it's difficult to avoid touching the surface when opening the lid and adjusting the temperature control. I also found that the lid, unless lifted all the way up, would close. At one point, my coworker Karen barely avoided getting branded with coil marks when she slid in a pizza.

Pizzas cooked with the Pizza Bella varied in consistency. The first pizza was the best. It had a fairly impressive bottom crust, with an unevenly cooked top—some spots were nearly burnt, while others were barely cooked at all. After removal of each pizza the machine has to reheat, or the next one will cook up wimpy.

ILLUSTRATION BY TONY DELUZ/PHOTOGRAPH BY DAVID HENDERSON

Shaping Foolproof Meringues

Pastry teacher Flo Braker adds sugar in three stages, pipes the meringues immediately, and uses small "test" meringues to check for doneness.

∾ BY JACK BISHOP ∾

Although the ingredients could not be simpler or less expensive, many home cooks shy away from meringues because they think they are too sweet or too temperamental, according to California-based pastry teacher Flo Braker, author of *The Simple Art of Perfect Baking* (Chapters, 1992). Braker dispenses easily with the first objection; unlike the supersweet meringues she remembers from her Indiana childhood, Braker's recipe has just enough sugar to ensure that the meringues harden properly but not so much that they are cloying. On the second point, Braker concedes that meringues can

> *"Meringues are great home desserts because of their keeping qualities,"* says Braker, who saves a tin of them in the pantry to make impromptu desserts.

be fickle, but offers a number of tips to eliminate the guesswork, even on rainy days.

Troubleshooting Tips

"It's the simplest recipes that sometimes cause the most confusion," Braker says, "and when people have trouble with meringues, it is usually because the most basic thing has gone wrong." First, she says, meringues must be piped or shaped immediately after they are made. Even a short rest can allow the moisture from the egg whites to separate and form a thin syrup that causes the whites to deflate.

Braker also adds the sugar to the meringues in three stages to produce maximum volume and optimum texture. Most of the granulated sugar is added early in the recipe so that it has a chance to dissolve, but two tablespoons are folded in with the confectioners' sugar to keep it from clumping.

The most common complaint that Braker hears from her students is that their meringues never "set up" in the oven. This, she says, is due to a misunderstanding: "Meringues are not supposed to harden completely in the oven." While low heat will dry them out, meringues do not become hard and crisp until they have had a chance to cool for five or ten

---

CLASSIC MERINGUE

Makes 2 large disks or 8 individual shells

4 tablespoons plus ⅓ cup granulated sugar
⅔ cup confectioners' sugar
½ cup (about 4 large) egg whites, at room temperature

1. Sift 2 tablespoons granulated sugar with confectioners' sugar; set aside.

2. Place egg whites in large bowl of electric mixer. Using whisk attachment, whip them on low speed just until frothy. Increase speed to medium, sprinkle in 2 tablespoons reserved granulated sugar, and continue whipping to soft peaks. Gradually add ⅓ cup reserved granulated sugar; continue whipping to stiff, glossy peaks. Stop mixer; rub some meringue between your fingers. If smooth, proceed to next step. If still grainy, continue beating until smooth.

3. Sprinkle sifted powdered-sugar mixture (and ground ginger and cinnamon if making Free-Form Meringue Shells; *see* page 13) over meringue; fold in with rubber spatula until just incorporated. Immediately continue with one of the recipes on page 13.

---

minutes. Therefore, Braker always makes a few small "test" meringues with leftover whipped egg whites. When she thinks the large disks or individual shells might be done, she removes one of these test meringues and lets it cool before evalu-

---

FOR LARGE MERINGUE DISKS AND CAKE

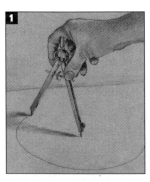

1. Use a compass to trace circles on parchment paper. If a compass is unavailable, use household items like lids or ramekins as guides to trace around.

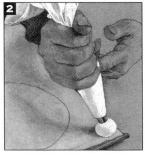

2. Before forming the meringue shapes, pipe out or spoon a small quantity (about ½ teaspoon) of meringue into each corner of the parchment paper to keep it in place as you work.

3. Beginning in the center of the traced circle, pipe meringue in a continuous, widening spiral until it reaches the edge of the circle. Hold the pastry bag perpendicular to the baking sheet, 1½ to 2 inches from the area you are piping. Apply continuous pressure as you pipe.

4. Spread 2 cups of strawberry ice cream over each frozen disk with a flexible metal spatula. Return the disk to the freezer for 30 minutes or until the ice cream is firm.

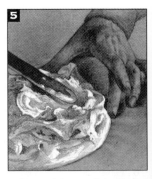

5. Spread 1 cup of vanilla ice cream over the strawberry ice cream on the large disk. Return the disk to the freezer until the ice cream is firm.

ating its texture. If the test meringue is done, so are the others.

The two desserts that Braker makes with her classic meringue recipe illustrate just some of the possibilities. When using large disks as cake layers, Braker uses a pastry bag to achieve uniform height. Piping also affords more precise control and is a must if making more intricate shapes.

Free-form shells, which can be shaped with the back of a spoon, can be filled with seasonal fruits for elegant but easy desserts. Since the shells are a bit thicker than the disks, they will take longer to dry out in the oven and may turn ivory or even champagne in color. "Very slight browning is caused by the caramelization of some of the sugar and only increases the flavor in the shells," says Braker. If the meringues become tan or darker, though, your oven temperature is too high and should be lowered.

ALMOND MERINGUE CAKE WITH STRAWBERRY AND VANILLA ICE CREAM
Serves 8 to 10

If you have any meringue left after piping the two disks, make a few dessert shells. To soften the ice cream, place it in the refrigerator about thirty minutes before needed. And remember, not all of the ice cream is needed at the same time. If you need ice cream softened in a hurry, you can also microwave it on the defrost setting, checking it every thirty seconds at first, and then every fifteen seconds as it reaches the softened state.

    Vegetable cooking spray
⅓ cup fine-chopped almonds
1 recipe Classic Meringue (*see* page 12)
1 quart strawberry ice cream, softened slightly
1 quart vanilla ice cream, softened slightly
1½ cups sliced almonds, toasted
    Fresh strawberries for garnish (optional)

1. Adjust oven rack to lower middle position; heat oven to 225 degrees. Line large baking sheet with parchment paper. Use a compass to make 8-inch and 6½-inch circles on parchment paper - (*see* illustration 1). Lightly spray each circle with cooking spray to ensure easy removal of meringues. Fit large pastry bag with ½-inch plain decorating tip.

2. Fold chopped almonds into Classic Meringue recipe. Immediately scoop meringue into prepared pastry bag. Follow instructions in illustrations 2 and 3 to secure paper and pipe meringue circles. Pipe a couple of 1½-inch disks with any excess meringue. These extra meringues are used to test for doneness.

3. Bake meringues until one of the test samples releases easily from paper and snaps crisply after 5 minutes of cooling, 60 to 80 minutes. Once sample is crisp when tested, remove baking sheet from oven and place on cooling rack until meringue disks are room temperature, about 30 minutes. Carefully remove cooled meringues from paper. Place larger disk on 9-inch round piece of cardboard or removable tart-pan bottom. Place smaller disk on similar surface. Freeze both disks for 30 minutes. (Can also be stored in an airtight container up to 2 weeks; upon removal, freeze the disks before adding topping.)

4. Follow illustrations 4 through 8 to assemble cake. Return cake to freezer for at least 4 hours or up to 1 day. About 15 minutes before serving, transfer cake to serving platter and garnish with strawberries. Use knife to cut cake into wedges and serve immediately.

FREE-FORM MERINGUE SHELLS FILLED WITH STRAWBERRIES AND PAPAYA
Serves 8

To form these meringue shells, you don't need a pastry bag or decorating tips, just a regular tablespoon. Once made, these meringue shells make an impressive, quick dessert filled with fruit, ice cream, or mousse.

    Vegetable cooking spray
1 recipe Classic Meringue (*see* page 12)

with ¼ teaspoon ground ginger and ⅛ teaspoon ground cinnamon
1 pint strawberries, hulled and sliced lengthwise
2 tablespoons sugar
1 teaspoon grated zest from small orange
1 small papaya, peeled, halved, and seeded; each half halved crosswise and sliced thin

1. Adjust oven racks to low and middle positions; heat oven to 225 degrees. Line two large baking sheets with parchment paper. Use a compass or 4-inch biscuit cutter to make four 4-inch circles on each paper (*see* illustration 1). Lightly spray each circle with cooking spray to ensure easy removal of meringues.

2. Place ½-teaspoon dollop of meringue in corners of each baking sheet to hold paper in place. Drop ½ cup meringue in center of each circle (illustration 9). With back of spoon, carefully spread meringue inside each circle. Continue to use back of spoon to make an indentation in meringue center, forming a decorative cup about ¼-inch thick in center and 1-inch high around edge (illustration 10). Shape a couple of 1½-inch disks with the spoon and remaining meringue. These extra meringues are used to test for doneness.

3. Bake meringues, switching positions of baking sheets after 30 minutes, until one of test samples releases easily from paper and snaps crisply after 5 minutes of cooling, 60 to 80 minutes. Once sample is crisp when tested, remove baking sheets from oven and place on cooling racks until meringues are room temperature, about 30 minutes. Carefully remove cooled meringues from paper. Set aside until ready to fill. (Can be stored in an airtight container up to 2 weeks.)

4. Toss berries, sugar, and orange zest in small bowl; let stand until light syrup forms, about 30 minutes. Add papaya and toss gently.

5. Place one meringue shell on each serving plate. Divide fruit and syrup among shells. Serve immediately. ∎

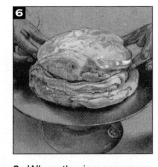

6. When the ice cream on the large disks is frozen, carefully slide the smaller meringue disk, ice-cream side up, on top of the ice-cream layers on the large disk.

7. Spread the remaining vanilla ice cream over the top and sides of the cake. Move the spatula from the bottom upward to contour the top and create the dome shape. Return the dessert to the freezer until the ice cream is firm.

8. Hold the cake in one hand directly over a baking pan containing the nuts. Use the other hand to gently press the nuts into the ice cream. The nuts can be secured by pressing them gently into the ice cream with a flexible metal spatula.

FOR INDIVIDUAL DESSERT SHELLS

9. Free-form meringue shells can be created without piping. Use the back of a spoon to carefully spread about ½ cup of meringue inside each traced circle.

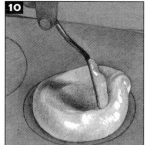

10. Still using the spoon, form an indentation in the center and a decorative edge around the side of each shell.

Tea-Smoked Chicken

Using a heavy pot, tinfoil, and a meat thermometer, you can get the full flavor of this traditional dish by smoking it indoors on top of your stove.

≈ BY DOUGLAS BELLOW ≈

By combining the flavoring and cooking processes, tradition-ally done as separate steps, it takes only an hour and a half to create a dish that used to take days.

Most recipes for the classic Chinese dish called tea-smoked duck involve five separate processes. First the bird is mar-inated in spices, next it is smoked, then it is steamed to actually cook it, then it is air-dried to add texture, and finally it is deep-fried to crisp the skin. While each of these steps adds something to the finished product, few cooks today are able to spend the day and a half to six days that it takes to complete them all.

After smoking many chickens as well as ducks, I found that by making two adjustments it is pos-sible to get the subtle flavors and textures of this dish with a relatively simple one-step cooking process. First, the bird is smoked for a longer time over an aromatic mixture; this combines into one step the flavoring and cooking normally achieved by marinating, smoking, and steaming. Second, duck is replaced by chicken, which makes it pos-sible to eliminate the drying and deep-frying that were needed to deal with the layer of fat that lies under the skin of a duck.

In this shortened method, we cook the bird on an improvised smoker on top of the stove. The smoker is made from a foil-lined pot with a foil lid, and a rack that suspends the chicken over a smoking mixture. While the aroma of the smok-ing might seem like a drawback, it is actually quite pleasant and certainly is no more invasive than frying or broiling.

Once you conquer any ini-tial fears you may have about building a small fire on top of your stove, you can get a very juicy and flavorful bird with an absolute minimum of preparation and cleanup. And once you have done it a couple of times, the whole setup process, from pulling your bird out of the grocery bag to starting the cooking, will take you no more than ten minutes. The cooking itself will take only about an hour and twenty minutes if you are using a four-pound bird.

The Smoking Mixture
In addition to the chicken, which should weigh between three and a half and four and a half pounds in order to fit nicely into the pot, you will also need a smoking mixture that will smolder in the bottom of the pot and fla-vor the meat as it cooks. This mixture consists of four ingredients: rice, brown sugar, tea, and spices. Each of these plays an important role in the cooking and flavoring process.

As the brown sugar heats, it begins to caramelize, forming various compounds, some of which are very volatile and enter the air as smoke. These give the bird a bittersweet, caramel flavor.

Like the sugar, the rice adds flavor. But it also has an added function—it absorbs the moisture that the sugar creates as it caramelizes as well as the moisture the bird gives off as it cooks. This is crucial because you want the smoking mixture to be as dry as possible so that you get smoke, not steam.

The tea provides most of the flavor in the smoke. Not only does it flavor the bird as the smoke is absorbed, but also, as the bird releases moisture, the tea particles settle on the bird and actually make tea on the skin and in the cavity of the bird. The tea colors the skin a beautiful, glossy, mahogany color and also serves as a sort of marinade as the bird cooks.

To see what differences in flavor they might provide, I tried three different types of tea—a reg-ular Chinese black tea, an orange pekoe, and a smoked Chinese tea called Lapsang souchong. While all three gave a good flavor, each had its advantages. The orange pekoe gave the best fragrance to the kitchen, while the Lapsang sou-chong gave the smokiest flavor to the meat. In the end I decided I liked this latter option best be-cause, when combined with the traditional Chinese flavorings of cloves, star anise, and citrus peel, it gave the chicken the strongest flavor. However, almost any loose tea will work, and you should feel free to experiment with your own tea and spice combinations. Cinnamon, ginger, and tangerine peel, for example, are possible substi-tutes for the spices that I chose.

Making a Smoker
For smoking, you will need a large Dutch oven or wok, some heavy-duty aluminum foil, and a rack to hold the bird. Each of these should have certain characteristics.

The pot needs to be large enough to hold the bird, the rack, and the smoking material; it also needs to be made of a fairly heavy material. There is no liquid in this recipe; only the aluminum foil protects the surface of the pot. Therefore, the pot needs to be able to withstand a good ninety min-utes of high heat. Because of this, it is probably not a good idea to use a nonstick or glazed pan; it may be ruined. Most woks are sufficiently large and durable, and many also come with a rack for steaming; the only potential problem with using a wok is that, if yours is well seasoned, the long exposure to high heat may burn away the ingrained oil, ruining the "nonstick" surface. If you regularly scrub out your wok after using it, however, the heat should be no problem at all since you will have already removed the oil by washing. Instead of a wok, I chose an old cast-iron Dutch oven (about twelve-quart capacity) made for camping. It worked just as well, although it was a bit smaller than my wok.

To seal the pot, use heavy-duty aluminum foil, preferably an eighteen-inch-wide roll. Since the foil completely surrounds the bird, it also protects your pot. By the end of the cooking the smoking mixture will have become a mass of molten sugar and burned rice; you can simply remove the foil and throw this mess away inside the foil.

When placing the bird on a rack above the smoking mixture, remember that the goal is to keep the bird suspended in the middle, with air on all sides. For most pots, that will mean that the rack should stand up off the bottom of the pan about an inch and the chicken should have about an inch of room on the sides and on top. Somewhat smaller air spaces will not affect the cooking time or the flavor, but the color might be affected. If the foil actually touches the chicken's skin, the skin will tend to be splotchy.

If you don't have a rack that fits your wok, or if you are using a Dutch oven, there are any number of improvised racks you can make. Perhaps the easiest method is to take two empty cans the size tuna fish comes in, remove the labels and both ends, and lay metal skewers across them to make a rack (illustration 2).

Before completely sealing the chicken in the foil, stick a meat thermometer through the foil lid into the leg or thigh (illustration 3) so you can tell when the bird is done. Other methods of checking doneness—such as looking at the juices, or moving the leg—can't be used because they would require unsealing the smoker.

Cooking the Chicken

The most critical part of cooking the chicken is being sure you are cooking it at the right temperature. The smoking mixture should be giving off a steady amount of smoke without going out or burning too quickly. The best way to judge this is to take a look at the hole through which the thermometer is inserted. You should see a thin, steady stream of smoke coming out. If there is no smoke, turn the heat up; if the smoke is billowing out, turn the heat down slightly.

Be aware that the pot gets quite hot, and that during cooking you will hear a lot of simmering and hissing. Don't worry. I have done this many times, and nothing terrible has ever happened. I don't suggest making this recipe, however, when you're not going to be around to check on it.

One slight drawback of this method compared with the traditional methods is that the bird is smoked for considerably longer, which means more smoke in your kitchen. To minimize this problem, I tried butchering the bird before cooking it, thinking that this would decrease smoking time. It did accomplish that, but the meat tended to become tough and dried out too quickly. Leaving the bird whole not only provided a better-looking finished product, but also a very well cooked and juicy bird. I decided it was well worth the relatively small additional amount of smoke in the kitchen.

One final note regarding a second drawback of this method, the condition of the skin. The finished chicken should have an attractive bronze or brown color, and a very moist interior. But by the end of the cooking process, some of the moisture from the chicken will have dripped into the bottom of the pot and steamed the bird. This tends to leave the skin a bit moist instead of crisp. If you are a fan of skin—although fewer and fewer people are these days (I still am)—simply coat the bird with a little sesame oil after smoking and put it in a preheated 450-degree oven. In less than five minutes the skin should crisp nicely, and its color should become even richer.

STOVE-TOP TEA-SMOKED CHICKEN
Serves 4 to 6

  ½ cup rice, any kind
  ⅓ cup light brown sugar

STEPS TO STOVE-TOP COOKING

1. Line a heavy-duty soup kettle or wok with at least two sheets of heavy-duty aluminum foil, leaving a couple of inches sticking up over the top.

2. Spread the dry smoking mixture evenly over the bottom of the covered pot and place the rack on top of the mixture. If you do not have a rack that fits into your wok or pot, you can make one by laying two metal skewers across two empty cans the size tuna fish comes in.

3. Lay the trussed chicken on top of the rack or skewers. Use another sheet of heavy-duty foil to tent the chicken; crimp it together with the foil that lines the pot or wok until you are halfway around the pot, then insert a meat thermometer through the foil and into the leg or thigh section of the bird.

4. When thermometer is in place, complete crimping the top sheet of foil to the bottom sheet in order to completely seal the smoker.

  ⅓ cup loose tea, preferably
       Lapsang souchong
  6 whole cloves
  3 star anise pods
  1 strip orange zest
  1 chicken, 3½ to 4½ pounds, rinsed and
       patted dry
       Salt and ground black pepper
       Sesame oil (optional)

1. Line large soup kettle, Dutch oven, or wok with at least two long sheets of heavy-duty aluminum foil so that there is a 2- to 3-inch rim of foil all the way around pot (*see* illustration 1).

2. Spread rice, sugar, tea, cloves, anise, and orange zest evenly over bottom of pan. Set wire rack over these, making sure that there will be about an inch of space all around chicken (any less and it will not brown well). Alternatively, set two empty tuna fish cans (tops, bottoms, and labels removed) on opposite sides of pot, and bridge them with two metal skewers (illustration 2).

3. Rub chicken cavity and skin with salt and pepper. Use 3-foot length of kitchen twine to tie legs together. Run twine around thighs and under wings on both sides of bird, pull it snug, and tie firm knot at neck; snip off excess twine.

4. Place trussed chicken on rack or skewers (illustration 3). Use layer of heavy-duty foil to make a tent shape over chicken; crimp this foil to about halfway around rim of foil lining wok or pot. Stick instant-read thermometer through foil lid and into the leg or thigh and finish crimping top piece of foil to completely seal the smoker (illustration 4).

5. Heat pot over high heat until tea mixture begins to smoke. Once smoking starts, reduce heat to medium-high. Smoke bird, making sure a thin, steady stream of smoke emerges from opening made by meat thermometer, until chicken registers 170 degrees, 45 minutes to 1½ hours, depending on size of bird. Once chicken is done, carefully remove pot from heat, unseal foil, and remove chicken. (If you want to crisp the skin, simply coat the cooked chicken with a little sesame oil and roast it in a 450-degree oven for about 5 minutes.)

6. Let chicken rest 10 minutes, carve, and serve. For cleanup, fold foil back on itself to reseal; cool foil ball to room temperature, then discard. ■

Douglas Bellow lives and cooks in Cambridge, Massachusetts.

Simple Cake Decorating

Decorating a birthday or other special-occasion cake does not need to be a major production. Below are some simple techniques from cake wizard Rosemary Littman that you can do quickly and easily with a pastry bag and a little know-how.

To ensure a neat finished cake, Littman advises that you write the message on the cake top first before applying other designs. That way, if you make a mistake, you can remove it, re-ice the top, and try again.

After writing the message on top of the cake, place the wide swags, pipe a top border, and finish by piping the bottom border. Also, keep a damp dish towel nearby to wipe clean the decorative opening of the tube. ∎

TO FIT A NEW PASTRY BAG WITH A PLASTIC COUPLER

A new pastry bag may have to be cut away at the pointed end in order to fit a metal decorating tube (tip) and/or a plastic coupler. Using a coupler allows you to change tubes without having to empty the pastry bag. *DO NOT* cut away too much or the tube, coupler, and icing will slip through the opening.

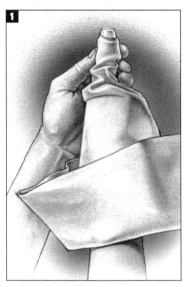

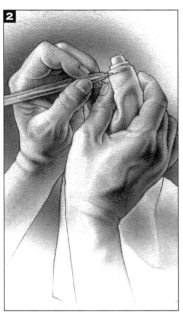

1. Unscrew the ring. Insert the larger cone-shaped piece (coupler), pointed end first, up into the narrow end of the pastry bag, pushing it in tightly.

2. With your fingernail or a pen, mark a line between the first and second groove (thread).

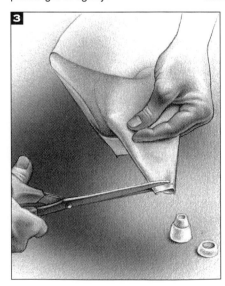

3. Remove the coupler, and cut away the bag at the mark with sharp scissors. Reinsert the coupler to expose the threads. Place a metal decorating tube over the coupler, and screw the ring tightly to secure the tube. (When fitting larger tubes, follow the same instructions, except for step 2. Instead, with a pen, mark the bag halfway up the decorating tube. Cut the bag away at this mark, and reinsert the tube, exposing approximately half of it.)

TO FILL AND HOLD A PASTRY BAG

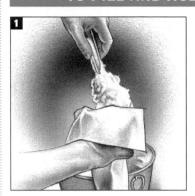

1. Make about a 3-inch cuff at the top of the pastry bag. With one hand, hold the bag open under the cuff, and with the other hand, fill the bag half full using a rubber spatula. Pack the frosting into the bag to eliminate air spaces. Pull the cuff back to its original position, and press the edges of the bag against the spatula as you remove it.

2. Twist the bag just above the icing, and grip it slightly in the curve of your hand between your thumb and forefinger. Consider this grip to be a "lock." A gentle pressure from the other fingers of that hand squeezes the icing out of the tube, while you use your other hand to guide the bag.

SIDE SWAGS

This should be done before a top border is applied.

1. Use a large cookie cutter, jar lid, or plastic cup. Place a piece of tape across it, making sure that the edge of the tape falls directly across the middle to create an open semicircle. This semicircle will be your guide.

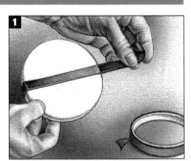

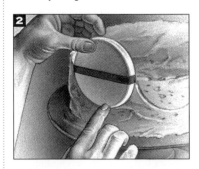

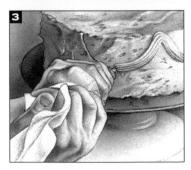

2. Mark off sections around the cake by lining up the tape with the top edge of the cake and pressing the open semicircle into the icing.

3. Pipe stars or swirls over these semicircles to create a side-swag design.

ILLUSTRATIONS BY HARRY DAVIS

BORDERS

To give a cake a finished look, add borders to the top edge and to the bottom edge where the cake meets the platter. To keep the borders and swags uniform, pipe a small section of border at a time. Stop and turn the cake a few degrees, and repeat the process until you've made the border all the way around.

SHELL BORDER

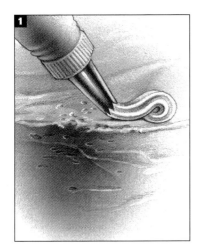

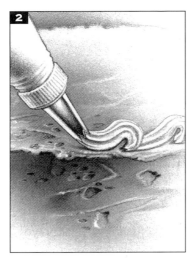

1. Hold the pastry bag at a 45-degree angle. Using medium pressure, squeeze out a puff of icing. As you move to the left, lessen your pressure on the bag to make a "tail." Stop the pressure and release the tube.

2. Make another puff, overlapping it onto the end of the first "tail," and again, move to the left and relax pressure to create another "tail." Repeat this to create a shell border all the way around the cake.

ZIGZAG BORDER

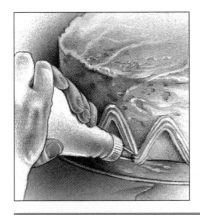

Hold the pastry bag at a 45-degree angle with the tube touching the cake's bottom edge. Using steady pressure, move along the edge, squeezing the icing in an up-and-down movement, being careful not to go too high. After you have gone 3 or 4 inches, stop squeezing at a point where the tube is near the platter. Repeat this process until you have gone completely around the cake and joined the last stroke to the first.

PRACTICE WRITING

When writing, thin the icing with a few drops of water or extract to make it flow more smoothly. Write your message (in block or cursive writing) on a piece of paper. Tape the paper to a flat surface and cover it with a sheet of clear acetate or plastic. Practice going over the message several times. Keep wiping the icing away and trying again until you are confident. When making printed letters, hold the bag vertically. When making cursive letters, tilt the bag a little as you write.

BASKET WEAVE

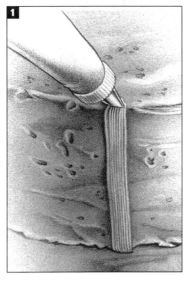

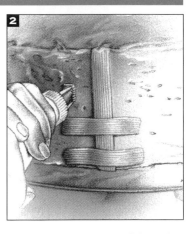

1. Make a vertical line from the bottom of the cake to the top of the cake.

2. Starting at the base of the cake, make short, equal-length, horizontal strokes over the vertical line, leaving a space between each stroke that is the same width as the stoke itself. Continue until you reach the top edge of the cake.

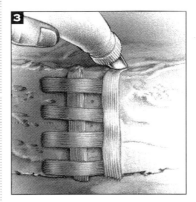

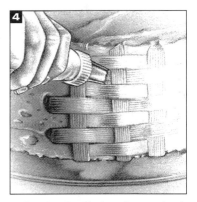

3. Moving to the right, make another vertical line from the bottom to the top of the cake, covering the right ends of the short strokes you just made. Then make a third vertical line, covering the left ends of the horizontal strokes.

4. Starting just below the top horizontal stroke, make a series of equal-length horizontal strokes that go over the left and right vertical lines. Repeat this pattern, fitting the strokes together to create a basket-weave effect.

ROSETTES AND STARS

Rosettes and stars are made with the pastry bag at a sharp angle. When repeating rosettes and stars, space each new one so that it touches the previous existing one.

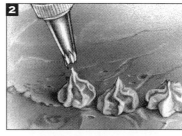

1. Rosettes are made by squeezing out a tiny circle of icing, never changing the angle at which the bag is hold.

2. Stars are made by squeezing out a bit of icing, letting up on the pressure, then immediately lifting the tube.

All-Purpose Birthday Cake

For a white cake with perfect, fine-grained texture, don't beat the egg whites prior to mixing.

∽ BY STEPHEN SCHMIDT ∽

White layer cakes have been the classic type of birthday cake for over a hundred years, and to my mind they remain the most delectable choice for this festive (if sometimes slightly depressing) occasion. White cake is simply a basic butter cake made with egg whites instead of whole eggs. The whites produce the characteristic color, and they also make the cake soft and fine-grained, a bit like pound cake but much lighter and more delicate. Unfortunately, the white cakes that I have baked over the years, although good enough, always fell short of my high expectations. They came out a little dry and chewy—one might say cottony—and I noticed that they were riddled with tunnels and small holes. What was I doing wrong?

Early on, I suspected my mixing method might be to blame. I had always mixed white cakes according to standard cookbook procedure—that is, I had creamed the butter and sugar, added the flour and milk alternately, and finally folded in stiffly beaten egg whites. Because this mixing method brings the flour into direct contact with liquid, it encourages the flour to form the elastic protein gluten. When beaten, gluten forms a stretchy net of ropelike fibers that not only make the cake tough, but also press the air cells together into holes and tunnels. Cookbook recipes generally recommend deft, gentle handling of the batter in order to minimize gluten formation, but it seemed that no matter how little I beat or how delicately I folded, my cakes did not improve.

In trying to avoid an "overglutenized" cake batter, I ordinarily use the so-called two-stage mixing method outlined by Rose Levy Beranbaum in *The Cake Bible* (Morrow, 1988). This method entails creaming the flour, butter, and sugar together (rather than just the butter and sugar) before adding the eggs and other liquid ingredients. Because the flour is mixed with butter at the start, it is partially waterproofed, and thus less prone to develop gluten. In the case of white cake, however, I could not bring myself to try this method because it uses unbeaten eggs, and every traditional recipe for white cake calls for stiffly beaten egg whites folded into the batter at the end. Surely the cake's special texture depended on beating the whites first, I thought. So I stuck with my old method and tried to improve the results by

Today's white cake is a delicate offshoot of fancy pound cakes from the nineteenth century.

fiddling with the proportions. Into the garbage went a dozen cakes.

Luckily, I happened upon a recipe called Old-Fashioned White Cake in the 1943 edition of *The Joy of Cooking*. The recipe called for working butter into the flour with one's fingertips, as in the making of pie crust, and then whisking in beaten egg whites. I was intrigued: Here was a two-stage white cake, but with the beaten egg whites I thought were necessary. Upon testing, the cake indeed proved to be more tender than the others I had made, and it also had a finer crumb. After a few more experiments, I eventually arrived at a white cake that I thought very good—but, alas, still not quite perfect. There were still those holes.

I was stumped, and I might have stayed stumped if I had not been paying particularly close attention one day while I was folding egg whites into a soufflé batter. As the rubber spatula drew the egg whites up from the bottom of the bowl and over the top of the batter, I was struck by how coarse and bubbly the whites were, even though they were not overbeaten and had seemed perfectly smooth and thick when taken from the mixer just moments before. Could it be that beaten egg whites, instead of promoting an ethereal texture in white cakes, actually formed large air pockets and caused those unsightly holes?

I tried the "old-fashioned" recipe again, only this time I simply mixed the egg whites with the milk before beating them into the flour-and-butter mixture. The results were fantastic. The cake was

not only fine-grained and holeless, but to my surprise, it was also larger and lighter than the ones I'd prepared with beaten whites. And the method couldn't be simpler, quicker, or more nearly failureproof. The two-stage method had proved, after all, to be the way to go.

Of course I was curious to know the reason for this surprising outcome, so I did some boning up on egg whites. Apparently, beating has something of the same effect on egg whites that cooking does. Both beating and heating cause some of the individual protein strands to uncoil, whereupon they bump into each other and start linking up into an increasingly tight, dense web. It is this linking process that causes cooked whites to coagulate and beaten whites to stiffen. The problem, then, with putting beaten egg whites into a batter is that the whites have, in this respect, already been partially cooked. Because of this, the whites do not mix well with the rest of the batter and tend instead to create large air pockets when the cake bakes. Unbeaten egg whites, on the other hand, mix easily with the rest of the ingredients. When, during baking, they set and stiffen, they provide the structure necessary to hold the fine air bubbles beaten into the batter by creaming. The result is a wonderfully velvety cake, perfect for that birthday person.

CLASSIC WHITE LAYER CAKE WITH BUTTER FROSTING AND RASPBERRY-ALMOND FILLING
Two-Layer Cake: Serves 12

If you have forgotten to bring the milk and egg white mixture to room temperature, set the bottom of the glass measure containing it in a sink of hot water and stir until the mixture feels cool rather than cold, around 75 degrees. Cake layers can be wrapped and stored for one day; frosting can be covered with plastic wrap and set aside at room temperature for several hours. Once assembled, the cake should be covered with an inverted bowl or cake cover and refrigerated. Under its coat of frosting, it will remain fresh for two to three days. Bring it to room temperature before serving. There is enough frosting to pipe a border around the base and top of the cake. If you want to decorate the cake more elaborately, you should make one and a half times the frosting recipe. You may also substitute lemon curd for the raspberry jam in the filling.

Classic White Cake

    2 tablespoons solid vegetable shortening
    2 heaping tablespoons all-purpose flour
       for flouring pans
    1 cup milk, at room temperature
    ¾ cup egg whites (about 6 large or
       5 extra large) at room temperature
    2 teaspoons almond extract
    1 teaspoon vanilla extract
    2¼ cups plain cake flour
    1¾ cups sugar
    4 teaspoons baking powder
    1 teaspoon salt
    12 tablespoons unsalted butter, softened

Butter Frosting

    ½ pound (2 sticks) unsalted butter,
       softened
    1 pound (4 cups) confectioners' sugar
    1 tablespoon vanilla extract
    1 tablespoon milk
       Pinch salt

Raspberry-Almond Filling

    ½ cup (2½ ounces) blanched slivered
       almonds, toasted and chopped coarse
    ⅓ cup seedless raspberry jam

1. *For the cake:* Set oven rack in middle position. (If oven is too small to cook both layers on a single rack, set racks in upper-middle and lower-middle positions.) Heat oven to 350 degrees. Coat bottom and sides of two 9-inch-by-1½-inch or -2-inch round cake pans with 1 tablespoon shortening each. Sprinkle 1 heaping tablespoon of all-purpose flour into each pan; roll pans in all directions to coat. Invert pans and rap sharply to remove excess flour.

2. Pour milk, egg whites, and extracts into 2-cup glass measure, and mix with fork until blended.

3. Mix cake flour, sugar, baking powder, and salt in bowl of electric mixer at slow speed. Add butter; continue beating at slow speed until mixture resembles moist crumbs, with no powdery ingredients remaining.

4. Add all but ½ cup of milk mixture to crumbs and beat at medium speed (or high speed if using handheld mixer) for 1½ minutes. Add remaining ½ cup of milk mixture and beat 30 seconds more. Stop mixer and scrape sides of bowl. Return mixer to medium (or high) speed and beat 20 seconds longer.

5. Divide batter evenly between two prepared cake pans; using rubber spatula, spread batter to pan walls and smooth tops. Arrange pans at least 3 inches from the oven walls and 3 inches apart. (If oven is small, place pans on separate racks in staggered fashion to allow for air circulation.) Bake until cake needle or toothpick inserted in the center comes out clean, 23 to 25 minutes.

6. Let cakes rest in pans for 3 minutes. Loosen from sides of pans with a knife, if necessary, and invert onto greased cake racks. Reinvert onto additional greased racks. Let cool completely, about 1½ hours.

7. *For the frosting:* Beat butter, confectioners' sugar, vanilla, milk, and salt in bowl of electric mixer at slow speed until sugar is moistened. Increase speed to medium (high if using handheld mixer); beat, stopping twice to scrape down bowl, until creamy and fluffy, about 1½ minutes. Avoid overbeating, or frosting will be too soft to pipe.

8. *For the filling:* Before assembling cake, set aside ¾ cup of the frosting for decoration. Spread small dab of frosting in center of cake plate to anchor cake, and set down one cake layer. Combine ½ cup of remaining frosting with almonds in small bowl and spread over first layer. Carefully spread jam on top, then cover with second cake layer. Spread frosting over top and sides of assembled cake. Pipe reserved frosting around perimeter of cake. (*See* pages 16 and 17 for decorating ideas.) ∎

Stephen Schmidt is the author of *Master Recipes* (Ballantine, 1987.)

CAKE BAKING 101

Over the years, nonbaking friends (some of whom literally use their ovens as sweater cupboards) have asked me for surefire recipes for birthday cake. I have given them recipes that I thought simply could not fail, and—guess what—they failed, often stupendously. Here's how you can avoid their mistakes:

Check your oven temperature with an oven thermometer, available at any hardware or kitchenware store. If your oven is too hot, the sides of the cake will set before the middle does, and the cake will hump or even crack. If your oven is too cold, the air will escape from the air cells in the batter before the batter begins to "set," and the cake will have a coarse texture and may even fall.

Use round cake pans measuring nine inches across and one and one-half or two inches deep. If your pans are too large, they overheat the rim of the cake, causing the same sorts of problems that an overheated oven does. I don't have to tell you what happens if your pans are too small. The pans should have absolutely vertical sides and be made of sturdy aluminum. Disposable foil pans make burnt frisbees, not cakes.

Grease the pans with shortening—not butter—and grease and flour them generously. Butter is largely protein solids and water. As it melts it may leave greaseless gaps to which your cake can stick. Do not be afraid to slather on the shortening; you will end up eating practically none of it. Flour is necessary to hold the shortening in place as the pan heats and melts the fat. Without the flour, the batter is likely to get through the layer of melted shortening and adhere to the pan.

Use cake flour. All-purpose flour contains too much protein and too little starch for white cake. It will yield a tough, low-lying final result. I know cake flour can be hard to find, but some store in your area is sure to have it. It comes in a box and is often passed over because it looks like a cake mix. Buy the plain kind, not self-rising, which has leavening and salt added. Many cookbooks suggest substitutes for cake flour, but they don't really work.

Have all the ingredients, especially the butter, at room temperature. Ice-cold ingredients do not emulsify well, which leads to a dense cake, and cold butter, of course, will not mix into the batter at all. On the other hand, the ingredients should not be warm, or the air cells in the butter will simply dissolve. An instant-read thermometer makes cake baking a breeze. Everything should register between sixty-five and seventy-five degrees.

Measure the flour correctly. My recipe is based upon the dip-and-sweep method. Empty the flour into a container, then shake the container to settle the flour. Dip in a cup made for dry measures, scoop out a heaping cupful, and level the top with a straight edge. Do not shake, tap, or pack the cup. If the cup is not completely filled on the first try, dump the contents back into the container, give the container a shake to resettle it, and try again.

Use fresh baking powder. As soon as a can of baking powder is opened, the acid and alkali components begin to react. There is significant deterioration within a few months, so when you open the can, write the date on it. When the baking powder is three months old, throw it out.

When arranging the cake layers in the oven, be sure to place the pans at least three inches apart and three inches away from the oven walls. Cakes placed too close to one another will rise toward each other and will end up lopsided. Cakes placed too close to the oven walls won't rise as high—sometimes they will rise quite a lot less—on the side nearest the wall. Both phenomena have the same cause. The part of the cake exposed to the most heat will set first, and thus will rise less than a cooler part. Cakes placed close to each other insulate one another from heat where they're closest and thus rise more there. Cakes set close to the oven walls become overheated on that side and thus rise less there.

Perfect Pork Roast

Roast, rest, and roast again is the formula for a pork roast that is juicy and succulently tender.

~ BY STEPHEN SCHMIDT ~

The ideal method requires allowing the roast to rest on the counter between sessions in the oven.

Twenty years ago pork was very fatty, so most authorities recommended roasting the meat to an internal temperature of 180 degrees to render out the fat. Unfortunately, this also had the effect of making the roast stringy and dry. In the last fifteen years, as pigs have been bred ever leaner, I and many other cooks have adopted much lower doneness temperatures. While this lighter cooking prevents stringiness, it does not ensure perfection—you can have a non-stringy piece of pork that is still dry as a bone.

The cooking of meat might be compared to the wringing of a wet towel. When the internal temperature of meat rises beyond 130 degrees, or "medium rare," its protein strands begin to link together to form a sort of helter-skelter web, a process that is called "coagulation." As the temperature increases still further, the strands shrink and bind together ever more tightly. As this process continues, the meat hardens, and fat and juice are squeezed out like water being wrung from a towel. In the case of most meats—for example, turkey or chicken breast and, to a lesser extent, veal—serious hardening and drying do not occur until the internal temperature surpasses 160 degrees, or "well done."

Pork, however, is different. Even when removed from the oven at an internal temperature of as low as 140 degrees, pork roasts feel decidedly hard to the touch. As the meat rests prior to carving, during which time its internal temperature

rises another 10 degrees or so, it becomes harder still. Anyone who has cooked a pork roast has witnessed the dire consequence of this process: All of the wonderful juices that should be inside the meat are instead squeezed out onto the platter.

Armed with this knowledge, I embarked on a search for the perfect pork-roasting method. I was aware at the outset that doneness temperature was not the only factor to be considered. The trick had to lie in bringing the pork to doneness in some special manner that prevented the unfortunate hardening and the ensuing loss of juice.

Searching for the Ideal Technique

In my first series of experiments, I focused on the effectiveness of various standard roasting procedures for pork center loin (*see* "What Is the Pork Center Loin?" page 21). Before trying anything else, I wanted to compare the results of covered roasting at a moderately low temperature (325 degrees) and uncovered roasting at a relatively high temperature (400 degrees). I used to swear by the former procedure, but over the years I had begun to suspect that the latter method produced substantially the same results.

My experiments confirmed my impressions. Taken out of the oven at an internal temperature of 145 degrees and allowed to rise to a temperature of around 155 degrees during a fifteen-minute rest, both roasts exuded a good deal of juice as they rested, and still more when they were carved. They both made acceptable eating, but the texture was not ideal. The meat was hard and a little dry, and it seemed to squeak against my teeth when chewed.

In three subsequent tests, I tried roasting at a very low temperature, around 200 degrees, which I hoped might produce a soft, moist roast. Unfortunately, it did not. I prepared one roast covered in a heavy casserole, another uncovered in a roasting pan, and a third under a two-inch-thick shell of moistened kosher salt, as some people like to do when roasting beef. Cooked to 145 degrees and allowed a fifteen-minute rest, all three roasts came out much the same as the first two roasts I had made: harder and drier than ideal.

I finally resorted to trying a yogurt-based mari-

nade, but it seemed to have virtually no effect even though I let the roast sit in it for a full three days. I had no more tricks up my sleeve—except one. Six years ago I had clipped a recipe that intrigued me but seemed just a little too odd to work. It involved roasting the pork at 475 degrees for thirty minutes, letting it rest for thirty minutes outside the oven, and then roasting it a second time at 325 degrees for twenty to twenty-five minutes, or until it reached an internal temperature of 137 degrees, the temperature at which the trichina parasite, in the highly unlikely event it should be present, is killed.

I followed the recipe as written, and the results were perfect. Instead of having a hard, squeaky mouth-feel, the meat was soft, succulent, and almost gelatinous, like a first-rate veal chop. Even more surprising, the roast had leaked no more than a tablespoon of juice during its rest, leaving the meat extremely moist.

The Mystery Explained

Next I tested the procedure using bone-in roasts. Because bone-in cuts always take longer to cook than boneless ones, I extended the initial high-heat cooking of the first roast from 30 to 40 minutes. Twenty minutes into its second roasting, this piece of meat registered 160 degrees so I yanked it out of the oven. As I had feared, it was overcooked. In preparing the second roast, I did not, of course, extend the initial cooking time. Unfortunately, neither did I improve on my results. To my complete amazement, this roast also registered 160 degrees twenty minutes into its second roasting. I pulled it out of the oven, let it rest, then carved it. In most sections, it was overcooked, but in some parts, particularly around the bones, it was virtually raw!

Deciding that the bones were the cause of all my woes, I boned the last of the three roasts. This time I took the temperature of the roast just ten minutes into its second cooking. It already registered close to 150 degrees, so I took the meat out. This roast was a little juicier than the first two, but it was still overdone. More surprising, it simply did not have the same soft, succulent quality as the roast I had made using my ideal method. Instead it was firm—and squeaky—in the manner of pork roasts cooked by conventional methods.

At this point I sought the counsel of food scientist Shirley Corriher. I had been working under the assumption that the purpose of double cooking is somehow to "shock" the meat, but Corriher was convinced that the method works on a much more basic principle. During the initial high-temperature roasting, she said, the outside of the meat absorbs a great deal of heat. When the roast is first taken out of the oven, the center is still virtually raw, but it undergoes considerable cooking during the thirty-minute rest as the heat stored in the outside penetrates the interior portions by conduction. However, the heat absorbed by the outside of the roast is not quite sufficient to fully cook the middle, so the roast has to be cooked a second time. This second cooking is conducted at a lower temperature so the outer portions of the roast do not get overdone. During the second roasting and precarving rest, the heat keeps flowing toward the center, finishing the cooking. Corriher explained further that heating the roast gently by conduction allows the proteins to hook together loosely, which keeps the meat soft and prevents juice from being squeezed out.

To me, this makes perfect sense. Most cooks agree that nearly all protein-based foods—meats, fish, eggs, milk, and cheese—are at their tender best when removed from the oven before they are fully cooked. This is because, once taken from the heat source, these foods continue to cook by the pure conduction of "stored heat." While foods on the stove or in an oven cook by a combination of heat types (including conduction, convection, and radiation), conduction, Corriher pointed out, is the gentlest type of heat. It promotes the loosest linking of the meat proteins, making for the tenderest texture and the least juice loss. Since much of the cooking of my ideal pork roast took place by pure conduction, the final results were quite logical.

Corriher put her finger on something else I had been doing wrong. When I cooked the successful roast, I had correctly taken the meat directly from the refrigerator to the oven. And, because the center of the meat was very cold, it never reached a temperature at which juice loss becomes serious (around 135 degrees) during the initial high-heat roasting. On the other hand, during my round of tests with the bone-in meat, in order to encourage the flavor of the seasonings to penetrate, I had let all three roasts stand at room temperature for several hours before putting them into the oven. Having higher-temperature meat to begin with resulted in the pork cooking through to the center during the initial high-heat roasting. Thus, the proteins linked tightly, toughening and drying the meat. The second cooking only made a bad situation worse.

Armed with Corriher's insights, I cooked two more boneless roasts. In both cases I took the meat directly from the refrigerator (the internal temperature was around 40 degrees) to the oven. The first roast I cooked for exactly thirty minutes at 475 degrees and allowed to rest for exactly thirty minutes. Its temperature when removed from the oven was 110 degrees, and while resting its temperature soared to 135 degrees. I then roasted it at 325 degrees for twenty minutes, whereupon it reached an internal temperature of 150 degrees, which rose to 160 degrees after a fifteen-minute rest.

This roast was much like the first successful one I had cooked, which is to say, excellent.

WHAT IS THE PORK CENTER LOIN?

The pork center loin runs along one side of the backbone from the hip bone to the (shoulder) blade bone. It comprises the center loin muscle plus, at the blade end, small parts of various shoulder muscles, which are redder and more fibrous than the loin muscle itself.

The part of the center loin that lies closest to the shoulder—about two-thirds of the total—consists of rib chops; the remainder of the center loin is made up of loin chops. Although the tenderloin is not, properly speaking, a part of this cut, it is sometimes left attached to bone-in loins.

The entire pork center loin weighs between ten and a half and twelve and a half pounds bone-in and five and a half to seven and a half pounds boned. With the bone left in, it is often labeled "pork center roast" at supermarkets; a boneless roast may be called a "boneless pork roast center."

Do not buy "rib end" or "loin end" pork roasts. These are cut just beyond the center loin, from the blade and hip ends, respectively. Both of them have many bones and muscle separations, and the meat can be chewy.

LOIN END

RIB END

← PORK CENTER LOIN →

TYING THE ROAST

1. Take a piece of twine about four times the length of the roast and knot it around one end of the roast. Then make a "lasso" by forming the fingers of one hand into a circle and running the twine around them.

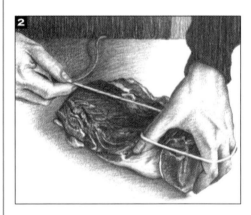

2. Widen the lasso just enough to slip it around the roast.

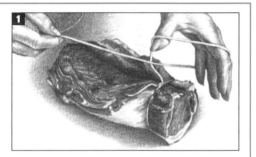

3. Pull the loop tight several inches down the roast from the first loop, then straighten the twine that now encircles the roast.

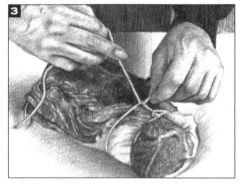

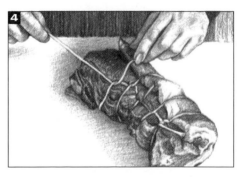

4. Continue this process until the entire roast has been firmly tied.

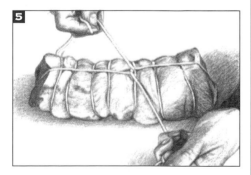

5. Turn the roast over, run another length of twine from end to end, and tie firmly.

However, I would have liked it just a little less done. Thus, I was prepared to give the second roast a much briefer second cooking. But this roast proved to be a little thicker and heavier than the first, and it reached an internal temperature of only 95 degrees after the initial high-heat roasting and 115 degrees after its thirty-minute first rest. It then required nearly thirty minutes to reach a temperature of 145 degrees during its second low-temperature roasting, and it rose to only 155 degrees during its rest before carving. This one was a little pink—which I don't mind at all—and absolutely perfect.

This last set of experiments taught me a very valuable lesson. The length of time of the second roasting can vary considerably depending on even slight size differences in the roast, and even a few minutes too long in the oven can significantly affect the results.

GARLIC-STUDDED ROAST PORK LOIN
Serves 4 to 6

A thin, flat pork loin roast will overcook. To avoid this overcooking, tie the roast yourself following the illustrations on page 21, or have the butcher perform the task for you.

    2   teaspoons dried thyme
    ¼   teaspoon ground cloves or allspice
    2   teaspoons salt
    1   teaspoon ground black pepper
    2   large garlic cloves, peeled and cut
        into slivers
    1   boneless center loin pork roast (about
        2¼ pounds), fat trimmed to about
        ⅛-inch thick; roast tied with heavy
        twine into tight cylinder and dried
        with paper towel

1. Mix thyme, cloves or allspice, salt, and pepper. Coat garlic slivers in spice mixture. Poke slits in roast with point of paring knife; insert garlic slivers. Rub remaining spice mixture onto meat. Wrap roast in foil; refrigerate 2 to 24 hours (can be refrigerated up to three days).

2. Adjust oven rack to center position and heat to 475 degrees. Take meat directly from refrigerator and place on cake rack set in shallow roasting pan. Roast exactly 30 minutes.

3. Remove meat from oven; immediately reduce oven temperature to 325 degrees. Insert instant-read meat thermometer at one end of roast, going into thickest part of the center (temperature will range from 80 to 110 degrees); let roast rest at room temperature, uncovered, for exactly 30 minutes. (At this point roast's internal temperature will range from 115 to 140 degrees.) After this 30-minute rest, remove meat thermometer, return meat to oven, and roast until meat thermometer inserted in thickest part of roast reaches an internal temperature of 145 degrees, 15 to 30 minutes longer, depending on roast's internal temperature at end of resting period. Since roast may cook unevenly, take temperature readings from a couple of locations, each time plunging thermometer to center of meat and waiting 15 seconds.

4. Let roast stand at room temperature, uncovered, for 15 to 20 minutes to finish cooking. (The temperature should register between 150 and 155 degrees.) Slice meat thin and serve with one of the sauces that follow.

RED PEPPER–BASIL SAUCE WITH BALSAMIC VINEGAR
Makes about 1 cup

    1½ tablespoons olive oil
    1   small onion, chopped
    1   large red pepper, cored, seeded, and
        chopped
    ½   cup chicken stock or low-salt canned
        chicken broth
    1   medium garlic clove, minced
    ¼   cup finely shredded fresh basil leaves
    1–2 teaspoons balsamic vinegar
        Salt and ground black pepper

Heat oil in small saucepan over medium heat. Add onion; sauté until softened, about 3 minutes.

Reduce heat to low. Add red pepper; cover and cook, stirring frequently, until very tender, 15 to 20 minutes. Transfer mixture to food processor fitted with steel blade. Add stock; process until pureed. Return mixture to saucepan. Add garlic; simmer to blend flavors, adding a little water if sauce is too thick, about 5 minutes. Stir in basil and season with balsamic vinegar and salt and pepper to taste.

COUNTRY MUSTARD-SHALLOT SAUCE WITH THYME
Makes about 1 cup

    2   tablespoons unsalted butter
    4   medium shallots, minced
    ¾   cup dry white wine or dry vermouth
    1   cup chicken stock or low-salt
        canned chicken broth
    ¾   teaspoon minced fresh thyme leaves, or
        ¼ teaspoon dried thyme, crumbled
    ¼   cup whole-seed ("country-style")
        prepared mustard
    1–2 tablespoons unsalted butter, softened
        (optional)

Heat butter in medium skillet over medium-high heat until foam subsides. Add shallots; sauté until softened, 3 to 4 minutes. Add wine; boil until nearly evaporated, 8 to 10 minutes. Add stock and thyme; boil until reduced by a third, about 5 minutes. Remove pan from heat and stir in mustard, then optional butter.

TOMATO-ROSEMARY CREAM SAUCE
Makes about 1 cup

If serving the roast pork loin with this sauce, substitute two teaspoons dried rosemary, pulverized, or two tablespoons, minced fresh rosemary for the thyme in the spice rub.

    1   tablespoon olive oil
    2   medium shallots, minced
    1   large tomato, peeled, seeded, and
        chopped
    3   tablespoons dry white wine or dry
        vermouth
    ½   cup chicken stock or low-salt canned
        chicken broth
    ¼   cup heavy cream
    ½   teaspoon minced fresh rosemary, or
        heaping ¼ teaspoon dried rosemary,
        pulverized
        Salt and ground black pepper

Heat oil in medium saucepan over medium-high heat. Add shallots; sauté until softened, 3 to 4 minutes. Add tomato; cook until softened and rendered of most of its juice, about 5 minutes. Add wine; cook until wine and tomato juice completely evaporate. Add stock, cream, and rosemary; continue to boil until sauce is reduced by half and lightly thickened, about 5 minutes. Season to taste with salt and pepper. ∎

Stephen Schmidt is the author of *Master Recipes* (Ballantine, 1987)

COOKING BONE-IN ROASTS

Bone-in roasts require a considerably longer cooking time than boneless ones. Unfortunately, much of this cooking must be done in the oven, by direct heat, rather than on the counter, by conduction. Thus, bone-in roasts become firmer than boneless roasts and leak more juice. The flavor of the roast as a whole is not improved by cooking the meat on the bone. I would always opt for a boneless roast.

If you want to cook a bone-in roast, choose a rib section piece weighing about four pounds or a loin section piece weighing three and a half pounds. (If the tenderloin is attached to the loin section roast, the purchase weight should be around four pounds. But remove the tenderloin before roasting, as it tends not to cook through.)

You will also need to make a few changes in the master recipe if you're working with a bone-in roast. Extend both the initial high-heat roast and the first rest from thirty to thirty-five minutes. You will note that the internal temperature after the first roasting will be about 75 degrees—or twenty to thirty degrees lower than is typical when using this same method with boneless roasts—but it will shoot up to nearly 120 degrees during resting due to all the heat stored in the bones. During its second, low-heat roasting, bring the pork to an internal temperature of 145 degrees, which will take forty to fifty minutes. Let the meat rest for twenty minutes, during which time the temperature will rise to around 155 degrees, and then carve.

Spring Vegetable Salads

Flavorful salads feature spring's tender young vegetables.

~ BY DEBORAH MADISON ~

Vegetables make good salads virtually any time of year but are perhaps especially welcome in spring, when new shoots and stalks finally begin to appear. Leeks, fennel, the first sweet and mild garlic, asparagus, and greens such as dandelions and arugula come on well ahead of summer's tomatoes and cucumbers.

ASPARAGUS VINAIGRETTE WITH SIEVED EGG AND PICKLED PINK ONIONS
Serves 6

The pink onions and sieved egg make this salad utterly springlike in appearance. You only need a quarter cup or so of the pickled onions, but the leftovers are great in salads or sandwiches.

Salt and ground black pepper
½ teaspoon sugar
½ cup white wine vinegar plus
   1 tablespoon for vinaigrette
1 small red onion, sliced thin and
   separated into rings
⅓ cup minced fresh Italian parsley leaves
2 teaspoons minced fresh tarragon leaves
1 tablespoon drained capers
1 strip zest and 1 tablespoon juice from a
   small orange; zest sliced thin and
   blanched 10 seconds, then minced
½ teaspoon Dijon-style mustard
¼ cup olive oil
1½ pounds fresh asparagus, rinsed and ends
   snapped
1 hard-boiled egg, peeled, white diced
   fine, yolk left whole for sieving

1. Mix ½ teaspoon salt, ¼ teaspoon pepper, sugar, and ½ cup vinegar in nonreactive bowl. Put onion slices in colander in sink; pour boiling water over them. Add warm onions to vinegar mixture with enough cold water to cover. Let stand until onions are pink, about 15 minutes. Set aside.

2. Put parsley, tarragon, capers, and orange zest in small bowl with pinch of salt; stir in juice and 1 tablespoon vinegar. Whisk in mustard, then slowly whisk in oil. Adjust seasonings and set aside.

3. Bring 1 inch water to boil in soup kettle. Put asparagus in steamer basket, then carefully place basket in kettle. Cover and steam over medium-high heat until asparagus spears bend slightly when picked up, 4 to 5 minutes. Transfer asparagus to clean kitchen towel to dry.

4. Arrange asparagus on platter. Spoon vinaigrette over it. Lift ¼ cup or so of onion rings from liquid and scatter over asparagus. Sprinkle diced egg white over asparagus, then push yolk through sieve so that it falls evenly over salad. Serve.

FENNEL AND OLIVE SALAD WITH CREAMY TARRAGON VINAIGRETTE
Serves 4

For a more filling salad, serve with thin garlic croutons spread with tapenade and topped with finely diced hard-boiled egg.

1 tablespoon crème fraîche or sour cream
2 tablespoons olive oil
1 tablespoon lemon juice and
   1½ teaspoons minced lemon zest
   from a small lemon
1 tablespoon minced fresh parsley leaves
2 small fennel bulbs (about 4 ounces
   each), stalks and fronds removed;
   2 teaspoons fronds, minced and
   reserved; bulbs trimmed, halved, and
   sliced thin crosswise
Salt and ground black pepper
2 cups frisée leaves, arugula, or mixed
   small salad greens, rinsed and dried
Niçoise olives, for garnish

1. Whisk crème fraîche, oil, and juice together in medium-size bowl. Add lemon zest, parsley, reserved minced fennel fronds, and salt and pepper to taste. Toss with sliced fennel bulb. (Can be covered and refrigerated up to 2 hours.)

2. Arrange salad greens on plate. Mound fennel salad on top of greens, garnish with olives, and serve.

ARUGULA SALAD WITH GARLIC CROUTONS, GRUYÈRE, AND HARD-BOILED EGGS
Serves 4

Dandelion greens, also available in early spring, can be substituted for the arugula in this recipe.

2 thin slices cut from large round loaf of
   sourdough bread
7 tablespoons olive oil
1 large garlic clove
   Salt
1½ tablespoons sherry vinegar
1 large shallot, minced
½ pound arugula, stemmed, washed
   thoroughly, and dried (about 6 cups)
   Ground black pepper
2 hard-boiled eggs, peeled and quartered
12 thin shavings of Gruyère cheese

1. Adjust oven rack to highest position and heat broiler. Brush bread with about 2 tablespoons of the oil; broil bread, turning once, until toasted on both sides. Rub toasted bread with garlic, then break each piece into large pieces to make croutons.

2. Mash the same garlic clove with ¼ teaspoon salt in small bowl until smooth; whisk in vinegar, then remaining oil, and finally shallots.

3. Heat this vinaigrette in small saucepan until hot. Pour hot dressing over greens in large serving bowl; toss lightly to coat. Add croutons and plenty of pepper; toss again. Arrange egg quarters and cheese shavings over greens and serve immediately.

BROCCOFLOWER AND CELERY SALAD
Serves 6 to 8

Cauliflower can be very nice in spring and may be substituted for the broccoflower in this recipe.

1 medium garlic clove
   Salt and ground black pepper
1 hard-boiled egg, peeled, yolk left
   whole, white cut into small dice
3 tablespoons sherry vinegar
6 tablespoons olive oil
1 small head broccoflower (about
   2 pounds), cut into small florets, stalk
   sliced thin
2 cups stemmed watercress, chopped
   coarse
3 small scallions, sliced thin
1 cup celery heart and leaves, cut into
   small dice
1 small green bell pepper, cut into small
   dice
12 pimiento-stuffed green olives, halved
1 tablespoon drained capers
½ cup whole fresh Italian parsley leaves

1. In small bowl, mash garlic clove with ¾ teaspoon salt, ¼ teaspoon pepper, and egg yolk until smooth. Stir in vinegar, then whisk in oil. Dressing should be a little on the tart side.

2. In a large serving bowl, toss broccoflower with remaining ingredients, including egg white; add salt and pepper to taste. Add vinaigrette and toss again. Adjust seasonings and serve.

Deborah Madison is the author of several cookbooks, including *The Savory Way* (Bantam, 1990) and *The Greens Cookbook* (Bantam, 1986). ∎

The Virtues of Bread Crumbs

For crispy bread crumbs that add flavor and texture, cut stale bakery French bread into pieces the size of black beans and bake in a 325-degree oven.

∼ BY GAYLE PIRIE AND JOHN CLARK ∼

Small bread crumbs have a texture like sawdust and contribute only bulk, but larger ones add a satisfying crunch.

Crisp, browned, homemade bread crumbs have many more culinary uses than simply adding filler to meat loaves or providing a coating. They can dress up a tossed salad, provide texture to creamy scrambled eggs, enrich pastas, and delicately enhance vegetables that need a little crunch.

To discover the best way to make bread crumbs, we searched for the correct bread, the best cooking method, the ideal oven temperature, and the right fat to cook in.

After testing fifteen types of bread, we found that supermarket wheat, white, multigrain, nut, and rye breads are not suitable for making crumbs. The biggest problem with these sandwich breads is that they are highly refined. In addition to having a "processed" taste, this also means that they have a high sugar content. This added sugar is considered a virtue by marketers, since it retards the development of gluten, keeping the bread soft and tender for days. But it is a vice when making bread crumbs. By the time these loaves get stale enough to make into crumbs, all you can really make from them is a fine powder that dissolves quickly on your tongue, the opposite effect of what you want.

We found that the best crumb is made from a good quality bread that has no strong flavor. Leftover sweet or sourdough French baguette bread from your local bakery will give you the best tasting, crispest bread crumbs.

Part of the beauty of using stale French bread is that you may not have to go to a store looking for it; you're likely to already have some in your pantry ready to use. Bread that is two to three days old is ideal for making bread crumbs because it has become quite firm but still retains *some* moisture, which is important in controlling the size of the crumbs. Bread that is four days old or older will be so dry that it will be pulverized by the cutting blades, yielding an unusable "powder" instead of individual crumbs. Bread that is one day old or less, on the other hand, will probably need to be dried in an oven before it can be made into crumbs.

When you make crumbs at home, you want them irregular and coarse, roughly the size of dried black beans, so they contribute texture as well as richness to your food. You can also vary the size of bread crumbs for each dish, letting the specific food for which you are using them be your guide. Remember, though, that when bread crumbs are too fine, with the sawdustlike texture of manufactured crumbs, they will contribute nothing to your gratin or sautéed vegetables except bulk and an insipid texture.

There are several ways to create crumbs (*see* "Three Easy Ways to Make Bread Crumbs," page 25). When using a food processor, which is the fastest and easiest way, it is important to monitor crumb size closely. Coarse crumbs, the size of dried black beans, are made in twenty to forty-five seconds, depending on the type and age of the bread. Generally, the older the bread, the longer it takes to turn it into crumbs. But again, be careful; crumbs that are overprocessed will be too fine.

After testing various cooking methods, we found using an oven was the clear winner for ease and consistency. Microwaving is absolutely out of the question because the crumbs never brown; they simply dry out. Crumbs can be sautéed, but this requires more attention than using an oven and is more likely to result in burned crumbs.

For oven browning, we tested various temperatures and cooking times. We found that baking in a standard 325-degree oven for twelve minutes proved the most successful method. At 275 degrees, the crumbs took twice as long to bake and were desiccated and hard, as opposed to baked and crisp; they were also pale and visually unappealing. In a 350-degree oven, the crumbs cooked quickly but very unevenly. Despite cautious stirring while baking, the smaller crumbs burned.

We prepared bread crumbs with olive oil, butter, margarine, vegetable oil, safflower oil, and peanut oil to see which fat worked best. Margarine and vegetable and safflower oils resulted in heavy, greasy crumbs. Good-quality olive oils and butter gave us the best results. Peanut oil turned out to be a fine substitute if butter or olive oil is not part of your diet.

The delicate flavors of extra virgin olive oils are often lost when baked with the crumbs; in fact, the high heat of baking can change them to a bitter flavor. Due to both this and the high cost, you're better off to save extra virgin olive oil for dishes in which its flavors can be detected. For overall great flavor, we recommend you use a good-quality olive oil or butter. In general, butter will give the crumbs a richer flavor while olive or peanut oil will contribute a much lighter flavor.

FREEZING BREAD CRUMBS

Our grandmother kept a bag of bread crumbs in the freezer at all times so she could pull them out to add crunch to dishes. This seemed so convenient that we decided to investigate it. We found that, while crumbs are best if used fresh, they can be frozen and stored for over a month if you seal them tightly in a plastic bag or some other airtight container so they don't pick up moisture or unwanted flavors from the freezer. When we tasted bread crumbs after two months in the freezer, we found they had lost their flavor. So we recommend that if you want to store crumbs in the freezer, you do so for no longer than a month to ensure they still have their flavor.

PHOTOGRAPH BY ERIC ROTH

Choose the one that best suits the dish you're making.

The last key to perfect bread crumbs is not to bake them too far ahead of time. They are best right out of the oven but can be held for an hour or so in a 200-degree oven until you're ready to sprinkle them over your favorite dish. Just don't try to store them on the shelf in a plastic bag.

MASTER RECIPE FOR TOASTED BREAD CRUMBS
Makes 1 cup (4 to 6 servings)

If you're serving a complex dish like a saucy meat or vegetable pasta or an elaborately filled omelette, this basic recipe is the one to use. When your dish needs flavor as well as texture, consider one of the variations that follow this recipe.

 1 cup fresh bread crumbs, coarse or medium (*see* illustrations for techniques)
 1½ tablespoons olive oil or melted butter
 ¼ teaspoon kosher salt or pinch of table salt

Adjust oven rack to center-low position and heat oven to 325 degrees. Mix bread crumbs with oil and salt to coat evenly. Spread in single layer on small baking sheet. Bake crumbs, stirring once after 5 minutes, until golden brown, about 12 minutes. Sprinkle warm crumbs over finished dish, allowing 2 to 3 tablespoons per person.

TOASTED BREAD CRUMBS WITH MARJORAM, THYME, AND LEMON ZEST

Follow Master Recipe for Toasted Bread Crumbs, stirring ½ teaspoon minced lemon zest, ½ teaspoon minced fresh thyme leaves, and ¼ teaspoon minced fresh marjoram leaves into toasted bread crumbs as they come out of oven. These are particularly nice with steamed or poached fish.

TOASTED BREAD CRUMBS WITH RED PEPPER FLAKES AND GARLIC

Follow Master Recipe for Toasted Bread Crumbs, stirring ¼ teaspoon hot red pepper flakes and ¼ teaspoon minced fresh garlic into bread crumbs as they come out of oven. Top sautéed vegetables or grilled meat with these spicy bread crumbs.

TOASTED BREAD CRUMBS WITH WHITE WINE AND BUTTER

Follow Master Recipe for Toasted Bread Crumbs, using melted butter rather than olive oil, and adding 2 tablespoons white wine with the butter and salt. Bake until crumbs are golden brown, about 4 minutes longer than in Master Recipe. Serve with steamed clams or braised fish.

TOASTED BREAD CRUMBS WITH CRACKED BLACK PEPPER

Follow Master Recipe for Toasted Bread Crumbs, adding ½ teaspoon of coarsely ground black pepper with the olive oil and salt. While these bread crumbs have a deep, black pepper taste, the baking softens the "heat" of the peppercorn flavor.

ILLUSTRATIONS BY NENAD JAKESEVIC

THREE EASY WAYS TO MAKE BREAD CRUMBS

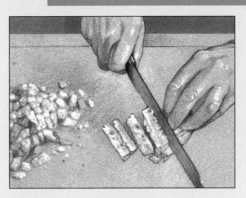

BY HAND

To make bread crumbs by hand, use a sharp bread knife to slice the bread ⅜-inch thick. Cut these slices into ⅜-inch strips, or *batons*, then cut these into cubes and chop the crumbs to the desired size.

GRATER

Though they will be finer textured, bread crumbs can be made with a box grater. Simply rub the firm bread against the largest holes of the grater.

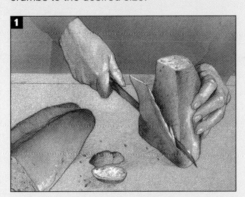

FOOD PROCESSOR

1. Slice off and discard the tough and often overbaked bottom crust.

2. Cut the trimmed loaf into 1½-inch cubes, then pulse the cubes in a food processor to the desired crumb size.

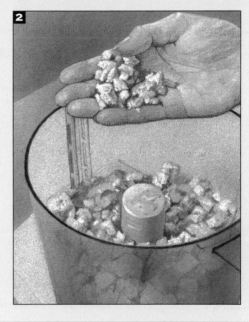

SPAGHETTI WITH FENNEL AND BREAD CRUMBS
Serves 6

 ¼ cup olive oil
 3 medium onions, sliced thin
 3 medium garlic cloves, finely chopped
 2 medium fennel bulbs, sliced thin
 2 tablespoons minced fresh oregano leaves or 2 teaspoons dried oregano
 ½ teaspoon hot red pepper flakes
 Salt
 1 pound spaghetti
 1 recipe Toasted Bread Crumbs (*see* above)
 Parmesan cheese (optional)

1. Heat oil in a large sauté pan over medium heat. Add onions and sauté until softened, about 5 minutes. Add garlic, fennel, oregano, pepper flakes, and salt to taste. Continue to cook over medium heat until fennel softens, 5 to 7 minutes longer.

2. Meanwhile, bring 1 gallon water to boil in large soup kettle. Add 1 tablespoon salt and spaghetti. Cook until spaghetti is al dente, 7 to 9 minutes. Drain, reserving ¼ cup of cooking water. Return spaghetti to kettle.

3. Add fennel mixture to spaghetti; toss to combine, adding enough reserved water to keep mixture moist. Adjust seasoning. Transfer portion of spaghetti to each of six pasta bowls. Sprinkle each with portion of toasted bread crumbs and top with Parmesan cheese, if desired. Serve immediately. ∎

John Clark and Gayle Pirie are San Francisco–based chefs and international restaurant consultants currently writing a cookbook on eggs.

Rating Vanilla Extracts

An all-star tasting panel found little difference between imitation vanilla and the most expensive brand. Does quality really make a difference?

⌁ BY JACK BISHOP ⌁

The reason that we do blind tastings at *Cook's Illustrated* is so we can provide you with recommendations based on our own personal experiences, rather than on what "everybody says." Sometimes the results confirm common wisdom, and sometimes, as in this tasting, they fly in the face of our expectations.

Most of us are dedicated fans of expensive, deliciously aromatic vanillas. But when the test results were in, it turned out that the differences among vanilla extracts disappeared during cooking. We found this so surprising that we ran a second blind testing—and came up with the same result.

In every food tasting we do, our first step is to taste the products by themselves. We almost always find a broad range of quality among samples tested; this held true when we tasted eleven vanilla extracts "as is."

But when testing ingredients such as extracts, which are not meant to be consumed alone, we also hold a second round of testing in which we use each sample to bake or cook something, then taste the resulting food. Ordinarily, we find a similar range of quality in this test as well. For instance, chocolates that were favored in a plain tasting (*see* November/December 1994 issue) made considerably better cakes than chocolates that rated poorly in the plain tasting. But when we ran the second-round test with vanilla, the results were a shock—it made little or no difference which vanilla was used.

A Surprising Dual Tasting

The first question we faced when organizing the tasting was how to taste the extracts. Since they are so potent (by law, the alcohol content of vanilla extract must be at least 35 percent), it is difficult to appreciate their differences when they are sampled alone. We asked industry experts and found that they usually sample vanilla by mixing it into milk to see how a particular batch might perform in ice cream, the leading commercial use for extract.

This seemed like a good way for our panel of baking experts to evaluate the leading supermarket and gourmet brands, so we followed suit. Our tasters were easily able to pick out superior brands when the extracts were diluted in eight parts milk to one part vanilla. Some extracts were gray, others brown; some were clear, others cloudy; some had a woody nose, while others smelled more like butterscotch or chemicals.

However, when the vanillas were tasted in

Most vanilla extract is made by steeping costly vanilla beans from Madagascar in alcohol.

shortbread cookies made with just flour, butter, and sugar, it was impossible to identify significant differences among the samples. Tasters who had loathed imitation vanilla when they tasted it in plain milk chose the cookies made with imitation vanilla as their favorite. Likewise, vanillas that had seemed clearly superior when tasted in milk (the same two brands were rated as favorites by every single taster) were impossible to pick out in cookies.

We were so surprised by this result that we held a second blind testing of vanilla extracts with members of the *Cook's Illustrated* editorial staff. Once again, tasters found distinct differences among vanillas when tasted in milk, but little or no difference among cookies baked with different vanillas. In a vanilla custard made with just milk, egg yolks, and sugar, only Tahitian vanilla, an entirely different bean, stood out as unique.

How can we explain this apparent discrepancy? First of all, unlike most ingredients that we have conducted blind tastings of, vanilla extract is used in extremely small quantities. Cookie and custard recipes call for only minute amounts of vanilla, usually around one percent of the total volume of ingredients. At such low concentrations, most differences among extracts are simply impossible to detect. The fact that vanilla extract contains so much alcohol, which evaporates during baking or when stirred into a hot custard, further complicates the task of tasting vanilla in a real setting.

Some Differences Prevail

Despite the less-than-clear results, our tasting did

reveal a few interesting facts. First of all, vanilla extract made at home by steeping beans in quality brandy for one month was judged to be decidedly inferior to commercial brands. Even though we followed the government standards for pure extract, a ratio of beans to liquid that manufacturers must follow, our homemade extract was anemic-tasting and not worth the effort or money. Homemade extract was the most expensive and least favorite sample in the tasting.

Our second major finding was that many people actually enjoy, or at least don't mind, the flavor of imitation extract. Imitation extract is derived from wood pulp and is chemically treated to resemble natural vanilla; it has an unmistakable flavor and aroma. When tasted in milk, most tasters thought this flavor was "fake" or "odd," while a few described it as "rich" or "nutty." However, when used in a custard or cookies, the imitation extract was actually preferred by several tasters. In particular, the custard made with imitation extract seemed to have more vanilla flavor than custards made with real extracts. Our natural aversion to imitation products, coupled with the modest cost difference between real and imitation vanilla, prevents us from recommending that you buy imitation extract.

The last major finding of our research has to do with Tahitian vanilla extract. Almost two-thirds of the world's supply of vanilla beans comes from Madagascar, an island off the eastern coast of Africa. Several high-end manufacturers make single-variety extracts from Madagascan beans (also known as Bourbon vanilla beans) as well as from beans from Mexico and Tahiti. Most extracts, however, are made with a blend of beans from various tropical locations.

Since some companies make several extracts, each from beans grown in a distinct region, we decided to limit the original tasting with our expert panel to extracts made with Madagascan beans (the most popular kind) as well as blended extracts presumably made from beans from several unnamed sources.

In the second tasting with members of the editorial staff of the magazine, we included "varietal" extracts made by Nielsen-Massey, each made with beans from a single source— Madagascar, Mexico, and Tahiti. When we tasted these extracts in milk, the differences were immediately apparent. The Tahitian extract was flowery, even musky, and easily distinguished from the Mexican and Madagascan extracts. Tahitian beans are a hybrid that originated spontaneously on a few islands in the South Pacific. Beans grown in every other part of the world, including Mexico and Madagascar, are from the same species.

We then tasted these three extracts in shortbread and in a stirred custard. As in the initial tasting, the differences among the cookies were too subtle to distinguish, despite the fact that the Mexican extract was deemed overly alcoholic and inferior when tasted in plain milk. The floral character of the Tahitian extract was also gone. Baking eliminated any identifying characteristics in these varietal extracts. However, the flavor of the Tahitian extract came through loud and clear in the stirred custard and provoked wildly diverging views. Some tasters responded favorably to the "flowery nose" while others thought the flavor was "too strong to be real" or just plain "horrible."

Despite the varied opinions, everyone agreed Tahitian vanilla extract was different. For custards and other desserts, such as mousses, fruit sauces, and ice creams, which don't involve baking, you may want to try Tahitian extract to see if you like the flavor. You may not love the results, but you will notice a difference. ∎

RATING VANILLA EXTRACTS

EXTRACTS TASTED IN MILK

Vanillas are listed here in order of preference based on the results of tasting them in a solution of eight parts milk to one part vanilla. In addition to the author, our tasting panel included Katherine Alford, a cooking teacher and writer; Rose Levy Beranbaum, baking expert and author of *The Cake Bible* and several other cookbooks; Stephanie Lyness, teacher and cookbook author; Nick Malgieri, director of the baking program at Peter Kump's New York Cooking School and author of several dessert cookbooks; Richard Sax, author of *Classic Home Desserts* and several other cookbooks; and Stephen Schmidt, author of the forthcoming *Dessert America, A History of American Baking*.

Since we were unable to detect differences among cookies and custards made with the following extracts, these ratings are somewhat tentative. However, you certainly cannot go wrong with the two top-rated extracts. McCormick, the best-selling brand, is readily available in supermarkets; Nielsen-Massey, a leading "gourmet" brand, actually costs less than McCormick since it can be purchased in larger quantities.

Nielsen-Massey Madagascar Bourbon Pure Vanilla Extract, $11 for eight ounces. This "murky," dark brown liquid with "sweet, well-rounded" flavor received three first-place votes and two second-place votes. Some tasters felt the alcohol content was a bit high. However, the flavor was described as "smooth," "buttery," and "even a bit chocolaty." *Available in gourmet stores and by mail from the Williams-Sonoma catalog (800-541-2233).*

McCormick Pure Vanilla Extract, $7.69 for four ounces. This "slightly cloudy" liquid with "good, strong" flavor received two first-place votes and two second-place votes. Tasters used an array of positive adjectives to describe it, including "floral," "buttery," "rounded," "mildly sweet," and "complex." All thought the vanilla flavor was quite clear. *Available in supermarkets.*

Spice Islands Pure Vanilla Extract 100% Bourbon Vanilla, $6.69 for four ounces. Although generally deemed to have a "pleasant, mild" flavor, most tasters also felt the flavor was a "bit faint" or "flat." Some tasters picked up a "floral" nose; others found the aroma "camphorlike" or "medicinal." *Available in supermarkets.*

Scotts Madagascar Bourbon Pure Vanilla Extract, $7 for four ounces. This "medium brown" vanilla is a "tiny bit murky" right from the bottle. Most tasters found the flavor to be somewhat "sweetish," with several comments on the "pleasant, vanilla nose." Others thought the flavor was "rubbery," "medicinal," "oddly floral," or "a bit like plastic." *Available by mail from the King Arthur Flour Baker's Catalogue (800-827-6836).*

Cook's Pure Vanilla Extract, $6.40 for four ounces. Several tasters thought this clear extract was "overly alcoholic" and "bitter." Others commented on the "butterscotch" flavor, which was also interpreted as "slightly medicinal." *Available in gourmet stores and by mail from A Cook's Wares (412-846-9490).*

International Gourmet 100% Pure Vanilla Extract, $5.50 for five ounces. This "perfectly clear" extract is "medium brown" with a "hint of red." Tasters were generally put off by the strong aroma, which was described as "plastic, like a beach ball," and "rubbery." Although a few tasters had somewhat positive reactions, like "nutty" and "candyish," most found this extract "weird" and "bitter as all hell." *Available by mail from Lorann Oils (800-248-1302).*

McCormick Premium Quality Imitation Vanilla Extract, $4.19 for four ounces. This product is a blend of 20 percent real extract and 80 percent imitation. Evidently, the small amount of real vanilla in this "clear," "grayish brown" liquid is enough to fool some but not most of our tasters. While two tasters detected a "nutty quality" reminiscent of hazelnuts or walnuts, others were reminded of "cough syrup" or "sawdust." *Available in supermarkets.*

Durkee Pure Vanilla Extract, $6.05 for four ounces. This "clear" extract is "medium brown" in color. Several tasters thought this sample had a "harsh, alcoholic nose." The flavor was deemed to be "rubbery," "a bit smoky," or "disgusting, just like Band-Aids." *Available in supermarkets.*

La Cuisine Distilled Vanilla Essence, $11 for two ounces. This product comes from Grasse, center of the French perfume business. Instead of using alcohol to extract flavor from vanilla, the beans are distilled into a thick brown liquid with tiny black specks of vanilla seeds. This essence is two to three times stronger than regular extract and was tasted in such a way as to compensate for this added strength. Although some professionals swear by this product, our tasters thought the flavor was "pleasant enough but not really vanilla." The high sugar content elicited comments such as "highly caramelized" and "tastes like a Sugar Daddy." The intense "floral nose" also threw tasters for a loop. Certainly the odd one in the lot. *Available by mail from La Cuisine Kitchenware (800-521-1176).*

Wagner's Natural Vanilla Extract, $4.25 for four ounces. The unusual "grayish" color of this "clear" extract was distressing to many panelists. "Blackish hue" and "dirty water appearance" did not inspire much confidence. Not one taster picked up a hint of vanilla. Instead tasters were reminded of "cough drops," "chemicals," "ginger," "petroleum," and "smoke." Needless to say, none of these associations prompted a positive response. *Available in gourmet stores.*

Homemade Vanilla Extract, about $12 for eight ounces. We used the same amount of beans that manufacturers do (13.35 ounces per gallon of liquid) but were unable to extract much vanilla flavor, despite steeping the beans for a month in brandy. This extract was deemed "oddly pale" and "anemic." Tasters also thought it was "overly alcoholic" and "harsh,"

EXTRACTS USED IN BAKING
Even to Experts, They're All the Same

When vanillas were tasted in shortbread cookies and in vanilla custard, even our panel of experts could tell little or no difference between the most expensive extracts and imitation vanilla made from wood pulp.

Rating Handheld Mixers

For the best all-around hand mixer, choose the KitchenAid; if you already have a countertop mixer for heavy tasks, the $10 Salton is your best choice.

～ BY SHARON KEBSCHULL BARRETT ～

There many kitchen tasks—from beating egg whites to whipping heavy cream—that are most easily done with a handheld mixer. All of them could be done by hand or with a countertop mixer, but the first method is more time-consuming and the second involves the inconvenience of dragging out a relatively heavy piece of equipment. It's far easier just to grab the hand mixer, plug it in wherever you happen to be working, and mix away. For this reason (as well as because of their relatively low price) hand mixers are still a popular kitchen appliance. In 1993, the latest year for which statistics are available, over six million hand mixers were sold, compared to a mere one million countertop mixers.

Like most kitchen appliances, hand mixers have undergone a number of transformations in the past few years. The major innovation has been a redesign of the beaters used with these mixers. Although some of the mixers (and not just the cheap ones) still come with the old-fashioned beaters that have a thick post down the middle, others now have a newer style of beaters with thin, curved wires. The wire beaters are a great improvement; their open center makes them far easier to clean, and they performed better and faster in virtually every test I ran.

Dave Becker, senior product manager for top-rated KitchenAid, says the company developed the new style of beaters a few years ago using computer modeling. When tested in its laboratories, the new beaters outperformed the old-style blade, driving food down to the bottom of the bowl, thus reducing splattering and improving mixing.

The Tests

I ran four tests (egg whites, whipping cream, mashed potatoes, and cookie dough) with each mixer, plus a fifth test (bread) for those that came with dough-hook attachments. All of the mixers were able to beat egg whites and whip cream well, and mashed potatoes didn't faze any of them too much, although some left a few lumps. But if you frequently make stiff doughs, you should choose your hand mixer carefully—making a peanut-butter cookie dough separated the workhorses from the wimps.

It was at this point that the differences between old-style and new-style beaters came to the fore. The post beaters on some mixers quickly got clogged; some of the machines bucked against the stiff dough while others slowed considerably. Only one smelled like it was burning, though, and all the mixers produced acceptable doughs in the end, but at the price of a very sore arm. This leads to another important design element to look for—a handle that slants up toward the front of the mixer, as opposed to a handle that sits parallel to the top of the mixer. The slanted handles fit the hand much better and reduce arm stress.

Overall, the $65 KitchenAid mixer was the clear winner. It was out in front in mixing speed, power, and comfort. It could handle stiff cookie doughs, but its maker doesn't pretend, as some do, that it can take

---

RATING HAND MIXERS

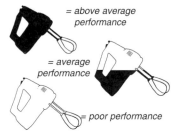

= above average performance

= average performance

= poor performance

The mixers were evaluated based on the following characteristics and are listed in order of preference. Prices are suggested retail. For information on purchasing the top models, see Sources and Resources on page 32.

Egg whites: Two whites were beaten on low speed for fifteen seconds, then the speed was increased a notch every ten seconds. Smoothly beaten whites that didn't look gritty and achieved a decent volume without splattering were best.

Whipping cream: One cup of cream was whipped on low speed for fifteen seconds, then the speed was increased a notch every ten seconds. Mixers that produced whipped cream with a good volume and a smooth texture without splattering were rated highest.

Mashed potatoes: Three-fourths of a pound of cooked potatoes were whipped for thirty seconds on the highest speed possible without splattering. Mixers that produced smoothly whipped potatoes were given top ratings.

Cookie dough: Mixers had to cream butter and sugar, then incorporate some flour, some peanut butter, and more flour for a recipe that made four dozen cookies. Mixers that could incorporate the flour without sending it flying and could maneuver through a stiff dough without slowing down or bucking got a top rating.

Dough hook: Mixers with hooks were evaluated for speed and ease of kneading with French bread dough. None of these mixers could knead dough easily and well.

Ease of cleaning: High marks went to mixers with no seams or openings on the underside and with modern, wire beaters without center posts.

Mixer	Price	Weight	Handle Type	Speeds	Egg Whites	Whipping Cream	Mashed Potatoes	Cookie Dough	Ease of Cleaning
KitchenAid Ultra Power Plus KHM5TB	$65	2 lb. 1.5 oz.	Curved	5-speed	above average	above average	above average	above average	above average
Farberware Power Plus D2730	$45	2 lb. 10 oz.	Curved	Continuous	above average	above average	above average	average	poor
Krups Power-Mix 745	$55	2 lb. 2.5 oz.	Curved	3-speed	above average	above average	above average	above average	above average
Sunbeam Mixmaster 2485	$25	2 lb. 3.0 oz.	Curved	6-speed	above average	above average	above average	average	poor
Salton MX-2	$10	1 lb. 11.5 oz.	Straight	5-speed	above average	above average	above average	average	above average
Rival 455S	$36	2 lb. 3.0 oz.	Curved	5-speed	above average	above average	above average	above average	poor
Braun Multi-Mix M820	$65	2 lb. 0.5 oz.	Curved	3-speed	poor	above average	average	average	poor
Hamilton Beach 45310	$25	2 lb. 4.5 oz.	Straight	5-speed	average	above average	poor	average	poor
Black & Decker Power-Pro M205S	$53	2 lb. 6.0 oz.	Curved	5-speed	poor	above average	average	poor	above average

Like so many gadgets, cordless mixers don't live up to their billing. I tested the Cuisinart CM3 and the Black & Decker 9220 HandyMixer, the two most widely available cordless mixers, both of which come with a recharging base for a counter or wall. The Cuisinart uses two post-style beaters, while the Black & Decker has a single beater, plus a whisk and a drink-mixing attachment.

Both mixers performed adequately in whipping egg whites and cream, but the Black & Decker met its match with mashed potatoes, and the Cusinart was barely able to move cookie dough.

At $53 for the Black & Decker and $59 for the Cuisinart, these machines are not bargains and, in my opinion, are not worth the frustration they cause. However, if you really must have a cordless mixer—if, for example, you have a kitchen where the outlets are not near the work surfaces—I recommend the Cuisinart.

on anything as stiff as bread dough. Cooks who want the power to do that, but who like the convenience of a hand mixer, should consider buying the $10 Salton, a best buy, then spending their savings on a countertop mixer.

In addition to beater style, speed settings were an important point of comparison among the mixers. Too often, the slow speed was not slow enough and sent clouds of flour into the air and slung whipping cream across the kitchen. Few of the machines had problems with a high speed that wasn't fast enough, although some of them struggled to maintain that speed with cookie dough. Five different speeds seems like an ideal range of choices; the three-speed Krups, for example, needs an intermediate setting between first and second, as second moves much too fast. Some mixers, among them the Krups, have a "pulse" setting, which helps in incorporating flour slowly but is useless when whipping cream or egg whites since it splatters them just as badly as a high-speed setting. The KitchenAid and Salton machines had well-set low and high speeds, but the Farberware, which had other problems, had the best speed settings. Its "variable speeds," a variation on the standard five speeds, are set on a continuous dial, giving the cook real control.

Many of the mixers are unnecessarily difficult to clean. Old-fashioned mixers and, unfortunately, many new ones have seams that run down the middle of their undersides, perfectly located for catching any gunk that flies up from the bowl and keeping it there for all eternity. I looked for mixers that had the new wire beaters, for quick cleaning, and no seams or openings on the bottom. Finally, I considered in my rat-

ings whether the mixers could stand on their back ends when their beaters were full of dough and how well-balanced the mixers felt in use—some that were very heavy on the beater end quickly became uncomfortable to operate.

Attachments

Some of the mixers came only with standard beaters, while others came with a variety of attachments. Whisks for egg whites and cream proved very successful. The Rival's whisk, for example, could be detached just before the whites were fully beaten and used by hand to finish the beating; this allowed me to avoid overbeating the egg whites, which would be easy to do with this mixer's fast speeds. A rod to turn a mixer into a hand blender (to be used for mixing drinks or sauces) is another one of the more useful attachments. The Braun wins the attachment war, with a hand blender and beaker, dough hooks, and a food chopper. However, all these attachments could not make up for the Braun's poor performance in several of the tests.

The dough hooks that came with some of the mixers proved to be the biggest disappointments. None of them could knead bread adequately. Invariably, the dough just flopped up the sides of the bowl when we tried to knead it. Cooks who want to avoid the physical exertion that hand kneading requires won't do so with a hand mixer, and the end product won't be as good as it would be if kneaded by hand or with a countertop mixer. To avoid hand kneading, either buy a countertop mixer or try using a food processor. ■

Sharon Kebschull Barrett recently graduated from Peter Kump's New York Cooking School.

KitchenAid: (Best Mixer) Very quiet and well-balanced with a comfortable handle. Slow speed is slow, and fast, truly fast. Beaters have a superior design.

Farberware: Despite cleaning problems, this ranks above the Krups because of its variable speeds, which give excellent control via a continuous dial.

Krups: Low speed is truly low, but mixer needs an intermediate speed between first and second. Has considerable trouble with thick mixtures.

Sunbeam: Good at egg whites, cream, and potatoes, but low speed is too fast for cookie dough. Beaters get clogged.

Salton: (Best Buy) Small post beaters make this mixer hard to clean, but otherwise a good choice. Too light to stand on its back end when beaters are full of dough.

Rival: Comes close to being a good mixer, but low speed is too fast. Back end is too narrow to stand reliably when beaters are full of dough.

Hamilton Beach: Post beaters and indentations along the underside make this mixer hard to clean. Very loud, and low speed sends flour flying.

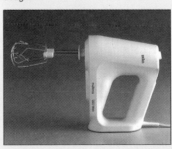

Braun: Comes with many attachments, including food chopper plus hand-blender rod and beater, but instructions aren't always clear. Mixer is heavy to hold and has an unpleasantly thick handle. Bucks a bit when mixing cookie dough.

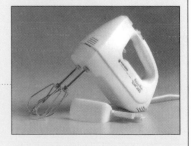

Black & Decker: Slow speed is far too fast, and machine lacks enough strength to mix cookie dough smoothly. Front end is heavy and a bit bulky.

"Vacation" Whites You Can Live With

We taste the white wines you're most likely to find when the selection is poor, and find an acceptable handful.

∾ BY MARK BITTMAN ∾

It's happened to every wine drinker who takes a summer vacation: You have to buy white wine in a convenience store, an ill-stocked supermarket, or one of those ramshackle package stores that specializes in wine coolers and cheap vodka. Asking a clerk for help is out—France, California, sauvignon, chardonnay, Mouton Cadet, Mouton Rothschild—it's all the same to him. You are on your own, and you'll likely encounter something produced by Gallo, Mondavi, or Sutter Home; an Italian white or two, and the French standard, Mouton Cadet. In short, you are not going to make any brilliant discoveries.

It was an attempt to aid the traveler in this distressing situation that inspired this tasting, a roundup of the best-selling, most widely available, least expensive white wines, the stuff you're most likely to find under the flashing Budweiser sign in that remote resort. We compiled this list with the help of Frank Walters, research director of *Impact* and *Market Watch*, two publications that track trends and sales.

Remember: These are white wines you probably wouldn't buy in your hometown but which you're sometimes forced to buy on the road. And the results were at least mildly encouraging.

But the bad news first: We included a ringer, the Trimbach Pinot Blanc, a well-made white that sells for a price comparable to that of most of the other wines here but which is not as widely available. Not surprisingly, it swept the field.

Unfortunately, you're not going to find Trimbach Pinot Blanc in your Vermont hideaway or your Montana chalet. And the rest of the bad news is that some of the wines we tasted were real dogs—bring one of these to your boss's summer house, and you're looking at a pay cut.

There are many facets of a good wine, and inexpensive wines may have none of them. Even assuming that there is no fraud involved (using cheap chenin blanc in place of more expensive chardonnay, for example), a chardonnay grape grown on unpruned, high-yield vines, in chemically fertilized soil, is not going to give you much flavor. Blend that grape with up to 25 percent of some nameless grape whose flavor approximates that of stale water, vinify it using fast, inexpensive methods, and you can still label the wine "Chardonnay," sell it for $6, and, presumably, make a profit. Some of the wines below probably go this route.

But not all. At least one was something you might actually consider purchasing for your home table. This wine, the 1993 Sebastiani Country Chardonnay, was a well-balanced, pleasant white that compares favorably to the best of the inexpensive country wines from France or Italy that are on sale at your local well-stocked wine merchants. At $5.50 a bottle, it's a good buy. And if that weren't enough, we uncovered no fewer than six other widely sold white wines ranging in price from just over $4 to $9 that no more than one of our tasters described in wholly negative terms. This is not a recommendation to substitute these wines for your favorite inexpensive white. But if you encounter one in a faraway land, you can purchase it without fear of embarrassment. ∎

BLIND TASTING RESULTS

As usual, the wines in our tasting were judged blind by a panel made up of both wine professionals and amateur wine-lovers. In the judging, seven points were awarded for each first-place vote; six for second; five for third; and so on. These wines were all purchased in the Northeast; prices will vary somewhat throughout the country. Within each category, the wines are listed in order, based on the number of points scored.

1993 Sebastiani Country Chardonnay

RECOMMENDED:
....

1992 Trimbach Pinot Blanc, $7.99. "Lively and smooth, with a hint of sweetness," wrote one taster. "The real thing," wrote another. "If it's under $10, it's a steal." From Alsace.

1993 Sebastiani Country Chardonnay, $5.49. "Light, but with a pleasant bite, and distinctively chardonnay"; "clean, fresh, and fruity." No taster had a bad word to say about this wine.

ACCEPTABLE:
....

1993 Duboeuf Chardonnay, $5.99. "Seems more natural than most"; "some nose, no middle, halfway decent finish." Generally an undistinguished but also unflawed French wine.

1991 Ernest and Julio Gallo Sauvignon Blanc, $4.25. "Has fruit and balance, but boring"; "light and innocuous"; "no fruit, no acid, no flavor." Note the price; you can't get much lower and still call it wine.

1993 Jadot Macon Villages, $8.99. Wide range of comments, from "love that nose, and nice and dry" (this written by a francophile) to "this is real garbage." Overall, it was reasonably well liked.

1993 Sutter Home Sauvignon Blanc, $5.49. "Distinctive, but whether good or bad is debatable." As above, comments ran the gamut, but the tone was generally positive.

1992 Mouton Cadet, $7.49. One taster found this wine "penetrating" and "delicious" and ranked it as his top choice. Most found it "not horrible, but not worth drinking."

1993 Glen Ellen Proprietor's Reserve Chardonnay, $4.99. This wine neither excited nor revolted anyone. In sum: "Off dry; no major flaws; acceptable."

NOT RECOMMENDED:
....

1992 Mondavi Woodbridge Sauvignon Blanc, $5.49. "Undistinguished"; "no fun." Fewer downright negative comments than the wines that follow, but little on the upside either.

Ernest and Julio Gallo Chardonnay, NV, $4.59. On the whole, people found this wine "overly sweet" and one thought it was "terrible." "Soda pop."

1992 Walnut Crest Maipo Valley Chardonnay, $4.99. The consensus was that this wine, which is from Chile, was "bland, bitter," and "stinky," but a couple of our tasters found it "fresh" and "not bad."

1990 Concha y Toro Sauvignon Blanc, $4.49. "Chemical nose"; "all kinds of weird sensations on the palate." The best anyone could say about this Chilean wine was that it was "boring."

1993 Bolla Soave, $6.99. The renegade taster who ranked Mouton Cadet number one picked this as his second favorite: "Lovely, elegant, and long." But nearly everyone else found it "closed," "awful," or "vile." (Personally, I wouldn't chance it.)

Corvo Salaparuta, NV, $7.99. In sum: "Yuk."

The Occasional Vegetarian
Karen Lee with Diane Porter
Warner, $24.95

Karen Lee writes for people who want to eat meatless meals several nights a week and argues that structuring a meal where meat is not on the plate is a challenge, requiring not only the elimination of meat but an entirely new approach to meal planning. Lee has been ambitious enough to attempt such an approach, with much success.

She begins by identifying four structures for vegetarian meals: dinners with a featured entree; composed plates of three or four side dishes as the entree; buffets; and a series of sequentially served small dishes. Recipes are divided into eleven categories, such as pastas, beans, grains, and soups. Each dish is accompanied by an explanation of how it can be incorporated into one or more of the four meal structures.

Chino Caponata, for example, is made with wok-charred eggplant, tomato sauce, soy sauce, sherry vinegar, chili oil, roasted red peppers, capers, and oregano. Lee suggests that it can be spread on toast, tossed with pasta, or served as a side dish on a buffet or composed plate. Like other recipes I tested, this demonstrated Lee's deft hand at mixing and matching various ethnic ingredients—all of which can be found at a basic supermarket—in healthy dishes.

Chino Caponata is bursting with flavor and contains about one teaspoon of oil per serving as a pasta sauce or side dish, even less when served as a dip or spread. Ginger Lentil Stew follows the same principles. Tiny French lentils are combined with aromatics such as carrots, celery, and leeks but get a decidedly non-European boost from fresh ginger, soy sauce, and cumin. The result tastes great and contains less than one teaspoon of oil per serving.

But Lee is not a slave to counting grams of fat (there are no nutrition counts in this book). Most recipes could pass muster with the food police, but none of the eight dishes I tested are ascetic by any standards. Fennel and Orange Salad with Herb-Lime Vinaigrette calls for olive oil dressing, sparingly used. Spinach Soufflé cuts fat by relying on extra egg whites and low-fat milk but still contains two yolks, a little butter, and a dusting of Parmesan cheese. Low-Fat Ginger Cake, with just four tablespoons of vegetable oil, tastes as good as any gingerbread-type cake I have made with a stick or two of butter. (Its incredibly moist texture is achieved by adding honey and molasses.)

Recipes are easy to execute, and ingredient lists are short. For instance, "Cream" of Carrot Soup contains just seven ingredients but has a rich, deep flavor. Whole-Grain Fried Rice, with six ingredients, is highly seasoned with soy sauce, scallions, carrots, and sesame seeds.

If more vegetarian efforts were like *The Occasional Vegetarian,* few Americans would have trouble giving up meat altogether, let alone for a few nights a week.

—*Jack Bishop*

The Bold Vegetarian
Bharti Kirchner
HarperPerennial, $16

Like *The Occasional Vegetarian,* this is a book for nonfanatics. There is fat, there is sugar, there are butter and eggs. There is also a great deal of flavor, and much success.

Kirchner is a fan of "world cuisine." Thus, she gives us standard vegetarian recipes from everywhere (such as Korean Spinach Banchan) and combines Eastern and Western ingredients with nearly reckless abandon. Her garlic bread recipe, for example, contains roasted garlic blended with olive oil, salt, and fresh oregano or parsley. No surprises there, until you add the asafetida, a powerful Indian spice that changes everything. I liked the results, which were not only bold and inventive but tasty. Kirchner favors "exotic" spices in otherwise ordinary dishes, and her palate is good enough (and her recipe-testing diligent enough) to pull this off.

Some results were unimpressive. Crostini with Chutney, which contains mint-cilantro chutney, thyme, olive oil, garlic, and grated cheese, set my senses awhirl—it just didn't hang together.

But most of the recipes I tried were successful. Tomato Peanut Soup, in which a more-or-less basic tomato soup is enlivened with turmeric and peanut butter, was rich and flavorful. Warm Mustard Green Salad combines soy sauce, sesame oil, and capers in the dressing, a combination I had not had before, but rather liked. Indian Style Roast Potatoes creates a crisp, low-fat, high-flavor potato by combining asafetida, cumin, sugar, lime juice, and mango powder. Once you own the non-Western ingredients (which require about $10 and one trip to your Asian market), this and other like dishes are easy to prepare.

It's worth mentioning that *The Bold Vegetarian* is a collection of recipes rather than a strategy planner, but it's also worth mentioning that Kirchner's serving suggestions and variations make this a fairly complete package.

—*Mark Bittman*

The Vegetarian Feast
Martha Rose Shulman
HarperPerennial, $14

When Martha Rose Shulman wrote the original edition of *The Vegetarian Feast* in 1979, meatless meal planning was a radical concept and low-fat cooking was far from de rigueur.

In the introduction to this revised edition, Shulman says she often added cheese and nuts to the original recipes in order to increase their protein content. At that time, nutritionists warned that vegetarians needed to take special measures to ensure sufficient protein consumption.

Now those high-fat, high-protein recipes are out of date. Shulman has therefore gone back to the kitchen to retest every recipe in the book, reducing fat along the way and adding fifty new recipes. Her approach is moderate—dishes still have enough fat to taste good—but the reduction in fat is quite impressive.

Black Bean Enchiladas is a good illustration. The original recipe calls for one-half cup of oil, twelve ounces of cheddar cheese, and one-half cup of walnuts. The revised version uses just three tablespoons of oil and six ounces of cheese; it eliminates the nuts but remains rich and enjoyable.

Some recipes proved more difficult to rework. Shulman's recipe for potato pancakes (panfried in a mixture of melted butter and oil) has been replaced by Grated Potato Pie, a French-inspired crustless tart that bakes in the oven. The grated potatoes are still bound by eggs as well as olive oil and Parmesan. But while this dish is by no means meager, it is not as heavy as fried pancakes.

Shulman has compensated for new tastes as well. Her original book had only a few pasta recipes; the revised edition devotes a whole chapter to the subject. Pasta with Cottage Cheese Pesto and Broccoli is a creamy, light alternative to traditional pesto, a recipe for which appears in the revised edition pretty much unchanged.

Each of the recipes I tested was reliable and struck a harmonious balance between taste and health issues, far from a modest accomplishment. ■

—*Jack Bishop*

SOURCES
AND RESOURCES

Most of the ingredients and materials needed for the recipes in this issue are available at your local supermarket, gourmet store, or kitchen supply shop. The following are mail-order sources for particular items. Prices listed below are current at press time and do not include shipping or handling unless otherwise indicated. Contact companies directly to confirm up-to-date prices and availability.

HAND MIXERS

After testing eleven hand mixers (*see* story on page 28), we can make a couple of recommendations. Our top-rated KitchenAid 5-Speed Ultra Power Plus KHM5TB retails for $65, but is available at a discounted price of $55.50 from A Cook's Wares (211 37th Street, Beaver Falls, PA 15010; 412-846-9490). The Salton 5-Speed MX-2 is also a best buy since it costs just $10. Salton operates a consumer hot line (800-233-9054) that will direct callers to local retail sources for the company's products. The Cuisinart CM3, the better of the two cordless mixers we tested, is also available from A Cook's Wares for $59.50.

CAST-IRON POT FOR SMOKING

Although tea-smoked chicken (*see* page 14) can be prepared in a wok, we prefer to use a heavy-duty cast-iron pot. Lehman's Non-Electric Catalog (4779 Kidron Road, Kidron, OH 44636; 216-857-5757) sells a ten-quart, cast-iron Dutch oven for $52 that is ideal for smoking a good-size chicken.

CHINESE TEA AND SPICES FOR SMOKING

The smoked chicken recipe on page 15 calls for aromatic tea as part of the smoking mixture. We particularly like Lapsang souchong, a Chinese black tea smoked over pine embers to give it a rich, pungent flavor. This fine tea as well as dozens of others is available from The Republic of Tea (P.O. Box 1175, Mill Valley, CA 94942; 800-354-5530). A 3.5-ounce tin of

Lapsang souchong costs $8.50. Star anise, which is more aromatic than common anise seed, is often used in Asian cooking to flavor poultry and is an essential ingredient in the spice mixture for the tea-smoked chicken. Whole star anise may be available in markets that carry a broad selection of spices. It is also available by mail from Penzey's Spice House (P.O. Box 1448, Waukesha, WI 53187; 414-574-0277). Penzey's sells whole pieces and broken pieces as well as ground star anise powder. Broken pieces, which are fine for smoking mixtures, cost $3.99 for four ounces, half the price of whole pieces.

SOFT-SHELL CRABS

Fresh soft-shell crabs (*see* recipes on page 7) are a sure sign of warmer weather. During the peak season of late spring through summer, these crabs should be available in most parts of the country. If you have trouble finding soft-shells at your market, the Annapolis Seafood Market (1300 Forest Drive, Annapolis, MD 21403; 410-263-7787) will ship fresh crabs by the half dozen to your home by next-day air. The price of the crabs fluctuates and generally decreases during late spring and summer when the supply is most abundant.

PIZZA TOOLS

Making pizza at home (*see* page 8) can be easy if you have the right equipment. An oversized peel (paddle) is a must for sliding the pizza onto hot quarry tiles or a baking stone. We like the thin aluminum peels with heatproof wooden handles that are sold through the King Arthur Flour Baker's Catalogue (P.O. Box 876, Norwich, VT 05055; 800-827-6836). The catalog carries two peels—the larger one has a fourteen-inch-square blade; the smaller peel has a twelve-inch-square blade—both with twelve-inch handles. We recommend that you buy the larger peel ($14.95), which can also be used to slide risen loaves of bread into the oven. While you're at it, you may also want to order semolina for

dusting the pizza paddle. King Arthur sells semolina in a two-pound bag that costs $1.95 or a five-pound bag for $4.85.

KITCHEN TWINE

Tying the pork roast (*see* page 21) helps ensure even cooking and a superior appearance. Linen is the best material for kitchen twine since it will not burn in a hot oven. The Williams-Sonoma catalog (800-541-2233) sells a ninety-two-yard spool of French white linen for $5. The twine comes in a plastic dispenser with its own cutter.

MESH TEA BALLS

An astute reader recommended using a mesh tea ball instead of cheesecloth to enclose dried herbs for a bouquet *garni* (*see* page 4). These tea balls can also be filled with mulling spices for cider or wine. The Williams-Sonoma catalog (800-541-2233) carries a set of two tea balls that are one-and-three-quarters inches and two-and-one-half inches in diameter. Both balls come with chains with small hooks on their ends that can be attached to the rim of a pot to make removal quite easy. The set of two tea balls costs $6.50.

CAKE DECORATING SUPPLIES

Decorating a birthday cake requires a minimal investment in professional tools. Wilton Enterprises (2240 West 75th Street, Woodridge, IL 60517; 708-963-7100) is known among baking experts for its wide assortment of pastry supplies. Cardboard cake circles and boards allow you to frost and transport cakes with ease. Wilton carries circles in sizes ranging from six to sixteen inches as well as a number of rectangular shapes. For the recipe on page 18, choose the eight-inch circle, which is sold in a pack of twelve for $3.69. A revolving cake stand allows you to turn the cake as you frost it and holds the bottom of the cake off the counter so it is easier to frost every surface. Wilton sells an eleven-inch, circular, plastic cake stand for $10.49 as well as a

professional, heavy-duty, aluminum stand with a twelve-inch rotating plate. The plastic stand is fine for regular jobs, although larger cakes with many tiers, especially wedding cakes, should be frosted on the stronger metal stand, which costs $54.99. Wilton also carries a number of decorating sets with pastry bags, couplers, and tips. Expect to spend $6.99 for an eighteen-piece starter kit, which includes four metal tips, two couplers, and six disposable pastry bags. More complete kits, such as the fifty-two-piece Supreme Cake Decorating Set ($27.99), come with many more tips and bags.

FINE-MESH STRAINERS

Paula Wolfert, cookbook author and expert on Mediterranean cuisines, shared a Quick Tip with us (*see* page 5) that requires a small-mesh sieve. Such a sieve can also be used to keep seeds out of lemon juice or to skim fat from a pot of soup. We particularly like the German-made sieves available from Sur La Table (410 Terry Avenue, Seattle, WA 98109; 800-243-0852). These sturdy, round sieves have a wide, metal rim and a shallow indentation in the center. They come in eight different sizes ranging from two-and-one-half inches in diameter ($5.95) to nine inches in diameter ($19.95).

INSTANT-READ THERMOMETER

Several recipes in this issue depend on the accurate measurement of the internal temperature of meat. We are partial to digital thermometers but find that they are often very expensive. That's why we were pleased to discover the Cooper Pocket Thermometer. This thermometer has a five-inch stem and an easy-to-read LCD display. It measures temperatures from minus 40 degrees up to 450 degrees and shuts off automatically when not in use. The Cooper thermometer is available from Professional Cutlery Direct (170 Boston Post Road, Suite 135, Madison, CT 06443; 800-859-6994) and costs $39.95. ■

**GARLIC-STUDDED
ROAST PORK LOIN**
page 22

**FRESH TOMATO PIZZA WITH ARUGULA
AND PROSCIUTTO**
page 11

**ASPARAGUS VINAIGRETTE WITH
SIEVED EGG AND PICKLED ONIONS**
page 23

**FREE-FORM MERINGUE SHELLS WITH
STRAWBERRIES AND PAPAYA**
page 13

PANFRIED SOFT-SHELL CRABS ON A BED OF SPINACH
page 7

STOVE-TOP TEA-SMOKED CHICKEN
page 15

Frozen Hot Chocolate

Mix ½ cup unsweet-ened Dutch-process cocoa and ¾ cup sugar in a medium saucepan. Stir in 10 table-spoons low-fat (1 percent) milk to form a smooth paste, then stir in an additional 2 cups milk over low heat until sugar dissolves. Pour mixture into ice cube trays; cover and freeze for at least 6 hours. (Mixture can be frozen up to one week.) Break frozen cubes into chunks with a table knife. Process mixture with 2 tablespoons milk in a food processor fitted with a steel blade until smooth. Serve immediately in frosted goblets. If desired, garnish with candied orange zest. *Serves 6.*

COOK'S
ILLUSTRATED

How to Thicken Fruit Pies
Why Does Tapioca Outperform Corn Starch?

Secrets of Smoke-Cooking
Techniques for Covered Grills and Smokers

Creamy Sorbets
How Sugar and Alcohol Affect Texture

A Better Burger
The Right Meat and the Right Method

QUICK-COOKING ZUCCHINI

·

BEST RED WINES FOR GRILLED FOOD

·

SPICE RUBS

·

RATING BLENDERS

·

CRISP COLESLAW

$4.00 U.S./$4.95 CANADA

"Corn"
See page 22 for the best ways to cook corn.

ILLUSTRATION BY
BRENT WATKINSON

Bay-Scented Roasted Potatoes, adapted from *Robert Verge's Vegetables in the French Way* (Artisan, 1994) by Roger Verge

ILLUSTRATION BY
CRAIG NELSON
(Based on a photograph by
Bernard Touillon)

COOK'S
ILLUSTRATED

Publisher and Editor	CHRISTOPHER KIMBALL
Consulting Editor	MARK BITTMAN
Senior Editor	JOHN WILLOUGHBY
Food Editor	PAM ANDERSON
Senior Writer	JACK BISHOP
Articles Editor	ANNE TUOMEY
Managing Editor	MAURA LYONS
Assistant Managing Editor	TRICIA O'BRIEN
Copy Editor	GARY PFITZER
Editorial Assistant	KIM N. RUSSELLO
Test Cook	VICTORIA ROLAND
Art Director	MEG BIRNBAUM
Food Stylist	MARIE PIRAINO
Special Projects Designer	AMY KLEE
Marketing Director	ADRIENNE KIMBALL
Circulation Director	ELAINE REPUCCI
Ass't Circulation Manager	JENNIFER L. KEENE
Circulation Coordinator	JONATHAN VENIER
Circulation Assistant	C. MARIA PANNOZZO
Production Director	JAMES MCCORMACK
Production Assistants	SHEILA DATZ
	PAMELA SLATTERY
Ass't Computer Admin.	MATTHEW FRIGO
Production Artist	KEVIN MOELLER
V.P./General Manager	JEFFREY FEINGOLD
Controller	LISA A. CARULLO
Accounting Assistant	MANDY SHITO
Office Manager	JENNY THORNBURY
Office Assistant	SARAH CHUNG
Special Projects	FERN BERMAN

Cook's Illustrated (ISSN 1068-2821) is published bimonthly by Boston Common Press, 17 Station Street, Box 569, Brookline, MA 02147-0569. Copyright 1995 Boston Common Press. Second-class postage paid at Boston, MA, and additional mailing offices, USPS #012487. For list rental information, please contact Direct Media, 200 Pemberwick Rd., Greenwich, CT 06830; 203-532-1000. Editorial office: 17 Station Street, Box 569, Brookline, MA 02147-0569; (617) 232-1000, FAX (617) 232-1572. Editorial contributions should be sent to: Editor, Cook's Illustrated, 17 Station Street, Box 569, Brookline, MA 02147-0569. We cannot assume responsibility for manuscripts submitted to us. Submissions will be returned only if accompanied by a large self-addressed stamped envelope. Subscription rates: $24.95 for one year; $45 for two years; $65 for three years. (Canada: add $3 per year; all other countries: add $12 per year.) Postmaster: Send all new orders, subscription inquiries, and change of address notices to Cook's Illustrated, P.O. Box 59046, Boulder, CO 80322-9046. Single copies: $4 in U.S., $4.95 in Canada and foreign. Back issues available for $5 each. Printed in the U.S.A.

EDITORIAL

FOR THE SAKE OF CONVENIENCE

CHRISTOPHER KIMBALL

I have been attending the same church in Vermont since 1955, the year our family bought twenty acres from Charlie Bentley's father, up behind the old Woodcock place. The church, built in 1877, stands on the edge of a cornfield by the Green River, and if I sit in the right pew, I can look out over the pasture where we still harvest corn with a team of mules hitched to a mechanical corn binder.

Inside the church, things haven't changed much either. Hymns are played on an Estey pump organ made in the 1880s, and the carpet covering the foot pedals is now threadbare. The chandelier is Victorian but simple—gray metal scrollwork capped by large tulip globes. The pews themselves are original, made of oak that has turned dark over the years. It's a modest church—practical and spare—but it serves its purpose in the Yankee tradition of economy and function.

Since our town is without a restaurant or store, one of the church's functions is to serve as a meeting place. After the service, the congregation heads for the back room for coffee and gossip. Just a few weekends ago, I was working on my second biscuit when the town's last farmer came up and asked, "What do you hear about those electric bread machines?"

Now that was quite a question coming from a man whose toolbox contains a hammer, a pair of pliers, a grease gun, and a few yards of baling twine. He owns three vintage Farmall tractors (one of which he bought new in 1949); he knows how to keep them running and uses each for a specific purpose. One has the proper hydraulics for lifting up a baler, one has the proper floating hitch for getting equipment around a tight corner, and the third is the backup tractor—useful when a tire goes flat in the middle of haying. Like a good cook, he prefers his equipment simple and well made—he doesn't pay for extras. Yet, here he was, asking about a $250 piece of kitchen gadgetry that is supposed to replace the best tools any farmer can have: his hands.

Now, I've tried bread machines. I couldn't get a loaf with great crust and real texture, but I made a dozen loaves of pretty good sandwich bread. It was easy but still too complicated for the task at hand. I prefer things well made and simple, like our church. A few well-worn tools in experienced hands are preferable to another jig, another gadget, another extra. I don't need an electric steamer when I can throw a $7 steaming basket in any old pot; I don't bother getting out the food processor when I want to dice a single onion or chop a couple carrots. Yet, I use an electric knife sharpener (I never mastered the traditional whetstone method), I let my standing mixer knead all of my dough these days. I even cook my rice in an electric cooker, my most used and highest rated kitchen appliance. And I sometimes use a fancy electric ice cream machine, which has replaced the old White Mountain freezer we used when I was a kid. I sort of miss the noise, the rock salt, and the ice cubes, but it's a lot easier to plug in the newer model and walk away.

Like many people, I have romantic notions about food. I like to think that Vermont farmers make bread by hand and that they still cut corn with a team, not a tractor, but I can't help but notice the satellite dishes behind the barn. The old Yankee in me believes that life shouldn't be too easy—real satisfaction comes only from accomplishing difficult tasks. But New Englanders are nothing if not practical, cobbling together whatever works best, regardless of whether it's new or old. Perhaps a bread machine isn't all that out of place—Ben Franklin would have been proud to invent it—and it's a gadget that fits right in with hand-cranked corn strippers, the early "Rube Goldberg" stationary hay balers, the horse-powered oat threshers, and my favorite, the dog-powered washing machine (power was supplied by a dog walking on a treadmill—you could tell it was wash day because dogs were scarce).

So I put aside my romantic notions about Vermont and told that farmer to go out and buy a bread machine. I guess it will find a place in his kitchen among the banged-up aluminum pots, the jars of pickled tongue, and the sap buckets stacked in the corner. After all, I could hardly expect him to keep to the old ways when my kitchen has made more than a few nods to modern technology. But as we are softened and cosseted by the march of convenience, we diminish ourselves. And on the day that Vermont farmer passes into history, I will be poorer for it, having witnessed the end of an era, of a time when hard work, thrift, and self-reliance were the coin of the realm. I expect on that day to turn off the computer and head for the fields to do a hard day's work. And at night, I'll go to the kitchen to bake bread by hand, and share it with neighbors, a communion in remembrance of a man, a time, and a place that will have disappeared a little too conveniently for our own good. ∎

NOTES

FROM READERS

COOKWARE POLLUTION

*B*efore you give a clean bill of health to non-stick cookware (see *product review in the November/December 1994 issue*), you should know that the manufacturing process by which these pans are produced is extremely dirty. Substantial amounts of airborne toxins are generated—much, much more than for conventional cast iron. As usual, the basic rule applies: You don't get something for nothing.

ROSS ALLARD
Cary, NC

RESPONSES TO COUNTRY BREAD STORY

Our recent article on "Rustic Country Bread" (January/February 1995) generated a large volume of letters. Our tests with the La Cloche, an unglazed pottery oven covered by a bell-shaped dome, provoked some heated debate. Many readers were quite passionate in their defense of this enclosed cooking vessel. Here's a sampling of the letters we received and subsequent kitchen tests that we conducted. (Note that most bread recipes are better suited to La Cloche than is wet rustic bread dough. Read on for details about our tests.)

LA CLOCHE MAKER COMPLAINS

*I*am dismayed that you did not follow the instructions that came with your La Cloche, which my company manufactures. The bell portion should not be soaked since this product is made out of stoneware and has an absorption factor of less than 1 percent. Perhaps you thought that stoneware has the same properties as terracotta, which does need to be soaked. Secondly, the instructions call for removing the bell during the last ten minutes or so of baking. This produces an evenly browned bread that is very crusty with a superb crumb. The baking time for bread made in La Cloche is exactly the same as a loaf of the same size baked conventionally in the oven. I suggest that you try baking another loaf, and perhaps your kitchen will be filled with the ring of success.

STEVEN SCHWAB
President, Sassafras Enterprises
Chicago, IL

We went back to the kitchen and baked about one dozen loaves of our bread in La Cloche. We followed your instructions and were pleased with the results. Taking the lid off La Cloche during the last ten minutes of baking gave our bread a darker, crisper, crunchier crust. However, we did feel that the crumb was finer and more cakelike than when the bread was baked on hot tiles as recommended in our recipe. The larger holes in the crumb that we love were missing from loaves made in La Cloche. As for total baking times, we found a slight difference: Our bread required thirty-five to forty-five minutes in La Cloche as opposed to thirty-five to forty minutes on tiles.

MORE CLOCHE COMMENTS

*L*ike you, I was ready to give up on La Cloche until I realized I was not wedded to the base. Try this: Place the bell on tiles or a stone and allow it to heat up along with the stone. When your loaf is ready for the oven, peel it onto the stone and cover it with the preheated bell. My loaves brown very nicely even without steam when I do it this way. My bread is usually done after forty or forty-five minutes when I start with a 450-degree oven and lower the temperature to 425 degrees after peeling the bread.

Also, instead of adding hot water to a preheated pan, I simply place a pan filled with cold water in a cold oven. Preheat your oven and stone or tiles as usual. When your oven comes to temperature, you have a pan full of boiling water, an oven full of steam, and you haven't exposed yourself to burns or scalds.

PHILIP BARATTA
La Jolla, CA

We found that preheating the bell on tiles worked fine but proved to be a bit messier than the standard method recommended by the manufacturer. The standard method—sprinkle cornmeal in the bottom of La Cloche at room temperature, turn risen bread into bottom pan, cover with lid, and slide contraption into hot oven—was easier and produced excellent results.

As for our recommendation about adding hot water to a preheated pan on the shelf below the bread, we find that this method guarantees a burst of steam just as the bread begins to bake and helps ensure that the crust is crisp. Although the method you describe may be easier, it will not produce a burst of steam. Of course, no pan of water is needed when La Cloche is used.

LA CLOCHE TRICKS

*H*aving experimented with bread in much the same way as you, I want to lend my support to most of your findings. The one area where I have come up with different results is in the use of La Cloche. After some work, I am convinced that cloche baking is the next best thing to using a fancy oven with steam injection or a brick oven.

The trick is to preheat the oven as high as it will go, up to 550 degrees, spritz the inside of the bell and the loaf itself, then lower the oven to 500 degrees and bake for twenty-five minutes. Then, lower the temperature to 450 degrees to finish baking (another twenty-five to thirty minutes). Yes, the bread does take longer to bake because of the time it takes for the heat to penetrate the cloche, but I have been overwhelmed by the beautiful breads with perfect crusts I have made.

Two more tricks: Place an empty baking sheet on the lower shelf to shield the bottom of the bread from the heating element. This allows for a more even bake, though the bottom always seems to bake darker because of its contact with the clay. Also, when the bread appears to be done (golden brown and hollow-sounding when it is thwacked), about fifty to fifty-five minutes, remove the cloche from the oven but allow the bread to stay in it, covered, for another ten minutes to finish up, then remove the bread to a cooling rack.

DR. PETER REINHART
Santa Rosa, CA

Although our rustic country bread will burn if baked on tiles in an oven set above 450 degrees, we found that it can be baked in La Cloche in an oven set to 500 degrees for twenty-five minutes and then turned down to 450 degrees until done. This higher temperature scheme made a slight improvement in the crust as compared to baking bread straight through at 450 degrees in the La Cloche.

We tried your spritzing suggestions and could not detect any improvements when compared to unspritzed loaves. This, however, turns out to be an asset. There is no need to add water, either in a pan or by spritz bottle, to the oven cooking environment. Also, we found that loaves baked in La Cloche are usually quite attractive. The crust becomes a rich golden color whether or not the water is added.

We too were sometimes disturbed by the thickness of the bottom crust of loaves baked in La Cloche. Sliding a baking sheet on the shelf below La Cloche allowed the heat to circulate better and promoted a more evenly cooked crust. The baking sheet did add about five minutes to the cooking time, which resulted in a darker crust. Overall, we thought this refinement was very useful. Finally, we could not detect any benefit from cooling bread in La Cloche for any period of time. When bread reaches correct temperature (210 degrees), simply remove the loaf from La Cloche and cool it on a rack.

ARE OVEN TILES SAFE?

*I*n several articles, you recommend lining the oven rack with quarry tiles to create a crisp crust. I used tiles for a number of years until several people in the tile business told me that even unglazed tiles are often coated with sealers and other chemicals. Also, since most tiles are made in Mexico and overseas, there is little control over what is used in the production process. I now use a pizza stone to create a brick-oven effect but I wonder what you know about the safety issues connected to the use of tiles for cooking.

HEIDI YORKSHIRE
Portland, OR

We called a number of leading food scientists about this issue. All assured us that these tiles pose no known health dangers, but also cautioned that no specific research has been done in this area. Dr. Joseph Ponte of Kansas State University says that since the tiles are fired at such high temperatures during the manufacturing process, it stands to reason that any volatile compounds would be burned off at that point rather than in your oven. He said that quarry tiles fall into the GRAS (generally regarded as safe) category, although there are no studies that he is aware of to back up this classification. We also checked with the Food and Drug Administration. A spokesperson told us there are no studies or reports that indicate there is any danger posed by using quarry tiles in your oven.

MEASURING FLOUR

*M*any recipes call for sifted flour, but I am sometimes unclear about this term. For "1 cup sifted flour," do you fill a cup with flour, level it off, and sift it, or should you sift flour onto a work surface, scoop it into a cup, and level it off?

ANA STEIN
Oak Brook, IL

We receive a lot of letters asking how to interpret recipes that call for sifted flour. In recipes, "1 cup sifted flour" and "1 cup flour, sifted" are not the same thing. The former describes flour that has been sifted onto a work surface or a piece of paper, then spooned into a measuring cup and leveled off. By putting the word "sifted" after the flour, the second description indicates that the flour should be measured (dip the cup into the flour and sweep off the excess) and then sifted. Although this may seem like a fine point, a cup of flour measured before sifting weighs about five ounces versus just four ounces if measured after the flour has been sifted. Obviously, this difference is enough to affect results in your baking.

This distinction between directions placed before and after ingredients applies to all recipe writing. For instance, "½ cup basil leaves, chopped" and "½ cup chopped basil leaves" are not the same thing. The first phrase indicates that half a cup of basil leaves should be measured out and then chopped. The second phrase indicates that an unknown quantity of basil should be chopped and then measured to equal one-half cup. Again, the difference is definitely enough to affect the dish you are making.

GREENS NUTRITION

*P*am Anderson's article on quick-cooking strong-flavored greens (January/February 1995) could not have been more thorough. I believe her results are valid, and the suggested recipes should be delicious. However, I settle for a more conservative method of preparing greens that compromises a bit more color for better nutrition.

Consider the fact that during blanching, greens lose as much as 50 percent more of certain minerals and vitamins than they do when steamed. Shredding or chopping the greens further increases nutrient loss even though this shortens cooking time. While I realize that your goal was to produce cooked greens of maximum color and tenderness, readers should be advised of the nutrient loss. Just one more example: Greens lose only 10 to 20 percent of their vitamin C when microwaved, but up to 62 percent when boiled.

SUSAN ASANOVIC, R.D.
Wilton, CT

SLOW-COOKED POLENTA

*A*s a polenta fan, I read with great interest Sarah Fritschner's "Foolproof Polenta" (January/February 1995). Over the years I have wrestled with many of the problems she raises. My solution, although different from hers, relies on the same principle as the double-boiler method she advocates.

I prepare polenta in a slow cooker. In order to avoid dirtying a second pot, I tried putting boiling water in the slow cooker on the high setting, adding the cornmeal, and then trying to thicken the polenta. Since this method took forever, I gave up on it. Now, I combine the polenta and water in the traditional fashion on top of the stove, then transfer the mixture to the slow cooker on the low setting for the final cooking. Two or three hours seems to work well, with the occasional stir. I have even left the polenta overnight in the slow cooker when I want to cool and slice it for a layered and baked recipe. The only caveat for cooking polenta this long is that you should not stir the crust that forms on top into the polenta. I simply remove and discard it in the morning.

ROY PALMERI
Cambridge, MA

COUNTING CALORIES

*T*he caloric numbers in your fine bread article are in error. You claim that it takes 225 calories to turn a gram of ice into steam and only 120 calories to turn an equal amount of tap water into steam. Although you have the difference between the two conditions correct (105 calories), your numbers are too low. It takes 720 calories to turn one gram of ice at 0 degrees into steam (540). Assuming your tap water starts at 25 degrees, it takes 615 calories to turn one gram of room temperature water into steam.

ERNEST KULJIAN
Freestone, CA

Thank you for pointing out our math error. Our point that it takes much more energy to turn ice cubes (rather than hot water) into steam is still valid. Therefore, we still recommend that you pour hot water into a preheated pan in the oven to provide steam as bread bakes. ∎

WHAT IS IT?

I use this device to make cheese straws, but it may have other uses. Can you tell me a little about this tool and where I can buy a new one?

LILLIAN COOK
Portsmouth, VA

You own an old-fashioned cookie press. While many modern versions are made of plastic, yours is metal. To use the cookie press, you must fill the cylinder with soft cookie dough. In a modern version, a squeeze on the levered handle shoots dough through a blade in the bottom of the cylinder to form a shaped cookie. Interchangeable blades form different shapes. Your cookie press comes from Sweden. Instead of pressing on the handle to force dough through one of the blades, you simply turn the handle on your model. While modern presses with levers dispense dough in only one thickness, the knob on your press can be adjusted to regulate the thickness of the dough extruded through the bottom of the cylinder. La Cuisine Kitchenware (800-521-1176) can special-order this cookie press from Sweden. It is made of tin over steel, comes with four blades, and costs $14.50.

ILLUSTRATION BY DAN KROVATIN

Quick Tips

PROTECTING PIE CRUST RIMS

Two readers, Mark Smith of Alpharetta, Georgia, and Peggy Beals of Marshfield, Massachusetts, both wrote to suggest this method of protecting the rim of a pie during baking. Not only is it quicker and easier than cutting out strips of aluminum foil, it is also reusable.

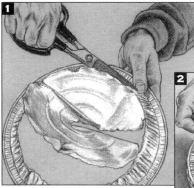

1. Cut the center out of a disposable foil pie plate.

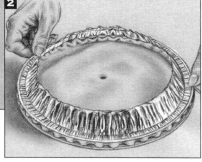

2. Place the trimmed pie plate, top side down, over the rim of the crust during baking.

REMOVING STUFFING EASILY

It's not always easy to scoop all the stuffing from the cavity of a fowl. Russ Webber of Visalia, California, recommends this procedure, which he learned from his wife. (*See* Sources and Resources, page 32, for more information.)

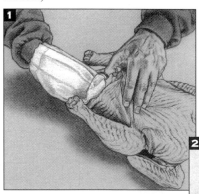

1. Make a cheesecloth bag by folding a piece of cheesecloth in half and sewing up the two sides. (To keep the top edge from fraying, machine-hem along the bag top, if you like.) Line the poultry cavity with the bag.

2. Fill the bag three-quarters full with the stuffing, then roast the bird as usual.

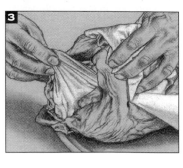

3. When the bird is done, simply remove the bag from the cavity. Since cheesecloth is permeable, the stuffing will have absorbed the juices of the fowl, and you will have a clean carcass to use for soup or stock.

GIVING YOUR CAKES A SILKY LOOK

Professionally decorated cakes always seem to have a molten, silky look. To get that same appearance in your homemade cakes, follow this tip from Amy Botticello of Arlington, Virginia.

1. Frost the sides and top of the cake and smooth out with a spatula as usual.

2. Use a hair dryer to "blow-dry" the frosted surfaces of the cake. The slight melting of the frosting gives it that smooth, lustrous appearance.

CLEANING COFFEE GRINDERS

Sarah Milstein of New York, New York, suggests using a pastry brush or one-inch paintbrush to clean coffee grinders. The brush can get around the metal blade in a blade grinder and also get into the corners of a mill grinder.

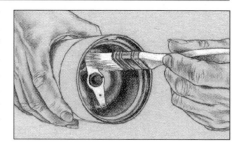

MAKING STEAMED SHRIMP GO FURTHER

Elizabeth Kupp of State College, Pennsylvania, recommends this method of "stretching" the amount of shrimp available; she discovered it one day when unexpected guests dropped by for dinner.

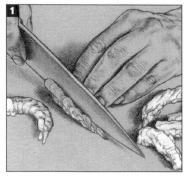

1. Peel and devein the shrimp, then halve them lengthwise and steam.

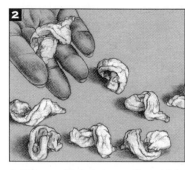

2. The cooked shrimp will curl into spirals and make for an attractive presentation.

ILLUSTRATIONS BY ALAN WITSCHONKE

MAKING DECORATIVE CITRUS SPIRALS

Sometimes during the summer you want to jazz up your cool fruit drinks. Here's a quick and colorful way to do so, suggested by Teina McConnell of Fort Worth, Texas.

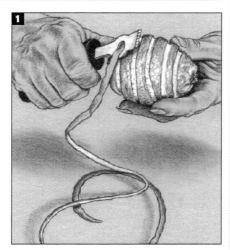

1. Before juicing citrus, use a citrus zester to score around the fruit and make a long strip of curly peel.

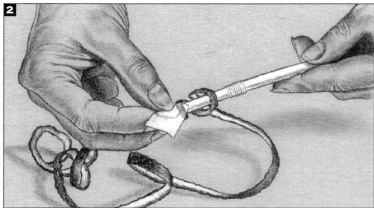

2. Tape the end of the strip of zest to one end of a skewer or plastic drinking straw.

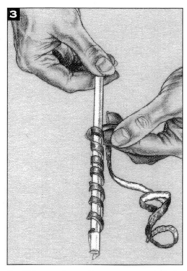

3. Wrap the citrus zest tightly around the rest of the skewer or straw, taping it at the other end.

4. Place the wrapped zest in the freezer. When serving lemonade, sangria, or other fruit drinks, remove the frozen spiraled zest from the skewer or straw, discard the tape, and use as a quick garnish.

MOISTENING PIE DOUGH

When making pie crust, it is often difficult to follow precisely the instructions to "sprinkle water evenly over the flour mixture 1 tablespoon at a time." To easily achieve the desired effect, follow this tip from Elvira Ceci of Woodbridge, Ontario.

1. Pour the entire recommended amount of water into a small spray bottle and spray as needed onto the flour mixture.

2. This allows you to use the minimum amount of water and distribute it evenly with little effort, stopping as soon as the dough holds together.

PREPARING FAVA BEANS

Fava beans are widely eaten around the Mediterranean, and can be found fresh in American markets during the summertime. When buying favas, look for pods that are bright green in color, with no signs of decay. Unlike green beans, which are best when crisp, the pods of fava beans should be soft; crispness is a sign of dried-out beans. To prepare fresh fava beans for cooking, follow these two steps:

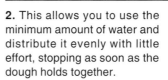

1. Remove the beans from the cushiony, foamlike outer pod.

2. The beans will be covered with a very pale green inner sheath. Although edible, this sheath is quite bitter in all but the youngest beans. Parboil the beans and peel the sheath off with a paring knife.

MEASURING EXTRACTS

When measuring out vanilla extract or other flavorings, follow the advice of Mary Ann Lee of Marco Island, Florida, and use a clean, plastic, measured dropper. This is not only an accurate way of measuring small amounts of liquid; it also avoids drips that are formed by pouring directly out of the bottle.

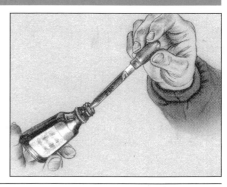

Thanks to our readers for Quick Tips: The editors of *Cook's Illustrated* would like to thank all of the readers who have sent us their quick tips. We have enjoyed reading every one of them, and have learned a lot. Keep them coming. We will provide a one-year complimentary subscription for each quick tip that we print. Send a description of your special technique to *Cook's Illustrated,* P.O. Box 569, Brookline Village, MA 02147-0569. Please write "Attention: Quick Tips" on the envelope and include your name, address, and daytime phone number. Unfortunately, we can only acknowledge receipt of tips that will be printed in the magazine. In case the same tip is received from two readers, the one postmarked first will be selected. Also, be sure to let us know what particular cooking problems you would like us to investigate in upcoming issues.

How to Thicken Fruit Pies

Testing shows that tapioca is the thickener of choice for fruit pies with delicate texture and bright, fresh fruit flavor.

BY CHRIS KIMBALL

For many years I have tried using flour and corn starch to thicken fresh blueberry or strawberry-rhubarb pies, but the results have been uniformly poor. Either I ended up with a pie from which the filling slid out like melted cheese when I cut it, or I had to use so much thickener that the bright, fresh flavor of the fruit was adulterated. Nothing worked.

So I decided to do a kitchen test to determine the best thickener. I baked four separate batches of blueberries. Each started with three cups of blueberries combined with one teaspoon of lemon juice and one-half cup of sugar. Then I added two tablespoons of four different thickeners, one to each batch: corn starch, wheat flour, tapioca, and arrowroot.

The corn starch thickened well, but at a price: It yielded dull fruit, lacking in bright flavor and noticeably less acid. As a result, the mixture tasted sweeter and heavier. The flour resulted in fruit that was similarly unsatisfying in appearance and taste, and it also had another failing: Two tablespoons was not enough to firm up the fruit well. To give flour another chance, I ran a test using four tablespoons. This time, the fruit was gummy and almost inedible. As it turns out, this is because flour, unlike the other three thickeners, contains proteins and other components as well as starch. As a result, it takes at least twice as much flour by volume to create the same degree of thickening as corn starch. This amount of flour will adversely affect your cherry or blueberry pie—you can taste it.

By contrast, the samples of fruit thickened with the root starches, arrowroot and tapioca, were clear and bright in appearance, and the flavor of the fruit came through clearly. Of the two, tapioca showed a bit more thickening power and was therefore my favorite.

Testing Tapioca

Based on this initial testing, I eliminated flour and corn starch as possible thickeners for fruit pies. I then pitted instant tapioca versus arrowroot in a head-to-head test. I baked two blueberry pies, each one using six cups of fruit and four tablespoons of one of these thickeners.

Again, both pies had a pleasing appearance, but the one thickened with tapioca turned out considerably thicker. As an additional benefit, tapioca is also cheaper than arrowroot—an 8-ounce box costs about $2.49 whereas a 1.87-ounce jar of McCormick's arrowroot costs $3.89.

During additional testing I found that the amount of tapioca should be varied depending on the juiciness of the berries. If you like a juicier pie, three tablespoons of tapioca is an adequate amount for six cups of fresh blueberries, for example. If you like a really firm pie with no juices, five tablespoons is the correct amount. When the test kitchen at Kraft was queried about their tapioca-heavy back-of-the-box recipe, the people there explained that they like to operate with a large margin of safety—that is, they suggest using a large amount of tapioca (four tablespoons Minute Tapioca to four cups of fruit) to be absolutely sure that the pie firms up properly. I like some juice and therefore opt for the lower quantity recommended in the Classic Blueberry Pie recipe at right.

When I made a lattice-top pie, however, I ran into trouble. I found that the tapioca on top of the fruit baked into hard bits that felt like eating Tic-Tacs. For an open or lattice pie, therefore, I suggest mixing all of the tapioca with three-quarters of the fruit, filling the pie, and then adding the balance of the fruit on top.

By the way, if you find only pearl tapioca in your pantry, just place it in a spice grinder, blender, or food processor and grind away. Now you have "instant" tapioca. The other solution, suggested by one manufacturer, is to allow pearl tapioca to soak in water before using. However, when I tested this method, I found that the tapioca's thickening powers were greatly diminished because it had already sucked in about as much water as it could handle before baking began. Since high heat does increase the ability of a thickener to absorb water, the pie did thicken somewhat, even with this partially hydrated tapioca, albeit at a greatly reduced rate. As a result, I don't recommend presoaking; just use quick-cooking tapioca if you can.

The Effects of Sugar and Acid

In addition to choosing a thickener, I needed to test the theories that both sugar and acidity adversely affect the thickening process. I found that, despite the fact that sugar does sop up the water that is necessary to the thickening process, this property had no effect when making fruit pies. The reason for this is simple: The proportion of sugar is low enough that it actually absorbs little water, leaving plenty of available water for the thickening agent to do its work.

The situation is similar with acid, which in general will inhibit thickening by causing the starch molecules to break into shorter lengths. In a lemon meringue pie, for example, this can create problems, so the lemon juice is usually added after thickening occurs. However, in a fruit pie containing only two teaspoons of juice per six cups of fruit, the home cook need not worry.

I also discovered that it is important to let fruit pies sit and cool, as this will allow the juices to thicken. A fresh fruit pie will not completely set until it comes to room temperature (allow at least one hour).

CLASSIC BLUEBERRY PIE

Makes one 9-inch pie, serving 6 to 8

The amount of sugar and tapioca you use is relative, depending on the fruit's quality and your taste. If you prefer a less sweet pie or if the fruit is especially sweet, use the lower sugar amount. If you like your pie juices fairly thick, or if the fruit is really juicy, then opt for the higher amount of tapioca. If you are using frozen fruit, measure it frozen, but let it thaw before filling the pie. If not, you run the risk of partially cooked fruit and undissolved tapioca.

Pie Dough

- 2¼ cups all-purpose flour, plus extra for dusting
- 1 teaspoon salt
- 2 tablespoons sugar
- 11 tablespoons chilled unsalted butter, cut into ¼-inch pieces
- 7 tablespoons chilled all-vegetable shortening
- ⅓–⅜ cup ice water

Blueberry Filling

- 3 pints (6 cups) blueberries, rinsed and picked over
- ¾–1 cup sugar
- 2 teaspoons juice and 1 teaspoon zest from small lemon
- ¼ teaspoon allspice
  Pinch nutmeg
- 3–4 tablespoons quick-cooking tapioca
- 2 tablespoons unsalted butter, cut into small pieces

1. Mix flour, salt, and sugar in food processor fitted with steel blade. Scatter butter pieces over flour mixture, tossing to coat butter with a little flour. Cut butter into flour with five 1-second pulses. Add shortening and continue to cut it in until flour is pale yellow and resembles coarse cornmeal with butter bits no larger than small peas, about four more 1-second pulses. Turn mixture into medium bowl.

2. Sprinkle all but 1 tablespoon of the ice water over mixture. With blade of rubber spatula, use folding motion to mix. Press down on dough with broad side of spatula until dough sticks together, adding up to 1 tablespoon of remaining ice water if dough does not come together. Divide dough into two balls, one slightly larger than the other. Flatten each into 4-inch-wide disk. Dust lightly with flour, wrap separately in plastic, and refrigerate at least 30 minutes.

3. Remove dough from refrigerator; let stand at room temperature to soften slightly, about 10 minutes. Heat oven to 400 degrees. Toss fruit with sugar, lemon juice and zest, spices, and tapioca; let stand for 15 minutes.

4. Roll larger dough disk on lightly floured surface into 12-inch circle, about ⅛-inch thick. Transfer and fit dough into 9-inch Pyrex pie pan, leaving dough that overhangs the lip in place. Turn fruit mixture, including juices, into pie shell. Scatter butter pieces over fruit. Refrigerate until ready to top with remaining dough.

5. Roll smaller disk on lightly floured surface into 10-inch circle. Lay over fruit. Trim top and bottom dough edges to ½ inch beyond pan lip. Tuck this rim of dough underneath itself so that folded edge is flush with pan lip. Flute dough in your own fashion, or press with fork tines to seal. Cut four slits at right angles on dough top to allow steam to escape. If pie dough is very soft, place in freezer for 10 minutes before baking.

6. Place pie on baking sheet; bake until top crust is golden, 20 to 25 minutes. Reduce oven temperature to 350 degrees and continue to bake until juices bubble and crust is golden brown, 30 to 40 minutes longer.

7. Transfer pie to wire rack; let cool to almost room temperature so juices have time to thicken, from 1 to 2 hours.

STRAWBERRY-RHUBARB PIE

Follow instructions for Classic Blueberry Pie, using 3 cups hulled and sliced strawberries and 3 cups rhubarb, trimmed and cut into 1-inch pieces, instead of blueberries. Substitute 1 tablespoon orange zest for lemon zest, omit allspice

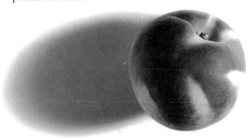

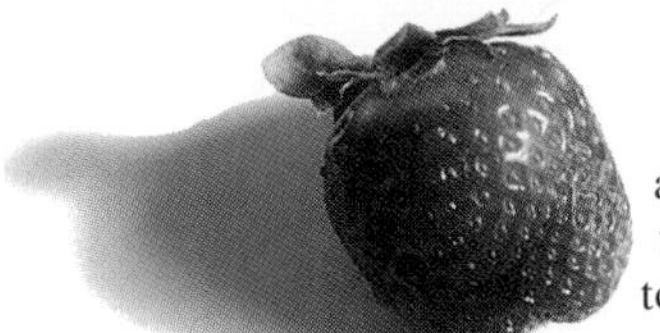

and nutmeg, and add ¼ teaspoon vanilla extract to fruit mixture.

PEACH PIE

Follow instructions for Classic Blueberry Pie, using 6 cups (about 3 pounds) peeled, pitted, and sliced peaches instead of blueberries. Substitute ½ cup brown sugar for ½ cup of the granulated sugar (leave remainder as granulated). Increase pinch nutmeg to ¼ teaspoon and add 1 tablespoon minced crystallized ginger and ¼ teaspoon salt to peach mixture.

CHERRY PIE

Follow instructions for Classic Blueberry Pie, using 6 cups of pitted fresh or frozen cherries instead of blueberries. Decrease allspice from ¼ to ⅛ teaspoon, and omit nutmeg. Add ⅛ teaspoon cinnamon, ⅛ teaspoon almond extract, and 1 tablespoon brandy to fruit mixture. Note: With sour cherries you should use the higher amount of sugar and tapioca. ∎

WHAT IS TAPIOCA?

You can usually tell where a starch comes from by its name. Thus, corn starch is made from corn, rice starch from rice, wheat starch from wheat, and arrowroot comes from the root of the arrowroot plant. But tapioca, our favorite thickener for fruit pies, is not quite so obvious: It comes from the root of the cassava plant. Also called "manioc," this plant is grown throughout most of the tropical world and is harvested when its roots are about six to twelve inches long. The starchy root can be boiled and eaten, and in many countries it takes the place of rice or potatoes in the diet.

To make what we know as tapioca, the starch is separated from the plant and cellulose material in the root. Pearl tapioca is made from tapioca starch that is heated into pearls. To create Minute Tapioca, the starch is partially gelatinized and then pasted together into pellets to improve its thickening powers. While we usually don't think of processing food as necessarily a good thing, with the case of tapioca, it results in a much more usable product.

STARCH SCIENCE

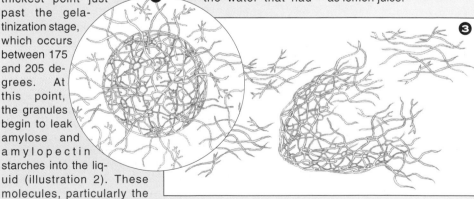

Starch occurs in granules (see illustration 1). These granules are essentially insoluble in their natural state, and only begin to absorb water with the introduction of energy in the form of heat. As the water begins to seep into the granules, they swell and begin to bump into one another, so that the mixture thickens. The solution reaches its thickest point just past the gelatinization stage, which occurs between 175 and 205 degrees. At this point, the granules begin to leak amylose and amylopectin starches into the liquid (illustration 2). These molecules, particularly the long amylose chains, form a web that traps the swollen granules, thickening the liquid even further.

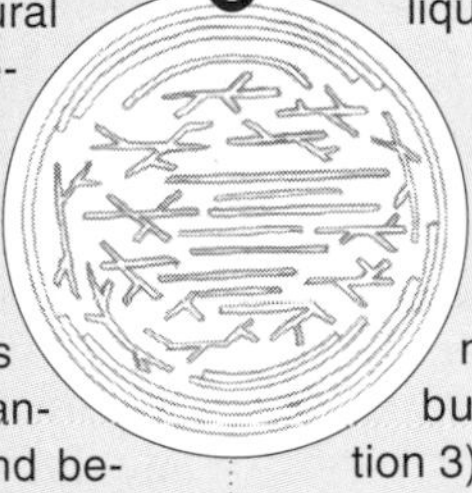

At a temperature somewhere near boiling, however, the granules have swollen to their maximum size and burst open (illustration 3). This bursting has two consequences: It allows most of the starch molecules to escape, and it also forces the water that had been absorbed by the granule to escape back into the mixture. As a result, the mixture begins to thin out again.

Obviously, this is not desirable, so manufacturers further process starches, such as Minute Tapioca, to avoid bursting granules. This preserves a creamier, more pleasant texture during thickening. The processing also makes starches less likely to have their thickening properties impaired by acids such as lemon juice.

How to Quick-Cook Zucchini

Either salt and drain or shred and squeeze this vegetable before sautéing, or slice it lengthwise and throw it on the grill.

∼ BY JACK BISHOP ∼

Given zucchini's ability to take over a garden, it's no surprise that cooks have devised dozens of ways to use this vegetable in everything from breads to pasta sauces. For this article, I wanted to answer a single question: Assuming that you have several pounds of zucchini in the garden or in the refrigerator, what are the best ways to turn it into a side dish?

I focused my attention and experiments on the three main steps involved in making zucchini: selection, preparation, and cooking. My recommendations in each area are strongly influenced by the main problem that confronts the cook when preparing zucchini—its wateriness. Zucchini is 95 percent water (among vegetables, only lettuce contains more water) and will become soupy if it is just thrown into a hot pan.

If zucchini cooks in its own juices, it will not brown. But since browning gives zucchini (as well as other foods) a rich, sweet flavor, I wanted to figure out a way to rid zucchini of some of its water before cooking. I also suspected that water was responsible for another problem I've often encountered when cooking zucchini. I've sometimes found that thick slices of zucchini are soft on the outside but firm and crunchy in the middle after cooking. I wanted to devise a method to ensure that the zucchini was evenly cooked throughout.

Selection and Preparation Tips

The first precautions against wateriness must take place in the supermarket. Size and firmness are the most important factors when purchasing zucchini. I find when it comes to commercially grown zucchini, the smaller ones are more flavorful and less watery than larger ones. Smaller zucchini also have fewer seeds. I look for zucchini that weigh less than eight ounces, and ideally less than six ounces. Mammoth zucchini may be fine as boats for a vegetable stuffing, but they are not my first choice for quick side dishes. Of course, all zucchini no matter their size should be firm with no soft spots.

The second issue is preparation. Many cookbooks recommend salting zucchini in order to draw out some of the moisture before cooking. The chemistry behind this reaction is quite sim-

To Shred Zucchini for Sautéing

1. Shred trimmed zucchini on the large holes of a box grater or in a food processor fitted with the shredding disk.

2. Wrap shredded zucchini in towels to squeeze out the excess liquid, then proceed immediately with sautéing.

To Slice Zucchini for Sautéing

3. Slice trimmed zucchini into ¼-inch-thick rounds, sprinkle with salt, and set aside for 30 minutes. Rinse and thoroughly dry before sautéing.

To Slice Zucchini for Grilling

4. Slice trimmed zucchini lengthwise into ½-inch-thick strips and proceed immediately with grilling.

ple. Water inside the zucchini is attracted to areas of higher ion concentration on the salted surface. The same reaction occurs with salt-cured meats.

After conducting about a dozen tests with salting, I found two methods for eliminating some of the water from zucchini before cooking. Sliced zucchini tossed with one and a half teaspoons of kosher salt per pound shed about twenty percent of its weight after sitting for thirty minutes. Almost three tablespoons of water was thrown off by the zucchini, further confirmation that the salt

was drawing out water. Although salting is not worth it unless you have thirty minutes to let the zucchini sit, I found that longer periods (I tried up to three hours) did not increase the amount of moisture extracted.

As you might expect, various amounts of salt were more or less effective. However, even after rinsing I thought zucchini sprinkled with more than one and a half teaspoons of kosher salt per pound was too salty after cooking. I found that one and a half teaspoons of salt delivered the maximum results while not adversely affecting flavor—as long as the zucchini was rinsed and thoroughly dried just before cooking.

If you don't have the time to salt the zucchini before sautéing, there is another option. Moisture from grated zucchini can be extracted manually by simply wrapping the shredded vegetable between several layers of paper towels or a large kitchen towel and squeezing (see illustrations 1 and 2). In fact, I was able to reduce the weight of shredded zucchini by 25 percent (more than salting ever achieved) by firmly squeezing it in paper towels. Since sliced zucchini has so much less surface area, this manual method for water extraction does not work. I tried weighting sliced and salted zucchini between two pans and also tried pressing on it by hand, but very little water actually came out.

I also tried extracting moisture from shredded zucchini by placing it in batches in a potato ricer with a very fine disk. This method was equally effective at removing water but tended to crush and bruise the zucchini. My first choice for removing water from grated zucchini is thus the towel-drying method.

In addition to salting, there is some controversy about soaking zucchini before cooking. Many Italian cookbooks claim that soaking zucchini "freshens" their flavor. In my tests, I found no difference between zucchini soaked in cold water for thirty minutes before slicing or shredding and zucchini that was simply washed.

My recommendation is to skip the soaking unless the zucchini is particularly dirty. In this case, soak for five minutes in a bowl of cold water.

The final step in making zucchini is the choice of cooking method. Since I was looking for ways to make quick side dishes, slower methods like roasting or stewing were not considered. Furthermore, moist cooking methods like boiling and steaming do nothing to counteract the wateriness of zucchini or to promote browning, so they are not my first choice.

Zucchini benefits most from dry-heat cooking methods like grilling and broiling, since liquid in the vegetable evaporates, causing the delicate flavor to become concentrated. In fact, when grilling, it is not necessary, or even desirable, to remove liquid by salting. Given the intense heat of the grill, I find that the high moisture content in the zucchini actually helps prevent the vegetable from scorching over hot coals. In effect, the water allows the zucchini to cook through without becoming incinerated. Also, since the cooking surface on a grill is open, water simply drops down onto the coals rather than sitting in a skillet. So much evaporation occurs during grilling over a hot fire that salting is not an issue.

Sautéing, however, is another matter. Even in a blazing hot pan, the zucchini will soon start to steam in its own juices. Water must be drained out before sautéing, either by slicing and salting or by shredding and squeezing.

The recipes below illustrate three techniques for handling zucchini. Since the flavoring agents can be easily altered, use these recipes as master techniques for preparing zucchini as a quick side dish. Several possible variations are listed, but these recipes lend themselves to endless last-minute improvisation.

SHREDDED ZUCCHINI SAUTÉ WITH GARLIC AND HERBS
(Master Recipe)
Serves 4

A shredding and drying technique is the best choice when you are pressed for time and want to cook zucchini indoors. Use any fresh herb on hand, varying the amount depending on its intensity. For instance, use two tablespoons of basil, parsley, or chives but just one tablespoon of oregano, thyme, or tarragon.

- 3 tablespoons olive oil
- 4 medium zucchini (about 1 ⅓ pounds), rinsed, trimmed, shredded, and squeezed dry (*see* illustrations 1 and 2, page 8)
- 2 medium garlic cloves, minced
- 1–2 tablespoons minced fresh herb leaves, such as parsley, basil, tarragon, or mint
- Salt and ground black pepper

Heat oil in 10-inch (preferably nonstick) skillet over medium-high heat. Add zucchini and garlic; cook, stirring occasionally, until zucchini is tender, about 7 minutes. Stir in herbs and salt and pepper to taste. Serve immediately.

SHREDDED ZUCCHINI AND CARROT SAUTÉ WITH GARLIC AND HERBS

Follow Master Recipe for Shredded Zucchini Sauté with Garlic and Herbs, substituting two

medium peeled and shredded carrots for one of the zucchini.

CREAMED ZUCCHINI WITH HERBS

Follow Master Recipe for Shredded Zucchini Sauté with Garlic and Herbs, substituting an equal amount of butter for olive oil. Omit garlic. Add ¼ cup heavy cream along with herbs; simmer briefly until cream is absorbed.

ZUCCHINI FRITTATA WITH PARMESAN AND HERBS

Heat broiler. Beat six large eggs with 3 tablespoons grated Parmesan cheese in medium bowl; set aside. Follow Master Recipe for Shredded Zucchini Sauté with Garlic and Herbs, stirring fully cooked zucchini mixture into eggs. Heat 2 additional teaspoons oil in the now empty skillet over medium heat. Add zucchini-egg mixture; cook until frittata is almost set, 4 to 5 minutes. Slide skillet under broiler and cook until frittata is set and top is browned. Do not let frittata burn. Flip onto serving plate. Serve hot or at room temperature.

SAUTÉED ZUCCHINI WITH LEMON AND HERBS
(Master Recipe)
Serves 4

Salt causes zucchini rounds to release excess water. This important extra step helps the zucchini to sauté rather than stew in its own juices. I found quarter-inch slices the perfect thickness. Thinner slices fall apart during cooking; thicker slices require a longer salting time. Use any fresh herb, varying the amount depending on its intensity. (Use more of the soft-leaved herbs such as mint, basil, or parsley, and less of the more intense ones such as oregano, thyme, or rosemary.) If you do not have kosher salt on hand, use a teaspoon or so of regular table salt.

- 4 medium zucchini (about 1⅓ pounds), rinsed, trimmed, and sliced crosswise into rounds about ¼ inch thick (*see* illustration 3, page 8)
- Kosher salt
- 3 tablespoons olive oil
- 1 small onion or 2 large shallots, minced
- 1 teaspoon grated zest and 1 tablespoon juice from 1 medium lemon
- 1–2 tablespoons minced fresh herb leaves
- Ground black pepper

1. Place zucchini slices in colander and sprinkle with 2 teaspoons salt. Set colander over bowl until about ⅓ cup water drains from zucchini, about 30 minutes. Rinse and thoroughly dry zucchini.

2. Heat oil in large skillet over medium heat. Add onions or shallots; sauté until almost softened, about 3 minutes. Increase heat to medium-high; add zucchini and lemon zest and sauté until zucchini is golden brown, about 10 minutes.

3. Stir in lemon juice and herbs, and season with pepper to taste. Adjust seasonings and serve immediately.

SAUTÉED ZUCCHINI WITH WALNUTS AND HERBS

Follow Master Recipe for Sautéed Zucchini with Lemon and Herbs, omitting lemon zest and juice and adding 2 tablespoons toasted chopped walnuts along with herbs.

SAUTÉED ZUCCHINI WITH OLIVES AND LEMON

Follow Master Recipe for Sautéed Zucchini with Lemon and Herbs, adding ¼ cup chopped Kalamata olives along with lemon juice and using thyme or oregano as the herb.

SAUTÉED ZUCCHINI WITH PANCETTA AND PARSLEY

Follow Master Recipe for Sautéed Zucchini with Lemon and Herbs, omitting olive oil. Add 2 ounces pancetta or bacon slices, cut into a small dice, to skillet before adding onions. When fat renders, add onions and continue with recipe. Omit lemon zest and juice, and use parsley as the fresh herb.

GRILLED ZUCCHINI SALAD WITH TOMATOES AND BASIL
Serves 6

Grilled zucchini can also be marinated in a vinaigrette made with red wine vinegar. Feel free to use any fresh herb on hand in the dressing. Grilled zucchini can be served right from the grill as a simple side dish with grilled meats, poultry, or fish.

- 6 medium zucchini (about 2 pounds), rinsed, trimmed, and sliced lengthwise into ½-inch-thick strips (*see* illustration 4, page 8)
- ¼ cup olive oil
- Salt and ground black pepper
- 2 tablespoons balsamic vinegar
- 2 large ripe tomatoes, cored and cut into thin wedges
- 2 tablespoons minced fresh basil leaves

1. Heat grill. Lay zucchini on large baking sheet and brush both sides with 2 tablespoons of the oil. Sprinkle generously with salt and pepper.

2. When grill rack is hot, use stiff wire brush to scrape surface clean. Grill zucchini until dark grill marks are visible on one side, 2 to 3 minutes. Turn and continue to grill until other side is marked, about 2 minutes. Remove from grill and cool briefly.

3. Whisk remaining 2 tablespoons oil with balsamic vinegar, ½ teaspoon salt, and ¼ teaspoon pepper. Toss tomatoes and basil with dressing in large bowl.

4. Cut grilled zucchini into 1-inch pieces. Toss with tomatoes and dressing. Adjust seasonings and serve. (Can be covered and set aside at room temperature for up to 3 hours at this point.) ■

Thin-Sliced Salmon Rolls with Couscous Filling

Pound a piece of fish—in this case salmon fillet—until it is thin, and you have the perfect wrapper for a stuffing of grains and seasonings.

~ BY MARK BITTMAN ~

It's about time some creative chef came up with a new way to wrap a fillet of fish around a filling before cooking it. Too often, restaurants—and cookbooks, for that matter—offer something like "baked stuffed fish," in which a fillet, usually one of flounder or some other relatively uninteresting fish, is wrapped around an unappetizing filling containing crabmeat, cheese, and bread crumbs. The resulting dish is an overly rich, gooey mess in which all the flavor of the fish is lost.

Michael Lomonaco, head chef at the renowned '21' Club in midtown New York, has developed a much better way. He begins with a center cut of boneless salmon, then cuts it into three not-too-thin horizontal slices. He sandwiches the slices between two sheets of plastic wrap, then gently pounds them into a thickness of between an eighth and a quarter of an inch. This technique, which has long been used for veal or boneless chicken breasts, translates perfectly to many meaty fish—not only salmon, but tuna and swordfish as well.

It results in a paillard that can not only be wrapped around any filling you like, but used for carpaccio (see "Fast Salmon Carpaccio," page 11).

Lomonaco proceeds by laying one of a variety of light, complementary stuffings on each of the paillards. In this instance, he chose one made of cooked cabbage, shiitake mushrooms, couscous, and seasonings. Using the plastic wrap, he rolls each of the salmon sheets tightly; at this point they can be refrigerated for several hours. When ready to cook, he quickly sautés the rolls (since the filling is cooked, it's just a matter of searing the fish), builds a light sauce based on the pan juices, Pernod, tomato, and tarragon, and serves the rolls on a bed of sautéspinach.

The resulting dish is not only attractive and impressive, but light and delicious. Furthermore, it can be made from start to finish in about an hour (if the stuffing is prepared in advance, the whole process takes about thirty minutes). Served with bread and/or another carbohydrate, it is the centerpiece of a deceptively elegant meal.

"There are no difficult techniques whatsoever involved in preparing this dish," says Lomonaco. "Just choose a thin-bladed carving, boning, or fillet knife to cut the fillet into three pieces, and work slowly." It helps if the fish is very cold before you begin cutting the slices; since salmon is a fatty fish, you might even consider putting it in the freezer for thirty minutes or so to firm it up even more. When making the slices, press the fish firmly to the table with your free hand to maintain an even thickness.

When it comes to pounding, the job is even easier. Says Lomonaco, "You can use almost anything to pound the salmon slices: a meat mallet, of course, or a rubber mallet, a rolling pin, even a small sauté pan." When you are pounding, use a very light touch, not only because the fish tears more easily than meat, but also because you are *not* trying to make the slices as thin as possible. In fact, you are just looking for circles or rectangles

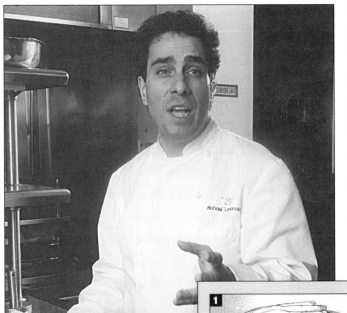

Michael Lomonaco, chef at New York's "21" Club, uses fish as a wrapper to create a dish that is tasty, healthful, and unusual enough to be festive.

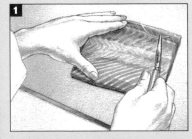

1. Start with a 5-to-6-inch-long center-cut salmon fillet. Check for any remaining pin bones (the long bones that run down the center of the fillet) and remove them with tweezers or needle-nose pliers.

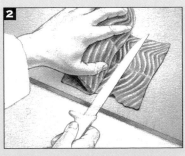

2. Holding a thin-bladed boning or fillet knife parallel to the work surface, cut the fillet from the skin, leaving as little of the meat on the skin as possible.

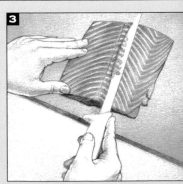

3. Use the knife to remove any of the dark, fatty tissue that remains on the skin side of the fillet.

PHOTOGRAPHS BY VINCENT LEE

of about seven or eight inches across, which means a thickness of just under a quarter of an inch (for carpaccio, you can pound the fish a bit thinner). If you do tear the salmon while you're pounding it, it's virtually self-sealing: Just overlap some of the flesh around the hole and pound gently.

Once the salmon fillets are flattened, you can refrigerate them for a few hours, still in their plastic covers, or roll them up right away. Once again, this is an extremely simple procedure, which will take you less than a minute or two per roll once you get going. The filling Lomonaco has chosen here is just one of an almost infinite number of possibilities: Almost any combination of grains and vegetables will serve nicely: spiced bread crumbs, rice, or kasha, cabbage scented with Asian spices, spinach with ginger and garlic (in which case the rolls might be placed on a bed of rice), and so on.

The reduction sauce, made at the last minute, after the rolls have been sautéed and are resting at low temperature in the oven, can also be varied greatly. Lomonaco uses Pernod—an anise-scented liqueur—complemented by tarragon, which also has a bit of licorice flavor to it, but as he notes, "You could also go with dry vermouth, ginger, and coriander, for example, or red wine and *herbes de Provence,* or a tiny bit of gin and some crushed juniper berries." It makes sense, of course, to match the flavorings in the sauce to those in the stuffing, but since salmon is such a full-flavored dish—one that can stand up to a range of seasonings—the number of options is really quite impressive.

In short, this is a series of techniques on which you can build any number of dishes simply by varying the filling and sauce ingredients. "I use these same techniques over and over again," says Lomonaco. "They're basic and simple, but they allow me to create a lovely, flavorful dish beginning with any number of raw ingredients."

SHIITAKE-STUFFED SALMON ROLLS WITH TARRAGON-TOMATO SAUCE
Serves 6

If you do not have two large skillets, cook the salmon rolls in two batches, keeping the cooked rolls warm while the remaining rolls cook. If you like, serve the salmon on a bed of spinach that has been sautéed with olive oil and garlic.

Shiitake Stuffing
2 tablespoons olive oil
1 small onion, cut into small dice
3 medium shallots, minced
2 large garlic cloves, minced
1 pound fresh shiitakes or other mushrooms, cleaned and sliced thin
2 large Napa cabbage leaves, shredded fine (about 1 cup)
½ cup dry white wine
1 cup cooked couscous (follow package instructions)
2 tablespoons minced fresh thyme leaves
Salt and ground black pepper

2 1-pound 5-to-6-inch-long center-cut salmon fillets, each fillet cut into three pieces and pounded (*see* illustrations 1 through 5, pages 10 and 11)
2 tablespoons olive oil, plus extra for brushing

Tarragon-Tomato Sauce
½ cup Pernod
1 cup dry white wine
1 large tomato, seeded and diced (about 1 cup)
¼ cup minced fresh tarragon leaves
4 tablespoons unsalted butter
Salt and ground black pepper

1. *For the stuffing:* Heat oil in large skillet over medium-high heat. Add onions and shallots; cook until partially softened, 2 to 3 minutes. Add garlic; cook until onions completely soften, 1 to 2 minutes longer. Add mushrooms; sauté until nicely browned, about 8 minutes. Add cabbage; cook until wilted, about 2 minutes. Add wine; simmer for 1 minute. Reduce heat to low, add couscous, and cook until all liquid has been absorbed. Stir in thyme, and season to taste with salt and pepper. Cool to room temperature.

2. Following illustrations 6 and 7, fill and roll salmon. Cover and refrigerate until ready to cook. (Can be refrigerated up to 4 hours.)

3. Heat broiler. Season salmon rolls with salt and pepper; brush tops with oil. Heat 1 tablespoon of oil in each of two large, nonstick skillets over medium-high heat. Add three rolls to each skillet; cook until nicely browned on bottom side, about 2 minutes. Remove each skillet from heat, then broil (about 3 inches from heat source) until browned on top. Carefully transfer rolls from each skillet and keep warm.

4. *For the sauce:* To one of the skillets, add Pernod and simmer until nearly evaporated, about 3 minutes. Add wine; simmer until reduced by half, about 5 minutes. Add tomatoes and tarragon; simmer until tomatoes have cooked into the sauce, about 3 minutes longer. Swirl in butter to create smooth, creamy sauce; season to taste with salt and pepper.

5. Carefully transfer salmon rolls to warm dinner plates. Drizzle portion of warm sauce over each roll and serve immediately. ■

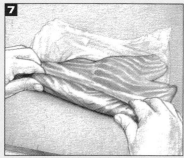

FAST SALMON CARPACCIO

If you are certain that your salmon is spanking fresh (or if it was properly handled frozen salmon), you can turn the pounded salmon fillets into carpaccio. Cut each pounded section in half, lay it on a plate, and garnish it simply, with a sprinkling of a fragrant extra-virgin olive oil, some high-quality balsamic vinegar, and a bit of minced red onion and/or capers; or more elaborately, with some lime segments, a dice of avocado, fresh tomato, and red onion, minced cilantro, basil, and chives, and a bit of olive oil and lime juice. Serve immediately.

1. Beginning one-third of the way down the thickness of the fillet, cut an even slice, holding the fish firmly in place with your free hand. Repeat so that you wind up with three pieces of even thickness.

5. Place each slice between two pieces of plastic wrap and pound gently, using a meat mallet, rubber mallet, rolling pin, or small sauté-pan. Pound the fish until it is 7 or 8 inches across in both directions.

6. Remove the top piece of plastic, but leave the fish on the bottom piece; make sure the line of its backbone is perpendicular to your body. Spoon a portion of filling onto the center of the fillet. Spread the filling along the center of the fish.

7. Use the plastic wrap to roll the fish fairly tightly, making sure you don't get any of the wrap caught in the roll.

No More Watery Coleslaw

To avoid watery slaw, salt and drain the cabbage before mixing.

❧ BY PAM ANDERSON WITH KAREN TACK ❧

Despite its simplicity, two things have always bothered me about my coleslaw: the pool of watery dressing at the bottom of the bowl after a few hours, and the salad's sharpness, regardless of the kind or quantity of vinegar I used. My slaw always seemed to taste better when I tried it again the next day, but by then the dressing was the consistency of milk.

Also, even though the food processor proved efficient for making large quantities of coleslaw, I always wanted to avoid the machine setup and cleanup for a measly half cabbage. And because I found hand-shredding such a small amount of cabbage to be a more tedious process than cleaning lettuce, tossed salad usually won out for family meals.

So, with these problems in mind, we began our coleslaw tests. First, we wanted to keep the cabbage from watering down the dressing; second, we wanted to make the salad piquant without tasting too sharp; and finally, we wanted to find out if there was an easier way to hand-shred cabbage.

Shred, Slice, Sliver, or Grate?

We started with cabbage shredding first. After experimenting with shredding the cabbage by hand, on a box grater, with a mandolin-style gadget, and with the steel blade, slicing disk, and grating disk on a Cuisinart food processor (as well as trying two additional specialty slicing disks), we determined that the slicing disk original to the food processor was indeed the best shredding tool for large jobs (see "Testing Ways to Shred Cabbage," page 13). For a half cabbage or less, though, we preferred a sharp chef's knife and the shredding technique shown in illustrations 1 through 3, page 13. The resulting cabbage shreds were long and thin, perfect for coleslaw.

Separating the leaves when using this technique made us realize we could separate them the same way for the food processor. Rather than having to cut the cabbage to fit through the feeder tube, we simply separated the cabbage-quarter stacks, whose leaves we could then roll to fit through the tube.

For those who prefer a more chopped slaw, it's simple to cut the hand-shredded cabbage into a fine dice. Simply turn the shreds crosswise and chop fine. The food processor did not serve well

Green and red cabbage should be salted before mixing, but Savoy and Napa have a different structure and become too limp when salted.

for this finer degree of cutting. Running the cabbage through the grating disk caused it to be chewed up and rough, while the cabbage chopped with the food processor's steel blade was inconsistent—some pieces chopped fine, others barely chopped, and all of them bruised.

Icy Plunge or Salt and Dry?

While most recipes instruct the cook to toss the shredded cabbage immediately with dressing, a few add an extra step. Either the shredded (or merely quartered) cabbage is soaked in ice water for crispening and refreshing, or it is salted, drained, and allowed to wilt (see "Where There's Salt, There's Water" below).

Cabbage soaked in ice water was crisp, plump, and fresh. If looks were all that mattered, this cabbage would have scored high next to the limp, salted cabbage in the neighboring colander. But its good looks were deceiving. Even though we drained the cabbage and dried it thoroughly, the dressing didn't really adhere. Furthermore, within minutes, the cabbage shreds started to lose their recently acquired water, so an even larger puddle of water diluted the creamy dressing. The stiff cabbage shreds were strawlike, making them difficult to fork and even more difficult to get into the mouth without leaving a creamy trail.

Quite unlike the ice-water cabbage, the salted shreds lost most of their liquid while sitting in the salt, leaving the cabbage wilted but pickle-crisp. Since the cabbage had already lost most of its own liquid, there was little or no liquid for the salt in the dressing to draw out. We had found the solution to the problem of watery dressing. In addition, having less water in it, the cabbage took on more of the dressing's flavors, and unlike the stiff, icy shreds, this limp cabbage was also easier to eat.

We did discover that the salting process leaves the cabbage a bit too salty, but a quick rinse washes away the excess salt. After the cabbage has been rinsed, just pat it dry with paper towels and refrigerate it until ready to combine it with the dressing. If the coleslaw is to be eaten immediately, rinse it quickly in ice water rather than tap water, then pat it dry. Coleslaw, at least the creamy style, should be served cold.

WHERE THERE'S SALT, THERE'S WATER

Vegetables that soak in ice water crisp up, while salted and drained vegetables go limp. Food scientist and cooking teacher Shirley Corriher says this phenomenon results from cell structure: "Vegetable cells are filled with liquid, but the cell walls are semipermeable, allowing liquid to flow into and out of the cell. Depending on where the salt quantity is greater, that's where the water flows."

Cabbage is a pretty tough vegetable, but when soaked in ice water, its shreds become even stiffer and crisper. In this case, the cabbage cells contain more salt than the ice water. The ice water is drawn into the cabbage cells, causing the shreds to plump up. Watching a scored radish blossom into a radish rose when soaked in ice water is an even more dramatic example of this principle.

When shredded cabbage is salted, on the other hand, the salt outside the cabbage is greater than the salt contained in the cells. The cell water is drawn out by clinging salt. This partially dehydrated cabbage is limp but still crisp.

The Acid Test

Having figured out how to keep the cabbage from watering down the dressing, we were ready to tackle the dressing's acidity problem. We found a few creamy coleslaw recipes in which the cabbage was tossed with sour cream only, or a combination of mayonnaise and sour cream—no vinegar. Although we were looking for ways to tone down the tang, a mix of sour cream and mayonnaise proved too mild for our taste. Other recipes called for lemon juice rather than vinegar. Although the lemon juice–flavored coleslaw was pleasantly tart, it lacked the depth that vinegar could offer.

Recalling "Quick Homemade Pickles," an article featured in the September/October 1994 issue of *Cook's Illustrated,* we decided to give low-acidity rice wine vinegar a try. We drizzled a bit of rice vinegar over the mayonnaise-tossed cabbage and found its mild acidity perfect for coleslaw.

Although there are several styles of coleslaw, the two that follow are classics—one mild and creamy, the other sweet-and-sour. Adjust either recipe to your taste. If sour cream is a must for your creamy slaw, then substitute it for some or all of the mayonnaise. Add green pepper or celery, red onions, or apples. Try caraway seeds or fresh dill, radishes or nuts.

SWEET-AND-SOUR COLESLAW
Serves 4

Since rice wine vinegar tends to mellow, you may want to use cider vinegar if making the slaw a day ahead. The presence of the sugar in this recipe keeps you from having to rinse off salt from the cabbage, as is ordinarily the case.

- 1 pound (about ½ medium head) red or green cabbage, shredded fine or chopped (6 cups), (*see* illustrations at right)
- 1 large carrot, peeled and grated
- ½ cup sugar
- 2 teaspoons kosher salt or 1 teaspoon table salt
- ¼ teaspoon celery seeds
- 6 tablespoons vegetable oil
- ¼ cup rice wine vinegar
  Ground black pepper

1. Toss cabbage and carrots with sugar, salt, and celery seeds in colander set over medium bowl. Let stand until cabbage wilts, at least 1 hour and up to 4 hours.
2. Pour draining liquid from bowl; rinse bowl and dry. Dump wilted cabbage and carrots from colander into bowl.
3. Add oil and vinegar; toss to coat. Season with pepper to taste. Cover and refrigerate until ready to serve. (Can be refrigerated 5 days.)

CURRIED COLESLAW WITH APPLES AND RAISINS
Serves 6

Follow recipe for Sweet-and-Sour Coleslaw, adding 1 teaspoon curry powder, 1 medium apple, peeled and cut into small dice, and ¼ cup raisins (optional) with oil and vinegar.

CREAMY COLESLAW
Serves 4

If you like caraway or celery seed in your coleslaw, you can add one-quarter teaspoon of either with the mayonnaise and vinegar. You can shred, salt, rinse, and pat the cabbage dry a day ahead, but dress it close to serving time.

- 1 pound (about ½ medium head) red or green cabbage, shredded fine or chopped (6 cups) (*see* illustrations below)
- 1 large carrot, peeled and grated
- 2 teaspoons kosher salt or 1 teaspoon table salt
- ½ small onion, minced
- ½ cup mayonnaise
- 2 tablespoons rice wine vinegar
  Ground black pepper

1. Toss cabbage and carrots with salt in colander set over medium bowl. Let stand until cabbage wilts, at least 1 hour and up to 4 hours.
2. Dump wilted cabbage and carrots into the bowl. Rinse thoroughly in cold water (ice water if serving slaw immediately). Pour vegetables back into colander, pressing, but not squeezing on them to drain. Pat dry with paper towels. (Can be stored in a zipper-lock bag and refrigerated overnight.)
3. Pour cabbage and carrots back again into bowl. Add onions, mayonnaise, and vinegar; toss to coat. Season with pepper to taste. Cover and refrigerate until ready to serve. ∎

TESTING WAYS TO SHRED CABBAGE

We tried every way we could think of to shred cabbage, from food processors to box graters to mandolin-style slicers to every variety of hand shredding. Box graters tore and bruised the cabbage; mandolin-style slicers did a decent job, but some had no adjustment to control the thickness of slices, which made it hard to get consistently thin shreds.

In the end, we found the food processor most efficient for big jobs. We preferred using the #4 slicing disk that comes with the Cuisinart machine. When hand-shredding for smaller jobs, we found that slicing halved cabbages was too awkward, and slicing quartered cabbage gave us pieces that were too short. As a result, we opted for the method shown below.

SHREDDING BY HAND

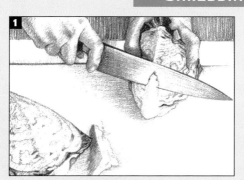

1. Quarter, then core the cabbage.

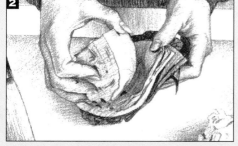

2. Separate the cabbage quarters into stacks of leaves that flatten when pressed lightly.

3. Use a chef's knife to cut each stack of cabbage diagonally into thin shreds. To chop the cabbage, turn the pile of shredded cabbage crosswise, then cut the cabbage shreds into a fine dice.

SHREDDING IN A FOOD PROCESSOR

To shred cabbage in a food processor, follow steps 1 and 2 under "Shredding by Hand." Roll the leaves crosswise and place them in the feeder tube. Using the slicing disk and pressing lightly on the pusher, shred the cabbage. Repeat with the other stacks.

A Better Burger

Settle for nothing but ground chuck. Season it simply, then shape it with a light hand. Grill it outside, or sear it indoors.

∽ BY PAM ANDERSON WITH KAREN TACK ∽

You don't need to be reminded of the billions served. Human beings eat a lot of hamburgers. You don't need a lot of explanation. Most hamburgers seem merely to satisfy hunger, rather than give pleasure. Too bad, because making an exceptional hamburger isn't hard or time-consuming. We're sure fast-food chains have good reasons for not offering hand-formed, 100 percent ground-chuck burgers, but home cooks do not.

If you have the right ground beef, the perfect hamburger can be ready in under fifteen minutes, assuming you season, form, and cook it properly. The biggest difficulty for many cooks, though, may be finding the right beef.

Chuck It

In order to test which cut or cuts of beef cook into the best burger, we ordered chuck, round, rump, sirloin, and hanging tenderloin, all ground to order with 20 percent fat. (Although we would question fat percentages in later testing, we needed a standard for these early tests. From our experience this percentage seemed right.) After a side-by-side taste test, we quickly concluded that most cuts of ground beef are pleasant but bland when compared to the robust, beefy-flavored ground chuck. Pricier ground sirloin, for example, cooked up into a particularly boring burger.

So pure ground chuck—the cut of beef that starts where the ribs end and moves up to the shoulder and neck, ending at the foreshank—was the clear winner. We were ready to race ahead to seasonings, but before moving on we stopped to ask ourselves, "Will cooks buying ground chuck from the grocery store agree with our choice?" Our efforts to determine whether grocery store ground chuck and ground-to-order chuck were even remotely similar took us along a culinary blue highway from kitchen to packing plant, butcher shop, and science lab.

According to Susan Perenti, assistant director of the National Live Stock and Meat Board, only beef's fat percentage is checked and enforced at the retail level. If a package of beef is labeled 90 percent lean, then it must contain no more than 10 percent fat, give or take a point. Retail stores are required to test each batch of ground beef, make the necessary adjustments, and keep a log of the results. Local inspectors routinely pull ground beef from a store's meat case for a fat check. If the tested meat is not within 1 percent of the package sticker, the store is fined.

Whether a package labeled ground chuck is, in fact, 100 percent ground chuck is a different story. First, we surveyed a number of grocery store meat department managers, who said that what was written on the label did match what was in the package. For instance, a package labeled "ground chuck" would contain only chuck trimmings. Same for sirloin and round. Only "ground beef" would contain mixed beef trimmings.

We got a little closer to the truth, however, by interviewing a respected butcher in the Chicago area, who spoke candidly. Of the several grocery stores and butcher shops he had worked at over the years, he had never known a store to segregate meat trimmings. In fact, in his present butcher shop, he sells only two kinds of ground beef—sirloin and chuck. He defines ground sirloin as ground beef (mostly but not exclusively sirloin) that's labeled 90 percent lean, and chuck as ground beef (including a lot of chuck trimmings) that's labeled 85 percent lean.

According to Perenti, only meat ground at federally inspected plants is guaranteed to match its label. At these plants an inspector checks that labeled ground beef actually comes from the cut of beef named on the label, and that the fat percentage is correct. To most retailers, though, specific cuts of ground beef can only be guaranteed to equal specific fat percentages.

Grind It to Order

Since retail ground beef labeling is deceptive, we suggest buying a chuck roast and having the butcher grind it for you. Even at a local grocery store, the butcher was willing to grind to order, but she cautioned that butchers at larger grocery store chains might not be so willing. Some meat, she adds, always gets lost in the grinder, so count on losing a bit (2 to 3 percent).

Because mass-ground beef can also be risky, it made theoretical sense to recommend grinding beef at home for those who want to reduce further their odds of eating beef tainted with *E. coli*. It didn't make much practical sense, though. Not all cooks own a grinder. And even if they did, we thought it was demanding far too much setup, cleanup, and effort for a dish meant to be so simple.

To see if there was an easier way, we tried hand-chopping and food-processor grinding. The hibachi-style, hand-chopping method was just as time-consuming and more messy than the traditional grinder. The meat must be sliced thin, then cut into cubes—before you go at it with two chef's knives. The fat doesn't evenly distribute, meat flies everywhere, and unless your knives are razor sharp, it's difficult to chop through the meat. What's worse, you can't efficiently chop more than two burgers at a time. And the resulting cooked burger could have been mistaken for chopped steak.

The food processor performed a surprisingly good meat-grinding job. We thought the steel blade would raggedly chew the meat, but to our surprise, it was evenly chopped and fluffy (see "Food Processor As Grinder," page 15, for more details).

For those who buy a chuck roast for grinding, we found the average chuck roast to be about 80 percent lean. To check its leanness, we bought a chuck roast—not too fatty, not too lean—and ground it in the food processor. We took our ground chuck back to the grocery store for the butcher to check its fat content in the Univex Fat Analyzer, a machine the store uses to check each batch of beef it grinds. A plug of our ground beef scored an almost perfect 21 percent fat when tested in the fat analyzer.

Marlis Belensky, test kitchen director at the National Live Stock and Meat Board, recommends leaner cuts of chuck—from the shoulder or arm—for grinding. "The closer you move to the rib," she warns, "the fattier the roast. Cuts like the blade roast are probably too fatty for grinding."

Up to this point, all of our beef had been ground with approximately 20 percent fat. A quick test of burgers with less and more fat helped us to decide that 20 percent fat, give or take a few percentage points, was good for burgers. Any higher fat percentage, and it's left in the pan. Any lower, and you start compromising the beef's juicy, moist texture.

Less Is Best

When to salt (and pepper) the meat may seem like an unimportant detail, but when making a dish as simple as a hamburger, little things matter. We tried seasoning the meat at four different times during the process. Our first burger was seasoned before the meat was shaped, the second burger was seasoned right before cooking, the third after each side was seared, and the fourth after the burger had been fully cooked.

Predictably, the burger that had been seasoned throughout was our preference. All the surface-seasoned burgers were the same. You got a hit of salt right up front, then the burger went bland. It was clear that the thin surface area was well seasoned, but the majority was not.

Though we preferred seasoning the meat before shaping, we wondered how salt would affect the meat if patties were formed then refrigerated before cooking. We were afraid that salt would cause the patties to leach out their liquid or cause the meat to toughen. But even patties left in the refrigerator for a couple of days leaked little blood, nor did we notice any textural or taste difference in the patties once they were cooked.

We tried other seasonings and culinary tricks. Most were distracting; a few were intriguing.

Minced onions and bread crumbs made the burger taste like meatloaf, while garlic made it taste like a meatball begging for red sauce. One recipe suggested mixing a bit of milk into the meat. As we suspected, the milk did nothing for the flavor, and the sugar in the milk caused the patty to burn during cooking. Another recipe recommended adding beef broth to old meat to mask unwanted flavors. Perhaps our meat was too far gone, but we don't think anything could mask the flavor of stale beef. Some recipes promised a juicier burger by adding ice water to the meat, but the juiciness had its price. The meat, in both raw and cooked form, was mushy. Another tip—ice chips placed in the center of the patty—certainly kept the burger rare but left a hole in its place. We never did get the point of the ice trick. If you want a rare burger, just don't cook it as long.

For those who like their burgers well done, we found that poking a small hole in the center of the patty before cooking did help the burger center to get done before the edges dried out. And for those who love cheese, we liked grating it into the raw beef as opposed to melting it on top. Since the cheese was more evenly distributed, a little went much further than the big hunk on top.

Pat It, Then Throw It in the Pan
With fresh-ground chuck, seasoned with salt and pepper, we moved into shaping and cooking. To defy the overpacking and overhandling warning you see in many recipes, we thoroughly worked a portion of ground beef before cooking it. The well-done burger exterior was dense like a meat pâté, and the less well-done interior was compact and pasty.

It's pretty hard to overhandle a beef patty, though, especially if you're trying not to. Once the meat has been divided into portions, we found tossing the meat from one hand to another helped bring it together into a ball without overworking it (*see* illustration 1). From there, pressing the ball of meat into a patty with the fingertips not only gave it surface texture, it also flattened it, again without overworking the meat (illustration 2).

For our taste, a four-ounce burger seemed a little skimpy. A five-ounce portion of meat patted into a nice size burger—a scant four inches in diameter and just shy of one inch thick. Just the right size for a bun.

No cooking method surpasses grilling, but we were awfully fond of the thick-crusted burgers we were able to cook in a well-seasoned cast-iron skillet. We didn't need any fat or salt in the pan to keep the burgers from sticking. Like a good loaf of bread, the perfect burger should display a crisp, flavorful crust that protects a moist, tender interior. Both grilling and pan-broiling delivered this kind of burger. Traditional broiling did not offer the contrast in texture we were looking for.

Whether you are grilling or pan-broiling, we make two suggestions. First, make sure the grill rack or pan is hot before adding the meat. If not, the hamburger will not develop that crucial crusty exterior. Second, avoid the temptation to continually flip the burger during cooking. Follow the cooking times in the recipe below, setting a timer if you like. When the buzzer goes off, flip the burger. When the buzzer goes off again, pull that burger confidently from the heat.

A BETTER BURGER
Serves 4
You can grill this burger, or pan-broil it in a twelve-inch cast-iron or nonstick skillet or a stovetop grill pan.

1¼ pounds 100 percent ground chuck

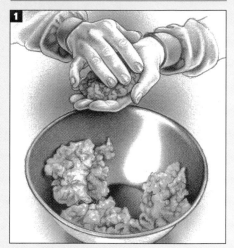

¾ teaspoon salt
¼ teaspoon ground black pepper
Buns and desired toppings

1. Break up chuck to increase surface area for seasoning. Sprinkle salt and pepper over meat; toss lightly with hands to distribute seasoning. Divide meat into four equal portions (5 ounces each); with cupped hands, toss one portion of meat back and forth to form loose ball (*see* illustration 1 above). Pat lightly to flatten into 1-inch-thick burger, 3½ to 4 inches across, using fingertips to create pocked, textured surface (illustration 2). Repeat with remaining portions of meat.

2. If grilling, heat enough coals to make hot fire. When coals are hot and covered with white ash, spread them in single layer. Position grill rack and lid; heat until rack is very hot, about 5 minutes. Place burgers on rack; cover and grill, turning once, to desired doneness as follows: 3 minutes per side for rare, 4 minutes per side for medium-rare, 5 minutes on first side and 4 minutes on second side for medium, and 5 minutes per side for well done. If pan-broiling, heat skillet over medium-high heat. When skillet is hot (drops of water flicked into it evaporate immediately), add patties and cook, turning once, to desired doneness, using same times as if grilling. Serve immediately with buns and desired toppings. ∎

FOOD PROCESSOR AS GRINDER

Even though I own a meat grinder, I don't regularly grind meat at home. The setup, breakdown, and washing up for a two-pound chuck roast is just not worth the effort. Besides, hamburgers are supposed to be impromptu, fast, fun food. To my surprise, though, the food processor does a respectable grinding job, and it's much simpler than a grinder. The key is to make sure the roast is cold, that it is cut into small chunks, and that it is processed in small batches. For a two-pound roast, cut the meat into one-inch chunks. Divide the chunks into four equal portions. Place one portion of meat in the work bowl of the food processor fitted with the steel blade. Pulse the cubes until the meat is ground, fifteen to twenty one-second pulses. Repeat with the remaining portions of beef. Then shape the ground meat, as in illustrations 1 and 2 above—*P.A.*

Decorative Melon Carving

Carved melons can serve as easy-to-make, decorative, edible centerpieces. These simple melon carvings were created by Charles Grandon, executive chef at The Colonnade Hotel in Boston. Grandon recommends that you have the melons at room temperature before carving, since this makes them more pliable and thus easier to work with. He also suggests that having sharp knives makes the process much easier. For the purpose of these illustrations, a dark pen was used to draw shapes on the melons in order to make the process more clearly visible. When you mark the melon, however, you should simply use a knife or ballpoint pen to score the pattern so that lines do not show. ∎

CARVING A HONEYDEW TO RESEMBLE A LOTUS FLOWER

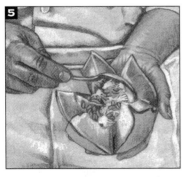

1. Starting about one-quarter of the way down the side of the melon from one pole, draw a curve in the shape of an elongated, reverse S, as shown.

2. Draw a second curve mirroring the first curve, meeting at the top to form a petal shape (resembling an onion dome on a Russian Orthodox church). Continue all around the melon creating an odd number of points, usually three or five depending on the size of the melon.

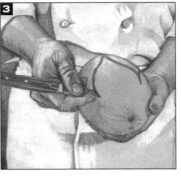

3. Using a paring knife, cut through the melon along the lines you have drawn. Make sure you cut all the way through the flesh as well as the rind.

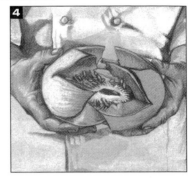

4. Pull the melon halves apart, using gentle pressure. If the melon does not separate easily, use your paring knife again to make sure your cuts were complete.

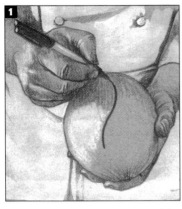

5. Scoop out the seeds with a spoon, being careful to leave the flesh intact. Cut a narrow slice off the pole of each half of the melon so that the bottom surface is flat.

6. Draw the petal pattern two more times, one inside the other, on the inside of each individual petal. Use the tip of a paring knife to score the pattern you have just drawn. Make sure you go all the way through the rind, but do not cut deeply into the flesh underneath.

7. Use the paring knife to separate the skin from the flesh, cutting in a downward motion from the tip of the petal to the base. Repeat with all petals.

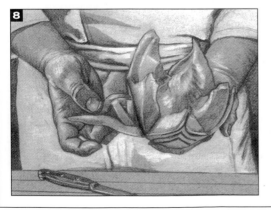

8. Grasp the rind of each petal and gently pull back. The design you have scored should "pop" out gently. If it does not, rescore with the paring knife, then pull out.

9. Fill the center of the finished melon with sorbets and fruits.

ILLUSTRATIONS BY TONY DELUZ

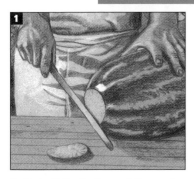

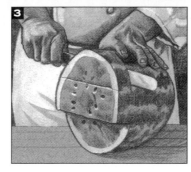

1. Cut off the bottom of the melon on each side to create a flat base. Be careful not to cut through to the red flesh. Cut the melon in half vertically (not through the poles of the melon). Set one half aside.

2. Using a carving knife, make a vertical cut into the exposed top of the melon half you are using, about a third of the way from one side. This cut should be about 1 inch to 1½ inches deep (approximately the width of the blade of a standard carving knife). Make a similar cut a third of the way from the other side.

3. Set the melon on its side. Using the carving knife, slice down from the side of the melon to the cut that you have just made, separating a one-third round of the melon. Repeat on the other side.

4. Stand the melon back up on its base. Use the carving knife to round off the edges of the basket "handle," as shown.

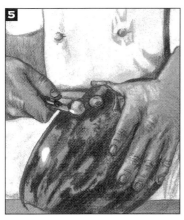

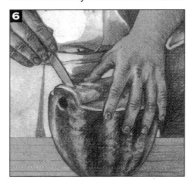

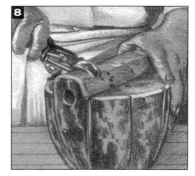

5. Using a sturdy melon-baller, cut a round hole into the side of each handle, piercing all the way through the rind to the flesh.

6. Use a paring knife to separate the skin from the flesh all the way around the melon. This will create a cleaner edge when you scoop out the flesh.

7. To create the effect of the staves of a wooden basket, use a paring knife (or a channel knife) to cut out narrow vertical channels around the melon, just deep enough to expose the light green of the rind. Do this about every 4 to 6 inches all the way around the melon.

8. Use an ice cream scoop to scoop out rounded balls of the watermelon flesh. Use a back-and-forth, rounding motion to scoop out completely round sections rather than the usual truncated orbs. Set these scoops of melon aside.

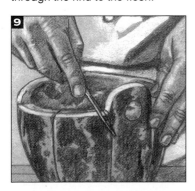

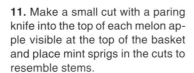

9. Use a paring knife to further define the handles by making a V-shaped notch at the base of the handle on either side.

10. Place the melon "apples" back into the basket, saving the most perfectly rounded ones for the top. (If you wish, you may scoop out the unused half of the melon and add these scoops as well for an overflowing basket.)

11. Make a small cut with a paring knife into the top of each melon apple visible at the top of the basket and place mint sprigs in the cuts to resemble stems.

12. The finished product can be used as a centerpiece or a dessert.

Smoke-Cooking

Whichever smoking device you use, the keys to smoke-cooking are maintaining a constant low temperature and keeping that smoke flowing.

∼ BY CHERYL ALTERS JAMISON AND BILL JAMISON ∼

Smoke-cooking yields a hearty, husky smoke flavor, evoking summer campfires. Unlike grilling, in which food is directly exposed to the heat of fire, in smoke-cooking the food is moved away from the flame so that the temperature is reduced to a level just above what the meat should register inside when it is done. This slow, indirect cooking tenderizes tough cuts—a major consideration in the past—and also allows time for the flavor of wood smoke to infuse the food, the effect usually sought today.

While the cooking temperature is low compared to grilling, it's high enough to fully cook meat. When doing smoke-cooking, also known as "hot smoking," most cooks maintain a temperature range between 200 and 250 degrees, a prudent level that gets the right results. Some experienced cooks who have complete confidence in their smokers and thermometers will go as low as 170 or 180 degrees, easily a safe internal temperature for pork, but it's not a good idea on the most common kinds of equipment. This is simply because the ideal temperature for bacteria growth is between 70 and 140 degrees. So, unless you are very sure of your equipment's ability to maintain a constant and relatively exact temperature, it is best to stay well out of that range.

In all cases, though, the cooking temperature stays at least two or three times higher than in smoke-curing, or "cold smoking," a process in which a combination of salt and smoke is used to preserve food rather than cook it. Smoke-curing temperatures vary but usually hover around 100 degrees or less. This type of smoking is a flavoring method rather than a true cooking method.

Another difference between smoke-cooking and this smoke-curing process is that smoke-cooking doesn't require brining. Therefore you don't end up with the heavy salt taste sometimes associated with smoked fish and meat. Since smoke-cooking does little or nothing for preservation, however, cooks should be aware that leftovers must be refrigerated.

Smoke and Supporting Flavors

A second critical element in smoke-cooking, in addition to a low cooking temperature, is an ample and appropriate use of wood in the fire. When people smoke-cook the old way, with whole logs, they generate a thick cloud of wood smoke. Unfortunately, few of us have pits in our backyard that are large enough to accommodate entire logs. It's impossible to replicate the same smoke density using a charcoal, gas, or electric heat source, but you'll want to lean as far in that direction as possible by starting with a generous amount of wood chunks and chips, then adding more as necessary to maintain a steady stream of smoke while the food cooks.

Not just any wood will do, though. Avoid softwoods such as pine, spruce, and cedar, since they give off pitch and impart a turpentine-like flavor to food. Instead, use hardwoods such as hickory, oak, maple, mesquite, alder, or cherry. These woods are sold in chips and chunks at stores that carry outdoor cooking supplies. To produce smoke, you soak the wood in water for a minimum of thirty minutes—preferably longer—so the chips and chunks will smolder in the fire instead of flame.

The kind of wood you use can affect the flavor of food, but the impact is minimal until after several hours of intense smoking in a real log fire. We experimented with hickory, mesquite, and cherry chips and found only subtle differences between them after moderately short cooking periods. It was not until we got into the five-hour-plus range that differences in wood made substantial differences in flavor.

The most effective way to add new layers of flavor in smoke-cooking is one of the oldest: the application of spices in the form of dry rubs, pastes, and marinades. We found all three of these flavoring methods to be more successful than another widely discussed alternative: adding herbs and other seasonings to the water pan in a smoker. We came to this conclusion after trying two experiments involving significant amounts of sage, a potent herb. In the first test, we cooked a chicken breast in an electric water smoker with three bunches of fresh sage in the water. In the second, we supplemented the herb with copious quantities of beer, onion, and mustard, also strong flavors. We got a nuance of taste in both instances but spent much more money—for less compelling and controllable results—than we would have on a paste or marinade.

Home Smoking Equipment

The biggest recent development in backyard smoke-cooking is an explosion in the availability of home equipment. Until the past decade, you had to build your own smoker or adapt a covered charcoal grill for the purpose. Those remain options, but other possibilities also abound now, including log-burning barbecue pits, new styles of wood ovens, and increasingly popular water smokers (see Sources and Resources, page 32, for sources for smokers). Among the alternatives, the majority of outdoor cooks use a water smoker or

charcoal grill, so we decided to focus on the characteristics and capabilities of those two options.

Water smokers generally operate on either electricity or charcoal. In each case, the heat source is at the bottom of the smoker, just below a water pan, which in turn rests below one or two grates for food. The water helps to keep the temperature low and adds moisture to food that could otherwise dry out during the slow smoking process. While the domed lid of the smoker may contain an imprecise temperature gauge, from our experience, it seldom provides useful readings. We place a grill or oven thermometer on the top grate to check the actual cooking temperature.

After several years of working with both a charcoal and electric water smoker, we've concluded that the electric models are more reliable, easier to use, and less expensive in the long run. While they do cost more than charcoal versions initially—$70 compared to $50 in one major national catalog—fuel expenses close up the difference quickly. Our charcoal smoker, a best-selling brand, requires a minimum of five pounds of briquettes to maintain a proper cooking temperature for just a few small items, and most of a large bag of charcoal for something like a turkey.

The charcoal smoker also fluctuates in temperature, firing up higher than ideal for smoking and then dropping steadily over several hours to a level that's ultimately too low. You have to track the temperature throughout the cooking process in order to assess cooking times, and also perhaps to ensure that you are staying within proper ranges. We prefer the consistency of the electric smokers. Ours maintains a steady 230 degrees all day, though individual experience may vary somewhat depending on differences in climate, equipment, and even extension cords.

Both kinds of water smokers enjoy significant advantages over the charcoal grills for smoke-cooking, however. While a kettle-style covered grill can do a better job with a fatty cut of meat, such as a pork butt, which benefits from dehydration and shrinkage, water smokers equal them or excel with all other foods. Just as important perhaps, grills are designed principally for high-heat cooking, not slow smoking, so you have to work against the grain. It often takes patience and dedicated practice to master the process.

The key to success with the kettle-style grill, for us at least, is a thermometer. You can use either a candy thermometer, if you have one with a head that faces outward, or a thermometer specifically made for grilling, such as those available from the Weber Company (see Sources and

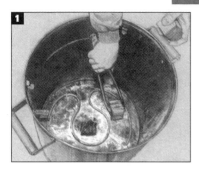

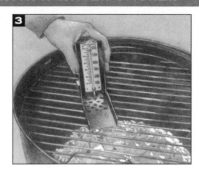

Two hours or more before you plan to start cooking, place wood chunks in a pan of water to soak. For every hour of projected cooking time, soak three or four large chunks.

Electric water smokers should be plugged in about thirty minutes before you plan to start cooking. If you are using a charcoal water smoker, ignite briquettes in the charcoal pan thirty minutes before cooking. Use the quantity of briquettes recommended by the manufacturer for the projected cooking time. Because you start with a substantial amount of charcoal, you seldom need to add more later in the cooking process.

When the smoker is ready to cook, use long-handled tongs to place three soaked wood chunks in the fire, avoiding direct contact with the coils on the electric smoker (see illustration 1). Line the water pan with aluminum foil, position the pan in the smoker, and fill it with water (illustration 2).

Place an oven or grill thermometer on the top cooking grate (illustration 3). Use a high-quality, accurate candy thermometer or a thermometer specially made for smoking. Check the temperature when you place the food on the grate (illustration 4); it should be about 200 degrees. Cover the smoker.

Check the temperature every two hours, at least initially while you're learning about your smoker, and also when you remove food. Note patterns, so you can make adjustments in cooking times based on the operation of your smoker. Be aware that you lose heat when you lift the lid, so don't do it any more than is necessary to have a good sense of the internal cooking temperature.

At the same time that you check the temperature, or at least every three hours, pour water carefully through the grates to refill the water pan. Wood needs to be replenished more often but usually doesn't require lifting the lid. Add three soaked wood chunks to the fire (illustration 5) whenever the smoke stream disappears, or at least once every hour.

Two hours or more before you plan to start cooking, place wood chunks and chips in a pan of water to soak. For every hour of projected cooking time, soak two chunks and a generous handful of chips.

About forty-five minutes before you plan to start cooking, remove the top grate from the grill and heat twenty-five charcoal briquettes in a chimney starter (sold at outdoor supply stores)

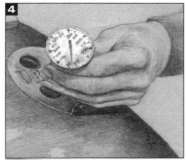

until all the coals are covered with white ash. Alternatively, stack the briquettes on one side of the bottom grate and heat them there. Line a standard-size loaf pan with aluminum foil, fill it two-thirds full of water, and place it on the bottom grate opposite the charcoal.

Close all except one of the vents underneath the grill and use long-handled tongs to spread the heated briquettes in a single layer on the bottom grate, concentrating them directly above the open vent (see illustration 1). Arrange the coals so they are touching but not overlapping, situated to provide a bed for the wood pieces. Place a handful of soaked wood chips and two of the chunks on the briquettes (illustration 2).

Replace the top grate. Place the food you are cooking directly over the pan of water, on the far side of the grill from the charcoal (illustration 3). Put the lid on the grill, with the top vent positioned above the food and fully opened.

Insert the probe end of a candy thermometer or grilling thermometer into the top vent of the grill (illustration 4), placing the tip as close as possible to the cooking area without touching the food. The head should hold the thermometer in place and be clearly visible.

Maintain a temperature as close as possible to 225 degrees. If the temperature stabilizes above 250 degrees, partly close the grill's vent beneath the charcoal, leaving a crack for air circulation. Open it again gradually as the temperature drops. (Watch the stream of smoke coming through the top vent. If the smoke dies out before the food is cooked, start with more wood next time, adding one or two extra chunks on the edge of the charcoal.)

If you are planning to cook for longer than one hour, begin heating additional charcoal after thirty minutes. When the temperature starts dropping below 220 degrees, remove the grill lid and top grate, and add six or seven coals to the fire with long-handled tongs, plus enough wood chips and chunks to replenish the initial supply (illustration 5). Repeat the process as needed over a long cooking period. You can also drop wood chips into the fire through the top grate any other time the lid is off, but because of the heat loss, we don't advise removing the cover for that purpose alone, unless the smoke stream has disappeared. Note that each time you take the lid off the grill, it will add ten minutes or more to your total cooking time.

Resources, page 32). The probe of the thermometer should go into the vent on the lid (*see* illustration 4 in "How to Smoke-Cook with a Kettle-Style Grill," page 19). That way, you can measure the cooking temperature without having to lift the cover, which you want to avoid as much as possible because it releases a lot of the already low heat inside and makes your cooking results less predictable.

Using the thermometer, experiment with the amount of charcoal and wood you need to establish an appropriate smoking temperature, and keep records on how long the fuel maintains that level. If the food requires much more than one hour of cooking time, you will likely have to remove the lid to add more preheated coals and wood, reducing the temperature temporarily. Various factors can further affect the situation, including outside air temperature, wind, altitude, humidity, and the type of charcoal that you use.

"How to Smoke-Cook with a Kettle-Style Grill" (page 19) suggests strategies that work for us, but you may need to fine-tune them to fit your circumstances.

Even when smoke-cooking is a challenge, the outcome justifies the effort. Food takes on a woodsy resonance that cannot be matched in any other way, a distinctive flavor deeply rooted in the American heritage. For taste and tradition both, it's an experience to savor.

SMOKED PORK CHOPS WITH FENNEL-MUSTARD RUB
Serves 6

6 1-inch-thick center loin or center rib pork chops (about 3 pounds)
2 tablespoons Spice Rub for Pork (*see* page 21)
¾ teaspoon salt

1. Rub each pork chop with 1 teaspoon spice rub, then sprinkle with salt. Let rubbed chops stand, loosely covered, in refrigerator for 2 to 3 hours. (Can be sealed in a plastic bag and refrigerated for 2 to 4 days.)

2. Following instructions for grill or smoker setup (*see* "How To Smoke-Cook with a Kettle-Style Grill" or "How To Smoke-Cook with a Water Smoker," page 19), soak wood chunks and set up grill or smoker.

3. Smoke pork chops until chops are firm but not hard, about 1½ hours. Serve.

SMOKED SALMON WITH CORIANDER-PEPPER RUB
Serves 6

6 center-cut salmon fillets (6 ounces each)
1½ tablespoons Spice Rub for Oily Fish (*see* page 21)
½ teaspoon salt

1. Rub each salmon fillet with ¾ teaspoon spice rub, then sprinkle with salt. Let rubbed salmon stand, loosely covered, at room temperature for 30 minutes. (Can be covered and refrigerated overnight if fish is fresh.)

2. Following instructions for grill or smoker setup (*see* "How To Smoke-Cook with a Kettle-Style Grill" or "How To Smoke-Cook with a Water Smoker," page 19), soak wood chunks and set up grill or smoker.

3. Smoke salmon until just opaque, about 1½ hours. Serve.

SMOKED TURKEY BREAST WITH GINGER-CARDAMOM RUB
Serves 10 to 12

1 turkey breast (about 5 pounds)
3 tablespoons Spice Rub for Chicken (*see* page 21)
1 teaspoon salt

1. Rub turkey breast all over with the spice rub, then sprinkle with salt. Cover and refrigerate rubbed turkey breast for 2 to 3 hours. (Can be covered and refrigerated overnight.)

2. Following instructions for grill or smoker setup (*see* "How To Smoke-Cook with a Kettle-Style Grill" or "How To Smoke-Cook with a Water Smoker," page 19), soak wood chunks and set up grill or smoker.

3. Smoke turkey breast until meat thermometer registers 165, about 6 to 7 hours. Remove from grill or smoker and let rest at least 15 minutes. Carve and serve. (Can be cooled to room temperature, wrapped in plastic, and refrigerated up to 3 days.) ∎

Cheryl Alters Jamison and **Bill Jamison** are the authors of *Smoke & Spice* (Harvard Common Press, 1994), a guide to cooking with smoke.

SMOKE-COOKING TIMES

Since smoking is not an exact science, the times listed here are approximate. They may vary depending on a number of factors, including equipment, outside air temperature, wind, altitude, humidity, and the type of fuel you use.

To add layers of flavor to smoked foods, rub them before cooking with one of the dry rubs on page 21 or marinate them in your favorite marinade.

FOOD	APPROXIMATE COOKING TIME
BEEF	
Brisket (4-pound flat cut)	4½–5 hours
Tenderloin (2 pounds)	Sear first, then 1½ hours (medium rare)
Flank Steak (1¼ pounds)	45–60 minutes (medium rare)
PORK	
Spareribs (3-pound slab)	5–6 hours
Baby Back Ribs (1½-pound slab)	3 hours
Chop (½-inch thick)	1 hour
Spareribs (3-pound slab)	5–6 hours
Tenderloin (12 ounces)	Sear first, then 1½ hours
POULTRY	
Whole Chicken (3½ pounds)	3½–4 hours
Boneless Skinless Chicken Breast (6 ounces)	30 minutes
Turkey Breast (5 pounds)	6–7 hours
SEAFOOD	
Swordfish Steak (10 ounces)	30–45 minutes
Tuna Steak (1-inch thick)	15–20 minutes (medium rare)
Salmon Fillet (1½ pounds)	30–45 minutes
Shrimp in Shells (medium size)	10–15 minutes
Scallops (Bay)	8–12 minutes
VEGETABLES	
Onion (large, halved)	50–70 minutes
Sweet Potato (8 ounces, whole)	2 hours

Spice Rubs

Make-ahead spice blends provide deep flavor with practically no effort.

~ BY CHRIS SCHLESINGER AND JOHN WILLOUGHBY ~

Rubbed onto the outside of foods, spice blends will encourage the formation of a deeply browned crust filled with complex, concentrated flavors. They are also a healthful alternative to traditional sauces since they contain no fat at all.

Spice rubs can be used with virtually any type of food, and in general you can mix and match rubs and foods with abandon. However, there are a couple of general guidelines to follow when choosing a spice mix for a particular food. First, you must take into account the size of the food item to be cooked and make the rub stronger or lighter accordingly. For example, a rub designed for the outside of a whole chicken should be more potent than one for a relatively thin chicken breast or thigh. Second, you need to match strength to strength in terms of taste, that is, use earthier spices for meat, lighter ones for fish and chicken. Also, keep in mind that spices like cumin and coriander are good "bulk" spices for rubs, while aromatic spices like cloves and cinnamon need to be used lightly.

Spice rubs actually function as a kind of dry marinade. As such, they have several advantages over their traditional wet counterparts.

Since they are composed almost solely of spices, they provide stronger flavors than marinades, which typically comprise oil and an acidic liquid with some spices added to the mix. Rubs also stick better to the surface of foods than marinades, which again gives them an edge when it comes to intensifying flavor.

The technique involved in using spice rubs could not be simpler. Just take small handfuls of the spice mix that you have chosen and rub it over the entire surface of the food to be cooked, using a bit of pressure to make sure the spices actually adhere to the food. No need for brushes, either—bare hands are the best way to apply these mixtures. You can put the rubs on food several hours before you begin to cook, or five minutes before, and the effect will be about the same.

You will notice that most of these rubs do not contain salt. However, you should sprinkle the food liberally with salt before applying the rubs. Contrary to the common wisdom that allowing meat to sit with salt on it causes the juices to leak out, this process actually adds a deeper flavor to the meat.

All the rubs below will keep for about six weeks if they are tightly covered and stored in a cool, dark place.

ALL-PURPOSE BARBECUE RUB
Makes about 1 cup

This rub, adapted from *Big Flavors of the Hot Sun* (Morrow, 1994), is a little sweet, a little hot, with just a hint of clove. It can be used on just about anything that you plan to barbecue, that is, to cook over low, indirect heat for a long period of time. For large red-meat roasts, such as leg of lamb or standing rib, increase the cayenne pepper from one teaspoon to one tablespoon and substitute one teaspoon cinnamon for the ground cloves.

- ½ cup paprika
- 2 tablespoons ground cumin
- 2 tablespoons mild chili powder
- 2 tablespoons ground black pepper
- 1 teaspoon cayenne pepper
- ½ teaspoon ground cloves

Mix all ingredients in small bowl.

SPICE RUB FOR STEAKS AND CHOPS
Makes about ⅔ cup

Season beef steaks and lamb chops generously with this pungent rub.

- ¼ cup black peppercorns
- ¼ cup white peppercorns
- 2 tablespoons coriander seeds
- 2 tablespoons cumin seeds
- 1½ teaspoons hot red pepper flakes
- 1½ teaspoons ground cinnamon

1. Toast peppercorns, coriander, and cumin over medium heat in small skillet, shaking pan occasionally to prevent burning, until first wisps of smoke appear, 3 to 5 minutes. Remove from heat, cool to room temperature, then mix with pepper flakes and cinnamon.

2. Grind to powder in spice grinder or with mortar and pestle.

SPICE RUB FOR PORK
Makes about 1 cup

For large roasts like a fresh ham or pork shoulder, you may want to add cayenne pepper or hot red pepper flakes to the mix.

- ¼ cup fennel seeds
- ¼ cup cumin seeds
- ¼ cup coriander seeds
- 1 tablespoon cinnamon
- 2 tablespoons ground mustard
- 2 tablespoons brown sugar

1. Toast fennel, cumin, and coriander over medium heat in small skillet, shaking pan occasionally to prevent burning, until first wisps of smoke appear, 3 to 5 minutes. Remove from heat, cool to room temperature, then mix with remaining ingredients.

2. Grind to powder in spice grinder or with mortar and pestle.

SPICE RUB FOR OILY FISH
Makes about 1 cup

Rub this aromatic mixture onto salmon, mackerel, or bluefish fillets.

- ¼ cup fennel seeds
- ¼ cup crushed coriander seeds
- ¼ cup white peppercorns
- 10 whole cloves
- 6 whole star anise

1. Toast fennel, coriander, and peppercorns over medium heat in small skillet, shaking occasionally to prevent burning, until first wisps of smoke appear, 3 to 5 minutes. Remove from heat, cool to room temperature, then mix with remaining ingredients.

2. Grind to powder in spice grinder or with mortar and pestle.

SPICE RUB FOR CHICKEN
Makes about 1¼ cups

- 3 tablespoons ground cardamom
- 3 tablespoons ground ginger
- 2 tablespoons ground turmeric
- 2 tablespoons ground cumin
- 2 tablespoons ground coriander
- 1 tablespoon ground allspice
- 3 tablespoons ground black pepper
- 2 tablespoons cayenne pepper
- 1 teaspoon ground cloves
- 3 tablespoons ground fenugreek (optional)

Mix all ingredients in small bowl. ∎

Chris Schlesinger and **John Willoughby** are the coauthors of several cookbooks, including *Big Flavors of the Hot Sun* (Morrow, 1994).

Cooking Corn on the Cob

What really matters is when the corn was picked and how it's been stored.

∼ BY PAM ANDERSON WITH KAREN TACK ∼

Neither of us grew up in corn country, so we thought people who wouldn't pick corn until their cooking water started to boil were a bit fanatical. What we've since tasted for ourselves is that the corn's maturity on the stalk and the time since it was picked are, in fact, about the only things you really have to worry about.

Corn-buying etiquette requires the customer to trust the farmer's expertise. It's not unusual to see signs asking customers not to pull down the husks before purchase. So what's a consumer to do? According to Dr. Charles McClurg, extension vegetable specialist at the University of Maryland, most of us basically have to rely upon a producer we can trust, but can use "the fingernail test" after purchasing to verify ripeness.

Immature corn kernels are not filled out, and there are deep furrows between each row. The kernel, when pricked with the nail, is juicy but not milky. Kernels of peak corn, however, are filled out so that there is no space between the rows; milky corn juice explodes from the pricked kernel. Kernels of overripe corn are completely filled out, many of them starting to "dimple," or cave in. When pricked with the nail, the kernel is dry and "doughy."

Once you have your corn in hand, you must choose a cooking method. Before starting this article, we thought that one cooking technique would shine. After running corn through the paces, though, we discovered that almost all cooking methods—steaming, boiling, grilling, even microwaving—are great ways to cook corn.

As is often the case, the simplest method of cooking corn—boiling it—had the most questions associated with it. Should part of the water be re-placed with milk? Should the water be seasoned with salt, with sugar, or nothing at all?

Using a mixture of milk and water as the boiling medium had advantages, but on the whole we decided against it because the milk seemed to mask the corn's clear, sweet flavor. Our main beef with boiling corn in milk, though, was scrubbing the burner dish from the milk overflow and scouring the milk-coated pot interior. After all, one of the beauties of boiled corn is hanging up the pot as soon as you've drained the corn.

Corn kernels boiled in salted water were predictably tougher than those boiled in unsalted water. According to Howard Hillman, author of *Kitchen Science* (Houghton Mifflin, 1989), trace amounts of calcium in salt toughen the kernel skin during cooking.

Sugar-seasoned water brought out the natural sweetness of corn the same way that salted water enhances the flavors of other vegetables. For most varieties of corn, we liked boiling it in lightly sweetened water. With the new sugar-enhanced varieties, however, we felt that the extra sugar pushed them into the dessert category.

Regardless of cooking technique, corn cooked in the husks consistently picked up the pleasant, fermented, earthy smell of the grassy husk, a flavor that appeals to some, though not to others. Although husks are optional when steaming, boiling, or microwaving, they become a natural protective covering when grill-roasting or oven-roasting. For both these cooking methods, leave the corn in the husk rather than wrapping the shucked corn in foil. Corn that is cooked in its husk must be silked and soaked for thirty minutes prior to cooking or, as we found out, the corn kernels will dry out before cooking through.

Keeping Corn Fresh

The best course of action is to cook corn right after it is picked. The second it is picked, corn starts converting its starches to sugars. It also continues "breathing"—taking in oxygen and giving off CO_2. For those who can't cook their corn right after it is picked, or even right after buying, Don Schlimme, food scientist at the University of Maryland, has a method of extending corn's life by slowing down its breathing.

To keep corn usably fresh for up to two weeks, begin by making ice water and adding two drops of Chlorox bleach and one drop of lemon juice to each gallon. (These trace amounts of bleach and lemon juice lower the pH of the water, killing microbes more completely and quickly.) Shuck and silk fresh-picked corn and drop the ears into the ice water. After at least fifteen minutes, remove the ears from the water, drain, and package in gallon-size zipper-lock storage bags with a thickness of between 0.8 mils and 1.75 mils (thin enough to allow oxygen to permeate). Seal the bag and store the corn in the coldest section of the refrigerator for up to two weeks. Each of the following recipes serves four.

BOILED CORN ON THE COB

If you want to serve more than one ear per person, remove cooked ears from the pot, add another four ears to the boiling liquid and let them cook while the first batch is being eaten. If the corn you are serving is one of the new super-sweet varieties, omit the sugar from the water.

    4   teaspoons sugar
    4   ears corn, silked and soaked in water
        for 30 minutes (*see* illustrations)
        or completely husked
        Butter
        Salt and ground black pepper

Bring 1 gallon water and sugar to boil in large pot. Add corn; return to boil and cook until tender, 5 to 7 minutes. Drain and serve with butter, salt, and pepper to taste.

MICROWAVED CORN ON THE COB

Place four silked or husked ears of corn on large plate; cover tightly with microwavable plastic wrap and microwave on high power for 10 minutes. Leaving plate covered with plastic wrap, let stand 3 to 4 minutes longer. Serve with butter, salt, and pepper to taste.

STEAMED CORN ON THE COB

Set a steamer basket in a large pot with about 1 inch of water. Bring to boil; carefully place four silked or husked ears of corn in basket. Cover and steam over high heat until tender, 7 to 10 minutes. Remove from basket with tongs and serve immediately with butter, salt, and pepper to taste.

GRILLED CORN ON THE COB

Heat grill. When grill is hot, place four silked ears of corn that have been soaked in water to cover for at least 30 minutes on grill rack. Grill over high heat, turning corn by quarter turns, until husks char, 15 to 20 minutes. ∎

SILKING WITHOUT HUSKING

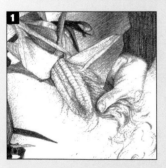

1. To remove silk, pull husks a little over halfway down. Remove silk, rinsing under cool, running water to wash away silk sticking to the ear.

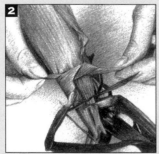

2. Pull husks back over the ear. Tie with a thin strip of husk or with kitchen twine. Soak in cold water to cover for at least 30 minutes.

ILLUSTRATIONS BY DAN BROWN

How to Make Crab Cakes

Use Atlantic blue crab with a minimum of binder, chill, then pan-fry.

∾ BY REGINA SCHRAMBLING ∾

My first taste of sweet crabmeat, sedulously picked out of hard shells at a seafood shack in Chincoteague, Virginia, set off a search that lasted ten years and took me from the Chesapeake Bay to Key West, with innumerable stops in between. Unfortunately, I consumed far too many crab-flecked dough balls before realizing I always found the best crab cakes at home.

Since then, I've experimented endlessly with dozens of recipes. But my first breakthrough came when I realized that, for great crab cakes, the bottom line is top-quality crabmeat.

Over the years I've tried several varieties of this sweet seafood: canned like tuna (the dregs); fresh pasteurized in a can (watery and bland); frozen Alaska king crab (stringy and wet); and lesser grades of the fresh stuff from the Chesapeake. But eventually I became an advocate of top-of-the-line crab, and that means Atlantic blue crab, the kind that is labeled "jumbo lump." This variety costs a couple of dollars a pound more than other types of crab, but, since a one-pound container is enough to make generous crab cakes for four, in my opinion it's money well spent.

Fresh lump blue crab is available year-round but tends to be most expensive from December to March. The meat should never be rinsed, but it does need to be picked over to remove any shells or cartilage the processors may have missed.

Once I had figured out what type of crab to use, my next task was to find the right binder. None of the usual suspects worked for me: Crushed saltines were a pain to smash small enough, potato chips added an overkill of richness, and fresh bread crumbs blended into the crabmeat a little too well texturally. Finally I settled on fine dry bread crumbs. You can either make your own (*see* "The Virtues of Bread Crumbs," May/June 1995) or use the unseasoned kind found in most supermarkets. They have no overwhelming flavor and are easy to mix in. The trickiest part is knowing when to stop; crab cakes need just enough binder to hold them together but not so much that the filler overwhelms the seafood. I started out using three-quarters of a cup of crumbs but ended up reducing that to two tablespoons for my final recipe. Cooks who economize by padding out their pricey seafood with bread crumbs will end up with dough balls, not crab cakes.

Other ingredients I've adopted are equally basic. Good, sturdy Hellmann's mayonnaise keeps the crabmeat moist (a homemade blend can be too liquid), and a whole egg, unbeaten, makes the crab, crumbs, and seasoning meld together both before and during cooking.

Classic recipes call for spiking crab cakes with everything from Tabasco to Worcestershire sauce, and those are both fine. But I've decided the best blend of tradition and trendiness is Old Bay seasoning combined with freshly ground white pepper and a tablespoon or more of chopped fresh herbs.

Just as essential as careful seasoning is careful mixing. I've found a rubber spatula works best, used in a folding motion rather than stirring. This is important because you want to end up with a chunky consistency. Those lumps aren't cheap.

Once I had the crab cake base down, I still had trouble keeping the cakes together as they cooked. My last breakthrough came when I tried mixing and shaping the cakes in advance for a dinner party, then chilling them until the guests arrived. As little as half an hour in the refrigerator made an ocean of difference: The cold firmed up the cakes so that they fried into perfect plump rounds without falling apart. I have since kept them chilled, tightly wrapped, for up to twenty-four hours.

I also tried different cooking methods. After baking, deep-frying, and broiling, I settled on frying in a cast-iron skillet over medium-high heat. This method is fast and also gives complete control over how brown and how crisp the cakes get. I first tried frying in butter, but it burned as it saturated the crab cakes. Cut with vegetable oil, it was still too heavy and made a mess of the pan. The ideal medium is plain old vegetable oil: It can be heated without burning and smoking, creates a crisp crust, and never obstructs the crab flavor.

PAN-FRIED CRAB CAKES WITH OLD BAY SEASONING
Serves 4

The amount of bread crumbs you add will depend on the crabmeat's juiciness. Start with the smallest amount, adjust the seasonings, then add the egg. If the cakes won't bind at this point, then add more bread crumbs, one tablespoon at a time.

- 1 pound jumbo lump crabmeat, picked over to remove cartilage or shell
- 4 scallions, green part only, minced (about ½ cup)
- 1 tablespoon chopped fresh herb, such as cilantro, dill, basil, or parsley
- 1½ teaspoons Old Bay seasoning
- 2 tablespoons or up to ¼ cup fine dry bread crumbs
- ¼ cup mayonnaise
- Salt and ground white pepper
- 1 large egg

Crab cakes require no accompaniment beyond a shot of hot sauce, but a creamy dip is also a good choice.

- ¼ cup flour
- 4 tablespoons vegetable oil

1. Gently mix crabmeat, scallions, herb, Old Bay, bread crumbs, and mayonnaise in medium bowl, being careful not to break up crab lumps. Season with salt and white pepper to taste. Carefully fold in egg with rubber spatula until mixture just clings together.

2. Divide crab mixture into four portions and shape each into a fat, round cake, about 3 inches across and 1½ inches high. Arrange on baking sheet lined with waxed paper; cover with plastic wrap and chill at least 30 minutes. (Can refrigerate up to 24 hours.)

3. Put flour on plate or in pie tin. Lightly dredge crab cakes. Heat oil in large, preferably nonstick skillet over medium-high heat until hot but not smoking. Gently lay chilled crab cakes in skillet; pan-fry until outsides are crisp and browned, 4 to 5 minutes per side. Serve hot, with or without following sauce.

CREAMY DIPPING SAUCE
Makes about ½ cup

- ¼ cup mayonnaise
- ¼ cup sour cream
- 2 teaspoons minced chipotles (smoked jalapeños)
- 1 small garlic clove, minced
- 2 teaspoons minced fresh cilantro leaves
- 1 teaspoon juice from 1 small lime

Mix all ingredients in small bowl. Cover and refrigerate until flavors blend, about 30 minutes. Serve with crab cakes or other fried fish. ∎

Regina Schrambling is the author of *Squash: A Country Garden Cookbook* (Collins-SanFrancisco, 1994).

Secrets of Creamy Fruit Sorbets

Forget about gelatin, egg whites, or corn syrup. The key to smooth, silky sorbets is plenty of sugar and a bit of alcohol.

~ BY JACK BISHOP ~

My goal was simple. Restaurant sorbets are invariably creamy and silky. They literally melt in your mouth, almost like ice cream. The sorbets I had been making at home since I bought an electric ice cream machine two years ago tasted fine, but their texture was overly icy. I wanted to figure out why.

I began by talking to chefs and reading through dozens of cookbooks, especially those by chefs, for recipe ideas. Most chefs and home cooks, myself included, reserve the term "sorbet" for frozen desserts without cream or milk. Sorbets are basically fruit and sugar, and that was the definition I decided to adopt.

I found a surprising number of possible solutions to the icy sorbet dilemma. They involved the use of the following ingredients either singly or in combination: gelatin, egg whites, jam, corn syrup, confectioners' sugar, superfine sugar, and alcohol. So I plotted out a methodical course for testing each of these variables using a simple sorbet recipe with fresh orange juice.

Trial and Error

Gelatin originally seemed to be the most promising of the possible additions. I tried a recipe from *The Joy of Cooking* that called for soaking gelatin in cold water and then adding that mixture to hot sugar syrup and fruit juice. As this mixture cooled, it started to gel and become gloppy-looking. I was not too optimistic. To my surprise, the sorbet emerged from the ice cream machine as a firm, white mass that scooped beautifully and had almost no iciness. Unfortunately, there was an unmistakable gumminess to it. No matter how I used gelatin (I tried several more variations, including heating the gelatin and beating it in a food processor to break it up), it gave the sorbet an unpleasant, rubbery quality.

Many French cookbooks I consulted suggested folding egg whites into the mix. Some authors folded lightly beaten whites into the sorbet mixture just before churning; others made an Italian meringue by slowly incorporating hot sugar syrup into egg whites beaten to soft peaks. After seven attempts at adding egg whites in various forms, I concluded they do nothing to prevent iciness. Egg whites beaten to soft peaks will make the ice crystals a bit smaller and give the sorbet a texture akin to newly fallen snow. However, the texture will never be creamy or smooth.

A few odd recipes suggested using jam to improve the texture. This logic proved correct, but the implementation was not practical. The cellular material from fruit pulp, especially the pectin, can act as a lubricant. (In this respect, I found that berry sorbets are softer and creamier than citrus sorbets because the whole fruit, which includes a fair amount of pectin, is being used.) When I tried adding marmalade to orange sorbet, the texture improved a bit. But after more tests, I realized that it was really the extra sugar in the jam that was responsible for ninety percent of the improvement in texture. Since adding plain sugar is much easier than calculating how much sugar is in a given jar of jam, I gave up on jam.

My last major area of concentration was the sweetener possibilities. I saw a number of recipes that used corn syrup. Could its thick, viscous quality carry over to the sorbet? The answer was no, and I found that when used in large amounts, corn syrup masks the fruit flavor. Next I tried confectioners' sugar and was surprised to detect graininess in the sorbet. I attributed this to the cornstarch, which is added to confectioners' sugar to keep it from clumping. I found superfine sugar to perform the same as regular sugar; it is not worth using unless you have some on hand.

Perfect Results and Some Refinements

Things really started to change when I turned to a recipe in a twenty-year-old book by Julia Child. She advocates the use of egg whites in some recipes in *The Way to Cook* (Knopf, 1989), but I liked the "more concentrated sherbet" recipe published in *From Julia Child's Kitchen* (Knopf, 1975). Although this sorbet was too sweet and runny for my taste, it was smooth and creamy. While most of the previous recipes I had consulted used one-quarter cup of sugar per cup of fruit, in this French recipe, Child used two-thirds of a cup of sugar per cup of fruit.

This high sugar concentration, simple as it is, turned out to be the solution to creamy sorbets. Sugar controls the texture (*see* "How to Retard Freezing" below): Add more sugar, and the texture improves. Everything else is just a smoke screen. Once I figured this out, the rest of my work was simple. I found that by using one-half cup of sugar per cup of fruit (give or take a few tablespoons depending on the fruit), I was able to achieve the desired result: smooth, creamy texture without cloying sweetness.

Even with reducing the sugar in Child's recipe, the sweetness proved pretty intense, but I discov-

---

HOW TO RETARD FREEZING

Water freezes at thirty-two degrees. Add sugar (or any substance that dissolves in water), and the freezing point is lowered. The more sugar that is added, the lower the freezing point becomes. Why does a lower freezing point make the sorbet taste less icy? We asked Shirley Corriher, cooking teacher and our food science advisor, to explain.

As a sorbet freezes, the water in the mixture forms ice crystals, and the sugar syrup that is left behind gradually becomes more concentrated. These sugar molecules make it harder for the remaining water molecules to bond, which thus lowers the freezing point. At some point, the remaining sugar syrup becomes so concentrated that it just won't freeze at the temperatures found in an ice cream machine or home freezer.

Unfrozen syrup keeps the sorbet soft and scoopable. In effect, the syrup lubricates the ice crystals and makes them less icy on the tongue. In addition, water in a high-sugar solution tends to form smaller crystals than water in a plain solution. These smaller crystals translate into a smoother feeling on the tongue. Corriher says that alcohol works in the same way by lowering the freezing point of the sorbet mixture.

What does this mean in the kitchen? Depending on how much sugar and alcohol are added to a sorbet, it can freeze as hard as ice cubes or remain slushy. The trick to making a creamy sorbet is to add enough sugar to keep it scoopable right from the freezer but not so much sugar that the sorbet is syrupy. Of course, the amount of sugar in the fruit itself has an effect on this process, which means that lemon sorbet needs more added sugar than pineapple sorbet. As for alcohol, I add a little to help keep the sorbet soft but not so much that you can taste it.

PHOTOGRAPHS BY DAVE HENDERSON

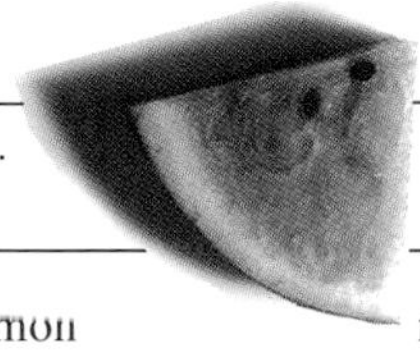

FRUIT	PREPARATION TO YIELD 2 CUPS FRUIT PUREE OR JUICE	SUGAR	LEMON JUICE	ALCOHOL
Apple	Use 2 cups cider.	¾ cup plus 1 tablespoon	2 tablespoons	1 tablespoon vodka, rum, or apple brandy
Blueberry	Puree 2½ cups berries with ½ cup cold water until smooth.	1 cup	2 tablespoons	1 tablespoon vodka
Grapefruit, red	Grate 2 teaspoons zest from two large grapefruits; combine with 1½ cups fresh-squeezed juice and ½ cup cold water.	1 cup plus 1 tablespoon	None	1 tablespoon vodka or Campari
Lemon	Grate 2 teaspoons zest from three large lemons; combine with ½ cup fresh-squeezed juice and 1½ cups cold water.	1¼ cups	None	1 tablespoon vodka
Mango	Peel and pit three medium mangoes. Puree flesh with ½ cup cold water until smooth.	¾ cup plus 1 tablespoon	2 tablespoons	1 tablespoon vodka
Orange	Grate 2 teaspoons zest from five large oranges; combine with 2 cups fresh-squeezed juice.	1 cup minus 1 tablespoon	1 tablespoon	1 tablespoon vodka or orange brandy
Peach	Peel and pit six medium peaches. Puree flesh with ½ cup cold water until smooth.	1 cup minus 1 tablespoon	2 tablespoons	1 tablespoon vodka or peach brandy
Pineapple	Stem, peel, quarter, and core one small pineapple. Puree flesh until smooth. Strain out stringy fibers.	¾ cup	1 tablespoon	1 tablespoon vodka or rum
Raspberry Blackberry Strawberry	Puree 3 cups berries with ½ cup cold water until smooth. Strain out seeds.	1 cup	1 tablespoon	1 tablespoon vodka or berry liqueur
Watermelon	Peel and seed 2½ pounds fruit. Puree flesh until smooth.	1 cup minus 1 tablespoon	2 tablespoons	1 tablespoon vodka or Campari

ered that adding up to two tablespoons of lemon juice to nonacid fruits helps to balance the sweetness. At this level, the lemon flavor is not detectable. Mildly acidic fruits need a smaller boost, a tablespoon or so of lemon juice. Lemons and limes do not require additional acid.

I also found that adding a tablespoon of high-proof alcohol improves the texture of the sorbets and permits a slight reduction in the amount of sugar. Tasteless vodka is my first choice, although any complementary brandy or eau-de-vie can be used. I tried white wine but found that because of its lower alcohol content, I had to use several tablespoons to achieve much of an effect on texture. At that concentration, the flavor of the wine became noticeable. This is fine in some sorbets—for instance, lemon sorbet with two or three tablespoons of white wine is lovely—but not appropriate in every case.

In the course of my research, I was also able to eliminate the hot sugar syrup step advocated by most chefs. Instead of heating sugar and water until the sugar dissolves, I simply mix the sugar right into the fruit juice or puree. Mixing on and off for several minutes is enough to dissolve the sugar—thus avoiding having to raise the temperature of the mix well above one hundred degrees (as happens when a hot sugar syrup is combined with the fruit) and incur hours of waiting time before processing the sorbet. In fact, if you mix the sugar and fruit substance over a bowl of ice water, sorbets can be ready to freeze about ten minutes after you walk into the kitchen.

A final note on ice cream machines. I tried my recipes in two electric ice cream machines (see Sources and Resources, page 32, for our recom-mendation) as well as a hand-operated Donvier, one of several canister-in-the-freezer models now on the market. The constant churning of the electric paddle makes better sorbets than hand-churning in a Donvier.

MASTER TECHNIQUE FOR FRUIT SORBETS
Serves 4

This recipe can be used to make any fruit sorbet. See the chart above for directions on preparing the fruit puree or juice. Since vodka is tasteless, it can be used with any fruit, but other suggestions appear above. For fruits not listed, follow directions for a similar fruit. For example, follow the lemon recipe to make lime sorbet. (*See also* "Sugar Content in Selected Fruits" at right.)

　　2　cups fruit puree or juice
¾–1¼　cups sugar
　0–2　tablespoons lemon juice
　　1　tablespoon vodka or other alcohol

1. Prepare fruit puree or juice as directed in chart above.
2. Combine fruit puree or juice, sugar, lemon juice, and alcohol in large bowl. Stir on and off for several minutes until sugar has dissolved. (To speed chilling process in step 3, combine ingredients in a metal bowl set over a larger bowl filled with ice water.) Rub finger along bottom of bowl to see if sugar has dissolved.
3. Pour mixture into small container. Seal and refrigerate until mixture is no more than 40 degrees. (If mixture has been stirred over a bowl of ice water, it may already be cold enough, and this step may be omitted.)
4. Pour chilled mixture into container of an ice cream machine and churn until frozen.
5. Scoop frozen sorbet into a container. Seal and transfer container to freezer for several hours to allow sorbet to firm up. (Sorbet can be kept frozen for up to 3 days.) ■

SUGAR CONTENT IN SELECTED FRUITS

The sugar content in fresh fruit differs according to the specific variety (some apples are naturally sweeter than others) and ripeness (ripe fruit contains more sugar than unripe fruit). Below is a list of the average sugar content in some common fruits based on figures in Harold McGee's *The Curious Cook* (North Point, 1990). To make sorbets with fruits not listed in the chart above, find a fruit in the chart with a corresponding sugar level and acidity and replace one fruit with the other.

Apple: 13%	Mango: 11%
Apricot: 9%	Orange: 11%
Blackberry: 8%	Papaya: 8%
Blueberry: 11%	Peach: 9%
Cantaloupe: 7%	Pear: 10%
Cherry: 14%	Pineapple: 13%
Grapefruit: 6%	Plum: 11%
Honeydew: 10%	Raspberry: 7%
Lemon: 2%	Strawberry: 7%
Lime: 1%	Watermelon: 9%

Tasting Barbecue Sauces

Designer sauces come out on top in a dual taste test, while sauces heavy in starch and corn syrup bring up the rear.

～ BY DOUGLAS BELLOW ～

Take a look in just about any refrigerator in America, and you will find some type of barbecue sauce. Although this uniquely American concoction started out years ago as a component of traditional barbecuing, it has evolved over the years into a kind of all-purpose summertime condiment for grilled meat and fowl.

This metamorphosis has come about largely because most of us do not have the time or the facilities to cook true barbecue. In this time-honored process, fairly large cuts of meat are first flavored with a dry rub or marinade, then hot-smoked at very low temperatures in a drum or pit for eight to twelve hours with an occasional basting of a second sauce, and finally served with a finishing sauce.

These days, instead of barbecuing, we are far more likely to grill meat quickly. Most of us don't make our own sauces either. Instead, we purchase bottled barbecue sauce off the shelf—and then ask it to accomplish all of the steps of traditional barbecue at once. We throw the meat into it to marinate, cook the meat in it, and serve the meat in more of it. This is often why store-bought sauces contain liquid smoke. They hope to substitute for long hours of smoking using concentrated smoky flavor. The liquid smoke also lets us get a sort of barbecue taste on oven-baked foods, although there is really no substitute for a live fire. (*See* "Secrets of Liquid Smoke," at right.)

It is important to keep in mind that store-bought barbecue sauce is based on what barbecue veterans define as a "finishing sauce," painted onto the barbecued meat after it comes off the heat. This is quite different from the basting sauce, which is made from a thin liquid to keep the meat moist during the long cooking. The basting sauces used in the traditional process never contain either sugar or tomato because these two ingredients tend to burn easily, leaving a bitter, charred taste.

For the same reason, you should not use store-bought sauces as a marinade, because then the sauce will burn when the meat is on the heat. Instead, brush purchased sauce onto your meat during the last few minutes that it is on the grill. Let it heat and cook a little bit, but be careful not to let it burn. Pass more of the sauce for dipping during

the meal, if you want. If you want to marinate your meat, use vinegar, oil, and spices instead.

So, now that we know the best way to use store-bought barbecue sauce, which is the one to buy?

To determine that, we held a blind tasting of a range of store-bought sauces. Given that there are many completely different styles among hundreds of different sauces manufactured in this country, the most difficult question that faced us in creating this tasting was which sauces to include.

As a start, we decided to limit the tasting to the tomato-based sauces, since they are far and away the most popular, and represent what most Americans picture when they think "barbecue sauce." Of course, we still had to narrow the field dramatically. We started with six of the top selling brands available in supermarkets throughout the country. We then ordered another five representative tomato-based sauces from different parts of the country. Smaller, regional favorites seemed appropriate contestants due to the strong local nature of barbecue itself. While these particular regional sauces came highly recommended by various sources, it is best to view them as representative of a very large number of possible choices. Not only are there other great tomato-based sauces out there, but whole other categories of sauce to try. We simply had to limit ourselves.

The sauces were tasted blind in two different ways. First, we tasted them just as they come out of the bottle. Second, we grilled chicken breasts, basting them in generous amounts of sauce for the final few minutes on the grill, allowing the sauces to caramelize but not burn or char. Since there is no orthodox set of guidelines about what barbecue sauce should be, tasters were asked to describe the sauces carefully and try to define the aspects of the sauces that they found most and least appealing.

Tasters Reject Starch and Corn Syrup

While there was general agreement between the two tastings, they were not equally definitive. The raw tasting produced a very clear ranking of likes and dislikes. When it came to tasting the sauces cooked on chicken, however, tasters found the

differences to be less pronounced.

This does not dilute the fact that there are definitely large differences between sauces. When tasting sauces alone, our tasters tended to choose the most expensive products, which also tend to be the spiciest ones with the strongest flavors. The three top choices have three very distinct flavors, coming, in fact, from three very different barbecue traditions, but are similar in that none of them is sweet, smoky, or ketchupy, and that all are manufactured by smaller, local sauce companies.

In the cooked test, preferences were still clear, but not by as large a margin. The sweeter, thicker, and often less expensive sauces tended to fare better than they had when tasted raw. Tasters agreed that this was largely due to the fact that the thicker sauces tended to adhere better to the chicken, so their tastes came through better than some of the pricier, thinner sauces.

When we checked the ingredients of the individual sauces, we found that two substances, corn syrup and starch, were consistently associated with low ratings. Of all the sauces tasted, only three list "food starch" among the primary ingredients. These same sauces were also the only ones that list corn syrup as their number one ingredient. Not coincidentally, these three—KC Masterpiece, Kraft Thick 'N Spicy, and Open Pit—were considered overly sweet and gooey by tasters, and ended up as three of the four lowest-rated sauces. (The fourth sauce of this group, Bone Suckin' Sauce, suffered with tasters from the fact that it is a very different style from all the other sauces, with a strong honey flavor.)

It seems, then, that the home cook has a choice. If you are really interested in sauces, it is worth trying out the smaller, more flavorsome, and somewhat more expensive regional brands such as Mad Dog, Gates, or Stubb's. We would suggest this particularly if you plan to use the sauce as a traditional dipping sauce, where you will get a lot of the raw flavor on your food. If, however, you just want something with which to baste meat while it is on the grill to add some flavor, or if you like somewhat sweeter and thicker sauces, there are some good options for a lot less money, with Bull's-Eye leading that pack. ∎

SECRETS OF LIQUID SMOKE

Many cooks avoid liquid smoke because they assume it's full of unhealthful chemicals. Fortunately for those who want to approximate the taste of smoke without the effort, liquid smoke is actually an all-natural product. Produced by burning hickory hardwood, condensing the smoke, and filtering it to remove all impurities, it is certified "natural" by the Food and Drug Administration.

The tasting was conducted at The Blue Room in Cambridge, Massachusetts. In addition to the author, the tasting panel included Chris Schlesinger, chef/owner of The Blue Room, East Coast Grill, and Jake & Earl's Dixie BBQ (these latter two also in Cambridge); Rob Halpin, chef/manager at Rudy's restaurant in Somerville, Massachusetts; Tommy King, barbecue pit-master at Redbones, also in Somerville; Lisa Lamme, owner of Le Saucier, a Boston retail store specializing in hot sauces; Sam

Sokol, manager of Harvest Restaurant in Cambridge, Massachusetts; Al Stankus, radio personality and coauthor of *Jazz Cooks* (Stewart, Tabori, and Chang, 1992); Peter Sagansky, a wine consultant; and two members of the *Cook's Illustrated* editorial staff. Panelists tasted all sauces plain and then brushed on grilled chicken breast during the last few minutes of cooking. Sauces are listed in order of preference as determined by their combined score from the two tests. ∎

| Mad Dog | Gates | Stubb's | Bull's-Eye | Lea & Perrin's | Heinz Thick & Rich | Larry Forgione's Barbecue Sauce | KC Masterpiece | Kraft Thick 'N Spicy | Bone Suckin' Sauce | Open Pit |

HIGHLY RECOMMENDED

Mad Dog (Best Sauce), $5.99 for nineteen ounces. Mad Dog, made in Boston, was the strong overall winner of the tasting. It is a thick, dark brown, and spicy sauce, with a "strong flavor of tomato paste." Mad Dog was the only sauce that scored in the top three in both the raw and cooked tests. Raw, our tasters liked its heat combined with its sweetness—"fruity fig beginning, with a long spicy aftertaste." This is a complicated sauce, with tamari, molasses, and liquid smoke among its ingredients, and it retained its powerful flavors after cooking.

RECOMMENDED

Gates, $5.99 for eighteen ounces. Gates is a strong, flavorful sauce from Kansas City. It is bright red with a "pungent, musty, and vinegary smell." Tasters picked out the flavors of chile powder, pepper, and celery seed. So much seed, in fact, that some tasters were distracted, calling it "gritty." Gates showed very well in both the raw and cooked tastings, with its salty, vinegary, and spicy flavors holding up well against the cooked chicken.

Stubb's, $5.99 for eighteen ounces. Stubb's, a very thin, orange sauce from Texas, barely edged out Mad Dog to win the raw tasting. Tasters liked the "balance of vinegar, spice, and sweetness" and "the kick at the end." Most felt Stubb's was a very high-quality, "natural-tasting" sauce. However, Stubb's disappeared in the cooked test, scoring rather poorly. Tasters said that they "couldn't taste it" (probably due to its thinness), although those who could find the flavors still complimented them.

Bull's-Eye (Best Buy), $2.29 for eighteen ounces. Bull's-Eye was the higher scorer among the national brands. It is a thick, sweet, dark brown sauce with a large dose of liquid smoke. While no taster felt that Bull's-Eye had excellent flavor, most tasters felt that it represented their impression of "what barbecue sauce should be." Many said it was like "what they grew up on." Bull's-Eye showed well in both categories, with its "smokiness" drawing attention during the raw tasting, and its "sweetness and coverage" proving noteworthy during the cooked test. Bull's-Eye does not have exceptional flavor, but it is a good quick fix for food, a clear best buy.

ACCEPTABLE

Lea & Perrin's, $2.29 for eighteen ounces. L & P is sweet, dark, and very thick. A few tasters noticed the flavor of Worcestershire sauce, although most felt that, other than some added "smoke," it was fairly "one-dimensional." L & P did modestly well among the sweet sauce fans in both the raw and cooked tastings, although one or two said they thought it tasted "mass-produced."

Heinz Thick & Rich, $1.29 for eighteen ounces. Unsurprisingly, nearly all of the tasters described Heinz as looking "disturbingly like ketchup." Despite the strong flavor of tomatoes and vinegar, most tasters felt that Heinz Thick & Rich was "too sweet." It did moderately well in the raw tasting, but tasters felt that the "vinegar and sweetness added little to chicken." Some felt that its texture seemed fake, or "emulsified," which made the sauce seem "cheap."

Larry Forgione's Barbecue Sauce, $4.95 for 7.5 ounces. This is a completely organic sauce made by American Spoon Foods, a company in Michigan that is a collaboration between famed chef Larry Forgione and food consultant Justin Rashid. This thin, salsa-textured sauce was the only one in the tasting with no sugar. Raw, most tasters felt it was "too weak," "flat," "plain," or "too subtle." It did do surprisingly well in the cooked test, however, although it seems that this was largely due to its distinctiveness from other sauces. Comments tended not to compliment the flavor, but instead went more along the lines of "at least it is interesting."

KC Masterpiece, $2.19 for eighteen ounces. KC Masterpiece is certainly not a masterpiece. "Sweet" and "smooth," with a "touch of smoke," and not much else. Turmeric is listed as an ingredient, but its flavor was undetectable. Raw, tasters felt that this sauce was not only too sweet, but "unbalanced" and "gummy." Like Larry Forgione's Barbecue Sauce, KC Masterpiece also did substantially better in the cooked tasting, where the sweetness was balanced by the salt of the chicken.

DON'T BOTHER

Kraft Thick 'N Spicy, $1.29 for eighteen ounces. Kraft Thick 'N Spicy is a sweet, fruity, ketchupy barbecue sauce. Our tasters found flavors of "lemon," "margarita" (lime), and "pineapple." Kraft Thick 'N Spicy was also characterized by its "strange orange-red color" and "very little nose." Most testers liked neither the taste nor the texture—"gloppy sweet," "like bad jelly," "gooey," and "don't expect it to do much for cooked food" (which it didn't).

Bone Suckin' Sauce, $5.99 for sixteen ounces. Bone Suckin' Sauce is a very sweet, thin, red sauce from North Carolina. Bone Suckin' Sauce did rather poorly in both tests at least partially due to its distinct difference from other sauces. Tasters found the texture "thin and loose" or even "watery" and were taken aback by the dominant flavor of honey. A few sweet-sauce fans felt it might make a "good dipping sauce" but also felt that "it did not cover cooked meat well."

Open Pit, $1.39 for eighteen ounces. Open Pit did poorly in both tests. It is a thick, "orangy red" sauce with a sweet flavor. Nearly all of the tasters felt that the color, when cooked, looked "weird," "strange," or "artificial" to the point of being distracting. Testers tasted either no flavor at all or a "sweet pickled flavor" like "relish" or "cooked strawberry jelly."

Blenders Prove Useful Tools

Our newfangled test winner can grate cheese, make pesto, puree hot soup, and "frappe" a chocolate milk shake.

∽ BY JACK BISHOP WITH SARAH REYNOLDS ∽

Blenders have come a long way from soda shops and ice cream parlors. While all of the models that we tested excel at such basic tasks as making a milk shake, manufacturers have tried to add new functions—everything from ice crushing to grating cheese—in order to keep this "old-fashioned" appliance current. The widespread acceptance of food processors in the 1980s sparked many of these changes in blender design. Although manufacturers have kept the basic structure the same (a glass jar sits on a motor that drives a rotating metal blade at the bottom of the jar), blades have been reconfigured (some blades are extremely thick while others are thin and razor-sharp) and blender jars have been reshaped (some jars are still tall and narrow while others are wider and shorter).

In addition to these changes, some companies have experimented with touch pads (a smooth surface is much easier to wipe clean than one cluttered with a dozen raised buttons). Some have tried to muffle the roaring sound while others have expanded the pulse function to include a high-energy (multispeed) function that adds extra power at any speed. One blender even has an automatic pulse (that goes on and off repeatedly until the button is pressed again) while a few retain the old-fashioned single-speed pulse.

Given the many changes in blender technology—and the fact that some six million Americans bought blenders for home use in 1994—we decided to evaluate the culinary potential of six "contemporary" blenders and see which were really worth purchasing. We found that some features are clearly more useful than others. A multispeed pulse is better than a single-speed pulse function, for example. However, touch pads that are hard to engage are not an improvement over regular buttons. Likewise, a wide

---

RATING BLENDERS

The six blenders were evaluated based on the following characteristics and are listed in order of preference. (For information on purchasing top models, *see* Sources and Resources, page 32.)

Capacity: Maximum amount that can be held in a blender jar. Larger jars were preferred. Note that blenders should never be filled to the top, so the figures here are intended for comparison only.

Speeds: Number of speeds and type of pulse function. We found the range between highest and lowest speeds to be more important than the number of individual speeds. A multispeed pulse function that worked at each speed was preferred over a separate single-speed pulse button.

Crushed ice: Some blenders could not crush ice without adding cold water and were rated poor. Those that could crush a few cubes (about six or so) were rated fair. One blender could handle a dozen cubes at once and received the top rating in this area.

Frozen drink: We combined one sixteen-ounce can of frozen margarita mix with one cup of water and three cups of ice cubes. Blenders that made a perfectly smooth drink with no ice chunks were rated good.

Milk shake: We combined one cup of milk with two large scoops of ice cream and two tablespoons of chocolate syrup. Every blender passed this test with flying colors by making a thick, smooth shake.

Grated cheese: We grated one-half cup of Parmesan cheese that had been cut into half-inch chunks. Blenders able to produce powdery grated cheese with no remaining chunks were favored here.

Pesto: We added one-half cup of olive oil, one-third cup of pine nuts, one-third cup of grated Parmesan cheese, one peeled garlic clove, and two cups of packed basil leaves and blended until smooth. Blenders able to produce a smooth pesto without distinct pieces of garlic or basil were favored. Note that all machines performed this task best when oil was added to the blender before the solid ingredients.

Pureed soup: We added two cups of cooked potatoes, carrots, and onions along with two cups of hot broth. Blenders able to puree soup without lumps or leaking were preferred.

■ = *good performance*    = *fair performance*    = *poor performance*

Blender	Price	Capacity	Speeds	Crushed Ice	Frozen Drink	Milk Shake	Grated Cheese	Pesto	Pureed Soup
Krups PowerX Plus 239	$50	7 cups	14 with multispeed pulse	fair	good	good	fair	good	poor
Waring Touch Blend TB201	$78	5½ cups	4 with single-speed automatic pulse	fair	good	good	good	good	poor
Cuisinart Vari-Speed Blender CB-4	$96	7 cups	13 with multispeed pulse	poor	good	good	fair	fair	poor
KitchenAid Classic 3-Speed Blender KSB3WH	$119	7 cups	3 with multispeed pulse	good	good	good	fair	poor	poor
Hamilton Beach Blend Master 54200	$50	6½ cups	14 with single-speed pulse	poor	fair	good	fair	fair	poor
Oster Designer 12-Speed Osterizer Power Blend 4102	$60	6 cups	12 with multispeed pulse	poor	good	good	poor	fair	poor

jar design may make the blender more sturdy, but it can also keep foods too far from the blade.

After working with dozens of bunches of basil, pounds of Parmesan, and gallons of soup, we cannot say that a "new" blender is an essential piece of kitchen equipment. After all, there are other tools that can grate cheese (a Mouli, for instance), puree soup (an immersion blender), and make pesto (a mini-food processor). However, one good blender can perform all of these tasks and more. If you are already inclined to buy a blender to make milkshakes or frozen drinks, you may as well purchase one with the widest range of culinary applications.

Narrowing the Field

As with most appliances that we test, there are literally hundreds of models on the market. Blenders are generally divided into two categories—those made specifically for use in bars (sometimes with stainless steel jars and often only one or two speeds) and those made for the kitchen (with glass jars and a range of speeds). We focused on the latter category and chose top models from the leading manufacturers.

In addition to general design and construction, we evaluated the performance of blenders on a number of particular tasks. We made milk shakes and frozen margaritas and also tried to crush ice in all of the blenders. Bar blenders generally do a much better job with ice, but all of the kitchen blenders that we tested should have been able to crush small amounts, at least according to the accompanying literature. In truth, only one blender (the KitchenAid) really crushes ice well. Two other blenders (the Krups and Waring) can crush some ice, but not more than six or eight cubes at once. Three other blenders cannot crush any ice at all.

For our culinary tests, we chose tasks that we hate to do in a food processor: grate a small amount of Parmesan cheese until powdery, make a small amount of pesto, and puree hot soup. (While we love our sturdy food processors, they never grate cheese fine enough, they leak when hot liquid is added to the bowl, and are too large to make a small amount of pesto.) Some blenders were able to handle all three jobs (pureeing soup was the easiest), while others faltered, especially when grating cheese.

The Results

After completing these six tests, it was clear which blenders we want to own. The Krups and Waring were able to perform all six tasks. The Cuisinart, KitchenAid, and Hamilton Beach each struggled with at least one task but are acceptable choices, while the Oster was unable to complete three of the six tests and is unacceptable.

On design issues, the Krups is the clear winner. This blender has the widest range of speeds with a truly low speed as well as a "power burst" button for top-notch pulsing. An easy-to-use dial adjusts the speed smoothly and makes cleanup quick since there aren't a dozen little buttons that can trap dirt. On the down side, this blender only does a fair job at grating cheese (the texture was pebbly rather than powdery). On the definite plus side, the Krups blender is so quiet you can actually have a conversation when it is on. The reasonable price is an added bonus.

The Waring blender actually outperformed the Krups model in a couple of areas — it made the finest grated cheese and smoothest pesto — but is rated second overall based on its annoying "high-tech" design. The touch-pad buttons are difficult to lock into place. The capacity of this blender is also too small. An automatic pulse function, which turns the blender on and off until the button is disengaged, is a nice feature, but it only works at one speed. Despite these flaws, the Waring blender is still a good second choice because it works well in spite of the design kinks.

The Cuisinart is incredibly noisy, and the plastic lid was warped and difficult to snap into place on the model we tested. The KitchenAid is a great ice crusher but left several small chunks after grating cheese for one minute and made the worst pesto, with large strips of basil and chunks of garlic. The culprit is the wide jar design, which makes the blender especially well balanced but also allows food to stray far from the blade.

The Hamilton Beach is another step down in quality. Fourteen speeds cover only half the territory of the three speeds in the KitchenAid. In addition, the blender left large chunks of cheese ungrated, struggled to crush the ice for the frozen drink, and failed to incorporate all of the basil into the pesto. Also, the design is not user-friendly.

The Oster blender seems to have a lot less power than the other models. Cheese stuck under the blade, and the blender began to emit a burning rubber smell during our tests. As for the pesto, the garlic was sliced (not minced), and the entire mixture was too chunky. ∎

TESTERS' COMMENTS

Krups (Best Blender): Excellent design and good performance in most areas make this blender the top choice.

Waring: An overly complicated design drops this blender to second place despite good performance at most tasks.

Cuisinart: Performance varied greatly on this blender with a limited range of speeds and an airplanelike roar.

KitchenAid: By far the best ice crusher in the bunch, but the culinary abilities of this blender are uneven.

Hamilton Beach: Mediocre performance plus confusing design make this blender an unappealing choice.

Oster: A poor range of speeds and subpar performance drop this weak blender to the back of the pack.

The Best Red Wines for Grilled Food

The common wisdom about what you should drink with grilled food turns out to be common tomfoolery.

∽ BY MARK BITTMAN ∽

Grilled foods, say many experts, are the perfect foil for "rough, hearty" red wines. Something about that charred flavor is supposed to complement wine that, under other circumstances, would suck your tongue right out of your mouth. As a result of this advice, many people—myself included—have gone blithely about buying young, rough, hearty red wines to serve with grilled vegetables, tuna, and steaks.

But that doesn't mean that such wine is the ideal partner for grilled food. In an attempt to determine what style of wine really *is* the right partner, we gathered a variety of styles of red wines and served them, with grilled foods, to a group of tasters. We tried to keep the price of these wines down—around half were $10 or less—which eliminated anything really grand. To keep the field relatively contained, we avoided wines made from cabernet sauvignon and pinot noir, the two most esteemed red wine grapes, whose wines are almost never recommended for grilled foods.

Instead, we concentrated on those reds that many people think of first: red (not pink) zinfandels, inexpensive wines from Spain, Portugal, and Australia, the latest bargain from Italy, something from southern France, and some trendy California selections. As a last-minute inspiration, we included the California wine that beat the wines of southern France in a tasting we held earlier this year.

The menu was simple: grilled vegetables, shrimp, steak, and chicken, cooked with a light brushing of olive oil. A variety of sauces were made available, ranging from a fiery mustard-horseradish to soy-ginger to parsley pesto. Our goal here was to give our tasters a wide range of flavors, the experience you have at many outdoor meals, and part of the rationale behind recommending blitzkrieg reds. As usual, the fifteen wines were poured blind, in flights of three; the only change was that they were poured while people were eating.

As they often do, our results ran counter to what we would have expected: The most rough-and-tumble wines, the wines that I, at least, would have been most inclined to serve with grilled foods, were nowhere near the top. Our winners were vigorous, fruity wines, not quite light but certainly not heavyweights. Almost to a person, our tasters were going for a style that was not similar to the food but rather served as a counterpoint to it. The two winners, for example, are both bright versions of wines that can also be made in a darker style: The Ravenswood Zinfandel is a lightly oaked, fruity zin, while the Cline is a southern France–style wine but mostly made from the ebullient carignane grape rather than a heavier variety.

In fact, it isn't until the fifth-ranked wine that we come to the rough style that we expected to do well. The Ridge Zinfandel and Vietti Barbera that tied for fifth place are wines that are difficult to drink without food but quite decent with it. Still, they were no match, in this tasting, for the lightweights that finished above them. It will be argued that the Ridge, especially, will become much more accessible in years to come, yet this is the type—and age—of wine that is frequently recommended to consumers (and has been recommended to me) despite the fact that it is too young. ∎

BLIND TASTING RESULTS

As usual, the wines in our tasting were judged by a panel made up of both wine professionals and amateur wine lovers. In the judging, seven points were awarded for each first-place vote; six for second; five for third; and so on. The wines were all purchased in the Northeast; prices will vary somewhat throughout the country. Within each category, wines are listed based on the number of points scored.

In general, Highly Recommended wines received few or no negative comments; Recommended wines had predominantly positive comments; Not Recommended wines had few or no positive comments.

HIGHLY RECOMMENDED

1993 Ravenswood Vintners Blend California Zinfandel, $9. This light, fruity zin was a runaway winner, with four out of ten first-place votes and eight of ten in the top five spots.

1990 Cline Côtes d'Oakley, Contra Costa County, $7. Also light and fruity, the winner of our March/April "Rhône" wine tasting continues to impress.

1993 Georges Duboeuf Domaine des Rosiers Moulin-a-Vent, $11.50. This Beaujolais did well: "Meaty and intense, with plenty of fruit," and "great with this food."

RECOMMENDED

1992 La Vieille Ferme Reserve Côtes du Rhône, $9. A not-too-big Rhône wine: "Slightly rough, but spices and nice fragrances come through."

1992 Ridge California Lytton Springs Zinfandel, $18. Some found this too young wine "pungent" and "medicinal." But to others, it was rich and lovely.

1989 Vietti Barbera d'Alba Bussia, $16. A "strong" wine, but a "good companion to food," according to some. "Shallow and too tannic," thought others.

1992 Rosenblum Cellars Sonoma County Old Vines Zinfandel, $13. Its adherents found this "bold, rugged, and forceful." Detractors called it "a high-tannin, no-fruit medicine."

N.V. Marietta Cellars Sonoma County Old Vine Red, Lot #14, $9. Received a first-place vote from a veteran taster, who found it "young, fruity, and lovely, with finesse." Few agreed.

1993 Ca' del Solo California Big House Red (Bonny Doon), $10. This also received a single first-place vote, from a taster who said it was "fruity and rich, with good balance." Others called it "antiseptic."

NOT RECOMMENDED

1990 Taurino Salice Salentino Riserva, $8. Some described this Chianti-like wine as "smooth, but not fascinating," but most found it to have a "nice nose but quite disappointing in the mouth."

1993 Rosemount Estate South Australia Shiraz, $9. "Fruit and spice, pleasant enough," was the most positive comment this elicited. Three tasters, without consulting, found it salty!

1987 Quinta do Carmo Alentejo Red (Portugal), $16. "Dry, rough, and very tannic."

1989 Lar de Barros Tinto Reserva (Spain), $10. "Thin and dull," with "more acid than fruit."

1991 Phelps California Vin du Mistral, $13. "Thin, tannic, and very simple."

1990 Guigal Gigondas (France), $15. "Dry," "rough," "raw," and "commonplace."

BOOK
REVIEWS

Delia Smith's Summer Collection
Delia Smith
Viking, $22.95

Like most Americans, I'd not heard of Delia Smith before reviewing this book. Smith, who's been setting Brits at ease in the kitchen for twenty years, has a large (five million books sold), loyal following. Frequent appearances on the BBC and her comprehensive book, *Delia Smith's Complete Illustrated Cookery Course*, have earned her a reputation as a foolproof recipe writer who explains "not only how, but why."

How unfortunate, then, that Smith makes her debut in this country with this, her fourth book, a lightweight collection of mostly Mediterranean and American recipes. Her new book features dishes that have been around long enough to become mainstream here—Pasta Puttanesca; Caesar Salad; Tomato, Mozzarella and Basil; and Pesto. There's a healthy shot of well-worn American recipes too—American Muffins, All-American Half-Pounders, and Deb's Iced Tea.

Other than a short introduction written to her new American audience, the book is only a *collection* of recipes. All the culinary wisdom of her earlier books is simply not here. Except for the introduction, she's writing as if to trusted old friends, not making herself known to new ones. It's Julia Child trying to sell *And Company* to an audience who's never heard of *Mastering the Art of French Cooking*.

I found her recipes easy to follow, but not flawless. Caledonian Ice Cream, a frozen vanilla base with caramelized oatmeal chunks, was made by churning sweetened and lightly whipped heavy cream. By the time the cream was frozen, though, the butterfat had separated from the milk solids, making the ice cream grainy with fat. I decided against making Smith's four-and-a-half-pound leg of lamb, which she roasts in a 375-degree oven for two and a half hours and promises it will carve up pink. (An hour would be more than enough.) On the other hand, her Sri Lankan Curry was as good as any I've eaten, and her Twice-Baked Goat's Cheese Soufflés were brilliant.

Smith has unfortunately been dubbed "the Martha Stewart from across the pond." She's not nearly as slick as Stewart, so those looking for another entertaining mentor will surely be disappointed. And those seeking her brilliant kitchen wisdom will be equally disappointed by this merely competent collection.

—Pam Anderson

Gather 'Round the Grill
George Hirsch with Marie Bianco
William Morrow, $20

With all the talk about funding for public television, I thought it might be interesting to look at the self-proclaimed "hottest new star" on the PBS culinary roster. *Grilling with Chef George Hirsch* was carried by 225 PBS stations last year and, according to his press material, was the "most talked-about new cooking show of 1994." A second season, with thirty-two episodes, is currently on the air.

In conjunction with the new season, Hirsch has written *Gather 'Round the Grill*. The book contains thirty-two seasonal menus, one of which will be demonstrated on each show. After testing eight recipes, I can only conclude that the camera is not telling the whole story.

The hook is quite simple. Hirsch prepares everything from soups to desserts on the grill. While some of the traditional grill fare (meats, vegetables, etc.) that I tested was fine, I don't see the point of making apple pie or pumpkin crème brûlée over a live fire.

Some examples: The custard for Chocolate Cream Pie thickens on the grill and is then poured into a prebaked store-bought pie shell. Because the saucepan was so far from the heat source on my gas grill, it took forty-five minutes to bring the milk to a boil and then thicken the custard. (This process takes fifteen minutes on a stove.) Even more infuriating was the instruction to bring the custard "to a boil." As might be expected, the custard curdled into long strands of scrambled eggs and was unusable.

In the same vein, Hirsch grills escarole leaves and adds them to a simple Escarole Soup with cannellini beans. Leafy greens, even if they are brushed with oil, don't really shine on the grill. In addition, the canned beans were added too early to the soup. After simmering for thirty minutes, they disintegrated.

Not everything I tested was so bad. Chili-Rub Flank Steak with Corn Salsa was excellent, although marinating the meat for two days seems excessive when a few hours will give the meat an excellent flavor.

Although Hirsch's enthusiasm for grilling and willingness to put "uncommon" fare such as bananas, chile peppers, pizza, and potatoes over hot coals is admirable, spotty directions and some just plain stupid ideas (deep-frying squid in a pot of hot oil on a grill seems excessively risky) are

serious flaws. His work is simply not up to the standards set by Julia Child, Pierre Franey, or Jeff Smith—public television veterans who know how to cook.

—Jack Bishop

A Well-Seasoned Appetite
Molly O'Neill
Viking, $24.95

I liked Molly O'Neill's *New York Cookbook*, and I like *A Well-Seasoned Appetite* also. The first, a collection of other people's recipes, had a vibrant, almost electric character. O'Neill's new book is, on the other hand, almost soothing and introspective. Essays that reflect the mood of the author and the subject matter combined with the selection of hip but generally simple recipes, confirm—to me at least—that O'Neill is among the best of this generation's American food writers.

During my first go-round, I thought that a certain portion of the recipes was on the too-simple side, but when I passed slowly through the book, I found that even these—Basic Corn on the Cob, for example—contained valuable information.

Fall Vegetable Salad was brilliant; oven-drying four vegetables took forever, of course, but was easy enough (you can do them all at once, just removing them from the oven at different times). And the result was a deceptively simple-looking salad with knockout flavor—the kind of thing I love in restaurants, made doable at home. A squash dish—a braise of acorn squash (I used butternut) with apples, cider, and butter—was also quite clever and flavorful.

Other than cheeseburgers, I am not wild about meat-and-cheese combos, so perhaps the lamb and feta pairing was not a wise choice to test. But my guests and I agreed that although the recipe produced a nicely cooked rack of lamb, we would have preferred a coating of garlic, bread crumbs, and parsley. Other recipes delighted me by delivering on their promises; not only is O'Neill's selection brilliant, everything here works.

A Well-Seasoned Appetite is organized by seasons, which has the disadvantage of assuming that you'll always want to make beef stew in the fall rather than in the winter. But within each section recipes are grouped logically and, after all, there is an index. Chances are you'll find this cookbook most useful if you browse the prose and dog ear the pages with recipes you find appealing—there will be plenty. ∎

—Mark Bittman

SOURCES
AND RESOURCES

Most of the ingredients and materials necessary for the recipes in this issue are available at your local supermarket, gourmet store, or kitchen supply shop. The following are mail-order sources for particular items. Prices listed below were current at press time and do not include shipping or handling unless otherwise indicated. We suggest that you contact companies directly to confirm up-to-date prices and availability.

BEST BLENDERS
We tested six blenders from leading manufacturers (see page 28) and have two clear favorites to recommend. The Krups PowerX Plus 239 is our first choice. A Cook's Wares (412-846-9490) sells this blender, which not only performs very well but is also the quietest one we have ever used, for $50. The Waring Touch Blend TB201 also performed extremely well in our tests. Although the design is not our favorite, this model is still a good choice. Contact the manufacturer's customer service department (203-379-0731) to locate a retail source in your area or to place an order directly with the factory.

STURDY GRATERS
Shredding zucchini on the large holes of a metal grater is a quick way to prepare this summer vegetable without salting (see page 8). Some graters will bend under pressure so it's important to have a heavy-gauge metal grater on hand. We like the sturdy stainless steel German graters carried by the Sur La Table catalog (800-243-0852). We particularly like the combination grater with large and small holes as well as a slicing blade. (Use the large holes to grate zucchini.) This grater costs $9.95.

FRESH CRABMEAT AND SEASONING
The best crab cakes are made with meat from Atlantic blue crabs, and the Chesapeake Bay is the number one location for this crustacean. Although summer is high season, it may be difficult to obtain this species in some parts of the country, especially in the West. Pacific Dungeness crab can be used, but with slightly different results. Chesapeake Express (1129 Hope Road, Centreville, MD 21617; 800-282-2722) ships fresh blue crabmeat from May through October. A pound of jumbo lump crab costs $25, while a pound of back-fin meat is $21. There is a three-pound minimum, and overnight shipping costs $12. Pasteurized crabmeat is also available during the summer as well as the winter. Unopened pasteurized crabmeat will last for months in the refrigerator and is preferable to fresh crabmeat that has been frozen. Chesapeake Express also sells a crab seasoning mix known as J.O. Seafood Seasoning, which is similar to the famed Old Bay seasoning. A sixteen-ounce can of this blend of herbs and spices costs $5.

PASTRY BOARD
When a pie recipe (see page 6) says to roll the dough out into a nine-inch circle, it can be a hassle to search for a tape measure, especially if your hands are covered with flour. That's why we like a large, wood pastry board with dimensions for various sizes imprinted on the surface. The board measures sixteen by twenty-two inches and has rulers imprinted on all four sides as well as circular rings that can be used to measure out dough for an eight-, nine-, or ten-inch pie. This board is available through the Sur La Table catalog (800-243-0852) and costs $19.95.

ELECTRIC ICE CREAM MACHINE
There have been a number of new products introduced since we last evaluated ice cream machines in the July/August 1993 issue. We found that making sorbets (see page 24) and ice creams at home is easiest with an electric ice cream machine. The only problem is cost. Our top-rated ice cream maker, the Simac machine from Italy, for example, costs $500. Until recently, the only other alternative to electric was a canister-type model such as the popular Donvier. (A metal container filled with special coolant can be frozen overnight and then slipped into this hand-crank model.) Now, there is a third choice that combines the power of an electric machine with the low cost of the frozen insert models. The new Krups La Glacière automatic ice cream maker works like a Donvier (a separate canister must be frozen overnight) except that the ice cream is churned electrically and not by hand. Constant churning means that more air is beaten into sorbets and ice creams and thus their texture is better. While nothing will beat the convenience of the Simac (no canisters to freeze), the price of the Krups is just $60, about the same as a manual Donvier. The Krups ice cream machine is currently available through the Williams-Sonoma catalog (800-541-2233).

SPICES FOR RUBS
The majority of supermarkets and gourmet stores have a good supply of whole spices. However, there are a few items used in the spice rub recipes on page 21 that may prove a bit more difficult to locate. Penzeys Spice House (P.O. Box 1448, Waukesha, WI 53187; 414-574-0277) carries hundreds of whole and ground spices. Some items that you may need include coriander seeds ($1.99 for four ounces), cumin seeds ($2.49 for four ounces), fennel seeds ($1.49 for four ounces), and star anise ($7.79 for four ounces). You may also want to consider purchasing a separate mill for grinding spices. When we rated coffee grinders earlier this year (see January/February 1995 issue), we particularly liked the Bosch blade grinder (Model MKM 6) for crushing whole spices. This mill retails for about $25 but is sold under the Starbucks label through its catalog (800-782-7282) for $19.95.

SMOKING EQUIPMENT
Our test kitchen prefers convertible smokers that contain a removable electric element. Either electricity or charcoal and wood can be used to power these smokers. We tested the recipes on page 19 with the Meco 5030 smoker. This three-foot-tall smoker comes with two racks for food, a drip pan, and a removable electric coil. To locate a retail source in your area that carries Meco products, call the company's consumer hotline at 800-251-7558. The suggested retail price for this model is $89.99. Smoking and grilling enthusiasts should also know about products available directly from Weber, a leading manufacturer of outdoor cooking equipment. Weber sells hickory and mesquite wood chunks in five-pound bags ($3.50) and ten-pound bags ($7). Hickory and mesquite chips are sold in one-and-a-half-pound bags ($1.20) and in three-pound bags ($2). Finally, you will need a good thermometer that can measure the heat in your smoker as well as the internal temperature of the food you are cooking. The Weber replacement thermometer ($14.99) fits most grills and smokers and can be used as an instant-read thermometer in foods. All Weber items may be ordered by calling 800-446-1071.

CORN-ON-THE-COB DISHES
Tired of corn rolling around or off dinner plates? Porcelain dishes that are deep enough to cradle an ear of corn are the solution. The dishes allow corn to be rolled for easy buttering, and the ends allow for clearance of corn holders. The Williams-Sonoma catalog (800-541-2233) sells a set of four white porcelain corn dishes for $20. A dozen nickel-plated brass corn holders are available for $15.

POULTRY STUFFING BAG
The quick tip on page 4 shows how to turn cheesecloth into a poultry stuffing bag. If you're not much of a sewer, you can purchase a washable, canvas poultry stuffing bag. It's available from the Cookery Ware Shop (Peddler's Village, P.O. Box 106, Lahaska, PA 18931; 215-794-8477) for $4.25. ∎

SMOKED PORK CHOP page 19
WITH SWEET-AND-SOUR COLESLAW
page 13

LEMON SORBET AND
STRAWBERRY SORBET
page 25

CHERRY PIE
page 7

PAN-FRIED CRAB CAKES WITH
OLD BAY SEASONING
page 23

GRILLED ZUCCHINI SALAD WITH TOMATOES AND BASIL
page 9

A BETTER BURGER page 15
WITH BOILED CORN ON THE COB page 22

Bay-Scented Roasted Potatoes

Peel, wash, and dry eight medium boiling potatoes. Starting at one end of potato and moving to the other end, make a crosswise slit every half inch. Cut fifteen or so bay leaves lengthwise into thirds. Stick a piece of bay leaf into each slit. Place potatoes in an oiled baking dish. Pour ¾ cup boiling chicken stock or low-sodium chicken broth over the potatoes, drizzle with ½ cup olive oil, then sprinkle potatoes with salt. Bake at 350 degrees until potatoes are tender and brown and cooking liquid has evaporated, about 40 minutes. Serve, removing bay leaves prior to eating.

NUMBER SIXTEEN

OCTOBER 1995

COOK'S
ILLUSTRATED

One Recipe, Three Cheesecakes

Creamy, Fluffy, or Extra-Dense

Chicken in the Pot

Sauté, then Braise for Easy, Foolproof Chicken

The Best Northern Cornbread

Two Milks and Two Leavenings Yield Light, Golden Cornbread

Testing Kitchen Scales

Electronic Models Justify the Price

THE BEST BAKED APPLE

RATING COCOAS

RANKING INEXPENSIVE MERLOTS

HOW TO SAUTÉ FISH FILLETS

$4.00 U.S./$4.95 CANADA

"Apples"
See page 12 for
the best way
to bake an apple.

ILLUSTRATION BY
CRAIG NELSON

Brandied Fall Fruits
adapted from
The Glass Pantry
(Chronicle Books, 1994)
by Georgeanne Brennan

ILLUSTRATION BY
CAROL FORTUNATO

COOK'S
ILLUSTRATED

Publisher and Editor CHRISTOPHER KIMBALL

Consulting Editor MARK BITTMAN

Senior Editor JOHN WILLOUGHBY

Food Editor PAM ANDERSON

Senior Writer JACK BISHOP

Articles Editor ANNE TUOMEY

Managing Editor MAURA LYONS

Assistant Managing Editor TRICIA O'BRIEN

Assistant Editor ADAM RIED

Copy Editor GARY PFITZER

Editorial Assistant KIM N. RUSSELLO

Test Cook VICTORIA ROLAND

Art Director MEG BIRNBAUM

Food Stylist MARIE PIRAINO

Special Projects Designer AMY KLEE

Marketing Director ADRIENNE KIMBALL

Circulation Director ELAINE REPUCCI

Ass't Circulation Manager JENNIFER L. KEENE

Circulation Coordinator JONATHAN VENIER

Circulation Assistant C. MARIA PANNOZZO

Production Director JAMES McCORMACK

Production Assistants SHEILA DATZ
PAMELA SLATTERY

Ass't Computer Admin. MATTHEW FRIGO

Production Artist KEVIN MOELLER

Vice President JEFFREY FEINGOLD

Controller LISA A. CARULLO

Accounting Assistant MANDY SHITO

Office Manager TONYA ESTEY

Office Assistant SARAH CHUNG

Special Projects FERN BERMAN

Cook's Illustrated (ISSN 1068-2821) is published bimonthly by Boston Common Press, 17 Station Street, Box 569, Brookline, MA 02147-0569. Copyright 1995 Boston Common Press. Second-class postage paid at Boston, MA, and additional mailing offices, USPS #012487. For list rental information, please contact Direct Media, 200 Pemberwick Rd., Greenwich, CT 06830; 203-532-1000. Editorial office: 17 Station Street, Box 569, Brookline, MA 02147-0569; (617) 232-1000, FAX (617) 232-1572, email cooksill@aol.com. Editorial contributions should be sent to: Editor, Cook's Illustrated, 17 Station Street, Box 569, Brookline, MA 02147-0569. We cannot assume responsibility for manuscripts submitted to us. Submissions will be returned only if accompanied by a large self-addressed stamped envelope. Subscription rates: $24.95 for one year; $45 for two years; $65 for three years. (Canada: add $3 per year; all other countries: add $12 per year.) Postmaster: Send all new orders, subscription inquiries, and change of address notices to Cook's Illustrated, P.O. Box 59046, Boulder, CO 80322-9046. Single copies: $4 in U.S., $4.95 in Canada and other countries. Back issues available for $5 each. PRINTED IN THE U.S.A.

EDITORIAL

FREEDOM OF CHOICE

CHRISTOPHER KIMBALL

On a recent trip to southern California, I found myself in a large Vietnamese neighborhood only a few miles from Disneyland. I stopped in at a shopping center restaurant that offered special pork vitals soup (*Chad Long*), eel hot pot (*Lau Long*), goat with curried onion and coconut milk (*De Xao Lan*), salted pickled plum drink (*Xi Muoi*), and pennyworth leaves drink (*Rau Ma*). I tried one of the goat curries, which was excellent, a grilled eel dish that was heavy on bones and light on meat, one of the traditional "pho" soups, which was highly aromatic and delicious, and the salted plum drink, evidently an acquired taste.

After lunch, I drove across the street (in southern California you cannot walk across the street without ending up as roadkill) to a huge Vietnamese supermarket. The produce display was prodigious, including chayoky squash (a small, round squash), Vietnamese celery (very thin and delicate), five kinds of mint, seven kinds of basil, galangal (a gingerlike root), fresh turmeric, panai leaves, white bittermelon, and miniature Thai eggplant. In the meat and fish department, shoppers were snapping up pork snouts, skate wings, fish balls of varying colors, jumbo prawns, belt fish, goby fish, Taiwan milk fish, apple snails, live stone crab, and frozen mud fish. I also found ten brands of coconut milk, salted duck eggs, pickled young grape in jars, and young tamarind leaf. It was like dying and going to heaven—the ultimate gourmet supermarket.

But the exhilaration of new foods was accompanied by profound culture shock. I felt like a recent Russian immigrant in Queens, suddenly confronted with a thousand choices. Where to live? What car to drive? Whether to subscribe to *The New York Times* or *Daily News?* Would I cook mud fish or German carp? Should I buy bittermelon or miniature Thai eggplant? As I grow older, I find abundance problematic. There is something intimate about making do with what is available, finding yet another way to prepare kidney beans, cook a chicken, or expand on my August repertoire of corn soup, corn fritters, corn relish, corn muffins, and corn pudding. Yet, the lure of a shop with ten types of fresh fish is as strong as the lure of Disney World to my seven-year-old.

I often wonder if choice and happiness are good companions. As Chris Schlesinger, coauthor of *The Thrill of the Grill*, says, you can't like both Texas and North Carolina barbecue. If you mention a tomato-based sauce east of Raleigh, you'll need to do some quick explaining. And I was thrilled to read *Silicon Snake Oil*, in which a pioneering computer hacker describes why he has given up the endless choices available on the Internet for a more circumscribed existence based in the real world. Another friend of mine, a doctor in the Ayurvedic tradition of India, offers his own theory of modern life. We are living in a time of Vata imbalance, he says, a period in which we are aggravated by a flood of choices, which leads to a loss of vitality.

In the kitchen, we also have to make choices. Perhaps over time, chayoky squash or miniature eggplant will creep into my repertoire, but, for now, I am suspicious of the benefits of the culinary superhighway. That's why I don't care much for tasting menus when I eat out, preferring to choose one dish rather than flitting from one bite to the next. That's also why my wife and I have turned off our home computer and unplugged the television. The kids read books, run around the house, fight, get bored, play games, and make too much noise. There are evenings when we feel like Homer and Marge Simpson, a frightening admission, but there is something oddly endearing about that family because their cartoon existence is chaotic, absurd, and entirely banal—that is, comfortably familiar.

At the end of my trip, I had dinner with Marion Cunningham, a friend and cookbook author. We always eat at the same restaurant, sit at the same table, and order roast chicken with potatoes and baked custard for dessert. Like old friends, we find deep satisfaction in the familiar. Although open to change, Marion, like all great home cooks, has made choices, spending time wisely in the kitchen, cooking what suits her. For each of us, there is a type of cooking that has a deep connection with our view of ourselves. It may be goat curry or may be pot roast, but good cooks know that, sooner or later, they have to limit their repertoire. Are we disappointed that Julia Child isn't teaching Thai cooking or that Marcella Hazan isn't an expert on beaten biscuits? Of course not.

Yet the memory of that Vietnamese supermarket is difficult to erase. The mint. The jumbo prawns. The stone crab. I am tempted to join the culinary revolution and leave behind what could be considered the relatively parochial cooking of New England. But perhaps making the right choice is more important than having many choices. And for me, that choice is to be loyal to the traditions, the people, and the foods of my childhood. ∎

NOTES FROM READERS

GUARANTEED PROOFING

I live in a large Victorian home with a chilly, drafty kitchen, which can make getting bread to rise a challenge in the winter. I have learned that I can obtain superb results using my dishwasher as a proof box. I run a wash cycle until there is about one inch of hot water in the machine. I turn the dial to the dry setting for a short time and then place the bowl with the dough on the rack. I leave the door unlatched to prevent accidental starting of the wash cycle. After I have punched down the dough and placed it in bread pans, I once again activate the dry cycle for a short time and place the pans back in the dishwasher for the final rise. I always get excellent results.

SAM SMITH
Salamanca, NY

Strange as it sounds, we found that this method works well, especially in a cold, drafty kitchen. We could never get an inch of water to stand in the bottom of our dishwasher, though, so we developed this variation: Run an empty dishwasher through the wash cycle. When the dry cycle starts, place the bowl containing the dough on the bottom rack, close the dishwasher, and let rise.

This method trims about twenty minutes from the first rise, which takes two hours in our cool (sixty-six-degree) kitchen. The temperature in our dishwasher was ninety-eight degrees when the dough was placed in the machine and about eighty degrees when the dough was removed. Of course, the air inside the dishwasher was quite moist, which also promoted a speedy rise. We found a similar savings of time with the second rise.

STORING COFFEE BEANS

I enjoyed your coffee article (January/February 1995 issue). Could you discuss storing coffee beans? I put them in an airtight container and place them in the freezer. I take out the appropriate amount just before grinding. Is this the best way to keep beans fresh or would some other method be better?

EDWARD GING
Pittsburgh, PA

This issue generates plenty of controversy among coffee professionals. Everyone agrees that beans must be stored in an airtight container. Oxygen will cause flavor in beans to deteriorate, so this is imperative. Most experts also agree that storing beans at room temperature on the counter away from sunlight is ideal. In the refrigerator or freezer, the oil on the beans can congeal. When it comes time to make coffee, the congealed oils may result in a cup of espresso with less foamy light brown crema on top, for instance. We have also found that fresh, room temperature beans make coffee with slightly more flavor than frozen or refrigerated beans.

However, these differences are small and may not be detected by every coffee drinker. The deciding factor should be how fast you plan on using the beans. Room temperature storage requires quick use of the beans. Within a week or two, flavor starts to go downhill as exposure to oxygen takes its toll. Storing beans in the freezer (it offers more protection than the refrigerator without additional risk) will slow down this process. Therefore, if you buy beans every week or two, keep them on the counter. If you buy beans less often, keep them in the freezer.

COMMENTS ON EDITORIAL

I am spurred to write by your thought-provoking editorial in the March/April 1995 issue. While I love the ritual aspects of 240 million people eating the same menu on Thanksgiving, I find it quite unattractive as a model for the rest of the year. I quite agree with your wonderfully Emersonian declaration of our common ground. Where I differ from you is the idea of what the best thing we can share is.

Personally, I rarely sound the diversity gong, and I understand the real threats to our national security when litchi nuts, mozzarella, and kiwis end up together in blue corn tortillas. But I fear even more strongly the dangers of an undifferentiated culinary banality. This is too well exemplified by the numbers of hamburgers this nation consumes simultaneously.

Indeed, I feel that the current culinary renaissance is a reassuring vital sign, culturally speaking. Nothing lets us know we are alive and happy more effectively than a new and positive experience. There is certainly a great difference between what the food media would have us believe is happening in up-to-date kitchens and the realities of modern life. But for the sensible cook who won't be driven to master the cooking of the Caucasus this season, a dish here, an ingredient there, is exactly what the good life in an American kitchen should be all about. The potent and exotic flavors of Mexican peppers, soy sauce, and Moroccan preserved lemons, to name a few, are actually ideal for incorporation into the expeditious cuisine you so rightly claim as the norm, and ingredients I would hate to live without.

STEPHEN LYLE
New York, NY

SPICE GRINDER

I have used Steve Johnson's braised lamb shanks recipe a number of times since I read your article (January /February 1995 issue), and everyone to whom I serve it loves it. I have settled for the most part on the version that includes the North African spices. You recommend the use of a spice grinder. I have exhausted all my resources in seeking one, including all the kitchen stores around here. Nowhere do I find a spice grinder. Pepper mills are useless for many spices. A mini-Cuisinart does a passable job, but I still hanker for a spice grinder. Where did you get yours?

JAMES SMITH RUDOLPH
Ann Arbor, MI

When we call for a spice grinder in a recipe, we are referring to an electric coffee mill that has been set aside specifically for the purpose of grinding whole spices. An inexpensive blade grinder (about $20 to $25) will do the job nicely. We recommend that you not grind coffee beans in the same machine. The beans will pick up some odd flavors if you do. For this reason, we call the grinder in our kitchen reserved for spices, a spice grinder. Sorry for the confusion.

As for a specific model, when we tested these grinders (see "Rating Electric Coffee Grinders" in the same issue as the lamb shanks story), we found the Bosch Model MKM 6 to be a slight favorite, although all of these cheap grinders were deemed adequate. The Starbucks catalog (800-782-7282) sells the Bosch grinder under its own label for $19.95.

CRÈME BRÛLÉE QUESTIONS

I would like to thank you for Gene Freeland's "Perfect Crème Brûlée" story in the March/April 1995 issue. He explained why many of my attempts at crème brûlée have ended up less than perfect. However, after reading the article, I was still left with one question. I sometimes add fresh raspberries or sliced strawberries to the ramekins before pouring in the cream and egg yolk mixture. Does the acidity or pectin content of these fruits affect the thickening ability or final texture of the custard?

I was also surprised that Mr. Freeland did not

mention a salamander in his experiments with caramelizing the sugar topping. While not a common item, salamanders are available in many specialty kitchen shops. I have found that these branding devices form paper-thin crusts of perfectly caramelized sugar, and, because they work so quickly, they make it unnecessary to rechill the custard at the end.

MORT O'SULLIVAN
New York, NY

Shirley Corriher, our food science expert, says that adding fruit to the ramekins can be cause for some concern. The acidity in raspberries or strawberries will cause the egg proteins to unwind faster (this process is called "denaturing"). Once the egg proteins have unwound, they will hook up and cause the custard to set. When adding fruit to crème brûlée, watch the custards as they bake and be prepared to remove them several minutes early from the oven. Also, at very high levels, acidity can cause the custard to curdle. This is more of a problem in recipes that rely on milk. The high fat content of heavy cream, which is used in our crème brûlée recipe, should prevent curdling. By the way, the pectin in the fruit is not a concern.

As for salamanders, we agree that they work extremely well (as do butane torches), but we wanted to develop a recipe that could be made without special equipment. If you would like to use a salamander to caramelize the sugar topping, La Cuisine Kitchenware (800-521-1176) carries two models. Its classic French salamander has a long handle and sturdy metal plate. A Spanish model has a shorter handle and a thinner metal plate. The heavy-duty French salamander costs $40 while the lighter-weight version, which is fine for occasional home use, costs $8.50.

To use either salamander, simply place the metal disk on a red-hot burner until it is quite hot. Lightly place the hot disk on the sugared top of each crème brûlée until it is caramelized. As you note, there is no need to rechill custards if a salamander is used to caramelize their tops.

BALSAMIC VINEGAR FRAUD

*A*s *a balsamic vinegar addict, I read your balsamic vinegar tasting story (March/April 1995 issue) with more than considerable interest. One aspect of the more expensive brands that I feel you should have covered is that of fraudulent age claims. Unfortunately, the only part of this rip-off that you did mention (some cheap balsamic vinegars are nothing more than flavored red wine vinegar) is just the tip of the iceberg. In far too many instances, legitimate "tradizionale" vinegars are receiving bogus "aging" at some stage of handling. This type of vinegar is sold as being a certain age, and this fictional age is used to justify a high price.*

I have been taken in by three different approaches to the same scam. The first involved a bottle labeled "ten years old," the second involved a salesclerk explaining another bottle's ancient pedigree, and the third involved an age

printed on the price tag. For instance, when one retailer I work with asked the wholesaler for a written statement authenticating a claim of "fifty years old" on a price tag, the wholesaler would only indicate that the bottle contained vinegar at least twelve years old but had a reputation of being at least twenty-five years old. Subsequent investigations indicated quite convincingly that there is no reliable method of having any of the producers of balsamic vinegar certify that any bottle of their product contains vinegar of a particular age.

It is noteworthy that while some of the reviewed vinegars are being sold as "twenty-five years old" or "more than ten years old," your magazine was not led astray to the point of mentioning age as a price-determining factor. With a product as popular and as unregulated as balsamic vinegar, there is ample opportunity for fortunes to be made from a gullible public.

NAME WITHHELD

We agree that the marketing of balsamic vinegar is plagued with misrepresentations and sometimes outright fraud. We mentioned in our article the scam of passing off sweetened red wine vinegar as balsamic vinegar since this practice affects the cheaper products (under $10) that constitute the bulk of the market. However, you are correct to point out that more expensive vinegars can also be marketed in a less-than-forthright manner.

Part of the problem has to do with the way balsamic vinegar is traditionally made. Unlike wine, which is usually aged in one cask and then bottled, traditional balsamic vinegar is aged in a series of casks, often with vinegars from different harvests and years being mixed or "topped up" to create the final product. To earn the designation "tradizionale," the base vinegar must be at least twelve years old. Given the formal acceptance process necessary to earn this designation, we are fairly confident that all traditional balsamic vinegar is really twelve years old.

However, claims above this level are not subject to regulation and hence depend on the integrity of the manufacturer, importer, wholesaler,

and retailer. While this is not to say that "twenty-five-year-old" vinegar may not be that old, the American consumer has no guarantee in this area. Our advice: Buy from a reputable source, and pay high prices for something that tastes good, not just for something that is supposed to be very old.

UNSALTED BUTTER FOR GREASING PANS

*A*lthough your answer about the differences between salted and unsalted butter (Notes from Readers, September/October 1994) was most interesting, a major reason for using unsalted butter was overlooked. Unsalted butter will not cause sticking. Cookies made with unsalted butter will not stick to baking sheets and cake pans rubbed with unsalted butter and then floured will release cakes beautifully.

JOHANNA STEPHENS
Tucson, AZ

MICROWAVE GARLIC BEFORE ROASTING

*W*ith regard to your article on poaching and then roasting garlic (September/October 1993 issue), I have developed a simplified method that eliminates the step of poaching in a saucepan and shortens the roasting time.

Prepare the garlic as directed (remove the papery skins and trim one-half inch from the tip end of each head), pour one-eighth inch of milk into a small plate or bowl, place the garlic cut side down in the milk, cover the garlic with an inverted bowl, and microwave it on low power for five to ten minutes, depending on how many heads of garlic you are working with. (The "reheat" function on my microwave works perfectly for this job.) After microwaving, roast the garlic in a 350-degree oven, cut side up, basting the heads with some of the milk and one-half teaspoon of olive oil per head of garlic. Reduce the roasting time from one hour in your recipe to about thirty minutes. Heaven. ∎

ADAM GOLD
Woodinville, WA

WHAT IS IT?

I have enclosed a picture of an item that I possess. It is a mystery as to what its purpose may have been. Can you enlighten me? This tool is made of hardwood, about twelve inches long, and the plunger extends another five inches. The bottom of the center shaft is metal, and the area where the shaft goes into the base is also lined with metal.

DWIGHT PETTERSON
Warwick, RI

You own a German bottle corker, which can be used to cork wine or vinegar bottles. To use this device, place the bottom of the corker over the top of a bottle that has been filled and

is ready to be sealed. Next, place a cork in the metal-lined well at the top of the base. Depress the plunger to push the cork down through a tunnel that exists in the base of the corker. As the cork moves through this tunnel, it is compressed so that it will fit into the opening at the top of the bottle. Once the cork goes into the bottle, it will expand again to create a tight seal. La Cuisine Kitchenware (323 Cameron Street, Alexandria, VA 22314; 800-521-1176) imports a very similar device from Germany. The cost is $40.

Quick Tips

MAKING MANAGEABLE DEVILED EGGS

As "finger food," deviled eggs are slippery, awkward to grasp, and a bit too big for the mouth. Linda-Marie Loeb of Belvere, California, suggests this method of making them both easier to serve and more attractive.

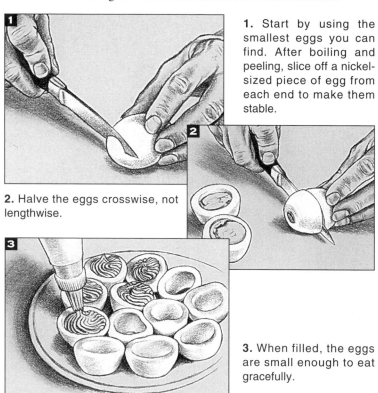

1. Start by using the smallest eggs you can find. After boiling and peeling, slice off a nickel-sized piece of egg from each end to make them stable.

2. Halve the eggs crosswise, not lengthwise.

3. When filled, the eggs are small enough to eat gracefully.

GRATING HARD CHEESES

Grating hard cheeses with a hand-held grater is efficient, but it often creates a mess on the counter. Mrs. Johann Komurek of Getzville, New York, wrote us with this tip for making the process neater.

1. Before you begin grating, wrap a piece of plastic wrap around the bottom of the grater and secure it with a rubber band.

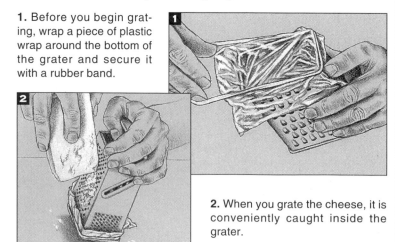

2. When you grate the cheese, it is conveniently caught inside the grater.

REMOVING LEAVES FROM CABBAGE

As fans of stuffed cabbage know, removing leaves from a head of cabbage without tearing them is a daunting task, even after parboiling. Daphne Keller of Red Bank, New Jersey, suggests this method.

1. Use a sharp paring knife to cut around the core at the base of the cabbage.

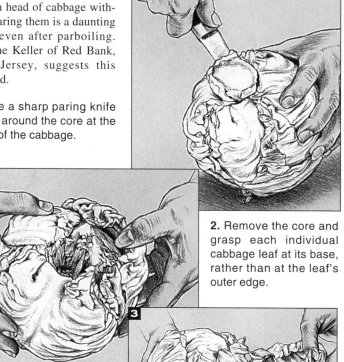

2. Remove the core and grasp each individual cabbage leaf at its base, rather than at the leaf's outer edge.

3. Gently lift the cabbage leaf from the cabbage.

DRYING LARGE QUANTITIES OF GREENS

Scores of readers have written us to suggest this tip for drying large quantities of lettuce or other greens easily.

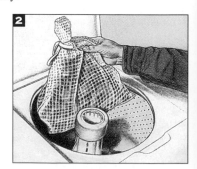

1. Place washed greens in a zippered pillowcase cover or net mesh bag.

2. Place the pillowcase or mesh bag in the washing machine on the spin cycle. When the cycle is done, the greens will be thoroughly dried.

ILLUSTRATIONS BY ALAN WITSCHONKE

MESS-FREE PIPING

For a "no-muss, no-fuss" way to fill and refill your pastry bag, take a tip from Mindy Arbo of Winchester, Massachusetts.

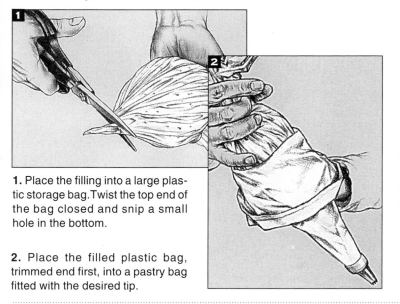

1. Place the filling into a large plastic storage bag. Twist the top end of the bag closed and snip a small hole in the bottom.

2. Place the filled plastic bag, trimmed end first, into a pastry bag fitted with the desired tip.

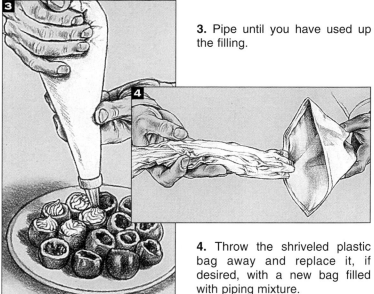

3. Pipe until you have used up the filling.

4. Throw the shriveled plastic bag away and replace it, if desired, with a new bag filled with piping mixture.

COOLING SUSHI RICE

Quick cooling leaves a nice sheen on sushi rice and also prevents it from overcooking, but traditional hand fanning takes a lot of effort. We suggest you follow this tip from Gordon Wing of Albany, California, and use an electric fan to cool the rice after cooking and dressing it with rice vinegar.

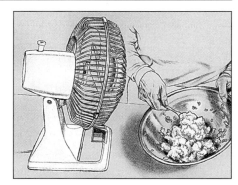

POURING BOILING WATER INTO A PAN IN THE OVEN

Putting boiling water into a pan in the oven when baking bread helps achieve the desired crust. Unfortunately, this can lead to scalding or burning yourself if you are not careful. Laton Maner of Williamsburg, Virginia, suggests using a copper watering can with a long spout to solve this problem. This method also works perfectly when adding water to a bain-marie.

FORMING GNOCCHI

In "The Secrets of Gnocchi" (March/April 1995), we suggested using a butter paddle to give the gnocchi the desired ridged shape. Pamela Czerwin of Oceanside, New Jersey, suggests an alternative—an unused hair pick. Because hair picks are made of plastic, dough tends not to stick to them, and because their teeth are so long, you will get nice, deep, even grooves with any size of gnocchi.

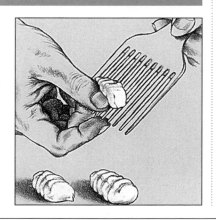

SEPARATING FAT FROM PAN DRIPPINGS

Barbara Robbins, a biochemist from Corvallis, Oregon, suggests using this laboratory trick to separate pan drippings more easily from fat when making a pan sauce. Pour all the liquid from the roasting pan into a glass measuring cup, then carefully slip a transparent bulb baster beneath the clear layer of fat and pull the amber juices into the baster.

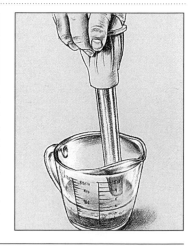

Thanks to our readers for Quick Tips: The editors of *Cook's Illustrated* would like to thank all of the readers who have sent us their quick tips. We have enjoyed reading every one of them, and have learned a lot. Keep them coming. We will provide a one-year complimentary subscription for each quick tip that we print. Send a description of your special technique to *Cook's Illustrated,* P.O. Box 569, Brookline Village, MA 02147-0569. Please write "Attention: Quick Tips" on the envelope and include your name, address, and daytime phone number. Unfortunately, we can only acknowledge receipt of tips that will be printed in the magazine. In case the same tip is received from two readers, the one postmarked first will be selected. Also, be sure to let us know what particular cooking problems you would like us to investigate in upcoming issues.

Cheesecake: One Recipe, Three Textures

Soft and creamy, light and fluffy, or firm and dense. Varying the oven temperature and using whole or separated eggs make all the difference.

≈ BY PAM ANDERSON WITH KAREN TACK ≈

Some dishes have universal standards of perfection—a well-made omelette, a crisp, buttery croissant, a full-flavored chicken soup. Cheesecake is not among these dishes. For most fans, perfect cheesecake has more to do with texture than flavor. Some cheesecakes are firm and dense, like a classic New York–style cheesecake. Others are rich, lush, and creamy, almost like a thick custard. Still others are as light and airy as meringue. Each style has its own following. One person's lush is another's wimpy; one person's fluffy is another's spongy; and one's dense is another's dry.

It was clear from the beginning that there could be no single ideal cheesecake recipe. In our informal cheesecake polls, all three textural styles came up as favorites. Our goal was to develop a basic cheesecake whose texture could be altered with a simple ingredient change or baking method. To better understand exactly what affects cheesecake's texture, we tested the key ingredients—cream cheese, eggs, cream, and sour cream—as well as a variety of baking methods and temperatures. After three days of testing, not only had we come up with the lush, creamy cheesecake we preferred, we had also figured out how to lighten the texture or make it more dense to suit other preferences.

In order to clearly determine the role of each ingredient, we made all cakes from a simple one-pound cream cheese recipe with sugar, eggs, vanilla, and a little lemon zest. They were all baked in disposable eight-and-one-half-inch cake pans in a three-hundred-degree oven until the cake perimeter jiggled and its center was not quite set. Once we developed the cheesecake formula, we switched to a two-pound cream cheese recipe and springform pans to determine the best baking methods, times, and temperatures.

Regular Philly Cheese, Please

Since cream cheese is, after all, the cornerstone in cheesecake, we started with this ingredient. We tested cakes made with fresh cream cheese and regular Philadelphia brand commercial cream cheese, as well as Philadelphia's Neufchatel (one-third less fat), light (50 percent less fat), and no-fat cream cheeses.

Fresh cream cheese was not available locally, so we resorted to mail order at $5.50 per pound plus overnight mail charges. Although this softer, creamier, tangy cheese was our first choice for spreading over a bagel, it proved too unstable for baking. Unlike any of the other cakes, the one made with fresh cream cheese baked up grainy, having broken or curdled slightly. The fresh cheese was simply too fragile for baking. (*See* "Cream Cheese Heresy," page 8.) Philadelphia brand cream cheese, on the other hand, was firmer and denser in texture than fresh cream cheese. Baked exactly the same way, this cake was smooth and creamy, superior to cake made with fresh cream cheese.

Unlike real cream cheese that melts like butter in your mouth, low-fat and no-fat varieties cling to the tongue. The cakes made from these cheeses also baked differently from those made with regular cream cheese. The Philly Neufchatel brand, which is whiter, softer, and more watery than regular cream cheese, baked more quickly as well. Even though it was pulled from the oven ten minutes sooner than any of the other cheesecakes, it cracked. The cake made with this cheese was also harder and more crumbly than that made with regular cream cheese.

Philly no-fat cream cheese developed a rubbery skin and several mudlike shallow cracks during baking. Underneath the skin, the cake was soft and chalky in texture with an unpleasant artificial taste. Of all the cakes we made during those three days, it was the only one we actually threw away. And although not nearly as bad as the no-fat cream cheese version, the light cream cheese cake tasted artificial as well. It was deceptively creamy at first, but an unmistakable dustiness lingered on the tongue.

One Egg, Two Eggs, Three Eggs, Four

Egg quantity differed with cheesecake recipes. To see just how many eggs a cheesecake would need, we made cakes with virtually every egg combination that made sense, starting with a cheesecake

With a few simple varations in our basic recipe, you can make cheesecake that is (from rear) fluffy, creamy, or firm.

made with all egg whites and ending with one made with all yolks. We should have used blindfolds to taste these cheesecakes, for their hues ranged from vivid yellow to pale cream, corresponding directly to egg quantity.

What we learned from our egg experiments is that a good cheesecake needs a combination of egg whites and yolks. The all-egg-white cheesecake was dry. Fortunately, the other extreme—an all-yolk cheesecake—didn't produce the best result either. The all-yolk cakes, and the ones made with whole eggs plus extra yolks, seemed to push this dessert into the custard category. The cakes were rich, heavy, and pleasantly eggy—but hardly cheesecake. Two whole eggs (four for a two-pound cream cheese recipe) made the cake creamy and tender without tasting overly rich and custardy.

It made sense that folding whipped egg whites into the batter would lighten the cheesecake's texture. So, during our egg tests, we confirmed our suspicions. Instead of beating whole eggs into the batter, we separated the eggs, beating the yolks into the cream cheese and sugar, then folding in the whipped whites just before baking. Though our master recipe was still in process, we could see that this technique of whipping the egg whites and folding them into the batter led to a light and airy texture, one of the three textures we were looking for.

The simple cream cheese–only cakes we had

been baking were perfect for testing individual ingredients, but as a dessert, they were lacking. Their relatively dry texture needed softening, and their flat flavor needed rounding. Our next set of tests—adding different ratios of sour cream and heavy cream to the cheesecake batter—made us realize the importance of these two supporting ingredients.

A Little Help from Some Friends

We had hoped to develop a cheesecake formula using either just cream or just sour cream because we didn't want a recipe calling for small quantities of each unless it was really necessary. But we found that it was.

In an attempt to drop the sour cream from our recipe, we tried substituting lemon juice. The resulting cake was pleasant, but too distinctly lemon-flavored.

Another option, topping the cheesecake with sour cream rather than incorporating it into the batter, seemed to us an extra step designed exclusively for hiding those unsightly center cracks. Our plan was to lose the cracks, not cover them up.

So we went back to experimenting with various ratios of these two ingredients. Cream gives cheesecake that velvety, smooth texture, but too much of it and you begin to mask the cream cheese flavor. Sour cream supports the underlying tang of the cream cheese, but, if overdone, it takes over as the dominant flavor. You need a little of each—cream for texture and sour cream for flavor. Too much of both and you end up with a rich, characterless dessert. After many experiments (see "Too Much of a Good Thing," below) we ended up using one-quarter cup of each.

Water Bath, Right Path

Now that we had a good batter, we wanted to keep it from baking up grainy and cracked. From previous cheesecake testing, we were water bath converts. We already knew that a water bath protects a cake from harsh, direct heat that can cause it to overcook, crack, and sink. But we also knew that this method has its drawbacks. The springform pan has be lined with heavy-duty foil. If the water level exceeds the foil lining or if the foil rips, wa-

ter seeps between the foil and pan, and the cake can become waterlogged. These water leaks occur more often than you might think.

If there were a better way, we were open. Would baking the cake over a pan of water work just as well as a water bath, or bain-marie? Would a dry method at a lower heat turn out as velvety-textured a cake as a bain-marie? Here was our chance to find out.

Starting with the more straightforward cooking methods, we baked three different cakes at 325 degrees for one hour. We baked the first cake in a dry oven. The second cake was baked over a pan of water placed on the rack below. The third cake was baked in a water bath. Predictably, the dry-

baked cheesecake puffed up like a soufflé, developing hairline cracks around the perimeter toward the end of baking. Its top was quite brown. As it cooled, though, it developed that familiar center crack. We tasted the cake at room temperature. A large area around the perimeter of the cake was as grainy as a broken hollandaise—the eggs had clearly overcooked. Only the very center of the cake was smooth and creamy.

The cheesecake baked over the pan of water was a step up from the dry-baked cake. Like the dry cake, it developed hairline cracks around perimeter. It souffléed throughout, though, not just around the edges. As it cooled, it developed only a tiny, center crack. Its surface was cream-colored with a few brown spots. The very outer edges of the cake were overcooked, but the large center area was soft and creamy.

The cake baked in the water bath was perfect—no cracks, no sinking, no spotting. Its texture around the outer edges was just as creamy as it was in the center.

Just to be sure that the differences in texture did not result from differences in baking time, we baked the same recipe for forty-five, fifty-five, sixty-five, and seventy-five minutes. The forty-five-minute version was unpleasantly goopy with no mixture of flavors. The fifty-five- and sixty-five-minute versions were both very good, with the flavors fully mixed and the cheesecake well set. Even the seventy-five-minute version was not unacceptable, a bit dryer but still well within range. It was clear that differences in cheesecake texture were not a function of cooking time but of other factors.

TOO MUCH OF A GOOD THING

To figure out just what ratio of cream cheese, cream, and sour cream make the ideal cheesecake, we analyzed and tried out a range of published cheesecake recipes.

CREAM CHEESE	SOUR CREAM	HEAVY CREAM	TESTERS' COMMENTS
1 pound	1 cup	none	Not bad, but too spongy. Needs cream to soften.
½ pound	1 cup	none	Sour cream too dominant. Borders on pasty.
⅓ pound	⅔ cup	⅔ cup	Pleasant, but cream cheese starts to get lost.
1 pound	none	6 tablespoons	Cream masks cream cheese. Lacks tart aspect.
¾ pound	¾ cup	6 tablespoons	Again, cream cheese flavor is lost.
½ pound	½ cup	2 tablespoons	Very sweet, custardy as opposed to cheesy.
1 pound	none	2 tablespoons	Very nice, lacking only a touch of tartness
1 pound	2 tablespoons	2 tablespoons	Ideal balance with real cream cheese flavor.

1. To prepare a spring-form pan for a water bath, cover the bottom and sides with heavy-duty aluminum foil. Place it in a roasting pan.

2. Set the roasting pan in an oven, then fill the pan with boiling water so it comes halfway up the side of the springform pan.

Finally, for the ultimate in long, slow baking, we tried an eight-hour water bath version in a two-hundred-degree oven. Although it was perfectly smooth with no cracks or coloring, it developed a thick top skin during baking. This baking method wasn't our favorite, but we at least discovered that a cheesecake baked for this long wasn't ruined.

A number of recipes instruct the cook to leave the cake in a turned-off oven once it has cooked. This technique, they say, keeps the cake from deflating. Although we never had problems with cheesecake deflation, we came to like this method for a different reason. We turned off the oven when the cake was just slightly underdone in the center. The tame heat of the turned-off oven allowed our cakes to fully set without overcooking.

Or Bake It High (Then Low) and Dry

We were almost there. We had the lush and creamy and the light and fluffy cakes perfected, but we had not come up with a crack-free, smooth-textured, dense cheesecake. We knew that moist heat could not deliver this style of cheesecake. It needed gentle, dry heat to evaporate some of the cake's moisture without overcooking the eggs. So we tried baking cakes for less time and at lower temperatures. Reduced oven time still delivered cracked cakes. Lower oven temperatures produced cakes that were not creamy enough to compete with our soft, lush cakes but not dense enough to offer a contrast. We finally decided to try the absurd.

During my research, I had come across a really odd baking method in *Villas at Table* (Harper & Row, 1988). In his recipe for Lindy's Cheesecake, author Jim Villas instructs the cook to bake the cake dry in a blistering five-hundred-degree oven for the first twelve minutes, then two hundred degrees for one hour longer. So skeptical were we of this method that we at first decided not even to waste the cream cheese. If cakes crack under more moderate conditions, we reasoned, then how could a cake baked in this environment stand a chance? But, we ended up following Villas's instructions, reducing the five-hundred-degree time

to ten minutes to compensate for a lesser amount of cream cheese in our recipe. After ten minutes, we peered in at a beautifully puffed cake. We held the oven door open until the inside reduced to two hundred degrees and baked the cake for another hour. The finished cake was beautiful. The high heat had caused the graham cracker crumbs to brown nicely and the eggs to puff. The low heat had gently cooked the cake, keeping the eggs from overcooking. The dry heat had allowed the cake to slowly dehydrate, creating that dense yet creamy texture we were seeking. Finally, we had a cheesecake to suit every taste.

RICH AND CREAMY CHEESECAKE
Serves 12 to 16

1	tablespoon unsalted butter, melted
3	tablespoons graham cracker crumbs
2	pounds cream cheese
1¼	cups sugar
4	large eggs
1	teaspoon zest from small lemon, minced
2	teaspoons vanilla extract
¼	cup heavy cream
¼	cup sour cream

1. Adjust oven rack to middle position and heat oven to 325 degrees. Line bottom of 9-inch springform pan with foil, tuck foil underneath pan bottom, assemble pan, then pull foil around side of pan (*see* illustrations 1 and 2, page 7). Brush bottom and sides with butter. Sprinkle crumbs over bottom. Tilt pan in all directions to coat evenly with crumbs. Cover pan underneath and along sides with sheet of heavy-duty foil (illustration 1, left) and set in large roasting pan. Bring kettle of water to boil for water bath.

2. Meanwhile, beat cream cheese in bowl of electric mixer until smooth. Gradually add sugar and beat on medium speed until sugar dissolves, about 3 minutes. Add eggs, one at a time, beating until just incorporated and scraping down after each addition. (If you don't scrape down the bowl after each egg, cream cheese that sticks to the bowl will ultimately show up as lumps in the batter.) Add zest and vanilla and beat until just incorporated. Remove bowl from mixer; stir in cream and sour cream.

3. Pour batter into prepared pan. Set roasting pan on oven rack and pour enough boiling water to come about halfway up side of springform pan (illustration 2, left). Bake until perimeter of cake is set, but center jiggles like Jell-O when pan is tapped, 55 to 60 minutes. Turn off heat and leave oven door ajar, using a long-handled kitchen fork or spoon to hold it open for 1 hour longer. Remove springform pan from water bath and set on wire rack; cool to room temperature. Cover and refrigerate until chilled, at least 4 hours. (Can be refrigerated up to 4 days.)

Light and Airy Cheesecake. Follow recipe for Rich and Creamy Cheesecake, separating eggs. Add yolks, rather than whole eggs, at instructed time. Continue with recipe, stirring in cream and sour cream. Beat egg whites to soft peaks. Fold whites into batter, pour into prepared pan, and bake, reducing cooking time to 45 to 50 minutes.

Dense and Firm Cheesecake. Follow recipe for Rich and Creamy Cheesecake, disregarding instructions for water bath. Bake cake at 500 degrees for 10 minutes. Reduce oven temperature to 200 degrees (leave oven door open until oven temperature reduces). Bake until cheesecake perimeter is set but center jiggles like Jell-O when pan is tapped, about 1 hour longer. Continue with cooling instructions in basic recipe. ∎

CREAM CHEESE HERESY

These days it is a culinary axiom that the purest, freshest ingredients make the best end product. However, when it comes to cream cheese used in cheesecakes, that is not the case.

Cream cheese is a very soft, very high-fat, cow's milk cheese prepared from either cream alone or, more typically, a mixture of cream and milk. In addition, most commercial cream cheese contains something lacking in fresh cream cheese—stabilizers that extend shelf life and thicken the cheese. In our baking tests, these stabilizers meant that commercial cream cheese yielded a cake texture clearly preferable, that is to say smoother and creamier, to that of the cake made with fresh, unstabilized cream cheese. The lesson? Fresh cream cheese is great to spread on your bagel or make dips, but if you aim to bake a smooth, rich cheesecake of excellent texture, stick with mainstream, commercial brands.

6-Minute Broccoli

The best way to prepare broccoli is to steam/boil it for less than seven minutes. After that, it starts to lose texture and flavor.

~ BY CHRISTOPHER KIMBALL ~

Broccoli can be boiled, steamed, sautéed, or stir-fried. After trying each of these methods many times, I finally settled on a combination of boiling and steaming. This method came out on top for two reasons: because it is fast (only the stalks are being boiled, so no need to bring a large pot of water to boil) and because the boiled stalks and steamed florets cook at slightly different rates, yielding bright color, firm florets, and thoroughly cooked stalks.

I also found that broccoli has an internal clock, one that starts ticking at almost exactly seven minutes of cooking time. At this point, chemical changes begin to occur that cause an initial undesirable loss of color and texture. This loss intensifies as cooking continues. By nine minutes, the stems and florets have become quite discolored and the texture mushy. At ten minutes, the broccoli is almost inedible—the florets fall apart, the color is mud green, and the flavor is sulfurous.

This deterioration is due to two distinct actions: heat and acid. As broccoli is heated during cooking, the chlorophyll begins to break down, resulting in a change of color and texture. In addition, all vegetables contain acids, which leach out during cooking, creating an acidic environment that also contributes to the breakdown of the chlorophyll. None of this is an issue, however, if broccoli is not cooked passed the magic witching point of seven minutes.

I also tested seven other procedures commonly used in cooking broccoli: presoaking in water (no difference); presoaking with sugar and salt (sweeter but not more flavorful); presoaking in acidulated water (no difference); cutting an "X" in the base of the stems and stalk prior to cooking (no difference); adding stale bread to the cooking liquid to reduce the broccoli odor (yielded wet bread with undiminished broccoli odor); boiling with the top of the pot on and off (it takes about one minute longer with the top off; the old wives' tale about allowing "gases to escape" is just that); and tying broccoli together and standing it up in boiling water (just try getting a bunch of broccoli to stand up straight!). Thus, none of these variations were improvements.

I did find, though, that there was another important factor: properly preparing broccoli prior to cooking. If you strip the stalk, it will cook at almost the same rate as the florets and become, as I discovered in my testing, perhaps the most flavorful and tender part of the vegetable.

Start by cutting the head off at the point at which the stems (attached to the florets) meet the stalk. I prefer to leave the florets in manageable clusters. If the stems are very thick, some cooks peel them with a small paring knife. To do this, position the blade at the base of the stem and cut just under the skin, pulling the blade toward the floret. Most cooks don't bother with this step, however, finding the slightly more sinewy texture of unpeeled stems acceptable.

The stalks, however, do need preparation, as they are covered with a tough layer of cellulose. First, cut off the woody end of the stalk. Now, with a paring knife, trim away one-eighth inch of outer peel to reveal the tender, whitish green core underneath. It's crucial to remove all of the tough green skin; otherwise the stalks will take longer to cook than the florets. (Do not try to peel the stalk with a vegetable peeler—it will not remove enough of the outer skin for a tender stalk.) If the stalk is relatively straight, simply stand it vertically on the cutting surface and cut downwards. For more irregular stalks, hold the stalk with one hand and then peel towards you. Lastly, cut the stalk in half lengthwise and then into bite-size pieces about an inch or so in length.

STEAMED/BOILED BROCCOLI
Serves 4

The florets and stalk are cooked simultaneously with two different methods. The thick stalks simmer in the cooking liquid, while the more delicate florets, set over the stalks, steam.

   1½ pounds broccoli
       Salt

1. Rinse broccoli and separate stalks from florets at points where floret stems meet stalk. Peel stalks by trimming away one-eighth inch of outer peel. Cut in half lengthwise and then into bite-size pieces. Separate florets into smaller sections and, if desired, peel stems.

2. Bring 1 inch water to boil in 11- or 12-inch sauté pan. Season with ½ teaspoon salt or to taste. Add broccoli stalks, then place florets over stalks, making sure florets don't sit in water. Cover and simmer until broccoli stalks are just tender, 5 to 6 minutes. Drain and serve immediately. If sautéing or stir-frying broccoli after this initial cooking stage, reduce cooking time to 3 to 4 minutes.

Steaming/boiling broccoli makes it easy to cook stalks and florets to proper doneness at the same time.

STIR-FRIED BROCCOLI WITH ORANGE SAUCE
Serves 4

Orange Sauce
   3 tablespoons juice and 1½ teaspoons zest from small orange
   ¼ teaspoon sugar
  1½ tablespoons chicken stock
   2 teaspoons light soy sauce
       Salt
   ½ teaspoon cornstarch

   2 tablespoons plus ½ teaspoon vegetable oil
   1 recipe Steamed/Boiled Broccoli (*see left*), cooked for 3 to 4 minutes only
   1 medium scallion, minced
   1 medium garlic clove, minced
   1 teaspoon minced fresh ginger

1. *For the sauce:* Mix all ingredients in small bowl; set aside.

2. Heat large skillet over high heat. When skillet is very hot, add 2 tablespoons oil; turn skillet so pan bottom is evenly coated. When oil starts to smoke, add broccoli and stir-fry until fully cooked and heated through, about 1½ minutes. Push broccoli to sides to make center well. Add scallion, garlic, and ginger, then drizzle remaining oil over these ingredients. Remove pan from heat; toss scallion mixture with broccoli. Return to heat; add sauce and stir until it completely coats broccoli and thickens slightly. ∎

Twice-Cooked Duck

Bruce Cost demonstrates a two-step Chinese method that draws the fat out of a duck by steaming and then crisps the skin by roasting.

～ BY JACK BISHOP ～

"Westerners still cook duck like the cavemen, by basically putting the duck in a fire," says author, restaurateur, and Asian food expert Bruce Cost. "The Chinese take advantage of the layer of fat on a duck to affect the skin and meat. Their technique is much more sophisticated."

Anyone who has roasted a duck and filled the kitchen with thick smoke understands Cost's point. Roasting will eventually render most of the fat, but too often at the price of charred skin and meat that has lost all of its moisture.

"In the West, we often treat duck just like chicken, but they are really very different," says Cost, who runs two Bay Area restaurants, Ginger Island in Berkeley and the Ginger Club in Palo Alto. Cost employs a two-step Chinese technique that uses steam to melt away the fat, followed by a short roasting period to crisp the skin. Cost says that, unlike Peking Duck, this preparation emphasizes both the skin and meat.

Season, Then Steam

Cost starts by seasoning the skin and inside cavity of the duck (*see* illustration 1, below). The recipe that follows relies on a traditional Chinese spice combination although other variations, including Western seasonings, are possible. (*See* "Alternative Flavors," page 11, for suggestions.) The toasted spices are combined with salt and half of this mixture is rubbed on the duck. The other half is served with the cooked duck.

After rubbing the duck with the spice mixture, the next step is to let the bird dry and "cure" slightly. In traditional Chinese kitchens, this would involve hanging the duck to air-dry for up to a day. Cost uses a simpler technique. He places a rack on top of a deep roasting pan and then rests the duck on the rack (illustration 2). As long as the pan is fairly deep, plenty of air will circulate underneath the duck, causing the skin to dry out and become highly seasoned with the spice mixture. Four hours is the minimum time that Cost allows for drying; overnight is the maximum.

The next step is steaming. A sixteen-inch wok or large Dutch oven fitted with a rack are the best options. The duck is placed on the rack above the boiling water (illustration 3). After about one hour, the skin becomes taut as the fat underneath melts into the simmering water below. When the skin begins to pull away from the joints on the wing (illustration 4), the meat is fully cooked. "The best part about steaming is that it causes the seasonings to melt into the meat, basting the bird with flavor," says Cost. "Steaming also makes the meat very tender and juicy." Losing most of the fatty layer beneath the skin is an added benefit.

Smoke If Desired, Then Roast

Cost's next step is to cool the steamed duck and to brush the skin with dark soy sauce to help give it a better color when it is roasted. At this point, the duck can be wrapped in plastic and refrigerated overnight. To prepare an elegant weeknight dinner, simply pull the duck from the refrigerator, roast it for thirty-five minutes, and serve.

Those who wish to may also smoke the duck before it is roasted, an intermediate step that adds a somewhat different character to the duck (*see* "Adding Smoky Flavor," page 11). With or without the smoking step, the final part of this technique is quick-roasting at a high heat to brown and crisp the skin and heat the meat through. Cost says to let the duck cool to room temperature after steaming (or smoking) and before placing it in the hot oven. "If duck is at room temperature, the oven heat hits the skin and crisps it right up."

As soon as the skin is brown and sizzling, you should remove the duck from the oven, cover it with foil, and allow it to rest for ten to twenty minutes before carving. Carve the duck into small pieces according to the Chinese method outlined in the illustrations on page 11.

TWICE-COOKED DUCK WITH ASIAN FLAVORINGS
Serves 4

As an alternative to the spice mixture that appears in this recipe, you could serve the duck with hoisin sauce and Asian pancakes or steamed white buns. If you go with the seasonings provided here, serve the duck with vegetables in a Western-style meal. Those who do not have kosher salt can substitute one tablespoon of regular table salt. (*See* Sources and Resources, page 32, for information on mail-ordering spices.)

PREPARING STEAMED/ROASTED DUCK

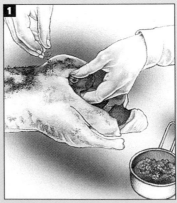

1. Rub half of the seasoned salt mixture over the skin and inside cavity of the duck.

2. Set a rack on top of a deep roasting pan. Place the duck on top, making sure that air can circulate underneath. Set the duck aside in a cool, airy place for 4 hours to dry out the skin and allow the seasonings to penetrate.

3. Set a rack in a large, 16-inch wok or a wide, deep pot. Fill the bottom with water and bring it to a boil. Place the duck back side up on rack, making sure the duck rests one inch above the water.

4. After the duck has steamed for fifty or sixty minutes, the skin will become taut. Look at the wing to see if it has steamed long enough. The skin should have started to pull away from joints, and the meat will be exposed.

4 whole star anise
2 teaspoons Szechuan peppercorns
1 large piece cassia bark or 1 small
    cinnamon stick
2 tablespoons kosher salt
4 thick slices unpeeled ginger
1 cup fresh cilantro leaves
1 duck (about 4½ pounds), thawed,
    rinsed, and patted dry (giblets
    reserved for another use)
1 teaspoon dark soy sauce

1. Toast star anise, peppercorns, and cassia bark or cinnamon stick in dry skillet just until they start to smoke. Grind in spice mill and combine with salt. Rub half the mixture over outside and inside cavity of duck (*see* illustration 1, page 10). Set aside remaining mixture.

2. Place ginger slices and cilantro in duck cavity. Set duck on rack above roasting pan and leave uncovered in cool, airy place for at least 4 hours or overnight (illustration 2, page 10).

3. Bring several inches of water to boil in large, 16-inch wok or wide, deep pot fitted with rack one inch above water level. Place duck, back side up, on rack (illustration 3, page 10). Cover pot and steam over high heat, adding more boiling water if necessary, until skin becomes taut and starts to pull away from joints on wings, 50 to 60 minutes (illustration 4, page 10).

4. Cool to room temperature and brush skin with soy sauce. (Duck can be wrapped in plastic and refrigerated up to 1 day. Bring to room temperature before roasting.)

5. Heat oven to 400 degrees. Place duck on rack inside roasting pan. Roast until skin is crisp and quite brown, 35 to 40 minutes. Remove from oven, cover with foil, and let rest for 10 to 20 minutes. Carve, following illustrations at right. Serve, using reserved portion of spice mixture as seasoned salt. ∎

Bruce Cost prepares duck according to a two-step Chinese method.

ADDING SMOKY FLAVOR

"Smoking this duck is definitely optional, but it gives the bird a nice flavor," says author and restaurateur Bruce Cost. To accomplish this, Cost lines a large wok or Dutch oven with aluminum foil and places three-quarters of a cup of raw white rice and six tablespoons each of black tea and sugar in the bottom of the pan. He sets the steamed duck (brushed with soy sauce) on a rack above the mixture and then covers the inside of the lid with foil, crimping the bottom and top pieces of foil together to seal in the duck and protect the pan from burning. (*See* "Tea-Smoked Chicken," May/June 1995, for more details on setting up a stove-top smoker.)

Cost turns the heat to high and waits for smoke to appear. He smokes the duck for ten minutes, turns off the heat, and leaves the wok covered for thirty to forty minutes, depending on how much smoke flavor he wants to impart. At this point, the smoked duck can be cooled, wrapped in plastic, and refrigerated for a day before roasting and serving. Since the smoking step is merely for flavor (steaming and roasting do the cooking), you can smoke the duck for as much or as little time as you want. The times that Cost recommends will give the duck a lightly smoky flavor with a nice hint of sweetness.

ALTERNATIVE FLAVORS

Bruce Cost often varies the seasonings used to cure the duck. Here are some recommendations for other mixtures, but feel free to make up your own combinations.

Rosemary-Sage Salt: Mix 2 tablespoons each minced fresh rosemary leaves and sage leaves with 2 tablespoons kosher salt and 2 teaspoons ground black pepper. Rub half the mixture over outside and inside cavity of duck; reserve other half for use at table. Place fresh rosemary sprigs in cavity instead of ginger and cilantro.

Three-Seed Salt: Toast 1 tablespoon each cumin, coriander, and fennel seeds in dry skillet until they start to smoke. Grind toasted seeds and combine with 2 tablespoons kosher salt. Rub half the mixture over outside and inside cavity of duck; reserve other half for use at table. Place fresh ginger and cilantro leaves in cavity as in master recipe.

CARVING DUCK, CHINESE STYLE

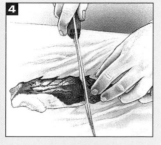

1. Cut off the wings at the third joint to separate them from the body; split the wings at the joints if desired.

2. Cut around the legs, probing into the thigh joint with a knife to pop out the leg. Cut the thigh joint to remove leg and thigh in one piece.

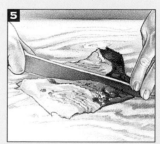

3. Hold the leg/thigh piece by the drumstick and cut through the joint between them. Split the thigh into two pieces and slice the meat off the drumstick.

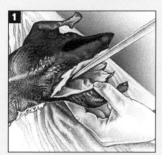

4. Slice between the back and breast and then along the side of the breastbone to peel off the entire breast in one piece.

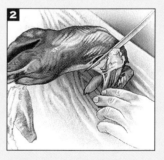

5. Slice the breast crosswise into three or four pieces. Repeat this process with the other breast.

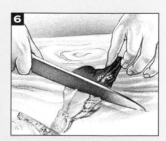

6. Turn the duck over and split the backbone down the middle. Cut each side into three pieces containing crisp skin and pockets of "oyster" meat for nibbling.

The Best Baked Apple

Choose the right apple variety, then bake it uncovered at 350 degrees.

∿ BY DEDE WILSON ∿

To allow steam to escape and keep apples from bursting, remove a strip of skin around the apple's stem end with a vegetable peeler.

Baked apples are a comforting, old-fashioned dish—simple to make and usually calling for no more than a few ingredients. Despite their simplicity, however, there are traps that may befall cooks. For example, the unwary may find themselves with a baked apple that is sweetened or seasoned improperly or, more commonly, with an apple that collapses and loses its shape during baking. Fortunately, both pitfalls are easy to avoid—the latter one being particularly dependent on using the right variety of apple.

I thus set out to determine which variety would make the best baked apple, as well as to decide what ingredients would best support the apple in this role. The process involved constructing a very basic master recipe with which I could determine which varieties baked the best. From that point I planned to limit the final number of varieties to five, and using all of them, start to change the ingredients and preparation techniques to come up with the best master recipe as well as some good variations.

The Best Apple

In order to establish which varieties of apple I would test, I consulted cookbooks and spoke with a number of apple experts including academics as well as apple growers. Several varieties were mentioned more than once, by books and experts alike, as the baking apples of choice: Rome Beauty, Cortland, Granny Smith, and Golden Delicious being the common four. McIntosh were widely believed not to be good bakers, as the flesh is often mushy when cooked. A few other varieties were mentioned as good bakers by the apple growers, most notably Baldwin, a deep red, firm variety, Ida Red, revered by many of these growers as the best baking apple, and Northern Spy, probably a close second in their esteem.

Armed with these opinions, I tested nine different apple varieties, searching for ones that retained a nice, round shape after baking. According to Wes Autio, Professor of Pomology at the University of Massachusetts, and Mark McLellan, Chairman of Food Science and Technology at Cornell University, some varieties of apples have a higher calcium content than others. This makes for a round baked apple because higher levels of calcium help retain the integrity of the cell wall structure during baking. Of course, in my tests I was searching for apples that not only held their shape but that were tasty as well.

In this testing, I tried to use apples of uniform size, with the median being eight ounces. I peeled a strip of skin off of the top of each to allow steam to escape, then washed and dried the apples, cored the centers, leaving the bottoms intact, and placed two of each variety in a nine-inch pie plate. To that I added two tablespoons of granulated sugar for each apple, sprinkling the sugar over and inside the fruits, and poured enough water into each dish to come up one-half inch in the plate. I baked them in a 350-degree oven until tender, usually between forty-five and fifty-five minutes, basting during the baking time. I determined them to be done by piercing with a knife. I aimed for a tender flesh, not al dente, but I tried not to let the skins burst, which would indicate that they were overcooked. Take note that I did not add any butter or cinnamon to these test batches, as I really wanted to test the flavor of the apples themselves.

The results of several days of testing are summarized in "Rating Baking Apples" on page 13. I ended up choosing Northern Spy, Cortland, and Golden Delicious as my favorites, based on their availability as well as their appearance and flavor.

The Best Technique

The second part of the testing involved using various combinations of techniques and ingredients with my chosen apples.

My first experiment involved baking apples covered with foil, both for the entire baking time as well as for half the baking time. The foil encouraged faster baking and also softened the skins a little more, but it also prevented the cider that I used as baking liquid from concentrating in flavor and reducing in texture. When the apples were baked uncovered, on the other hand, some of the liquid evaporated, and the sugar, along with the natural sugars in the cider, began to caramelize and make a nice syrupy sauce. Even covering the apples for just part of the baking time discouraged caramelization, so uncovered baking turned out to be a better choice.

Next I tried baking at varying oven temperatures. In preliminary trials I baked several apples at 325, 350, 375, and 400 degrees. It was clear that at 325 degrees, not only was a longer cooking time needed, but too much of the liquid evaporated during the process; by the time the apples were baked to the proper consistency, hardly any sauce was left. Also, the extended time in the oven encouraged the colors of the apples to fade a bit more and dried out the apple's flesh. With the higher temperatures of 375 and 400 degrees, the apple skins were more prone to splitting, and the flesh texture was harder to control. At 400 degrees, in fact, the skins burst well before the inside of the apple was tender. So, 350 degrees proved to be the best baking temperature by far, allowing the cook to keep tabs on the tenderness of the apple and preserve enough of the juice for the sauce.

As for flavoring ingredients, I found that the

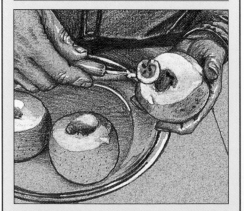

EASY APPLE CORING

The easiest way to core a whole apple thoroughly is with a melon baller, so long as you are careful not to puncture the blossom end.

PHOTOGRAPH BY DAVE HENDERSON/ILLUSTRATION BY TONY DELUZ

addition of cider and cinnamon greatly improved the flavor of the apples. In fact, I have come to think of cider and cinnamon as the salt and pepper of the basic baked apple. I also baked a few apples with nutmeg and cloves, spices often used with apples in other recipes, but found that they overpowered the apple flavor. In the same way, I found that adding butter to the baked apples, which many recipes call for, altered the apple flavor in a way I did not think was beneficial. More importantly, upon cooling, the butter solidified and became an unappetizing, waxy, hard fat floating in the sauce. This situation is only true, however, of the basic master recipe. Some of the recipes with a stuffing inside the apple do require butter as a binder.

CIDER-BAKED APPLES WITH CINNAMON SUGAR
Serves 4

Serve these baked apples warm with whipped cream, ice cream, vanilla yogurt, or crème fraîche.

    4 large apples, about 2 pounds total (*see* chart for apple choices, below), with strip of skin peeled from stem end, then rinsed, dried, and cored (*see* illustration, page 12)
    ½ cup sugar
 ½–1 teaspoon cinnamon
    1 cup apple cider (preferably unfiltered) or enough to come ½ inch up side of pan.

1. Heat oven to 350 degrees. Place apples in 9-inch Pyrex pie pan or 8-inch-square baking pan. Mix cinnamon and sugar, adding more cinnamon if desired, then sprinkle over and inside apple cavities. Pour cider in pan.

2. Bake apples, basting every 15 minutes, until tender when pierced with thin, sharp knife or cake tester, 45 to 55 minutes. Be careful not to overbake, or skins will split, causing apples to lose their shape. Serve warm. (Can be cooled to room temperature, covered, and refrigerated for 2 days. Reheat before serving.)

BREAKFAST BAKED APPLES WITH YOGURT AND GRANOLA

Follow recipe for Cider-Baked Apples with Cinnamon Sugar, substituting brown sugar for sugar and adding 1 teaspoon vanilla extract to cider before pouring over apples. Serve with granola and vanilla yogurt.

HONEY-BAKED APPLES WITH CRÈME FRAÎCHE

Follow recipe for Cider-Baked Apples with Cinnamon Sugar, making following changes: Substitute equal amount of honey for sugar and equal amount water for cider. Eliminate cinnamon and instead place large strip of lemon zest in each apple cavity. Squeeze juice of 1 lemon over apples. Serve fruit warm with a dollop of crème fraîche.

WALNUT-RAISIN BAKED APPLES WITH MAPLE SYRUP

Follow recipe for Cider-Baked Apples with Cinnamon Sugar, filling each apple cavity with ¼ of a mixture made of ¼ cup each dark raisins and chopped walnuts and 4 teaspoons softened butter. Substitute maple syrup for sugar.

RUM-BAKED APPLES WITH MASCARPONE AND ALMONDS

Follow recipe for Cider-Baked Apples with Cinnamon Sugar, filling each apple cavity with ¼ of a mixture made of 3 ounces almond paste, 3 tablespoons sugar, 2 tablespoons dark rum, and 1 tablespoon softened butter. Omit cinnamon and sprinkle with only 5 tablespoons sugar. Mix ½ cup mascarpone cheese with 1 tablespoon sugar and 1 teaspoon dark rum. Serve warm apples with dollop of sweetened mascarpone. ∎

Dede Wilson is a freelance author living in western Massachusetts. She is currently writing a book on wedding cakes.

RATING BAKING APPLES

Aside from Red Delicious, Golden Delicious, and Granny Smith, no other apples are reliably available nationwide, according to the International Apple Institute. Of these three varieties, Golden Delicious rated very well in our testing, so if you cannot find any of the other more esoteric varieties, you should always be able to find the Goldens. Try some of the recipes with your own local apples, and do some comparing yourself.

	APPLE VARIETY	FLAVOR	FLESH TEXTURE	VISUAL APPEAL	AVAILABILITY	FINAL RECOMMENDATION
	BALDWIN	Excellent, sophisticated, winelike flavor	Soft, yielding	Retained round shape and red color nicely	Hard to find; usually available from small, local orchards	Best flavor and highly recommended but hard to find; worth seeking out
	CORTLAND	Cinnamon-like and pleasant, slightly acidic	Soft, a bit mushy	Red color held up well as did round shape; red-tinged flesh	Common in New England and Mid-Atlantic states	Recommended—easy to find in New England, unique cinnamon flavor
	GOLDEN DELICIOUS	Buttery, rich flavor	Very tender	OK—golden color	Nationwide	Highly recommended because of flavor, texture, and availability
	GRANNY SMITH	Tart	Dry, coarse	Unappetizing green-brown color	Nationwide	Not good—fleshy and too dry
	IDA RED	Good flavor—bright and clear	Soft, yielding	Good—retained shape and color	Mostly New England	Highly recommended for flavor and texture if you can get it
	MCINTOSH	Dull, lackluster	Too mushy	Not good—did not retain round shape	Most states	Not recommended—dull flavor, mushy texture
	NORTHERN SPY	Great flavor—mellow with a bite	Tender and buttery texture	Pretty good—nice large, round apples with red and gold color	Hard to find; usually available from small, local orchards	Excellent flavor but hard to find
	RED DELICIOUS	Uninteresting	Dry	Retained shape and color	Nationwide	Not recommended—too dry
	ROME BEAUTY	Dullest flavor—no distinctiveness	Firm, dry flesh	Very red skin; kept shape very well	Common in New England	Not recommended—worst flavor

Bread Salads

Day-old, good-quality bread can be recycled in Mediterranean-style salads.

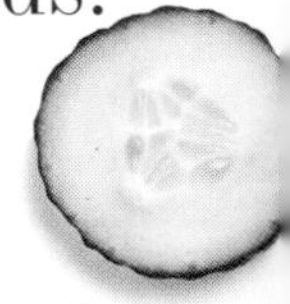

∼ BY JULIA DELLA CROCE ∼

Bread links us with our past and with our spirit. To the Italians and other peoples of the Mediterranean, bread is holy; it is almost unthinkable to throw it away. It is not surprising, then, that there are so many uses for bread throughout the Mediterranean. One of the most delightful and perhaps surprising dishes that evolved in this part of the world is the use of stale bread for salads.

Such thrifty salads are superb dishes not only because, for many of them, the oven needn't be turned on, but because they allow flavorful and fresh tomatoes to be fully experienced, along with fragrant mint, parsley, and fresh cilantro. Another crucial ingredient is high-quality, extra-virgin olive oil. Because the dry bread so readily absorbs moisture, much of the flavor of the dish is derived from the dressing. Mind that so-called "pure" olive oil, which is actually refined, will not impart sufficient flavor to the dressing.

Last but not least, fundamental to the success of these salads is the quality of bread. Sliced white bread, or airy supermarket bread that is highly refined and becomes rock-hard within a few days simply won't do. Ideally, bread used in bread salads should not contain sugar or sweeteners of any kind, which would conflict with the savory nature of the ingredients. Nor should it include such ingredients as raisins or nuts. What the bread should have is a sturdy texture and good wheaty flavor. In addition, it must be dampened first. The extent of dampening is determined by the dryness of the bread; if the bread receives too much dampening, it will collapse into a soggy mess from the anointment of water or dressing.

Because the bread becomes soggy fairly quickly, none of these salads should be made very much in advance of serving (*see* individual recipes for suggested preparation ahead of time). The best approach is to assemble all of the salad ingredients in advance (in the case of the *fattoush*, toast the bread), then combine the ingredients just before serving.

BREAD SALAD WITH TOMATOES, HERBS, AND RED ONIONS
Serves 4

My father's mother made this salad when her life as an immigrant was still difficult, and there was little else to eat besides stale bread. Despite its most humble origins, this salad is delicious. The bread must be coarse peasant bread or any sturdy Italian-style bread. Other breads will not hold up to being dressed with oil and vinegar and combined with tomatoes, which are full of water. Also, don't use sweetened breads. If the tomatoes are ripe and the olive oil is particularly flavorful, you can omit the vinegar, moistening the bread with a tablespoon or two of water instead.

1 pound day-old coarse peasant bread or sturdy Italian-style bread, crusts removed, cut or torn into 1-inch cubes (about 6 cups)
½ cup extra-virgin olive oil
3 tablespoons red wine vinegar
2 large, vine-ripened tomatoes or 4 plum tomatoes, seeded and cut into medium dice
½ red onion, sliced paper-thin
2 tablespoons torn fresh basil or mint leaves
2 teaspoons whole fresh oregano leaves
1 tablespoon minced fresh Italian parsley leaves
½ teaspoon salt
¼ teaspoon ground black pepper

Place bread cubes in shallow bowl. Mix oil, vinegar, tomatoes, onion, and half of herbs in medium bowl. Let stand for flavors to develop, about 10 minutes, then add to bread, along with remaining herbs, and toss well. Season with salt and pepper or to taste. If bread still seems dry, sprinkle 1 or 2 tablespoons water to rehydrate it a bit. Serve. (If sturdy bread is used, salad can be covered and set aside up to 2 hours.)

PITA BREAD SALAD WITH CUCUMBERS, CHERRY TOMATOES, AND FRESH HERBS
Serves 6

I learned this simple version of *fattoush* many years ago from a Lebanese friend. It is dressed with the juice of fresh lemons instead of vinegar, which gives the salad a lovely, refreshing tartness. While draining the cucumbers is an extra step, it keeps the salad from becoming soggy.

½ seedless Dutch cucumber (skin intact) or 1 regular cucumber (peeled, and seeded), cut into small dice
Salt and ground black pepper
1 foot length Syrian flat bread or four 6-inch pita breads, several days old, torn into ½-inch pieces
1 pint cherry tomatoes, halved, or 2 large vine-ripened tomatoes, chopped coarse
6 scallions, trimmed and sliced thin, including 2 inches of green
¼ cup minced fresh mint leaves
¼ cup minced fresh cilantro or parsley leaves
½ cup extra-virgin olive oil
6 tablespoons juice from 2 large lemons

1. Heat oven to 375 degrees. Put cucumber in colander; sprinkle with ¼ teaspoon salt. Place weight (such as zipper-lock bag filled with water) over cucumbers; drain to release most of liquid, about 30 minutes. Rinse and pat dry.

2. Put bread pieces on baking sheet; bake until crisp but not browned, 5 to 7 minutes. Transfer to large bowl; add cucumber, tomatoes, scallions, and herbs, and toss well. In small bowl, combine oil and juice and salt and pepper to taste. Add to large bowl, toss again, and serve immediately.

BREAD SALAD WITH ROASTED PEPPERS AND SICILIAN OLIVES
Serves 4 to 6

Sourdough or a sturdy peasant bread is needed for this salad. Airy, unsubstantial bread will become soggy very quickly.

1 pound sturdy Italian bread, crusts removed, cut or torn into 1-inch cubes (about 6 cups)
2 bell peppers, one red and one yellow, roasted, stemmed, seeded, and cut into ½-inch strips
½ cup extra-virgin olive oil
¼ cup cider vinegar
1 small red or white onion, quartered and sliced thin
1 medium scallion, trimmed and sliced thin, including 2 inches of green
3 tablespoons pitted and sliced green olives
1 tablespoon minced fresh oregano leaves
½ teaspoon salt
¼ teaspoon ground black pepper

1. Mix bread cubes and pepper strips in large bowl; set aside.

2. Mix oil, vinegar, onion, scallion, olives, oregano, salt, and pepper in medium bowl; let stand for flavors to develop, about 10 minutes. Add dressing to bread and peppers; toss to combine. If bread still seems dry, sprinkle in 1 or 2 tablespoons water to rehydrate it a bit. Serve. (If sturdy bread is used, salad can be covered and set aside up to 2 hours.) ■

Julia della Croce is a writer, cooking teacher, and the author of five cookbooks, including *The Vegetarian Table: Italy* (Chronicle, 1994).

PHOTOGRAPHS BY DAVE HENDERSON

Quick and Easy Brioche

Skip the sponge process and first rise, but still have a light, delicious pastry.

BY NICK MALGIERI

Flaky, buttery, and readily adaptable to a variety of forms and accompanying flavors, brioche dough has long been a favorite of professional bakers. Most home bakers tend to shun this rich dough, however, because preparing it in the traditional method is very time-consuming. It requires waiting for a sponge to rise, mixing more flour into the sponge, waiting again for the resulting dough to rise, and chilling the dough—until finally it is ready to use.

The process of making brioche dough may be considerably shortened, however, by eliminating the sponge in favor of a one-step mixing method and by shortening or eliminating the preliminary rising. Only the final rising before baking must be maintained, since it is essential to the texture and flavor of the pastry.

It is the richness of brioche dough that allows these shortcuts. In lean, simple doughs such as bread doughs, which are made up of only flour, water, yeast, and salt, extended fermentation time develops both flavor and structure. In more complex doughs that contain sugar as well as relatively large amounts of fat in the form of eggs, butter, and/or oil, fermentation largely contributes aeration. Letting a rich dough rise only once, just before it is baked, gives the dough the appropriately light texture it needs before the heat of baking further expands the air cells in the dough.

Best of all, if you don't have time to use the dough immediately, you can leave it in the refrigerator for up to twenty-four hours before shaping it, letting it rise, and baking, a factor that makes this dough even more convenient.

QUICK BRIOCHE
Makes enough for any of the recipes on pages 16 and 17

1 envelope (about 2½ teaspoons) active dry yeast
½ cup warm milk (about 110 degrees)
2¼ cups unbleached all-purpose flour
6 tablespoons unsalted butter, cut into 6 pieces
3 tablespoons sugar
½ teaspoon salt
2 large eggs

1. In small bowl, whisk yeast into milk, then stir in 1 cup of flour. Cover with plastic wrap and set aside.

2. Put butter, sugar, and salt in workbowl of food processor fitted with metal blade. Pulse at 1-second intervals, scraping sides of bowl several times, until mixture is soft and smooth. Add eggs, one at a time, and process after each addition until fully incorporated (even though mixture may look curdled). Add remaining 1¼ cups flour and yeast mixture from step 1, scraping sides of workbowl with rubber spatula. Pulse at 1-second intervals to form soft, smooth dough. Then process continuously for 15 seconds.

3. Turn dough (sticky at this point) out onto generously floured work surface and knead until smooth and elastic. Proceed with one of following recipes, or, if making Brioche Plum Tart or Brioche Loaf, proceed directly to pages 16 and 17.

The fillings that follow may be used for the Brioche Ring on page 16. For a really simple filling, spread a scant cup of your favorite jam over the dough before rolling it into a cylinder. The final pastry cream recipe can be used with the Raspberry Brioche Shortcake on page 17.

ALMOND FILLING WITH CURRANTS
Makes enough for Brioche Ring
For the almond paste, you may substitute one-half cup of blanched almonds ground to a paste in the food processor along with one-quarter cup of sugar, one-half teaspoon of almond extract, and one teaspoon of water.

⅔ cup currants
4 ounces almond paste, cut into ½-inch pieces
¼ cup sugar
1 yolk, plus 1 egg
4 tablespoons unsalted butter, softened
¼ cup flour

1. Cover currants with water in small saucepan. Bring to boil over medium heat, then immediately drain and spread currants on plate lined with paper towels.

2. Process paste and sugar in workbowl of food processor fitted with steel blade until combined. Add yolk, then egg, pulsing until smooth after each addition. Add butter; continue to pulse until smooth. Add flour; pulse until just absorbed. Transfer to small bowl, stir in currants, then refrigerate until ready to use.

CINNAMON-WALNUT FILLING
Makes enough for Brioche Ring
1 cup toasted walnut or pecan pieces
½ cup sugar

1 teaspoon ground cinnamon
1 egg, plus 1 yolk
4 tablespoons unsalted butter, softened
¼ cup flour
½ cup raisins or currants

1. Process ½ cup of the nuts to paste in workbowl of food processor fitted with steel blade. Add sugar; pulse to mix. Add cinnamon, egg plus yolk, butter, and flour; pulse until smooth.

2. Transfer to small bowl; fold in remaining ½ cup nuts and the raisins. Refrigerate until ready to use.

ORANGE-FLAVORED CREAM CHEESE FILLING
Makes enough for Brioche Ring

1 package (8 ounces) cream cheese
¼ cup sugar
1 egg
1 teaspoon zest from 1 small orange
1 teaspoon vanilla extract
2 tablespoons flour

Process cream cheese with sugar in workbowl of food processor fitted with steel blade until smooth. Add remaining ingredients; pulse until fully incorporated and smooth. Refrigerate until ready to use.

LIGHTENED PASTRY CREAM
Makes enough for Raspberry Brioche Shortcake

⅓ cup flour
½ cup sugar
Pinch salt
1½ cups milk
4 egg yolks
3 tablespoons orange liqueur
¾ cup heavy whipping cream

Mix flour, sugar, and salt in nonreactive saucepan. Whisk in milk, then yolks over medium-low heat. Whisk constantly until mixture thickens and comes to full boil, about 15 minutes. Remove from heat; whisk in liqueur. Transfer to medium nonreactive bowl and place plastic wrap directly over surface to keep skin from forming. Refrigerate until cold. Just before assembly of shortcake, whip cream to stiff peaks and fold into existing mixture. ∎

Nick Malgieri directs the baking program at Peter Kump's New York Cooking School and is the author of the forthcoming *How to Bake* (HarperCollins, 1995).

Brioche Desserts

The Quick Brioche dough on page 15 can be used to form any of the desserts pictured here, following the step-by-step illustrations. For the Brioche Ring, choose any one of the three fillings on page 15. Each filling recipe makes enough for one ring. ■

BRIOCHE PLUM TART

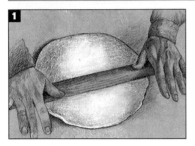

1. Turn Quick Brioche dough (one recipe) into a greased bowl. Cover it with plastic wrap and refrigerate for 1 hour. Halve the dough. Transfer one half to a floured work surface; refrigerate the remaining half for another use. Roll the dough to an 11- or 12-inch disk. (If the dough does not roll easily, chill it for 30 minutes, then reroll.)

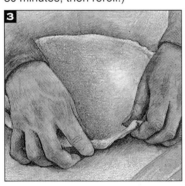

3. Fold the dough about ½ inch under around the perimeter of the disk. Cover the dough with greased plastic wrap until it puffs slightly, 20 to 30 minutes. Adjust the oven rack to the center position and heat the oven to 375 degrees.

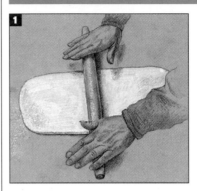

2. Transfer the disk to a greased, parchment-lined cookie sheet. Place a 10- or 11-inch plate or pan on the dough in order to mark a perfect circle on it.

4. Meanwhile, rinse, quarter, and pit 2 pounds of Italian prune plums, and mix ¼ cup of sugar and 2 teaspoons of cinnamon together. Arrange the plum quarters close together in concentric circles on the risen dough; sprinkle them with cinnamon sugar. Bake until the crust is golden brown and the fruit is cooked, about 20 minutes. Transfer the cookie sheet to a wire rack and let it cool to room temperature.

5. Brush the cooled tart with apricot glaze (¾ cup of apricot preserves that have been heated with 2 tablespoons of water, then strained). Sprinkle the tart edge with ¼ cup of toasted, sliced almonds and confectioners' sugar.

BRIOCHE RING

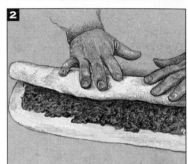

1. Turn Quick Brioche dough (one recipe) into a greased bowl. Cover it with plastic wrap and refrigerate for 1 hour. Make one of the fillings on page 15. Roll the chilled dough into an 8-by-18-inch rectangle. Spread the dough evenly with filling, leaving a ½-inch border on the long side farthest from you.

3. Mark the cylinder top at 1½-inch intervals, then use scissors to cut almost, but not quite all the way through the cylinder .

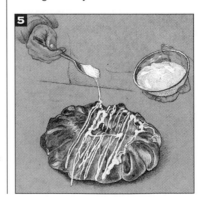

2. Beginning at the long side nearest you, roll the dough into a tight cylinder. Transfer the cylinder, seam side down and coiling it to fit, onto a cookie sheet lined with greased parchment or waxed paper. Cover it with greased plastic wrap and refrigerate until firm, about 15 minutes.

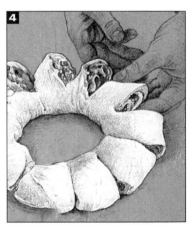

4. Turn each piece of dough, cut side up. Cover the dough with greased plastic wrap and let it rise until almost doubled, about 1 hour. While the dough is rising, adjust the oven rack to the center position and heat the oven to 350 degrees. Bake the ring until it is golden brown, 35 to 40 minutes.

5. Place the cookie sheet on a wire rack until it is cool enough to handle, then slide the ring onto the rack and cool it to room temperature. Mix 1 cup of confectioners' sugar with 2 tablespoons of milk. Drizzle this icing over the cooled ring.

ILLUSTRATIONS BY ANATOLY

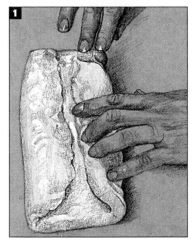

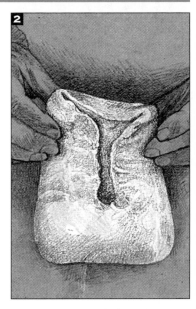

1. Grease an 8½-by-4½-by-2¾-inch loaf pan; line the pan bottom with parchment or waxed paper, then grease the paper. Press Quick Brioche dough (one recipe) into a 9-by-5-inch rectangle, with the short end facing you. Fold each long side about 1 inch in toward the center; press firmly to seal.

2. Fold the top half of the dough toward the center.

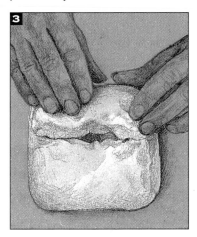

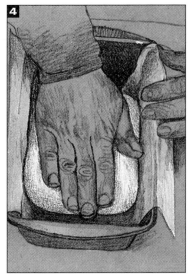

3. Fold the bottom half of the dough up past the seam; pinch it to seal.

4. Place the dough in the pan, seam side down. Flatten the dough top with the palm so that it fills the pan evenly. Cover the pan with greased plastic wrap; let the dough rise about 1 inch above the pan rim. Adjust the oven rack to the center position and heat the oven to 350 degrees while the dough is rising.

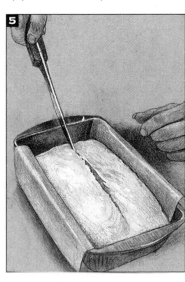

5. Using a razor blade or a sharp knife, slash the dough down the center, leaving about 1 inch unslashed at either end. Bake until golden brown, about 40 minutes. Transfer the pan to a wire rack; let it cool for 5 minutes. Turn the loaf out of the pan onto the rack; let it cool to room temperature on its side.

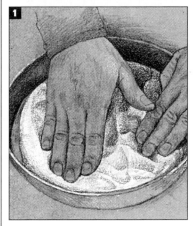

1. Press Quick Brioche dough (one recipe) into a greased 9- or 10-by-2-inch layer cake pan. Cover it with greased plastic wrap and let it almost double in size, about 1 hour. While the dough is rising, start preparing Lightened Pastry Cream (page 15) and adjust the oven rack to the center position and heat the oven to 350 degrees.

2. Bake until the brioche is golden brown, 25 to 30 minutes. Transfer it to a wire rack and let it cool for 5 minutes. Turn the brioche out onto the rack and cool it to room temperature. Slice off the top quarter of the brioche and reserve it.

3. Cut around the circumference, leaving a ½-inch border and making sure not to cut a hole in the bottom of the brioche.

4. With a paring knife and fingers, hollow out the brioche. Place it on a serving plate and sprinkle on 2 tablespoons of orange-flavored liqueur.

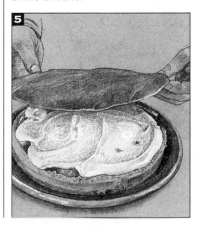

5. Spoon half the pastry cream into the hollowed out brioche. Sprinkle 1 pint of raspberries over the cream, then spoon the remaining pastry cream over the raspberries. Brush another 2 tablespoons of the liqueur over the inside of the reserved brioche top and place it over the pastry cream. (The shortcake can be refrigerated approximately 4 hours ahead.) Dust the shortcake with confectioners' sugar.

Chicken in the Pot

Sautéing chicken pieces and then braising them with vegetables produces both perfectly cooked white and dark meat.

~ BY RONNIE FEIN ~

Like almost everyone else these days, I'm always looking for versatile, nearly effortless recipes that don't take much time. That way I can cook them during the week or fancify them up a bit to serve to company on the weekend. Perhaps my favorite of these all-purpose recipes is what I call "Chicken in the Pot."

Unlike the classic French recipe of this name, which calls for a mature stewing hen stuffed with forcemeat and poached in stock for hours, my modern version is something of a cross between sautéed chicken and braised chicken, cooked and served with vegetables. It's a meal-in-one, done in about forty-five minutes and using only one pan. Because chicken's mild flesh matches well with delicate seasonings and vegetables but also stands up superbly to bold spices and hearty ingredients, you can vary the recipe in almost endless ways.

Choosing the Chicken and the Pot

When I set out to create a quick and adaptable one-pot Chicken in the Pot recipe, I wanted to make use of the virtues of both sautéing and braising. But since sautéing usually calls for a cut-up broiler/fryer, while braising is best done with an older, tougher, whole bird, the first decision I had to make was what kind of chicken to use.

I knew that if I wanted to prepare a meal in less than an hour, I'd need to go with the cut-up broiler/fryer. A whole chicken simply takes too long. Broiler/fryers come in several sizes. I found that the smaller ones, weighing in at two and one-half to three pounds, tasted fine and took only twenty minutes to cook through. However, when I tried larger chickens, weighing about three and one-half pounds, they proved an even better choice. Even though I had to brown the pieces in batches so that the recipe consequently took longer, I found that the meat was juicier and that the vegetables, seasonings, and fluids had more time to lend flavors to each other, giving the dish a richer, more harmonious taste. I also tried using only white meat and only dark meat, both of which worked fine. I also tried using a large roaster, but didn't like the results. First, it was more difficult to cut the bird into pieces—and you can't purchase precut parts as you can with a broiler/fryer. Second, the meat took longer to cook, so the white portions were too dry and the vegetables were mush by the time the meat cooked through completely. Finally, the roaster rendered much more fat after the initial browning. That's something nobody wants these days. Getting rid of the fat required too much effort too.

Because my family consists of white-meat eaters, I tried the dish using only breasts and wings. Lucky us, it worked, without any change in time, temperature or method. Dark meat pieces also cooked about the same way, except there was more fat in the pan after browning the pieces. No matter, because you spill off all but a film of fat before you add the vegetables anyway. Basically, this easygoing recipe works perfectly well with a whole cut-up chicken or any parts you like, about three and one-half pounds worth.

I then set about trying to make Chicken in the Pot in several different kinds of cookware. What I discovered is that you don't need any special equipment, only a skillet and lid, to make this recipe. The skillet can be any old twelve-inch or fourteen-inch skillet, as long as it is heavy. (Thin, lightweight cookware cooks unevenly and can cause scorching.)

Even so, given a choice, I prefer some cookware to others. For example, I found that by using a deep, straight-sided, twelve-inch sauté pan or a Dutch oven, there was less spatter on the stovetop. I also preferred the results from my anodized aluminum and pressure-cast aluminum pans; the chicken browned beautifully in both. Nonstick cookware other than the pressure-cast aluminum variety was just okay. It didn't brown the chicken as well. I do not use cast-iron or regular aluminum cookware for this recipe because it calls for wine, and those metals react with wine or other acids, causing an off-taste in the food. As far as the lid goes, any tight fitting cover will do.

The Cooking Process

The first decision to be made about the actual cooking was whether or not to brown the chicken. When you sauté chicken, you always brown it first, but you can prepare braised chicken without doing so. I tried it both ways and concluded that browning was better, even though it added about fifteen minutes to the recipe. Browning the chicken gave it a deeper, almost "nutty" taste and crisped the skin. While the skin doesn't stay crisp, the initial searing gives it an enduring resilience that's texturally pleasing. Unbrowned skin was flabbily soft. Those who are concerned with fat content can easily remove the skin before serving. I prefer this approach to cooking without the skin, since when I tried the latter idea, the flesh of the chicken tightened up around the edges during cooking.

Having thus decided to brown the chicken, my cooking began by heating a small amount of fat in the pan—about two tablespoons is adequate for one chicken. I tried to cut down on this amount and use cooking spray, but the skin burned and the flesh just beneath became stringy. I tried various combinations of butter, butter and oil, olive oil, and so on and found that the all-butter version was most tasty. A problem existed, however: Butter burns easily. I didn't want to make the effort to clarify the butter, so I used the old standby combo of butter and oil. It worked perfectly: a rich, buttery flavor and no burning. The all-vegetable oil

When making Chicken in the Pot, be sure to place the vegetables on top of the chicken after sautéing; that way, they won't be crushed by the meat and will render their juices to the chicken.

PHOTOGRAPH BY DAVE HENDERSON

version was fine, just not as enticing to the palate.

Many sautéed and braised chicken recipes call for flouring the chicken before browning it, so I tried that to see what additional benefits it might provide. The results were disappointing. Although the pan gravy was an attractive color, this was the only asset of the process. Flouring caused the chicken to absorb more fat (none remained to spill off before adding the vegetables to the pan) and gave the finished chicken a gritty surface. In deciding to eliminate flouring, I found it essential to dry the chicken thoroughly before adding it to the pan, or the water caused excess spattering.

When the butter has melted and begins to look foamy, the pan is hot enough to receive the chicken. I found that if you don't wait for the pan to heat adequately, two things happen. First, the chicken absorbs too much fat. Second, it doesn't brown properly because heat rising in the flesh causes a "steam" effect. To brown chicken well, you have to keep the heat moderately high, enough to hear a sizzle.

Although you cook the vegetables separately in a classic chicken sauté, my goal was to use only one pan. At first I cooked the vegetables in the fat left in the pan after browning the chicken. It was terrific. In an effort to cut the fat, though, I tried spilling off almost all the pan fat before sautéing the vegetables. That worked beautifully although I had to watch the ingredients carefully and stir them often to prevent scorching.

Chicken in the Pot is so accommodating, you can use just about any vegetable. I began with some basics: carrots, mushrooms, and onions. Sometimes I substituted leeks for the onions and liked that better, but this is a matter of taste. Whichever vegetables you use, it is important that you put them on top of the chicken pieces when you return the chicken to the pan. That way, they won't be crushed by the weight of the meat and will stay attractive. Second, when placed on top of the chicken the vegetables render their juices to the meat below, assuring that the chicken will be soft and succulent. When I tried keeping the vegetables at the bottom, which was a little easier, I wound up with mush and too little pan fluid.

I experimented quite a bit with the amount of liquid to add. I was looking for just enough to bathe and baste the meat and vegetables in about a half hour, like a sauté, yet little enough so that it would have an intense, concentrated flavor, like a slow-cooking braise. I started by using a cup of liquid but found the resulting pan gravy too thin and lacking in flavor. Half a cup turned out to be perfect. Of course, you will need to change the amount if you vary the vegetables in the recipe. For example, more watery vegetables such as mushrooms, tomato, zucchini, and yellow squash render more liquid so you may need less fluid to begin with. On the other hand, ingredients such as potatoes, beans, dried fruit, and dried mushrooms absorb liquid during cooking, so you will need to increase the amount of fluid with which you start.

The type of liquid you use is a matter of taste. I used white wine in the master recipe because I found it tastier than stock. You need not bother

preheating the liquid; there is so little that its temperature is irrelevant.

After you add the liquid, it's time to lower the heat. To assure the meat will be braise-soft with sauté-quickness, the ingredients must cook just below a simmer. Too high a flame and the chicken will contract like a rubber band; too low and the meat will still be cooking when the vegetables are over the hill.

It is also a good idea to baste the ingredients three to four times during cooking. When I didn't do that, the flavors didn't seem as well blended. For this reason, it is more convenient to complete the cooking on top of the stove. However, if you're short on stovetop space, you can finish the dish in a preheated three-hundred-degree oven. In that case, you'll need a heatproof-handled pan. Either way, the chicken will cook through in about twenty-five minutes.

When the dish is done, you've got an unpretentious, savory meal of tender meat, flavor-rich vegetables, and about three-quarters to one cup of fragrant juices you can serve over cooked rice, polenta, egg noodles, or any other starch you choose. There's no need to reduce the liquids unless you prefer to glaze the chicken and vegetables instead of using the pan juices as a sauce. In that case, remove the chicken and the vegetables to a serving platter and keep them warm while you boil the pan fluids until they look syrupy. It takes about a minute or two.

CHICKEN IN THE POT WITH CARROTS, MUSHROOMS, AND THYME
Serves 4
If you like, you can substitute two medium leeks for the onion in this recipe. To prepare leeks, trim the dark green leaves and root end, keeping the base intact. Quarter each leek lengthwise and rinse thoroughly. Rice pilaf makes a nice accompaniment. You can make this dish in a smaller sauté pan, but you will then need to brown the chicken in batches.

 1 chicken (3 to 4 pounds), rinsed, patted dry, and cut into 8 pieces
 ½ teaspoon salt
 ¼ teaspoon ground black pepper
 1 tablespoon butter
 1 tablespoon vegetable oil
 1 large onion, sliced
 4 medium carrots, halved crosswise, then halved or quartered lengthwise depending on thickness
 8 ounces domestic mushrooms, cleaned and halved if large
 3 large thyme sprigs (1½ teaspoons fresh leaves) or ½ teaspoon dried thyme
 ½ cup dry white wine

1. Sprinkle chicken with salt and pepper. Heat butter and oil in 12-inch sauté pan over medium-high heat. When butter foaming subsides, add chicken; sauté until browned on both sides, moving around to brown evenly, 10 to 15 minutes. Remove from pan and set aside.

2. Discard all but thin film of fat from pan. Add onion, carrots, and mushrooms; sauté, stirring frequently to prevent scorching, until pan juices evaporate, 4 to 5 minutes.

3. Return chicken and accumulated juices to pan, moving vegetables to top. Add thyme sprigs and wine; bring to boil. Lower heat, cover, and barely simmer until chicken is cooked through, basting three or four times, about 25 minutes. Place portion of chicken on each plate; top with vegetables. Ladle juices over both chicken and vegetables and/or accompanying starch and serve immediately.

CHICKEN IN THE POT WITH TOMATOES, BLACK OLIVES, AND CAPERS
Serve with polenta or pasta
Follow recipe for Chicken in the Pot with Carrots, Mushrooms, and Thyme, making the following changes: Omit carrots. Add 1 garlic clove, minced, once pan juices have evaporated. Once chicken is returned to pan, add 1 can (28 ounces) plum tomatoes, drained, halved, seeded, and chopped coarse; 3 tablespoons each minced fresh parsley and basil leaves; ½ cup black olives, pitted and chopped coarse; and 2 teaspoons drained capers. Decrease wine to ¼ cup using hearty red wine instead of white.

CHICKEN IN THE POT WITH TURNIPS AND NORTH AFRICAN SPICES
Serve with steamed couscous
Follow recipe for Chicken in the Pot with Carrots, Mushrooms, and Thyme, making the following changes: Substitute 2 turnips, sliced ¼-inch thick, then cut into ½-inch strips, for the mushrooms. Add 1 garlic clove, minced, once pan juices have evaporated. Once chicken is returned to pan, add ¼ teaspoon cayenne pepper, ¼ teaspoon ground cumin, ¼ teaspoon ground cinnamon, and ⅛ teaspoon ground coriander, along with 1 cup cooked chickpeas. Substitute ½ cup chickpea cooking liquid for wine in recipe.

CHICKEN IN THE POT WITH POTATOES AND INDIAN SPICES
Serve with cooked white rice
Follow recipe for Chicken in the Pot with Carrots, Mushrooms, and Thyme, making the following changes: Substitute 3 medium all-purpose potatoes, peeled and cut into 1-inch chunks, for the mushrooms. Add 2 garlic cloves, minced, and 1 tablespoon fresh ginger, minced, once pan juices have evaporated. Once chicken is returned to pan, add 1 teaspoon ground cumin, ½ teaspoon ground turmeric, ½ teaspoon ground coriander, ⅛ teaspoon cayenne pepper, pinch of ground cinnamon, and ¼ teaspoon salt. Substitute ½ cup plain, unflavored yogurt mixed with ⅓ cup chicken stock for the wine, and rather than bring liquid to boil, bring it barely to simmer. Add 1 cup thawed frozen peas in last 3 minutes of cooking. ■

Ronnie Fein is a Connecticut-based cooking teacher and the author of *The Complete Idiot's Guide to Cooking Basics* (Alpha Books, 1995).

The Best Northern Cornbread

After testing scores of recipes, we find that the best cornbread is made with stone-ground cornmeal, two leavenings, and two types of milk.

~ BY JUDY MONROE ~

The version of cornbread most popular in the North is golden brown, fluffy, and slightly sweet, a first cousin to cake.

While all cornbreads are quick to make and bake, there are two very distinct types: Northern and Southern. Southerners use 100 percent white cornmeal, and they like their cornbread crumbly, dry, and flat—about one inch thick. Most Northerners prefer sweeter, lighter, and higher golden cornbreads, which they achieve by adding a little sugar and combining white flour and yellow cornmeal. Both types of cornbreads sport a brown crust, although Southern cornbread crusts are also crisp and crunchy.

In perfecting homemade Northern cornbread, I aimed for a high-rising, moist cornbread, one with a rich corn taste and handsome golden color. Among other things, I wanted to find the right proportion of cornmeal to flour, the correct type and amount of chemical leavening, and the ideal amount of sugar for a batch of cornbread. After baking forty-three batches of cornbread, I uncovered some surprises as I experimented with the ingredients, mixing techniques, and baking temperatures and times.

The Dry Ingredients
I first tested all aspects of the five dry ingredients. I found that the order in which these ingredients—cornmeal, flour, leavening agent, sugar, and salt—go into the mixing bowl didn't matter, but the proportion of cornmeal to flour definitely did.

The best flavor, texture, and rise resulted from a 1:1 ratio of cornmeal to all-purpose flour. If I added more cornmeal, the texture coarsened, and the cornbread baked flatter. Using more flour than cornmeal resulted in a less intense corn flavor and a cakelike texture.

Cornbreads made with stone-ground or water-ground cornmeal tasted better and had a more varied and therefore interesting texture than those made with my supermarket standards, Quaker Enriched and Degerminated Cornmeals (*see* "Grinding It Right," page 21). In addition, not only I, but also my fourteen tasters, all from the Midwest and the South, failed to detect any taste differences between cornbreads made with yellow versus white cornmeal. Cornbreads made with blue cornmeal, however, did taste more earthy, with a very faint bitterness, a taste which I personally did not like as well.

All-purpose, unbleached flour easily won out over plain cake flour and whole wheat flour. All-purpose flour yielded the tallest cornbreads. I didn't try bleached flour. The whiteness of bleached flour is unnecessary in yellow cornbread. Cake flour produced a doughy cornbread that collapsed. Whole wheat flour masked some corn flavor and made the cornbread too dense and gritty.

I thought I liked a fairly sweet Northern cornbread. I sure changed my mind fast. The recipes I examined ranged from one tablespoon of sugar to eight, so I started with two and adjusted up and down. More sugar made the cornbreads taste like a dessert bread. In test batches without sugar, though, I missed it. I substituted honey, molasses, and light brown sugar for the granulated sugar, but I did not like the taste. In the end, the perfect taste to me was four teaspoons of sugar for a batch of cornbread.

The leavening that I used would depend, I knew, on whether I used milk or buttermilk in the mixture, so I postponed a final decision on that dry ingredient. Finally, in tests with and without salt, I found that adding one-half teaspoon helped bring out the corn flavor and balanced the sweetness.

The Wet Ingredients
I had now assembled my dry ingredients. At this point, most cornbread recipes instruct the cook to add the wet ingredients—egg, milk, and fat—to the dry ones. I first tested for the number of eggs. Two eggs tasted the best to me. Three eggs rated as too eggy. One egg baked into a fine cornbread, but I missed the extra eggy flavor. The eggs added moisture and helped the cornbread rise higher; the yolks contributed to the golden interior and rich taste.

My next set of tests focused on buttermilk and milk. Buttermilk contributed a rich, luscious taste that highlighted the corn flavor, although the texture became coarser and heavier. Using buttermilk clearly moved the cornbread to bread status, away from any hint of dessert. Cornbreads made with milk tasted fine but lacked richness, although the lighter texture and softer yellow color were appealing. To remedy this, I decided to use a combination of buttermilk and milk.

My hunch worked. A half milk and half buttermilk combination baked into the best cornbread, with a wonderful taste, light texture, handsome yellow-gold interior, high rise, and a brown crust with some crunch.

Next, I tested the fats. Butter outranked the other contenders. Vegetable oil, vegetable shortening, and margarine tasted boring and lackluster, and none of my tasters liked the lard. A couple of tasters (myself included) enjoyed the flavor of bacon fat at first, but after a few more bites, found it overpowering. I discovered that I liked a cornbread that is fairly lean on the butter. Two tablespoons of butter for a batch of cornbread tasted the best to me. More than that was too heavy and started to interfere with the corn flavor. Cornbread made with less lacked richness.

Most recipes instruct the cook to add the melted butter last. Is this necessary? I wondered. To find out, I tried several experiments. First I creamed the softened butter, then added the remaining ingredients. The top of the cornbread looked pebbled and less appetizing. Next, I melted the butter, then stirred in all the other ingredients. The cornbread was heavy and too moist. Finally, I added the melted butter last. This method produced the best tasting and most attractive cornbread. I detected no difference when I used hot or warm melted butter as long as I mixed it in fast.

Armed with my basic ingredients and their order into the mixing bowl, I then asked two questions. How long do I mix the batter, and with what? I learned to mix quickly, just to combine the dry and wet ingredients, and then add another ten or twelve strokes to distribute the melted butter quickly and evenly. As for the proper tool, I found that a fork left clumps of dry cornmeal at the bottom of the bowl, while a whisk, egg beaters, or electric mixer were overkill. I rated a wooden spoon or a scraper as the best and easiest-to-use tools.

Chemical Leavenings: Soda or Powder?

To obtain the light texture and high rise of Northern cornbread, some type of chemical leavening such as baking soda or baking powder is required. These leavenings, when mixed with the other ingredients, release a gas—carbon dioxide—that causes the batter to bake up light and high. The air beaten into the eggs and combined ingredients is not enough to sufficiently rise Northern cornbread batter during baking.

As I experimented with baking soda and baking powder, the two typical leavenings for cornbread, I discovered that three or four teaspoons of baking powder produced the tallest cornbreads, but ones that lacked some corny taste. Cornbreads made with 100 percent baking soda sported darker, golden brown and brown tops and a stronger array of interior colors: deeper golden or yellow overall color, with flecks of deep orange and yellow.

Hoping to achieve a bread with the color provided by baking soda and the high rise caused by baking powder, I combined the two chemical leavenings. After tinkering with various amounts of each, I found what I was looking for. Two teaspoons of baking powder plus one-half teaspoon of baking soda yielded a tall rise, golden color, and the best taste. When I increased the baking soda, I noted a mushy, soapy taste, which meant that the available acid in the batter was not neutralizing the extra leavening, so I stuck with the one-half teaspoon.

Baking Refinements

With my recipe now in hand, I looked at three final variables: the fat to grease the pan, the type of baking pan, and oven temperature. My goal was a Northern cornbread with an evenly browned crust, a golden brown color, and a moist interior. I tested an assortment of fats: vegetable shortening, vegetable spray, margarine, lard, bacon fat, and butter. The best flavored crusts resulted from the animal fats. I ended up choosing butter since it ranked number one in taste.

A crisp, crunchy crust is an essential feature of Southern-style cornbread, so a cast-iron skillet is the preferred pan for cooking it. For the more tender Northern cornbreads, however, metal baking pans are the best choice. I tried using a glass pan, but my cornbread overbaked around the edges. After testing round and square metal pans, I opted for the square version because it has more capacity than a round pan. Because of this, cornbreads baked in a round pan rose higher but were too moist.

As for oven temperature, I found that cornbreads baked at 350 degrees and 375 degrees had very thick, heavy crusts because they took a long time to form. Moving into the 400-degree range, I found that a 425-degree oven baked the best Northern cornbread. At this higher temperature, the crust formed more quickly and the whole cornbread baked faster, resulting in a crisper crust and lighter-textured cornbread.

GOLDEN NORTHERN CORNBREAD
Makes 9 servings

This cornbread is moist and light, with the rich taste of corn. Use stone-ground or water-ground cornmeal for the best taste and texture. Either yellow or white cornmeal bakes into a handsome, delicious cornbread.

    1 cup yellow or white stone-ground or
         water-ground cornmeal
    1 cup all-purpose flour
    2 teaspoons baking powder
  ½ teaspoon baking soda
    4 teaspoons sugar
  ½ teaspoon salt
    2 large eggs
  ⅔ cup buttermilk
  ⅔ cup milk
    2 tablespoons unsalted butter, melted,
         plus extra softened butter for
         greasing pan

1. Adjust oven rack to center position and heat to 425 degrees. Grease a 9-by-9-by-2-inch metal pan.

2. Stir cornmeal, flour, baking powder, baking soda, sugar, and salt in large bowl. Push dry ingredients up side of bowl to make a well.

3. Crack eggs into well and stir lightly with wooden spoon, then add buttermilk and milk. Stir wet and dry ingredients quickly until almost combined. Add melted butter; stir until ingredients are just combined.

4. Pour batter into greased pan. Bake until top is golden brown and lightly cracked and edges have pulled away from side of pan, about 25 minutes.

5. Transfer pan to wire rack to cool slightly, 5 to 10 minutes. Cut cornbread into squares and serve warm. (Pan can be wrapped in foil up to 1 day. Reheat cornbread in a 350-degree oven for 10 to 15 minutes.)

GOLDEN CORNBREAD WITH CHEDDAR

Follow recipe for Golden Northern Cornbread, omitting sugar. After adding butter, quickly fold in 1 cup (2½ ounces) shredded cheddar or Monterey Jack cheese.

GOLDEN CORNBREAD WITH JALAPEÑOS

Follow recipe for Golden Northern Cornbread, omitting sugar. After adding butter, quickly fold in one small jalapeño, seeded and minced, for mild chile flavor. For bolder heat use up to two jalapeños that have been minced but not seeded.

GOLDEN CORNBREAD WITH BACON

To end up with ½ cup bacon needed for this recipe, cut 8 ounces sliced bacon into small dice, then fry until well browned and crisp. Drain, cool, then set aside until ready to fold into batter. Follow recipe for Golden Northern Cornbread, omitting sugar. After adding butter, quickly fold in crumbled bacon bits. ∎

Judy Monroe is a St. Paul, Minnesota–based food writer and author of three cookbooks.

GRINDING IT RIGHT

The large commercial mills use huge steel rollers to grind dent corn (a hard, dry corn) into cornmeal. But some smaller mills scattered around the United States do grind with millstones; some still use water as the energy source. The smaller millers often choose not to degerm, or remove all the germ, cleanly. This makes their product closer to a whole-grain cornmeal. The higher moisture and oil content of their cornmeal causes it to go rancid within two to four weeks. If you buy some, wrap it tightly in plastic or put it into a moisture-proof container, then refrigerate or freeze it. Degerminated cornmeals such as Quaker's store for a year, if kept dry and cool.

According to Dr. Elwood Caldwell, Director of Scientific Studies at the American Association of Cereal Chemists, no nutritional difference exists between stone-ground and water-ground cornmeal versus steel-ground meal. However, there are still reasons to buy stone-ground or water-ground cornmeal. First, the texture of cornbreads made with these meals is more interesting since the cornmeals are not a uniform grind. More importantly, I found that cornbreads made with stone-ground and water-ground brands tasted much better than those made with the standard Quaker cornmeals. However, this doesn't mean that cornmeal labeled as stone-ground or water-ground is an automatic guarantee of good taste and texture. Some brands I tested were finely ground; others were more irregular. One of the more expensive stone-ground cornmeals I tested rated "fair" and "poor" in taste.

So what is a consumer to do? Well, for the most corny taste, hunt for cornmeals containing lots of the tasty germ. Caldwell suggests this quick test: Pour some cornmeal onto a clean table or plate. Squeeze it in your hand and try to heap it up. If it clings together and stays in a little pile, then some germ remains. If it settles back or does not cling together, the cornmeal contains no germ. The Quaker cornmeals rolled around like tiny marbles and immediately poured out of my hand. When I squeezed the stone-ground and water-ground cornmeals, all passed the test.

Sautéing Fish Fillets

Choose the right pan, get it good and hot, and judge your cooking time by the thickness of the fish.

~ BY KATHERINE ALFORD ~

Sautéing, a quick cooking technique, is an ideal way to handle a wide variety of fish. It is particularly suited for mild flatfish fillets, adding a delicate, crispy texture and flavor you can't get with other techniques. But sautéing fish can be intimidating to the uninitiated cook, particularly if the fish sticks to the pan or falls apart.

Years ago, as a young cook at the Quilted Giraffe, I remember being awed by the Zen-like elegance of a master sauté cook, Hillary Gregg. It seemed that any fish he cooked had that perfect measure of golden crust encasing a juicy center. I learned that the key to his success lay in an uncomplicated routine: a properly heated pan, a light lubrication of fat, and patience. Gregg showed me how foods sautéed in tentative heat were slow to brown and ran the risk of steaming and overcooking.

For this article, I wanted to establish a consistent method that I could use with different fish. I limited my tests to filleted, white-fleshed fish. I classified them by thickness: thin, meaning about one-half inch thick, including sole and flounder; medium thick, meaning about three-quarters inch thick, including snapper and sea bass; and thick, meaning about one inch thick, including catfish and scrod.

Preparing to Sauté

My first test was to see if the type of pan used made any difference when sautéing. To find out, I sautéed two-ounce pieces of lemon sole in nonstick, stainless steel, cast-iron, and rolled steel pans. I knew from past experience that the key was to preheat the pan. When food is added to a cold pan, it is a guarantee that it will stick and cook unevenly. When choosing a pan for sautéing, it is important that it be of a heavy enough material to conduct the heat uniformly.

I heated the pans for three minutes over moderate heat, or until a drop of water beaded up and evaporated in about twenty seconds, before adding the fat. When ready to sauté, I raised the heat to high, added one teaspoon of canola oil, and then added a small fish fillet. This test confirmed that as long as the pan is heated and the fish cooked with moderate to high heat, there is almost no difference in the end result. Each piece of fish was browned and moist, and didn't stick in the pan.

There was, however, a slight aspect to pay attention to when working with the nonstick pans. Fat beaded up on the surface, and the temptation was to add more fat to evenly cover it. To make sure that the fish was lubricated by the fat, I dragged it through the oil before laying it in the lubricated pan. I then tried another approach for adding fat to the nonstick pans. I brushed the fish with the fat, then put the fish into an unlubricated pan. Even with this limited amount of fat, the fish browned and was moist. It was a bit of an odd way to sauté—without the gratifying sound of food sizzling in the pan—but it was ideal for reduced fat cooking. Another advantage of nonstick pans is their reliable surface, which helps build confidence when learning to sauté.

How much fat do you need if you're not going with the nonstick method? This depends on the size and number of fillets being cooked. For a single fillet about seven to eight inches long and three to four inches wide, in an eight- to nine-inch sauté pan, one teaspoon of fat was sufficient. However, when I cooked more than one fillet in the same pan, I discovered I needed about a tablespoon of fat to accommodate them. The weight of the fillets didn't seem to matter as much as the surface area covered by the fish. I found overall that less fat when sautéing was better. Too much fat coming up the sides of the fish made the crust a tough shell and the fish greasy. If you need to add fat while cooking, the best way is to drizzle it down the side of the pan so it doesn't cool things down.

I was also curious to see if the type of fat used made a significant difference. I sautéed the different thicknesses of fish fillets in butter, olive oil, flavorless canola oil, and a combination of butter and oil. (I eliminated using clarified butter due to the extra work that it adds to an otherwise quick procedure.)

All the fats produced satisfactory results, each with a distinct advantage. Butter was by far the tastiest and gave the fish a gorgeous golden crust. There is a disadvantage cooking with butter, however: Its smoke point is lower than vegetable oils, and it can burn easily. This can be problematic when cooking a thick piece or one with a breading. Butter is an ideal medium for sautéing thin fillets. To get the best results with butter, heat the pan over moderate heat, then add the butter. It will melt, then foam up. If you add the fish fillet

When sautéing fillets that taper down to a thin tail, fold the tail over to ensure even cooking. Also be sure the sauté pan you use is large enough to comfortably hold the fillets in a single layer without crowding.

just as the foam subsides, you catch the butter at the proper temperature for sautéing. If the butter burns and smokes, the pan is too hot; wipe out the pan and start again.

Next I tested both pure and extra-virgin olive oils. Both were perfectly suitable for sautéing the fish. Not surprisingly, the extra-virgin complemented the fish with a sweeter, fuller, more complex flavor than the pure. Although the olive oils produced a crust on the fish, they did not give the same rich appearance as the butter.

The canola oil was the most versatile of the bunch. Its high smoke point allowed it to take prolonged heat, making it suitable for thin or thick fillets and breadings. Canola contributes no flavor to the fish, which can be an advantage when pairing it with mild sauces.

My last test involved a thick fillet of scrod with canola oil and butter. I heated the pan, lightly lubricated it with oil, and then added the fish. I cooked it until it was just turning brown and then added about a teaspoon of butter. Here I had the perfect blend of canola's high temperature and butter's flavor. This was the solution for thicker fillets.

I also compared fish fillets cooked salted and peppered to those seasoned after cooking. Fish browned better and had a fuller flavor when it was salted immediately before cooking rather than af-

PHOTOGRAPH BY DAVE HENDERSON

ter, and unsalted fish was more likely to stick. According to food chemistry expert Shirley Corriher, the salt draws moisture from the fish, which speeds caramelization, as well as providing a thin buffer zone, making the fish less likely to stick. However, it is important not to salt the fish in advance, which pulls too much moisture from the fish, causing it to steam instead of sauté.

When preparing to sauté, check that your pan can properly accommodate the fish. The fillets should lie flat and uncrowded in the pan. In my testing, if a fish snuck up the side of the pan, it stuck and fell apart when flipping over. Since some flat fish fillets can be quite large, it is better to cut them before cooking so they lie flat. Another trick to fit fillets that taper down to a thin tail and avoid overcooking the thinner portion is to fold the tail under so the piece is all the same thickness. When sautéing three or four fillets, you may need to use two pans.

Some fish fillets are sold with the skin on. This is helpful when cooking because it holds the fish together while it cooks. However, fish sautéed with the skin on can curl inconveniently. To avoid this, I scored the skin with a sharp knife at one-and-one-half-inch intervals. When the fish is cooked on the skin side, press it down with a spatula for twenty seconds or so until it lies flat.

For all fillets, thick or thin, I found that cooking them first on the smooth, rounded side, not the skin side, was better. The trick is to brown them undisturbed on the first side, in the fresh fat and with assertive heat, until the edges and a thin border on the fillet turn opaque. Resist the temptation to check the food constantly. All that activity cools the food down, meaning that the fish won't brown and will be more likely to stick to the pan. (As Gregg would say, "Just let it cook.") Before turning the fillets over, give the pan a shake to make sure they are free. If a fillet does stick, don't scrape it off the bottom of the pan; instead, let it cook a bit longer. Most times the fish sticks because it hasn't had a chance to form its protective crust. Once the crust is formed, it will shake loose. If you have a troublesome piece, drizzle in a bit of fat and cook it for thirty seconds to a minute more, then briskly slip a spatula under it.

Although I usually prefer fish sautéed without breading, I also wanted to see what effect different breadings would make. I tried various coatings: flour, bread crumbs, eggs, milk, buttermilk, and cornmeal. Flour, although commonly suggested for sautéing fish, added a pasty coating. Floured fish is less likely to stick to the pan, but with practice the same effect can be achieved by properly heating the pan. If you do need to flour fish, dust only the side that goes into the pan first.

I then tried flounder dredged in flour and egg. This coating browned nicely and contributed a pleasant, eggy taste with a downy instead of crisp coating. Fillets dipped in flour, egg, and bread crumbs made a crisp shell. This kept the fish particularly moist, compared with fillets dredged in bread crumbs alone. I compared fish cooked with fresh bread crumbs versus dried bread crumbs, and I preferred the fresh. They absorbed less fat and kept their brittle shell longer. With fresh bread crumbs you have the added benefit of choosing a gutsy-flavored bread, like a sourdough, instead of the insipid store-bought varieties. I experimented with cornmeal and buttermilk and found I loved buttermilk's acidic edge. When choosing cornmeal for a bread coating, I preferred the crunchy shell of a polenta grind cornmeal (instant was fine) versus standard cornmeal.

When breading fillets for sautéing, first dry and season them with pepper. Spread the coatings in flat-rimmed dishes or bowls large enough to accommodate the fish. To avoid breading your fingers in the process, try to use one hand when dipping the fish in the wet ingredients and the other for dry (see illustrations 1 and 2, below). Shake off any excess coating from the fish before dipping into the next coating. Excess breading can burn in the pan. You need more fat when sautéing a breaded fish, about two tablespoons per medium pan. With a breading, cook the fish at a more moderate pace so as not to scorch the coating. When sautéing three to four fillets, you may need to use two pans.

Timing

How long to cook your fillets is important. With thin pieces, a minute too long, and the fish will flake, fall apart, and be dry. With thick pieces, a minute shy, and they can be raw.

After testing fillets one-half inch thick, I learned that the best method was to brown the fish over an assertive heat, then to flip them over, turn the heat down to moderate, and cook for one minute. Then turn the pan off. The fish will continue to cook with the residual heat of the pan, but is modulated by the cooling as well. The second side may be slightly less brown than the first side, but on the very thin fillets, if you crisp both sides, you run the risk of overcooking the fish.

For thick fillets, I tried browning them and then finishing them in a 350-degree oven, but the crust got soggy. The best technique was to brown the fish over high to medium-high heat, and then flip it over and continue cooking over medium heat.

To check that the fish is done, poke it with your finger. It should feel firm but not flake. If the fish falls into dry flakes, it's been overcooked.

After timing over twenty-five different fillets for this article, I was surprised to find that the timing was consistent with the Canadian method of ten minutes cooking per inch of thickness. I thought that this would overcook the fish, but cooking over high heat first and then moderating it for the latter part of the cooking did, in fact, cook one-half-inch fillets within four to five minutes and one-inch-thick fillets within nine to eleven minutes. To gauge how long to cook the fish, measure it at its thickest

MESS-FREE BREADING

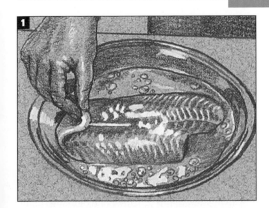

1. To avoid getting breading all over your fingers, use one hand when dipping the fish in the wet ingredients.

2. Dip the fish in the dry ingredients with the other hand, then shake off any excess coating.

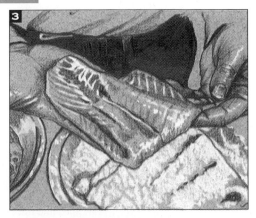

3. After breading fillets, fold the tail end up so that the fillet is a more even thickness.

point and estimate eight to ten minutes per inch. If the fish is held while a pan sauce is made, it is important to remember that it will continue to cook as it rests.

SAUTÉED THIN FISH FILLETS
Serves 4

For these thin, flat fillets, such as sole or flounder, you can fold the thin tail end under (*see* illustration 3, page 23). This step will enable you to fit all four fillets in one large skillet rather than having to heat up two.

1½ pounds thin fish fillets, rinsed and dried with paper towels, skin scored at one-and-one-half-inch intervals
   Salt and ground black pepper
2 tablespoons unsalted butter, oil, or combination of two

Heat one large or two medium skillets over medium heat until drop of water beads up and evaporates, 2 to 3 minutes. Increase heat to medium-high; add butter and/or oil to pan (or 1 tablespoon to each pan). Season fish with salt and pepper to taste. When foaming subsides (if using butter) or oil starts to shimmer, add fillets, skin side up, to the pan or pans. Cook until golden brown, 2 to 3 minutes, occasionally shaking pan gently to keep fillets from sticking. Turn fish with spatula. If fillet is very thin, turn heat off immediately, allowing residual heat from pan to finish cooking fish. If fish is a little thicker, continue to cook over medium-high heat for 1 minute, then turn off heat and allow residual heat to finish cooking it. Serve immediately with one of the pan sauces that follow.

SAUTÉED MEDIUM-THICK FISH FILLETS

Medium-thick fish measure about three-quarters inch thick and include fish like striped bass and snapper.

Follow recipe for Sautéed Thin Fish Fillets, using oil or combination oil and butter and increasing cooking time on first side to 3 to 4 minutes and

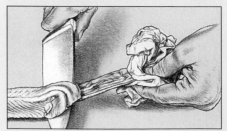

MAKING SKINNING EASIER

To more easily remove the skin from a fish fillet, start at the end of the tail, then slide your knife along between the skin and flesh of the tail until you can grab hold of the skin. Use this "handle" to help separate the skin from the flesh.

cooking time on second side to 2 to 3 minutes.

SAUTÉED THICK FISH FILLETS

This category of fish includes those measuring at least one inch thick. Larger flaked fish, such as scrod, tend to fall apart easily during cooking. I found cutting the fillets into individual portions made them easier to turn and therefore less likely to fall apart. If the fillets look like they will crowd the pan, use two skillets rather than one. You want to ensure they brown, not steam.

Follow recipe for Sautéed Thin Fish Fillets, using oil or combination butter and oil and increasing cooking time on first side to 5 to 6 minutes over high to medium-high heat and cooking time on second side to 4 to 5 minutes over medium heat. Add 1 extra teaspoon butter to pan when you turn fish.

QUICK PAN SAUCES FOR SAUTÉED FISH

Pan sauces are one of the rewards of sautéing. When making them, keep the fats used in the dish complementary; for example, a warm vinaigrette will complement fish sautéed in olive or neutral oils but will fight with fish sautéed in butter. Cream sauces enhance fish sautéed in butter.

WARM BALSAMIC VINAIGRETTE WITH HERBS
Serves 4

3 tablespoons balsamic vinegar
1 medium garlic clove, minced
2 tablespoons minced fresh parsley leaves
1 tablespoon minced fresh thyme leaves
½ teaspoon kosher salt
   Ground black pepper
⅓ cup olive oil

1. Whisk vinegar with garlic, parsley, thyme, and salt, as well as pepper to taste; slowly whisk in olive oil. Set aside.
2. Add vinaigrette to hot pan once fish has been sautéed and removed, and any juices set aside. Bring to simmer and continue simmering 1 minute. Pour in reserved juices. Spoon over fish and serve.

HORSERADISH AND CIDER CREAM SAUCE
Serves 4

1 shallot, minced
   Butter (if necessary for sautéing)
¼ cup cider
4 teaspoons cider vinegar
⅔ cup heavy cream
2½ tablespoons prepared horseradish
   Salt and ground black pepper
1 tablespoon minced fresh parsley leaves

Add shallot to warm pan once fish has been sautéed and removed, and any juices set aside;

add bit of butter if pan is dry. Sauté over medium heat until almost softened, 1 to 2 minutes. Increase heat to high; add cider and vinegar and reduce to thin syrup, 2 to 3 minutes. Add cream, horseradish, and reserved juices; simmer until sauce thickens, 1 to 2 minutes. Season with salt and pepper to taste. Spoon sauce over fish, sprinkle with parsley, and serve.

PROVENÇAL TOMATO SAUCE WITH BASIL AND ORANGE
Serves 4

2 garlic cloves, minced
½ small onion, minced
   Oil (if necessary for sautéing)
¼ cup white wine
½ teaspoon fennel seeds, cracked
½ teaspoon zest from small orange
⅓ cup clam juice or fish stock
⅔ cup tomato puree
   Pinch saffron threads, crumbled
2 tablespoons minced fresh basil leaves
   Salt and ground black pepper

Add garlic and onion to warm pan once fish has been sautéed and removed, and any juices set aside; add bit of oil if pan is dry. Sauté over medium heat until almost softened, about 3 minutes. Add wine, fennel, and zest, then clam juice, puree, saffron, and reserved juices. Simmer until slightly thickened, 2 to 3 minutes. Stir in basil and season to taste with salt and pepper. Spoon warm sauce over fish and serve.

MUNG BEAN SAUCE WITH GINGER, CILANTRO, AND SOY
Serves 4

If you like a more brothy sauce, you can omit the cornstarch in this recipe.

2 teaspoons minced fresh ginger
⅛ teaspoon hot red pepper flakes
   Oil (if necessary for sautéing)
2 cups drained mung bean sprouts
⅓ cup clam juice or fish stock
1 tablespoon soy sauce or tamari
1 teaspoon fresh lime juice
¾ teaspoon honey
½ teaspoon cornstarch, dissolved in 2 tablespoons water
3 tablespoons minced fresh cilantro leaves
2 scallions, sliced thin, trimmed

Add ginger and red pepper to warm pan once fish has been sautéed and removed, adding bit of oil if pan is dry. Sauté over medium heat until fragrant, about 30 seconds. Increase heat to high and add sprouts to pan; toss over high heat until slightly wilted, about 1 minute. Add clam juice, soy sauce, lime juice, and honey; bring to boil. Add dissolved cornstarch; return to boil to thicken. Stir in cilantro and scallions. Spoon over fish and serve. ■

Katherine Alford is a cooking teacher and freelance writer living in New York City.

ILLUSTRATIONS BY ALAN WITSCHONKE

The Best Baked Potato

After baking hundreds of spuds, we find that the traditional method is best—so long as you open up the potatoes immediately after baking.

In the world of June Cleaver, potatoes were baked at 350 degrees because they were put into the oven along with the roast, which cooked at 350 degrees.

The world has changed a lot since Wally and the Beav sat down to dinner. The evening meal has become a hastier project. Stir-fries, sautés, and "à la minutes" have crept into the territory once held by roasting.

To go along with this new, quicker cooking style, I decided to try to find a faster—or even just a better—route to baked potatoes. Along the way, I baked all-purpose potatoes, Yukon Golds, and Idaho-grown Russets. I tried baking them poked and unpoked, greased and ungreased, with ends dipped in salt, microwaved all the way, microwaved and finished in the oven, baked with gadgets that are supposed to decrease cooking time, and baked at various temperatures. And, against the wishes of all the potato experts in the world, I also tried baking them in foil.

After all this experimentation, what I discovered was that the traditional slow baking is best, mainly because of the effect it has on the skin. The skin of a potato baked at 350 degrees for an hour and fifteen minutes simply has no peer. Just under the skin, a well-baked potato will develop a substantial brown layer. This is because the dark skin absorbs heat during cooking, and the starch just inside the skin is broken down into sugar and starts to brown. All good cooks know that browning adds flavor to everything from layer cakes and bread crust to roasted meat and onions. If you love baked potato skin, this is definitely your method.

Potatoes cooked at 400 and 450 degrees will indeed cook faster—at 450 they may even cook in forty-five minutes—but because they cook for a shorter time, the inner browned layer isn't as even or as flavorful as it is with the slower roast method. In addition, the skin isn't quite as thick and chewy. Cooked long enough to develop chewy skin at these higher temperatures, the inner, browned layer becomes thick and unpleasant, and somewhat overbrowned.

I also tried starting potatoes at 500 degrees for ten minutes and then turning the oven down to 350 degrees, but again, this method failed to promote even browning. Oiling the skin causes a potato to cook somewhat more quickly. But baking at 400 degrees for an hour does not develop the same great skin or browning that can be achieved by cooking longer, oiled or not, at 350 degrees.

Thus, unfortunately, the perfect potato takes the longest to cook. Also, be forewarned: The most important step to a fluffy potato is opening it wide when it's hot and letting the steam escape to the air rather than being trapped in the potato. Letting the potato sit a while after baking, or providing a too-small opening, will steam the potatoes and cause their flesh to become more dense: Any special character you could have gotten from the more expensive Russets will disappear.

So no matter what method you choose for baking your potato, from microwaving to slow baking at 350 degrees, opening the potato wide is critical to great-tasting flesh. A microwaved potato (*see* "Quicker Baked Potato," below) will need a minute or so of standing time; after it has stood, pierce it with a fork and open it wide.

MASTER RECIPE FOR OVEN-BAKED POTATO
Serves 4

4 7-ounce Idaho Russet potatoes

Heat oven to 350 degrees. Scrub potatoes well to remove dirt. Place on middle rack of oven, and bake 75 minutes. Remove from oven and pierce with fork to create dotted "X." Press in at ends of potato to push flesh up and out. ∎

Sarah Fritschner is the food editor of the *Louisville Courier-Journal* and is the author of *The Express Lane Cookbook* (Chapters Publishing Ltd., 1995).

To open a baked potato, make a dotted "X" on the top with the tines of a fork, then press in at the ends of the potato to push the flesh up and out. The more steam that comes out, the better.

POTATO BAKING TIPS

✱ The expensive metal pokers that you stick into potatoes to decrease cooking time do not seem to have that effect, but they do make cooking time more uniform, so that a potato always cooks in the same amount of time at a given temperature.

✱ Cutting the ends off a potato and dipping them in salt makes for crusty, salty ends, but doesn't measurably alter baking time or flakiness.

✱ Though a potato has never exploded in my oven, I've heard of it happening. Poking the potato before baking will prevent this, but it does not measurably affect the amount of moisture retained by the potato. The flesh of a potato that has been poked seems just as dry as that of one that has not been. However, it is a good idea to poke a hole or two in any potato you are going to microwave, since explosions are more common there.

✱ High-moisture boiling potatoes and Yukon Golds will bake just fine, but they don't produce the fluffy, dry texture that you'll get from Russet Burbanks.

✱ Foil-wrapped potatoes are a notion perpetuated by mediocre steak houses that want to be able to keep potatoes warm indefinitely. Foil is an insult to potatoes; it holds the steam in, causing limp, damp skins and dense flesh.

QUICKER BAKED POTATO

In the course of my tests, I discovered that the microwave, properly used, can make the process shorter. Despite my preconceived notions, microwaves do not create a potato with insipid, dense flesh. When cooked properly, the flesh of a microwaved potato comes out pretty well. What's missing is the delicious browned layer under the skin and the chewy, dry skin that skin lovers covet.

Microwave directions call for cooking a seven-ounce potato for four minutes on high power, changing the position of the potato halfway through cooking. You must increase the cooking time by four minutes for each additional potato.

I found that cooking potatoes for half the recommended microwave time, then finishing them in a 450-degree oven for twenty minutes, produced a potato with fluffy, dry flesh, some browning, and a pretty good skin. If you're in a hurry, this half-and-half method is the best way to produce a delicious potato. Rubbing the skin with oil did not seem to change the cooking time, so you can leave out that step.

Dutched vs. Natural Cocoas

Our panel preferred dutched cocoas in hot chocolate but found that natural and dutched cocoas were equally appropriate in brownies.

∽ BY ALICE MEDRICH AND JACK BISHOP ∽

In the last twenty years, a seductive array of European desserts has enriched the American baker's repertoire and expanded our use of chocolate as an ingredient. Flourless chocolate tortes, chocolate mousse, and chocolate truffles have taught us to use nibbling-quality semisweet and bittersweet chocolates in dessert making.. (*See* "Are Expensive Chocolates Worth the Money?" November/December 1994.)

It's easy to forget that Americans once baked almost exclusively with unsweetened chocolate and cocoa powder—the stuff of great American classics like brownies, fudge, and devil's food cake. As sophisticated as we have become about chocolate, many cooks are confused about cocoa. How is this powder related to chocolate and what are the differences between regular and dutched cocoas?

Cocoa is derived from chocolate liquor—the professional term for unsweetened baking chocolate. Chocolate liquor is made from cocoa beans scooped from the pods of the tropical cacao tree. The beans are fermented, roasted, shelled, and then ground into a molten paste. This paste is half fat (cocoa butter) and half cocoa solids; nothing else is added. The paste is hardened in molds and can be remelted for use in baking.

Cocoa powder is chocolate liquor that has been pressed to remove half to three-quarters of its fat and then pulverized. A hydraulic press, designed by the Dutchman C. J. Van Houten in the nineteenth century, removes fat while leaving solids behind. Cocoa has a strong chocolate flavor and is easy to incorporate into other ingredients.

To Dutch or Not to Dutch

In addition to designing the cocoa press, Van Houten also developed a process to reduce the natural acidity in chocolate and make it more digestible. Untreated chocolate is mildly acidic, which is indicated by its pH value of between 5.2 and 5.6, about the same as black coffee. By adding a small amount of an alkaline solution, usually potassium carbonate, to either the shelled cocoa beans or chocolate liquor, Van Houten was able to raise the pH to about 7 (neutral) or slightly higher. This technique, called "dutching" or

Cocoa beans such as those shown may be "dutched" to reduce their natural acidity.

"Dutch processing," has a number of side effects. Dutching darkens the color of the cocoa, mellows its flavor, and was thought to improve its ability to dissolve in liquid. (This last trait has since been proven to be a myth.) Today, European cocoas are generally dutched while American supermarket cocoas are not, although American manufacturers make dutched cocoa for professional use.

Of course, the effect of dutching on flavor is the most interesting issue for the home cook. With this in mind, we structured our tasting not only to determine which cocoas have the best flavor but also to make some conclusions about the merits of dutching. We conducted two separate tastings with our panel of experts. In the first tasting, cocoas were sampled in hot milk sweetened with a small amount of sugar. Five leading natural cocoas (all American brands) were pitted against seven leading dutched cocoas (four European brands and three American specialty brands).

Dutch-process cocoas took the first six places in the hot chocolate tasting. One possible reason for this outcome is color. Dutched cocoas yielded hot chocolates with a rich, warm brown color, while hot chocolates made with natural cocoa were pale or washed-out-looking. The natural assumption would be that darker cocoas have more chocolate flavor, and our tasters may have been guided, at least in part, by this. However, because the natural acids in the chocolate have been neutralized, the flavor of dutched cocoa is generally considered to be more mellow.

So were the eyes of our tasters fooling their taste buds? Not necessarily. Many tasters found the natural cocoas to be overly bitter or harsh when tasted in hot chocolate. In contrast, dutched cocoas were more rounded and smooth. It may be that the mellow quality of the dutched cocoas made it easier for the chocolate flavor to come through in the hot chocolates, while the acidity in the natural cocoas blocked out the chocolate flavor in this application.

Which Cocoa for Baking?

Most cooks use cocoa in baking, so we also wanted to design a second test with this in mind.

Since the pH values of dutched and natural cocoas are so different, most recipe writers specify a leavener based on the cocoa used in the recipe. For example, cakes with acidic natural cocoa usually call for alkaline baking soda because an alkali is needed to produce carbon dioxide. Conversely, recipes with Dutch-process cocoa, which is neutral or slightly alkaline, generally use baking powder, which contains both an acid and alkali. In order to avoid this issue, we decided to test cocoas in a brownie recipe without leavening or acidic ingredients. The results were quite different than in the first tasting of hot chocolates.

Our top cocoa, the dutched Van Leer from New Jersey, showed well in both the hot chocolate and brownie tastings. However, a number of Dutch-process cocoas that performed well in the hot chocolate tasting were less favorably judged in the brownie tasting. In contrast, several natural cocoas that had been poorly rated in the hot chocolate tasting made excellent brownies.

A couple of theories. The harshness that bothered tasters when they sampled hot chocolates made with natural cocoa was impossible to detect in brownies made with so much more sugar and other ingredients. In fact, this harsh quality may have been interpreted as "full-flavored" in the brownies. We suspect that some of the mellow dutched cocoas simply faded in the brownies.

Another point to consider is familiarity. American desserts, like brownies, have typically been made with natural cocoa. Taste memories from our childhood would favor natural cocoas in this context. In fact, many of the brownies made with dutched cocoas tasted fine but were not "brownielike" in the opinion of our tasters.

The brownie tasting demonstrated that the choice of a particular cocoa in baking is complicated and probably more dependent on the leavener used in the recipe and the amount of sugar and fat (recipes with more sugar and fat should favor more assertive natural cocoas), as well as the quality of the cocoa itself. In any case, since the dutched Van Leer cocoa tied for first place among the brownies and took second place in the hot chocolate tasting, you can hardly go wrong with this brand. All of the recommended cocoas will deliver decent results in baking, while the recommended dutched cocoas are your best bet for dairy-based preparations like hot chocolate. ∎

Alice Medrich is the author of *Chocolate and the Art of Low-Fat Desserts* (Warner Books, 1994).

PHOTOGRAPH COURTESY OF THE CHOCOLATE MANUFACTURERS ASSOCIATION

Twelve unsweetened cocoas were tasted blind in hot chocolate made with whole milk, cocoa, and a little sugar as well as brownies made with sugar, butter, eggs, cocoa, flour, vanilla, and salt. The tastings were conducted independently of each other at Chez Panisse in Berkeley, California. In addition to the authors, the panel included author and pastry teacher Flo Braker; cookbook author Marion Cunningham; Narsai David, KCBS radio food news editor; cookbook author Carol Field; Emily Luchetti, cookbook author and pastry chef at Stars in San Francisco; Tom Roach, owner of Tom's Cookies in San Francisco; Lindsey Shere, pastry chef at Chez Panisse and cookbook author; cookbook author Marlene Sorosky; Kathleen Stewart, of the Downtown Bakery and Creamery in Healdsburg, California; and Carolyn Beth Weil, owner of The Bakeshop in Berkeley.

The cocoas are listed in order of preference based on their combined scores in the two tastings. Figures for pH and percentage of cocoa butter were supplied by the manufacturers. Prices are based on supermarket purchases in California or mail-order sources where indicated. Most mail-order cocoas are sold in bulk to gourmet stores and shipped to consumers in any quantity desired.

Number of mugs/brownie plates indicates finish in hot chocolate/brownie tastings. 12 symbols indicates 1st place, 1 symbol indicates last (12th) place

HIGHLY RECOMMENDED COCOA

This cocoa ranked at the top of both tastings.

Van Leer 120 Cocoa (Jersey City, New Jersey), pH 6.8–7.2, 22–24% cocoa butter, $5 per pound. This dutched cocoa was the only sample that finished at the top of both tastings. "Dark, reddish brown" cocoa made a "rich, enticing" cup of hot chocolate that tasters described as "clean," "well-balanced," "fruity," and "chocolaty." Brownies were "fairly dark" with a "wonderful flavor" and "strong hints of coffee." Available by mail from New York Cake (800-942-2539).

RECOMMENDED COCOAS

These cocoas were rated highly in one but not both tastings.

Pernigotti Cocoa (Italy), pH 6.8–7.2, 20–22% cocoa butter, $10.50 for 13.5-ounce tin. This "dark, reddish brown" Dutch-process cocoa made a "rich," "intense" cup of hot chocolate. Several panelists detected a "vanilla note" (label says .1% pure vanilla is added) as well as "an unusual sweetness." Brownies were "nearly black" and had a "roasted flavor" that some panelists enjoyed but others thought was "unbrownie-like." Dark color did not track with "mild" chocolate flavor. Available by mail from Williams-Sonoma (800-541-2233).

Valrhona Cocoa (France), pH 7.8–8.2, 21% cocoa butter, $6 per pound. This Dutch-process cocoa won the hot chocolate tasting but fared poorly among brownies. "Rich, dark brown" cocoa made "most flavorful" hot chocolate with "pleasant, bittersweet" quality. "Almost black" brownies were "disappointingly flat" with an "alkaline flavor" that was also described as "off-tasting" or "almost like coconuts." Most tasters thought chocolate flavor in brownies was "too tepid." Available by mail from New York Cake (800-942-2539).

Merckens Premium Natural Cocoa (Mansfield, Massachusetts), pH 5.4–5.8, 22–24% cocoa butter, $3 per pound. Hot chocolate made with this "fairly light" cocoa elicited two kinds of reaction: "pale and not very chocolaty" or "not as dark but sweet and mild." There was more agreement about brownies: "nice and chocolaty," "hints of fruit and coffee," and "excellent." Available by mail from the King Arthur Flour Baker's Catalogue (800-827-6836).

Hershey's Cocoa (Hershey, Pennsylvania), pH 5.3–5.9, 10–13% cocoa butter, $2.59 for 8-ounce tin. This popular natural cocoa is great for brownies but not for hot chocolate. "Very pale," "pinkish brown" cocoa made a "very mild," "weak" cup of hot chocolate. In contrast, brownies had "good chocolate flavor" that was described as "rich," "full," and "smooth." Available in supermarkets.

Droste Cocoa (Holland), pH not available, 20% cocoa butter, $3.85 for 8.8-ounce box. This "medium-color" Dutch-process cocoa was judged consistently in the two tastings. Hot chocolate was "rich even through the finish" with a "good, strong flavor" that reminded several tasters of coffee or nuts. Brownies were deemed "good but not great" with "decent chocolate flavor" that some panelists interpreted as "sort of bland." Available in supermarkets.

Bensdorp Royal Dutch Cocoa (Holland), pH 6.8–7.2, 23% cocoa butter, $3.78 per pound. "Good roasted flavor" in hot chocolate made with this "medium-dark" cocoa with some hints of "fruitiness." A few panelists thought this "off, fruity flavor" was out of place in brownies. Comments ranged from "burnt paper" and "hints of coconut" to "fairly chocolaty" and "decent." Available by mail from Dairy Fresh Chocolates (617-742-2639).

Guittard High-Fat Natural Cocoa (Burlingame, California), pH 5.3–5.9, 22–24% cocoa butter, $3.50 per pound. This very light cocoa made "very pale" hot chocolate. Flavor was described as "flat," with "odd floral notes." Brownies were more warmly received with comments like "intense" and "good cocoa flavor." Available by mail from Paradigm Foodworks (800-234-0250).

Merckens Premium Dutch Cocoa (Mansfield, Massachusetts), pH 7.1–7.5, 10–15% cocoa butter, $3 per pound. "Rich, dark color" of hot chocolate "tracked nicely with good chocolate flavor." Brownies were received with less enthusiasm with comments like "not very chocolaty" and "a little off." Available by mail from the King Arthur Flour Baker's Catalogue (800-827-6836).

COCOAS NOT RECOMMENDED

These cocoas finished at the bottom of both tastings.

Nestlé Cocoa (Glendale, California), pH 5.3, 11.5–13.5% cocoa butter, $2.19 for 8-ounce tin. This very light natural cocoa finished last among hot chocolates. Hot chocolate was "extremely pale," "harsh," "chemical-like," and "astringent." Brownies earned slightly better marks with comments like "ordinary but not bad" and "old-fashioned brownies." Available in supermarkets.

Ghirardelli Premium Unsweetened Cocoa (San Leandro, California), pH 5.0–5.6, 22–24% cocoa butter, $3.69 for 10-ounce tin. This popular "gourmet" brand of natural cocoa finished next-to-last in both tastings. Cocoa was deemed "fairly light" and made a "washed-out," "flat-tasting" hot chocolate "with little real chocolate flavor." Brownies were not much better with comments like "sweet but no chocolate flavor." Available in supermarkets.

Guittard Jersey Cocoa (Burlingame, California), pH 7.0–7.3, 22–24% cocoa butter, $3.50 per pound. This fairly light Dutch-process cocoa fared poorly in both tastings. Hot chocolate "doesn't taste much like chocolate," with "bitter aftertaste" and "acrid, licorice flavor." Brownies earned similarly negative comments, such as "metallic or tinny flavor," "peculiar," and "plain and bland." Available by mail from Paradigm Foodworks (800-234-0250).

For Kitchen Scales, Go Electronic

Digital electronic scales are far superior to traditional mechanical models—but high performance comes at a price.

~ BY JACK BISHOP WITH SANDY RAY ~

Americans are not accustomed to weighing ingredients, but weighing is essential for precision. Many European cookbooks list ingredients by weight, and professional bakers on both sides of the Atlantic weigh ingredients for best results.

One example proves the wisdom of weighing. Depending on the way that flour is packed into a measuring container, one cup can weigh less than four ounces or more than five ounces. An ounce may not seem like much. However, in a recipe with three cups of flour, the difference could be as much as three ounces, almost an extra cup.

You can walk into any housewares store in the mall and pick up a cheap scale for $10 or $15, but will it be any good? Is a bad scale worse than no scale at all? And what about dieters? More and more of us are trying to control portions. If that's your goal, you need a scale that can distinguish between four and five ounces of meat.

For these reasons, we decided to evaluate a number of kitchen scales on the market. There are two main types of scales for home use—mechanical and electronic. Each has its advantages and disadvantages.

Mechanical scales operate on a spring and lever system. When an item is placed on the scale, internal springs are compressed. The springs are attached to levers, which move a needle on the scale's display (a ruler with lines and numbers printed on a piece of paper and glued to the scale). The more the springs are compressed, the further the needle moves along the ruler. Mechanical kitchen scales are fairly cheap, costing as little as $10 and rarely more than $40.

Electronic kitchen scales rely on a "capacitive" system for measuring weight. These scales have two plates that are clamped at a fixed distance. The bottom plate is stationary; the top plate is not. When food is placed on the platform attached to the top plate, the distance between the plates changes slightly as the platform is depressed. The movement of the top plate (no more than a thousandth of an inch) causes a change in the flow of electricity in the scale's circuitry. This change is translated into a weight and expressed in numbers displayed on the face of the scale. Electronic scales start at around $50 (sometimes less on sale) but can cost more than $100.

Although we think a scale is an essential piece of kitchen equipment, we don't think there is any need to spend $100 or more. We limited our testing to widely available models from top manufacturers that cost less than $70. This ceiling allowed us to test a number of basic electronic scales as well as numerous mechanical scales.

Go Electronic

First and foremost a scale must be accurate. We used calibrated laboratory weights to judge accu-

---

RATING KITCHEN SCALES

Four electronic and nine mechanical scales were evaluated based on the following criteria and are listed in order of preference within each category. If cost is not a concern, we prefer the electronic scales, which are a must for precise measurement of ingredients for baking or dieting. The top three electronic scales are all recommended. These scales are fairly similar, although there are some differences in capacity, design, and price.

Among mechanical scales, only the top three scales are recommended, with varying degrees of enthusiasm. In general, precision must be weighed against capacity and ease of use when deciding among the mechanical scales.

Price: Suggested retail prices are listed. (*See* Sources and Resources, page 32, for mail-order outlets for top scales.)

Capacity: Scales with greater capacity (up to eleven pounds) are preferred over scales unable to measure the weight of a chicken or roast.

Measuring Increments: Smallest increment that the scale can measure. Scales able to measure smaller increments are preferred. Increments on some electronic scales become larger at higher weights; the figure listed is for low weights.

Accuracy: We used laboratory weights to measure the accuracy of each scale. Most scales (including all of the electronic models) were quite accurate although a few mechanical models seem to have been poorly calibrated at the factory.

Precision: Some scales are easier to read and hence better suited to precise measurements, especially of small quantities. For instance, scales with very closely spaced measuring lines were downgraded since it was hard to tell the difference between three and four ounces.

Design: Scales with large measuring areas are preferred since it is easier to weigh a large piece of meat or use your own bowl to hold loose ingredients. Scales with larger attachments (bowls or trays) for weighing ingredients are also preferred.

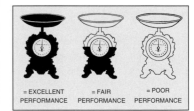

= EXCELLENT PERFORMANCE = FAIR PERFORMANCE = POOR PERFORMANCE

	Price	Capacity	Measuring Increments	Accuracy	Precision	Design
ELECTRONIC SCALES						
EKS Electronic Kitchen Scale 6005	$65	11 lb./5 kg.	¼ oz./5 grams			
Terraillon Electronic Food Scale BE 225	$50	4.4 lb./2 kg.	⅛ oz./2 grams			
Cuisinart Precision Electronic Scale SA 110	$70	6.6 lb./3 kg.	¼ oz./5 grams			
Soehnle Domino Electronic Kitchen Scale 8036	$56	4.4 lb./2 kg.	¹⁄₁₀ oz./2grams			
MECHANICAL SCALES						
EKS Kitchen Mix Bowl Scale 51	$19	11 lb./5 kg.	¼ oz./5 grams			
Soehnle Domo Baking & Domestic Scale 1310	$35	11 lb./5 kg.	1 oz/50 grams			

	Price	Capacity	Measuring Increments	Accuracy	Precision	Design
Mechanical Scales continued:						
Terraillon Automatic Scale BA 2000	$25	5 lb./2 kg.	½ oz./10 grams			
Guzzini SpaceSmart	$30	4.5 lb./2 kg.	1 oz./20 grams			
Soehnle Prima Baking & Domestic Scale 1309	$24	4.5 lb./2 kg.	1 oz./20 grams			
Terraillon Automatic Scale CB5	$30	10 lb./5 kg.	1 oz./20 grams			
Polder Household Scale 802	$22	11 lb./5 kg.	1 oz./100grams			
Braun Multipractic Scale UKW 1	$20	4.5 lb./2 kg.	1 oz./20 grams			
Polder Recipe Scale 1230	$12	4.5 lb./2 kg.	1 oz./20 grams			

racy and, with a few exceptions, found all the scales tested to be accurate. Precision, however, is another matter. The tightly spaced lines on most mechanical scales make it quite difficult to distinguish between four ounces and four and one-half ounces. All of the electronic scales can measure down to one-quarter ounce or less, but mechanical scales (with two exceptions) weigh in one-ounce increments. For this feature alone, electronic scales are the better choice.

There are several more good reasons to spend the extra money on an electronic scale. Weight is expressed in numbers on a digital display whereas with a mechanical scale, the user must judge where the needle falls, which is not always easy when the ruler is small and it measures with both grams and ounces.

The "add-and-weigh" feature touted on the packages of most mechanical scales is false hype. All of the electronic scales tested have a tare function (a small button) that resets the scale to zero when ingredients are already on the scale. On a mechanical scale, you must physically reset the scale to zero by turning the base or using the knob to bring the needle back down to zero. You can then add more ingredients and weigh them, but this "feature" is so cumbersome it's useless.

In addition, electronic scales are much more compact than mechanical scales (most are no more than an inch thick) and can be stored in a drawer. Electronic scales do require batteries, but all four models tested have an automatic shut-off feature to conserve energy.

The EKS electronic scale is our top choice, in part because of its eleven-pound capacity. We also liked several other scales with a maximum capacity of only five or six pounds. However, since these scales cannot weigh a large chicken or roast, they did not receive our top rating.

Mechanical Choices

If you decide that $50 or $60 is too much to spend on an electronic scale, there are better and worse mechanical scales. In fact, while three of the four electronic scales tested would be welcome additions to our kitchens, most of the mechanical scales tested are not worth the money. One recurring problem is how the scales are set to zero. On some models, the base of the scale must be rotated until the needle is lined up with the zero. On other models, a small knob (usually on the side or back of the scale) must be turned to bring the needle down to zero.

The two worst scales (the Braun Multipractic and Polder 1230) have very loose turning bases. The slightest motion and the needle is no longer set to zero. In effect, the needle has to be set back to zero before every use. This is not to suggest that all mechanical models with knobs are superior. We could accept either design as long as the base or knob was quite tight and somewhat difficult to move.

The EKS 51 is the best mechanical scale because of its eleven-pound capacity and extra-large mixing bowl attachment. A knob on the back sets the scale to zero and has enough tension to keep the needle still when the scale is jiggled. ∎

ELECTRONIC SCALES

For those willing to spend the money, the EKS Electronic is our top pick. Buyers looking for the best value should cosider the Terraillon Electronic. If ease of use and accuracy are lesser considerations than economy, the EKS 51 is the best of the mechanical scales.

BEST BUY

Terraillon Electronic: The base is a bit small on this well-made scale, but the price is certainly right.

BEST ELECTRONIC

EKS Electronic: This scale has everything: large capacity, roomy weighing base, and a big digital display.

Cuisinart: A solid choice with a large base and digital display. Switching from grams to ounces is difficult.

Soehnle Domino: Not recommended. Base and bowl too small; switching from grams to ounces is tricky.

MECHANICAL SCALES

BEST MECHANICAL

EKS 51: Given the low cost and accuracy, this high-capacity scale is a good choice.

Soehnle Domo: Not as accurate or precise as other top mechanicals but a good bet, especially for its large capacity.

Terraillon 2000: Reading through a magnifying lens is tricky but gives the most precision among mechanicals.

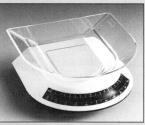

Guzzini SpaceSmart: Not very precise or accurate but still a cut above lower-rated scales.

Soehnle Prima: Scale has a tiny base with a large measuring cup attachment that is good for liquids but not solids.

Terraillon CB5: This fairly accurate scale is hard to read since numbers are so scrunched together.

Polder 802: Poorly made with a needle that must be unstuck after every use. Imprecise, especially in grams.

Braun Multipractic: The slightest jiggle gives an inaccurate measurement. Base and bowl are tiny.

Polder 1230: Extremely hard to read at low increments; base and weighing dish are too small. Not very accurate.

Ranking Inexpensive Merlots

Merlot is becoming increasingly popular, but it's a case of "buyer beware"; while there are certainly some good inexpensive merlots, bad ones abound.

∼ BY MARK BITTMAN ∼

Merlot is the grape that is being planted at the fastest rate in California—faster than cabernet sauvignon, chardonnay, and zinfandel (and even faster than viognier, the increasingly popular white grape, which will be the subject of a future *Cook's Illustrated* tasting). Theoretically at least, it's easy to explain why merlot is so popular: At its best, this noble red grape produces a sturdy, full-bodied wine, which, when made into some of the best wines of Bordeaux, commands top dollar in France and elsewhere.

But you could, of course, say the same of cabernet sauvignon, the red grape that forms the basis for the vast majority of great and very good red wines of Bordeaux. What's the difference?

The difference, it seems, is time. Cabernet sauvignon requires a good deal of time to mellow; great wines made from it are rarely drunk before they are ten years old. And even in California, home of softer wines, cabernet can be off-putting when it is young. Merlot, however, matures much more quickly, becoming approachable at a younger age; that's why it's the grape of choice for blending with cabernet, something the French began to appreciate about two hundred years ago. It smoothes out the rough edges and makes the wine more charming when young and somewhat fruitier when mature. Ten years ago (a little more, in some rare instances), the majority of California winemakers realized all of this; that's when Meritage wines—red wines that combined cabernet, merlot, and other grapes in the style of Bordeaux (see "Rating California's Best Reds," January/February 1995)—began to come into style.

At about the same time, it was recognized that "straight," that is, unblended, merlot could appeal to the American palette when it was quite young. This has had one important advantage to the winemaker: The shorter the storage time, the less money spent on holding the wine until it matures. In the case of merlot, the wine can be released in as little as eighteen months after the harvest. Many of the wines we tasted (in April 1995), including our winner, were from the 1993 vintage—which is not much more time than is required to *make* a credible red wine, let alone age it.

Merlot, therefore, can be a moneymaker, which explains not only why it is being planted in California but in Australia, Italy, Chile, and anywhere else the climate will support the grape. All of this helps to keep the price of merlot down, which makes it even more appealing to many consumers.

Unfortunately, as we discovered in our tasting

of fourteen under-$10 merlots from around the world, really great merlot cannot be made in such a short time. Although we found some more-than-decent wines selling for as little as $5, and a real champion at $7, they were far from great. And, unfortunately, we also uncovered a slew of wines that were mediocre and worse.

Clearly, we have recommendations to make when it comes to buying an inexpensive merlot; chances are good you'll be pleased with any of the top six wines, one of which costs just $5. But,

given that there are literally scores of merlots for sale in the $10-and-under price range, the unfortunate result of our tasting is that it failed to reveal any pattern. We cannot generalize that "California merlot is reliable" (some is quite good, but some is not); or "stick with names that you know" (three of our bottom four finishers were wines with well-known names); or "avoid the 1992 vintage" (both the 1992 and 1993 vintages did equally well). It's just too soon to begin to generalize about the new, inexpensive merlots. ■

1993 HACIENDA CLAIR DE LUNE

BLIND TASTING RESULTS

As usual, the wines in our tasting were judged by a panel made up of both wine professionals and amateur wine lovers. In the judging, seven points were awarded for each first-place vote; six for second; five for third; and so on. The wines were all purchased in the Northeast; prices will vary somewhat throughout the country. Within each category, wines are listed based on the number of points scored.

In general, Highly Recommended wines received few or no negative comments; Recommended wines had predominantly positive comments; and Not Recommended wines had few or no positive comments.

VERY HIGHLY RECOMMENDED

1993 Hacienda Clair de Lune, California, $7. A runaway winner, with nearly 50 percent more points than the second-place wine. Six out of ten tasters put this in first or second place; all tasters placed it in the top seven. Why? "Pretty nose, great fruit, lovely on the palate." This is the merlot most California winemakers would like to produce.

HIGHLY RECOMMENDED

1993 Forest Glen, California, $10. "Ripe, rich," wine with "too much oak," but "lovely and fruity."

1992 Glen Ellen, California, $5. Note the price; this wine was just beat out by the one above. "Nice balance—some spice, sweet with soft tannins," and "eminently drinkable."

1992 Fetzer Eagle Peak, California, $8.50. A hint of what serious, well-made, but inexpensive California merlot might taste like: "Varietal, with nice wood; more grip and finish than most." Could hold in bottle for a couple of years.

1992 Beautour, Napa Valley, $9. Generally liked by most, who appreciated its "soft tannins" and "good balance." This wine will probably improve over time.

1992 Napa Ridge, North Coast, $9. From the winery whose inexpensive pinot noir stunned our tasters in 1993. "Nice, round wine, with some structure and good fruit."

RECOMMENDED

1993 Rosemount Estate, South Australia, $10. Comments ranged from "pleasant, cherrylike, and fruity" to "little finish, little fruit, too simple."

1990 Château Jonqueyres Bordeaux Supérieur, $9. "Leathery, underwhelming fruit, but with a real nose" and "way too tannic with fruit hidden; could be good someday." Perhaps too "French" a wine to include here.

1993 Grand Cru, California, $8. "Stinky nose, quite vegetal," but "nice structure" and "very classy wine."

1992 Mezza Corona, Trentino, $7. Our lone Italian entry. "Subtle, spicy, with good mouth feel," but somehow "dusty" and "sour."

NOT RECOMMENDED

1992 Concha y Toro, Chile, $5.50. Its one admirer found it "subtle and pleasant." Most detected a "garbagey" aroma, and some thought it downright "putrid."

1993 Sutter Home, California, $6. One taster found this wine "nice and fruity." Others said it had "little fruit," "no tannins," or "no flavor."

N.V. Vendange, California, $5. "Odd," "sour," "thin," and "vegetal." "Tastes like motor oil."

1993 Duboeuf, Vin de Pays D'Oc, $6. Although most found this "bitter, hot" or "insubstantial," some credited it with a "pleasant, inoffensive" character. Such comments did not earn points.

BOOK
REVIEWS

Book of Tarts
Maury Rubin
William Morrow, $20

Maury Rubin is a television producer-turned-pastry chef who operates the City Bakery in New York. By combining a penchant for fresh seasonal fruits with an equally modern philosophy of minimalist, avant-garde design (sorry, no piped roses or glazed fruit), Rubin has tried to reinvent traditional French pastry, albeit with a humorous American twist. It works—his tarts taste like Paris but look like Frank Lloyd Wright.

Rubin has assembled forty of his favorite recipes, all of which make six individual tarts. Individual tarts may seem like extra work (and they are), but the results are impressive. And, as anyone who has tried to cut up a nine-inch tart filled with custard knows, individual tarts are much easier to serve.

Rubin offers easy-to-follow instructions for the shells. I tried three versions—Standard Tart Dough, Chocolate Tart Dough, and Candied Ginger Tart Dough—and all were excellent. The standard recipe (the basis for most of the others) is the most forgiving pastry dough I have ever handled—it never sticks, can be stretched extremely thin, and can even be rerolled.

The tart fillings are extremely basic—usually nothing more than a few complementary ingredients. I was wowed by Summer Fruit Tart with Lemon Cream. The simple lemon custard took ten minutes to prepare, and the pairing of blackberries and honeydew melon is striking. Sake-Spiked Plum Tart with Ginger is an inventive combination, perfectly matched with the Candied Ginger Tart Dough. The World's First Stuffed Raspberry Tart (melted bittersweet chocolate is piped into raspberries, which are piled on top of lightly sweetened whipped cream) is witty but simple.

The only disappointment was Chocolate Custard Infused with Ethiopian Coffee Beans. The ingredients seemed right—coffee-infused heavy cream, bittersweet chocolate, and egg yolks—but the technique was flawed. The custard was too runny and needed to be cooked for a minute or two after the yolks were added.

All in all, though, Rubin has put together an impressive collection that offers plenty of fine baking for the patient home cook. Best of all, his pastry philosophy seems in step with the times—take the best ingredients and then present them in the simplest but most pleasing manner possible.

—*Jack Bishop*

In a Shaker Kitchen:
100 Recipes from the Shaker Tradition
Norma MacMillan
Simon & Schuster, $25

Few groups in history were more orderly, fastidious, and quality-conscious than the Shakers, the English-turned-American sect whose simply designed furniture epitomizes nineteenth-century Americana. (Few groups held odder beliefs, either; the Shakers practiced celibacy and, as a not very surprising result of this behavior, have all but died out.)

Shaker food was simple but varied, and two aspects of it made it superior to that of much of the rest of the country: One, unlike most other farmers, who took their best products to market and lived on what was left, the Shakers cooked their prime ingredients. And two, Shaker cooking, for whatever reason—perhaps because so many minds worked on each dish (they lived and cooked communally)—was inventive.

For this reason, it still seems fresh and appealing, as is demonstrated in Norma MacMillan's glossy, full-color book, which contains not only near-perfect food photography using Shaker implements as props, but a handful of historic photos and drawings. In looks, *In a Shaker Kitchen* is top-notch.

The basic but appealing recipes work, too. Chicken Breasts with Fried Apples took me less than thirty minutes to prepare, and the addition of apple cider, lemon zest, and a bit of heavy cream made it a luxurious weeknight dish. Potato Cakes with Rosemary is the type of side dish you now see at tony restaurants all over the country; the recipe itself is perfect. Scented Leaf Rolls, "scented" with butter and herbs, were sensational although I wish that food processor directions were included for the dough.

Other recipes were equally satisfying. The lone downside to this book—that many of the recipes (which are relatively few in number to begin with) can be found readily elsewhere—is actually not as damning as it might seem. Apple Pie, for example, although quite simple, contains a bit of rose water, a nice, different touch; Rice Pudding is topped with a delicious Boiled Cider Syrup; Meat Loaf contains a load of fresh herbs; and so on.

This is a simple, traditional cookbook that demonstrates once again that real old-fashioned American cooking is far better than we were led to believe during the middle of this century.

—*Mark Bittman*

The New Southern Cook
John Martin Taylor
Bantam, $27.95

I received the galley release of John Martin Taylor's *The New Southern Cook* about the time that George Wallace publicly apologized for attacking the Civil Rights movement in Alabama thirty years ago. Wallace's public penance clearly marked the death of the Old South; coincidentally, here was Taylor arguing persuasively that a culinary New South is on the move. In his introductory essay, Taylor calls the new South "international, the new melting pot." He talks of free-range veal farms in Virginia, truffle sites and goat's milk dairies in Georgia, and sturgeon harvesting/caviar processing further down the coast.

Although Taylor's introduction argues dramatic culinary change in the South, many of the recipes do not support this thesis. Celeriac and Fennel Soup with Italian Sausage; Cucumber-Yogurt Salad; Tabbouleh; and Roasted Pepper, Onion, and Endive Salad suggest only that Southerners have developed a taste for Mediterranean and Middle Eastern food like the rest of the country. Furthermore, recipes like The Best Cornbread, The Best Grits, Country-Fried Steak with Mashed Potatoes and Gravy, and Fried Chicken offer little evidence of any melting in the Southern pot. This is unalloyed Old South.

Even though they might not be evidence of a cultural change, some of Taylor's recipes are strong. The Best Cornbread as well as The Best Grits were some of the best I'd ever sampled. Hoppin' John Salad, the traditional dish of black-eyed peas and rice turned into a salad, was fresh and flavorful with jalapeños, red onion, fresh herbs, and lemon vinaigrette.

But other recipes were off. Goat Cheese Biscuits were dry, and Chicken Pie, flavored almost entirely with onions and boiled eggs, wasn't worth eating. In Spicy Shrimp and Asparagus, a salad for four, Taylor instructs us to toss in two cups of mayonnaise—an obvious error.

When George Wallace sings "We Shall Overcome," it's fairly clear the Old South is dead. What the New South will become, however, seems less than clear. John Martin Taylor tempts us with a promising introduction that is not borne out in his recipes. His informative essay with a few supporting recipes would have made a much more effective magazine article than a book. ■

—*Pam Anderson*

SOURCES
AND RESOURCES

Most of the ingredients and materials needed for the recipes in this issue are available at your local supermarket, gourmet store, or kitchen supply shop. The following are mail-order sources for special items. The prices listed below are current as of press time but do not include shipping or handling unless otherwise indicated. Contact companies directly to confirm up-to-date prices and availability.

BEST KITCHEN SCALES
We tested thirteen electronic and mechanical scales for the story on page 28. The EKS Electronic Kitchen Scale 6005 has a large weighing surface, an eleven-pound capacity, and easy-to-read digital display. This top-rated scale is available at Williams-Sonoma stores nationwide for $65. If you do not live near one of these stores, call the company's customer service department (800-541-1262), and it will put you in touch with a store that can ship a scale to you. Scales are not sold through the company's catalog division. The second-rated Terraillon Electronic Food Scale BE 225 retails for $50 but is available at a discount of $42.50 from A Cook's Wares catalog (412-846-9490). A Cook's Wares also discounts the third-rated Cuisinart Precision Electronic Scale SA 110 from its regular retail price of $70 to $65. Although mechanical scales are less precise than electronic versions, there were several clear winners. The top-rated EKS Kitchen Mix Bowl Scale 51 is accurate and has an eleven-pound capacity. It is available at Williams-Sonoma stores nationwide and costs $19. The second-rated Soehnle Domo Baking and Domestic Scale 1310 is available from Zabar's (212-787-2000) for a discounted price of $26.98. The third-rated Terraillon Automatic Scale BA 2000 is available from A Cook's Wares for a discount of $21.30.

SPRINGFORM PAN
The cheesecake recipes on page 8 must be prepared in a nine-inch springform pan. We recommend that you use a springform pan with a very tight seal and sturdy spring latch. The Sur La Table catalog (800-243-0852) carries an especially practical nine-inch springform pan that comes with two different bottom inserts. The flat bottom is perfect for baking a cheesecake or layer cake. The fluted tube bottom can be used to bake a coffee cake or a kugelhopf. This German-made pan costs $9.95 and has a large, heavy-duty side spring that keeps the pan from leaking even when it is placed in a water bath.

CORNMEAL BY MAIL
Cornbread (see page 20) has the best taste and texture when made with stone-ground or water-ground cornmeal that contains some of the germ. Since stone-ground and water-ground cornmeal contain much of the germ, they have a higher oil content than supermarket brands and tend to go rancid more quickly. Store these whole cornmeals in the refrigerator or freezer to prolong freshness. The King Arthur Flour Baker's Catalogue (800-827-6836) carries whole yellow, blue, and white cornmeal, all ground with the germ. The cornmeal comes in two-pound bags and costs $2.35 for yellow cornmeal, $3.35 for blue cornmeal, and $4.25 for white cornmeal. King Arthur also sells whole yellow and blue corn, which you can grind yourself if you have your own grain mill.

MAIL-ORDER DUCK
Bruce Cost's duck recipe on page 10 can be successfully made with any supermarket duck. However, many supermarkets do little duck business and do not have a fast turnover. You may want to order a duck from your butcher or from a specialty meat and poultry company like D'Artagnan (800-327-8246) to guarantee freshness and high quality. D'Artagnan sells whole Long Island-style Pekin ducks (which is what Cost recommends for his recipe) for $1.95 per pound plus shipping. A D'Artagnan Pekin duck weighs about five pounds, has never been frozen, and is raised without stimulants or chemicals. D'Artagnan also sells Mallard ducks ($25 each), a farm-raised variety of the same breed found in the wild. This rare duck has very dark meat, weighs about two pounds, and is available only during the fall. D'Artagnan also sells Muscovy ducks ($4.95 per pound), large birds that can weigh up to eight pounds, and a Moulard duck ($4.15 per pound), a cross between a Pekin and Muscovy duck that weighs about eight pounds. Moulards are known for their especially meaty red breasts. Their legs are well suited to making duck confit.

ASIAN SPICES
The duck recipe on page 10 requires a number of spices sold in Asian grocery or gourmet stores. These spices are also available by mail from Penzeys Spice House (P.O. Box 1448, Waukesha, WI 53187; 414-574-0277). Penzeys sells whole star anise, which has a strong, spicy, licorice flavor that works nicely with the duck. Four ounces costs $7.79. The company also carries Szechuan peppercorns. Although not a true peppercorn, this reddish, dried berry has an aromatic, mildly peppery quality. Penzeys sells four ounces of the peppercorns for $4.49. The final ingredient in the spice rub for the duck is cassia bark. Cassia is actually a type of cinnamon native to Southeast Asia; it has a strong, sweet flavor. True cinnamon comes from Sri Lanka, has a more complex flavor than cassia, and is generally a little less potent. Penzeys sells several types of cinnamon, including Chinese cassia cinnamon, which would be a good choice for the spice rub. It is sold in one-half-inch chunks and is stronger and spicier than the variety sold in supermarkets, most of which is also cassia. Four ounces of Chinese cassia costs $2.99.

LARGE CASSEROLE DISH
The Chicken in the Pot recipes on page 19 should be prepared in a pan that is wide enough to permit all the chicken to be sautéed at one time and deep enough to hold all the vegetables and liquid. An added plus is that it's an attractive pan that can be brought to the table. Enameled cast-iron cookware such as Le Creuset meets all of these criteria. This French cookware is thick enough to ensure even heating, and the bright, enameled exteriors are suited to the stovetop as well as the table. A Cook's Wares catalog (412-846-9490) sells Le Creuset cookware at a discount. A 6.5-quart oval oven (which can be used to prepare any of the chicken recipes) retails for $200 but is on sale for $116. Other Le Creuset pans are also discounted, some up to 55 percent.

MELON BALLER
A melon baller is the best tool for partially coring apples for the baked apple recipes on page 13. We especially like the long, oval scoop on the French melon baller carried by the J.B. Prince Company (212-302-8611). This plain oval scoop (item number D309-A) has a fairly long handle and a scoop that measures about one and one-quarter inches long. This melon baller costs $8.40.

BOUTIQUE APPLES
Among supermarket apples, Golden Delicious are the best choice for the baked apple recipes on page 13. However, many specialty varieties available at farm stands or local orchards are just as good, if not better. We particularly like Northern Spy, Cortland, and Baldwin apples when baked. If you cannot find any of these varieties in your area, they are available by mail from Dwight Miller Orchards (R.D. 2, P.O. Box 835, Putney, VT 05346; 802-254-9158). This Vermont orchard grows about fifty apple varieties. Apples are packed in boxes and sold in increments of fifteen. A minimum order of fifteen apples costs between $16 and $18 (depending on the mailing address) and includes shipping. An order of forty-five apples costs between $36.50 and $42.50. ∎

**FISH FILLET WITH
PROVENÇAL TOMATO SAUCE** page 24

BRIOCHE PLUM TART
page 16

**PITA BREAD SALAD WITH
CUCUMBERS, CHERRY TOMATOES,
AND FRESH HERBS** page 14

**RICH AND
CREAMY CHEESECAKE**
page 8

**CHICKEN IN THE POT WITH CARROTS,
MUSHROOMS, AND THYME** page 19

**TWICE-COOKED DUCK WITH
ASIAN FLAVORINGS** page 10

Brandied Fall Fruits

Peel and core four slightly underripe pears and two firm apples, then cut them lengthwise into slices 1 inch thick. Stem one small bunch purple and one small bunch green grapes. Combine 3 cups brandy and 3 cups sugar in large, nonreactive saucepan and bring to boil over high heat. Reduce heat to low and simmer, stirring, until sugar dissolves, 2 to 3 minutes. Add fruit and simmer additional 2 to 3 minutes, or until fruit is tender. Remove fruit from mixture and pack into glass jars, adding enough hot syrup to cover, and put on lids. Refrigerate at least 4 weeks to meld flavors, opening lids briefly every few days. Will keep about 4 months in refrigerator.

NUMBER SEVENTEEN

DECEMBER 1995

COOK'S
ILLUSTRATED

Perfect Prime Rib
Sear It First, Then
Roast It Long and Low

Smoked Salmon
Taste Test
Inexpensive American
Brand Beats High-
Priced Competition

Rating And Using
Electric Pasta
Makers
Top Models Rated
Plus Tips and Recipes

The Best Pecan Pie
Pralinelike Flavor and
Crisp Crust

RUSTIC HOLIDAY
STUFFINGS
•
OLD-FASHIONED
GINGERBREAD
•
RATING PINK SPARKLERS
•
BEST POTATO GRATIN

$4.00 U.S./$4.95 CANADA

TABLE
OF CONTENTS

"Pears and Nuts"

ILLUSTRATION BY
BRENT WATKINSON

Smoked Salmon on Endive Boats, adapted from *Williams-Sonoma Hors d'Oeuvres & Appetizers* (Time-Life, 1992)

ILLUSTRATION BY
CAROL FORTUNATO

COOK'S
ILLUSTRATED

Publisher and Editor CHRISTOPHER KIMBALL

Consulting Editor MARK BITTMAN

Senior Editor JOHN WILLOUGHBY

Food Editor PAM ANDERSON

Senior Writer JACK BISHOP

Articles Editor ANNE TUOMEY

Editorial Production Director MAURA LYONS

Assistant Managing Editor TRICIA O'BRIEN

Assistant Editor ADAM RIED

Copy Editor GARY PFITZER

Test Cook VICTORIA ROLAND

Art Director MEG BIRNBAUM

Food Stylist MARIE PIRAINO

Special Projects Designer AMY KLEE

Marketing Director ADRIENNE KIMBALL

Circulation Director ELAINE REPUCCI

Ass't Circulation Manager JENNIFER L. KEENE

Circulation Coordinator JONATHAN VENIER

Circulation Assistant C. MARIA PANNOZZO

Production Director JAMES MCCORMACK

Project Coordinator SHEILA DATZ

Production Coordinator PAMELA SLATTERY

Systems Administrator MATTHEW FRIGO

Production Artist KEVIN MOELLER

Vice President JEFFREY FEINGOLD

Controller LISA A. CARULLO

Accounting Assistant MANDY SHITO

Office Manager TONYA ESTEY

Special Projects FERN BERMAN

Cook's Illustrated (ISSN 1068-2821) is published bimonthly by Boston Common Press Limited Partners, 17 Station Street, P.O. Box 569, Brookline, MA 02147-0569. Copyright 1995 Boston Common Press Limited Partners. Second-class postage paid at Boston, MA, and additional mailing offices, USPS #012487. For list rental information, please contact Direct Media, 200 Pemberwick Road, Greenwich, CT 06830; (203) 532-1000. Editorial office: 17 Station Street, P.O. Box 569, Brookline, MA 02147-0569; (617) 232-1000, FAX (617) 232-1572, email: cooksill@aol.com. Editorial contributions should be sent or emailed to: Editor, *Cook's Illustrated*. We cannot assume responsibility for manuscripts submitted to us. Submissions will be returned only if accompanied by a large self-addressed stamped envelope. Subscription rates: $24.95 for one year; $45 for two years; $65 for three years. (Canada: add $3 per year; all other countries: add $12 per year.) Postmaster: Send all new orders, subscription inquiries, and change of address notices to *Cook's Illustrated*, P.O. Box 7444, Red Oak, IA 51591-0444. Single copies: $4 in U.S., $4.95 in Canada and other countries. Back issues available for $5 each. PRINTED IN THE U.S.A.

EDITORIAL

FACES FROM THE PAST

My introduction to New York's meat district was ten years ago, when I filmed a video on butchering starring Jack Ubaldi, the founder of the Florence Meat Market.

At that time, West 14th Street was the center of the universe for meat wholesalers. Walk past the thick plastic flaps at the entrance of any establishment and you were hit with a blast of chilled air and a faint sweet-and-sour undercurrent, not unpleasant but always a reminder of the trade. Forequarters and hindquarters hung on giant hooks

CHRISTOPHER KIMBALL

gliding on overhead rails, moving into line, waiting for the butchers with narrow, well-honed knives held like daggers. The floor was concrete and almost frozen with a slick layer of water, fat, and bits of meat. On this stage, the butchers moved about with a determined but casual rhythm. The faces of those men were more developed than those you see uptown—expressive features set hard by time and experience.

I recently returned to 14th Street. Today, the wholesalers are mostly gone, replaced by the same monotonous crates of Kry-O-Vac cuts that you see all over the East Coast, boxed and shipped directly from Omaha. The Eastern Meat Market, one of the few survivors, is still breaking down kosher meat with a small crew. The shell of the loin with the chine bone is now "175"—a numerical designation that has taken the place of the local vernacular. Say goodbye to club steaks, Newport steaks, franken, deckel. They will be forgotten over time, just as we can no longer name the different types of horse-drawn carriages—cabriolets, coupes, phaetons, and surreys.

Our small town in Vermont is also changing. When I walk our property, I find stone walls and cellar holes way up in the woods, put there by nineteenth-century sheep farmers. At the height of the town's population, we had seven schools, two stores, three churches, two sawmills, and an assortment of factories making clothespins, oyster barrels, brush backs, and cheese, plus a gristmill, a flaxmill, and two blacksmith shops. Today, none of these buildings are standing except the Methodist church (we outlasted the Congregationalists) and the number two schoolhouse, which is no longer in use. The population has dropped from 1,187 in 1810 to about 250 full-time residents today.

But I miss the faces most of all. It is said that you can't do anything about the face you're born with, but you make the face you die with. Today, faces are homogenized and soft, the highlights removed. But back in the 1950s there were still faces that looked like coarse woodcuts—open, expressive faces, some aggressive, others impish, some sly, and others severe. I will never forget the face of old Fred Woodcock, with his empty stare and drooping handlebar mustache, and the shifty, squinty-eyed look of Herbie the hired hand, who showed up in the summers for haying. He died two years ago up in Rutland—found frozen in the cab of a parked semi.

Each year we lose a bit of our culinary past as well. Who knows the difference between a buckle and a grunt, a fool and a pandowdy, a crisp and a cobbler? If you'd walked across this country a hundred years ago, you probably wouldn't have eaten the same biscuit twice. Some would be beaten, some made with cream, some with butter, and others with buttermilk. Today you can walk into any fancy eatery from San Diego to Maine and get the same plate of grilled swordfish or the same repertoire of fresh pastas. We have come a long way from the ersatz food of the 1960s, but it seems that cooking is no longer a grassroots movement born of necessity. It's a top-down cuisine, invented by food writers, chefs, and restaurateurs, marketed by food magazines and cooking shows.

Last summer I was teaching our six-year-old daughter to ride a bike. After endless unsuccessful outings, she hopped on one last time and took off unexpectedly down the dirt road, hair lifted by the wind, face ablaze with anticipation, quickly rounding the corner by our neighbor's horse barn. For a moment, I stood there frozen, realizing that something had ended. Part of her childhood was now over, her face already much changed from the early snapshots in the family album. I told myself that it isn't her childhood that needs to be preserved, it's the joyful intimacy that should remain in all things from parents to kids, from cooks to food, from butchers to their trade. I silently wished her Godspeed and good fortune and slowly walked down the road, eyes stinging with tears, hoping I would hear her call out my name one last time as she rode away. ∎

NOTES

FROM READERS

MORE ON DUALIT TOASTERS

In your March/April 1995 "Notes from Readers," a reader commented on how disappointed he was with the performance of the Dualit toaster that you had panned in an earlier article on toasters. I have more bad news for you: They are being recalled.

I work part-time at Williams-Sonoma, and we have received notice from Waring, the U.S. distributor for Dualit, that there are potentially serious problems with the Electronic Dualit Toasters (models CTS2E/DOM-11EA36 and CTS4E/DOM-11EA42). According to the letter, any interruption in power to the toaster (such as a power failure or even just quickly unplugging and replugging the toaster) may cause the toaster to turn itself on and stay on until someone resets the timer or unplugs the toaster.

Customers can contact the store where they purchased the toaster or work out a repair/return plan with Waring by calling 800-831-3960.

JANINE SCIARAPPA
Boston, MA

TRADITIONAL ROESTI

Having grown up and learned to cook (home-style) in the German-speaking part of Switzerland, I would like to comment on your roesti article in the January/February 1995 issue. Your piece is a good overview on the preparation of this traditional Swiss German dish. But I have to take exception to the statement "don't bother to precook the potatoes." Yes, you can make something roestilike using raw potatoes, but it won't be traditional roesti. There is a clear texture and flavor difference between the two methods that is hard to describe but easy to taste. The author calls the cake made from raw potatoes "moist" and having a "fresh potato flavor." Most Swiss probably would not be so complimentary and would call it "raw-tasting." Traditional roesti made from boiled and cooled-down potatoes (they're easier to grate when cold and seem to absorb a bit less butter) are creamier in texture and mellower in taste.

PETER BAENZIGER
Kalamazoo, MI

DUSTING BREAD WITH CORNMEAL

I read your bread article in the January/February 1995 issue with delight. Long have I wondered how to produce thick-crusted, chewy peasant breads. You recommend spreading your pizza paddle or bread peel with cornmeal (and it has to be a lot for this wet dough) to make sliding the dough onto the baking stone easier. The only problem is that cornmeal goes flying everywhere, burning in the oven and setting off my smoke alarm. To avoid this, I sprinkle cornmeal on the dough before I invert it onto the paddle. I then have the right amount and most of it sticks to the dough, rather than flying into my oven.

MICHAEL WHITE
Missoula, MT

Our kitchen testers loved your idea, which does solve the annoying problem of ending up with a cornmeal coating on the bottom of the oven. This trick is especially helpful with our sticky country bread dough, but we use it with pizza dough as well as other breads.

CLEANING BURR COFFEE GRINDERS

If you use a burr-type coffee grinder (as recommended in your article on coffee grinders in the January/February 1995 issue), the cogs and other parts eventually become clogged with oil from the coffee beans. To clean off the accumulated oil, I simply grind raw rice in the coffee grinder. Of course, discard any coffee that comes out as well as the oil-tinged rice.

ELAINE HOFBERG
Los Angeles, CA

We found that running about one-quarter cup of long-grain rice through our burr grinder was enough to loosen and remove the residual coffee grounds stuck in the cogs. The rice turns into a fine gray powder, a sign that it is picking up dark grounds as it works its way through the grinder. Since some rice may be left behind, we recommend running a few tablespoons of old coffee beans through the cogs just to clear out any remaining rice particles. Your grinder is now clean and ready to start grinding fresh beans.

ANOTHER WAY TO COOK POLENTA

I enjoyed your article on polenta (January/February 1995 issue) and would like to share another nontraditional method that I found in the Monday to Friday Cookbook *by Michele Urvater (Workman, 1991, revised 1995). This method requires very little work and does not take nearly as long as the double-boiler method you describe.*

Urvater recommends heating some olive oil (about one-quarter cup per cup of cornmeal although I'm sure less would work) over medium heat. Add the cornmeal and stir for about one minute to coat and toast the grain. Then add water (four cups per cup of cornmeal) and whisk as it comes to a boil. Once it simmers, cover and lower the heat. The polenta should be done in about twenty minutes.

I realize this method may be "disqualified" due to the addition of olive oil, but it sure works well. It's very easy, and the polenta behaves like polenta cooked any other way—mushy at first, firm when cooled.

JENNY BRYAN
Irvine, CA

Adding olive oil to the polenta makes it less likely to form lumps, so the method you describe yields lovely polenta. As you suggested, we found that as little as one tablespoon of oil per cup of cornmeal was enough to coat the granules and keep them from lumping together. A few thoughts, though. Even at this reduced level, the oil can still be tasted. Although this might be welcome in some dishes, it may seem odd if you want to add butter and cheese, for instance. Also, polenta made with oil is fairly soft and does not firm up quite as well as polenta made with just cornmeal, water, and salt.

COOKING BRISKET IN A FOIL POUCH

Your article on beef brisket (March/April 1995) was fascinating. I have been cooking brisket for thirty-five years with raves and kudos. My method for slow-cooking brisket in a foil pouch is as follows: I trim a whole or center-cut brisket. I then lay out two pieces of heavy-duty aluminum foil and join them together by folding over the edges three times. I then add another sheet of foil on top of the seam to make sure that the liquid does not leak out. I then place the brisket on top of the foil and add seasonings (soy sauce, Worcestershire sauce, garlic powder, ground celery seed, and any other spices I feel like). I then carefully pour red wine around the outside of the meat and wrap up the brisket tightly. (I use what I call a "drug-store wrap" because a tight seal is the key to this process.) I place the foil-wrapped brisket in a 300-degree oven and bake for six to seven hours. I remove the brisket from the oven and let it rest for thirty minutes. I then open the package and cut the meat across the grain. I improve the gravy and serve.

The whole point of this "no-peek" method is to steam/roast the brisket in a tightly sealed environment for perfect tenderness and taste. I have never used a thermometer since piercing the foil would defeat the logic of this method. Anyway, it's a guaranteed winner.

PAT VANDEVER
Scottsdale, AZ

We tried this method in our kitchen, using our original seasonings. The meat was extremely tender and tasty, although a tad on the dry side (a problem with every brisket recipe, it seems). We found that this foil pouch method works best if the pouch is built on top of a baking sheet. We laid out the foil as you suggested over a large baking sheet, added our meat, seasonings, and liquid, then sealed up the packet. As you note, heavy-duty foil is essential. We tried a thinner foil and found that the pouch leaked badly.

CLEANING A BLENDER

*I*n the March/April 1995 issue you published a tip for cleaning a food processor bowl. This prompted me to send the following tip for cleaning a blender. This trick really works, cleaning even underneath the blade.

Begin by filling the dirty blender container one-half to three-quarters full with water and then add a little dishwashing detergent. Put the container back on the blender stand, cover, and blend. Remove the container from the stand, rinse with hot water, and you've got a clean blender.

MARGARET MCNEIL
Memphis, TN

BRISKET UNDER PRESSURE

*A*s a retired fluvial hydraulic engineer, your scientific article on cooking brisket aroused my curiosity. Why can't we have our cake and eat it too? I wondered what could be done with cooking under pressure, say fifteen pounds per square inch. This will produce almost exactly the author's "reduced" oven temperature of 250 degrees. It is quite possible that pressure will increase the rate of conversion of collagen to gelatin, and, more importantly, it will decrease the rate of moisture loss. Of course, there is no way of establishing the initial high temperature in your recipe of 500 degrees (about 665 psi) so it will take somewhat longer to reach the internal temperature plateau of 160 degrees.

I tried my theory in a double-boiler pressure cooker because I did not want to dilute the potential gravy with the steam water. This was particularly pertinent as I had no experience using a pressure cooker for very long cooking times—so I did not know what my steam water loss might be. To be safe, I used an excessive amount of water in the bottom of a double boiler that had lost its handle. It fit neatly into my Presto pressure cooker.

I seared a small first-cut brisket (2.15 pounds) and deglazed the pan with red wine. I then placed the brisket and juices in the inner pan and assem-

bled the pressure cooker. I cooked the brisket for two hours and then cooled the pan until the pressure valve opened. The meat was quite tender but still a little on the dry side. I think this process has real potential but needs fine tuning.

RICHARD SHAW
Richmond, TX

FRESH WATER FOR TEA

A frequent kitchen warning is to use only freshly boiled water for tea because it "still has the oxygen in it." But I thought that all the free oxygen has fled the water by the time it reaches 200 degrees. What's the correct thinking on this?

CHRISTOPHER GRAY
New York, NY

Freshly boiled water from the cold (not hot) tap should be used to make tea because it does contain more dissolved oxygen than either water from the hot tap or reheated, previously boiled water. You are right that as water heats, it loses oxygen. However, this is a gradual process that is accelerated in water that has been sitting in a hot water heater for some time or water that has already been boiled. Water with less oxygen will make tea that is a little flat tasting. The difference is quite small but may be noticeable to real tea connoisseurs. Another reason not to use hot tap water or reheated water is that the water may pick up some off flavors from a hot water heater or a tea kettle over time. You may even pick up some metallic notes in your tea.

LAMB SHANK TIPS

I would like to offer additional techniques and tips on the excellent article by Steve Johnson on "Braising Lamb Shanks" that appeared in the January/February 1995 issue. When buying lamb shanks, ask the butcher to "crack" or cut the shank bones. This serves two purposes: First, it allows the marrow to be released and flavor the sauce; second, smaller shank pieces allow better

fitting and arranging in the pan. Another good idea is to place the shanks in the freezer for a short time before trimming. When the shanks are partially frozen, it is easier to shave off the exterior fat and white fell.

I brown my shanks on an outdoor grill over mesquite charcoal. I prefer grilling over browning in the pan for two reasons. First, on the grill, the mesquite charcoal smoke permeates and flavors the meat; second, extra fat is expelled from the meat, falls, and drains on the charcoals, thus avoiding further contact between the meat and dissolved fat. This procedure renders the shanks practically fat-free.

The final step in the meat preparation before braising is to microwave the browned shanks for five minutes in white wine. I use one cup of wine for every four or five shanks. This process further tenderizes the shanks from within.

ZE'EV VERED
Moraga, CA

Thank you for your insightful tips. We asked our butcher to crack several lamb shanks—he sawed through the bones but left the meat attached to form elbowlike pieces. Although we couldn't really taste or see any extra marrow in the sauce, this technique certainly makes sense as a good way to release this flavorful lamb essence.

We also tried freezing the shanks before trimming the fat. We found a period of thirty to sixty minutes was enough to firm up the fat, making it easier to remove. Next we tried browning the shanks on the grill. You certainly end up with less fat in the pan with this method. However, lighting a grill fire for just five minutes of browning seems like a lot of work, especially since grilling for such a short time doesn't impart all that much flavor. Of course, if you have an indoor or gas grill, the effort would be worthwhile, especially for those concerned with removing as much fat as possible from the shanks.

Lastly, we liked the effect that microwaving the shanks in wine had on the meat. This quick poaching makes the meat even more tender. ■

WHAT IS IT?

I have had this knife with a long, very flexible blade in my kitchen for years, and I am not sure how to use it. The blade is quite thin and bends much more than any other knife I own. The edge of the blade has hollowed-out ovals. Any ideas what this knife does and why it has this funny design?

JUDY JOHNSON
Chicago, IL

You own a special smoked salmon slicer. All smoked salmon slicers have long, thin blades that are extremely flexible. This flexibility allows you to bend the knife and glide the blade along the skin while keeping your hand in a comfortable position. The salmon slicer that you own has a special added feature: a granton (or scalloped) edge. The tiny, oval-shaped, hollowed-out areas on the blade minimize the surface area of the knife that comes in contact with the fish. Since smoked salmon is so oily and sticky, the less surface area that actually touches the fish, the less tearing of the delicate flesh that will occur. To slice smoked salmon, slide the blade parallel to the work surface to make your cuts. Slices should be so thin that you can see the blade of the knife through them. Professional Cutlery Direct (800-859-6994) carries a number of smoked salmon slicers, including a Forschner slicer with a twelve-inch, granton-edged blade and molded plastic handle. This knife costs $39.95.

Quick Tips

FOLDING EGG WHITES GENTLY

Folding egg whites uniformly into other ingredients without deflating the whites is always a challenge. Clara Palton of Duluth, Minnesota, suggests this easy, quick method.

1. Fit a handheld mixer with only one beater, set it at the lowest speed, and beat the egg whites into the mixture with a folding motion.

2. This method is thorough but gentle enough to keep the whites from deflating.

MAKING THIN SUGAR COOKIES

Marla Hagerty of Huntsville, Alabama, suggests that, for very thin, crispy sugar cookies, you roll out the dough on a cookie sheet covered with parchment paper, cut the cookies with the desired cutter, top with another sheet of parchment paper, and freeze. When ready to bake, pop out the shapes like paper dolls.

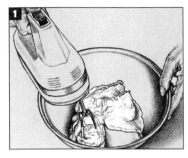

FILLING STUFFED MANICOTTI

Getting the filling into stuffed shells or manicotti can be a tedious and frustrating chore. After she had a baby, Nancy Hughes of Jacksonville, North Carolina, discovered a tool that makes this task easy.

1. Fill the bowl of a long-handled infant spoon with the desired filling.

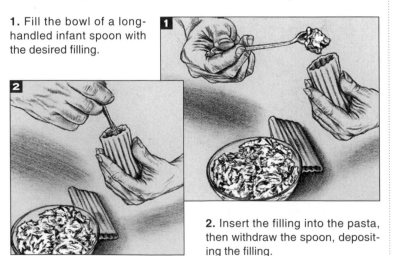

2. Insert the filling into the pasta, then withdraw the spoon, depositing the filling.

FREEZING STOCK IN CONVENIENT PORTIONS

Homemade stock improves the flavor of everything from rice to stews. But since many recipes call for only a small amount of stock, home cooks often find themselves defrosting a large container of stock just to get the cup or so they need. Barbra Letts of Longmont, Colorado, offers this tip to solve the problem.

1. Ladle the stock into oversized, nonstick muffin tins, each of which holds just under one cup of stock, and freeze.

2. When the stock is frozen, twist the muffin tin in the same manner as you twist an ice tray, tapping the bottom with a butter knife to loosen if necessary. Place the frozen cubes in a plastic bag, seal tightly, and use as needed.

AVOIDING THE BURN OF CHILE PEPPERS

To work with very hot, fresh chile peppers such as habañeros without burning your hands, David Joachim of Binghamton, New York, recommends using a chef's knife and a serrated-tip grapefruit spoon.

1. Holding the chile in place with the grapefruit spoon, slice the chile lengthwise with the chef's knife.

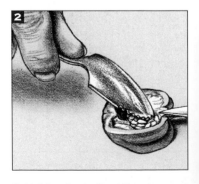

2. Holding the knife at the stem end of the chile, use the grapefruit spoon to scrape out the seeds and ribs.

ILLUSTRATIONS BY ALAN WITSCHONKE

PUREEING HEADS OF GARLIC

Susan Doss of Plano, Texas, suggests this tip for extracting the "meat" from a head of roasted garlic.

1. Cut about ¼ inch from the end of a head of roasted garlic. Place the garlic tip side down, in a potato ricer.

2. The extruded garlic is nicely pureed, while the peel remains inside the ricer.

TRANSFERRING PIE CRUST

Over the years, cooks have developed many methods for transferring pie crust into the pie pan. Richard Carr of Woodstock, Connecticut, suggests this method, which is particularly effective.

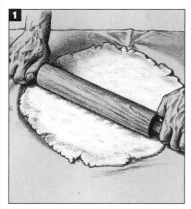

1. Roll out the crust on a floured pastry cloth or sheets of waxed paper, as shown here.

2. Fold the waxed paper over so that the dough forms a half-circle.

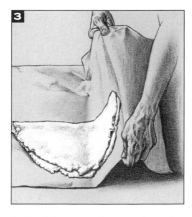

3. Fold the waxed paper from the other side so the dough forms a quarter-circle.

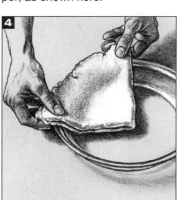

4. Transfer the quarter-circle of dough from the waxed paper to a pie plate, placing the dough point in the exact center of the pan.

5. Unfold the dough halfway.

6. Finally, unfold the dough completely. The open dough is centered and wrinkle-free.

REHYDRATING DRIED INGREDIENTS

Dried ingredients such as mushrooms or chile peppers often have to be rehydrated before use. Maggie Carter of Downey, California, has come up with a foolproof method. Place the mushrooms or other dried ingredients in a glass measuring cup and cover with warm water. Place a custard cup over the dried ingredients, then fill the cup with water. This keeps the ingredients completely submerged so they rehydrate evenly.

BETTER FRIED CHICKEN

Anita Searles of Austin, Texas, wrote to suggest putting several pieces of celery, with leaves, into the oil when frying chicken. Our Food Editor tried this tip and found that it produced more beautifully colored and better-tasting fried chicken every time she did it.

Thanks to our readers for Quick Tips: The editors of *Cook's Illustrated* would like to thank all of the readers who have sent us their quick tips. We have enjoyed reading every one of them, and have learned a lot. Keep them coming. We will provide a one-year complimentary subscription for each quick tip that we print. Send a description of your special technique to *Cook's Illustrated,* P.O. Box 569, Brookline Village, MA 02147-0569. Please write "Attention: Quick Tips" on the envelope and include your name, address, and daytime phone number. You can also email us at cooksill@aol.com. Unfortunately, we can only acknowledge receipt of tips that will be printed in the magazine. In case the same tip is received from two readers, the one postmarked first will be selected. Also, be sure to let us know what particular cooking problems you would like us to investigate in upcoming issues.

The Best Pecan Pie

Patiently sleuthing through dozens of recipe variations, we finally create a pie with silky smooth texture, rich pralinelike flavor, and a crisp crust.

~ BY STEPHEN SCHMIDT ~

Getting the filling of a pecan pie just right requires a precise balance of butter, eggs, brown sugar, and corn syrup.

As much as I like pecan pie, I have a couple of problems with the dessert. First, like many other people, I find the pie, at least as it is typically made, too sweet, both in an absolute sense and in relation to its other flavors, which are overwhelmed by the sugariness.

My other major complaint has to do with texture. Pecan pies too often turn out to be curdly and separated, and the weepy filling turns the bottom crust soggy and leathery. The fact that the undercrust usually seems underbaked to begin with doesn't help matters.

I first began to get a handle on the curdling issue several years back while researching and testing chess pies, a specialty of the South. Descended from a common source (*see* "Pecan Pie Ancestry," page 8), chess and pecan pies are structurally similar. They are both custards, albeit custards of an especially sugary, buttery kind. The main difference between the two desserts is that chess pies usually contain some milk or cream and thus are opaque and creamy while pecan pies typically do not and therefore are translucent and jellylike.

Both pecan and chess pies have always frustrated me. My pies always turned out grainy and weepy while those served to me by expert Southern bakers were wonderfully soft and smooth, almost like cream pies. After much questioning of the recipe contributors, I discovered the reason for their success. They take their pies out of the oven much sooner than I did, while the center is barely thicker than raw egg white. The pies continue to cook after they are removed from the oven, as heat travels from the edges to the middle by conduction. And since pecan and chess pies are composed largely of sugar and butter, cooling serves to make them still more solid.

Unfortunately, gauging the right moment at which to take these pies out of the oven remained a chancy thing for me. Too often I found the edges of my pie had become curdly, and occasionally I erred on the other side and ended up with a pie that was still runny in the middle. As I embarked on this article, the first thing that I wanted to accomplish was to discover a foolproof means of baking my pecan pies to smooth, silky perfection.

I first stirred up a batch of my favorite pecan pie filling, which is made with sugar and corn syrup. Then I baked tarts filled with the mixture at various temperatures. A hot oven (375 degrees and above) was, predictably, a disaster. The edges of the tarts reared up and solidified before the centers had even thickened. A moderate oven (325 to 350 degrees), the temperature at which I had baked my pies previously, was better but still frequently resulted in curdled edges. A slow oven (250 to 300 degrees) turned out to be the best, yielding tarts with nicely thickened centers but without hardened edges. There was a problem, however. Tarts baked at very low temperatures took so long to firm up that the crusts turned soggy, even when the shells were thoroughly prebaked and glazed with egg yolk. Furthermore, the filling tended to separate into a jellylike layer on the bottom and a frothy cap. At this point, I remembered that old recipes—and indeed some modern ones as well—specify heating the filling first. When I tried this, I cut the baking time by close to half and fixed the problems of soggy crust and separated bottom.

The Great Filling Mystery

Once I had resolved the issues of the texture and the soggy crust, I expected smooth sailing on the rest of my voyage to a perfect pecan pie. I already had what I considered to be the perfect proportions for chess pie—six tablespoons butter, one and one-third cups sugar, three eggs, and two-thirds cup milk. Made according to this formula, chess pie has just the right balance of sweetness as well as a delicious buttery flavor and light but firm consistency. All I had to do to make a great pecan pie, I reasoned, was to reduce the milk so the pie would seem jellylike rather than creamy. Then, to give my pecan pie a rich, pralinelike flavor, I would use dark brown sugar instead of white. It all sounded so simple.

But it wasn't.

I thought that I might be able to cut the creaminess by reducing the milk by half. As it turned out I was right, but I was not happy with the consis-

---

Many pecan pies are marred by bad crusts. Sogginess is not the only problem. Too often, some of the filling manages to leak through the pastry, fusing the crust to the pan and making it impossible to cut neat slices. Prebaking the crust is essential, and glazing the crust with egg yolk adds extra insurance against leaks. The following dough is especially good for prebaked crusts because it resists shrinking and shriveling during prebaking, yet the crust is flaky and delicious.

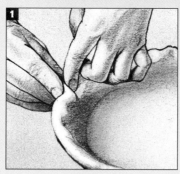

1. After pressing the dough into the pan and trimming it, flute the edges with your fingers.

2. Cover the dough with a sheet of heavy-duty aluminum foil, pressing it against the crust.

3. Use a fork to prick holes through the aluminum foil on the bottom and sides of the pan.

PIE SHELL FOR PECAN PIE
For a 9-inch single pie shell

1¼ cups all-purpose flour, plus extra for dough and surface
2 tablespoons confectioners' sugar
½ teaspoon salt
8 tablespoons chilled unsalted butter, cut into ¼-inch pats
2 tablespoons vegetable shortening, frozen solid and cut into small pieces
1 large chilled egg white, thoroughly mixed with ice water (about 2 tablespoons) to equal ¼ cup
1 large egg yolk beaten with ⅛ teaspoon water

1. Mix flour, sugar, and salt in food processor fitted with steel blade. Scatter butter and shortening over dry ingredients and pulse until mixture resembles coarse cornmeal, 10 to 15 seconds. Turn mixture into medium bowl.

2. Sprinkle egg white mixture over flour mixture and, with blade of rubber spatula, use folding motion to mix. Press down on dough with broad side of spatula until dough sticks together. Shape dough into ball with hands, then flatten into 4-inch disk. Dust dough lightly with flour, wrap tightly in plastic wrap, and place in refrigerator for at least 1 hour or up to 2 days.

3. Roll dough on lightly floured surface into 13-inch circle and transfer to 9-inch pie pan, preferably glass. Press dough into corners and sides of pan, being careful not to stretch dough. Trim edges of dough to make ½-inch overhang. Tuck overhanging dough under so that folded edge is flush with rim of pan. Flute edge (*see* illustration 1).

4. Chill shell until firm, about 1 hour. Prick sides and bottom with fork and line entire shell with heavy-duty aluminum foil, pressing foil firmly against shell and extending it over fluted rim (illustration 2). Prick foil with fork (illustration 3) and return shell to refrigerator while oven is heating.

5. Adjust oven rack to center position and heat oven to 400 degrees. Bake, pressing once or twice with mitt-protected hands, if necessary, to flatten any puffing, until crust is firmly set, about 15 minutes. Remove foil and continue to bake until bottom begins to color, about 10 minutes longer. Remove from oven, brush sides and bottom with egg yolk, and return to oven until yolk glazes over, about 1 minute longer.

---

tency. Made with such a high proportion of sugar, my pecan pie did not set firmly enough, and when I cut through the carapace of pecans on top, the filling squished out the sides. I am embarrassed to reveal how many different attempts I made to fix this consistency problem. Suffice it to say that all failed, even the addition of flour or cornstarch, neither of which, I learned, is effective in thickening a filling when the pie is baked at a low temperature and allowed to finish its cooking outside the oven.

In any event, cutting the milk by half brought on another problem. The pie tasted way too sweet. To make the pie less sugary I tried increasing the butter to two whole sticks, but the butter gave the filling a sticky-creamy consistency that I didn't really like. I was able to fix the stickiness by adding more eggs, but now the pie was simply creamy—and so rich that no one could eat more than a bite or two.

Those who bake pecan pies and are familiar with the usual recipes are surely wondering at this point why I didn't try replacing the milk with corn syrup, a standard ingredient in pecan pies. The answer, simply, is that I identified the syrup with the pie's excessive sweetness. But after untold failed experiments, I had no other recourse. Most of the cookbook authorities that I consulted agreed that corn syrup had roughly half the sweetness of sugar. Thus, to get a pecan pie that had roughly the same sweetness as the chess pie I liked so much, I reasoned that I should replace the milk in my chess pie recipe with an equal amount of syrup and reduce the sugar by one-third cup, yielding a formula of six tablespoons butter, one cup brown sugar, three eggs, and two-thirds cup syrup.

I was skeptical, however, that a pie so buttery, sugary, and syrupy would set. I decided to compromise. I reduced the butter to four tablespoons and used light brown sugar instead of dark, reasoning that light brown would have an effect on thickness midway between that of white and dark brown. The pie did set, but I found the flavor indistinct and the sweetness level just a little too high. To fix these problems I tried substituting dark corn syrup for light. The resulting pie was not excessively sweet, but I really didn't like the caramel-like flavor of the dark syrup.

Clearly I was hankering after that pralinelike taste that only dark brown sugar gives. I reinstated the deleted two tablespoons of butter to offset sweetness, put in dark brown sugar and light syrup, increased the vanilla—another component of that praline flavor—and held my breath. The pie set. It was not too sweet. And it had a lovely taste. But was it perhaps just a little too firm? I thought it was. I baked another, increasing the corn syrup just a tiny bit, to three-quarters cup, and found myself, at last, satisfied.

There are, I know, many people who find pecan pie, no matter how it is made, intrinsically too sweet and otherwise not to their taste. To them I recommend the variations that follow, par-

To avoid burning butter while melting it, place it in a pan held in a skillet of simmering water.

---

ticularly the chesslike Buttermilk Pecan Pie with Raisins, which may be my favorite pie in the whole world.

PERFECT PECAN PIE
Serves 8

If you want warm pie, cool the pie thoroughly, then cut and warm it in a 250-degree oven for about twenty minutes.

 1 9-inch baked pie shell (*see* recipe, page 7)
 6 tablespoons unsalted butter, cut into 1-inch pieces
 1 cup packed dark brown sugar
 ½ teaspoon salt
 3 large eggs
 ¾ cup light corn syrup
 1 tablespoon vanilla extract
 2 cups pecans (8 ounces), toasted and chopped into small pieces

 1. Adjust oven rack to center position, and heat oven to 275 degrees. Place pie shell in oven if not already warm.
 2. Melt butter in medium heatproof bowl set in skillet of water maintained at just below simmer. Remove bowl from skillet; mix in sugar and salt with wooden spoon until butter is absorbed. Beat in eggs, then corn syrup and vanilla. Return bowl to hot water; stir until mixture is shiny and warm to the touch, about 130 degrees. Remove from heat; stir in pecans.
 3. Pour mixture into warm shell; bake until center feels set yet soft, like gelatin, when gently pressed, 50 to 60 minutes. Transfer pie to rack; let cool completely, at least 4 hours. Serve pie at room temperature or warm, with lightly sweetened whipped cream or vanilla ice cream.

TRIPLE CHOCOLATE CHUNK PECAN PIE
Serves 8

 1 9-inch baked pie shell (*see* recipe, page 7)
 3 tablespoons unsalted butter, cut into 1-inch pieces
 ¾ cup packed dark brown sugar
 ½ teaspoon salt
 2 large eggs
 ½ cup light corn syrup
 1 teaspoon vanilla extract
 1 cup pecans (4 ounces), toasted and chopped into small pieces
 2 ounces each semisweet chocolate, milk chocolate, and white chocolate, cut into ¼-inch pieces

Follow recipe for Perfect Pecan Pie, scattering chocolate pieces over pecan mixture once it has been poured into shell, then gently pressing them into filling with back of spoon. Increase baking time to 55 to 65 minutes.

BUTTERMILK PECAN PIE WITH RAISINS
Serves 8

To make a buttermilk chess pie, omit the nuts and raisins. Serve at room temperature or lightly chilled.

 1 9-inch baked pie shell (*see* recipe, page 7)
 6 tablespoons unsalted butter, cut into 1-inch pieces
 1⅓ cups granulated sugar
 ½ teaspoon salt
 3 large eggs
 ⅔ cup buttermilk
 ½ cup pecans (2 ounces), toasted and chopped into small pieces
 ½ cup raisins, chopped fine

Follw recipe for Perfect Pecan Pie, beating in buttermilk for the corn syrup and vanilla. Stir in raisins along with pecans.

MAPLE PECAN PIE
Serves 8

More liquid than corn syrup, maple syrup yields a softer, more custardlike pie. Toasted walnuts can be substituted for pecans.

 1 9-inch baked pie shell (*see* recipe, page 7)
 4 tablespoons unsalted butter, cut into 1-inch pieces
 ½ cup granulated sugar
 ¼ teaspoon salt
 3 large eggs
 1 cup pure maple syrup, preferably Grade B or Grade A dark amber
 1½ cups pecans (6 ounces), toasted and chopped into small pieces

Follow recipe for Perfect Pecan Pie, beating in maple syrup for the corn syrup and vanilla. ∎

Stephen Schmidt is the author of the forthcoming *Dessert America*, to be published by William Morrow.

PECAN PIE ANCESTRY

Both pecan and chess pies are descended from a class of seventeenth-century confections known as "cheesecakes." These early pies were made by boiling beaten eggs in milk until the mixture scrambled. The resulting "curd" was drained from the "whey" and beaten to a fluff, then combined with raw eggs, milk or cream, butter, sugar, and flavorings and baked in a pastry crust.

By 1900, most American bakers had moved on to a slightly more modern cheesecake, in which raw eggs, milk or cream, butter, sugar, and flavorings were baked in a pastry crust until the filling set into a thick jelly or "cheese." The cheesecakes were most often flavored with lemon. A second common type of custard cheesecake, made without milk or cream, often went by the name of "transparent pudding" because its filling was clear and shiny rather than opaque.

Until the mid-nineteenth century, American bakers prepared all custard cheesecakes with roughly equal weights of eggs, butter, and sugar, which resulted in fillings that were rich and melting but not terribly sweet. However, after the Civil War, as tastes and notions of economy changed, cooks more or less halved the butter and doubled the sugar.

At around the same time, the terms "cheesecake" and "pudding" rapidly went out of fashion, and desserts baked in pastry crusts came to be called simply "pies." Lemon cheesecakes and puddings thus became lemon pies, which eventually evolved into modern lemon meringue pies as cooks cut back on the butter and eggs still further by substituting water and cornstarch. The other cheesecakes and puddings, meanwhile, became chess pies, "chess" being a shortened form of "cheese." Pecan pies are simply chess pies with nuts. Today, most people make "transparent" pecan pies, without milk or cream, but many creamy, chess-type pies with pecan and other nuts still survive in the South.

PHOTOGRAPHS BY DAVE HENDERSON

Roast Turkey Revisited

We find that, with decreased brining strength and a lower oven temperature, the method we developed for small turkeys works just as well for larger birds.

∼ BY PAM ANDERSON WITH KAREN TACK ∼

I haven't touched another turkey since that hot summer of 1993 when we roasted more than thirty of them for the November/December issue (*see* "The Holiday Turkey Perfected"). During those many tests, we discovered two essential keys: Turkey tasted better if it was first brined in salt water, and the breast didn't overcook (always an issue when cooked conventionally) if the turkey was rotated during roasting.

Back in '93, we roasted only smaller, twelve- to fourteen-pound turkeys. Obviously, when you cooked as many as we did, the smaller the better. When number thirty-something emerged from the oven looking good and tasting even better, we quit. We had taken the experiment as far as we could. We knew, however, that many Thanksgiving birds are necessarily larger—and we got many calls from readers wondering how to adapt our method for bigger birds. So we decided to revisit the subject this year, but this time using turkeys in the eighteen to twenty-pound bracket.

Less Salt, Tastes Great

In our original experiments, we settled on a four-hour brining time, but it meant that cooks had to get up with the chickens to brine *and* roast their Thanksgiving turkey. Given the increased roasting time of a larger bird, this method would have had cooks arising in the middle of the night.

If we decreased the brine strength, we wondered, might we achieve a convenient overnight brine? Our original brine called for two pounds of salt with a four-hour brining time. This time around, we reduced the salt to one pound and increased the brining time to eight hours. The time schedule proved more convenient, and the resulting roasted turkeys and gravies tasted pleasantly seasoned. (Just be sure not to resalt the turkey before roasting, and don't salt the giblet broth.)

Next we adjusted the roasting technique. Turning a twenty-pound bird on its side the way we could with the ten- and twelve-pounders was just asking for trouble. Even if it were possible, most ovens aren't big enough for a really large turkey to sit wing side up. Our smaller birds did not brown evenly without the extra turns, but the larger turkeys, given their longer roasting times, browned evenly with just one flip—from breast side down to breast side up.

Echoing our '93 experience, roasting temperature became our real challenge. Because of the turkeys' large size, we found that roasting at 350 and 400 degrees tended to overcook the exterior by the time the interior was done. We eventually found that roasting these large turkeys at 250 degrees breast side down, then breast side up produced the most evenly cooked turkeys. To brown the skin, we increased the oven temperature to 400 degrees for the final hour of roasting.

Originally we recommended roasting the turkey on a V-rack set over a perforated broiler pan. Because we were cooking the smaller birds at a high temperature, we found the pan juices evaporated quickly, causing the vegetables to burn. We recommended a perforated broiler pan that would allow the turkey juices to drip down while keeping the liquid from evaporating as quickly. This helped, but more liquid still needed to be added and the perforated lid prohibited the cook from checking the amount of liquid in the pan. We now prefer a simpler solution: Roast the turkey on a V-rack set in a heavy-duty roasting pan. When more water is needed (which is now easy to see), just add it.

We've also decided that you don't need to add stock to the pan during roasting. Water, cooked with the pan vegetables and turkey drippings, makes a flavorful enough liquid to mix with the giblet broth.

ROAST TURKEY WITH
GIBLET PAN SAUCE
Serves 18 to 20

1   large turkey (18 to 20 pounds gross weight), rinsed thoroughly, giblets, neck, and tail piece removed and set aside
1   pound salt (about 1 cup table salt or 2 cups kosher)
1   bay leaf
3   medium onions, chopped coarse
1½ medium carrots, chopped coarse
1½ celery stalks, chopped coarse
6   thyme sprigs
1   tablespoon butter, melted, plus extra for brushing and basting turkey
3   tablespoons cornstarch

1. Place turkey in large stockpot or clean bucket. Add 2 gallons water and salt. Refrigerate or set in very cool (40 degrees or less) spot for 8 hours.

2. Remove turkey from salt water and rinse both cavities and skin under cool running water for several minutes until all traces of salt are gone.

3. Meanwhile, reserving liver, put giblets, neck, and tail piece, bay leaf, and one-third each of onions, carrots, celery, and thyme in large saucepan. Add 6 cups water and bring to simmer, skimming foam from surface as necessary. Bring to boil, then simmer, uncovered, to make a flavorful broth, about 1 hour (add reserved liver during last 5 minutes of cooking). Strain broth (setting giblets, neck, and tail aside), cool to room temperature, and refrigerate until ready to use. (You should have about 1 quart of broth.) Remove meat from neck and tail, cut giblets into medium dice, and refrigerate until ready to use.

4. Heat oven to 250 degrees. Toss another third of the onions, carrots, celery, and thyme with 1 tablespoon butter and place in body cavity. Bring legs together and perform simple truss (*see* "The Holiday Turkey Perfected," November/December 1993).

5. Scatter remaining vegetables and thyme in roasting pan; pour 1 cup water over vegetables. Set heavy-duty V-rack, adjusted to widest setting, in pan. Brush entire breast side of turkey with butter, then place turkey, breast side down, on V-rack. Brush entire back side of turkey with butter.

6. Roast 3 hours, basting back side every hour or so and adding small quantities of water if vegetables look dry. Remove pan from oven (close oven door); baste with butter. With wad of paper toweling in each hand, turn breast side up. Continue to roast 1 hour, basting once or twice. With turkey still in oven, increase oven temperature to 400 degrees; roast until skin has browned and internal temperature of legs and breast registers about 165 degrees, about 1 hour longer. Transfer turkey to platter; let rest 20 to 30 minutes.

7. Meanwhile, strain pan drippings into large saucepan (discard solids) and skim fat. Return roasting pan to stove and place over two burners set on medium heat. Add reserved broth to roasting pan, and using wooden spoon, stir to loosen brown bits. When juices start to simmer, strain into saucepan containing pan drippings along with reserved giblets; bring to boil. Mix cornstarch with 3 tablespoons water and gradually stir into pan juices. Bring to boil; simmer until sauce thickens slightly. Carve turkey; serve sauce passed separately. ∎

Salt brining makes for a better tasting turkey.

Foolproof Genoise

Master baker Rose Beranbaum uses clarified butter and mixes cornstarch with flour to solve problems with this egg-leavened cake.

∼ BY JACK BISHOP ∼

Most Americans are comfortable making butter cakes, which are leavened chemically, usually with baking powder. But when it comes to genoise, a European sponge cake leavened by egg foam, all bets are off.

Maybe it's the name (a French take on a cake from Genoa, Italy), or maybe it's the reliance on egg foam; either way, genoise has a reputation for being fickle. "But genoise has so many uses that bakers should really know how to make it," argues Beranbaum. She especially likes to use genoise for cakes that will be covered with a frosting that must be refrigerated. "Butter cakes stiffen up like cardboard in the refrigerator, but genoise remains tender," she explains. And, because genoise-based cakes can be refrigerated, they are perfect for holiday occasions when you want to bake in advance.

Overall, a syrup-soaked genoise has twice the eggs, half the flour and butter, and the same amount of sugar as a standard yellow cake. When compared to other sponge cakes, the biggest difference is the eggs, which are separated for most American-style sponge cakes but beaten whole for a genoise.

"There's so much mystery surrounding genoise, but it's really a simple cake," says famed cake baker Rose Levy Beranbaum.

In the standard genoise recipe, eggs and sugar are beaten over warm water until thick and foamy. The eggs must be warm (so they will hold more air) but not so hot that they curdle. Melted butter and flour are folded in, and the batter is poured into a pan and baked. Sounds easy enough, but as with other sponge-type cakes (angel food, for example), there is plenty of room for error, especially if the egg foam is deflated.

Secrets for Success

Beranbaum, author of numerous cookbooks including the much-acclaimed *The Cake Bible* (Morrow, 1988), has developed a number of "tricks" to ensure perfect results when making genoise. The first issue is the butter. "There is really very little butter in this cake, so you want it to have as much flavor as possible," says Beranbaum. Her answer is clarified brown butter, which adds a rich, nutty flavor that regular melted butter does not have.

The next secret is the flour. Because of its lower protein content, cake flour makes tenderer, finer cakes than all-purpose flour. However, Beranbaum takes this one step further by cutting cake flour with a large quantity of corn starch, further reducing the protein content of the flour and making her genoise especially tender and finely textured.

Finally, when it comes to handling the beaten eggs, Beranbaum has figured out how to keep the foam from deflating. After the eggs and sugar are warmed and beaten, Beranbaum uses a long-handled skimmer with large holes to fold in the flour/cornstarch mixture. This device incorporates the flour without deflating the beaten eggs.

The cake is baked in a single layer—crusts are removed for better syrup absorption—and then split because the texture is finer and the rise more even than if the batter were divided into two pans before baking. (*See* illustrations 1 through 5, below, for tips on crust removal and splitting the cake into two layers.) You then sprinkle the split layers with a flavored soaking syrup. Classic recipes use a brush to distribute the syrup, but Beranbaum finds that this method can loosen crumbs on the trimmed layers. A small bulb baster (illustration 6) or medical syringe lets you distribute the syrup over the layers without actually having to touch the cake.

Buttercream Basics

Traditional buttercream is made by heating sugar and water to the soft ball stage (238 degrees) and then incorporating the syrup into beaten egg yolks. You then add butter and flavorings to finish off this rich, creamy frosting. Of course, many cooks are wary of sugar syrups and with good reason—they can be temperamental and require precise measurement of temperature.

Beranbaum has gotten around these issues by developing a variation on the classic recipe,

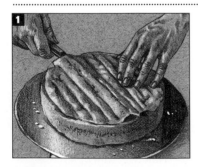

1. The crusts must be removed so that they don't prevent the syrup from being absorbed. Use a long serrated knife to trim a thin layer from the cake top.

2. The bottom crust is thinner than the top crust and can be scraped away with the serrated knife.

3. With the cake on a revolving stand, hold the serrated knife against the side of the cake at its midpoint and slowly turn the stand to make a shallow groove all the way around the cake.

4. Slide the knife into the groove and use a side-to-side motion to slice the cake in half. Keep one hand on top of the cake to steady it and check occasionally to make sure the knife is still in the groove.

PHOTOGRAPH BY VINCENT LEE

which she calls Neoclassic Buttercream. Instead of sugar and water, the syrup is made by boiling corn syrup and sugar. When the corn syrup–sugar mixture comes to a full rolling boil, the syrup has reached the correct temperature, which eliminates the need for a candy thermometer. This recipe also makes it unnecessary to wash down the sides of the pan to prevent graininess or crystallization—as soon as the sugar dissolves, this syrup is smooth.

Beranbaum also offers frosting tips that can be used with any cake. "The biggest problem people have when frosting is that they pick up crumbs from the cake," says Beranbaum. "It's better to load on more frosting than to add it in small amounts." A back-and-forth motion (without lifting up) keeps the spatula pressed against the cake and prevents crumbs from being picked up. Once the surface (either the top or side) is covered, Beranbaum uses the edge of a spatula to remove excess frosting. Placing the cake on a stand and turning it slowly to move the spatula around the cake also ensures an even layer of frosting.

GRAND MARNIER CAKE WITH NEOCLASSIC ORANGE BUTTERCREAM
Serves 8 to 10

To measure the sifted flour called for in this recipe, lightly spoon and mound it into a one-half cup measure and sweep off the excess with a long, flat spatula. Orange oil, the superconcentrated essence of many oranges, delivers a powerful orange flavor in the buttercream. Rose Levy Beranbaum prefers Boyajian orange oil. You may substitute two tablespoons of Grand Marnier, but the flavor will be less intense. The buttercream is easier to make with a hand mixer but can also be prepared in a standing mixer. If using a standing mixer, add a small amount of hot syrup to the yolks with the mixer turned off, then beat them on high for five seconds. Continue adding more syrup in this way until all of the syrup has been beaten into the yolks. The cake, syrup, and buttercream can be made well in advance of assembling, and the frosted cake can be refrigerated for up to five days, perfect for holiday entertaining. Remove it from the refrigerator one hour before serving to soften the buttercream slightly.

Classic Genoise
- 4 tablespoons unsalted butter
- 1 teaspoon vanilla extract
- ½ cup sifted cake flour
- 6 tablespoons cornstarch
- 4 large eggs
- ½ cup granulated sugar

Grand Marnier Soaking Syrup
- ¼ cup plus 1½ teaspoons sugar
- 2 tablespoons Grand Marnier or other orange-flavored liqueur

Neoclassic Orange Buttercream
- 6 large egg yolks
- ¾ cup granulated sugar
- ½ cup light corn syrup
- 1 pound unsalted butter, softened
- 1 tablespoon grated zest from 1 orange
- 1 teaspoon orange oil

1. *For the genoise:* Adjust oven rack to center position and heat oven to 350 degrees. Grease 9-by-2-inch round cake pan. Line bottom with parchment paper; grease paper as well. Dust pan lightly with flour; tap out excess.

2. Melt butter in small heavy saucepan over medium heat. When butter looks clear, continue to cook, watching carefully, until solids drop and begin to brown. Immediately pour through fine strainer or strainer lined with cheesecloth. Return clarified browned butter (there should be 3 tablespoons) to medium bowl, add vanilla, and keep warm by covering.

3. Sift flour and cornstarch together; set aside. Heat eggs and sugar in large mixing bowl set over saucepan of simmering water (do not let bottom of bowl touch water), stirring constantly to prevent curdling, until lukewarm. Using whisk attachment on standing mixer, beat on high speed until egg mixture triples in volume, about 5 minutes.

4. Thoroughly whisk scant cup of egg mixture into warm butter; set aside. Turn half of flour mixture into sieve; sift over remaining egg batter. Fold gently, but rapidly, with large skimmer or whisk. Repeat with remaining flour, folding until flour is no longer visible. Fold in egg-and-butter mixture until just incorporated.

5. Immediately pour batter into prepared pan. Bake until cake starts to pull away from sides, 25 to 35 minutes. (Do not open oven door until cake is almost done, or it could fall.) Meanwhile, grease two cake racks.

6. Immediately loosen cake from side of pan with small metal spatula and invert at once onto rack. Remove parchment and invert cake again onto second rack. Let cool completely. (Genoise can be wrapped in plastic and stored at room temperature for 2 days, refrigerated for 5 days, or frozen for 2 months.)

7. *For the syrup:* Combine sugar and ½ cup water in small saucepan; bring to rolling boil over medium heat, stirring constantly. Remove from heat, cover tightly, and let cool completely. Pour syrup into measuring cup; add liqueur and additional water to bring liquid to ¾ cup. (Syrup can be refrigerated in airtight container for 1 month.)

8. Following illustrations 1 through 6, below, halve cake crosswise and sprinkle each layer with syrup.

9. *For the buttercream:* Grease 1-cup glass measuring cup and place it near stovetop.

10. Beat yolks in large bowl with electric hand mixer until light in color, about 4 minutes.

11. Meanwhile, mix sugar and syrup in small saucepan. Cook over low heat, stirring constantly, until sugar dissolves and mixture comes to rolling boil. The entire surface should be covered with moving bubbles. (If mixture boils before sugar dissolves, remove from heat and stir until sugar dissolves before continuing to cook.) Immediately pour syrup into prepared measuring cup.

12. Beat syrup into yolks in steady stream, scraping any syrup clinging to glass measure into bowl. (Do not pour syrup onto beaters or it will spin to sides of bowl.) Continue beating until mixture is completely cooled.

13. Gradually beat in softened butter, zest, and oil until smooth. (Buttercream can be covered and stored at room temperature for 6 hours or refrigerated in airtight container for 1 week. Bring to room temperature before use.)

14. Following illustrations 7 and 8, below, assemble the cake, then frost cake with buttercream. ∎

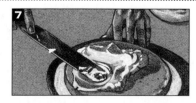

5. Slide a greased removable bottom from a tart or quiche pan between the layers and lift off the top.

6. Place the layer on a piece of plastic wrap and use a small bulb baster or large medical syringe to sprinkle syrup over the layer. Cover the layer with a second piece of plastic wrap, gently flip it over, pull back the plastic and sprinkle the other side with syrup. Repeat the process with the second layer.

7. Place dab of frosting in center of 9-inch cardboard round. Center one layer on round and place the round on cake stand. Place 1 cup buttercream in center of layer. Use long frosting spatula to spread buttercream without lifting up. Remove excess buttercream with side of spatula. Freeze cake for 3 minutes.

8. Remove the cake from the freezer. Place the unfrosted layer on the greased tart pan bottom and slide it onto the frosted bottom layer, making sure that the layers are aligned. Frost the top and sides.

Perfect Prime Rib

For a roast that's as pink, juicy, and tender at the surface as it is in the center, sear it first, then roast it long and low.

∾ BY PAM ANDERSON WITH KAREN TACK ∾

By cooking a simply tied roast at a low oven temperature, the home cook can duplicate the finest restaurant prime rib.

A prime rib is a little like a turkey: You probably cook only one a year, usually for an important occasion, almost always for a crowd. Although you know there are alternative cooking methods that might deliver a better roast, they're too risky. You don't want to be remembered as the cook who carved slices of almost raw standing rib, or the host who delayed dinner for hours waiting for the roast to get done. Rather than chance it, you stick with the standard 350 degrees for X minutes per pound. A roast cooked this way, you decide, will at least not embarrass you.

This story began last Christmas, because I was the cook who gambled the $40 standing rib roast and Christmas dinner memories. I ordered a prime rib roast from the butcher. Instructions taped onto the butcher paper read, "Roast in a 500-degree oven for *thirty-five* minutes (five minutes per pound). Turn oven heat off and let roast stand for exactly one hour. Do not open oven door once oven has been turned off." The butcher promised a memorable medium-rare roast by following these instructions. This method sounded so odd, I couldn't resist giving it a shot. Since a few of my guests liked their meat closer to well than rare, I increased the oven time to six minutes per pound (forty-two minutes total) and fired up the oven.

I recognized the drawbacks of this method fairly quickly. The oven was occupied for the final hour and a half or so before dinner—a potential problem for single-oven owners. Smoking fat triggered the kitchen smoke alarm at the thirty-minute mark, so cooks must disengage the smoke alarm, turn on the fan, and brace themselves for a smoky kitchen. Despite these obstacles, the prime rib emerged from the oven looking a rich, dark brown. The roast carved into two medium-well slices, two medium slices, two medium-rare slices, and a couple of fairly rare center slices. So I gambled and at least broke even last holiday. Odds were pretty good, though, that I could do better.

Prime Temp

Other than using general terms like *juicy* and *tender*, we weren't exactly sure how to define perfect prime rib when we started testing, so we had no preconceived ideas about what techniques or methods would deliver a superior roast. In addition to our normal cookbook research, we decided to interview a few of the thousands of chefs who cook prime rib every day. Between what we found in books and what we learned from these chefs, we came up with a dozen or so fairly different methods. Although there were minor issues, such as whether the roast needed to be tied or whether it should be roasted on a rack, one big question needed answering: At what temperature should prime rib be roasted?

We started with oven temperatures. Suggested roasting temperatures ranged from a bold 425 degrees to a tepid 200. Other recipes recommended an initial high-temperature sear (450 to 500 degrees), then reducing the oven temperature to a more moderate temperature (350 degrees) for actual roasting. Testing the full range, we roasted prime ribs at the following temperatures:

Roast 1: *500 degrees for five minutes per pound, then left in the turned-off oven for two hours (a variation on the method I tried as described above)*
Roast 2: *500-degree preheat, immediately reduced to 350 degrees as the roast is placed in oven*
Roast 3: *425 degrees for the entire cooking time*
Roast 4: *450 degrees for the first half hour, then 350 degrees until done*
Roast 5: *350 degrees for the entire cooking time (with the roast placed on a rack over a pan of water as suggested by a respected restaurant chef)*
Roast 6: *325 degrees for the entire cooking time*
Roast 7: *250 degrees for the entire cooking time*
Roast 8: *200 degrees for the entire cooking time*

In addition to the disadvantages already discussed above about the roast cooked at 500 degrees at five minutes per pound, roast #1, left in the turned-off oven for two hours, was barely warm at carving and had grown cold before we could finish eating it.

To our minds, the only advantage to cooking meat over a pan of water, (*see* roast 5), was to prohibit dripping fat from spitting over the oven, but with the downward direction we were headed on the oven dial, sputtering fat was not a big problem.

All prime ribs roasted at oven temperatures exceeding 300 degrees were pretty much the same. Each slice of carved beef was well done around the exterior and medium towards the center, with a beautiful medium-rare pink center. We might have been tempted to report that roasting temperature doesn't much matter if we hadn't tried cooking prime rib at oven temperatures under 300 degrees. Certainly, the ribs cooked at 300 degrees and above all looked quite acceptable before carving especially when compared to the low-temperature prime ribs. We ended up with a surprise, however.

Love At First Bite, Not At First Sight

It's funny that we should end up preferring the prime rib roasted at 200 degrees because it certainly wasn't love at first sight. About halfway through this roast's cooking time, I wrote in my notes, "Though the meat looks virtually raw, the internal temperature registers a surprising 110 degrees, and very little of its fat has rendered." But we changed our minds quickly as soon as we carved the first slice. This roast was as beautiful on the inside as it was anemic on the outside. Unlike the roasts that cooked at higher temperatures, this one was rosy pink from the surface to the center—the juiciest and most tender of all the roasts we cooked. This was restaurant prime rib at its best.

Besides being evenly cooked, the prime rib roasted in a 200-degree oven had another thing going for it: Its internal temperature increased only a degree or two during its resting period.

ASK FOR IT BY NUMBER

Butchers tend to cut a rib roast, which consists of ribs six through twelve if left whole, into two distinct cuts. The more desirable of the two cuts consists of ribs ten through twelve (left illustration). Since this portion of the roast is closer to the loin end, it is sometimes called the "loin end." Other butchers call it the "small end" or the "first cut." Whatever it is called, it is more desirable because it contains the large, single rib-eye muscle and is less fatty. A less desirable cut, which is still an excellent roast, consists of ribs six to nine (right illustration), closer to the chuck end, and sometimes called the second cut. The closer to the chuck, the more multimuscled the roast be-

comes. Since muscles are surrounded by fat, this also means a fattier roast. While some cooks may prefer this cut because the fat adds flavor, in general, the more tender and more regularly formed loin end is considered the best.

According to butcher Ronnie Savenor, of Savenor's in Boston, the clearest way to indicate what you want is to ask for "the first three ribs from the loin end."—P.A.

The loin end rib roast includes ribs ten, eleven, and twelve.

The "second cut" rib roast includes ribs six through nine.

TIE IT UP

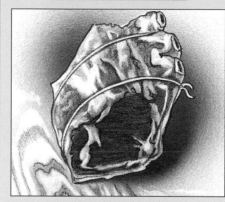

We didn't tie the first few prime ribs that we roasted. We found out pretty quickly, though, that unless the roast was tied, the outer layer of meat pulled away from the rib-eye muscle, causing the roast to look a little unattractive. Separated from the main roast, this outer flap of meat also tended to overcook. To solve this problem easily, tie the roast at both ends running parallel to the bone.

(Roasts are allowed to rest when they come out of the oven both to distribute the heat evenly and to allow the juices to reabsorb back into the outer layers of the meat.) A roast cooked to 128 degrees, for example, moved only to 130 degrees after a forty-five-minute rest.

Not so with the roasts cooked at higher temperatures. Their internal temperatures increased much more dramatically out of the oven. As a matter of fact, we noticed a direct correlation between oven temperature and the roast's post-cooking temperature increase. Prime ribs roasted at more moderate temperatures (325 to 350) increased, on average, fourteen degrees during resting. In other words, if pulled from the oven at a rare 126-degree internal temperature, these roasts had moved up to a solid medium (140 degrees) by the end of the resting period. Furthermore, the prime rib roasted at 425 degrees increased a whopping twenty-four degrees (from 119 to 143) during its rest. Those roasted at a lower 250 degrees crept only up only five degrees before carving. We considered this lower increase a definite advantage since we liked being able to pull the roast from the oven at the temperature we wanted it, rather than trying to speculate how many degrees the roast would jump during resting.

In addition to its more stable internal temperature, the prime rib roasted at 200 degrees also lost less weight during cooking than those roasted at higher temperatures. A six-and-three-quarter pound roast cooked in a 200-degree oven weighed just over six and one-quarter pounds when it came out of the oven, a loss of less than eight ounces. By contrast, similar roasts cooked in a 325-degree oven lost just over a pound while the roast cooked at 350 degrees lost one and one-half pounds. The prime rib cooked at 425 degrees lost

a shocking two pounds. Part of the weight loss is fat, but certainly a good portion is juice. This test confirmed our sense that the beef roasted at 200 degrees was indeed juicier than those roasted at the higher temperatures.

Since those at the Beef Council would not endorse an oven-roasting temperature under 300 degrees, we decided to check the safety of this low-

heat method before getting too sold on it. After conversations with a number of food scientists across the country, we determined that low-temperature roasting is as safe a cooking method as higher-temperature roasting. And though the odds of finding bacteria inside a prime rib roast are virtually nonexistent, the only way to guarantee a bacteria-free slab of prime rib is to cook it to

CARVE IT SIMPLY

Bringing the whole roast to the table and carving each slice from the rib is probably more festive, but to carve a prime rib simply, we found it easier to cut the roast from the bone, then slice the boneless meat.

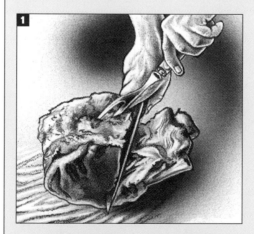

1. To carve, remove the twine and set the roast on a cutting board, rib bones perpendicular to the board. Using a carving fork to hold the roast in place, cut along the rib bones to sever the meat from the bones.

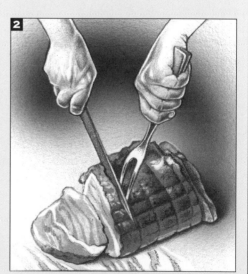

2. Set the roast cut side down; carve the meat across the grain into thick slices.

an internal temperature of 160 degrees, regardless of cooking method, low temperature or high. Unfortunately, at 160 degrees, the meat is gray, tough, and unappetizing.

The only thing that bothered us about the slow-roasted prime rib was its raw-looking, unrendered fatty exterior. By searing the meat on top of the stove before low-roasting it, though, we solved the problem of the unattractive look.

As unclear a term as "perfect prime rib" had been to us at the beginning, it was crystal clear the moment we carved off that first slab from our 200-degree roasted prime rib. We both immediately recognized it as the beef you get at a great prime rib restaurant. As it turns out, many prime rib restaurants slow-roast their meat. They use special ovens that roast the meat at 250 degrees until the meat reaches an internal temperature of 120 degrees. At that time, the oven heat is decreased to 140 degrees, causing the meat's internal temperature to increase to 130 degrees and re-

main there until ready to serve (up to twenty-four hours later). Unfortunately, few home cooks can use this method since most home oven thermostats do not go below 200 degrees. But by following the recipe below, home cooks can very closely approximate the superb prime rib served in the country's best restaurants.

Salt (For Once) Doesn't Make It Better

Because we had seen for ourselves salt's ability to improve certain foods (*see* "The Holiday Turkey Perfected," November/December 1993; "No More Watery Coleslaw," July/August 1995; and "Roast Turkey Revisited," page 9) and because we saw so many roast beef recipes promoting salt crusts and doughs, we felt certain salt would play a role in our perfect prime rib. Following some recipes and adapting others, we tested five salt-related methods, including covering a prime rib with three pounds of kosher salt before roasting, encasing it in a salt dough, covering it with a layer

of coarse sea salt and refrigerating it for twenty-four hours prior to roasting, and soaking it in a brine for nine hours prior to roasting.

None of the rib roasts were improved from the salting techniques. In fact, most of these roasts were clearly inferior. While we chipped through the thick layer of salt on the kosher salt prime rib to find a nicely browned roast, the salt had not penetrated past the surface. This roast was juicy, but the meat texture was firmer—not an advantage as far as we were concerned. When we asked ourselves if this roast was worth a box of salt, our answer was an emphatic "No."

The salt-dough–encased prime rib cooked quickly. In fact, when we checked it at two hours (the minimum cooking time for most of the roasts), it registered 140 degrees, and by the time we were ready to carve, it had already moved up to 160 degrees. We could find no reason to compensate for this overcooked state. The savings in oven time was wasted on making and rolling out the dough and blanketing it over the roast. And, since the dough ingredients simply get tossed after cooking, there is not even a payoff in terms of a stunning presentation.

The exterior of the meat covered with coarse sea salt was inedibly salty, while the interior of the meat was completely unaffected, but the real loser was the brined roast. The brining turned our fine-textured, tender prime cut into an ordinary, coarse and firm-textured, cheaper cut of beef. Our $5.29-per-pound roast tasted more like $2.59 brisket. The brine seemed to have penetrated a few inches into the meat, though we're not sure how it got there since the meat's weight before and after soaking were virtually identical.

PERFECT PRIME RIB
Serves 6 to 8

Even if you don't purchase the roast a week ahead of time as the instructions suggest, even a day or two of aging in the refrigerator will help.

> 1   3-rib standing rib roast (7 pounds), first cut (*see* "Ask for It by Number," page 13), aged (*see* "Aging Beef: Wet or Dry?" left), set at room temperature for 3 hours, and tied (*see* "Tie It Up," page 13)
>   Salt and ground black pepper

1. Adjust oven rack to low position and heat oven to 200 degrees. Heat large roasting pan over two burners set at medium-high heat. Place roast in hot pan and cook on all sides until nicely browned and about ½ cup fat has rendered, 6 to 8 minutes.

2. Remove roast from pan. Set wire rack in pan, then set roast on rack. Generously season with salt and pepper.

3. Place roast in oven and roast until meat registers 130 degrees (for medium-rare), about 3½ hours (or about 30 minutes per pound). Let stand 20 minutes (a bit longer is fine) before serving.

4. Transfer to cutting board and carve in accordance with "Carve It Simply," page 13. ∎

AGING BEEF: WET OR DRY?

I didn't realize how hard it was to find dry-aged beef until I set out to buy it. I had seen hanging beef carcasses at my local butcher's, so I assumed he sold at least some aged beef. When I called to order dry-aged prime rib for testing, though, he told me they carried only Kry-O-Vac- or wet-aged beef. His reasons were mostly financial.

Most butchers don't dry-age beef anymore because hanging quarters of beef take up too much refrigerator space for too long. During its aging process, dry-aged beef also dehydrates (loses weight) and requires trimming (loses more weight). That weight loss means less beef costs more money. Wet-aged beef loses virtually no weight during the aging process and it comes pre-butchered, packaged, and ready to sell. Since beef is expensive to begin with, most customers opt for the less expensive wet-aged beef.

Is there a difference between wet-aged and dry-aged beef? We think so. For our test, we ordered both a dry-aged and wet-aged prime rib roast from a restaurant supplier in Manhattan. The differences between the two roasts were clear-cut.

Like a good, young red

wine, wet-aged beef tasted pleasant and fresh on its own. When compared to the dry-aged beef, though, we realized its flavors were less concentrated. The meat tasted washed out. The dry-aged beef, on the other hand, engaged the mouth. It was stronger, richer, and gamier-tasting with a pleasant tang. The dry-aged and wet-aged beef were equally tender, but the dry-aged beef had an added buttery texture about it.

The aging process—wet or dry—causes beef to become tender. Enclosed in Kry-O-Vac, wet-aged beef is shut off from oxygen—the key to flavor development and concentration. Since availability and price pose problems, you may simply want to age beef yourself. It's just a matter of

making room in the refrigerator and remembering to buy the roast ahead of time.

To dry-age a prime rib, buy your roast up to one week early. Pat it dry and place it on a wire rack set over a paper-towel-lined cake pan or plate (*see* illustration below, left). Set the racked roast in the refrigerator and let it age until you are ready to roast it, three to seven days. (I left one in the refrigerator for nine days; the cooked roast was meltingly tender with big flavor.) Before roasting, shave off any exterior meat that has completely dehydrated (illustration below, right). Between the trimming and dehydration, count on a seven-pound roast losing a pound or so during a week's aging.—*P.A.*

To dry-age the prime rib, refrigerate it on a rack set over a paper-towel-lined cake pan for three to seven days.

Once the beef has aged, shave off the dehydrated exterior layer of the roast with a sharp knife.

ILLUSTRATIONS BY HARRY DAVIS

Fearless Phyllo

To avoid cracking and sticking, thaw phyllo dough slowly, keep it at room temperature, and brush it with melted or clarified butter.

~ BY DIANE KOCHILAS ~

Phyllo is easy to use, can be formed into myriad shapes, and works equally well in sweet and savory recipes. For all its versatility, though, phyllo is not without pitfalls.

Phyllo comes in very thin sheets that are either frozen or chilled. The single most important thing to know when working with the pastry is that it needs to be at room temperature when you use it. Most problems arise from packages that have been hastily thawed; sheets that are still cold will crack along the folds or may be stuck together at the corners.

If the package is frozen, it should be thawed slowly in the refrigerator overnight or for at least eight hours. Chilled phyllo should then be left out (still in the package) for two hours before using.

Unless there is a Greek or Middle Eastern food shop in your area, it is best to buy phyllo from a busy supermarket, where the product is likely to move quickly and therefore be fresher. Some manufacturers, such as Apollo, date their phyllo, so you can tell if it is fresh. Even if there is no date on the package, you know that phyllo is good and fresh if you can bunch up a sheet in your hand and open it again without its cracking.

Almost every phyllo recipe calls for brushing each layer of pastry with some sort of fat. In savory dishes a combination of oil and melted butter may be used, but butter provides richer flavor and crispier phyllo. For the crispiest results, the butter should be melted and clarified (milk solids, the white foam that is skimmed off when you clarify butter, can make the pastry burn).

Phyllo doesn't need to be brushed excessively with fat, however. A teaspoon of butter or oil per sheet is adequate if used with care, although the best results in terms of flavor and crispness are usually had with a slightly more generous use of fat, about half a tablespoon per sheet.

The filling recipes below can be used in any of the phyllo pastries on pages 16 and 17.

SPICED APPLE-RAISIN FILLING
Makes about 3½ cups

Although best used in the cigar-shaped and large triangle-shaped pastries, this filling can be used for other shapes as well. If using this filling for smaller pastries, cut the apples into a small dice and substitute currants for the raisins.

    3   large Granny Smith apples, peeled,
          cored, and sliced thin
    ½   cup dark or golden raisins
    ⅓   cup sugar
    1   tablespoon juice from small lemon
    1   teaspoon ground cinnamon
    ½   teaspoon ground cloves
          Pinch ground allspice
    2   tablespoons unsalted butter
    ½   cup dried bread crumbs

1. Mix apples, raisins, sugar, juice, and spices in large bowl.
2. Heat butter in medium skillet over medium heat. Add breadcrumbs and cook, stirring constantly, until golden brown, 2 to 3 minutes. Toss with apple mixture; set aside until ready to fill pastries.

SPINACH, LEEK, AND FETA FILLING
Makes about 2 cups

This recipe makes enough filling for the following: three to four dozen small triangles (about sixteen large triangles); eighteen small rolls (or four to six large rolls); four dozen small purses (or eight large purses); or about one dozen coils.

    2   tablespoons olive oil
    1   large leek, white part only, washed
          thoroughly and chopped fine
    1   box (10 ounces) frozen chopped
          spinach, thawed and
          squeezed dry
    ¼   cup minced fresh parsley leaves
    3   tablespoons minced fresh dill leaves
    ½   cup (2½ ounces) crumbled
          feta cheese
    1   large egg
    ¼   teaspoon grated nutmeg
          Salt and ground black pepper

1. Heat oil in large skillet over medium heat. Add leek; cook until softened, 6 to 8 minutes.
2. Meanwhile, mix spinach, parsley, dill, feta, and egg in medium bowl. Add cooked leek and season with nutmeg, salt, and pepper. Cover and refrigerate until ready to use.

CLASSIC BAKLAVA FILLING
Makes about 30 pastries

Baklava can be made with practically any combination of nuts or dried fruits. This filling can be used in any of the phyllo pastries.

    2   cups walnuts, minced
    2   cups almonds or pistachios, minced
    ½   cup currants
    3   tablespoons sugar
    1   tablespoon ground cinnamon
    ½   teaspoon ground cloves

Mix all filling ingredients in medium bowl. ■

Diane Kochilas is the author of *The Food and Wines of Greece* (St. Martins Press, 1990).

BUTTERING PHYLLO

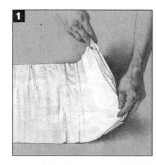

1. Fold a stack of phyllo sheets in half, forming a "book."

2. Fold the top left-hand half-sheet out and brush with butter. Brush all left sheets until you reach the center.

3. Without brushing the open middle sheet, "close" the book in the opposite direction from original fold.

4. Now fold the top sheet out as if opening the back cover of the book, and brush the right-hand sheets until you reach the middle again.

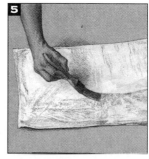

5. When the book is fully open again, brush the whole top sheet with butter.

Making Phyllo Pastries

~ BY DIANE KOCHILAS ~

You can use any of the fillings on page 15 to fill any of these pastries. Keep in mind that the process of brushing should be quick—three to four minutes at most—because phyllo dries out very quickly. When making any of these pastries, follow the layering procedure shown in step 1 of Phyllo Triangles, below, to keep the dough moist. Once you have filled and shaped your phyllo pastries, they may be frozen. Small pastries should be placed on a baking sheet for freezing. Brush the tops with butter, which helps to seal the phyllo against the moisture in the filling and will ultimately help to keep it crisp, then wrap the trays well with plastic wrap or foil. These frozen pastries can be baked or fried directly out of the freezer, without defrosting. ∎

PHYLLO TRIANGLES

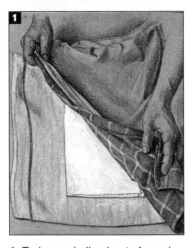

1. To keep phyllo sheets from drying out, cover them with either plastic wrap or two dish towels. Place a dry towel directly over the phyllo, then cover the dry towel with a damp towel.

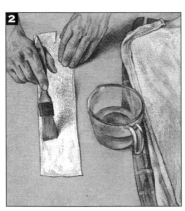

2. With the shortest end near you, brush a phyllo sheet with butter, then top it with a second sheet and brush it. Cut these sheets, lengthwise, to make two 6-inch wide double layer strips, then fold each strip in half lengthwise and brush the tops.

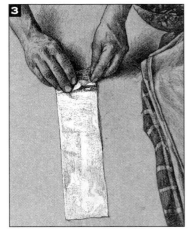

3. Place two rounded teaspoons of filling on the bottom left-hand corner. Fold up the phyllo to form a right-angle triangle.

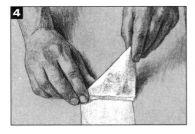

4. Continue folding up and over, flag-folding style, to end of strip.

5. Brush triangle with butter and place seam side down on an ungreased baking sheet. Bake in a 375-degree oven until golden, about 15 to 18 minutes.

For large Phyllo Triangles: Follow the instructions for Phyllo Triangles, using one phyllo sheet rather than two. Do not cut the pastry in half, but fold it over and brush the top with butter. Follow the folding instructions in illustrations 3 and 4, using 2 tablespoons of filling per triangle, then bake the triangles in a 325-degree oven until golden brown, 25 to 30 minutes.

PHYLLO ROLLS

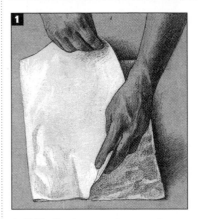

1. With the long end nearest you, brush one sheet of phyllo with butter, then fold it in half, crosswise. Brush the top with butter.

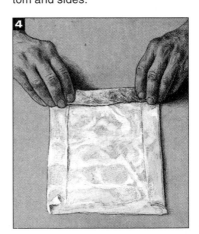

2. Spoon about 2 tablespoons of filling along the bottom edge, leaving a 1-inch border along the bottom and sides.

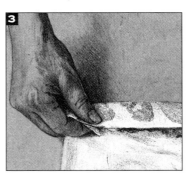

3. Fold the bottom of the dough over the filling.

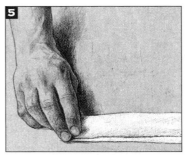

4. Fold in each side of the phyllo dough. Roll the phyllo up to form a cigar-shaped roll.

5. Brush the roll with butter and place it seam side down on an ungreased baking pan. Brush the top with butter. Bake in a 375-degree oven until golden, about 15 to 20 minutes.

For large Phyllo Rolls: Following illustrations 1 through 5 on page 15, brush a stack of five phyllo sheets with melted, clarified butter. Turn the stack so the short end is facing you. Spoon about ½ cup of filling along the bottom edge, leaving a 1½-inch border along the bottom and sides. Follow the instructions in steps 3 and 4 for Phyllo Rolls, using all five layers of the stacks to roll the filling. Bake in a 325-degree oven until golden brown, 25 to 35 minutes.

Coils can only be made with phyllo that is extremely fresh and pliable. If it cracks at all, it won't work. The fillings should be relatively dry, such as Spinach, Leek, and Feta Filling or Classic Baklava Filling.

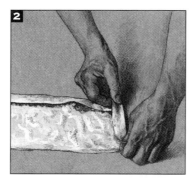

1. With the long end nearest you, brush a phyllo sheet with butter. Fold it in half, lengthwise, so that the fold is nearest you. Sprinkle the top surface with water, then spoon about 3 tablespoons of filling along the bottom edge, leaving a 1¼-inch border along the bottom and sides.

2. Fold the bottom of the phyllo over the filling; fold in the sides.

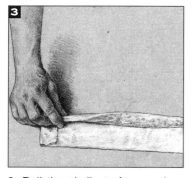

4. Keeping the phyllo seam side down, hold it by one end and gently roll it into a loose coil.

3. Roll the phyllo to form a cigar shape, as with Phyllo Rolls.

5. Push the coil together with cupped hands. Place all the coils you have shaped on an ungreased baking sheet. Brush the tops with butter or oil and bake in a 350-degree oven until golden, about 20 to 30 minutes.

2. Spoon two teaspoons of filling onto each square, brushing the border of each square with water.

1. Following illustrations 1 through 4, page 15, brush a stack of 4 phyllo sheets with butter. Using a ruler as a guide, cut the phyllo stack into twenty-four 2½-inch squares.

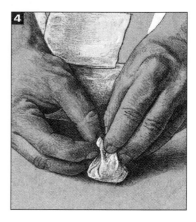

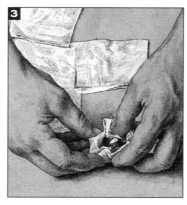

4. Pinch the corner together to form a sealed pouch. Brush each pouch with butter and place them 1 inch apart on an ungreased cookie sheet. Freeze for 10 minutes before baking. Bake in a 375-degree oven until golden, 12 to 15 minutes.

3. Gather the points of the square with two hands.

For large Phyllo Purses: Cut 6- or 8-inch squares and fill them with 4 to 5 tablespoons of filling. Bake in a 325-degree oven until golden brown, 20 to 25 minutes.

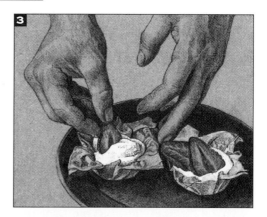

1. Following illustrations 1 through 4, page 15, brush a stack of 4 phyllo sheets with butter. Using a ruler as a guide, cut the phyllo stack into 5-inch squares. Grease a muffin tin. Push each stack into an individual muffin cup.

2. Fold the edges down or leave them sticking up for decoration. Bake the shells in a 325-degree oven until golden, about 8 to 10 minutes, watching carefully that the tips do not burn.

3. Remove the shells from the oven and let them cool in the muffin tin for 5 minutes. Spoon in sweet or savory filling.

How To Make Potato Gratin

For the easiest, most tender gratin, cook the potatoes on the stovetop in liquid,
then bake them in a shallow pan.

~ BY KATHERINE ALFORD ~

"Potato gratins, what a breeze," I thought to myself. "Slice up a couple of spuds, pour on some milk, put it in a warm oven, and forget about it until it is golden brown and bubbly." Forty pounds of potatoes and over thirty gratins later, I have found that everything from how thick you slice the potatoes to the type of pan you use makes a difference in this dish.

Potato gratins—also known as French dauphinois or Yankee scalloped potatoes—consist of thinly sliced potatoes covered by a liquid and baked in a wide, shallow baking pan until the potatoes are tender and the top gets a burnished crust. Most recipes follow the same procedure: Rub an ovenproof dish with garlic, brush it with butter, layer it with sliced potatoes, add seasonings and just enough liquid to cover the potatoes, and bake. But, as I discovered, within that definition lies plenty of room for personal taste.

The Slice, Not the Potato

My starting point was to find out whether the type of potato makes a difference in the finished product. I went to my cookbooks but found no consensus. Some adamantly preferred one type or another, and others were blasé. So I decided to try all the major varieties of potatoes, including all-purpose whites, boilers, yellow-fleshed, and new potatoes. All made tasty gratins, but I did find subtle variations in flavor or texture—waxy potatoes ended up firmer, for example, while floury baking potatoes were more tender. However, the differences were relatively slight, and I began to suspect that the way the potato is sliced is more significant than which type is used.

I had plenty of opportunity to test this theory. As I plowed through my mountain of tubers, peeling and slicing, I quickly discarded my knife as too slow. I tried a food processor but found that the resulting slices were uneven. Also, I had to cut the larger potatoes into awkward shapes to fit them into the feed tube. In the end, I was most satisfied with an inexpensive plastic slicer (*see* "Any Way You Slice It," page 19). With the aid of the mandolin and its handy safety guard, I could effortlessly slice the potatoes, which made

When slicing potatoes for use in gratins, don't store them in water to prevent oxidation since this pulls out all their starch and results in a bland gratin. Instead, peel and slice the potatoes only when you're ready to begin cooking.

putting a gratin together a snap.

Another advantage of the mandolin is its ability to slice the potatoes not only very evenly, but also very thinly. I found potatoes cut into one-sixteenth-inch slices soaked up the cooking liquid and melted into a cakelike texture. When sliced one-eighth-inch thick, however, they kept their shape throughout baking and ended up as distinct slices, bathed in sauce.

The Pan, the Temperature, and the Liquid

The pan in which you make gratin is an important consideration. A standard gratin dish is oval, ten to twelve inches long, and six to eight inches wide. As it turns out, the dimensions of the pan are more important than the material of which the pan is made. I cooked successful gratins in a variety of dishes, from classic enamel to earthenware to ovenproof glass—the key is that they were all shallow. Two to three layers of potatoes should come about three-quarters of the way up the sides of the pan so they cook evenly and have a broad surface area to brown.

Whatever kind of dish you use, the standard procedure calls for rubbing it with garlic prior to cooking. Although I have rubbed my share of dishes with cloves of garlic over the years, I've never been sure if it was merely an occult ritual or if it really contributed to the flavor of dish. In simple gratins, if I focused on the taste of garlic, there was a pleasant hint of it. But when heady Gruyère cheese was included in the dish, the garlic got lost. I found that the best way to get a stronger garlic punch was to smash the clove and vigorously rub it around the dish so that at least half of it was smeared on the surface, then let this dry a bit while I prepared the rest of the dish. I then minced the remaining garlic and tossed it into my cooking liquid, which fully perfumed the gratin.

I next turned my attention to oven temperature. I baked gratins at temperatures of 350, 400, and 450 degrees. I found that 350 was best, because at the higher temperatures, the slices on the top of the gratin tended to dry out and become tough. I also discovered that it helps to baste the top slices once or twice during the cooking so they stay moist and brown evenly.

Next, I made gratins using a variety of liquids, including whole milk, low-fat milk, half-and-half, heavy cream, meat broths, and water. The heavy cream had a tendency to break and become greasy, particularly at higher temperatures. The low-fat milk, on the other hand, was insipid while the whole milk was almost completely soaked up by the potatoes, leaving only a light curd between the layers. My favorite all-purpose, dairy cooking medium turned out to be half-and-half cooked at 350 degrees for about an hour. Gratins made this way had just the right balance of saturated potato and saucy liquid, without overwhelming the taste of the potato. They were also easy to prepare.

Not all gratins need to be made with dairy products, however, especially as we watch our fat consumption. One of the virtues of potato gratins is that they are delicious when made with flavorful broths and stocks. I was very pleased with the results I got with water as well. In fact, it was a recipe using water that led me to the particular cooking method that made the best gratins.

I had tried pouring cold liquids over the layered potatoes and baking them. Next, I tried heating the liquid first, which sped up the cooking process but didn't affect the overall result. I was intrigued by a technique used by Richard Olney in his justly famous Potato and Sorrel Gratin, included in Lydie Marshal's *Passion for Potatoes* (Harper, 1992). To make this gratin, Olney first puts potato slices and onions in a saucepan with barely enough salted water to cover them and then brings the mixture just up to a boil on top of the stove. As the water reaches a boil, it thickens beautifully to envelop the potatoes in a velvety sauce. The transformation of the liquid is a wonderful demonstration of food chemistry—the essential relationship of heat and starch is right there in the pot to see.

I adopted this basic technique of cooking the sliced potatoes in the cooking liquid before pouring both into the gratin dish. For my tests, I placed a pound of sliced potatoes, enough liquid to barely cover them, salt, and pepper into a saucepan and brought the liquid to a boil, stirring occasionally so the potatoes didn't scorch or stick. I next lowered the heat and simmered the mixture until the liquid thickened, then poured the potatoes into a baking dish and finished them in a 350-degree oven.

This method turned out to possess many benefits. It sped up the cooking process by heating the ingredients before baking, it made the assembly of the gratin much faster, and because the seasoning was added to the liquid, it ensured that the final product was evenly seasoned. The only seeming disadvantage was that the potatoes could not be fastidiously laid out in the dish in a harmonious pattern, a process I had always enjoyed. I was not sure that this method would satisfy my aesthetics. But I was pleased to find that the slices adhered together in a natural pattern, and I could easily fashion the top layer into a scalloped motif with a fork if I so desired.

Additional Tips

There are several ways to enhance the crust from which these dishes get their name (the French word *gratin* means "crust"). Dotting the top with butter aids the golden crust, as does cheese. A nice finish can also be achieved by pouring a thin layer of cream over the top of the gratin for the final twenty or thirty minutes of baking. This cap of cream browns evenly without greasy edges. I tried bread crumbs as well but found them superfluous. Incidentally, gratins made without cheese take longer to brown, so when the potatoes are tender, you can speed up the final browning by running the dish under a broiler.

Gratins can take on different characteristics by infusing the liquid with herbs or spices. Friendly pairings are bay leaf, thyme, basil, and tarragon, and in lighter gratins, I like to layer thin slices of vegetables. What I love best about potato gratins is that with a few simple variations, they can suit a wide variety of meals, seasons, and moods.

CLASSIC POTATO GRATIN
Serves 4 to 6
For a more pronounced crust, sprinkle three tablespoons of heavy cream or grated Gruyère cheese on top of the potatoes after forty-five minutes of baking.

    1   large garlic clove, peeled and smashed
    1   tablespoon butter, softened
    2¼ cups half-and-half
    1¼ teaspoons salt
    ⅛   teaspoon ground black pepper
        Pinch grated nutmeg
        Pinch cayenne pepper (optional)
    2   pounds potatoes, peeled and sliced
        ⅛-inch thick or less

1. Adjust oven rack to center position and heat oven to 350 degrees. Rub bottom and sides of 5- to 6-cup gratin dish or shallow baking dish with garlic. Mince remaining garlic and set aside. Once garlic in dish has dried, about 2 minutes, spread dish with half the butter.

2. Bring half-and-half, salt, pepper, nutmeg, cayenne (if desired), potatoes, and reserved garlic

to boil in medium saucepan over medium-high heat, stirring occasionally with wooden spoon (liquid will just barely cover potatoes). Reduce heat and simmer until liquid thickens, about 2 minutes.

3. Pour potato mixture into prepared dish; shake dish or use fork to distribute potatoes evenly. Gently press down potatoes until submerged in liquid; dot with remaining butter.

4. Bake until top is golden brown (basting once or twice during first 45 minutes) about 1 hour 15 minutes. Let rest 5 minutes and serve.

POTATO GRATIN WITH SWEET PEPPERS AND TOMATOES
Follow recipe for Classic Potato Gratin, increasing oven temperature from 350 to 375 degrees. Increase garlic from 1 to 2 large cloves. Substitute 2½ tablespoons olive oil for butter, using ½ tablespoon to coat baking dish. Heat remaining oil in medium saucepan and sauté reserved minced garlic with 1 onion, sliced thin, until soft and lightly browned, about 5 minutes. Add potatoes, liquid, and seasonings, substituting 1½ cups water and ½ cup dry vermouth for half-and-half and 3 tablespoons minced fresh basil leaves for nutmeg. Pour half of potato mixture into prepared dish; top with 1 red bell pepper, cored, seeded, and sliced thin. Add remaining potato mixture and cover with 5 plum tomatoes, sliced thin. Season with additional salt and pepper to taste and sprinkle with ¼ cup grated Parmesan cheese. Increase baking time to 1 hour 25 minutes.

POTATO GRATIN WITH BROTH AND PARMESAN
Follow recipe for Classic Potato Gratin, increasing oven temperature from 350 to 375 degrees. Increase garlic from 1 to 2 large cloves. Substitute equal amount chicken stock or low-sodium canned broth for half-and-half. Decrease salt to 1 teaspoon if using unsalted homemade stock or ½ teaspoon if using canned broth. Substitute one bay leaf for nutmeg. Sprinkle ¼ cup grated Parmesan on gratin after 45 minutes of baking.■

Katherine Alford is a cooking teacher and food writer living in New York.

The consistently thin, even potato slices that make great gratins are easy to achieve using a slicing device known as a mandolin. To determine the performance differences between the more and less expensive models, we sliced potatoes and lemons on a top-of-the-line French Bron mandolin costing $150, a $30 German Boerner V-Slicer, and a $5.50 Feemster Vegetable Slicer made in the United States.

First, it is important to purchase a slicer with a safety guard, which guides food onto—and protects your hands from—the blade. Whether expensive or not, all these contraptions have razor-sharp blades, and a slip of the finger could be dangerous. While the Feemster, for example, makes respectable slices and has a wide adjustment range, it comes without

a safety guard and is light and flimsy. We do not recommend it.

The expensive Bron mandolin is the heaviest and most solid. It has a safety guard and adjusts infinitely between one-sixteenth and one-half inch for slicing, thick and thin julienning, and waffle cutting. It sliced well, though we felt the blade on our brand new test model might be a bit dull. If durability tops your priority list and cost is less important, this model is a good choice. Many restaurant kitchens use it and consider it a workhorse for slicing.

The best of the three slicers we tested, however, was the Boerner V-Slicer. Though it is made of plastic and therefore probably less durable than a stainless-steel model, it does have a safety guard that spears the food to hold it in place and

also plunges it toward the blade, enabling you to safely slice the entire piece as the slicing action decreases its size. This feature helps minimize waste. Also, the edges of the safety guard are ridged, so you'll be able to feel them with your fingers even if you glance away. Another advantage of the V-Slicer is the angle of its blades. Food hits an angled blade less abruptly than it does a straight blade and is exposed to more blade area for a cleaner, easier slice. We found this to be a significant advantage. The V-Slicer has only two adjustments for slicing—thick (one-quarter inch) and thin (one-sixteenth inch)—but that should be sufficient for most home cooking. (*See Sources and Resources, page 32, for ordering information.*)

Feemster Vegetable Slicer

Boerner V-Slicer

Bron Mandolin

How to Cook Brussels Sprouts

Braising is the preferred way to prepare these "little cabbages," with microwaving a close second.

∼ BY PHYLLIS M. CAREY ∼

The taste of brussels sprouts is often maligned simply because the sprouts are not prepared properly. True, they can be bitter and limp if overcooked, but they can also be crisp, tender, and nutty-flavored when handled appropriately.

To find the best and simplest way to prepare brussels sprouts, I chose to investigate boiling, steaming, microwaving, and braising. The result I was looking for was a tender, not-too-bitter, attractively green-colored brussels sprout that could be prepared with little fuss.

I began my testing with boiling and steaming, the two most popular methods of cooking vegetables. Since bringing water to a boil can take up to twenty minutes, the added cooking time of eight to ten minutes—to reach just the right tenderness—meant that boiled brussels sprouts could take up to thirty minutes to prepare. That would be acceptable had the result been spectacular. I found, however, that boiling produced only a waterlogged, olive-green-colored, bitter sprout.

Steaming was next. Certainly, steaming is a great way to cook vegetables—fewer nutrients are washed away in the water, the vegetables keep their vibrant colors, and, since less boiled water is used, the cooking time is dramatically reduced. I was convinced that this would be the ideal cooking method for these "little cabbages." However, after several trials, I found that steamed brussels sprouts still had quite a bitter taste rather than the nutty flavor I sought, even when I was very careful not to overcook them.

If steaming wasn't the answer, what *would* produce the tender, tasty sprouts I desired? I considered the microwave, an appliance that, even microwave foes would agree, can beautifully prepare many varieties of vegetables. To find out, I added one-quarter cup of water to one pound of brussels sprouts and cooked them, covered, on high power for five to six minutes. They were perfect: green, tender, sweet, and nutty.

A problem arose, however, when I considered the fact that the quantity of brussels sprouts cooked in the microwave at any one time would determine how long they would take to cook. Unlike conventional cooking methods, even a modest adjustment in microwave cooking time could result in completely overcooked vegetables. For those accustomed to microwave cooking and familiar with such timing adjustments, this method would be the easiest and best for preparing sprouts. But what about those who don't know the intricacies of microwave cooking and don't feel comfortable winging it? An overcooked brussels sprout from the microwave oven is actually chewy. I felt I needed to continue my investigation.

Braising, which refers to cooking food with a small amount of liquid in a tightly covered pan, was the next and last cooking method I tried. As I thought about it, I realized that microwaved brussels sprouts actually *are* braised—rapidly. Perhaps cooking them on the stovetop would produce equally satisfying results. I braised one pound of sprouts on top of the stove, using only half a cup of water, cooking them until they were just tender enough to be pierced easily by the tip of a knife, about eight to ten minutes. This method met all the criteria I had established for the perfectly cooked brussels sprout by producing a tender, nutty-flavored, bright green vegetable.

Since braising in water was so successful, I decided to try braising in other liquids as well. First, I tried cooking the sprouts in unsalted butter, but found that it was difficult to regulate the heat with the lid on and still keep the butter from burning. They came out tasting fine but took longer to cook and required too much attention. Adding broth to the butter helped reduce the attention needed and produced a very green vegetable, but the taste was merely acceptable. Braising in chicken stock produced a sprout that didn't taste much different from the ones braised in water.

Overall, the tastiest brussels sprouts I cooked came from braising them in whipping cream, a classic French technique for cooking vegetables. I streamlined the preparation by simply placing the cleaned sprouts in a covered pan with the cream. Lightly seasoned with salt, pepper, and nutmeg, the finished sprouts absorbed most of the cream, creating a slightly sweet, nutty flavor that was in no way bitter. Because the results were so tasty, I almost hesitate to offer any additional ideas for preparing brussels sprouts. Alas, cooking this healthy vegetable in cream on a regular basis simply goes against the healthy lifestyle conscience. Save this method for the holidays when you can throw caution to the wind. For everyday, you can still produce wonderful sprouts by braising them in water.

The best brussels sprouts are available in late fall through early winter, peaking in late November. They are often associated with the holidays because of their short season. When buying brussels sprouts, choose those with small, tight heads, no more than one and one-half inches in diameter, for the best flavor. Larger sprouts can often be trimmed of loose leaves along the stem and still be quite good. However, because these larger sprouts are more robust, they cook best when cut in half.

Look for firm, compact, bright green brussels sprouts. Yellow or brown-tipped leaves usually indicate that they are older. Once purchased, keep the sprouts in a vented container in the refrigerator for no longer than four to five days.

PREPARING BRUSSELS SPROUTS

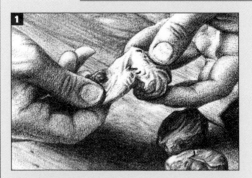

1. To prepare brussels sprouts for cooking, first peel off any loose or discolored leaves.

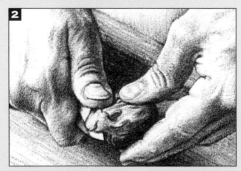

2. Use a paring knife to slice off the bottom of the stem end, leaving leaves attached.

ILLUSTRATIONS BY DAN BROWN

BASIC BRAISED BRUSSELS SPROUTS
Serves 3 to 4

Serve these tender brussels sprouts seasoned simply with ground black pepper and butter or in one of the following recipes.

   1 pound small, firm, bright green brussels sprouts, rinsed, with stem ends and discolored leaves removed (*see* illustration, page 20)
   ½ teaspoon salt

Bring sprouts, ½ cup water, and salt to boil in 2-quart saucepan over medium-high heat. Lower heat, cover, and simmer (shaking pan once or twice to redistribute sprouts) until knife tip inserted into a brussels sprout center meets no resistance, 8 to 10 minutes. Drain well and serve or continue with one of the recipes that follow.

GLAZED BRUSSELS SPROUTS WITH CHESTNUTS
Serves 4 to 6

To use fresh chestnuts, place the nuts in a saucepan, cover them with boiling water, and simmer them for twenty to thirty minutes. Alternatively, roast them in a 425-degree oven for twenty to twenty-five minutes until tender. Peel both the shell and the thin skin from the meat when they are cool enough to handle. If chestnuts are unavailable, substitute half a cup of toasted chopped hazelnuts.

   3 tablespoons unsalted butter
   1 tablespoon granulated sugar
   1 can (16 ounces) peeled chestnuts in water, drained (about 1½ cups)
   1 recipe Basic Braised Brussels Sprouts
      Salt and ground black pepper

1. Heat 2 tablespoons of the butter and sugar in medium skillet over medium-high heat until butter melts and sugar dissolves.

2. Stir in chestnuts. Turn heat to low and cook, stirring occasionally, until chestnuts are glazed, about 3 minutes.

3. Add remaining butter and sprouts; cook, stirring occasionally, to heat through, about 5 minutes. Season to taste with salt and pepper and serve.

SAUTÉED BRUSSELS SPROUTS WITH GARLIC AND PINE NUTS
Serves 4

This is an especially good way to prepare brussels sprouts for those unsure of their liking for this vegetable. Lots of garlic never hurts.

   2 tablespoons olive oil
   ¼ cup pine nuts
   2 large garlic cloves, minced
   1 recipe Basic Braised Brussels Sprouts, quartered after cooking
      Salt and ground black pepper

1. Heat oil in large skillet over medium heat. Add nuts; cook, stirring frequently, until nuts be-

PHOTOGRAPHS BY DAVE HENDERSON

What about that age-old idea of cutting a small "X" in the stem end of each brussels sprout before cooking? The idea behind this technique is to produce faster, more even cooking throughout by allowing the water or steam to penetrate the thicker stem end. If you have ever practiced this technique, you know that it is time-consuming to cut that little "X," especially since the sprouts are small and round and tend to roll away from the knife. I thought it would be worthwhile to see if this extra step was really necessary.

I carved an "X" into the bottom of half of each batch of brussels sprouts I tested—whether boiled, steamed, microwaved, or braised. While monitoring cooking times, I tested one sprout with an "X" and one without. Interestingly, I found that the sprouts with an "X" cut in the stem end did, indeed, seem to be more evenly cooked when tested early in the cooking, before the sprout was completely tender. However, by the time the sprout top was cooked through, it was impossible to tell the difference in the tenderness or cooking evenness between the marked and unmarked sprouts.

On-site tests conducted at *Cook's Illustrated* showed that the same result held true for other vegetables commonly carved with an "X" for even cooking: broccoli stems and pearl onions. Pearl onions cooked at exactly the same rate whether they had been marked or not while carved broccoli stalks tested slightly faster up to the three-minute point after which they showed no difference at all.

In other words, the notorious "X" appears to be a tenet of kitchen wisdom based on myth. Cutting an "X" into the stem end of a brussels sprout, broccoli stalk, or pearl onion has no effect on producing evenly cooked, tender vegetables.—*P.M.C.*

gin to brown, about 2 minutes. Add garlic; cook until softened, about 1 minute.

2. Stir in sprouts and cook, stirring constantly, until heated through, 2 to 3 minutes. Season to taste with salt and pepper and serve.

BRAISED BRUSSELS SPROUTS WITH TARRAGON-MUSTARD BUTTER
Serves 4

The mustard sauce in this recipe may separate and appear curdled after the brussels sprouts are added. If so, continue cooking, and it should come back together.

   4 tablespoons unsalted butter
   2 tablespoons Dijon mustard
   1 teaspoon dried tarragon leaves
   1 recipe Basic Braised Brussels Sprouts
      Salt and ground black pepper

1. Melt butter in medium skillet over medium heat. Whisk in mustard until smooth; add tarragon. Cook, stirring constantly, until bubbly, about 30 seconds.

2. Stir in sprouts, coating well with butter mixture. Cook, stirring frequently, until heated through, 3 to 4 minutes. Season to taste with salt and pepper and serve.

BRUSSELS SPROUTS BRAISED IN CREAM
Serves 4

Follow recipe for Basic Braised Brussels Sprouts, substituting 1 cup whipping cream for ½ cup water. Increase cooking time to 10 to 12 minutes.

Season with pinch grated nutmeg and ground black pepper and serve without draining.

BRAISED BRUSSELS SPROUTS WITH NUTMEG-SCENTED WHITE SAUCE
Serves 4

Scalding the milk makes it easier to blend in with the butter-flour mixture. There is little chance of lumping and the sauce comes to a boil more quickly as well.

   2 tablespoons unsalted butter
   2 medium shallots, minced
   1 tablespoon flour
   1 cup whole or 2 percent milk, heated to boiling
   ½ teaspoon salt
   ¼ teaspoon pepper
      Pinch ground nutmeg or to taste
   1 recipe Basic Braised Brussels Sprouts

1. Heat butter in medium saucepan over medium heat. Add shallots; sauté until just softened, about 2 minutes. Whisk in flour; continue to cook for 30 seconds.

2. Increase heat to medium-high; whisk in hot milk. Continue to whisk until mixture comes to boil. Reduce heat to medium and simmer until fully thickened, 1 to 2 minutes longer. Season with salt, pepper, and nutmeg.

3. Add sprouts to sauce; toss to coat. Simmer until heated through, about 2 minutes longer. Adjust seasonings and serve immediately.

Phyllis M. Carey is the author of *The Casual Gourmet; 50 Entertaining Menus.*

Old-Fashioned Gingerbread

For the best version of this traditional cake, use light molasses, equal parts of whole milk and buttermilk, and melt the butter before adding it to the batter.

∽ BY JUDY MONROE ∽

Gingerbread can be served right out of the oven, cooled to warm, or at room temperature, and will retain its moist texture for up to five days.

Despite its name, gingerbread is a cake rather than a bread, since it is tender, moist, and several inches thick. It is also a boon to busy cooks since a batch popped into the oven an hour or so before mealtime means warm gingerbread squares for dessert.

According to Bruce Cost, author of *Ginger: East to West* (Aris Books, 1989), gingerbread derives its name from medieval medicinal pastes and candies containing ginger. By the fourteenth century, honey and bread crumbs had been added, and gingerbread had come to resemble a dry, flat, sliceable bread. By the early seventeenth century, French and German cooks had added flour and eggs to the mix, producing something close to the modern version. The English continued to refine the recipe, adding the distinctive flavor of molasses, which was available to them in great quantities from their American colonies. Our American version of gingerbread, not surprisingly, follows the English mold.

My goal was to develop a traditional American gingerbread. The basic ingredients for spicy cake include some type of fat, sugar, eggs, a liquid such as milk or water, molasses, flour, a chemical leavener, and spices. Within these parameters, different types of gingerbread abound. Some are soft and cakey squares; others are more like breads and are baked in a loaf pan. For my recipe, I aimed for a sweet, moist, well-balanced spice cake with a slightly crispy top and crust. I found that small changes in ingredients made the difference between a dry, heavy cake versus a light, moist, pleasantly spicy gingerbread.

To carry out my experiments, I needed a basic recipe. My choice was between the two most common versions of cakelike gingerbreads—those made with hot water and those made with milk. After testing both, I chose the milk-based gingerbread as my starting point. It tasted richer and baked up moister because of the milk fat.

The Right Sweeteners
I next concentrated on finding the best type and blend of sweeteners. Most recipes called for a dry sugar—white, light brown, or dark brown—and a liquid sugar of some variety. To give every recipe its due, I tested gingerbreads made with four types of molasses—light, dark, black strap, and sorghum molasses—as well as cane sugar syrup, honey, corn syrup, and maple syrup.

The light-colored honey gingerbread received only so-so taste ratings from all of my eighteen testers. Corn syrup garnered few comments other than "bland" and "boring." Some tasters liked the maple syrup gingerbreads, but the taste was untraditional and too sweet.

I quickly discovered that, at least for American taste buds, molasses is a key gingerbread ingredient. It gives gingerbread an old-fashioned taste and deepens the overall flavor. But the type of molasses is crucial.

All types of molasses are extracted from cane sugar, but the darker types, including dark, black strap, and sorghum versions, undergo less processing. This gives them a more robust flavor and darker color. Because of their strong, assertive flavor, however, both black strap molasses and sorghum molasses gingerbreads scored poorly. In my taste ratings, light unsulphured molasses flew to the top. One cup gave the gingerbread a lovely brown color, moistness, and a rich, sweet taste. The runner-up was cane syrup. But while cane syrup gingerbreads were sweeter and lighter than those made with molasses, they lacked that satisfying molasses-flavor punch.

Once I settled on light molasses, I tested the dry sugars. Brown sugar showed up more often in gingerbread recipes than white sugar, and I assumed it tasted the best. My tests proved different. Molasses and white sugar were the best taste combination. Brown sugar, because it already contains molasses, added too much molasses flavor while the less assertive white sugar allowed the spices to dominate.

My next experiments centered on the fat, eggs, and milk. With bold-tasting molasses and the many spices, would a neutral vegetable fat rate well? The answer was a clear no, as butter decisively won this contest. The other contenders—vegetable oil, vegetable shortening, lard, and margarine—produced a less rich and tasty gingerbread.

I found that eight tablespoons of butter for an eleven-inch by seven-inch pan of gingerbread was just right. More made the gingerbread too heavy and rich. When I used less, the gingerbread was good, but drier. Some recipes instruct the cook to cream the softened butter, then beat in the sugar, molasses, eggs, and so on. Others tell the cook to melt the butter, then proceed. I found gingerbread made with melted butter to be a bit denser, but more moist and tender because the melted butter was evenly blended into the batter. Also, using melted butter made the mixing process easier and faster and avoided the risk of overbeating, which would have toughened the cake.

Next, I checked the egg requirement, trying first one egg and then two eggs per batch. Each produced good gingerbreads although two-egg gingerbread fell a little in the middle near the end of baking because of a bit too much moisture in the batter. A single egg gave me the best taste, height, and tenderness.

The Right Milk Combination
The remaining liquid ingredient I tested was milk. Buttermilk, another traditional gingerbread choice, was next on my list, plus sour cream and yogurt. At first, I was pleased with buttermilk gingerbread. The taste was rich and flavorful, although the texture was somewhat coarse. Buttermilk gingerbreads were also a darker brown, which some tasters rated as appealing. Regular milk, on the other hand, yielded gingerbreads with a softer color, finer texture, and higher rise, but they were also more bland and a mite drier. Gingerbreads made with sour cream and yogurt tasted less traditional, so I abandoned further tests.

Although the buttermilk seemed the best choice, the coarser texture and darker color bothered me. Also, by the second day, the buttermilk flavor in the stored gingerbreads started to dominate, which neither my tasters nor I liked. I wanted to achieve the light, fine texture and higher rise of the milk gingerbreads and the rich flavor of the buttermilk gingerbreads. Following a hunch, I tested mixtures of buttermilk and milk. Dozens of gingerbreads later, I hit on the right balance—half buttermilk and half whole milk. Both milks add richness, but the tang of buttermilk is balanced by the sweetness of regular milk. The milk-buttermilk combination baked into the best gingerbreads, with a wonderful taste, light texture, handsome brown color, and high rise. The crust and top, when cooled a little, crunched and melted in the mouth.

The Right Spices
I looked at over eighty gingerbread recipes, spanning nearly two centuries, and to my surprise, ran across several without any ginger! Gingerbread without ginger did not sound right—and when I tried the recipes, the cakes did not taste right.

An essential gingerbread ingredient, then, is ginger of some variety. Several recipes call for fresh ginger, and in combination with crystallized ginger, it makes a delicious gingerbread with a deep ginger flavor. The dried, ground version of the spice is more common in traditional gingerbread recipes, however, so I decided to stick with that for my master recipe.

Many recipes also include other spices, typically cinnamon, cloves, and nutmeg. After experimenting, I liked all these spices in my gingerbread, plus allspice and a little cocoa. I tried cardamom, a favorite spice in Scandinavian gingerbread but disliked its strong methanol taste. Although mace has a complex taste, I found it too subtle for gingerbread.

Generally, I preferred a pleasantly spicy gingerbread. For example, two tablespoons (six teaspoons) of ginger may be right for some, but I found this amount overpowering.

Other Dry Ingredients
Gingerbread requires a leavening such as baking powder or baking soda. When I first tested all buttermilk, one teaspoon of baking soda produced a gingerbread with good height, but somewhat coarse texture. When I tested milk-buttermilk combinations, I tinkered with the amounts of baking soda and baking powder. My goal was a gingerbread with a fine texture, high rise, and slightly crunchy top and sides. I got a high rise with two teaspoons of baking powder and only one-quarter teaspoon of baking soda, but the gingerbread was drier and less flavorful. I kept adjusting the proportion of baking powder to baking soda, but in the end, found that the best flavor

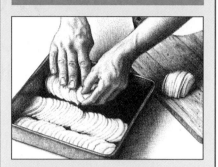

PLACING THE APPLES

For Apple Upside-Down Gingerbread (recipe at right), the apples should be peeled, halved, cut very thin, and fanned out so they overlap slightly in the pan.

came from using one-half teaspoon of baking soda to a little more than two cups of flour. I detected a mushy, soapy taste when I increased the baking soda, which meant that the available acid in the batter (from the molasses and buttermilk) was not neutralizing the extra leavening.

Since gingerbread is quickly mixed together, with minimal handling, all-purpose flour worked the best. These gingerbreads baked high with a fine texture. Cake flour is too soft for gingerbread and baked into a doughy mess while whole wheat flour made dense, coarse gingerbread.

When mixing the batter, a hand mixer, egg beater, wooden spoon, and whisk all worked quite well. The acid in the buttermilk and molasses inhibit gluten development and act as tenderizing agents. This means you can vanish any flour lumps, but do not overmix or the gingerbread will toughen. I ran across several recipes that alternated adding wet and dry ingredients, but this was overkill for a simple batch of gingerbread.

OLD-FASHIONED GINGERBREAD
Serves 8
For stronger ginger flavor, replace the dried ginger with three tablespoons grated peeled fresh gingerroot and three tablespoons minced crystallized ginger. If you prefer a lighter gingerbread cover loosely with aluminum foil during the last fifteen to twenty minutes of baking.

- 2¼ cups sifted, unbleached all-purpose flour
- ½ teaspoon baking soda
- ½ teaspoon salt
- 2 teaspoons ground dried ginger
- 1 teaspoon ground cinnamon
- ½ teaspoon ground cloves
- ½ teaspoon ground nutmeg
- ½ teaspoon ground allspice
- 1 teaspoon Dutch-processed cocoa
- 8 tablespoons unsalted butter, melted, then cooled to room temperature
- ¾ cup light unsulphured molasses
- ¾ cup granulated sugar
- ½ cup buttermilk
- ½ cup milk
- 1 large egg

1. Adjust oven rack to center position and heat oven to 350 degrees.
2. Whisk together flour, baking soda, salt, ginger, cinnamon, cloves, nutmeg, allspice, and cocoa in medium bowl.
3. Beat butter, molasses, sugar, buttermilk, milk, and egg in large bowl of an electric mixer

on low speed.
4. Add dry ingredients to liquid; beat on medium speed until batter is smooth and thick, about 1 minute, scraping down sides of bowl with rubber spatula as needed. Do not overmix. (If using the fresh ginger, batter will be lumpy.)
5. Working quickly, pour batter into nonstick 11-by-7-by1½-inch rectangular metal baking pan and smooth surface. (If you do not have a nonstick baking pan, then use no-stick cooking spray or solid vegetable shortening to grease pan sides and bottom, then dust with flour.)
6. Bake until top springs back when lightly touched, and edges have pulled away from the pan sides, about 35 to 45 minutes.
7. Set pan on wire cake rack and let cool 5 to 10 minutes. Serve hot, warm, or at room temperature. (Gingerbread can be wrapped in plastic wrap, then foil, and refrigeratored up to 5 days.)

APPLE UPSIDE-DOWN GINGERBREAD
Serves 8
For the apple topping: Grease sides of 11-by-7-by-1½-inch metal pan. Pour 4 tablespoons melted unsalted butter into pan; spread ¾ cup light brown sugar evenly over pan bottom. Peel, halve, core, and slice thin three tart baking apples (Granny Smith or Jonathan). Arrange slices, overlapping slightly upon brown sugar mixture (*see* illustration to left).

For the gingerbread: Follow Old-Fashioned Gingerbread recipe, pouring batter over apple slices. Increase baking time to 50 to 60 minutes. Let cake cool in pan 5 minutes, invert onto serving plate, cut into squares, and serve.

GINGERBREAD WITH DRIED FRUIT
Serves 8
Follow Old-Fashioned Gingerbread recipe, folding ¾ cup raisins, dried cranberries, *or* chopped prunes into batter.

ORANGE SAUCE FOR GINGERBREAD
Makes about 1¾ cups
Citrus complements gingerbread spices. Here, orange offers a refreshing change from the more traditional lemon-flavored sauce.

- 1⅓ cups juice plus 1 teaspoon zest from 4 large oranges
- ½ cup granulated sugar
- 4 teaspoons cornstarch
- ⅛ teaspoon salt
- 2 tablespoons unsalted butter
- 1 tablespoon juice from a small lemon

1. In small sauce pan bring orange juice, sugar, cornstarch, and salt to boil over medium heat, stirring constantly. Continue to cook until sauce is thick and clear, about 1 minute.
2. Remove from heat, then stir in butter, lemon juice, and zest. Serve hot, warm, or at room temperature over gingerbread squares. ∎

Judy Monroe is a St. Paul, Minnesota–based food writer and author of three cookbooks.

ILLUSTRATION BY DAN BROWN

Smoked Salmon Tasting

An inexpensive product from a small American producer tops our tasting.

⤳ BY JACK BISHOP ⤳

While most smoked salmon available these days is farm-raised, some wild smoked salmon is still available.

For most Americans, finding good-quality smoked salmon at a local market is a tough proposition—the available product is either of poor quality or does not turn over fast enough to maintain peak freshness.

As a result, most Americans must resort to mail order as their source of this special occasion food. Therefore, we decided to do a blind tasting of the many smoked salmons that are available by mail. Fortunately, the fish that topped our tasting is so inexpensive that, even with mailing costs, it is no more expensive than the product available in the best urban emporiums.

A Question of Species

There are several important species of salmon, among which Atlantic salmon is by far the most readily available on the East Coast. Fished almost to extinction in the wild, this species is now farmed all over the world. On the West Coast, there are many more alternatives, including not only farmed Atlantic but also wild varieties of native Pacific species. Each species has different characteristics, including color and fat content.

When it comes to smoking, the more oil in the fish the better. Salmon with too little fat dries out during smoking, resulting in a product more like salmon jerky than one with a creamy texture. For this reason, Atlantic salmon, which has the highest oil content, is the only choice in Europe and on the East Coast. Some locally farmed Atlantic salmon is smoked on the West Coast, as are native Pacific species, especially king and sockeye. But, for all intents and purposes, when you buy "smoked salmon" in most stores or by mail, you are buying smoked Atlantic salmon.

For this tasting, we assembled a representative group of salmon, including six domestic brands (from both coasts) and five European brands (from Norway, France, Ireland, and Scotland). We also sampled three different species (Atlantic, king, and sockeye), including both wild and farmed varieties of the Atlantic. While several of the smoked salmons that we tested are caught (or farmed) and smoked in the same general area, many are not. The winning smoked salmon, for example, comes from a smokehouse in New Jersey that purchases farmed Atlantic salmon from various sources.

The Smoking Process

So how does a whole fish become a side of smoked salmon? After the fish has been gutted and filleted, it undergoes two basic steps: curing and smoking. The sides of salmon can be dry-cured (rubbed with salt and perhaps sugar and other flavorings like herbs or spices) and left for several days in a very cool environment until much of the moisture has leached out of the fish. The other choice is wet-brining in which the fillets are soaked in a salt solution. Dry-curing takes much longer, but in either case the salt content of the fish must reach 5 percent (the legal minimum) in order to ensure that microbes cannot grow in the fish. Wet-brining results in a mushier texture. Professionals do not recommend it.

After the fish has been cured, it is smoked. A number of variables exist here, including temperature, type of wood, and length of smoking. For a soft, silky texture, salmon is cold-smoked at temperatures under 90 degrees (and often much lower). The length of time will affect the degree of smoke flavor imparted to the fish. Obviously, the type of wood is key. Smokehouses traditionally have used local woods: alder in the Pacific Northwest, hickory and fruitwoods in the Northeast, oak in Scotland, juniper in Norway. Of course, modern commerce has made it possible to use any wood in the world, but most companies still stick to the local tradition.

The Results

When evaluating smoked salmon, professionals look at a number of characteristics, including appearance, texture, and flavor. A primary characteristic of high-quality salmon is marbling. Like a good piece of beef, a side of smoked salmon should have thin bands of fat running throughout the flesh. If the salmon does not have enough fat, it will be tough and dry. The top-three-finishing salmons all had noticeable marbling.

SMOKED SALMON FROM NEW JERSEY?

I grew up in New Jersey and am used to hearing the jokes. But even I was surprised when a smoked salmon from New Jersey won our tasting. I decided to take a road trip.

Perona Farms, nestled in the hills of northwestern New Jersey, about fifty miles from Manhattan, is a family-run catering and restaurant business. Several years ago, chef Kirk Avondoglio, great-grandson of the farm's first proprietors, started smoking his own salmon to see if he could improve on the product the restaurant was purchasing. This side operation has turned into a million-dollar business supplying top chefs as well as savvy consumers who order by mail.

Avondoglio dry-cures fillets ("wet-brining is cheating," he says) for about ninety hours. He pokes each fillet (as if he were grilling a steak) to see if it is ready for the smokehouse. "No two pieces are the same, and adjustments must be made in the process to account for natural differences." His cure is a simple mixture of salt and sugar. The sugar adds some sweetness to the fish but also slows down the salting process. "I could finish the curing process much quicker without the sugar, but I like what it does for the fish," he explains. "The key to this whole process is finding the right cure; if you don't cure them right, the smoke won't do anything."

After the sides of salmon have been cured, they are placed in the smokehouse, a small ten-foot-high structure made of cinder blocks and an old industrial refrigerator door. Although some companies smoke for a day or longer, Perona Farms smokes for just six hours. "The key is keeping the temperature below 70 degrees, even lower if possible," says Avondoglio. He also keeps the collarbone in the fish until packaging time so that the salmon can be hung during smoking to ensure even distribution of the smoke flavor. He uses only oak, which he says gives the fish its "smooth taste."

So, beyond this, what's his secret? As far as I can tell, it's the individual attention each fish receives at this low-tech, artisanal operation. Impeccably fresh fish flown in from the finest farms in Maine, Canada, and Scotland doesn't hurt either.—*J.B.*

But in the final analysis, smoked salmon falls and rises on flavor. The traits here are smokiness, saltiness, sweetness, and fishiness. In general, professionals look for a clean, salmon flavor that is not overly fishy or oily. A hint of sweetness can be welcome, and while the fish should taste of salt and smoke, these flavors should not overwhelm the palate. Of course, these characteristics (especially the last two) are very subjective.

For this reason, we were surprised when the votes were tallied after the tasting. There was a clear consensus about most of the fish. The top three brands (all smoked domestically) start with farmed Atlantic salmon, which is then cured and smoked in small batches. The other two recommended brands come from Scotland, which many experts believe is home to the best smoked salmon in Europe. Oak is the wood of choice in

Scotland and generally gives salmon a lightly smoked flavor.

In general, salmon smoked from Europe is more expensive than domestic products. The two most expensive salmons in our tasting (from France and Ireland) ended up near the bottom of the rankings while the top choice was among the least expensive brands. This proves that you don't have to go broke to the buy the best. ∎

<hr>

RATING SMOKED SALMON

Eleven mail-order smoked salmons were tasted blind at Oceana restaurant in New York and are listed in order of preference based on the scores awarded by our judges. The salmon was presliced (with one exception) and vacuum-packed. The place designation in each listing refers to the site of the smokehouse; phone numbers are for mail-order departments. Prices are listed, along with overnight or two-day (for West Coast fish) shipping costs to Connecticut. (Shipping costs, of course, vary depending on the size of the order and destination and may include separate box charges that some companies add.)

In addition to the author and *Cook's Illustrated* Food Editor Pam Anderson, the panel included the following: Katherine Alford, a cooking teacher and writer; Rose Levy Beranbaum, cookbook author and consultant; Stephanie Crane, publicist for Oceana restaurant; Carmine Dellaporta, smoked fish buyer for Dean & Deluca; Dana Jacobi, food writer; Stephanie Lyness, food writer; Rick Moonen, executive chef at Oceana; Arthur Schwartz, food writer and radio host; and Michele Scicolone, cookbook author.

RECOMMENDED SALMONS
These salmons received positive comments from almost every taster.

Perona Farms Smoked Atlantic Salmon (Andover, New Jersey; 800-762-8569), $19.95 per pound plus shipping ($8.90 for 2.84-lb. side). The "very dark orange," "slightly oily" fillet had visible lines of fat, which several tasters saw as a sign of "good marbling." Most tasters appreciated the "good mouth-feel" of this "buttery, rich" salmon. The smoke (which is 100% oak) and salt were "light," and there was "no trace of fishiness." Some tasters did pick out "a hint of sweetness." A "great choice."

Sullivan Harbor Farm Smokehouse Smoked Salmon (Sullivan Harbor, Maine; 800-422-4014), $31.50 to $35 per pound, shipping included. This "red-brick-colored," "lightly marbled" fillet finished just behind the winner and picked up four first-place votes. The texture of this farmed Maine salmon was described as "firm" and "smooth" with some "slight dryness at edges." The flavor was "very smoky" with a "good hit of salt and sugar."

Gerard & Dominique European Style Smoked Salmon (Bothell, Washington; 800-858-0449), $20 per pound plus shipping ($12 for 2.35-lb. side). Farmed Atlantic salmon from this small West Coast operation was "firm" but "creamy" with a "silky, unctuous" quality that was also described as "nicely oiled." (The label says that olive oil is added during processing.) A few tasters wanted more smoke and/or salt, but most appreciated the mild flavor of this salmon.

Balducci Scottish Smoked Salmon (Scotland; 800-225-3822), $30 per pound plus shipping ($16 for 1.5-lb. side). The famed New York gourmet store imports wild Scottish salmon. The pale pink fish received three first-place votes. The texture was "smooth" and "moist." Most tasters felt there was a "good balance" of smoke, salt, and fish.

Mackenzie Limited Smoked Scottish Salmon (Scotland; 800-858-7100), $32.25 per pound plus shipping ($4.50 for 2-lb. side). Although this salmon did not receive as many top votes as others in this category, it was deemed a good if not great choice by almost every taster. The fillet was "pinkish orange" with "thick fat lines." The texture was "fatty" and "smooth" but a "bit too soft" for many tasters. Some panelists felt the smoke and salt were "balanced" while others thought this sample was "too mild" or "flat."

ACCEPTABLE SALMONS
These salmons received mixed reviews from tasters.

Scandia Fresh Smoked Norwegian Salmon (Norway; 203-838-2087),

$18.95 per pound plus shipping ($6.50 for 2.56-lb. side). The label says this salmon was farm-raised and then smoked with juniper. The texture was "softer than most" and was downgraded by many tasters. Oil beaded up on the surface, and most panelists complained of "fishy" flavor. Although not terrible, this fish was flawed.

Ducktrap River Fish Farm Kendall Brook Smoked Atlantic Salmon (Belfast, Maine; 800-828-3825), $30 to $40 per pound, shipping included (1.5- to 2-lb. side). This fairly expensive salmon had its admirers but, again, was far from stellar. The color was an "odd, brownish orange" with small, dark flecks (of herbs or ash?) on top. The very strong smoke flavor was a turn-on for some, a turn-off for others.

Portlock Alder Smoked Wild Sockeye Salmon (Seattle; 800-872-5666), $15.95 per pound plus shipping ($11.85 for two 1-lb. sides). This small, "reddish orange" fish was easily recognized as sockeye by experienced tasters. The texture was "extremely firm" but "a bit dry" due to the lower oil content in the species. The flavor was quite smoky, "almost like jerky." Some tasters responded positively to this "chewy," "heavily smoked" fish; others thought it was "weird."

SALMONS NOT RECOMMENDED
These salmons earned negative comments from most tasters.

Petrossian Paris Smoked Salmon (France; 212-245-2217), $42 per pound plus shipping ($25 for 2.5-lb. side). The most expensive salmon in the tasting (it's sliced by hand) is farmed in Norway, smoked in France, and then shipped to Petrossian boutiques around the globe. The texture was especially "satiny," but most tasters picked up a "biting," "chemical," or "sharp" flavor.

Fionn McCool Oak-Smoked Irish Salmon (Ireland; 212-684-4321), $35 per pound, shipping included (3.48-lb. side). The second-most expensive salmon in the tasting showed good marbling. However, the "mealy," "cottony," "chewy" texture was a real stumbling block for most panelists. The flavor got mixed reviews.

Portlock Nova Smoked Copper River King Salmon (Seattle; 800-872-5666), $17.25 per pound plus shipping ($11.85 for 1.5 lbs. of sliced salmon). Tasters were disappointed that this prized species from Alaska showed so poorly. Although smoked with alder wood, there were so many problems with the fish itself, it's hard to say what effect this had on the results. The color was "washed out," the texture was "mushy," "sticky," and "pasty," and the flavor was "way too fishy."

Rustic Holiday Stuffings

These bread stuffings can be cooked inside the bird or out.

BY LEA BERGEN

Chewy, rustic, slightly stale loaves of flavorful bread such as sourdough, whole wheat, or rye—used alone or in combination—create the foundation of these flavorful stuffing recipes.

To make croutons, cut the bread into half-inch cubes, trimming the crust if you wish. Preheat the oven to 350 degrees. Put the cubes on cookie sheets, turn off the oven, and let the cubes dry out in the oven overnight. If you need to make the cubes in a hurry, bake them in a 275-degree oven until crisp but not browned, from thirty to sixty minutes, depending on the bread's initial dryness.

Note that if you wish to pair the recipe for Roast Turkey on page 9 with any of these recipes, you will need to prepare all of the stuffing *outside* the bird. For each of these recipes, if baking outside the bird, drizzle an additional quarter cup of stock over the stuffing before baking.

HERB AND MUSHROOM STUFFING
Makes about 11 cups

- 3 tablespoons butter, plus extra for baking dish and foil
- 4 medium celery stalks, chopped coarse (about 2 cups)
- 3 medium onions, chopped coarse (about 3 cups)
- 10 ounces mushrooms, sliced thin (about 3 cups)
- 2 teaspoons dried sage
- 2 teaspoons dried thyme
- 1 teaspoon dried rosemary
- 1 teaspoon dried marjoram
- ¼ cup sweet sherry
- 2 large eggs, lightly beaten
- 1 cup chicken or turkey stock or low-sodium canned broth
- ½ cup heavy cream
- 1 teaspoon salt
- ½ teaspoon ground black pepper
- 8 cups dried bread cubes (French, sourdough, or whole wheat are good choices)
- ½ cup minced fresh parsley leaves

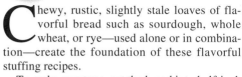

1. Heat butter in large skillet over medium high heat. Add celery and onions; sauté until softened, about 5 minutes. Add mushrooms; sauté until lightly golden and liquid evaporates, about 7 minutes. Add sage, thyme, rosemary and marjoram; sauté to blend flavors, 2 to 3 minutes. Add sherry; cook until reduced by half. Remove pan from heat; cool to room temperature.

2. Whisk eggs, stock, cream, salt, and pepper in large bowl. Add bread cubes, cooled vegetable mixture, and parsley; toss gently to mix.

3. Stuff turkey if desired; do so just before roasting. Turn remaining stuffing into buttered shallow baking dish; bake at 350 degrees, covered with buttered aluminum foil, until knife inserted into center feels warm to the touch, 25 to 40 minutes depending on amount of stuffing. Uncover and bake until top crisps slightly, 5 to 10 minutes.

CORNBREAD-APPLE STUFFING
Makes about 11 cups

- 8 ounces bacon, fried crisp, dried, and cut crosswise into ½-inch pieces, reserving 4 tablespoons drippings (optional)
- 4 tablespoons butter, plus extra for baking dish and foil
- 2 medium onions, chopped coarse (about 2 cups)
- 2 small stalks celery, chopped coarse (about 1 cup)
- 3 medium-large tart apples (such as Granny Smith), peeled and cut into ½-inch chunks (about 3 cups)
- 3 tablespoons minced fresh thyme
- 2 tablespoons minced fresh sage
- 2 large eggs, lightly beaten
- 1 cup heavy cream, chicken or turkey stock, or low-sodium canned broth
- 1 teaspoon salt
- ½ teaspoon ground black pepper
- 4 cups dried French bread cubes
- 4 cups crumbled cornbread
- 1 cup pecans, toasted, and chopped coarse
- ¼ cup minced fresh parsley leaves

1. Heat bacon drippings *or* butter in large skillet over medium-high heat. Add onions and celery; sauté until softened, about 5 minutes. Add apples, thyme, and sage; sauté until apples begin to soften, 5 to 7 minutes longer. Remove pan from heat and cool mixture to room temperature.

2. Whisk eggs, cream or stock, salt, and pepper in large bowl. Add bread cubes, cornbread, cooked bacon, vegetable mixture, pecans, and parsley; toss gently to coat.

3. Bake in accordance with step 3 of Herb and Mushroom Stuffing.

SAUSAGE AND PEAR STUFFING WITH CHESTNUTS AND PRUNES
Makes about 11 cups

- 3 tablespoons butter, plus extra for baking dish and foil
- 8 ounces bulk pork or chicken-and-apple sausage
- 1 medium onion, chopped coarse (about 1 cup)
- 2 firm pears, peeled and cut into ½-inch chunks
- 1 large tart apple (such as Granny Smith), peeled and cut into ½-inch chunks
- ¼ cup brandy
- 2 large eggs, lightly beaten
- 1½ cups chicken or turkey stock or low-sodium canned broth
- 1 teaspoon salt
- ½ teaspoon ground black pepper
- ⅛ teaspoon grated nutmeg
- 1 cup cooked, peeled chestnuts, fresh or canned (*see* note in Glazed Brussels Sprouts with Chestnuts recipe, page 21)
- 6 cups dried bread cubes (rye and whole wheat are good choices)
- ½ cup pitted prunes, cut into ½-inch pieces
- ½ cup walnuts, toasted and chopped coarse

1. Heat 1 tablespoon butter in large skillet over medium-high heat. Add sausage and cook, breaking meat up into small pieces, until no longer pink, 5 to 7 minutes. Transfer sausage to small bowl with slotted spoon; set aside. Discard fat; return skillet to burner. Heat remaining butter over medium-low heat; add onion and cook until soft, about 10 minutes. Add pears and apple; continue to cook over low heat until onion begins to brown, 10 to 12 minutes. Increase heat to high, add brandy, and cook until reduced by half. Remove pan from heat; cool mixture to room temperature.

2. Whisk eggs, stock, salt, pepper, and nutmeg in large bowl. Add sausage, cooled fruit mixture, chestnuts, bread cubes, prunes, and walnuts; toss gently to coat. Adjust seasonings to taste.

3. To bake, follow step 3 of Herb and Mushroom Stuffing. ∎

Lea Bergen is a restaurant consultant and food writer based in San Francisco.

PHOTOGRAPHS BY DAVE HENDERSON

Making Pasta Machines Work

Essential tips and tested recipes can eliminate the frustrating trial and error most cooks experience with these fickle electric machines.

~ BY TOM LACALAMITA ~

If you have ever used an electric pasta machine, you know that even the best intentions do not guarantee perfect results (see "Rating Electric Pasta Makers," page 28). There are many variables that affect the quality of the pasta, and understanding how to control these variables will enable you to achieve better results.

Commercial dried pasta is made from finely ground golden durum wheat flour, also called semolina or pasta flour. This flour has a high gluten content and produces pasta with a good bite. This flour can also be used to make fresh pasta. When water (the only other ingredient in commercial pasta) is added, the result is a fairly firm, chewy fresh pasta.

Most Americans (as well as Italians) prefer a softer texture when making fresh pasta. This consistency can be achieved by using all-purpose flour along with eggs for liquid. All-purpose flour has a much lower gluten content than durum wheat flour. Less gluten means the pasta will have a finer texture and softer bite. Eggs are used instead of water for several reasons. The fat in the eggs promotes softness and elasticity. A dough made with all-purpose flour and water would be gummy and never supple. The eggs also add richness and flavor to fresh pasta.

I find olive oil to be an essential addition to egg pasta made in an electric machine; it makes the dough smoother and easier to extrude. This stands in contrast to most traditional recipes without oil. Egg pasta with oil that is rolled through a hand-cranked machine can become slick and therefore more difficult to sauce. However, the dies on an electric pasta machine leave the surface fairly rough, so slickness is not an issue.

Kneading the Dough

As the dough (either with semolina or all-purpose flour) is mixed, the gluten comes into contact with the liquid ingredients, forming an interlocking network of elastic strands. This is what gives pasta its "bite." Since kneading allows the flour to absorb more water, do not overestimate how much liquid the flour requires to form a dough. A dough that appears dry can reach the right consistency with more kneading and no extra liquid.

For this reason, you should add one-half cup of the liquid ingredients to the flour as it mixes in the pasta machine, over the course of a minute or two. Let the machine continue to knead to bring more flour in contact with the liquid. You do not want the dough to knead too long since it will eventually form a large ball or balls too big to pass through the extruder tunnel. The dough should be crumbly, yet not dry. It should be extruded when it forms soft, pea-sized crumbs.

If after a couple of minutes the dough continues to look dry and pebbly, add more liquid, one tablespoon at a time. A dry dough can always be moistened by adding more liquid. Adding more flour to a wet dough does not work because the dough sticks to everything and gums up the rotating mixing arm.

While preparing the dough, soak the extruder die in a small bowl of hot tap water. This simple step is essential because hot water acts as a lubricant and facilitates extrusion. However, the first inch or two of extruded pasta may be a bit sticky due to the residual moisture on the die. Simply cut and discard these first few inches.

If the die appears to be buckling while extruding, stop the machine immediately. This is a definite indication that the dough is too dry or has not been kneaded sufficiently and is unable to pass through the openings in the die. Either let the dough knead longer or add additional liquid.

MASTER RECIPE FOR EGG PASTA
Makes 1 pound

- 3 large eggs
- 1½ teaspoons olive oil
- 3 cups unbleached, all-purpose flour, sifted
- ¾ teaspoon salt, plus extra for cooking

1. Place selected die in small bowl, cover with hot tap water, and set aside.
2. Place eggs and oil in glass measuring cup. Add enough water so that you have ¾ cup liquid. Beat with fork and set aside.
3. Remove die from hot water and install according to manufacturer's directions. Add flour and salt to mixing chamber. Turn on machine and slowly pour liquid ingredients through opening in cover, adding about ½ cup during first minute or two. Mix approximately 2 to 3 minutes, or until dough forms soft, pea-sized crumbs. If dough appears too dry, add remaining egg mixture, 1 tablespoon at a time, until pasta reaches proper consistency.
4. Switch machine to extrusion mode and extrude pasta. Use knife to slice off first 2 inches of pasta and discard. Continue to extrude and cut pasta at desired lengths with serrated knife. Set pasta aside on towels 30 minutes before using. (Pasta can be kept at room temperature for 2 hours or placed in a zipper-lock plastic bag and refrigerated for 12 hours or frozen for 1 month.)
5. Bring abundant water to boil in large pot. Add salt to taste and as much pasta as desired. Cook until al dente, 3 to 4 minutes if at room temperature or chilled, and about 5 minutes if frozen.

SPINACH PASTA
Makes 1 pound
Follow Master Recipe, decreasing eggs from 3 to 2. Mix eggs with oil and 1 tablespoon water. Add 5 ounces frozen chopped spinach, thawed and squeezed very dry, to flour and salt.

FRESH HERB PASTA
Makes 1 pound
Follow Master Recipe, adding ½ cup minced fresh herbs (Italian parsley, basil, mint, or any combination) to flour and salt.

DURUM WHEAT PASTA
Makes 1 pound
Follow Master Recipe, substituting ¾ cup water for 3 eggs. Omit oil and substitute durum flour for all-purpose flour.

Tom Lacalamita *is the author of* The Ultimate Pasta Machine Cookbook *(Simon & Schuster, 1994).*

TROUBLESHOOTING TIPS

Keep these points in mind as you work with an electric pasta machine:

- Add a little oil to egg pasta to increase its elasticity.
- Err on the dry side. More liquid can always be added, but a wet dough is a lost cause.
- Kneading hydrates the dough, so always mix well before adding more liquid.
- Do not extrude until the dough forms soft, pea-sized crumbs.
- Soak the die in hot water to facilitate extrusion.
- Discard the first inch or two of extruded pasta.
- Set the pasta aside for at least thirty minutes before cooking to relax the gluten.
- Strand pastas are your best bet.

Rating Electric Pasta Makers

These high-tech "wonders" mix, knead, and extrude pasta in minutes. But even expensive models have flaws, while cheap units fail miserably.

~ BY JACK BISHOP ~

Small appliance companies are hoping that electric pasta machines will be the next bread machine. With sales topping half a million units last year and still rising, many companies are slapping their logo on one of these high-tech units. The concept is simple: Dump in flour and eggs, and the machine will mix and knead the dough and then extrude it through a die. Different dies make different shapes, everything from spaghetti and fettuccine to lasagne or ziti.

The attraction is clear, but the performance of most models fell far short of my expectations. When I test kitchen equipment, I usually find a few recommended models with features I particularly like. Other models work fairly well and are acceptable choices. I rarely find more than one or two units that don't work as promised. With pasta machines, the opposite was true. None of the machines that I tested is ideal. The top-rated Simac is quite good and makes several kinds of great pasta. It's worth every penny to a pasta lover like myself, especially since I enjoy fresh spaghetti and fettucine, which cannot be made easily on my hand-cranked Atlas pasta machine. In addition, the Cuisinart and Creative Pasta Express X4000 are decent pasta makers, but several other units, while performing some tasks well, fail miserably at other basic chores. Overall, I had as many failures as successes, which makes choosing the right pasta maker imperative. Make the wrong decision, and you will store your machine in the basement.

So why are electric pasta makers so fickle? Two theories. First of all, many of these machines are not designed or built all that well. My hunch is that manufacturers have cut corners to keep costs down. The fact that I found a direct correlation between price and performance would seem to bear this out.

For example, the quality of the dies in many machines is poor. The two top-rated units, which come from the same factory in Italy and are priced over $225, have heavy brass dies through which the pasta is extruded. Other machines (priced from $90 to $180) come with cheap plastic dies. The brass dies simply make thinner (i.e., better) pasta. Lasagne extruded through a plastic die was invariably thick and unusable, and most of the fettuccine pushed through plastic dies was not as good as strands I can roll and cut in a hand-cranked pasta maker like an Atlas. Dough extruded through brass dies, however, did have the potential to outdo the Atlas. The spaghetti and fettuccine turned out by the Simac were better than anything I have ever made at home.

One thing that no die (either brass or plastic) could do was make decent tubular pasta. No matter what kind of dough I tried, when I cut off tubular shapes like ziti or rigatoni as they extruded, the ends invariably stuck together. Although it is possible to use a toothpick to pry apart the opening on each noodle, most cooks won't want to spend the time.

In addition to the problem of flimsy dies, many machines were not strong enough to withstand the intense pressure needed to complete

---

RATING PASTA MACHINES

■ = good performance

◩ = fair performance

□ = poor performance

Nine electric pasta machines were evaluated based on the following characteristics and are listed in order of preference. For purchasing information, *see* page 32.

Weight: Heavier machines proved sturdier than lighter ones and were preferred.
Dies: Although an assortment is a welcome feature, the quality is much more important. Heavy brass dies (with plastic backs) are far superior to flimsy all-plastic dies.
Cleanup: No machine is easy to clean. The Simac and Cuisinart machines have more parts with hard-to-reach places than other units and were downgraded.

Spaghetti: Most are able to extrude thin strands of spaghetti, something a manual machine rarely does well.
Fettuccine: Only the Simac makes paper-thin fettuccine. The Cuisinart is a distant second. All others could not equal the fettuccine made in a manual pasta maker.
Lasagne: No machine makes good lasagne. Most are too narrow (less than an inch across) and too fat (more than a sixteenth inch thick). The top three machines make strips less than a sixteenth inch thick and about two inches across—not lasagne but at least something usable for ravioli or tortellini, especially if thinned some more with a rolling pin.

PASTA MAKER	PRICE	WEIGHT	DIES	CLEANUP	SPAGHETTI	FETTUCCINE	LASAGNE
Simac PastaMatic MX 700	$229	16 lbs.	8 brass dies (7 for pasta)	◩	■	■	◩
Cuisinart Deluxe Pasta Maker DPM-3	$299	16 lbs.	7 brass dies (6 for pasta)	◩	■	■	◩
Creative Pasta Express X4000	$179	15 lbs.	18 plastic dies (14 for pasta)	◩	■	◩	◩
Popeil Automatic Pasta Maker	$149	9 lbs.	12 plastic dies (10 for pasta)	◩	■	◩	◩
Vitantonio Pasta Perfetto 900	$159	11 lbs.	8 plastic dies (all for pasta)	◩	■	◩	□
Farberware Pasta Pro D3015	$130	11 lbs.	10 plastic dies (all for pasta)	◩	■	◩	□
Maverick Pasta del Giorno MPM 6468	$90	10 lbs.	11 plastic dies (8 for pasta)	◩	■	◩	□
Creative Pasta Express X500	$99	10 lbs.	11 plastic dies (8 for pasta)	◩	◩	◩	□
Rival Pasta Chef PM 1000	$100	10 lbs.	10 plastic dies (9 for pasta)	■	◩	◩	◩

the extrusion process. In all models, ingredients are mixed and kneaded in one chamber. When the dough is ready, the user flips a switch and the dough starts to move through an extrusion tunnel or chamber. Most models have a thick, coil-like rod that slowly moves pieces of dough from the mixing chamber to the back of the die. When enough dough builds up against the back of the die, it is forced through the holes in the die. The user must then cut the pasta off at the desired length.

Many machines labored during the extrusion process. The front blew off one particularly flimsy model because the pressure was so great. Even kneading wet dough was too much for some machines, and their motors shut off automatically. The three top-rated machines are much more solid and sturdy than the others. These units weigh fifteen or sixteen pounds; all others weigh in at around ten pounds. Again, I found that you get what you pay for. More money buys a stronger machine that is less likely to stall during extrusion.

In addition to design flaws, I found that electric pasta makers are fickle due to the high level of experience required by the user. You can throw ingredients into a bread machine, walk away, and come back several hours later to a decent loaf. Electric pasta makers require constant attention during operation. The user (not the machine) decides when the dough has been kneaded enough and is ready to be extruded. This decision is crucial. Dry, underkneaded dough will yield crumbly, brittle pasta. Wet, overkneaded dough will back up in the extrusion chamber and yield sticky, gluey pasta—that is if the machine does not shut down first.

The difference between dry and wet pasta can be as little as a tablespoon of liquid. Unlike handmade pasta, which should come together in a smooth, silky mass, the dough in an electric machine must never reach this easily recognized stage. It must be crumbly enough that small pieces can move through the extrusion tunnel, but not so dry that the pasta will be brittle.

Some Conclusions

These negative comments do not mean you should not buy an electric pasta maker. Several models make lovely pasta, but they are all quite expensive. My clear first choice is the Simac. It slowly mixes and kneads the dough, which prevents the kind of overkneading that occurred in models with a fast-moving mixing arm. Although the mixing and extrusion process takes about twenty minutes (twice as long as some cheaper models), the results are superior. Also, the Simac pushed all the dough out of the mixing chamber and into the extrusion tunnel, something most units could not do. The spaghetti and fettuccine are superb—better than anything you can make by hand or with a hand-cranked pasta machine. On the downside, the Simac has more parts than other models and is particularly difficult to clean.

The second-rated Cuisinart comes from the same factory as the Simac but has some modifications and a higher price. I did not like the thicker fettuccine die included with this machine as much. On the plus side, the Cuisinart has the best manual.

The Creative Pasta Express X4000 is another step down in quality. Although very sturdy and fast, the plastic dies on this machine are not as good as the brass ones on the Simac or Cuisinart.

The Popeil, Vitantonio, and Farberware machines are all less solid and share similar strengths and weaknesses. Although all make excellent spaghetti, I can't recommend any of them. The lasagne dies on all three units are useless and the fettuccine is only so-so. The Popeil is the best of the lot, if only because it is quieter and the mixing arm does not trap as much dough in the chamber. Both the Vitantonio and Farberware machines (which are almost identical) are extremely loud and have trouble moving the pasta from the mixing chamber into the extrusion tunnel. Also, the fast-moving mixing arm promotes overkneading, especially since the arm continues to work the dough during extrusion.

The Maverick has the same strength (good spaghetti) and flaws, with an additional one: This machine makes even thicker fettuccine. The Creative Pasta Express X500 is also in this same general class but with the further problem that the spaghetti extrudes at an uneven pace so that some strands are much shorter than others. Finally, the Rival is a stripped-down variation on the Vitantonio and Farberware. Although the price is right, this machine has so little power that it stopped every time the dough was almost ready for extrusion. After six attempts, I gave up without ever extruding pasta from this lemon. ∎

Simac (Best Pasta Maker): The clear favorite with good performance and solid construction. Cleanup is a chore.

Cuisinart: From the same factory as the Simac but sold without the really thin fettuccine die. Why pay more for less?

Creative Pasta Express X4000: Very sturdy with a combination mixing blade and extruder coil. Would be great if the dies were better.

Popeil: Fine for spaghetti but not much else. An expensive one-purpose machine.

Vitantonio: A superfast mixing blade overkneads the dough and then fails to push it all into the extrusion tunnel.

Farberware: Similar design and performance as the Vitantonio, with the same deafening roar.

Maverick: Dough backs up in the extruding area, but the real downfall is the lower quality of the dies.

Creative Pasta Express X500: Inferior dies and uneven extrusion (some strands come out faster than others) are serious flaws.

Rival: Extremely poor performance (including having the front of the machine blow off) makes this flimsy model a real dog.

Rating Pink Sparklers

Rosé sparkling wines are notoriously expensive, and for no reason. Although a pricey wine led our pack, several wines costing half as much are good buys.

⌒ BY MARK BITTMAN ⌒

Pink and bubbly, sparkling rosé is the wine of true celebrations. This must explain, at least in part, why most of its producers feel justified in cranking up the price. When splurging for a serious party, a wedding, an important anniversary, or a brilliant New Year, who's going to quibble over a few dollars?

You will if you pick up a bottle of most $50 sparkling rosés and find yourself imbibing a sour-tasting concoction, one that cannot compare to the standard Champagnes from the same houses costing, in many cases, half that amount.

Now, you might get a glorious wine for that $50, but you also might get a better-than-decent one for a third the cost. As with "regular" Champagne, or with sparkling wine from anywhere in the world (Champagne is a district in France, which technically lends its name only to wines made there), the differences result from the grapes and the winemaking techniques, neither of which justifies a higher cost for rosés.

Making a sparkling rosé is little different from making any sparkling wine, with one exception: The winemaker must turn the wine from clear, or slightly golden, to pink or copper-colored. There are two ways to do this. One is to add red wine to the blend; the other is to let the grape juice remain in contact with the skins of red grapes during fermentation. Neither of these is especially challenging, and neither has much impact on flavor.

Producing rosé sparkling wines, then, involves the same process as producing any other sparkling wine. Grapes are pressed and fermented in the usual manner. Many sparklers-to-be are fermented again (malolactic fermentation) and blended with wines from other vintages and/or vineyards. They are then "dosed" with a bit of sweetened wine to which some yeast has been added, and bottled with a temporary cork. For the next few months or years, the bottles are turned occasionally ("riddled"), and then disgorged—the sediment ejected by the pressure released when the temporary cork is removed. In most cases, another "dosage" is added, the final cork is put in place, and the wine is stored until mature and bubbly.

This process, known as the *méthode champenoise,* is the one most commonly used, largely because it is not *that* expensive and because the two alternatives—one in which the wines are fermented in pressurized tanks, the other in which carbon dioxide is pumped into still wine (as in making soda)—rarely produce quality wines.

The point is that good rosé sparklers are good sparklers that happen to be pink. What became obvious in our tasting of fourteen rosé sparklers from all over the world, with prices ranging from $10 to $50, was that neither price nor producer was a good predictor of quality. Our top finisher was a grande dame of Champagne, but our second-place wine was a little-known product of the same region and, much more surprising, our fourth-place finisher was an el-cheapo California product made by a producer whose wines have not shown well in previous *Cook's Illustrated* tastings.

There's little logic here, but our panel was pleased by the overall results; although not unanimous, there was general agreement. Next year, with new blends, everything will undoubtedly be different. This year, however, you have fairly clear choices in a variety of price ranges, both for wines to look for and those to avoid. ∎

BLIND TASTING RESULTS

As usual, the wines in our tasting—held at Chamard Vineyards in Clinton, Connecticut—were judged by a panel made up of wine professionals and amateurs. In the judging, seven points were awarded for each first-place vote; six for second; five for third; and so on. The wines were purchased in the Northeast; prices will vary somewhat throughout the country, with European wines more expensive and American wines less expensive on the West Coast.

Within each category, wines are listed by points scored. Wines are from France unless otherwise noted. In general, Very Highly Recommended wines received only positive comments; Highly Recommended wines received few negative comments; Recommended wines had predominantly positive comments; Not Recommended wines received few or no positive comments.

LAURENT PERRIER, CUVÉE ROSÉ BRUT

CAPUCINE ROSÉ

VERY HIGHLY RECOMMENDED

Laurent Perrier, Cuvé e Rosé Brut, $50. Runaway winner with half again as many points as the next highest finisher. "Lovely flavor, soft bubble, great complexity" and "a terrific wine, with or without bubbles." Ten out of thirteen tasters put it in their top five choices, an almost unprecedented vote of confidence. Too bad you can't buy it for $9.99.

Capucine Rosé, $18. Little-known Champagne of good quality. "Spicy, well-balanced, with rich fruit" and "full-flavored."

HIGHLY RECOMMENDED

Schramsberg 1989 Brut Rosé (California), $25. "Subtle fruit, nice fizz—would be great to start a meal."

Korbel Brut Rosé (California), $12. Note price. Korbel's wines have not done well in previous *Cook's* sparkler tastings, but this one was found by some to have a "strong nose with good fruit." It garnered several high votes and was truly disliked by no one.

Roederer 1988 Brut Rosé, $50. Note price. "Superflavorful—the best," wrote one taster. Others liked this wine but didn't feel as strongly.

RECOMMENDED

Scharffenberger Brut Rosé (California), $21.

"Spicy, well-balanced, with good flavors," said the taster who ranked this first. Others found it "light, with no guts" or "sweet, with little flavor."

Roederer Estate Brut Rosé (California), $25. This California cousin of our fifth-ranked wine was found to be "nicely balanced, well-made, and mouthwatering" by some, but "drinkable, not notable" by others.

Veuve Cliquot 1985 Rosé Reserve, $50. Note price. Some said it was "lively and flavorful." Others found it "sour, bitter, astringent."

Berlucci Cuvé e Imperiale (Italy), $18. This wine drew neither much enthusiasm from its admirers nor much in the way of disparaging comments from its detractors.

Moet and Chandon 1988 Brut Impérial Rosé, $48. Note price. "Odd but enjoyable."

NOT RECOMMENDED

Mumm Cordon Rosé, $32. The taster who liked this most called it "drinkable." Others found it "not clean."

Freixenet Brut Rosé (Spain), $10. Comments ranged from "questionable" to "sad" to "awful."

Monte Rossa Rosé (Italy), $22. Two tasters ranked this third, but most found it "medicinal" or with a "bad aftertaste."

Argyle Rosé (Oregon), $15. From a producer of good pinot noir. This had a "big hit of fruit on the palate," said its sole admirer. Most said it was "indifferent."

BOOK
REVIEWS

The Everyday Cookbooks
Time-Life Books, $14.95 each

When this five-book series landed in my kitchen, I was immediately intrigued, primarily because of the Time-Life name. Many food professionals consider the books in the *Time-Life Illustrated Library of Cooking* to be cornerstones in their libraries. Although twenty-five years old, these single-subject books are still valuable resources for both information and recipes.

With such high expectations, I guess I was bound to be disappointed. There are some good dishes in this new collection, but the food lacks a unifying focus, a soul, if you will. My impression is that a bunch of test cooks developed six hundred recipes without much editorial or culinary oversight.

For instance, Linguine with Mediterranean Pasta Sauce was quick, low in fat, and delicious. However, I don't think a half pound of linguine will satisfy four people, even if two are kids.

Lemon-Herb Marinated Chicken Breasts is the kind of standard recipe found in many Italian cookbooks but was nonetheless both tasty and simple. However, the recipe calls for four boneless breast halves with the skin still on, something I rarely see in supermarkets. Since the skin protects the meat during grilling, I substituted four breasts with bones in, but I'm sure some cooks would buy boneless, skinless breasts and be disappointed by the results.

Couscous with Gingered Vegetables, a soupy collection of carrots, zucchini, and red bell peppers, makes a light main dish when ladled over couscous. Although technically fine, this recipe highlights a recurring problem with the book—the lack of headnotes. I was surprised by how brothy this dish was; I was expecting it to be more saladlike. A headnote easily could have alerted me to set the table with spoons instead of forks.

I might have overlooked these flaws if some dishes had not been outright duds. When I cooked Garlic Shrimp with Cuban Black Bean Salad, the flavors simply did not work and the dish was badly in need of some rice. Hoppin' John Salad was too hodgepodge for my taste: The rice and black-eyed pea salad was fine, but adding one-half pound of smoked ham just to bulk it up was a mistake, and four teaspoons of grated lemon zest in the dressing was definitely overkill.

While I found good food in these books, they could have benefited from considerably more kitchen work. This is especially true given that they're geared to cooks who don't want to anticipate problems and make adjustments as they try to get a weeknight dinner on the table.

—Jack Bishop

How to Bake
Nick Malgieri
Harper Collins, $35

Those who seek comprehensive, all-in-one volumes will welcome this hefty entry from the well-qualified Nick Malgieri, whose work often appears in these pages. Both concept and execution are top-notch: After testing more than a dozen recipes, I had *perhaps* one complaint (the baking time for a light cocoa quick bread was a tad long) and a dozen delicious baked goods.

These were not limited to desserts. Large sections are also devoted to semisweet and not-sweet items here, including a simple, easily executed pissaladière—the onion-topped pizza of Nice—gobbled up by my dinner guests, and Sicilian Eggplant Tarts, with olives, pine nuts, and raisins, gobbled up by me. There is a strong bread section as well, with a Rustic White Bread that is straightforward and successful. There are also quick breads, muffins, and scones.

Most of the book, though, is given over to baked desserts, an area in which Malgieri shines. His experience makes it possible for him to take matters that are covered in nearly all baking books and give them a fresh take, as he does with his half-page discussion of how to whip egg whites.

Best of all, however, are the variations that follow many recipes, which increase the value of the book enormously. For example, Hazelnut and Almond Dacquoise with Coffee Buttercream looks and tastes completely different than Pistachio Raspberry Meringue, but the techniques and ingredients used to make them are almost identical. Malgieri sums up how to make the latter, using the skeleton of the former, in a terse paragraph of text that is not only easy to follow but also works beautifully.

Finally, I appreciate that, although Malgieri is always looking for ways to improve technique, he doesn't mess around with ingredients much: Yes, you can make Buttermilk Corn Bread without three eggs and a half stick of butter, but it won't be as good as Malgieri's. My feeling has always been that baking is about richness; none of that has been sacrificed in *How to Bake*.

—Mark Bittman

The Joy of Coffee
Corby Kummer
Chapters, $22

Given America's surging interest in good coffee, it's no surprise that publishers have responded with so many books on the subject. A half-dozen new coffee titles now line my shelves. Most are a combination of coffee lore, brewing tips, and dessert recipes. *The Joy of Coffee* follows the same format but contains much more firsthand reporting and insightful brewing information than any of its competitors.

For example, Kummer starts at the source with a visit to a Costa Rican coffee plantation. His lively description of a tiring and not terribly fruitful stint as a bean picker is both entertaining and educational. Detailed sections on roasting and cupping (the process by which experts judge beans) are technical but still lively. Practical chapters on grinding and storing, brewing, espresso, types of beans, and caffeine round out the text.

I appreciated Kummer's lucid, informative writing on this complex subject, and was most grateful for his tell-it-like-it-is tone. For example, he calls heavily advertised Colombian coffee "at best...clean and neutral" and informs the reader that "it's hard to get a bad coffee from Costa Rica." For those confused by the multitude of new coffee gadgets, he states that only four pieces of equipment are "essential for superb drip coffee": a grinder, a measuring cup, a gold-washed metal filter, and a thermal carafe.

Although this book is really meant for the bedroom (that's where I do all my reading), I tested three of the forty-odd recipes, and all were fine. Most were developed by food consultant Lisë Stern, although a few come from Kummer's own kitchen and others were donated by master baker Flo Braker.

Kummer's Unbeatable Biscotti are drier than most classic almond biscotti (they bake for one and one-half hours) but quite good. Chock-Full-of-Nuts Chocolate Chip Cookies are made with pulverized oats and pecans, which give them a nutty, crunchy quality. Indispensable Snack Cake is quite simple and not terribly sweet, making it an excellent partner for coffee.

Few people will buy this book for the recipes alone, but they are a welcome companion to what is a well-written and informative discussion of the bean. ■

—Jack Bishop

SOURCES

AND RESOURCES

Most of the ingredients and materials needed for the recipes in this issue are available at your local supermarket, gourmet store, or kitchen supply shop. The following are mail-order sources for particular items. Prices listed below were current at press time and do not include shipping or handling unless otherwise indicated. We suggest that you contact companies directly to confirm up-to-date prices and availability.

ELECTRIC PASTA MACHINES
We tested nine models of electric pasta machines for the story on page 28 and can only wholeheartedly recommend the top two brands; a third model is a decent value but does not deliver the same level of performance. The Simac PastaMatic MX 700 is our clear favorite. The sturdy brass dies produce the best spaghetti and fettuccine we have ever made. The machine is remarkably sturdy and does the best job of kneading and extruding pasta. The Simac is available from the Williams-Sonoma catalog (800-541-2233) for $229. The Cuisinart Deluxe Pasta Maker DPM-3 is almost identical to the Simac (it comes from the same factory in Italy), but the fettuccine die is a bit thicker. This pasta maker is available from the Chef's Catalog (800-338-3232) for $299. If these two models are out of your price range, the third-rated Creative Pasta Express X4000 may be an option. Although the plastic dies are not as good as the metal dies on the top models, this machine is sturdy enough to handle kneading and extruding with ease. This pasta maker is sold through the King Arthur Flour Baker's Catalogue (800-827-6836) for $189 and may occasionally be discounted at department stores.

SELECT A SPUD
In the potato gratin article on page 18, we find that you can tailor the gratin to your mood by varying the thickness of the slices and the type of potato. Your local market may stock two or three kinds of potatoes, but for a greater selection, New Penny Farm (P.O. Box 448, Presque Isle, ME 04769; 800-827-7551) grows more than a dozen types and ships them in five-pound, ten-pound, or twenty-pound bags. Costs are the same for all varieties: $19.50 for a five-pound bag, plus $2 shipping; $24.50 for a ten-pound bag, plus $3 shipping; and $34.50 for a twenty-pound bag, plus $5 shipping. These shipping rates apply for addresses west of the Mississippi and change slightly with the seasons. There is no shipping charge for consumers east of the Mississippi.

SLICE A SPUD
Using a knife to cut potatoes into consistently thin, even slices can be a challenge. We tested different cutting methods for the potato gratin article on page 18 and determined that a mandolin does the job most easily (see sidebar on page 19). Variations in the design and materials of these devices abound, and prices run the gamut from about $6 to $150. A Cook's Wares (412-846-9490) sells two models that impressed us for different reasons. The $142 Bron Mandolin is made in France of sturdy, thick-gauge stainless steel and is designed for professional use. If you pop for this one, the chances are good that your grandchildren will use it to slice their spuds well into the twenty-first century. Somewhat less durable, correspondingly less expensive, and every bit as effective is the Boerner V-Slicer for $29.30. Though thickness adjustments are limited to only "thin" and "thick," this high-impact plastic device sports two angled stainless steel blades for excellent cutting performance. It should hold up just fine for home use.

BUT DON'T SLICE YOURSELF!
Mandolin blades are razor sharp and designed to remain so for years, so take real care when cleaning them. Using the Polar Bear Supreme protective glove, model FS301, will provide some extra protection against cuts. Originally designed for use in cleaning deli slicer blades and in the meat industry, the glove is made from yarn that combines three stainless steel strands with high-strength optical fibers. Though not absolutely indestructible (the manufacturer, Tom Thumb Glove/Golden Needles, cautions against using the glove on serrated or powered cutting tools, and we managed to cut through it with a sharp ten-inch chef's knife using considerable pressure), it offers significant added protection and peace of mind when cleaning your mandolin. Retail availability is limited because it is essentially a food-service industry product, but Boston-based Kitchen Arts (161 Newbury Street, Boston, MA 02116; 617-266-8701) will accept phone orders for the $22.95 glove from any U.S. location.

BATTER SKIMMERS
One of master baker Rose Levy Beranbaum's tricks for making a foolproof genoise (see Master Class on page 10) is to use a metal skimmer with fairly large holes (one-eighth-inch) to fold the dry ingredients into the egg foam. Two such skimmers, both stainless steel, are available from A Cook's Wares (412-846-9490): a four-and-three-quarter-inch diameter model by Amco for $10 and a $14.99 Henckels model with a slightly larger diameter and a black polypropylene handle.

DRIED CHESTNUTS
Like apples, fresh chestnuts are a culinary benefit of the colder autumn and winter months that factor into the recipes for Sausage and Pear Stuffing with Chestnuts and Prunes on page 26 and Glazed Brussels Sprouts with Chestnuts on page 21 in this issue. As an alternative to fresh chestnuts, which are available only for a short time each year, American Spoon Foods, Inc. (1668 Clarion Avenue, P.O. Box 566, Petoskey, MI 48770; 800-222-5886) sells eight-ounce bags of dried chestnuts for $5.95. These chestnuts come shelled and peeled, which is convenient for home cooks. They also keep well for a long time and can be ground into flour in a food processor or mill for use in baking. They rehydrate to roughly two and a half times their weight and volume and can be used just as you would fresh-cooked chestnuts.

NUTMEG AND GRINDERS
The flavor and scent of freshly grated nutmeg is a perennial sign of holiday baking and cooking—both sweet and savory. This issue of Cook's Illustrated alone calls for nutmeg in three recipes: Old-Fashioned Gingerbread on page 23, Classic Potato Gratin on page 19, and Sausage and Pear Stuffing with Chestnuts and Prunes on page 26. The best way to use this spice is to grind as much as you need for your recipe from whole nutmegs. Spices, Etc. (P.O. Box 5266, Charlottesville, VA 22905; 800-827-6373) sells packages of whole nutmegs in three sizes: 1.7 ounces for $2.60, 9 ounces for $6.40, and 20 ounces for $8. The company also sells three types of nutmeg grinders: a small stainless-steel grater (akin to the familiar box graters in concept) for $3.95, a clear acrylic model with a crank handle and storage space for whole nutmegs in the top (like some peppermills in appearance) for $17.95, and a model similar to the acrylic grinder but somewhat smaller and with a black plastic base for $14.95. For the path of least resistance (and flavor), Spices, Etc. also sells ground nutmeg.

CRYSTALLIZED GINGER
Crystallized ginger is a supreme treat for the ginger fiends among us, as well as a rich flavor boost in the Old-Fashioned Gingerbread recipe on page 23. Peeled slices of fresh ginger are cooked in sugar syrup and coated with granulated syrup, so the flavor is at once fiery and sweet. It is a natural for baking and the whole pieces dipped in chocolate are fantastic. A sixteen-ounce tin of crystallized ginger from Australia is available from the Williams-Sonoma Catalog (800-541-2233) for $11. ∎

PRIME RIB page 14 **AND**
BRAISED BRUSSELS SPROUTS page 21

PHYLLO TRIANGLES
page 16

CLASSIC POTATO GRATIN
page 19

PERFECT PECAN PIE
page 8

GRAND MARNIER CAKE WITH NEOCLASSIC
ORANGE BUTTERCREAM page 11

ROAST TURKEY page 9
WITH HERB AND MUSHROOM STUFFING page 26

Smoked Salmon–Filled Belgian Endive

Mix 6 ounces coarse-chopped smoked salmon with 2 tablespoons olive oil, 1 tablespoon lemon juice, 2 tablespoons snipped chives, and ¼ teaspoon ground white pepper. Cover and refrigerate until flavors blend, about 1 hour. Meanwhile, remove 6 to 8 outer leaves from each of 4 Belgian endives. Refrigerate. When ready to serve, stir 1 ounce (about 1 tablespoon) salmon roe into salmon mixture, and spoon a portion of the filling into each endive leaf. Arrange on a platter and serve. *Makes about 2 ½ dozen.*